Alex Haley taught himself to write during  Coast Guard. After retiring in 1959 – as its ~~Chief Journalist~~ – he became a magazine writer and interviewer before undertaking his first book, *The Autobiography of Malcolm X*. He has spent the twelve years since then researching and writing *Roots*.

Alex Haley
ROOTS

PICADOR

published by Pan Books

First published in Great Britain 1977 by
Hutchinson and Co Ltd ·
First published in Picador 1977 by Pan Books Ltd,
Cavaye Place, London SW10 9PG
This reset Picador edition first published 1978
11th printing 1979
© Alex Haley 1976
All rights reserved
A condensed version of a portion of this work first
appeared in *Reader's Digest*
© Reader's Digest Association Inc 1974
ISBN 0 330 25301 8
Set, printed and bound in Great Britain by
Cox and Wyman Ltd, Reading

DEDICATION

It wasn't planned
that *Roots*' researching and writing
finally would take twelve years.
Just by chance it is being published
in the Bicentennial Year of the United States.
So I dedicate *Roots* as a birthday offering to my country
within which most of *Roots* happened.

Acknowledgments

I owe deep gratitude to so many people for their help with *Roots* that pages would be required simply to list them all. The following are pre-eminent:

George Sims, my lifelong friend from our Henning, Tennessee, boyhood, is a master researcher who often travelled with me, sharing both the physical and emotional adventures. His dedicated combing through volumes by the hundreds, and other kinds of documents by the thousands – particularly in the U.S. Library of Congress and the U.S. National Archives – supplied much of the historical and cultural material that I have woven around the lives of the people in this book.

Murray Fisher had been my editor for years at *Playboy* magazine when I solicited his clinical expertise to help me structure this book from a seeming impassable maze of researched materials. After we had established *Roots'* pattern of chapters, next the story line was developed, which he then shepherded throughout. Finally, in the book's pressurized completion phase, he even drafted some of *Roots'* scenes, and his brilliant editing pen steadily tightened the book's great length.

The Africa section of this book exists in its detail only because at a crucial time Mrs DeWitt Wallace and the editors of the *Reader's Digest* shared and supported my intense wish to explore if my maternal family's treasured oral history might possibly be documented back into Africa where all black Americans began.

Nor would this book exist in its fullness without the help of those scores of dedicated librarians and archivists in some fifty-seven different repositories of information on three continents. I found that if a librarian or archivist becomes excited with your own fervour of research, they can turn into sleuths to aid your quests.

I owe a great debt to Paul R. Reynolds, doyen of literary agents – whose client I have the pleasure to be – and to Doubleday Senior Editors Lisa Drew and Ken McCormick, all of whom have patiently shared and salved my frustrations across the years of producing *Roots*.

Finally, I acknowledge immense debt to the griots of Africa – where today it is rightly said that when a griot dies, it is as if a library has burned to the ground. The griots symbolize how all human ancestry goes back to some place, and some time, where there was no writing. Then, the memories and the mouths of ancient elders was the only way that early histories of mankind got passed along . . . for all of us today to know who we are.

1

Early in the spring of 1750, in the village of Juffure, four days up-river from the coast of The Gambia, West Africa, a manchild was born to Omoro and Binta Kinte. Forcing forth from Binta's strong young body, he was as black as she was, flecked and slippery with Binta's blood, and he was bawling. The two wrinkled midwives, old Nyo Boto and the baby's Grandmother Yaisa, saw that it was a boy and laughed with joy. According to the forefathers, a boy first-born presaged the special blessings of Allah not only upon the parents but also upon the parents' families; and there was the prideful knowledge that the name of Kinte would thus be both distinguished and perpetuated.

It was the hour before the first crowing of the cocks, and along with Nyo Boto and Grandma Yaisa's chatterings, the first sound the child heard was the muted, rhythmic *bomp-a-bomp-a-bomp* of wooden pestles as the other women of the village pounded couscous grain in their mortars, preparing the traditional breakfast of porridge that was cooked in earthen pots over a fire built among three rocks.

The thin blue smoke went curling up, pungent and pleasant, over the small dusty village of round mud huts as the nasal wailing of Kajali Demba, the village alimamo, began, calling men to the first of the five daily prayers that had been offered up to Allah for as long as anyone living could remember. Hastening from their beds of bamboo cane and cured hides into their rough cotton tunics, the men of the village filed briskly to the praying place, where the alimamo led the worship: '*Allahu Akbar! Ashadu an lailahailala!*' (God is great! I bear witness that there is only one God!) It was after this, as the men were returning towards their home compounds for breakfast, that Omoro rushed among them, beaming and excited, to tell them of his first-born son. Congratulating him, all of the men echoed the omens of good fortune.

Each man, back in his own hut, accepted a calabash of porridge from his wife. Returning to their kitchen in the rear of the compound, the wives fed next their children, and finally themselves. When they had finished eating, the men took up their short, bent-handled hoes, whose wooden blades had been sheathed with metal by the village blacksmith, and set off for their day's work of preparing the land for farming of the groundnuts and the couscous and cotton that were the primary men's crops, as rice was that of the women, in this hot, lush savanna country of The Gambia.

By ancient custom, for the next seven days, there was but a single task with which Omoro would seriously occupy himself: the selection of a name for his first-born son. It would have to be a name rich with history and with promise, for the people of his tribe – the Mandinkas – believed that a child would develop seven of the characteristics of whomever or whatever he was named for.

On behalf of himself and Binta, during this week of thinking, Omoro visited every household in Juffure, and invited each family to the naming ceremony of the newborn child, traditionally on the eighth day of his life. On that day, like his father and his father's father, this new son would become a member of the tribe.

When the eighth day arrived, the villagers gathered in the early morning before the hut of Omoro and Binta. On their heads, the women of both families brought calabash containers of ceremonial sour milk and sweet munko cakes of pounded rice and honey. Karamo Silla, the jaliba of the village, was there with his tan-tang drums; and the alimamo, and the arafang, Brima Cesay, who would some day be the child's teacher; and also Omoro's two brothers, Janneh and Saloum, who had journeyed from far away to attend the ceremony when the drumtalk news of their nephew's birth had reached them.

As Binta proudly held her new infant, a small patch of his first hair was shaved off, as was always done on this day, and all of the women exclaimed at how well formed the baby was. Then they quieted as the jaliba began to beat his drums. The alimamo said a prayer over the calabashes of sour milk and munko cakes, and as he prayed, each guest touched a calabash brim with his or her right hand, as a gesture of respect for the food. Then the alimamo turned to pray over the infant, entreating Allah to grant him long life, success in bringing credit and pride and many children to his family, to his village, to his tribe – and, finally, the strength and the spirit to deserve and to bring honour to the name he was about to receive.

Omoro then walked out before all of the assembled people of the village. Moving to his wife's side, he lifted up the infant and, as all watched, whispered three times into his son's ear the name he had chosen for him. It was the first time the name had ever been spoken as this child's name, for Omoro's people felt that each human being should be the first to know who he was.

The tan-tang drum resounded again; and now Omoro whispered the name into the ear of Binta, and Binta smiled with pride and

10

pleasure. Then Omoro whispered the name to the arafang, who stood before the villagers.

'The first child of Omoro and Binta Kinte is named *Kunta*!' cried Brima Cesay.

As everyone knew, it was the middle name of the child's late grandfather, Kairaba Kunta Kinte, who had come from his native Mauretania into The Gambia, where he had saved the people of Juffure from famine, married Grandma Yaisa, and then served Juffure honourably till his death as the village's holy man.

One by one, the arafang recited the names of the Mauretanian forefathers of whom the baby's grandfather, old Kairaba Kinte, had often told. The names, which were great and many, went back more than two hundred rains. Then the jaliba pounded on his tan-tang and all of the people exclaimed their admiration and respect at such a distinguished lineage.

Out under the moon and the stars, alone with his son that eighth night, Omoro completed the naming ritual. Carrying little Kunta in his strong arms, he walked to the edge of the village, lifted his baby up with his face to the heavens, and said softly, *'Fend kiling dorong leh warrata ka iteh tee.'* (Behold – the only thing greater than yourself.)

2

It was the planting season, and the first rains were soon to come. On all their farming land, the men of Juffure had piled tall stacks of dry weeds and set them afire so that the light wind would nourish the soil by scattering the ashes. And the women in their rice fields were already planting green shoots in the mud.

While she was recovering from childbirth, Binta's rice plot had been attended by Grandma Yaisa, but now Binta was ready to resume her duties. With Kunta cradled across her back in a cotton sling, she walked with the other women – some of them, including her friend Jankay Touray, carrying their own newborns, along with the bundles they all balanced on their heads – to the dugout canoes on the bank of the village bolong, one of the many tributary canals that came twisting inland from the Gambia River, known as the

Kamby Bolongo. The canoes went skimming down the bolong with five or six women in each one, straining against their short, broad paddles. Each time Binta bent forward to dip and pull, she felt Kunta's warm softness pressing against her back.

The air was heavy with the deep, musky fragrance of the mangroves, and with the perfumes of the other plants and trees that grew thickly on both sides of the bolong. Alarmed by the passing canoes, huge families of baboons, roused from sleep, began bellowing, springing about and shaking palm-tree fronds. Wild pigs grunted and snorted, running to hide themselves among the weeds and bushes. Covering the muddy banks, thousands of pelicans, cranes, egrets, herons, storks, gulls, terns and spoonbills interrupted their breakfast feeding to watch nervously as the canoes glided by. Some of the smaller birds took to the air – ringdoves, skimmers, rails, darters, and kingfishers – circling with shrill cries until the intruders had passed.

As the canoes arrowed through rippling, busy patches of water, schools of minnows would leap up together, perform a silvery dance, and then splash back. Chasing the minnows, sometimes so hungrily that they flopped right into a moving canoe, were large, fierce fish that the women would club with their paddles and stow away for a succulent evening meal. But this morning the minnows swam around them undisturbed.

The twisting bolong took the rowing women around a turn into a wider tributary, and as they came into sight, a great beating of wings filled the air and a vast living carpet of seafowl – hundreds of thousands of them, in every colour of the rainbow – rose and filled the sky. The surface of the water, darkened by the storm of birds and furrowed by their flapping wings, was flecked with feathers as the women paddled on.

As they neared the marshy faros where generations of Juffure women had grown their rice crops, the canoes passed through swarming clouds of mosquitoes and then, one after another, nosed in against a walkway of thickly matted weeds. The weeds bounded and identified each woman's plot, where by now the emerald shoots of young rice stood a hand's height above the water's surface.

Since the size of each woman's plot was decided each year by Juffure's Council of Elders, according to how many mouths each woman had to feed with rice, Binta's plot was still a small one. Balancing herself carefully as she stepped from the canoe with her new baby, Binta took a few steps and then stopped short, looking with surprise and delight at a tiny thatch-roofed bamboo hut on stilts. While she was in labour, Omoro had come here and built it as a shelter for their son. Typical of men, he had said nothing about it.

Nursing the baby, then nestling him inside his shelter, Binta changed into the working clothes she had brought in the bundle on her head, and waded out to work. Bending nearly double in the water, she pulled up by the roots the young weeds that, left alone, would outgrow and choke the rice crop. And whenever Kunta cried, Binta waded out, dripping water, to nurse him again in the shadow of his shelter.

Little Kunta basked thus every day in his mother's tenderness. Back in her hut each evening, after cooking and serving Omoro's dinner, Binta would soften her baby's skin by greasing him from head to toe with shea tree butter, and then – more often than not – she would carry him proudly across the village to the hut of Grandma Yaisa, who would bestow upon the baby still more cluckings and kissings. And both of them would set little Kunta to whimpering in irritation with their repeated pressings of his little head, nose, ears and lips, to shape them correctly.

Sometimes Omoro would take his son away from the women and carry the blanketed bundle to his own hut – husbands always resided separately from their wives – where he would let the child's eyes and fingers explore such attractive objects as the saphie charms at the head of Omoro's bed, placed there to ward off evil spirits. Anything colourful intrigued little Kunta – especially his father's leather huntsman's bag, nearly covered by now with cowrie shells, each for an animal that Omoro had personally brought in as food for the village. And Kunta cooed over the long, curved bow and quiver of arrows hanging nearby. Omoro smiled when a tiny hand reached out and grasped the dark, slender spear whose shaft was polished from so much use. He let Kunta touch everything except the prayer rug, which was sacred to its owner. And alone together in his hut, Omoro would talk to Kunta of the fine and brave deeds his son would do when he grew up.

Finally he would return Kunta to Binta's hut for the next nursing. Wherever he was, Kunta was happy most of the time, and he always fell asleep either with Binta rocking him on her lap or bending over him on her bed, singing softly such a lullaby as,

My smiling child,
Named for a noble ancestor.
Great hunter or warrior
You will be one day,
Which will give your papa pride.
But always I will remember you thus.

However much Binta loved her baby and her husband, she also felt a very real anxiety, for Moslem husbands, by ancient custom, would often select and marry a second wife during that time when their first wives had babies still nursing. As yet Omoro had taken no other wife; and since Binta didn't want him tempted, she felt that the sooner little Kunta was able to walk alone, the better, for that was when the nursing would end.

So Binta was quick to help him as soon as Kunta, at about thirteen moons, tried his first unsteady steps. And before long, he was able to toddle about without an assisting hand. Binta was as relieved as Omoro was proud, and when Kunta cried for his next feeding, Binta gave her son not a breast but a sound spanking and a gourd of cow's milk.

3

Three rains had passed, and it was that lean season when the village's store of grain and other dried foods from the last harvest was almost gone. The men had hunted, but they had returned with only a few small antelopes and gazelle and some clumsy bushfowl, for in this season of burning sun, so many of the savanna's waterholes had dried into mud that the bigger and better game had moved into deep forest – at the very time when the people of Juffure needed all their strength to plant crops for the new harvest. Already, the wives were stretching their staple meals of couscous and rice with the tasteless seeds of bamboo cane and with the bad-tasting dried leaves of the baobab tree. The days of hunger had begun so early that five goats and two bullocks – more than last time – were sacrificed to strengthen everyone's prayers that Allah might spare the village from starvation.

Finally the hot skies clouded, the light breezes became brisk winds and, abruptly as always, the little rains began, falling warmly and gently as the farmers hoed the softened earth into long, straight rows in readiness for the seeds. They knew the planting must be done before the big rains came.

The next few mornings, after breakfast, instead of canoeing to their rice fields, the farmers' wives dressed in the traditional fertility costumes of large fresh leaves, symbolizing the green of growing things, and set out for the furrowed fields of the men. Their voices would be heard rising and falling even before they appeared as they chanted ancestral prayers that the couscous and groundnuts and other seeds in the earthen bowls balanced on their heads would take strong roots and grow.

With their bare feet moving in step, the line of women walked and sang three times around every farmer's field. Then they separated, and each woman fell in behind a farmer as he moved along each row, punching a hole in the earth every few inches with his big toe. Into each hole a woman dropped a seed, covered it over with her own big toe, and then moved on. The women worked even harder than the men, for they not only had to help their husbands but also tend both the rice fields and the vegetable gardens they cultivated near their kitchens.

While Binta planted her onions, yams, gourds, cassava and bitter tomatoes, little Kunta spent his days romping under the watchful eyes of the several old grandmothers who took care of all the children of Juffure who belonged to the first kafo, which included those under five rains in age. The boys and girls alike scampered about as naked as young animals – some of them just beginning to say their first words. All, like Kunta, were growing fast, laughing and squealing as they ran after each other around the giant trunk of the village baobab, played hide-and-seek, and scattered the dogs and chickens into masses of fur and feathers.

But all the children – even those as small as Kunta – would quickly scramble to sit still and quiet when the telling of a story was promised by one of the old grandmothers. Though unable yet to understand many of the words, Kunta would watch with wide eyes as the old women acted out their stories with such gestures and noises that they really seemed to be happening.

As little as he was, Kunta was already familiar with some of the stories that his own Grandma Yaisa had told to him alone when he had been visiting in her hut. But along with his first-kafo playmates, he felt that the best story-teller of all was the beloved, mysterious, and peculiar old Nyo Boto. Bald-headed, deeply wrinkled, as black as the bottom of a cooking pot, with her long lemongrass-root chewstick sticking out like an insect's feeler between the few teeth she had left – which were deep orange from the countless kola nuts she had gnawed on – old Nyo Boto would settle herself with much grunting on her low stool. Though she acted gruff, the children knew that she loved them as if they were her own, which she claimed they all were.

Surrounded by them, she would growl, 'Let me tell a story . . .'

'Please!' the children would chorus, wriggling in anticipation.

And she would begin in the way that all Mandinka story-tellers began: 'At this certain time, in this certain village, lived this certain person.' It was a small boy, she said, of about their rains, who walked to the riverbank one day and found a crocodile trapped in a net.

'Help me!' the crocodile cried out.

'You'll kill me!' cried the boy.

'No! Come nearer!' said the crocodile.

So the boy went up to the crocodile – and instantly was seized by the teeth in that long mouth.

'Is this how you repay my goodness – with badness?' cried the boy.

'Of course,' said the crocodile out of the corner of his mouth. 'That is the way of the world.'

The boy refused to believe that, so the crocodile agreed not to swallow him without getting an opinion from the first three witnesses to pass by. First was an old donkey.

When the boy asked his opinion, the donkey said, 'Now that I'm old and can no longer work, my master has driven me out for the leopards to get me!'

'See?' said the crocodile. Next to pass by was an old horse, who had the same opinion.

'See?' said the crocodile. Then along came a plump rabbit who said, 'Well, I can't give a good opinion without seeing this matter as it happened from the beginning.'

Grumbling, the crocodile opened his mouth to tell him – and the boy jumped out to safety on the riverbank.

'Do you like crocodile meat?' asked the rabbit. The boy said yes. 'And do your parents?' He said yes again. 'Then here is a crocodile ready for the pot.'

The boy ran off and returned with the men of the village, who helped him to kill the crocodile. But they brought with them a wuolo dog, which chased and caught and killed the rabbit, too.

'So the crocodile was right,' said Nyo Boto. 'It *is* the way of the world that goodness is often repaid with badness. This is what I have told you as a story.'

'May you be blessed, have strength and prosper!' said the children gratefully.

Then the other grandmothers would pass among the children with bowls of freshly toasted beetles and grasshoppers. These would have been only tasty tidbits at another time of year, but now, on the eve of the big rains, with the hungry season already beginning, the toasted insects had to serve as a noon meal, for only a few handfuls of couscous and rice remained in most families' storehouses.

4

Fresh, brief showers fell almost every morning now, and between the showers Kunta and his playmates would dash about excitedly outside. 'Mine! Mine!' they would shout at the pretty rainbows that would arc down to the earth, seeming never very far away. But the showers also brought swarms of flying insects whose vicious stinging and biting soon drove the children back indoors.

Then suddenly, late one night, the big rains began, and the people huddled inside their cold huts listening to the water pound on their thatch roofs, watching the lightning flash and comforting their children as the frightening thunder rumbled through the night. Between cloudbursts, they heard only the barking of the jackals, the howling of the hyenas, and the croaking of the frogs.

The rains came again the next night, and the next, and the next – and only at night – flooding the lowlands near the river, turning their fields into a swamp and their village into a mudhole. Yet each morning before breakfast, all the farmers struggled through the mud to Juffure's little mosque and implored Allah to send still *more* rain, for life itself depended upon enough water to soak deeply into the earth before the hot suns arrived, which would wither those crops whose roots could not find enough water to survive.

In the damp nursery hut, dimly lighted and poorly heated by the burning dry sticks and cattle dung patties in the earthen floor's shallow firehole, old Nyo Boto told Kunta and the other children of the terrible time she remembered when there were not enough big rains. No matter how bad anything was, Nyo Boto would always remember a time when it was worse. After two days of big rain, she told them, the burning suns had come. Although the people prayed very hard to Allah, and danced the ancestral rain dance, and sacrificed two goats and a bullock every day, still everything growing in the ground

17

began to parch and die. Even the forest's waterholes dried up, said Nyo Boto, and first wild fowl, and then the forest's animals, sick from thirst, began to appear at the village well. In crystal-clear skies each night, thousands of bright stars shone, and a cold wind blew, and more and more people grew ill. Clearly, evil spirits were abroad in Juffure.

Those who were able continued their prayers and their dances, and finally the last goat and bullock had been sacrificed. It was as if Allah had turned His back on Juffure. Some – the old and the weak and the sick – began to die. Others left town, seeking another village to beg someone who had food to accept them as slaves, just to get something into their bellies, and those who stayed behind lost their spirit and lay down in their huts. It was then, said Nyo Boto, that Allah had guided the steps of marabout Kairaba Kunta Kinte into the starving village of Juffure. Seeing the people's plight, he kneeled down and prayed to Allah – almost without sleep and taking only a few sips of water as nourishment – for the next five days. And on the evening of the fifth day came a great rain, which fell like a flood, and saved Juffure.

When she finished her story, the other children looked with new respect at Kunta, who bore the name of that distinguished grandfather, husband of Kunta's Grandma Yaisa. Even before now, Kunta had seen how the parents of the other children acted towards Yaisa, and he had sensed that she was an important woman, just as old Nyo Boto surely was.

The big rains continued to fall every night until Kunta and the other children began to see grown-ups wading across the village in mud up to their ankles and even to their knees, and even using canoes to paddle from place to place. Kunta had heard Binta tell Omoro that the rice fields were flooded in the bolong's high waters. Cold and hungry, the children's fathers sacrificed precious goats and bullocks to Allah almost every day, patched leaking roofs, shored up sagging huts – and prayed that their disappearing stock of rice and couscous would last until the harvest.

But Kunta and the others, being yet little children, paid less attention to the hunger pangs in their bellies than to playing in the mud, wrestling each other and sliding on their naked bottoms. Yet in their longing to see the sun again, they would wave up at the slate-coloured sky and shout – as they had seen their parents do – 'Shine, sun, and I will kill you a goat!'

The life-giving rain had made every growing thing fresh and luxuriant. Birds sang everywhere. The trees and plants were explosions of fragrant blossoms. The reddish-brown, clinging mud underfoot was newly carpeted each morning, with the bright-coloured petals and green leaves beaten loose by the rain of the night before. But amid all the lushness of nature, sickness spread steadily among the people of Juffure, for none of the richly growing crops was ripe enough to eat. The adults and children alike would stare hungrily at the thousands of plump mangoes and monkey apples hanging heavy on the trees, but the green fruits were as hard as rocks, and those who bit into them fell ill and vomited.

'Nothing but skin and bones!' Grandma Yaisa would exclaim, making a loud clicking noise with her tongue every time she saw Kunta. But in fact his grandma was almost as thin as he; for every storehouse in Juffure was now completely empty. What few of the village's cattle and goats and chickens had not been eaten or sacrificed had to be kept alive – and fed – if there was to be a next year's crop of kids and calves and baby chicks. So the people began to eat rodents, roots and leaves foraged from in and around the village on searchings that began when the sun rose and ended when it set.

If the men had gone to the forests to hunt wild game, as they frequently did at other times of the year, they wouldn't have had the strength to drag it back to the village. Tribal taboos forbade the Mandinkas to eat the abounding monkeys and baboons; nor would they touch the many hens' eggs that lay about, or the millions of big green bullfrogs that Mandinkas regarded as poisonous. And as devout Moslems, they would rather have died than eat the flesh of the wild pigs that often came rooting in herds right through the village.

For ages, families of cranes had nested in the topmost branches of the village's silk-cotton tree, and when the young hatched, the big cranes shuttled back and forth bringing fish, which they had just caught in the bolong, to feed their babies. Watching for the right moment, the grandmothers and the children would rush beneath the tree, whooping and hurling small sticks and stones upward at the nest. And often, in the noise and confusion, a young crane's gaping mouth would miss the fish, and the fish would miss the nest and come slapping down among the tall tree's thick foliage to the ground. The children would struggle over the prize, and someone's family would have a feast for dinner. If one of the stones thrown up by the children happened to hit a gawky, pin-feathered young crane, it would sometimes fall from the high nest along with the fish, killing or injuring itself in the crash against the ground; and that night a few families would have crane soup. But such meals were rare.

By the late evening, each family would meet back at their hut, bringing whatever each individual had found – perhaps even a mole or a handful of large grubworms, if they were lucky – for that night's pot of soup, heavily peppered and spiced to improve the taste. But such fare filled their bellies without bringing nourishment. And so it was that the people of Juffure began to die.

5

More and more often now, the high-pitched howling of a woman would be heard throughout the village. The fortunate were those babies and toddlers yet too young to understand, for even Kunta was old enough to know that the howling meant a loved one had just died. In the afternoons, usually, some sick farmer who had been out cutting weeds in his field would be carried back to the village on a bullock's hide, lying very still.

And disease had begun to swell the legs of some adults. Yet others developed fevers with heavy perspiration and trembling chills. And among all the children, small areas on their arms or legs would puff up, rapidly grow larger and painfully sore; then the puffed areas would split, leaking a pinkish fluid that soon became a full, yellow, stinking pus that drew buzzing flies

The hurting of the big open sore on Kunta's leg made him stumble while trying to run one day. Falling hard, he was picked up by his playmates, stunned and yelling, with his forehead bleeding. Since Binta and Omoro were away farming, they rushed him to the hut of Grandma Yaisa, who for a number of days now had not appeared in the nursery hut.

She looked very weak, her black face gaunt and drawn, and she was sweating under her bullock hide on her bamboo pallet. But when she saw Kunta, she sprang up to wipe his bleeding forehead. Embracing him tightly, she ordered the other children to run and bring her some kelelalu ants. When they returned, Grandma Yaisa tightly pressed together the skin's split edges, then pressed one struggling driver ant after another against the wound. As each ant angrily clamped its strong pincers into the flesh on each side of the cut, she

20

deftly snapped off its body, leaving the head in place, until the wound was stitched together.

Dismissing the other children, she told Kunta to lie down and rest alongside her on the bed. He lay and listened to her laboured breathing as she remained silent for some time. Then Grandma Yaisa's hand gestured towards a pile of books on the shelf beside her bed. Speaking slowly and softly, she told Kunta more about his grandfather, whose books she said those were.

In his native country of Mauretania, Kairaba Kunta Kinte had thirty-five rains of age when his teacher, a master marabout, gave him the blessing that made him a holy man, said Grandma Yaisa. Kunta's grandfather had followed a family tradition of holy men that dated back many hundreds of rains into Old Mali. As a man of the fourth kafo, he had begged the old marabout to accept him as a student, and for the next fifteen rains had travelled with his party of wives, slaves, students, cattle and goats as he pilgrimaged from village to village in the service of Allah and his subjects. Over dusty foot trails and muddy creeks, under hot suns and cold rains, through green valleys and windy wastelands, said Grandma Yaisa, they had trekked southwards from Mauretania.

Upon receiving his ordination as a holy man, Kairaba Kunta Kinte had himself wandered for many moons alone, among places in Old Mali such as Keyla, Djeela, Kangaba and Timbuktu, humbly prostrating himself before very great old holy men and imploring their blessings for his success, which they all freely gave. And Allah then guided the young holy man's footsteps in a southerly direction, finally to The Gambia, where he stopped first in the village of Pakali N'Ding.

In a short while, the people of this village knew, by the quick results from his prayers, that this young holy man had upon him Allah's special favour. Talking drums spread the news, and soon other villages tried to lure him away, sending messengers with offers of prime maidens for wives, and slaves and cattle and goats. And before long he did move, this time to the village of Jiffarong, but only because Allah had called him there, for the people of Jiffarong had little to offer him but their gratitude for his prayers. It was here that he heard of the village of Juffure, where people were sick and dying for lack of a big rain. And so at last he came to Juffure, said Grandma Yaisa, where for five days, ceaselessly, he had prayed until Allah sent down the big rain that saved the village.

Learning of Kunta's grandfather's great deed, the King of Barra himself, who ruled this part of The Gambia, personally presented a choice virgin for the young holy man's first wife, and her name was Sireng. By Sireng, Kairaba Kunta Kinte begot two sons – and he named them Janneh and Saloum.

By now, Grandma Yaisa had sat up on her bamboo pallet. 'It was then,' she said with shining eyes, 'that he saw Yaisa, dancing the seoruba! My age was fifteen rains!' She smiled widely, showing her toothless gums. 'He needed no king to choose his next wife!' She looked at Kunta. 'It was from my belly that he begot your papa Omoro.'

That night, back in his mother's hut, Kunta lay awake for a long time, thinking of the things Grandma Yaisa had told him. Many times, Kunta had heard about the grandfather holy man whose prayers had saved the village, and whom later Allah had taken back. But Kunta had never truly understood until now that this man was his father's father, that Omoro had known him as he knew Omoro, that Grandma Yaisa was Omoro's mother as Binta was his own. Some day, he too would find a woman such as Binta to bear him a son of his own. And that son, in turn . . .

Turning over and closing his eyes, Kunta followed these deep thoughts slowly into sleep.

6

Just before sundown for the next few days, after returning from the rice field, Binta would send Kunta to the village well for a calabash of fresh water, which she would use to boil a soup from whatever scraps she could find. Then she and Kunta would take some of the soup across the village to Grandma Yaisa. Binta moved more slowly than usual, it seemed to Kunta, and he noticed that her belly was very big and heavy.

While Grandma Yaisa protested weakly that she would soon feel well again, Binta would clean up the hut and arrange things. And they would leave Grandma Yaisa propped up on her bed, eating a bowl of soup along with some of Binta's hungry-season bread, made from the yellow powder that covered the dry black beans of the wild locust tree.

Then one night, Kunta awakened to find himself being shaken roughly by his father. Binta was making low, moaning sounds on her bed, and also within the hut, moving quickly about, were Nyo Boto and Binta's friend Jankay Touray. Omoro hurried across the village with Kunta, who, wondering what all this was about, soon drifted back to sleep on his father's bed.

In the morning, Omoro again awakened Kunta and said, 'You have a new brother.' Scrambling sleepily onto his knees and rubbing his eyes, Kunta thought it must be something very special to so please his usually stern father. In the afternoon, Kunta was with his kafo mates, looking for things to eat, when Nyo Boto called him and took him to see Binta. Looking very tired, she sat on the edge of her bed gently caressing the baby in her lap. Kunta stood a moment studying the little wrinkly black thing; then he looked at the two women smiling at it, and he noticed that the familiar bigness of Binta's stomach was suddenly gone. Going back outside without a word, Kunta stood for a long moment and then, instead of rejoining his friends, went off to sit by himself behind his father's hut and think about what he had seen.

Kunta continued sleeping in Omoro's hut for the next seven nights – not that anyone seemed to notice or care, in their concern for the new baby. He was beginning to think that his mother didn't want him any more – or his father, either – until, on the evening of the eighth day, Omoro called him before his mother's hut, along with everyone else in Juffure who was physically able, to hear the new baby given his chosen name, which was Lamin.

That night Kunta slept peacefully and well – back in his own bed beside his mother and his new brother. But within a few days, as soon as her strength had returned, Binta began to take the baby, after cooking and serving something for Omoro's and Kunta's breakfast, and spent most of each day in the hut of Grandma Yaisa. From the worried expressions that both Binta and Omoro wore, Kunta knew that Grandma Yaisa was very sick.

Late one afternoon, a few days later, he and his kafo mates were out picking mangoes, which had finally ripened. Bruising the tough, orange-yellow skin against the nearest rock, they would bite open one plump end to squeeze and suck out the soft sweet flesh within. They were collecting basketfuls of monkey apples and wild cashew nuts when Kunta suddenly heard the howling of a familiar voice from the direction of his grandma's hut. A chill shot through him, for it was the voice of his mother, raised in the death wail that he had heard so often in recent weeks. Other women immediately joined in a keening cry that soon spread all the way across the village. Kunta ran blindly towards his grandmother's hut.

Amid the milling confusion, Kunta saw an anguished Omoro and a bitterly weeping old Nyo Boto. Within moments, the tobalo drum was being beaten and the jaliba was loudly crying out the good deeds of Grandma Yaisa's long life in Juffure. Numb with shock, Kunta stood watching blankly as the young, unmarried women of the village beat up dust from the ground with wide fans of plaited grass, as was the custom on the occasion of a death. No one seemed to notice Kunta.

As Binta and Nyo Boto and two other shrieking women entered the hut, the crowd outside fell to their knees and bowed their heads. Kunta burst suddenly into tears, as much in fear as in grief. Soon men came with a large, freshly split log and set it down in front of the hut. Kunta watched as the women brought out and laid on the log's flat surface the body of his grandmother, enclosed from her neck to her feet in a white cotton winding cloth.

Through his tears, Kunta saw the mourners walk seven circles around Yaisa, praying and chanting as the alimamo wailed that she was journeying to spend eternity with Allah and her ancestors. To give her strength for that journey, young unmarried men tenderly placed cattle horns filled with fresh ashes all around her body.

After most of the mourners had filed away, Nyo Boto and other old women took up posts nearby, huddling and weeping and squeezing their heads with their hands. Soon, young women brought the biggest ciboa leaves that could be found, to protect the old women's heads from rain through their vigil. And as the old women sat, the village drums talked about Grandma Yaisa far into the night.

In the misty morning, according to the custom of the forefathers, only the men of Juffure – those who were able to walk – joined the procession to the burying place, not far past the village, where otherwise none would go, out of the Mandinkas' fearful respect for the spirits of their ancestors. Behind the men who bore Grandma Yaisa on the log came Omoro, carrying the infant Lamin and holding the hand of little Kunta, who was too frightened to cry. And behind them came the other men of the village. The stiff, white-wrapped body was lowered into the freshly dug hole, and over her went a thick woven cane mat. Next were thorn bushes, to keep out the digging hyenas, and the rest of the hole was packed tight with stones and a mound of fresh earth.

Afterwards, for many days, Kunta hardly ate or slept, and he would not go anywhere with his kafo mates. So grieved was he that Omoro, one evening, took him to his own hut, and there beside his bed, speaking to his son more softly and gently than he ever had before, told him something that helped to ease his grief.

He said that three groups of people lived in every village. First were those you could see – walking around, eating, sleeping and working. Second were the ancestors, whom Grandma Yaisa had now joined.

'And the third people – who are they?' asked Kunta.

'The third people,' said Omoro, 'are those waiting to be born.'

7

The rains had ended, and between the bright blue sky and the damp earth, the air was heavy with the fragrance of lush wild blooms and fruits. The early mornings echoed with the sound of the women's mortars pounding millet and couscous and groundnuts – not from the main harvest, but from those early-growing seeds that the past year's harvest had left living in the soil. The men hunted, bringing back fine, plump antelope, and after passing out the meat, they scraped and cured the hides. And the women busily collected the ripened reddish mangkano berries, shaking the bushes over cloths spread beneath, then drying the berries in the sun before pounding them to separate the delicious futo flour from the seeds. Nothing was wasted. Soaked and boiled with pounded millet, the seeds were cooked into a sweetish breakfast gruel that Kunta and everyone else welcomed as a seasonal change of diet from their usual morning meal of couscous porridge.

As food became more plentiful each day, new life flowed into Juffure in ways that could be seen and heard. The men began to walk more briskly to and from their farms, pridefully inspecting their bountiful crops, which would soon be ready for harvesting. With the flooded river now subsiding rapidly, the women were rowing daily to the faro and pulling out the last of the weeds from among the tall, green rows of rice.

And the village rang again with the yelling and laughing of the children back at play after the long hungry season. Bellies now filled with nourishing food, sores dried into scabs and falling away, they dashed and frolicked about as if possessed. One day they would capture some big scarab dung beetles, line them up for a race, and cheer the fastest to run outside a circle drawn in the dirt with a stick. Another day, Kunta and Sitafa Silla, his special friend, who lived in the hut next to Binta's, would raid a tall earth mound to dig up the blind, wingless termites that lived inside, and watch them pour out by the thousands and scurry frantically to get away.

Sometimes the boys would rout out little ground squirrels and chase them into the bush. And they loved nothing better than to hurl stones and shouts at passing schools of small, brown, long-tailed monkeys, some of which would throw a stone back before swinging up to join their screeching brothers in the topmost branches of a tree. And every day the boys would wrestle, grabbing each other, sprawling down, grunting, scrambling and springing up to start all over again, each one dreaming of the day when he might become one of Juffure's champion wrestlers and be chosen to wage mighty battles with the champions of other villages during the harvest festivals.

Adults passing anywhere near the children would solemnly pretend not to see nor hear as Sitafa, Kunta, and the rest of their kafo growled and roared like lions, trumpeted like elephants, and grunted like wild pigs, or as the girls — cooking and tending their dolls and beating their couscous — played mothers and wives among themselves. But however hard they were playing, the children never failed to pay every adult the respect their mothers had taught them to show always towards their elders. Politely looking the adults in the eyes, the children would ask, 'Kerabe?' (Do you have peace?) And the adults would reply, 'Kera dorong.' (Peace only.) And if an adult offered his hand, each child in turn would clasp it with both hands, then stand with palms folded over his chest until that adult passed by.

Kunta's home-training had been so strict that, it seemed to him, his every move drew Binta's irritated finger-snapping – if, indeed, he wasn't grabbed and soundly whipped. When he was eating, he would get a cuff on the head if Binta caught his eyes on anything except his own food. And unless he washed off every bit of dirt when he came into the hut from a hard day's play, Binta would snatch up her scratchy sponge of dried plant stems and her bar of homemade soap and make Kunta think she was going to scrape off his very hide.

For him ever to stare at her, or at his father, or at any other adult, would earn him a slap as quickly as when he committed the equally serious offence of interrupting the conversation of any grown-up.

26

And for him ever to speak anything but truth would have been unthinkable. Since there never seemed any reason for him to lie, he never did.

Though Binta didn't seem to think so, Kunta tried his best to be a good boy, and soon began to practise his home-training lessons with the other children. When disagreements occurred among them, as they often did – sometimes fanning into exchanges of harsh words and finger-snapping – Kunta would always turn and walk away, thus displaying the dignity and self-command that his mother had taught him were the proudest traits of the Mandinka tribe.

But almost every night, Kunta got spanked for doing something bad to his baby brother – usually for frightening him by snarling fiercely, or by dropping on all fours like a baboon, rolling his eyes, and stomping his fists like forepaws upon the ground. 'I will bring the toubob!' Binta would yell at Kunta when he had tried her patience to the breaking point, scaring Kunta most thoroughly, for the old grandmothers spoke often of the hairy, red-faced, strange-looking white men whose big canoes stole people away from their homes.

8

Though Kunta and his mates were tired and hungry from play by the time of each day's setting sun, they would still race one another to climb small trees and point at the sinking crimson ball. 'He will be even lovelier tomorrow!' they would shout. And even Juffure's adults ate dinner quickly so that they might congregate outside in the deepening dusk to shout and clap and pound on drums at the rising of the crescent moon, symbolic of Allah.

But when clouds shrouded that new moon, as they did this night, the people dispersed, alarmed, and the men entered the mosque to pray for forgiveness, since a shrouded new moon meant that the heavenly spirits were displeased with the people of Juffure. After praying, the men led their frightened families to the baobab, where already on this night the jaliba squatted by a small fire, heating to its utmost tautness the goatskin head of his talking drum.

Rubbing at his eyes, which smarted from the smoke of the fire,

Kunta remembered the times that drums talking at night from different villages had troubled his sleep. Awakening, he would lie there, listening hard; the sounds and rhythms were so like those of speech that he would finally understand some of the words, telling of a famine or a plague, or of the raiding and burning of some village, with its people killed or stolen away.

Hanging on a branch of the baobab, beside the jaliba, was a goatskin inscribed with the marks that talk, written there in Arabic by the arafang. In the flickering firelight, Kunta watched as the jaliba began to beat the knobby elbows of his crooked sticks very rapidly and sharply against different spots on the drumhead. It was an urgent message for the nearest magic man to come to Juffure and drive out evil spirits.

Not daring to look up at the moon, the people hurried home and fearfully went to bed. But at intervals through the night, the talk of distant drums echoed the appeal of Juffure for a magic man in other villages as well. Shivering beneath his cowskin, Kunta guessed that their new moon was shrouded, too.

The next day, the men of Omoro's age had to help the younger men of the village to guard their nearly ripened fields against the seasonal plague of hungry baboons and birds. The second-kafo boys were told to be especially vigilant as they grazed the goats, and the mothers and grandmothers hovered closer than they normally would over the toddlers and the babies. The first kafo's biggest children, those the size of Kunta and Sitafa, were instructed to play a little way out past the village's tall fence, where they could keep a sharp lookout for any stranger approaching the travellers' tree, not far distant. They did, but none came that day.

He appeared on the second morning – a very old man, walking with the help of a wooden staff and bearing a large bundle on his bald head. Spotting him, the children raced shouting back through the village gate. Leaping up, old Nyo Boto hobbled over and began to beat on the big tobalo drum that brought the men rushing back to the village from their fields a moment before the magic man reached the gate and entered Juffure.

As the villagers gathered around him, he walked over to the baobab and set down his bundle carefully on the ground. Abruptly squatting, he then shook from a wrinkled goatskin bag a heap of dried objects – a small snake, a hyena's jawbone, a monkey's teeth, a pelican's wingbone, various fowls' feet, and strange roots. Glancing about, he gestured impatiently for the hushed crowd to give him more room; and the people moved back as he began to quiver all over – clearly being attacked by Juffure's evil spirits.

The magic man's body writhed, his face contorted, his eyes rolled wildly, as his trembling hands struggled to force his resisting wand into contact with the heap of mysterious objects. When the wand's tip, with a supreme effort, finally touched, he fell over backwards and lay as if struck by lightning. The people gasped. But then he slowly began to revive. The evil spirits had been driven out. As he struggled weakly to his knees, Juffure's adults – exhausted but relieved – went running off to their huts and soon returned with gifts to press upon him. The magic man added these to his bundle, which was already large and heavy with gifts from previous villages, and soon he was on his way to answer the next call. In his mercy, Allah had seen fit to spare Juffure once again.

9

Twelve moons had passed, and with the big rains ended once again, The Gambia's season for travellers had begun. Along the network of walking paths between its villages came enough visitors – passing by or stopping off in Juffure – to keep Kunta and his playmates on the lookout almost every day. After alerting the village when a stranger appeared, they would rush back out to meet each visitor as he approached the travellers' tree. Trooping boldly alongside him, they would chatter away inquisitively as their sharp eyes hunted for any signs of his mission or profession. If they found any, they would abruptly abandon the visitor and race back ahead to tell the grownups in that day's hospitality hut. In accordance with ancient tradition, a different family in each village would be chosen every day to offer food and shelter to arriving visitors at no cost for as long as they wished to stay before continuing their journey.

Having been entrusted with the responsibility of serving as the village lookouts, Kunta, Sitafa, and their kafo mates began to feel and act older than their rains. Now after breakfast each morning, they would gather by the arafang's schoolyard and kneel quietly to listen as he taught the older boys – those of the second kafo, just beyond Kunta's age, five to nine rains old – how to read their Koranic verses and to write with grass-quill pens dipped in the black ink of bitter-orange juice mixed with powdered crust from the bottom of cooking pots.

When the schoolboys finished their lessons and ran off – with the tails of their cotton dundikos flapping behind them – to herd the village's goats out into the brushlands for the day's grazing, Kunta and his mates tried to act very unconcerned, but the truth was that they envied the older boys' long shirts as much as they did their important jobs. Though he said nothing, Kunta was not alone in feeling that he was too grown up to be treated like a child and made to go naked any longer. They avoided suckling babies like Lamin as if they were diseased, and the toddlers they regarded as even more unworthy of notice, unless it was to give them a good whack when no adults were watching. Shunning even the attentions of the old grandmothers who had taken care of them for as long as they could remember, Kunta, Sitafa, and the others began to hang around grownups of their parents' age in hopes of being seen underfoot and perhaps sent off on an errand.

It was just before the harvest came that Omoro told Kunta very casually, one night after dinner, that he wanted him up early the next day to help guard the crops. Kunta was so excited he could hardly sleep. After gulping down his breakfast in the morning, he almost burst with joy when Omoro handed him the hoe to carry when they set out for the fields. Kunta and his mates fairly flew up and down the ripe rows, yelling and waving sticks at the wild pigs and baboons that came grunting from the brush to root or snatch up groundnuts. With dirt clods and shouts, they routed whistling flocks of blackbirds as they wheeled low over the couscous, for the grandmothers' stories had told of ripened fields ruined as quickly by hungry birds as by any animal. Collecting the handfuls of couscous and groundnuts that their fathers had cut or pulled up to test for ripeness, and carrying gourds of cool water for the men to drink, they worked all through the day with a swiftness equalled only by their pride.

Six days later, Allah decreed that the harvest should begin. After the dawn's suba prayer, the farmers and their sons – some chosen few carrying small tan-tang and souraba drums – went out to the fields and waited with heads cocked, listening. Finally, the village's great tobalo drum boomed and the farmers leaped to the harvesting. As the jaliba and the other drummers walked among them, beating out a rhythm to match their movements, everyone began to sing. In exhilaration now and then, a farmer would fling his hoe, whirling up on one drumbeat and catch it on the next.

Kunta's kafo sweated alongside their fathers, shaking the groundnut bushes free of dirt. Halfway through the morning came the first rest – and then, at midday, happy shouts of relief as the women and girls arrived with lunch. Walking in single file, also singing harvest songs, they took the pots from their heads, ladled the contents into calabashes, and served them to the drummers and harvesters, who ate and then napped until the tobalo sounded once again.

Piles of the harvest dotted the fields at the end of that first day. Streaming sweat and mud, the farmers trudged wearily to the nearest stream, where they took off their clothes and leaped into the water, laughing and splashing to cool and clean themselves. Then they headed home, swatting at the biting flies that buzzed around their glistening bodies. The closer they came to the smoke that drifted towards them from the women's kitchens, the more tantalizing were the smells of the roasted meats that would be served three times daily for however long it took to finish the harvest.

After stuffing himself that night, Kunta noticed – as he had for several nights – that his mother was sewing something. She said nothing about it, nor did Kunta ask. But the next morning, as he picked up his hoe and began to walk out the door, she looked at him and said gruffly, 'Why don't you put on your clothes?'

Kunta jerked around. There, hanging from a peg, was a brand-new dundiko. Struggling to conceal his excitement, he matter-of-factly put it on and sauntered out the door – where he burst into a run. Others of his kafo were already outside – all of them, like him, dressed for the first time in their lives, all of them leaping, shouting, and laughing because their nakedness was covered at last. They were now officially of the second kafo. They were becoming men.

10

By the time Kunta sauntered back into his mother's hut that night, he had made sure that everyone in Juffure had seen him in his dundiko. Though he hadn't stopped working all day, he wasn't a bit tired, and he knew he'd never be able to go to sleep at his regular bedtime. Perhaps now that he was a grown-up, Binta would let him stay up later. But soon after Lamin was asleep, the same as always, she sent him to bed – with a reminder to hang up his dundiko.

As he turned to go, sulking as conspicuously as he thought he could get away with, Binta called him back – probably to reprimand him for sulking, Kunta thought, or maybe she'd taken pity on him and changed her mind. 'Your Fa wants to see you in the morning,' she said casually. Kunta knew better than to ask why, so he just said, 'Yes, Mama,' and wished her goodnight. It was just as well he wasn't tired, because he couldn't sleep now anyway, lying under his cowhide coverlet wondering what he had done now that was wrong, as it seemed he did so often. But racking his brain, he couldn't think of a single thing, especially nothing so bad that Binta herself wouldn't have whacked him for it, since a father would involve himself only with something pretty terrible. Finally he gave up worrying and drifted off to sleep.

At breakfast the next morning, Kunta was so subdued that he almost forgot the joy of his dundiko, until naked little Lamin happened to brush up against it. Kunta's hand jerked up to shove him away, but a flashing look from Binta prevented that. After eating, Kunta hung around for a while hoping that something more might be said by Binta, but when she acted as if she hadn't even told him anything, he reluctantly left the hut and made his way with slow steps to Omoro's hut, where he stood outside with folded hands.

When Omoro emerged and silently handed his son a small new slingshot, Kunta's breath all but stopped. He stood looking down at it, then up at his father, not knowing what to say. 'This is yours as one of the second kafo. Be sure you don't shoot the wrong things, and that you hit what you shoot at.'

Kunta just said, 'Yes, Fa,' still tongue-tied beyond that.

'Also, as you are now second kafo,' Omoro went on, 'it means you will begin tending goats and going to school. You go goatherding today with Toumani Touray. He and the other older boys will teach you. Heed them well. And tomorrow morning you will go to the schoolyard.' Omoro went back into his hut, and Kunta dashed away to the goat pens, where he found his friend Sitafa and the rest of his kafo, all in their new dundikos and clutching their new slingshots – uncles or older brothers having made them for boys whose fathers were dead.

The older boys were opening the pens and bleating goats were bounding forth, hungry for the day's grazing. Seeing Toumani, who was the first son of the couple who were Omoro's and Binta's best friends, Kunta tried to get near him, but Toumani and his mates were all herding the goats to bump into the smaller boys, who were trying to scramble out of the way. But soon the laughing older boys and the wuolo dogs had the goats hurrying down the dusty path with Kunta's kafo running uncertainly behind, clutching their slingshots and trying to brush the dirtied spots off their dundikos.

As familiar with goats as Kunta was, he had never realized how fast they ran. Except for a few walks with his father, he had never been so far beyond the village as the goats were leading them – to a wide grazing area of low brush and grass with the forest on one side and the fields of village farmers on the other. The older boys each nonchalantly set their own herds to grazing in separate grassy spots, while the wuolo dogs walked about or lay down near the goats.

Toumani finally decided to take notice of Kunta tagging along behind him, but he acted as if the smaller boy was some kind of insect. 'Do you know the value of a goat?' he asked, and before Kunta could admit he wasn't sure, he said, 'Well, if you lose one, your father will let you know!' And Toumani launched into a lecture of warnings about goatherding. Foremost was that if any boy's inattention or laziness let any goat stray away from its herd, no end of horrible things could happen. Pointing towards the forest, Toumani said that, for one thing, living just over there, and often creeping on their bellies through the high grass, were lions and panthers, which, with but a single spring from the grass, could tear a goat apart. 'But if a boy is close enough,' said Toumani, 'he is tastier than a goat!'

Noting Kunta's wide eyes with satisfaction, Toumani went on: Even a worse danger than lions and panthers were toubob and their black slatee helpers, who would crawl through the tall grass to grab people and take them off to a distant place where they were eaten. In his own five rains of goatherding, he said, nine boys from Juffure had been taken, and many more from neighbouring villages. Kunta hadn't known any of the boys who had been lost from Juffure, but he remembered being so scared when he heard about them that for a few days he wouldn't venture more than a stone's throw from his mother's hut.

'But you're not safe even inside the village gates,' said Toumani, seeming to read his thoughts. A man he knew from Juffure, he told Kunta, deprived of everything he owned when a pride of lions killed his entire herd of goats, had been caught with toubob money soon after the disappearance of two third-kafo boys from their own huts one night. He claimed that he had found the money in the forest, but the day before his trial by the Council of Elders, he himself had disappeared. 'You would have been too young to remember this,' said Toumani. 'But such things still happen. So never get out of sight of somebody you trust. And when you're out here with your goats, never let them go where you might have to chase them into deep bush, or your family may never see you again.'

As Kunta stood quaking with fear, Toumani added that even if a big cat or a toubob didn't get him, he could still get into serious trouble if a goat got away from the herd, because a boy could never catch a dodging goat once it got onto someone's nearby farm of couscous and groundnuts. And once the boy and his dog were both gone after it, the remaining flock might start running after the strayed one, and hungry goats could ruin a farmer's field quicker even than baboons, antelopes, or wild pigs.

By noontime, when Toumani shared the lunch his mother had packed for him and Kunta, the entire new second kafo had gained a far greater respect for the goats they had been around all of their lives. After eating, some of Toumani's kafo lounged under small trees nearby, and the rest walked around shooting birds with their students' untried slingshots. While Kunta and his mates struggled to look after the goats, the older boys yelled out cautions and insults and held their sides with laughter at the younger boys' frantic shoutings and dashings towards any goat that as much as raised its head to look around. When Kunta wasn't running after the goats, he was casting nervous glances towards the forest in case anything was lurking there to eat him.

In the mid-afternoon, with the goats nearing their fill of grass, Toumani called Kunta over to him and said sternly, 'Do you intend me to collect your wood for you?' Only then did Kunta remember how many times he had seen the goatherds returning in the evening, each of them bearing a headload of light wood for the night fires of the village. With the goats and the forest to keep an eye on, it was all Kunta and his mates could do to run around looking for and picking up light brush and small fallen limbs that had become dry enough to burn well. Kunta piled his wood up into a bundle as large as he thought his head could carry, but Toumani scoffed and threw on a few more sticks. Then Kunta tied a slender green liana vine about the wood, doubtful that he could get it onto his head, let alone all the distance to the village.

With the older boys observing, he and his mates somehow managed to hoist their headloads and to begin more or less following the wuolo dogs and the goats, who knew the homeward trail better than their new herdsmen did. Amid the older boys' scornful laughter, Kunta and the others kept grabbing at their headloads to keep them from falling off. The sight of the village had never been prettier to

Kunta, who was bone-weary by now; but no sooner had they stepped inside the village gates when the older boys set up a terrific racket, yelling out warnings and instructions and jumping around so that all of the adults within view and hearing would know that they were doing their job and that their day of training these clumsy younger boys had been a most trying experience for them. Kunta's headload somehow safely reached the yard of Brima Cesay, the arafang, whose education of Kunta and his new kafo would begin the next morning.

Just after breakfast, the new herdsmen – each, with pride, carrying a cottonwood writing slate, a quill, and a section of bamboo cane containing soot to mix with water for ink – trooped anxiously into the schoolyard. Treating them as if they were even more stupid than their goats, the arafang ordered the boys to sit down. Hardly had he uttered the words when he began laying about among them with his limber stick, sending them scrambling – their first obedience to his command not having come as quickly as he wanted. Scowling, he further warned them that for as long as they would attend his classes, anyone who made so much as a sound, unless asked to speak, would get more of the rod – he brandished it fiercely at them – and be sent home to his parents. And the same would be dealt out to any boy who was ever late for his classes, which would be held after breakfast and again just after their return with the goats.

'You are no longer children, and you have responsibilities now,' said the arafang. 'See to it that you fulfil them.' With these disciplines established, he announced that they would begin that evening's class with his reading certain verses of the Koran, which they would be expected to memorize and recite before proceeding to other things. Then he excused them, as his older students, the former goatherds, began arriving. They looked even more nervous than Kunta's kafo, for this was the day for their final examinations in Koranic recitations and in the writing of Arabic, the results of which would bear heavily upon their being formally advanced into the status of third kafo.

That day, all on their own for the first time in their lives, Kunta's kafo managed to get the goats unpenned and trotting in a ragged line along the trail out to the grazing area. For a good while to come, the goats probably got less to eat than usual, as Kunta and his mates chased and yelled at them every time they took a few steps to a new clump of grass. But Kunta felt even more hounded than his herd. Every time he sat down to sort out the meaning of these changes in his life, there seemed to be something he had to do, someplace he had to go. What with the goats all day, the arafang after breakfast and after herding, and then whatever slingshot practice he could fit in before darkness, he could never seem to find the time for any serious thinking any more.

11

The harvesting of groundnuts and couscous was complete, and the women's rice came next. No men helped their wives; even boys like Sitafa and Kunta didn't help their mothers, for rice was women's work alone. The first light of dawn found Binta with Jankay Touray and the other women bending in their ripe fields and chopping off the long golden stalks, which were left to dry for a few days on the walkway before being loaded into canoes and taken to the village, where the women and their daughters would stack their neat bundles in each family's storehouse. But there was no rest for the women even when the rice harvesting was done, for then they had to help the men to pick the cotton, which had been left until last so that it would dry as long as possible under the hot sun and thus make better thread for the women's sewing.

With everyone looking forward to Juffure's annual seven-day harvest festival, the women hurried now to make new clothes for their families. Though Kunta knew better than to show his irritation, he was forced for several evenings to tend his talky, pesty little brother Lamin while Binta spun her cotton. But Kunta was happy again when she took him with her to the village weaver, Dembo Dibba, whom Kunta watched in fascination as her rickety hand-and-foot loom wove the spindles of thread into strips of cotton cloth. Back at home, Binta let Kunta trickle water through wood ashes to make the strong lye into which she mixed finely pounded indigo leaves to dye her cloth deep blue. All of Juffure's women were doing the same, and soon their cloth was spread across low bushes to dry, festooning the village with splashes of rich colour – red, green, and yellow as well as blue.

While the women spun and sewed, the men worked equally hard to finish their own appointed tasks before the harvest festival – and before the hot season made heavy work impossible. The village's tall bamboo fence was patched where it was sagging or broken from the back-scratching of the goats and bullocks. Repairs were made on mud huts that had been damaged by the big rains, and new thatching replaced the old and worn. Some couples, soon to marry, required new homes, and Kunta got the chance to join the other children in stomping water-soaked dirt into the thick, smooth mud that the men used to mould walls for the new huts.

Since some muddy water had begun to appear in the buckets that were pulled up from the well, one of the men climbed down and found that the small fish that was kept in the well to eat insects had died in the murky water. So it was decided that a new well must be dug. Kunta was watching as the men reached shoulder depth in the new hole, and passed upward several egg-sized lumps of a greenish-white clay. They were taken immediately to those women of the village whose bellies were big, and eaten eagerly. That clay, Binta told him, would give a baby stronger bones.

Left to themselves, Kunta, Sitafa, and their mates spent most of their free hours racing about the village playing hunter with their new slingshots. Shooting at nearly everything – and fortunately hitting almost nothing – the boys made enough noise to scare off a forest of animals. Even the smaller children of Lamin's kafo romped almost unattended, for no one in Juffure was busier than the old grandmothers, who worked often now until late at night to supply the demands of the village's unmarried girls for hair-pieces to wear at the harvest festival. Buns, plaits, and full wigs were woven of long fibres picked carefully from rotting sisal leaves or from the soaked bark of the baobab tree. The coarser sisal hairpieces cost much less than those made from the softer, silkier fibre of the baobab whose weaving took so much longer that a full wig might cost as much as three goats. But the customers always haggled long and loudly, knowing that the grandmothers charged less if they enjoyed an hour or so of good, tongue-clacking bargaining before each sale.

Along with her wigs, which were especially well made, old Nyo Boto pleased every woman in the village with her noisy defiance of the ancient tradition that decreed women should always show men the utmost of respect. Every morning found her squatted comfortably before her hut, stripped to the waist, enjoying the sun's heat upon her tough old hide and busily weaving hairpieces – but never so busily that she failed to notice every passing man. 'Hah!' she would call out, 'Look at that! They call themselves men! Now, in *my* day, men were *men!*' And the men who passed – expecting what always came – would all but run to escape her tongue, until finally Nyo Boto fell asleep in the afternoon, with her weaving in her lap and the toddlers in her care laughing at her loud snoring.

The second-kafo girls, meanwhile, were helping their mothers and big sisters to collect bamboo baskets full of ripe medicinal roots and cooking spices, which they spread under the sun to dry. When grains were being pounded, the girls brushed away the husks and chaff. They helped also with the family washing, beating against rocks the soiled clothing that had been lathered with the rough, reddish soap the mothers had made from lye and palm oil.

The men's main work done – only a few days before the new moon that would open the harvest festival in all of The Gambia's villages – the sounds of musical instruments began to be heard here and there in Juffure. As the village musicians practised on their twenty-four-stringed koras, their drums, and their balafons – melodious instruments made of gourds tied beneath wooden blocks of various lengths that were struck with mallets – little crowds would gather around them to clap and listen. While they played, Kunta and Sitafa and their mates, back from their goatherding, would troop about blowing bamboo flutes, ringing bells, and rattling dried gourds.

Most men relaxed now, talking and squatting about in the shade of the baobab. Those of Omoro's age and younger kept respectfully apart from the Council of Elders, who were making their annual pre-festival decisions on important village business. Occasionally two or three of the younger men would rise, stretch themselves, and go ambling about the village with their small fingers linked loosely in the age-old yayo manner of African men.

But a few of the men spent long hours alone, patiently carving on pieces of wood of different sizes and shapes. Kunta and his friends would sometimes even put aside their slings just to stand watching as the carvers created terrifying and mysterious expressions on masks soon to be worn by festival dancers. Others carved human or animal figures with the arms and legs very close to the body, the feet flat, and the heads erect.

Binta and the other women snatched what little relaxation they could around the village's new well, where they came every day for a cool drink and a few minutes of gossip. But with the festival now upon them, they still had much to do. Clothing had to be finished, huts to be cleaned, dried foods to be soaked, goats to be slaughtered for roasting. And above all, the women had to make themselves look their very best for the festival.

Kunta thought that the big tomboyish girls he had so often seen scampering up trees looked foolish now, the way they went about acting coy and fluttery. They couldn't even walk right. And he couldn't see why the men would turn around to watch them – clumsy creatures who couldn't even shoot a bow and arrow if they tried.

Some of these girls' mouths, he noticed, were swelled up to the size of a fist, where the inner lips had been pricked with thorns and rubbed black with soot. Even Binta, along with every other female in the village over twelve rains old, was nightly boiling and then cooling a broth of freshly pounded fudano leaves in which she soaked her feet – and the pale palms of her hands – to an inky blackness. When Kunta asked his mother why, she told him to run along. So he asked his father, who told him, 'The more blackness a woman has, the more beautiful she is.'

'But why?' asked Kunta.

'Some day,' said Omoro, you will understand.'

12

Kunta leaped up when the tobalo sounded at dawn. Then he, Sitafa, and their mates were running among grown-ups to the silk-cotton tree, where the village drummers were already pounding on the drums, barking and shouting at them as if they were live things, their hands a blur against the taut goatskins. The gathering crowd of costumed villagers, one by one, soon began to respond with slow movements of their arms, legs, and bodies, then faster and faster, until almost everyone had joined the dancing.

Kunta had seen such ceremonies for many plantings and harvests, for men leaving to hunt, for weddings, births, and deaths, but the dancing had never moved him – in a way he neither understood nor was able to resist – as it did now. Every adult in the village seemed to be saying with his body something that was in his or her mind alone. Among the whirling, leaping, writhing people, some of them wearing masks, Kunta could scarcely believe his eyes when he saw tough old Nyo Boto suddenly shrieking wildly, jerking both of her hands before her face, then lurching backward in fear at some unseen terror. Snatching up an imaginary burden, she thrashed and kicked the air until she crumpled down.

Kunta turned this way and that, staring at different people he knew among the dancers. Under one of the horrifying masks, Kunta recognized the alimamo, flinging and winding himself again and again like some serpent around a tree trunk. He saw that some of those he had heard who were even older than Nyo Boto had left their huts, stumbling out on spindly legs, their wrinkled arms flapping, their rheumy eyes squinting in the sun, to dance a few unsteady steps. Then Kunta's eyes widened as he caught sight of his own father. Omoro's knees were churning high, his feet stomping up dust. With ripping cries, he reared backwards, muscles trembling, then lunged forward, hammering at his chest, and went leaping and twisting in the air, landing with heavy grunts.

The pounding heartbeat of the drums seemed to throb not only in Kunta's ears but also in his limbs. Almost without his knowing it, as if it were a dream, he felt his body begin to quiver and his arms to flail, and soon he was springing and shouting along with the others, whom he had ceased to notice. Finally he stumbled and fell, exhausted.

He picked himself up and walked with weak knees to the sidelines – feeling a deep strangeness that he had never known before. Dazed, frightened, and excited, he saw not only Sitafa but also others of their kafo out there dancing among the grown-ups, and Kunta danced again. From the very young to the very old, the villagers danced on through the entire day, they and the drummers stopping for neither food nor drink but only to catch fresh breath. But the drums were still beating when Kunta collapsed into sleep that night.

The festival's second day began with a parade for the people of honour just after the noon sun. At the head of the parade were the arafang, the alimamo, the senior elders, the hunters, the wrestlers, and those others whom the Council of Elders had named for their important deeds in Juffure since the last harvest festival. Everyone else came trailing behind, singing and applauding, as the musicians led them out in a snaking line beyond the village. And when they made a turn around the travellers' tree, Kunta and his kafo dashed ahead, formed their own parade, and then trooped back and forth past the marching adults, exchanging bows and smiles as they went, stepping briskly in time with their flutes, bells, and rattles. The parading boys took turns at being the honoured person; when it was Kunta's turn, he pranced about, lifting his knees high, feeling very important indeed. In passing the grown-ups, he caught both Omoro's and Binta's eyes and knew they were proud of their son.

The kitchen of every woman in the village offered a variety of food in open invitation to anyone who passed by and wished to stop a moment and enjoy a plateful. Kunta and his kafo gorged themselves from many calabashes of delicious stews and rice. Even roasted meats – goats and game from the forest – were in abundance; and it was the young girls' special duty to keep bamboo baskets filled with every available fruit.

When they weren't stuffing their bellies, the boys darted out to the travellers' tree to meet the exciting strangers who now entered the village. Some stayed overnight, but most tarried only a few hours before moving on to the next village's festival. The visiting Senegalese set up colourful displays with bolts of decorated cloth. Others arrived with heavy sacks of the very best quality Nigerian kola nuts, the grade and size of each determining the price. Traders came up the bolong in boats laden with salt bars to exchange for indigo, hides, beeswax, and honey. Nyo Boto was herself now busily selling – for a cowrie shell apiece – small bundles of cleaned and trimmed lemongrass roots, whose regular rubbing against the teeth kept the breath sweet and the mouth fresh.

Pagan traders hurried on past Juffure, not even stopping, for their wares of tobacco and snuff and mead beer were for infidels only, since the Moslem Mandinkas never drank nor smoked. Others who seldom stopped, bound as they were for bigger villages, were numerous footloose young men from other villages – as some young men had also left Juffure during the harvest season. Spotting them as they passed on the path beyond the village, Kunta and his mates would run alongside them for a while trying to see what they carried in their small bamboo headbaskets. Usually it was clothing and small gifts for new friends whom they expected to meet in their wanderings, before returning to their home villages by the next planting season.

Every morning the village slept and awakened to the sound of drums. And every day brought different travelling musicians – experts on the kora, the balafon, and the drums. And if they were flattered enough by the gifts that were pressed upon them, along with the dancing and the cheers and clapping of the crowds, they would stop and play for a while before moving on to the next village.

When the story-telling griots came, a quick hush would fall among the villagers as they sat around the baobab to hear of ancient kings and family clans, of warriors, of great battles, and of legends of the past. Or a religious griot would shout prophecies and warnings that Almighty Allah must be appeased, and then offer to conduct the necessary – and by now, to Kunta, familiar – ceremonies in return for a small gift. In his high voice, a singing griot sang endless verses about the past splendours of the kingdoms of Ghana, Songhai, and Old Mali, and when he finished, some people of the village would often privately pay him to sing the praises of their own aged parents at their huts. And the people would applaud when the old ones came to their doorways and stood blinking in the bright sunshine with wide, toothless grins. His good deeds done, the singing griot reminded everyone that a drumtalk message – and a modest offering – would quickly bring him to Juffure any time to sing anyone's praises at funerals, weddings, or other special occasions. And then he hurried on to the next village.

It was during the harvest festival's sixth afternoon when suddenly the sound of a strange drum cut through Juffure. Hearing the insulting words spoken by the drum, Kunta hurried outside and joined the other villagers as they gathered angrily beside the baobab. The drum, obviously quite nearby, had warned of oncoming wrestlers so mighty that any so-called wrestlers in Juffure should hide. Within minutes, the people of Juffure cheered as their own drum sharply replied that such foolhardy strangers were asking to get crippled, if not worse.

The villagers rushed now to the wrestling place. As Juffure's wrestlers slipped into their brief dalas with the rolled-cloth handholds on the sides and buttocks, and smeared themselves with a slippery paste of pounded baobab leaves and wood ashes, they heard the shouts that meant that their challengers had arrived. These powerfully built strangers never glanced at the jeering crowd. Trotting behind their drummer, they went directly to the wrestling area, clad already in their dalas, and began rubbing one another with their own slippery paste. When Juffure's wrestlers appeared behind the village drummers, the crowd's shouting and jostling became so unruly that both drummers had to implore them to remain calm.

Then both drums spoke: 'Ready!' The rival teams paired off, each two wrestlers crouching and glaring, face to face. 'Take hold! Take hold!' the drums ordered, and each pair of wrestlers began a catlike circling. Both of the drummers now went darting here and there among the stalking men; each drummer was pounding out the names of that village's ancestral champion wrestlers, whose spirits were looking on.

With lightning feints, one after another pair finally seized hold and began to grapple. Soon both teams struggled amid the dust clouds, their feet kicked up, nearly hiding them from the wildly yelling spectators. Dogfalls or slips didn't count; a victory came only when one

42

wrestler pulled another off balance, thrust him bodily upwards, and hurled him to the ground. Each time there came a fall – first one of Juffure's champions, then one of the challengers – the crowd jumped and screamed, and a drummer pounded out that winner's name. Just beyond the excited crowd, of course, Kunta and his mates were wrestling among themselves.

At last it was over, and Juffure's team had won by a single fall. They were awarded the horns and hooves of a freshly slaughtered bullock. Big chunks of the meat were put to roast over a fire, and the brave challengers were invited warmly to join the feasting. The people congratulated the visitors on their strength, and unmarried maidens tied small bells around all of the wrestlers' ankles and upper arms. And during the feasting that followed, Juffure's third-kafo boys swept and brushed to smoothness the wrestling area's reddish dust to prepare it for a seoruba.

The hot sun had just begun to sink when the people again assembled around the wrestling area, now all dressed in their best. Against a low background of drums, both wrestling teams leaped into the ring and began to crouch and spring about, their muscles rippling and their little bells tinkling as the onlookers admired their might and grace. The drums suddenly pounded hard; now the maidens ran out into the ring, weaving coyly among the wrestlers as the people clapped. Then the drummers began to beat their hardest and fastest rhythm – and the maidens' feet kept pace.

One girl after another, sweating and exhausted, finally stumbled from the ring, flinging to the dust her colourfully dyed tiko headwrap. All eyes watched eagerly to see if the marriageable man would pick up that tiko, thus showing his special appreciation of that maiden's dance – for it could mean he meant soon to consult her father about her bridal price in goats and cows. Kunta and his mates, who were too young to understand such things, thought the excitement was over and ran off to play with their slingshots. But it had just begun, for a moment later, everyone gasped as a tiko was picked up by one of the visiting wrestlers. This was a major event – and a happy one – but the lucky maiden would not be the first who was lost through marriage to another village.

13

On the final morning of the festival, Kunta was awakened by the sound of screams. Pulling on his dundiko, he went dashing out, and his stomach knotted with fright. Before several of the nearby huts, springing up and down, shrieking wildly and brandishing spears, were half a dozen men in fierce masks, tall head-dresses, and costumes of leaf and bark. Kunta watched in terror as one man entered each hut with a roar and emerged jerking roughly by the arm a trembling boy of the third kafo.

Joined by a cluster of his own equally terrified second-kafo mates, Kunta peered with wide eyes around the corner of a hut. A heavy white cotton hood was over the head of each third-kafo boy. Spying Kunta, Sitafa, and their group of little boys, one of the masked men dashed towards them waving his spear and shouting fearfully. Though he stopped short and turned back to his hooded charge, the boys scattered, squealing in horror. And when all of the village's third-kafo boys had been collected, they were turned over to slaves, who took them by the hand and led them, one by one, out the village gate.

Kunta had heard that these older boys were going to be taken away from Juffure for their manhood training, but he had no idea that it would happen like this. The departure of the third-kafo boys, along with the men who would conduct their manhood training, cast a shadow of sadness upon the entire village. In the days that followed, Kunta and his mates could talk of nothing but the terrifying things they had seen, and of the even more terrifying things they had overheard about the mysterious manhood training. In the mornings, the arafang rapped their heads for their lack of interest in memorizing the Koranic verses. And after school, trooping along behind their goats out into the bush, Kunta and his mates each tried not to think about what each could not forget – that he would be among Juffure's next group of hooded boys jerked and kicked out through the village gate.

They all had heard that a full twelve moons would pass before those third-kafo boys would return to the village – but then as men. Kunta said that someone had told him that the boys in manhood training got beatings daily. A boy named Karamo said they were made to hunt wild animals for food; and Sitafa said they were sent out alone at night into the deep forest, to find their own way back.

But the worst thing, which none of them mentioned, although it made Kunta nervous each time he had to relieve himself, was that during the manhood training a part of his foto would be cut off. After a while, the more they talked, the idea of manhood training became so frightening that the boys stopped talking about it, and each of them tried to conceal his fears within himself, not wanting to show that he wasn't brave.

Kunta and his mates had got much better at goatherding since their first anxious days out in the bush. But they still had much to learn. Their job, they were beginning to discover, was hardest in the mornings, when swarms of biting flies kept the goats bolting this way and that, quivering their skins and switching their stubby tails as the boys and the dogs rushed about trying to herd them together again. But before noon, when the sun grew so hot that even the flies sought cooler places, the tired goats settled down to serious grazing, and the boys could finally enjoy themselves.

By now they were crack shots with their slingshots – and also with the new bows and arrows their fathers had given them on graduating to the second kafo – and they spent an hour or so killing every small creature they could find: hares, ground squirrels, bush rats, lizards, and one day a tricky spurfowl that tried to decoy Kunta away from her nest by dragging a wing as if it had been injured. In the early afternoon, the boys skinned and cleaned the day's game, rubbing the insides with the salt they always carried, and then, building a fire, roasted themselves a feast.

Each day out in the bush seemed to be hotter than the day before. Earlier and earlier the insects stopped biting the goats to look for shade, and the goats bent down on their knees to get at the short grass that remained green beneath the parched taller grass. But Kunta and his mates hardly noticed the heat. Glistening with sweat, they played as if each day were the most exciting one in their lives. With their bellies tight after the afternoon meal, they wrestled or raced or sometimes just yelled and made faces at one another, taking turns at keeping a wary eye on the grazing goats. Playing at war, the boys clubbed and speared each other with thick-rooted weeds until someone held up a handful of grass as a sign of peace. Then they cooled off their warrior spirits by rubbing their feet with the contents of the stomach of a slaughtered rabbit; they had heard in the grandmothers' stories that real warriors used the stomach of a lamb.

Sometimes Kunta and his mates romped with their faithful wuolo dogs, which Mandinkas had kept for centuries, for they were known as one of the very finest breeds of hunting and guard dogs in all of

Africa. No man could count the goats and cattle that had been saved on dark nights from killer hyenas by the howling of the wuolos. But hyenas weren't the game stalked by Kunta and his mates when they played at being huntsmen. In their imaginations, as they crept about in the tall, sun-baked grass of the savanna, their quarry were rhinoceros, elephant, leopard, and the mighty lion.

Sometimes, as a boy followed his goats around in their search for grass and shade, he would find himself separated from his mates. The first few times it happened to him, Kunta herded up his goats as quickly as he could and headed back to be near Sitafa. But soon he began to like these moments of solitude, for they gave him the chance to stalk some great beast by himself. It was no ordinary antelope, leopard, or even lion that he sought in his daydreaming; it was that most feared and dangerous of all beasts – a maddened buffalo.

The one he tracked had spread so much terror throughout the land that many hunters had been sent to kill the savage animal, but they had managed only to wound it, and one after another, it had gored them with its wicked horns. Even more bloodthirsty than before with its painful wound, the buffalo had then charged and killed several farmers from Juffure who had been working on their fields outside the village. The famed simbon Kunta Kinte had been deep in the forest, smoking out a bee's nest to sustain his energy with rich honey, when he heard the distant drumtalk begging him to save the people of the village of his birth. He could not refuse.

Not even a blade of the dry grass crackled under his feet, so silently did he stalk for signs of the buffalo's trail, using the sixth sense that told master simbons which way animals would travel. And soon he found the tracks he sought; they were larger than any he had ever seen. Now trotting silently, he drew deeply into his nostrils the foul smell that led him to giant, fresh buffalo dung. And manoeuvring now with all the craft and skill at his command, simbon Kinte finally spotted the huge bulk of the beast himself – it would have been concealed from ordinary eyes – hiding in the dense, high grass.

Straining back his bow, Kinte took careful aim – and sent the arrow thudding home. The buffalo was badly wounded now, but more dangerous than ever. Springing suddenly from side to side, Kinte evaded the beast's desperate, stricken charge and braced himself as it wheeled to charge again. He fired his second arrow only when he had to leap aside at the last instant – and the huge buffalo crashed down dead.

Kinte's piercing whistle brought from hiding, awed and trembling, those previous hunters who had failed where he had gloriously succeeded. He ordered them to remove the huge hide and horns and to summon still more men to help drag the carcass all the way back to Juffure. The joyously shouting people had laid down a pathway of hides within the village gate so that Kinte would not get dust upon his feet. 'Simbon Kinte!' the talking drum beat out. 'Simbon Kinte!' the children shouted, waving leafy branches above their heads. Everyone was pushing and shoving and trying to touch the mighty hunter so that some of his prowess might rub off on them. Small boys danced around the huge carcass, re-enacting the kill with wild cries and long sticks.

And now, walking towards him from amid the crowd, came the strongest, most graceful, and most beautifully black of all the maidens in Juffure – indeed, in all of The Gambia – and kneeling before him, she offered a calabash of cool water; but Kinte, not thirsty, merely wet his fingers, to favour her, whereupon she drank that water with happy tears, thus showing to everyone the fullness of her love.

The clamouring crowd was spreading – making way for aged, wrinkled, grey-headed Omoro and Binta, who came tottering against their canes. The simbon permitted his old mother to embrace him while Omoro looked on, eyes filled with pride. And the people of Juffure chanted 'Kinte! Kinte!' Even the dogs were barking their acclaim.

Was that his own wuolo dog barking? 'Kinte! Kinte!' Was that Sitafa yelling frantically? Kunta snapped out of it just in time to see his forgotten goats bounding towards someone's farm. Sitafa and his other mates and their dogs helped to herd them up again before any damage was done, but Kunta was so ashamed that a whole moon went by before he drifted off into any more such daydreams.

14

As hot as the sun already was, the five long moons of the dry season had only begun. The heat devils shimmered, making objects larger in the distance, and the people sweated in their huts almost as much as they did in the fields. Before Kunta left home each morning for his goatherding, Binta saw that he protected his feet well with red palm oil, but each afternoon, when he returned to the village from the open bush, his lips were parched and the soles of his feet were dry and cracked by the baking earth beneath them. Some of the boys came home with bleeding feet, but out they would go again each morning – uncomplaining, like their fathers – into the fierce heat of the dry grazing land, which was even worse than in the village.

By the time the sun reached its zenith, the boys and their dogs and the goats all lay panting in the shade of scrub trees, the boys too tired to hunt and roast the small game that had been their daily sport. Mostly, they just sat and chatted as cheerfully as they could, but somehow by this time the adventure of goatherding had lost some of its excitement.

It didn't seem possible that the sticks they gathered every day would be needed to keep them warm at night, but once the sun set, the air turned as cold as it had been hot. And after their evening meal, the people of Juffure huddled around their crackling fires. Men of Omoro's age sat talking around one fire, and a little distance away was the fire of the elders. Around still another sat the women and the unmarried girls, apart from the old grandmothers, who told their nightly stories to the little first-kafo children around a fourth fire.

Kunta and the other second-kafo boys were too proud to sit with the naked first kafo of Lamin and his mates, so they squatted far enough away not to seem part of that noisy, giggling group – yet near enough to hear the old grandmothers' stories, which still thrilled them as much as ever. Sometimes Kunta and his mates eavesdropped on those at other fires; but the conversations were mostly about the heat. Kunta heard the old men recalling times when the sun had killed plants and burned crops; how it had made the well go stale, or dry, of times when the heat had dried the people out like husks. This hot season was bad, they said, but not as bad as many they could remember. It seemed to Kunta that older people always could remember something worse.

Then, abruptly one day, breathing the air was like breathing flames, and that night the people shivered beneath their blankets with the cold creeping into their bones. Again the next morning, they were mopping their faces and trying to draw a full breath. That afternoon the harmattan wind began. It wasn't a hard wind, nor even a gusty wind, either of which would have helped. Instead it blew softly and steadily, dusty and dry, day and night, for nearly half a moon. As it did each time it came, the constant blowing of the harmattan wore away slowly at the nerves of the people of Juffure. And soon parents were yelling more often than usual at their children, and whipping them for no good reason. And though bickering was unusual among the Mandinkas, hardly a daytime hour passed without loud shoutings between some adults, especially between younger husbands and wives like Omoro and Binta. Suddenly then nearby doorways would fill with people watching as the couple's mothers went rushing into that hut. A moment later the shouting would grow louder, and next a rain of sewing baskets, cooking pots, calabashes, stools, and clothes would be hurled out the door. Then, bursting out themselves, the wife and her mother would snatch up the possessions and go storming off to the mother's hut.

After about two moons, just as it had begun, the harmattan suddenly stopped. In less than a day, the air became still, the sky clear. Within one night, a parade of wives slipped back in with their husbands, and their mothers-in-law were exchanging small gifts and patching up arguments all over the village. But the five long moons of the dry season were only half over. Though food was still plentiful in the storehouses, the mothers only cooked small quantities, for no one, not even the usually greedy children, felt like eating much. Everyone was sapped of strength by the sun's heat, and the people talked less and went about doing only the things they had to do.

The hides of the gaunt cattle in the village were broken by lumpy sores where biting flies had laid their eggs. A quietness had come upon the scrawny chickens that normally ran squawking around the village, and they lay in the dust on their sides, with their wings fanned out and their beaks open. Even the monkeys now were seldom seen or heard, for most of them had gone into the forest for more shade. And the goats, Kunta noticed, grazing less and less in the heat, had grown nervous and thin.

For some reason – perhaps it was the heat, or perhaps simply because they were growing older – Kunta and his goatherding mates, who had spent every day together out in the bush for almost six moons, now began to drift off alone with their own small herds. It had happened for several days before Kunta realized that he had never before been completely away from other people for any real length of time. He looked across at other boys and their goats in the distance, scattered across the silence of the sunbaked bush. Beyond them lay the fields where the farmers were chopping the weeds that had grown in the moons since the last harvest. The tall piles of weeds they raked to dry under the sun seemed to wave and shimmer in the heat.

Wiping the sweat from his brow, it seemed to Kunta that his people were always enduring one hardship or another – something uncomfortable or difficult, or frightening, or threatening to life itself. He thought about the burning, hot days and the cold nights that followed them. And he thought about the rains that would come next, turning the village into a mudhole and finally submerging the walking paths until the people had to travel in their canoes from place to place where usually they walked. They needed the rain as they needed the sun, but there always seemed to be too much or too little. Even when the goats were fat and the trees were heavy with fruit and blossoms, he knew that would be the time when the last rain's harvest would run out in the family storehouses and that this would bring the hungry season, with people starving and some even dying, like his own dearly remembered Grandma Yaisa.

The harvest season was a happy one – and after that, the harvest festival – but it was over so soon, and then the long, hot dry season would come again, with its awful harmattan, when Binta kept shouting at him and beating on Lamin – until he almost felt sorry for his pest of a small brother. As he herded his goats back towards the village, Kunta remembered the stories he had heard so many times when he was as young as Lamin, about how the forefathers had always lived through great fears and dangers. As far back as time went, Kunta guessed, the lives of the people had been hard. Perhaps they always would be.

Each evening in the village now, the alimamo led the prayers for Allah to send the rains. And then one day, excitement filled Juffure when some gentle winds stirred up the dust – for those winds meant that the rains were soon to come. And the next morning, the people of the village gathered out in the fields, where the farmers set afire the tall piles of weeds they had raked up, and thick smoke coiled up over the fields. The heat was nearly unbearable, but the sweating people danced and cheered, and the first-kafo children went racing and whooping about, each trying to catch good-luck pieces of drifting, feathery flakes of ashes.

The next day's light winds began to sift the loose ashes over the fields, enriching the soil to grow yet another crop. The farmers now began chopping busily with their hoes, preparing the long rows to receive the seeds – in this seventh planting time through which Kunta had lived in the endless cycle of the seasons.

15

Two rains had passed, and Binta's belly was big again, and her temper was even shorter than usual. So quick was she to whack both her sons, in fact, that Kunta was grateful each morning when goat-herding let him escape her for a few hours, and when he returned in the afternoon, he couldn't help feeling sorry for Lamin, who was only old enough to get into mischief and get beaten but not old enough to get out of the house alone. So one day when he came home and found his little brother in tears, he asked Binta – not without some misgivings – if Lamin could join him on an errand, and she snapped 'Yes!' Naked little Lamin could hardly contain his happiness over this amazing act of kindness, but Kunta was so disgusted with his own impulsiveness that he gave him a good kick and a cuffing as soon as they got beyond Binta's earshot. Lamin hollered – and then followed his brother like a puppy.

Every afternoon after that, Kunta found Lamin waiting anxiously at the door in hopes that his big brother would take him out again. Kunta did, nearly every day – but not because he wanted to. Binta would profess such great relief at getting some rest from both of them that Kunta now feared a beating if he didn't take Lamin along. It seemed as if a bad dream had attached his naked little brother to Kunta's back like some giant leech from the bolong. But soon Kunta began to notice that some of the kafo mates also had small brothers tagging along behind them. Though they would play off to one side or dart about nearby, they always kept a sharp eye on their big brothers, who did their best to ignore them. Sometimes the big boys would dash off suddenly, jeering back at the young ones as they scrambled to catch up with them. When Kunta and his mates climbed trees, their little brothers, trying to follow, usually tumbled back to the ground, and the older boys would laugh loudly at their clumsiness. It began to be fun having them around.

Alone with Lamin, as he sometimes was, Kunta might pay his brother a bit more attention. Pinching a tiny seed between his fingers, he would explain that Juffure's giant silk-cotton tree grew from a thing that small. Catching a honey-bee, Kunta would hold it carefully for Lamin to see the stinger; then, turning the bee around, he would explain how bees sucked the sweetness from flowers and used it to make honey in their nests in the tallest trees. And Lamin began to ask Kunta a lot of questions, most of which he would patiently answer. There was something nice about Lamin's feeling that Kunta knew everything. It made Kunta feel older than his eight rains. In spite of himself, he began to regard his little brother as something more than a pest.

Kunta took great pains not to show it, of course, but returning homeward now each afternoon with his goats, he really looked forward to Lamin's eager reception. Once Kunta thought that he even saw Binta smile as he and Lamin left the hut. In fact, Binta would often snap at her younger son, 'Have your brother's manners!' The next moment, she might whack Kunta for something, but not as often as she used to. Binta would also tell Lamin that if he didn't act properly, he couldn't go with Kunta, and Lamin would be very good for the rest of the day.

He and Lamin would always leave the hut now walking very politely, hand in hand, but once outside, Kunta went dashing and whooping – with Lamin racing behind him – to join the other second- and first-kafo boys. During one afternoon's romping, when a fellow goatherd of Kunta's happened to run into Lamin, knocking him on his back, Kunta was instantly there, shoving that boy roughly aside and exclaiming hotly, 'That's my brother!' The boy protested and they were ready to exchange blows when the others grabbed their arms. Kunta snatched the crying Lamin by the hand and jerked him away from their staring playmates. Kunta was both deeply embarrassed and astonished at himself for acting as he had towards his own kafo mate – and especially over such a thing as a sniffling little brother. But after that day, Lamin began openly trying to imitate whatever he saw Kunta do, sometimes even with Binta or Omoro looking on. Though he pretended not to like it, Kunta couldn't help feeling just a little proud.

When Lamin fell from a low tree he was trying to climb one afternoon, Kunta showed him how to do it right. At one time or another, he taught his little brother how to wrestle (so that Lamin could win the respect of a boy who had humiliated him in front of his kafo mates); how to whistle through his fingers (though Lamin's best whistle was nowhere near as piercing as Kunta's); and he showed him the kind of berry leaves from which their mother liked to make tea. And he cautioned Lamin to take the big, shiny dung beetles they always saw crawling in the hut and set them gently outside on the ground, for it was very bad luck to harm them. To touch a rooster's spur, he told him, was even worse luck. But however hard he tried, Kunta couldn't make Lamin understand how to tell the time of day by the position of the sun. 'You're just too little, but you'll learn.'

Kunta would still shout at him sometimes, if Lamin seemed too slow in learning something simple; or he would give him a slap if he was too much of a pest. But he would always feel so badly about it that he might even let the naked Lamin wear his dundiko for a while.

As he grew closer to his brother, Kunta began to feel less deeply something that had often bothered him before – the gulf between his eight rains and the older boys and men of Juffure. Indeed, scarcely a day of his life that he could remember had ever passed without something to remind him that he was still of the second kafo – one who yet slept in the hut of his mother. The older boys who were away now at manhood training had always had nothing but sneers and cuffings for those of Kunta's age. And the grown men, such as Omoro and the other fathers, acted as if a second-kafo boy were something merely to be tolerated. As for the mothers, well, often when Kunta was out in the bush, he would think angrily that whenever he got to be a man, he certainly intended to put Binta in her place as a woman – although he did intend to show her kindness and forgiveness, since after all, she was his mother.

Most irritating of all to Kunta and his mates, though, was how the second-kafo girls with whom they had grown up were now so quick to remind them that they were thinking already of becoming wives. It rankled Kunta that girls married at fourteen rains or even younger, while boys didn't get married until they were men of thirty rains or more. In general, being of the second kafo had always been an embarrassment to Kunta and his mates, except for their afternoons off by themselves in the bush, and in Kunta's case, his new relationship with Lamin.

Every time he and his brother would be walking somewhere by themselves, Kunta would imagine that he was taking Lamin on some journey, as men sometimes did with their sons. Now, somehow, Kunta felt a special responsibility to act older, with Lamin looking up to him as a source of knowledge. Walking alongside, Lamin would ply Kunta with a steady stream of questions.

'What's the world like?'

'Well,' said Kunta, 'no man or canoes ever journeyed so far. And no one knows all there is to know about it.'

'What do you learn from the arafang?'

Kunta recited the first verses of the Koran in Arabic and then said, 'Now you try.' But when Lamin tried, he got badly confused – as Kunta had known he would – and Kunta said paternally, 'It takes time.'

'Why does no one harm owls?'

'Because all our dead ancestors' spirits are in owls.' Then he told Lamin something of their late Grandma Yaisa. 'You were just a baby, and cannot remember her.'

'What's that bird in the tree?'

'A hawk.'

'What does he eat?'

'Mice and other birds and things.'

'Oh.'

Kunta had never realized how much he knew – but now and then Lamin asked something of which Kunta knew nothing at all.

'Is the sun on fire?' Or: 'Why doesn't our father sleep with us?'

At such times, Kunta would usually grunt, then stop talking – as Omoro did when he tired of so many of Kunta's questions. Then Lamin would say no more, since Mandinka home-training taught that one never talked to another who did not want to talk. Sometimes Kunta would act as if he had gone into deep private thought. Lamin would sit silently near-by, and when Kunta rose, so would he. And sometimes, when Kunta didn't know the answer to a question, he would quickly do something to change the subject.

Always, at his next chance, Kunta would wait until Lamin was out of the hut and then ask Binta or Omoro the answer he needed for Lamin. He never told them why he asked them both so many questions, but it seemed as if they knew. In fact, they seemed to act as if they had begun to regard Kunta as an older person, since he had taken on more responsibility with his little brother. Before long, Kunta was speaking sharply to Lamin in Binta's presence about things done wrongly. 'You must talk clearly!' he might say with a snap of his fingers. Or he might whack Lamin for not jumping swiftly enough to do anything his mother had ordered him to do. Binta acted as if she neither saw nor heard.

So Lamin made few moves now without either his mother's or his brother's sharp eyes upon him. And Kunta now had only to ask Binta or Omoro any questions of Lamin's and they immediately told him the answer.

'Why is father's bullock's hide mat of that red colour? A bullock isn't red.'

'I dyed the hide of the bullock with lye and crushed millet,' replied Binta.

'Where does Allah live?'

'Allah lives where the sun comes from,' said Omoro.

16

'What are slaves?' Lamin asked Kunta one afternoon. Kunta grunted and fell silent. Walking on, seemingly lost in thought, he was wondering what Lamin had overheard to prompt that question. Kunta knew that those who were taken by toubob became slaves, and he had overheard grown-ups talking about slaves who were owned by people in Juffure. But the fact was that he really didn't know what slaves *were*. As had happened so many other times, Lamin's question embarrassed him into finding out more.

The next day, when Omoro was getting ready to go out after some palm wood to build Binta a new food storehouse, Kunta asked to join his father; he loved to go off anywhere with Omoro. But neither spoke this day until they had almost reached the dark, cool palm grove.

Then Kunta asked abruptly, 'Fa, what are slaves?'

Omoro just grunted at first, saying nothing, and for several minutes moved about in the grove, inspecting the trunks of different palms.

'Slaves aren't always easy to tell from those who aren't slaves,' he said finally. Between blows of his bush axe against the palm he had selected, he told Kunta that slaves' huts were roofed with nyantang jongo and free people's huts with nyantang foro, which Kunta knew was the best quality of thatching grass.

'But one should never speak of slaves in the presence of slaves,' said Omoro, looking very stern. Kunta didn't understand why, but he nodded as if he did.

When the palm tree fell, Omoro began chopping away its thick, tough fronds. As Kunta plucked off for himself some of the ripened fruits, he sensed his father's mood of willingness to talk today. He thought happily how now he would be able to explain to Lamin all about slaves.

'Why are some people slaves and others not?' he asked.

Omoro said that people became slaves in different ways. Some were born of slave mothers and he named a few of those who lived in Juffure, people whom Kunta knew well. Some of them were the parents of some of his own kafo mates. Others, said Omoro, had once faced starvation during their home villages' hungry season, and they had come to Juffure and begged to become the slaves of some-one who agreed to feed and provide for them. Still others – and he named some of Juffure's old people – had once been enemies and been captured as prisoners. 'They become slaves, being not brave enough to die rather than be taken,' said Omoro.

He had begun chopping the trunk of the palm into sections of a size that a strong man could carry. Though all he had named were slaves, he said, they were all respected people, as Kunta well knew. 'Their rights are guaranteed by the laws of our forefathers,' said Omoro, and he explained that all masters had to provide their slaves with food, clothing, a house, a farm plot to work on half shares, and also a wife or husband.

'Only those who permit themselves to be are despised,' he told Kunta – those who had been made slaves because they were convicted murderers, thieves, or other criminals. Those were the only slaves whom a master could beat or otherwise punish, as he felt they deserved.

'Do slaves have to remain slaves always?' asked Kunta.

'No, many slaves buy their freedom with what they save from farming on half share with their masters.' Omoro named some in Juffure who had done this. He named others who had won their freedom by marrying into the family that owned them.

To help him carry the heavy sections of palm, Omoro made a stout sling out of green vines, and as he worked, he said that some slaves, in fact, prospered beyond their masters. Some had even taken slaves for themselves, and some had become very famous persons.

'Sundiata was one!' exclaimed Kunta. Many times, he had heard the grandmothers and the griots speaking of the great forefather slave general whose army had conquered so many enemies.

Omoro grunted and nodded, clearly pleased that Kunta knew this, for Omoro also had learned much of Sundiata when he was Kunta's age. Testing his son, Omoro asked, 'And who was Sundiata's mother?'

'Sogolon, the Buffalo Woman!' said Kunta proudly.

Omoro smiled, and hoisting onto his strong shoulders two heavy sections of the palm pole within the vine sling, he began walking. Eating his palm fruits, Kunta followed, and nearly all the way back to the village, Omoro told him how the great Mandinka Empire had been won by the crippled, brilliant slave general whose army had begun with runaway slaves found in swamps and other hiding places.

'You will learn much more of him when you are in manhood training,' said Omoro – and the very thought of that time sent a fear through Kunta, but also a thrill of anticipation.

Omoro said that Sundiata had run away from his hated master, as most slaves did who didn't like their masters. He said that except for convicted criminals, no slaves could be sold unless the slaves approved of the intended master.

'Grandmother Nyo Boto also is a slave,' said Omoro, and Kunta almost swallowed a mouthful of palm fruit. He couldn't comprehend this. Pictures flashed across his mind of beloved old Nyo Boto squatting before the door of her hut, tending the village's twelve or fifteen naked babies while weaving baskets of wigs, and giving the sharp side of her tongue to any passing adult – even the elders, if she felt like it. 'That one is nobody's slave,' he thought.

The next afternoon, after he had delivered his goats to their pens, Kunta took Lamin home by a way that avoided their usual playmates, and soon they squatted silently before the hut of Nyo Boto. Within a few moments the old lady appeared in her doorway, having sensed that she had visitors. And with but a glance at Kunta, who had always been one of her very favourite children, she knew that something special was on his mind. Inviting the boys inside her hut, she set about the brewing of some hot herb tea for them.

'How are your papa and mama?' she asked.

'Fine. Thank you for asking,' said Kunta politely. 'And you are well, Grandmother?'

'I'm quite fine, indeed,' she replied.

Kunta's next words didn't come until the tea had been set before him. Then he blurted, 'Why are you a slave, Grandmother?'

Nyo Boto looked sharply at Kunta and Lamin. Now it was she who didn't speak for a few moments. 'I will tell you,' she said finally.

'In my home village one night, very far from here and many rains ago, when I was a young woman and wife,' Nyo Boto said, she had awakened in terror as flaming grass roofs came crashing down among her screaming neighbours. Snatching up her own two babies, a boy and a girl, whose father had recently died in a tribal war, she rushed out among the others – and awaiting them were armed white slave raiders with their black slatee helpers. In a furious battle, all who didn't escape were roughly herded together, and those who were too badly injured or too old or too young to travel were murdered before the others' eyes, Nyo Boto began to sob, ' – including my own two babies and my aged mother.'

As Lamin and Kunta clutched each other's hands, she told them how the terrified prisoners, bound neck-to-neck with thongs, were beaten and driven across the hot, hard inland country for many days. And every day, more and more of the prisoners fell beneath the whips that lashed their backs to make them walk faster. After a few days, yet more began to fall of hunger and exhaustion. Some struggled on, but those who couldn't were left for the wild animals to get. The long line of prisoners passed other villages that had been burned and ruined, where the skulls and bones of people and animals lay among the burned-out shells of thatch and mud that had once been family huts. Fewer than half of those who had begun the trip reached the village of Juffure, four days from the nearest place on the Kamby Bolongo where slaves were sold.

'It was here that one young prisoner was sold for a bag of corn,' said the old woman. 'That was me. And this was how I came to be called Nyo Boto,' which Kunta knew meant 'bag of corn'. The man who bought her for his own slave died before very long, she said, 'And I have lived here ever since.'

Lamin was wriggling in excitement at the story, and Kunta felt somehow even greater love and appreciation than he had felt before for old Nyo Boto, who now sat smiling tenderly at the two boys, whose father and mother, like them, she had once dandled on her knee.

'Omoro, your papa, was of the first kafo when I came to Juffure,' said Nyo Boto, looking directly at Kunta. 'Yaisa, his mother, who was your grandmother, was my very good friend. Do you remember her?' Kunta said that he did and added proudly that he had told his little brother all about their grandma.

'That is good!' said Nyo Boto. 'Now I must get back to work. Run along, now.'

Thanking her for the tea, Kunta and Lamin left and walked slowly back to Binta's hut, each deep in his own private thoughts.

The next afternoon, when Kunta returned from his goatherding, he found Lamin filled with questions about Nyo Boto's story. Had any such fire ever burned in Juffure? he wanted to know. Well, he had never heard of any, said Kunta, and the village showed no signs of it. Had Kunta ever seen one of those white people? 'Of course not!' he exclaimed. But he said that their father had spoken of a time when he and his brothers had seen the toubob and their ships at a point along the river.

Kunta quickly changed the subject, for he knew very little about toubob, and he wanted to think about them for himself. He wished that he could *see* one of them – from a safe distance, of course, since everything he'd ever heard about them made it plain that people were better off who never got too close to them.

Only recently a girl out gathering herbs – and before her two grown men out hunting – had disappeared, and everyone was certain

58

that toubob had stolen them away. He remembered, of course, how when drums of other villages warned that toubob had either taken somebody or was known to be near, the men would arm themselves and mount a double guard while the frightened women quickly gathered all of the children and hid in the bush far from the village – sometimes for several days – until the toubob was felt to be gone.

Kunta recalled once when he was out with his goats in the quiet of the bush, sitting under his favourite shade tree. He had happened to look upwards and there, to his astonishment, in the tree overhead, were twenty or thirty monkeys huddled along the thickly leaved branches as still as statues, with their long tails hanging down. Kunta had always thought of monkeys rushing noisily about, and he couldn't forget how quietly they had been watching his every move. He wished that now *he* might sit in a tree and watch some toubob on the ground below him.

The goats were being driven homewards the afternoon after Lamin had asked him about toubob when Kunta raised the subject among his fellow goatherds – and in no time they were telling about the things they had heard. One boy, Demba Conteh, said that a very brave uncle had once gone close enough to *smell* some toubob, and they had a peculiar stink. All of the boys had heard that toubob took people away to eat them. But some had heard that the toubob claimed the stolen people were not eaten, only put to work on huge farms. Sitafa Silla spat out his grandfather's answer to that: 'White man's lie!'

The next chance he had, Kunta asked Omoro, 'Papa, will you tell me how you and your brothers saw the toubob at the river?' Quickly, he added, 'The matter needs to be told correctly to Lamin.' It seemed to Kunta that his father nearly smiled, but Omoro only grunted, evidently not feeling like talking at that moment. But a few days later, Omoro casually invited both Kunta and Lamin to go with him out beyond the village to collect some roots he needed. It was the naked Lamin's first walk anywhere with his father, and he was overjoyed. Knowing that Kunta's influence had brought this about, he held tightly onto the tail of his big brother's dundiko.

Omoro told his sons that after their manhood training, his two older brothers Janneh and Saloum had left Juffure, and the passing of time brought news of them as well-known travellers in strange and distant places. Their first return home came when drumtalk all the way from Juffure told them of the birth of Omoro's first son. They spent sleepless days and nights on the trail to attend the naming ceremony. And gone from home so long, the brothers joyously embraced some of their kafo mates of boyhood. But those few sadly told of others gone and lost – some in burned villages, some killed by fearsome firesticks, some kidnapped, some missing while farming, hunting, or travelling – and all because of toubob.

Omoro said that his brothers had then angrily asked him to join them on a trip to see what the toubob were doing, to see what might be done. So the three brothers trekked for three days along the banks of the Kamby Bolongo, keeping carefully concealed in the bush, until they found what they were looking for. About twenty great toubob canoes were moored in the river, each big enough that its insides might hold all the people of Juffure, each with a huge white cloth tied by ropes to a tree-like pole as tall as ten men. Nearby was an island, and on the island was a fortress.

Many toubob were moving about, and black helpers were with them, both on the fortress and in small canoes. The small canoes were taking such things as dried indigo, cotton, beeswax, and hides to the big canoes. More terrible than he could describe, however, said Omoro, were the beatings and other cruelties they saw being dealt out to those who had been captured for the toubob to take away.

For several moments, Omoro was quiet, and Kunta sensed that he was pondering something else to tell him. Finally he spoke: 'Not as many of our people are being taken away now as then.' When Kunta was a baby, he said, the King of Barra, who ruled this part of The Gambia, had ordered that there would be no more burning of villages with the capturing or killing of all their people. And soon it did stop, after the soldiers of some angry kings had burned the big canoes down to the water, killing all the toubob on board.

'Now,' said Omoro, 'nineteen guns are fired in salute to the King of Barra by every toubob canoe entering the Kamby Bolongo.' He said that the King's personal agents now supplied most of the people whom the toubob took away – usually criminals or debtors, or anyone convicted for suspicion of plotting against the King – often for little more than whispering. More people seemed to get convicted of crimes, said Omoro, whenever toubob ships sailed in the Kamby Bolongo looking for slaves to buy.

'But even a king cannot stop the stealings of some people from their villages,' Omoro continued. 'You have known some of those lost from our village, three from among us just within the past few moons, as you know, and you have heard the drumtalk from other villages.' He looked hard at his sons, and spoke slowly. 'The things I'm going to tell you now, you must hear with more than your ears – for not to do what I say can mean your being stolen away forever!'

Kunta and Lamin listened with rising fright. 'Never be alone when you can help it,' said Omoro. 'Never be out at night when you can help it. And day or night, when you're alone, keep away from any high weeds or bush if you can avoid it.'

For the rest of their lives, 'even when you have come to be men,' said their father, they must be on guard for toubob. 'He often shoots his firesticks, which can be heard far off. And wherever you see much smoke away from any villages, it is probably his cooking fires, which are too big. You should closely inspect his signs to learn which way the toubob went. Having much heavier footsteps than we do, he leaves signs you will recognize as not ours: he breaks twigs and grasses. And when you get close where he has been, you will find that his scent remains there. It's like a wet chicken smells. And many say a toubob sends forth a nervousness that we can feel. If you feel that, become quiet, for often he can be detected at some distance.'

But it's not enough to know the toubob, said Omoro. 'Many of our own people work for him. They are slatee traitors. But without knowing them, there is no way to recognize them. In the bush, therefore, trust *no* one you don't know.'

Kunta and Lamin sat frozen with fear. 'You cannot be told these things strongly enough,' said their father. 'You must know what your uncles and I saw happening to those who had been stolen. It is the difference between slaves among ourselves and those whom toubob takes away to be slaves for him.' He said that they saw stolen people chained inside long, stout, heavily guarded bamboo pens along the shore of the river. When small canoes brought important-acting toubob from the big canoes, the stolen people were dragged outside their pens onto the sand.

'Their heads had been shaved, and they had been greased until they shined all over. First they were made to squat and jump up and down,' said Omoro. 'And then, when the toubob had seen enough of that, they ordered the stolen people's mouths forced open for their teeth and their throats to be looked at.'

Swiftly, Omoro's finger touched Kunta's crotch, and as Kunta jumped, Omoro said, 'Then the men's foto was pulled and looked at. Even the women's private parts were inspected.' And the toubob finally made the people squat again and stuck burning hot irons against their backs and shoulders. Then, screaming and struggling, the people were shipped towards the water, where small canoes waited to take them out to the big canoes.

'My brothers and I watched many fall onto their bellies, clawing and eating the sand, as if to get one last hold and bite of their own home,' said Omoro. 'But they were dragged and beaten on.' Even in the small canoes out in the water, he told Kunta and Lamin, some kept fighting against the whips and the clubs until they jumped into the water among terrible long fish with grey backs and white bellies and curved mouths full of thrashing teeth that reddened the water with their blood.

Kunta and Lamin had huddled close to each other, each gripping the other's hands. 'It's better that you know these things than that your mother and I kill the white cock one day for you.' Omoro looked at his sons. 'Do you know what that means?'

Kunta managed to nod, and found his voice. 'When someone is missing, Fa?' He had seen families frantically chanting to Allah as they squatted around a white cock bleeding and flapping with its throat slit.

'Yes,' said Omoro. 'If the white cock dies on its breast, hope remains. But when a white cock flaps to death on its back, then *no* hope remains, and the whole village joins the family in crying to Allah.'

'Fa—' Lamin's voice, squeaky with fear, startled Kunta, 'where do the big canoes take the stolen people?'

'The elders say to Jong Sang Doo,' said Omoro, 'a land where slaves are sold to huge cannibals called toubabo koomi, who eat us. No man knows any more about it.'

17

So frightened was Lamin by his father's talk of slave-taking and white cannibals that he awakened Kunta several times that night with his bad dreams. And the next day, when Kunta returned from goatherding, he decided to turn his little brother's mind – and his own – from such thoughts by telling him about their distinguished uncles.

'Our father's brothers are also the sons of Kairaba Kunta Kinte, for whom I am named,' said Kunta proudly. 'But our uncles Janneh and Saloum were born of Sireng,' he said. Lamin looked puzzled, but Kunta kept on explaining. 'Sireng was our grandfather's first wife, who died before he married our Grandma Yaisa.' Kunta arranged twigs on the ground to show the Kinte family's different individuals. But he could see that Lamin still didn't understand. With a sigh, he began to talk instead of their uncles' adventures, which Kunta himself had thrilled to so often when his father had told of them.

'Our uncles have never taken wives for themselves because their love of travelling is so great,' said Kunta. 'For moons on end, they travel under the sun and sleep under the stars. Our father says they have been where the sun burns upon endless sand, a land where there is never any rain.' In another place their uncles had visited, said Kunta, the trees were so thick that the forests were dark as night even in the daytime. The people of this place were no taller than Lamin, and like Lamin, always went naked – even after they grew up. And they killed huge elephants with tiny, poisoned darts. In still another place, a land of giants, Janneh and Saloum had seen warriors who could throw their hunting spears twice as far as the mightiest Mandinka, and dancers who could leap higher than their own heads, which were six hands higher than the tallest man in Juffure.

Before bedtime, as Lamin watched with wide eyes, Kunta acted out his favourite of all the stories – springing suddenly about with an imaginary sword slashing up and down, as if Lamin were one of the bandits whom their uncles and others had fought off every day on a journey of many moons, heavily laden with elephants' teeth, precious stones, and gold, to the great black city of Zimbabwe.

Lamin begged for more stories, but Kunta told him to go to sleep. Whenever Kunta had been made to go to bed after his father told him such tales, he would lie on his mat – as his little brother now would – with his mind making the uncles' stories into pictures. And sometimes Kunta would even dream that he was travelling *with* his uncles to all the strange places, that he was talking with the people who looked and acted and lived so differently from the Mandinkas. He had only to hear the names of his uncles and his heart would quicken.

A few days later, it happened that their names reached Juffure in a manner so exciting that Kunta could hardly contain himself. It was a hot, quiet afternoon, and just about everyone in the village was sitting outside his hut's doorway or in the shade of the baobab – when suddenly there came a sharp burst of drumtalk from the next village. Like the grown-ups, Kunta and Lamin cocked their heads intently to read what the drum was saying. Lamin gasped aloud when he heard his own father's name. He wasn't old enough to understand the rest, so Kunta whispered the news it brought: Five days of walking in the way the sun rose, Janneh and Saloum Kinte were building a new village. And their brother Omoro was expected for the ceremonial blessing of the village on the second next new moon.

The drumtalk stopped; Lamin was full of questions. 'Those are *our* uncles? Where is that place? Will our *fa* go there?' Kunta didn't reply. Indeed, as Kunta dashed off across the village towards the hut of the jaliba, he barely heard his brother. Other people were already gathering there – and then came Omoro, with the big-bellied Binta behind him. Everyone watched as Omoro and the jaliba spoke briefly, and Omoro gave him a gift. The talking drum lay near a small fire, where its goatskin head was heating to extreme tautness. Soon the crowd looked on as the jaliba's hands pounded out Omoro's reply that, Allah willing, he would be in his brothers' new village before the second next new moon. Omoro went nowhere during the next days without other villagers pressing upon him their congratulations and their blessings for the new village, which history would record as founded by the Kinte clan.

It wasn't many days before Omoro was to depart when an idea that was almost too big to think about seized upon Kunta. Was it remotely possible that his papa might let him share the journey? Kunta could think of nothing else. Noticing his unusual quietness, Kunta's fellow goatherds, even Sitafa, left him alone. And towards his adoring little brother, he became so short-tempered that even Lamin drew away, hurt and puzzled. Kunta knew how he was acting and felt badly, but he couldn't help himself.

He knew that now and then some lucky boy was allowed to share a journey with his father, uncle, or grown-up brother. But he also knew that such boys had never been so young as his eight rains, except for some fatherless boys, who got special privileges under the forefathers' laws. Such a boy could start following closely behind any man, and the man would never object to sharing whatever he had – even if he was on a journey lasting for moons – so long as the boy followed him at exactly two paces, did everything he was told, never complained, and never spoke unless spoken to.

Kunta knew not to let anyone, especially his mother, even suspect what he dreamed of. He felt certain that not only would Binta disapprove, but she would also probably forbid his ever mentioning it again, and that would mean Omoro would never know how desperately Kunta hoped he could go. So Kunta knew that his only hope lay in asking fa himself – if he could ever catch him alone.

There were soon but three days before Omoro was to leave, and the watchful, almost despairing Kunta was herding his goats after breakfast when he saw his father leaving Binta's hut. Instantly he began manoeuvring his goats into milling back and forth, going nowhere, until Omoro had gone on in a direction and to a distance that Binta surely wouldn't see. Then, leaving his goats alone, because he had to take the chance, Kunta ran like a hare and came to a breathless stop and looked up pleadingly at his father's startled face. Gulping, Kunta couldn't remember a single thing he had meant to say.

Omoro looked down at his son for a long moment, and then he spoke. 'I have just told your mother,' he said – and walked on.

It took Kunta a few seconds to realize what his father meant. 'Aieee!' Kunta shouted, not even aware that he had shouted. Dropping onto his belly, he sprang froglike into the air – and bolting back to his goats, sent them racing towards the bush.

When he collected himself enough to tell his fellow goatherds what had happened, they were so jealous that they went off by themselves. But by midday they could no longer resist the chance to share with him the excitement of such wonderful luck. By that time he had fallen silent with the realization that ever since the drumtalk message had come, his father had been thinking about his son.

Late that afternoon, when Kunta raced happily home and into his mother's hut, Binta grabbed him without a word and began to cuff him so hard that Kunta fled, not daring to ask what he had done. And her manner changed suddenly towards Omoro in a way that shocked Kunta almost as much. Even Lamin knew that a woman was absolutely never allowed to disrespect a man, but with Omoro standing where he could plainly hear her, Binta loudly muttered her disapproval of his and Kunta's travelling in the bush when the drums of different villages were reporting regularly of new people missing. Fixing the breakfast couscous, she pounded the pestle into the mortar so furiously that the sound was like drums.

As Kunta was hurrying out of the hut the next day – to avoid another whacking – Binta commanded Lamin to stay behind and began to kiss and pat and hug him as she hadn't done since he was a baby. Lamin's eyes told Kunta his embarrassment, but there was nothing either of them could do about it.

When Kunta was outside the hut away from his mother, practically every adult who saw him offered congratulations upon his being Juffure's youngest boy ever given the honour of sharing an elder's long journey. Modestly, Kunta said, 'Thank you,' reflecting his proper home-training – but once out in the bush beyond the sight of grown-ups, he pranced under an extra-large headbundle he had brought along to show his mates how well he balanced it – and would balance it the next morning when he strutted past the travellers' tree behind his father. It fell to the ground three times before he took as many steps.

On his way homewards, with many things he wanted to do around the village before leaving, Kunta felt a strange pull to visit old Nyo Boto before doing anything else. After delivering his goats, he escaped from Binta's hut as quickly as he could and went to squat before Nyo Boto's. Shortly she appeared in her doorway. 'I have expected you,' she said, inviting him inside. As usual, whenever Kunta visited her alone, the two of them just sat quietly for a while. He had always liked and looked forward to that feeling. Although he was very young and she was very old, they still felt very close to each other, just sitting there in the dim hut, each of them thinking private thoughts.

'I have something for you,' said Nyo Boto finally. Moving to the dark pouch of cured bullock's hide that hung from the wall by her bed, she withdrew a dark saphie charm of the kind that encircled one's upper arm. 'Your grandfather blessed this charm when your father went to manhood training,' said Nyo Boto. 'It was blessed for the manhood training of Omoro's first son – yourself. Your Grandma Yaisa left it with me for when your manhood training would start. And that is really this journey with your *fa*.' Kunta looked with love at the dear old grandmother, but he couldn't think of a right way to say how the saphie charm would make him feel that she was with him no matter how far away he went.

The next morning, returning from prayers at the mosque, Omoro stood waiting impatiently as Binta took her time completing the adjustment of Kunta's headload. When Kunta had lain awake too filled with excitement to sleep through the night, he had heard her sobbing. Then suddenly she was hugging Kunta so hard that he could feel her body trembling, and he knew, more than ever before in his life, how much his mother really loved him.

With his friend Sitafa, Kunta had carefully reviewed and practised what he and his father now did: first Omoro and then Kunta made two steps out into the dust beyond the doorway of his hut. Then, stopping and turning and bending down, they scraped up the dust of their first footprints and put it into their hunters' bags, thus insuring that their footprints would return to that place.

Binta watched, weeping, from her hut's doorway, pressing Lamin against her big belly, as Omoro and Kunta walked away. Kunta started to turn for a last look – but seeing that his father didn't, kept his eyes front and marched on, remembering that it wasn't proper for a man to show his emotions. As they walked through the village, the people they passed spoke to them and smiled, and Kunta waved at his kafo mates, who had delayed their rounding up of the goats in order to see him off. He knew they understood that he didn't return their spoken greetings because any talking now was taboo for him. Reaching the travellers' tree, they stopped, and Omoro added two more narrow cloth strips to the weather-tattered hundreds already hanging from the lower limbs, each strip representing the prayer of a traveller that his journey would be safe and blessed.

Kunta couldn't believe it was really happening. It was the first time in his life he would spend a night away from his mother's hut, the first time he would ever go farther from the gates of Juffure than one of his goats had strayed, the first time – for so many things. While Kunta was thus preoccupied, Omoro had turned and without a word or a backward glance, started walking very fast down the path into the forest. Almost dropping his headload, Kunta raced to catch up with him.

18

Kunta found himself nearly trotting to keep the proper two paces behind Omoro. He saw that almost two of his quick, short steps were necessary for each long, smooth stride of his father. After about an hour of this, Kunta's excitement had waned almost as much as his pace. His headbundle began to feel heavier and heavier, and he had a terrible thought: Suppose he grew so tired he couldn't keep up? Fiercely, he told himself he would drop in his tracks before that would happen.

Here and there, as they passed, snuffling wild pigs would go rushing into the underbush, and partridges would whirr up, and rabbits would bound for cover. But Kunta wouldn't have paid an elephant much attention in his determination to keep up with Omoro. The muscles below Kunta's knees were beginning to ache a little. His face was sweating, and so was his head; he could tell by the way his bundle began sliding off balance, a little bit one way or the other, and he kept having to put both his hands up there to readjust it.

Ahead, after a while, Kunta saw that they were approaching the travellers' tree of some small village. He wondered what village it was; he was sure he would know its name if his father said it, but Omoro had neither spoken nor looked back ever since they left Juffure. A few minutes later, Kunta saw dashing out to meet them – as he himself had once done – some naked children of the first kafo. They were waving and hallooing, and when they got closer, he could see their eyes widen at the sight of one so young travelling with his father.

'Where are you going?' they chattered, scampering on either side of Kunta. 'Is he your *fa*?' 'Are you Mandinka?' 'What's your village?' Weary as he was, Kunta felt very mature and important, ignoring them just as his father was doing.

Near every travellers' tree, the trail would fork, one leading on into the village and the other past it, so that a person with no business there could pass on by without being considered rude. As Omoro and Kunta took the fork that passed by this village, the little children exclaimed unhappily, but the grown-ups seated under the village baobab only threw glances at the travellers, for holding everyone's attention was a griot whom Kunta could hear loudly orating about the greatness of Mandinkas. There would be many griots, praise singers, and musicians at the blessing of his uncles' new village, Kunta thought.

The sweat began to run into Kunta's eyes, making him blink to stop the stinging. Since they had begun walking, the sun had crossed only half the sky, but his legs already hurt so badly, and his headload had become so heavy, that he began to think he wasn't going to make it. A feeling of panic was rising in him when Omoro suddenly stopped and swung his headload to the ground alongside a clear pool at the side of the trail. Kunta stood for a moment trying to control his unsteady legs. He clutched his headbundle to take it down, but it slipped from his fingers and fell with a bump. Mortified, he knew his father had heard – but Omoro was on his knees drinking from the spring, without a sign that his son was even there.

Kunta hadn't realized how thirsty he was. Hobbling over to the water's edge, he kneeled down to drink – but his legs refused the position. After trying again in vain, he finally lay down on his stomach, braced himself on his elbows, and managed to lower his mouth to the water.

'Just a little.' It was the first time his father had spoken since they left Juffure, and it shocked Kunta. 'Swallow a little, wait, then a little more.' For some reason, he felt angry towards his father. 'Yes, Fa,'

68

he intended to say, but no sound came. He sipped some cool water and swallowed it. Making himself wait, he wanted to collapse. After sipping a little more, he sat up and rested beside the pool. The thought passed through his mind that manhood training must be something like this. And then, sitting upright, he drifted off to sleep.

When he awakened with a start — how long had it been? — Omoro was nowhere to be seen. Jumping up, Kunta saw the big headload under a nearby tree; so his father wouldn't be far away. As he began to look around, he realized how sore he was. He shook himself and stretched. The muscles hurt, but he felt much better than he had. Kneeling for a few more gulps of water from the spring, Kunta noticed his reflection in the still surface of the pool — a narrow black face with wide eyes and mouth. Kunta smiled at himself, then grinned with all his teeth showing. He couldn't help laughing, and as he looked up — there was Omoro standing at his side. Kunta sprang up, embarrassed, but his father's attention seemed to be on other things.

In the shade of some trees, neither of them speaking a word, as the monkeys chattered and the parrots screeched above their heads, they ate some of the bread from their headloads, along with the four plump wood pigeons Omoro had shot with his bow and roasted while Kunta slept. As they ate, Kunta told himself that the first time there was any chance, he was going to show his father how well he too could kill and cook food, the way he and his kafo mates did out in the bush.

When they finished eating, the sun was three fourths across the sky, so it wasn't as hot when the headloads were retied and readjusted on their heads and they set out on the trail once again.

'Toubob brings his canoes one day of walking from here,' said Omoro when they had gone a good distance. 'Now is daytime when we can see, but we must avoid high bush and grass, which can hide surprises.' Omoro's fingers touched his knife sheath and his bow and arrows. 'Tonight we must sleep in a village.'

With his father, he need not fear, of course, but Kunta felt a flash of fright after a lifetime of hearing people and drums tell of disappearances and stealings. As they walked on — a little faster now — Kunta noticed hyena dung on the trail, its colour lily-white because hyenas with their strong jaws cracked and ate so many bones. And beside the path, their approach caused a herd of antelope to stop eating and stand like statues, watching until the humans had passed by.

'Elephants!' said Omoro a little later, and Kunta saw the surrounding trampled bush, the young saplings stripped to bare bark and limbs, and some half-uprooted trees the elephants had leaned on to push the topmost tender leaves downwards where they could reach them with their trunks. Since elephants never grazed near villages and people, Kunta had seen only a few of them in his life, and then only from a great distance. They had been among the thousands of forest animals that ran together, sounding like thunder, ahead of frightening black smoke clouds when a great fire had swept across the brushland once when Kunta was very young; but Allah's rain had put it out before it harmed Juffure or any other nearby villages.

As they trudged along the seemingly endless trail, it occurred to Kunta that just as people's walking feet made trails, so did spiders spin the long, thin threads they travelled on. Kunta wondered if Allah willed matters for the insects and the animals as He did for people; it surprised him to realize he never had thought about that before. He wished he could ask Omoro about it right now. He was even more surprised that Lamin hadn't asked him about it, for Lamin had asked him about even smaller matters than insects. Well, he would have much to tell his little brother when he returned to Juffure – enough to fill days out in the bush with his fellow goatherds for moons to come.

It seemed to Kunta that he and Omoro were entering a different kind of country than the one where they lived. The sinking sun shone down on heavier grasses than he had ever seen before, and among the familiar trees were large growths of palm and cactus. Apart from the biting flies, the only flying things he saw here were not pretty parrots and birds such as those that squawked and sang around Juffure, but circling hawks in search of prey and vultures hunting for food already dead.

The orange ball of the sun was nearing the earth when Omoro and Kunta sighted a thick trail of smoke from a village up ahead. As they reached the travellers' tree, even Kunta could tell that something wasn't right. Very few prayer strips hung from the limbs, showing that few of those who lived here ever left their village and that most travellers from other villages had taken the trail that passed it by. Alas, no children came running out to meet them.

As they passed by the village baobab, Kunta saw that it was partly burned. Over half of the mud huts he could see were empty; trash was in the yards; rabbits were hopping about; and birds were bathing in the dust. The people of the village – most of them leaning or lying about in the doorways of their huts – were almost all old or sick, and a few crying babies seemed to be the only children. Kunta saw not a person of his age – or even as young as Omoro.

Several wrinkled old men weakly received the travellers. The eldest among them, rapping his walking stick, ordered a toothless old woman to bring the travellers water and couscous: maybe she's a slave, thought Kunta. Then the old men began interrupting each other in their haste to explain what had happened to the village. Slave takers one night had stolen or killed all of their younger people, 'from your rains to his!' One old man pointed at Omoro, then at Kunta. 'We old they spared. We ran away into the forest.'

Their abandoned village had begun going to pieces before they could bring themselves to return. They had no crops yet, and not much food or strength. 'We will die out without our young people,' said one of the old men. Omoro had listened closely as they talked, and his words were slow as he spoke: 'My brother's village, which is four days distant, will welcome you, grandfathers.'

But all of them began shaking their heads as the oldest said : 'This is our village. No other well has such sweet water. No other trees' shade is as pleasant. No other kitchens smell of the cooking of our women.'

The old men apologized that they had no hospitality hut to offer. Omoro assured them that he and his son enjoyed sleeping under the stars. And that night, after a simple meal of bread from their head-loads, which they shared with the villagers, Kunta lay on his pallet of green, springy boughs, and thought about all he had heard. Suppose it had been Juffure, with everybody he knew dead or taken away – Omoro, Binta, Lamin and himself too, and the baobab burned, and the yards filled with trash. Kunta made himself think about something else.

Then, suddenly, in the darkness, he heard the shrieks of some forest creature caught by some ferocious animal, and he thought about people catching other people. In the distance he could also hear the howling of hyenas – but rainy season or dry, hungry or harvest, every night of his life, he had heard hyenas howling somewhere. Tonight he found their familiar cry almost comforting as he finally drifted off to sleep.

19

In the first light of dawn, Kunta came awake, springing onto his feet. Standing beside his pallet was a queer old woman demanding in a high, cracked voice to know what had happened to the food she had sent him for two moons ago. Behind Kunta, Omoro spoke softly: 'We wish we could tell you, Grandmother.'

As they hurried on beyond the village after washing and eating, Kunta remembered an old woman in Juffure who would totter about, peering closely into anyone's face and telling him happily, 'My daughter arrives tomorrow!' Her daughter had disappeared many rains before, everyone knew, and the white cock had died on its back, but all those she stopped would gently agree, 'Yes, Grandmother – tomorrow.'

Before the sun was very high, they saw ahead a lone figure walking towards them on the trail. They had passed two or three other travellers the day before – exchanging smiles and greetings – but this old man, drawing near, made it clear that he wanted to talk. Pointing from the direction he had come, he said, 'You may see a toubob.' Behind Omoro, Kunta nearly stopped breathing. 'He has many people carrying his headloads.' The old man said the toubob had seen him and stopped him, but only sought help in finding out where the river began. 'I told him the river begins farthest from where it ends.'

'He meant you no harm?' asked Omoro.

'He acted very friendly,' said the old man, 'but the cat always eats the mouse it plays with.'

'That's the truth!' said Omoro.

Kunta wanted to ask his father about this strange toubob who came looking for rivers rather than for people; but Omoro had bade farewell to the old man and was walking off down the footpath – as usual, without a glance to see if Kunta was behind him. This time Kunta was glad, for Omoro would have seen his son holding onto his headload with both hands while he ran painfully to catch up. Kunta's feet had begun to bleed, but he knew it would be unmanly to take notice of it, let alone mention it to his father.

For the same reason, Kunta swallowed his terror when, later that day, they rounded a turn and came upon a family of lions – a big male, a beautiful female, and two half-grown cubs – lounging in a meadow very near the path. To Kunta, lions were fearsome, slinking animals that would tear apart a goat that a boy permitted to stray too far in its grazing.

Omoro slowed his pace, and without taking his eyes from the lions, said quietly, as if sensing his son's fear, 'They don't hunt or eat at this time of the day unless they're hungry. These are fat.' But he kept one hand on his bow and the other by his quiver of arrows as they passed by. Kunta held his breath but kept walking, and he and the lions watched each other until they were out of sight.

He would have continued to think about them, and about the toubob, also somewhere in the area, but his aching legs wouldn't let him. By that night, he would have ignored twenty lions if they had been feeding at the place Omoro chose for them to spend the night. Kunta had barely lain down on his bed of soft branches before he was into a deep sleep – and it seemed only minutes before his father was shaking him awake in the early dawn. Though he felt as if he hadn't slept at all, Kunta watched with unconcealed admiration how swiftly Omoro skinned, cleaned and roasted their morning meal of two hares, which he had caught in night snares. As Kunta squatted and ate the tasty meat, he thought how he and his goatherding mates used up hours in catching and cooking game, and he wondered how his father and other men ever found time to ever learn so much – about everything there was to know, it seemed.

His blistered feet, and his legs, and his back, and his neck all began to hurt again this third day on the trail – in fact, his whole body seemed to be one dull ache – but he pretended that manhood training had already begun and that he would be the last boy in his kafo to betray his pain. When he stepped on a sharp thorn just before midday, Kunta bravely bit his lip to avoid crying out, but he began to limp and fall so far behind that Omoro decided to let him rest for a few minutes beside the path while they ate their afternoon meal. The soothing paste his father rubbed into the wound made it feel better, but soon after they began walking again, it began to hurt – and bleed – in earnest. Before long, however, the wound was filled with dirt, so the bleeding stopped, and the constant walking numbed the pain enough to let him keep up with his father. Kunta couldn't be sure, but it seemed to him that Omoro had slowed down a tiny bit. The area around the wound was ugly and swollen by the time they stopped that night, but his father applied another poultice, and in the morning it looked and felt good enough to bear his weight without too much pain.

Kunta noticed with relief, as they set out the next day, that they had left behind the thorn and cactus land they had been travelling through and were moving into bush country more like Juffure's, with even more trees and thickly flowering plants, and more chattering monkeys and multicoloured land birds than he had ever seen before. Breathing in the fragrant air made Kunta remember times when he had taken his little brother to catch crabs down along the banks of the bolong, where he and Lamin would wait to wave at their mother and the other women rowing homewards after work in their rice fields.

Omoro took the bypass fork at every travellers' tree, but each village's first-kafo children always raced out to meet them and to tell the strangers whatever happened to be the most exciting of the local news. In one such village, the little couriers rushed out yelling, 'Mumbo jumbo! Mumbo jumbo!' and considering their job done, fled back inside the village gate. The bypassing trail went near enough for Omoro and Kunta to see the townspeople watching a masked and costumed figure brandishing a rod over the bare back of a screaming woman whom several other women held. All of the women spectators were shrieking with each blow of the rod. From discussions with his fellow goatherds, Kunta knew how a husband, if enough annoyed by a quarrelsome, troublemaking wife, could go quietly to another village and hire a mumbo jumbo to come to his village and shout fearsomely at intervals from concealment, then appear and publicly discipline that wife, after which all of the village's women were apt to act better for a time.

At one travellers' tree, no children came out to meet the Kintes. In fact, there was no one to be seen at all, and not a sound was to be heard in the silent village, except for the birds and monkeys. Kunta wondered if slave takers had come here, too. He waited in vain for Omoro to explain the mystery, but it was the chattering children of the next village who did so. Pointing back down the trail, they said that village's chief had kept on doing things his people disliked until one night not long ago, as he slept, everyone had quietly gone away with all their possessions to the homes of friends and families in other places – leaving behind an 'empty chief', the children said, who was now going about promising to act better if only his people would return.

Since night-time was near, Omoro decided to enter this village, and the crowd under the baobab was abuzz with this exciting gossip. Most felt certain that their new neighbours would return home after they had taught their chief his lesson for a few more days. While Kunta stuffed his stomach with groundnut stew over steamed rice,

Omoro went to the village jaliba and arranged for a talking-drum message to his brothers. He told them to expect him by the next sundown and that travelling with him was his first son.

Kunta had sometimes daydreamed about hearing his name drum-sounding across the land, and now it had happened. It wouldn't leave his ears. Later, on the hospitality hut's bamboo bed, bone-weary as he was, Kunta thought of the other jalibas hunched over their drums pounding out his name in every village along their route to the village of Janneh and Saloum.

At every travellers' tree now, since the drums had spoken, were not only the usual naked children but also some elders and musicians. And Omoro couldn't refuse a senior elder's request to grant his village the honour of at least a brief visit. As the Kintes freshened themselves in each hospitality hut and then sat down to share food and drink in the shade of the baobab and silk-cotton trees, the adults gathered eagerly to hear Omoro's answers to their questions, and the first, second and third kafos clustered about Kunta.

While the first kafo stared at him in silent awe, those of Kunta's rains and older, painfully jealous, asked him respectful questions about his home village and his destination. He answered them gravely with, he hoped, the same dignity as his father did their fathers' questions. By the time they left, he was sure the villagers felt they had seen a young man who had spent most of his life travelling with his father along The Gambia's long trails.

20

They had tarried so long at the last village that they would have to walk faster and harder to reach their destination by sundown, as Omoro had promised his brothers. Though he sweated and ached, Kunta found it easier than before to keep his headload balanced, and he felt a new spurt of strength with each of the drumtalk messages that now filled the air with word of the arrival of griots, jalibas, senior elders and other important people in the town ahead, each representing such distant home villages as Karantaba, Kootacunda,

Pisania and Jonkakonda, most of which Kunta had never heard of. A griot from the Kingdom of Wooli was there, said the drums, and even a prince sent by his father, the King of Barra. As Kunta's cracked feet padded quickly along the hot, dusty trail, he was amazed at how famous and popular his uncles were. Soon he was all but running, not only to keep close behind the ever more rapidly striding Omoro, but also because these past few hours seemed to be taking forever.

Finally, just as the sun began to turn crimson on the western horizon, Kunta spotted smoke rising from a village not far ahead. The wide, circular pattern of the smoke told Kunta that dried baobab hulls were being burned to drive away mosquitoes. That meant the village was entertaining important visitors. He felt like cheering. They had arrived! Soon he began to hear the thunder of a big ceremonial tobalo drum – being pounded, he guessed, as each new personage entered between the village gates. Intermingling was the throb of smaller tan-tang drums and the shrieking of dancers. Then the trail made a turn, and there under the rising smoke was the village. And alongside a busy growth they saw a man who caught sight of them at the same instant and began to point and wave as if he had been posted there to await an oncoming man with a boy. Omoro waved back at the man, who immediately squatted over his drum and announced on it: 'Omoro Kinte and first son—'

Kunta's feet scarcely felt the ground. The travellers' tree, soon in sight, was festooned with cloth strips, and the original single-file trail had already been widened by many feet – evidence of an already popular and busy village. The pounding of the tan-tangs grew louder and louder, and suddenly the dancers appeared, grunting and shouting in their leaf-and-bark costumes, leaping and whirling and stamping out through the village gate ahead of everyone else, all of them rushing to meet the distinguished visitors. The village's deep-voiced tobalo began to boom as two figures came running through the crowd. Ahead of Kunta, Omoro's headbundle dropped suddenly to the ground, and Omoro was running towards them. Before he knew it, Kunta's own headbundle had dropped and he was running too.

The two men and his father were hugging and pounding each other. 'And this is our nephew?' Both men yanked Kunta off his feet and embraced him amid exclamations of joy. Sweeping them on to the village, the huge welcoming party cried out their greetings all around them, but Kunta saw and heard no one but his uncles. They certainly resembled Omoro, but he noticed that they were both somewhat shorter, stockier, and more muscular than his father. The older Uncle Janneh's eyes had a squinting way of seeming to look a long distance, and both men moved with an almost animal quickness. They also talked much more rapidly than his father as they plied him with questions about Juffure and about Binta.

Finally, Saloum thumped his fist on Kunta's head. 'Not since he got his name have we been together. And now look at him! How many rains have you, Kunta?'

'Eight, sir,' he answered politely.

'Nearly ready for manhood training!' exclaimed his uncle.

All around the village's tall bamboo fence, dry thornbushes were piled up, and concealed among them were sharp-pointed stakes to cripple any marauding animal or human. But Kunta wasn't noticing such things, and the few others of around his age who were there he saw only out of the corners of his eyes. He scarcely heard the racket of the parrots and monkeys above their heads, or the barking of the wuolo dogs underfoot, as the uncles took them on a tour of their beautiful new village. Every hut had its own private yard, said Saloum, and every woman's dry-foods storehouse was mounted directly over her cooking fire, so the smoke would keep her rice, couscous, and millet free of bugs.

Kunta almost got dizzy jerking his head towards this or that exciting sight, smell, or sound. It was both fascinating and confusing to overhear people speaking in Mandinka dialects that he couldn't understand beyond an occasional word. Like the rest of the Mandinkas – except for those as learned as the arafang – Kunta knew next to nothing of the languages of other tribes, even of those who lived nearby. But he had spent enough time around the travellers' tree to know which tribes were which. The Fulas had oval faces, longer hair, thinner lips, and sharper features, with vertical scars on their temples. The Wolof were extremely black and very reserved, the Serahuli lighter-skinned and small in stature. And the Jolas – there was no mistaking *them* – scarred their entire bodies, and their faces always seemed to wear a ferocious expression.

Kunta recognized people from all of these tribes here in the new village, but there were even more he didn't recognize. Some were haggling loudly with traders as they hawked their wares. Older women clamoured over tanned hides, and younger women bargained for hairpieces made from sisal and baobab. The cry 'Kola! Fine purple kola!' drew a cluster of those whose few remaining teeth were already orange-stained from chewing the nuts.

Amid friendly elbowing and pushing, Omoro was introduced to an endless stream of villagers and important persons from exciting places. Kunta marvelled at his uncles' fluent talking in the strange tongues they spoke. Letting himself drift into the shifting throng, knowing that he could find his father and uncles whenever he wanted to, Kunta soon found himself among the musicians who were playing for all who felt like dancing. Next he sampled the roast antelope and beef and the groundnut stew that the village women kept bountifully supplied on tables in the baobabs' shade for anyone who wanted it. It was all right as food went, Kunta thought, but not as tasty as the succulent harvest-festival dishes prepared by the mothers of Juffure.

Seeing some women over by the well talking excitedly about something, Kunta sidled over, his ears as wide as his eyes, and heard that a very great marabout was reported to be only about half a day's travel away on the trail, journeying with his party to honour the new village, since it had been founded by sons of the late holy man Kairaba Kunta Kinte. Kunta was thrilled anew to hear his own grandfather spoken of so reverently. Unrecognized by any of the women, he heard them chatter next about his uncles. It was time they travelled less and settled down to have wives and sons, one woman said. 'The only trouble they will have,' said another, 'is so many maidens eager to be their wives.'

It was almost dark when Kunta, feeling very awkward, finally approached some boys of around his own age. But they didn't seem to mind that he had hung around the grown-ups until now. Mostly, they seemed anxious to tell Kunta how their new village had come to be. 'All of our families became your uncles' friends somewhere during their travels,' said one boy. All of them had been dissatisfied with their lives where they were, for one reason or another. 'My grandfather didn't have enough space for all his family and his children's families to be close to him,' a boy said. 'Our bolong wouldn't grow good rice,' said another.

His uncles, Kunta heard, began telling friends they knew an ideal place where they were thinking of building a village. And the families of Janneh and Saloum's friends were soon on the trail with their goats, chickens, pets, prayer rugs and other possessions.

Soon it was dark and Kunta watched as the fires of the new village were lit with the sticks and branches that his new friends had collected earlier in the day. Because it was a time of celebration, they told him all the villagers and visitors would sit together around several fires, instead of the usual custom, which dictated that the men and the women and children would sit at separate fires. The alimamo would bless the gathering, they said, and then Janneh and Saloum would walk inside the circle to tell stories about their travels and adventures. In the circle with them would be the oldest visitor to the village, a senior elder from the distant upper-river of Fulladu. It was whispered that he had over a hundred rains, and would share his wisdom with all who had ears to hear.

Kunta ran to join his father at the fireside just in time to hear the alimamo's prayer. After it, no one said anything for a few minutes. Crickets rasped loudly, and the smoky fires cast dancing shadows upon the wide circle of faces. Finally, the leathery old elder spoke: 'Hundreds of rains before even my earliest memories, talk reached across the big waters of an African mountain of gold. This is what first brought toubob to Africa!' There was no gold mountain, he said, but gold beyond description had been found in streams and mined from deep shafts first in northern Guinea, then later in the forests of Ghana. 'Toubob was never told where gold came from,' said the old man. 'for what one toubob knows, soon they all know.'

Then Janneh spoke. Nearly as precious as gold in many places, he said, was salt. He and Saloum had personally seen salt and gold exchanged in equal weights. Salt was found in thick slabs under certain distant sands, and certain waters elsewhere would dry into a salty mush, which was shaped into blocks after sitting in the sun.

'There was once a *city* of salt,' said the old man. 'The city of Taghaza, whose people built their houses and mosques of blocks of salt.'

'Tell of the strange humpbacked animals you have spoken of before now,' demanded an ancient-looking old woman, daring to interrupt. She reminded Kunta of Grandmother Nyo Boto.

A hyena howled somewhere in the night as people leaned forward in the flickering light. It was Saloum's turn to speak. 'Those animals that are called camels live in a place of endless sand. They find their way across it from the sun, the stars and the wind. Janneh and I have ridden these animals for as long as three moons with few stops for water.'

'But many stops to fight off the bandits!' said Janneh.

'Once we were part of a caravan of twelve thousand camels,' Saloum continued. 'Actually, it was many smaller caravans travelling together to protect ourselves against bandits.'

Kunta saw that as Saloum spoke, Janneh was unrolling a large piece of tanned hide. The elder made an impatient gesture to two young men who sprang to throw onto the fire some dry branches. In the flaring light, Kunta and the others could follow Janneh's finger as it moved across a strange-looking drawing. 'This is Africa,' he said. The finger traced what he told them was 'the big water' to the west, and then 'the great sand desert', a place larger by many times than all of The Gambia – which he pointed out in the lower left of the drawing.

'To the north coast of Africa, the toubob ships bring porcelain, spices, cloth, horses and countless things made by men,' said Saloum. 'Then, camels, and donkeys bear those goods inland to places like Sijilmasa, Ghadames and Marrakech.' The moving finger of Janneh showed where those cities were. 'And as we sit here tonight,' said Saloum, 'there are many men with heavy headloads crossing deep forests taking our own African goods – ivory, skins, olives, dates, kola nuts, cotton, copper, precious stones – back to the toubob's ships.'

Kunta's mind reeled at what he heard, and he vowed silently that some day he too would venture to such exciting places.

'The marabout!' From far out on the trail, the lookout drummer beat out the news. Quickly a formal greeting party was lined up – Janneh and Saloum as the village's founders; then the Council of Elders, the alimamo, the arafang; then the honoured representatives of other villages, including Omoro; and Kunta was placed with those of his height among the village's young ones. Musicians led them all out towards the travellers' tree, timing their approach to meet the holy man as he arrived. Kunta stared hard at the white-bearded, very black old man at the head of his long and tired party. Men, women and children were heavily loaded with large headbundles, except for a few men herding cattle and, Kunta judged, more than a hundred goats.

With quick gestures, the holy man blessed the welcoming party and bade them rise from their knees. Then Janneh and Saloum were specially blessed, and Omoro was introduced by Janneh, and Saloum beckoned to Kunta, who went dashing up alongside them. 'This is my first son,' said Omoro, 'who bears his holy grandfather's name.' Kunta heard the marabout speak words in Arabic over him – which he couldn't understand, except for his grandfather's name – and he felt the holy man's fingers touching his head as lightly as a butterfly's wing, and then he went dashing back among those of his own age as the marabout went to meet the others in the welcoming party, conversing with them as if he were an ordinary man. The young ones in Kunta's group began to trail away and stare at the long line of wives, children, students and slaves who brought up the rear of the procession.

The marabout's wives and children quickly retired into guest huts. The students, taking seats on the ground and opening their head-bundles, withdrew books and manuscripts – the property of their teacher, the holy man – and began reading aloud to those who gathered around each of them to listen. The slaves, Kunta noticed, didn't enter the village with the others, Remaining outside the fence, the slaves squatted down near where they had tethered the cattle and penned the goats. They were the first slaves Kunta had ever seen who kept away from other people.

The holy man could scarcely move for all the people on their knees around him. Villagers and distinguished visitors alike pressed their foreheads to the dirt and wailed for him to hear their plaints, some of the nearest presuming to touch his garment. Some begged him to visit their villages and conduct long-neglected religious services. Some asked for legal decisions, since law and religion were companions under Islam. Fathers asked to be given meaningful names for new babies. People from villages without an arafang asked if their children might be taught by one of the holy man's students.

These students were now busily selling small squares of cured goathide, which many hands then thrust towards the holy man for him to make his mark on. A holy-marked piece of goatskin, sewn into a treasured saphie charm such as Kunta wore around his upper arm, would insure the wearer's constant nearness to Allah. For the two cowrie shells he had brought with him from Juffure, Kunta purchased a square of goathide and joined the jostling crowd that pressed in upon the marabout.

It ran through Kunta's mind that his grandfather must have been like this holy man, who had the power, through Allah, to bring the rain to save a starving village, as Kairaba Kunta Kinte had once saved Juffure. So his beloved grandmas Yaisa and Nyo Boto had told him since he was old enough to understand. But only now, for the first time, did he truly understand the greatness of his grandfather – and of Islam. Only one person, thought Kunta, was going to be told why he had decided to spend his precious two cowries and now stood holding his own small square of cured goatskin waiting his turn for a holy mark. He was going to take the blessed goatskin back home and turn it over to Nyo Boto, and ask her to keep it for him until the time came to sew it into a precious saphie charm for the arm of his own first son.

21

Kunta's kafo, galled with envy of his trip, and expecting that he would return to Juffure all puffed up with himself, had decided – without any of them actually saying so – to show no interest whatever in him or his travels when he returned. And so they did, thinking nothing of how heartsick it made Kunta feel to arrive home and find his lifelong mates not only acting as if he hadn't been away, but actually ending conversations if he came near, his dearest friend Sitafa acting even colder than the others. Kunta was so upset that he hardly even thought about his new infant brother, Suwadu, who had been born while he was away with Omoro.

One noon, as the goats grazed, Kunta finally decided to overlook his mates' unkindness and try to patch things up. Walking over to the other boys, who were sitting apart from him eating their lunches, he sat down among them and simply began talking. 'I wish you could have been with me,' he said quietly, and without waiting for their reaction, began to tell them about the trip.

He told how hard the days of walking had been, how his muscles had ached, about his fright in passing the lions. And he described the different villages he had passed through and the people who lived there. While he spoke, one of the boys jumped up to regroup his goats, and when he returned – without seeming to notice – sat down closer to Kunta. Soon Kunta's words were being accompanied by grunts and exclamations from the others, and before they knew it, just at that point in his story when he reached his uncles' new village, the time had come to drive the goats homewards.

The next morning in the schoolyard, all of the boys had to strain not to let the arafang suspect their impatience to leave. Finally out again with their goats, they huddled around Kunta, and he began to tell them about the different tribes and languages all intermingled in his uncles' village. He was in the middle of one of the tales of faraway places that Janneh and Saloum had told around the campfire – the boys hanging raptly on every word – when the stillness of the fields was broken by the ferocious barking of a wuolo dog and the shrill, terrified bleating of a goat.

Springing upright, they saw over the edge of the tall grass a great, tawny panther dropping a goat from his jaws and lunging at two of their wuolo dogs. The boys were still standing there, too shocked and scared to move, when one of the dogs was flung aside by the panther's sweeping paw – as the other dog leaped wildly back and forth, the panther crouched to spring, their horrible snarlings drowning out the frantic barking of the other dogs and the cries of the other goats, which were bounding off in all directions.

Then the boys fanned out, shouting and running, most trying to head off the goats. But Kunta bolted blindly towards his father's fallen goat. 'Stop, Kunta! *No!*' screamed Sitafa as he tried to stop him from running between the dogs and the panther. He couldn't catch him; but when the panther saw the two yelling boys rushing at him, he backed off a few feet, then turned and raced back towards the forest with the enraged dogs at his heels.

The panther stink and the mangled nanny goat made Kunta sick – blood was running darkly down her twisted neck; her tongue lolled out; her eyes were rolled back up in her head and – most horribly – her belly was ripped wide open and Kunta could see her unborn kid inside, still slowly pulsing. Nearby was the first wuolo dog, whining in pain from its gashed side and trying to crawl towards Kunta. Vomiting where he stood, Kunta turned, ashen, and looked at Sitafa's anguished face.

Dimly, through his tears, Kunta sensed some of the other boys around him, staring at the hurt dog and the dead goat. Then slowly they all drew back – all but Sitafa, who put his arms around Kunta. None of them spoke, but the question hung in the air: How is he going to tell his father? Somehow Kunta found his voice. 'Can you care for my goats?' he asked Sitafa. 'I must take this hide to my father.'

Sitafa went over and talked with the other boys, and two of them quickly picked up and carried off the whimpering dog. Kunta then motioned Sitafa to go away with the others. Kneeling by the dead nanny goat with his knife, Kunta cut and pulled, and cut again, as he had seen his father do it, until finally he rose with the wet hide in his hands. Pulling weeds, he covered over the nanny's carcass and the unborn kid, and started back towards the village. Once before he had forgotten his goats while herding, and he had vowed never to let it happen again. But it *had* happened again, and this time a nanny goat had been killed.

Desperately, he hoped it was a nightmare, and that he'd awaken now, but the wet hide was in his hands. He wished death upon himself, but he knew his disgrace would be taken among the ancestors. Allah must be punishing him for boasting, Kunta thought with shame. He stopped to kneel towards the way the sun rose and prayed for forgiveness.

Rising, he saw that his kafo had all the goats herded back together and were getting ready to leave the grazing area, lifting their headloads of firewood. One boy was carrying the injured dog, and two of the other dogs were limping badly. Sitafa, seeing Kunta looking towards them, put his headload down and started towards Kunta, but quickly Kunta waved him away again to go on with the rest.

Each footstep along the worn goat trail seemed to take Kunta closer to the end – the end of everything. Guilt and terror and numbness washed over him in waves. He would be sent away. He would miss Binta, Lamin, and old Nyo Boto. He would even miss the arafang's class. He thought of his late Grandma Yaisa, of his holy man grandfather whose name he bore, now disgraced; of his famous travelling uncles, who had built a village. He remembered that he had no headload of firewood. He thought of the nanny goat, whom he remembered well, always skittish and given to trotting off from the rest. And he thought of the kid not yet born. And while he thought of all these things, he could think of nothing but what he most feared to think of: his father.

His mind lurched, and he stopped, rooted, not breathing, staring ahead of him down the path. It was Omoro, running towards him. No boy would have dared tell him; how had he known?

'Are you all right?' his father asked.

Kunta's tongue seemed cleaved to the roof of his mouth. 'Yes, Fa,' he said finally. But by then Omoro's hand was exploring Kunta's belly, discovering that the blood soaking his dundiko wasn't Kunta's.

Straightening, Omoro took the hide and laid it on the grass. 'Sit down!' he ordered, and Kunta did, trembling as Omoro sat across from him.

'There is something you need to know,' said Omoro. 'All men make mistakes. I lost a goat to a lion when I was of your rains.'

Pulling at his tunic, Omoro bared his left hip. The pale, deeply scarred place there shocked Kunta. 'I learned, and you must learn. *Never* run towards any dangerous animal!' His eyes searched Kunta's face. 'Do you *hear* me?'

'Yes, Fa.'

Omoro got up, took the goat's hide, and flung it far off into the brush. 'Then that is all that needs to be said.'

Kunta's head reeled as he walked back to the village behind Omoro. Greater even than his guilt, and his relief, was the love he felt for his father at this moment.

22

Kunta had reached his tenth rain, and the second-kafo boys his age were about to complete the schooling they had received twice daily since they were five rains old. When the day of graduation came, the parents of Kunta and his mates seated themselves in the arafang's schoolyard beaming with pride in the very front rows, even ahead of the village elders. While Kunta and the others squatted before the arafang, the village alimamo prayed. Then the arafang stood and began looking around at his pupils as they waved their hands to be asked a question. Kunta was the first boy he chose.

'What was the profession of your forefathers, Kunta Kinte?' he asked.

'Hundreds of rains ago in the land of Mali,' Kunta confidently replied, 'the Kinte men were blacksmiths, and their women were makers of pots and weavers of cloth.' With each pupil's correct answer, all those assembled made loud sounds of pleasure.

Then the arafang asked a mathematical question: 'If a baboon has seven wives, each wife has seven children, and each child eats seven groundnuts for seven days, how many nuts did the baboon steal from some man's farm?' After much frantic figuring with grass-quill pens on their cottonwood slates, the first to yelp out the right answer was Sitafa Silla, and the crowd's shouting of praise drowned out the groans of the other boys.

Next the boys wrote their names in Arabic, as they had been taught. And one by one, the arafang held up the slates for all the parents and other spectators to see for themselves what education had achieved. Like the other boys, Kunta had found the marks that talk even harder to read than they were to write. Many mornings and evenings, with the arafang rapping their knuckles, they had all wished that writing was as easy to understand as the talking drum, which even those of Lamin's age could read as if someone standing beyond sight were calling out the words.

One by one now, the arafang asked each graduate to stand. Finally came Kunta's turn. 'Kunta Kinte!' With all eyes upon him, Kunta felt the great pride of his family in the front row, even of his ancestors in the burying ground beyond the village – most especially of his beloved Grandma Yaisa. Standing up, he read aloud a verse from the Koran's last page; finishing, he pressed it to his forehead and said, 'Amen!' When the readings were done, the teacher shook each boy's hand and announced loudly that as their education was complete, these boys were now of the third kafo, and everyone broke out into a loud cheering. Binta and the other mothers quickly removed the covers from the bowls and calabashes they had brought, heaped with delicious foods, and the graduation ceremony ended in a feast that soon emptied both.

Omoro was waiting the next morning when Kunta came to take the family's goats out for the day's grazing. Pointing to a fine young male and female, Omoro said, 'These two are your school-finishing present.' Almost before Kunta could stammer out his thanks, Omoro walked away without another word – as if he gave away a pair of goats every day – and Kunta tried very hard not to seem excited. But the moment his father was out of sight, Kunta whooped so loud that his new charges jumped and started running – with all the others in hot pursuit. By the time he caught up with them and herded them out to the fields, the rest of his mates were already there – showing off their *own* new goats. Treating them like sacred animals, the boys steered their charges to only the most tender grasses, already picturing the strong young kids they would soon produce, and the kids would have soon after, until each boy had a herd as large and valuable as his father's.

Before the next new moon appeared, Omoro and Binta were among the parents who gave away a third goat – this one to the arafang as an expression of gratitude for their son's education. If they had been more prosperous, they would have been glad to give even a cow, but they knew he understood that this was beyond their means, as it was beyond the means of everyone in Juffure, which was a humble village. Indeed, some parents – new slaves with nothing saved – had little to offer but their own backs, and their grateful gift of a moon's farm work for the arafang was graciously accepted.

The passing moons soon flowed into seasons until yet another rain had passed and Kunta's kafo had taught Lamin's kafo how to be goatherds. A time long awaited now drew steadily nearer. Not a day passed that Kunta and his mates didn't feel both anxiety and joy at the approach of the next harvest festival, which would end with the taking away of the third kafo – those boys between ten and fifteen rains in age – to a place far away from Juffure, to which they would return, after four moons, as men.

Kunta and the others tried to act as if none of them were really giving the matter any particular thought or concern. But they thought of little else, and they watched and listened for the slightest sign or word from a grown-up that had anything at all to do with manhood training. And early in the dry season, after several of their fathers quietly left Juffure for two or three days and just as quietly returned, the boys whispered tensely among themselves, especially after Kalilu Conteh overheard his uncle say that much-needed repairs had been made on the jujuo, the manhood-training village that had gone unused and exposed to weather and animals for almost five rains since the last training had been completed there. Even more excited whispering followed talk among their fathers about which elder might be selected by the Council of Elders to be the kintango, the man in charge of manhood training. Kunta and all of his mates had many times heard their fathers, uncles, and older brothers speaking reverently of the kintangos who had supervised their own manhood training many rains before.

It was just before the harvest season when all of the third-kafo boys reported to one another in a fever of excitement how their mothers had silently measured each of them with a sewing tape around his head and down to his shoulders. Kunta did his best to hide the vivid memory of that morning five rains before when, as brand-new little goatherds, he and his mates had been scared nearly out of their wits as they watched screaming boys under white hoods being kicked and jeered from the village by a band of terrifyingly masked, shrieking, spear-carrying kankurang dancers.

The tobalo soon boomed out the beginning of the new harvest, and Kunta joined the rest of the villagers in the fields. He welcomed the long days of hard work, for they kept him too busy and too tired to give much thought to what lay ahead. But when the harvesting was done and the festival began, he found himself unable to enjoy the music and the dancing and the feasting as the others did – as he himself had done for as long as he could remember. The louder the merriment, in fact, the unhappier he became until finally he spent most of the last two days of the festival sitting by himself on the banks of the bolong skipping stones across the water.

On the night before the last day of the festival, Kunta was in Binta's hut silently finishing his evening meal of groundnut stew with rice when Omoro walked in behind him. From the corner of his eye, Kunta glimpsed his father raising something white, and before he had a chance to turn around, Omoro had pulled a long hood down firmly over his head. The terror that shot through Kunta all but numbed him. He felt his father's hand gripping his upper arm and urging him to stand up, then to move backwards until he was pushed down onto a low stool. Kunta was grateful to sit, for his legs felt like water and his head felt light. He listened to himself breathing in short gasps, knowing that if he tried to move, he would fall off the stool. So he sat very still, trying to accustom himself to the darkness. Terrified as he was, it seemed almost a double darkness. As his upper lip felt the moist warmth of his breath inside the hood, it flashed through Kunta's mind that surely once such a hood had been thrust in the same way over his father's head. Could Omoro have been so frightened? Kunta couldn't even imagine that, and he felt ashamed to be such a disgrace to the Kinte clan.

It was very quiet in the hut. Wrestling the fear that knotted the pit of his stomach, Kunta closed his eyes and focused his very pores on trying to hear something, anything at all. He thought he heard Binta moving about, but he couldn't be sure. He wondered where Lamin was, and Suwadu, who surely would be making noise. He knew only one thing for sure: neither Binta nor anyone else was going to speak to him, let alone lift that hood off his head. And then Kunta thought how awful it would be if his hood *did* get lifted, for everyone would see how scared he really was, and perhaps therefore a boy unworthy of joining his kafo mates in manhood training.

Even boys the size of Lamin knew – since Kunta had told him – what would happen to anyone who showed himself too weak or cowardly to endure the training that turned boys into hunters, into warriors, into men – all within a period of twelve moons. Suppose he should fail? He began gulping down his fear, remembering how he had been told that any boy who failed the manhood training would be treated as a child for the rest of his life, even though he might look like a grown man. He would be avoided, and his village would never permit him to marry, lest he father others like himself. These sad cases, Kunta had heard, usually slipped away from their villages sooner or later, never to return, and even their own fathers, mothers, brothers and sisters would never mention them again. Kunta saw himself slinking away from Juffure like some mangy hyena, scorned by everyone; it was too horrible to think of.

After a time, Kunta realized that he was faintly hearing the drumbeats and the shouting of dancers in the distance. More time passed. What hour was it, he wondered. He guessed it must be near the sutoba hour, halfway between dusk and dawn, but after a few moments he heard the alimamo's high-pitched wailing for the village's safo prayer, two hours before midnight. The music ceased and Kunta knew that the villagers had stopped their celebrating and the men were hastening to the mosque.

Kunta sat until he knew the prayers must have been over, but the music didn't resume. He listened hard, but could hear only silence. Finally he nodded off, awakening with a start only a few moments later. It was still quiet – and darker under the hood than a moonless night. Finally, faintly, he was certain that he could hear the early yippings of hyenas. He knew that hyenas always yipped for a while before settling down to steady howling, which they would continue until early daybreak, sounding eerily far away.

During the harvest festival week, at the first streaks of daybreak, Kunta knew the tobalo would boom. He sat waiting for that to happen – for *anything* to happen. He felt his anger building, expecting the tobalo to sound at any moment – but nothing happened. He grated his teeth and waited some more. And then, at last, after jerking awake a few times, he dozed off into a fitful sleep. He all but leaped from his skin when the tobalo finally did boom. Under the hood, his cheeks were hot with embarrassment that he had fallen asleep.

Having become accustomed to the hood's darkness, Kunta could all but see the morning's activities from the sounds his ears picked up – the crowing of the cocks, the barking of the wuolo dogs, the wailing of the alimamo, the bumping of the women's pestles as they beat the breakfast couscous. This morning's prayer to Allah, he knew, would be for the success of the manhood training that was about to begin. He heard movement in the hut, and he sensed that it was Binta. It was strange how he couldn't see her, but he knew it was his mother. Kunta wondered about Sitafa and his other mates. It surprised him to realize that throughout the night, he hadn't once thought about them until now. He told himself that they must surely have had as long a night as he had.

When the music of koras and balafons began playing outside the hut, Kunta heard the sound of people walking and talking, louder and louder. Then drums joined the din, their rhythm sharp and cutting. A moment later, his heart seemed to stop as he sensed the sudden movement of someone rushing into the hut. Before he could even brace himself, his wrists were grabbed, and roughly he was snatched up from the stool and jerked out through the hut door into the all but deafening noise of staccato drums and screeching people.

Hands knocked him and feet kicked him. Kunta thought desperately of bolting away somehow, but just as he was about to try, a firm yet gentle hand grasped one of his. Breathing hoarsely under his hood, Kunta realized that he was no longer being hit and kicked and that the screaming of the crowd was suddenly no longer near by. The people, he guessed, had moved along to some other boy's hut, and the guiding hand that held his must belong to the slave Omoro would have hired, as every father did, to lead his hooded son to the jujuo.

The crowd's shouting rose to a frenzied pitch every time another boy was dragged from a hut, and Kunta was glad he couldn't see the kankurang dancers, who were making bloodcurdling whoops as they sprang high into the air brandishing their spears. Big drums and small drums – every drum in the village, it seemed – were pounding as the slave guided Kunta faster and faster between rows of people shouting on either side of him, crying out things like 'Four moons!' and 'They will become men!' Kunta wanted to burst into tears. He wished wildly that he could reach out and touch Omoro, Binta, Lamin – even the snivelling Suwadu – for it felt too much to bear that four long moons were going to pass before he would see again those he loved even more than he had ever realized until now. Kunta's ears told him that he and his guide had joined a moving line of marchers, all stepping to the swift rhythm of the drums. As they passed through the village gates – he could tell because the noise of the crowd began to fade – he felt hot tears well up and run down his cheeks. He closed his eyes tight, as if to hide the tears even from himself.

As he had felt Binta's presence in the hut, now he felt, almost as if it were a smell, the fear of his kafo mates ahead of and behind him in the line, and he knew that theirs was as great as his. Somehow that made him feel less ashamed. As he trudged on in the white blindness of his hood, he knew that he was leaving behind more than his father and his mother and his brothers and the village of his birth, and this filled him with sadness as much as terror. But he knew it must be done, as it had been done by his father before him and would some day be done by his son. He would return, but only as a man.

23

They must be approaching – within a stone's throw, Kunta sensed – a recently cut bamboo grove. Through his hood, he could smell the rich fragrance of bamboo freshly chopped. They marched closer; the smell became stronger and stronger; they were at the barrier, then through it; but they were still outdoors. Of course – it was a bamboo fence. Suddenly the drums stopped and the marchers halted. For several minutes, Kunta and the others stood still and silent. He listened for the slightest sound that might tell him when they had stopped or where they were, but all he could hear was the screeching of parrots and the scolding of monkeys overhead.

Then, suddenly, Kunta's hood was lifted. He stood blinking in the bright sun of mid-afternoon, trying to adjust his eyes to the light. He was afraid even to turn his head enough to see his kafo mates, for directly before them stood stern, wrinkled senior elder Silla Ba Dibba. Like all the other boys, Kunta knew him and his family well. But Silla Ba Dibba acted as if he had never seen any of them before – indeed, as if he would rather not see them now; his eyes scanned their faces as he would have looked at crawling maggots. Kunta knew that this surely was their kintango. Standing on either side of him were two younger men, Ali Sise and Soru Tura, whom Kunta also knew well; Soru was a special friend of Omoro's. Kunta was grateful that neither of them *was* Omoro, to see his son so scared.

As they had been taught, the entire kafo – all twenty-three boys – crossed their palms over their hearts and greeted their elders in the traditional way: 'Peace!' 'Peace only!' replied the old kintango and his assistants. Widening his gaze for a moment – careful not to move his head – Kunta saw that they stood in a compound dotted with several small, mud-walled, thatch-roofed huts and surrounded by the tall new bamboo fence. He could see where the huts had been patched, undoubtedly by the fathers who had disappeared from Juffure for a few days. All this he saw without moving a muscle. But the next moment he nearly jumped out of his skin.

'Children left Juffure village,' said the kintango suddenly in a loud voice. 'If men are to return, your fears must be erased, for a fearful person is a weak person, and a weak person is a danger to his family, to his village, and to his tribe.' He glared at them as if he had never seen such a sorry lot, and then turned away. As he did so, his two assistants sprang forwards and began to lay about among the boys with limber sticks, pummelling their shoulders and backsides smartly as they herded them like so many goats, a few boys apiece, into the small mud huts.

Huddled in their bare hut, Kunta and his four mates were too terrified to feel the lingering sting of the blows they had received, and too ashamed to raise their heads even enough to look at one another. After a few minutes, when it seemed that they would be spared from further abuse for a little while, Kunta began to sneak looks at his companions. He wished that he and Sitafa were in the same hut. He knew these others, of course, but none as well as his yayo brother, and his heart sank. But perhaps that's no accident, he reasoned. They probably don't want us to have even that small comfort. Maybe they're not even going to feed us, he began to think, when his stomach started to growl with hunger.

Just after sunset, the kintango's assistants burst into the hut. *'Move!'* A stick caught him sharply across the shoulders, and the scrambling boys were hissed at as they rushed outside into the dusk, bumping into boys from other huts, and under the flying sticks were herded with gruff orders into a ragged line, each boy grasping the hand of the boy ahead. When they were all in place, the kintango fixed them with a dark scowl and announced that they were about to undertake a night journey deep into the surrounding forest.

At the order to march, the long line of boys set out along the path in clumsy disarray, and the sticks fell steadily among them. 'You walk like buffalo!' Kunta heard close to his ear. A boy cried out as he was hit, and both assistants shouted loudly in the darkness, 'Who was that?', and their sticks rained down even harder. After that no boy uttered a sound.

Kunta's legs soon began to hurt – but not as soon or as badly as they would have done if he hadn't learned the manner of loose strid-ing taught him by his father on their trip to the village of Janneh and Saloum. It pleased him to think that the other boys' legs were surely hurting worse than his, for they wouldn't yet know how to walk. But nothing he had learned did anything to help Kunta's hunger and thirst. His stomach felt tied in knots, and he was starting to feel light-headed when at last a stop was called near a small stream. The reflection of the bright moon in its surface was soon set to rippling as the boys fell to their knees and began to scoop up and gulp down handfuls of water. A moment later the kintango's assistants com-manded them away from the stream with orders not to drink too much at once, then opened their headpacks and passed out some chunks of dried meat. The boys tore away at the morsels like hyenas,

Kunta chewed and swallowed so fast that he barely tasted the four bites he managed to wrest away for himself.

Every boy's feet had big, raw blisters on them, Kunta's as bad as any of the rest; but it felt so good to have food and water in his stomach that he hardly noticed. As they sat by the stream, he and his kafo mates began to look around in the moonlight at one another, this time too tired rather than too afraid to speak. Kunta and Sitafa exchanged long glances, but neither could tell in the dim light if his friend looked as miserable as he felt himself.

Kunta hardly had a chance to cool his burning feet in the stream before the kintango's assistants ordered them back into formation for the long walk back to the jujuo. His legs and head were numb when they finally came within sight of the bamboo gates shortly before dawn. Feeling ready to die, he trudged to his hut, bumped into another boy already inside, lost his footing, stumbled to the dirt floor – and fell deep asleep right where he lay.

On every night for the next six nights came another march, each one longer than the last. The pain of his blistered feet was terrible, but Kunta found by the fourth night that he somehow didn't *mind* the pain as much, and he began to feel a welcome new emotion: pride. By the sixth march, he and the other boys discovered that though the night was very dark, they no longer needed to hold the next boy's hand in order to maintain a straight marching line.

On the seventh night came the kintango's first personal lesson for the boys: showing them how men deep in the forest used the stars to guide them, so that they would never be lost. Within the first half moon, every boy of the kafo had learned how to lead the marching line by the stars, back towards the jujuo. One night when Kunta was the leader, he almost stepped on a bush rat before it noticed him and scurried for cover. Kunta was almost as proud as he was startled, for this meant that the marchers had been walking too silently to be heard even by an animal.

But animals, the kintango told them, were the best teachers of the art of hunting, which was one of the most important things for any Mandinka to learn. When the kintango was satisfied that they had mastered the techniques of marching, he took the kafo, for the next half moon, deep into the bush far from the jujuo, where they built lean-to shelters to sleep in between countless lessons in the secrets of becoming a simbon. Kunta's eyes never seemed to have been closed before one of the kintango's assistants was shouting them awake for some training session.

The kintango's assistants pointed out where lions had recently crouched in wait, then sprung out to kill passing antelope; then where the lions had gone after their meal and lain down to sleep for the rest of the night. The tracks of the antelope herd were followed backwards until they almost painted a picture for the boys of what those antelope had done through the day before they met the lions. The kafo inspected the wide cracks in rocks where wolves and hyenas hid. And they began to learn many tricks of hunting that they had never dreamed about. They had never realized, for example, that the first secret of the master simbon was never moving abruptly. The old kintango himself told the boys a story about a foolish hunter who finally starved to death in an area thick with game, because he was so clumsy and made so much noise, darting here and there, that all about him animals of every sort swiftly and silently slipped away without his even realizing that any had been near.

The boys felt like that clumsy hunter during their lessons in imitating the sounds of animals and birds. The air was rent with their grunts and whistles, yet no birds or animals came near. Then they would be told to lie very quietly in hiding places while the kintango and his assistants made what seemed to them the same sounds, and soon animals and birds would come into sight, cocking their heads and looking for the others who had called to them.

When the boys were practising bird calls one afternoon, suddenly a large-bodied, heavy-beaked bird landed with a great squawking in a nearby bush. 'Look!' one boy shouted with a loud laugh – and every other boy's heart leaped into his throat, knowing that once again that boy's big mouth was going to get them all punished together. No few times before had he shown his habit of acting before thinking – but now the kintango surprised them. He walked over to the boy and said to him very sternly, 'Bring that bird to me – alive!' Kunta and his mates held their breaths as they watched the boy hunch down and creep towards the bush where the heavy bird sat stupidly, turning its head this way and that. But when the boy sprang, the bird managed to escape his clutching hands, frantically beating its stubby wings just enough to raise its big body over the brushtops – and the boy went leaping after it in hot pursuit, soon disappearing from sight.

Kunta and the others were thunderstruck. There was clearly no limit to what the kintango might order them to do. For the next three days and two nights, as the boys went about their training sessions, they cast long glances at each other and then the nearby bush, all of them wondering and worrying about what had befallen their missing mate. As much as he had annoyed them before by getting them all beaten for things he'd done, he seemed never more one of them now that he was gone.

The boys were just getting up on the morning of the fourth day when the jujuo lookout signalled that someone was approaching the village. A moment later came the drum message: it was he. They rushed out to meet him, whooping as if their own brother had returned from a trek to Marrakech. Thin and dirty and covered with cuts and bruises, he swayed slightly as they ran up and slapped him on the back. But he managed a weak smile – and well he should. Under his arm, its wings and feet and beak bound with a length of vine, he held the bird. It looked even worse than he did, but it was still alive.

The kintango came out, and though speaking to that boy, he made it clear that he was really speaking to them all: 'This taught you two important things – to do as you are told, and to keep your mouth shut. These are among the makings of men.' Then Kunta and his mates saw that boy receive the first clearly approving look cast upon anyone by the old kintango, who had known that the boy would sooner or later be able to catch a bird so heavy that it could make only short, low hops through the bush.

The big bird was quickly roasted and eaten with great relish by everyone except his captor, who was so tired that he couldn't stay awake long enough for it to cook. He was permitted to sleep through the day and also through the night, which Kunta and the others had to spend out in the bush on a hunting lesson. The next day, during the first rest period, the boy told his hushed mates what a tortuous chase he had led, until finally, after two days and a night, he had laid a trap that the bird walked into. After trussing it up – including the snapping beak – he had somehow kept himself awake for another day and night, and by following the stars as they had been taught, had found his way back to the jujuo. For a while after that, the other boys had very little to say to him. Kunta told himself that he wasn't really jealous; it was just that the boy seemed to think that his exploit – and the kintango's approval of it – had made him more important than his kafo mates. And the very next time the kintango's assistants ordered an afternoon of wrestling practice, Kunta seized the chance to grab that boy and throw him roughly to the ground.

By the second moon of manhood training, Kunta's kafo had become almost as skilled at survival in the forest as they would have been in their own village. They could now both detect and follow the all but invisible signs of animals, and now they were learning the secret rituals and prayers of the forefathers that could make a very great simbon himself invisible to animals. Every bite of meat they ate now was either trapped by the boys or shot by their slings and arrows. They could skin an animal twice as fast as they could before, and cook the meat over the nearly smokeless fires they had learned to build by striking flint close to dry moss under light, dry sticks. Their meals of roasted game – sometimes small bush rats – were usually topped off with insects toasted crispy in the coals.

Some of the most valuable lessons they learned weren't even planned. One day, during a rest period, when a boy was testing his bow and one careless arrow happened to strike a nest of kurburungo bees high in a tree, a cloud of angry bees swarmed down – and once again all the boys suffered for the mistake of one. Not even the fastest runner among them escaped the painful stings.

'The simbon never shoots an arrow without knowing what it will hit,' the kintango told them later. Ordering the boys to rub one another's puffed and hurting places with shea tree butter, he said, 'Tonight, you will deal with those bees in the proper manner.' By nightfall, the boys had piled dry moss beneath the tree that held the nest. After one of the kintango's assistants set it afire, the other one threw into the flames a quantity of leaves from a certain bush. Thick, choking smoke rose into the tree's upper limbs, and soon dead bees were dropping around the boys by the thousands, as harmlessly as rain. In the morning, Kunta and his kafo were shown how to melt down the honeycombs – skimming off the rest of the dead bees – so that they could eat their fill of honey. Kunta could almost feel himself tingle with that extra strength it was said honey would give to great hunters when they were in need of quick nourishment deep in the forest.

But no matter what they went through, no matter how much they added to their knowledge and abilities, the old kintango was never satisfied. His demands and his discipline remained so strict that the boys were torn between fear and anger most of the time – when they weren't too weary to feel either. Any command to one boy that wasn't instantly and perfectly performed still brought a beating to the entire kafo. And when they weren't being beaten, it seemed to Kunta, they were being wakened roughly in the middle of the night for a long march – always as a punishment for some boy's wrongdoing. The only thing that kept Kunta and the others from giving that boy a beating of their own was the certain knowledge that they would be beaten for fighting; among the first lessons they had learned in life – long before coming to the jujuo – having been that Mandinkas must never fight among themselves. Finally the boys began to understand that the welfare of the group depended on each of them – just as the welfare of their *tribe* would depend on each of them one day. Violations of the rules slowly dwindled to an occasional lapse, and with the decline in beatings, the fear they felt for the kintango was slowly replaced by a respect they had felt before only for their fathers.

But still hardly a day would pass without something new to make Kunta and his mates feel awkward and ignorant all over again. It amazed them to learn, for example, that a rag folded and hung in certain ways near a man's hut would inform other Mandinka men when he planned to return, or that sandals crossed in certain ways outside a hut told many things that only other men would understand. But the secret Kunta found the most remarkable of all was sira kango, a kind of men's talk in which sounds of Mandinka words were changed in such a way that no women or children or non-Mandinkas were permitted to learn. Kunta remembered times when he had heard his father say something very rapidly to another man that Kunta had not understood nor dared to ask explained. Now that he had learned it himself, he and his mates soon spoke nearly everything they said in the secret talk of men.

In every hut as each moon went by, the boys added a new rock to a bowl to mark how long they had been gone from Juffure. Within days after the third rock was dropped in the bowl, the boys were wrestling in the compound one afternoon when suddenly they looked towards the gate of the jujuo, and there stood a group of twenty-five or thirty men. A loud gasp rose from the boys as they recognized their fathers, uncles, and older brothers. Kunta sprang up, unable to believe his eyes, as a bolt of joy shot through him at the first sight of Omoro for three moons. But it was as if some unseen hand held him back and stifled a cry of gladness – even before he saw in his father's face no sign that he recognized his son.

Only one boy rushed forwards, calling out his father's name, and without a word that father reached for the stick of the nearest kintango's assistant and beat his son with it, shouting at him harshly for betraying his emotions, for showing that he was still a boy. He added, unnecessarily, as he gave him the last licks, that his son should expect no favours from his father. Then the kintango himself barked a command for the entire kafo to lie on their bellies in a row, and all of the visiting men walked along the row and flailed the upturned backsides with their walking sticks. Kunta's emotions were in a turmoil; the blows he didn't mind at all, knowing them to be merely another of the rigours of manhood training, but it pained him not to be able to hug his father or even hear his voice, and it shamed him to know that it wasn't manly even to wish for such indulgences.

The beating over, the kintango ordered the boys to race, to jump, to dance, to wrestle, to pray as they had been taught, and the fathers, uncles and older brothers watched it all silently, and then departed with warm compliments to the kintango and his assistants, but not so much as a backward look at the boys, who stood with downcast faces. Within the hour, they got another beating for sulking about the preparation of their evening meal. It hurt all the more because the kintango and his assistants acted as if the visitors had never even been there. But early that night, while the boys were wrestling before bedtime – only halfheartedly now – one of the kintango's assistants passed by Kunta and said brusquely to him, under his breath, 'You have a new brother, and he is named Madi.'

Four of us now, thought Kunta, lying awake later that night. Four brothers – four sons for his mother and father. He thought how that would sound in the Kinte family history when it was told by griots for hundreds of rains in the future. After Omoro, thought Kunta, he would be the first man of the family when he returned to Juffure. Not only was he learning to be a man, but he was also learning many, many things he would be able to teach Lamin, as already he had taught him so many of the things of boyhood. At least he would teach him that which was permissible for boys to know; and then Lamin would teach Suwadu, and Suwadu would teach this new one whom Kunta had not even seen, whose name was Madi. And some day, Kunta thought as he drifted off to sleep, when he was as old as Omoro, he would have sons of his own, and it would all begin again.

24

'You are ceasing to be children. You are experiencing rebirth as men,' the kintango said one morning to the assembled kafo. This was the first time the kintango had used the word 'men' except to tell them what they weren't. After moons of learning together, working together, being beaten together, he told them, each of them was finally beginning to discover that he had two selves – one within him, and the other, larger self in all those whose blood and lives he shared. Not until they learned that lesson could they undertake the next phase of manhood training: how to be warriors. 'You know already that Mandinkas fight only if others are warlike,' said the kintango. 'But we are the finest warriors if driven to fight.'

For the next half moon, Kunta and his mates learned how to make war. Famous Mandinka battle strategies were drawn in the dust by the kintango or his assistants, and then the boys were told to re-enact the strategies in mock battles. 'Never completely encircle your enemy,' counselled the kintango. 'Leave him some escape, for he will fight even more desperately if trapped.' The boys learned also that battles should start in late afternoon, so that any enemy, seeing defeat, could save face by retreating in the darkness. And they were taught that during any wars, neither enemy should ever do harm to any travelling marabouts, griots, or blacksmiths, for an angered marabout could bring down the displeasure of Allah; an angered griot could use his eloquent tongue to stir the enemy army to greater savagery; and an angered blacksmith could make or repair weapons for the enemy.

Under the direction of the kintango's assistants, Kunta and the others carved out barbed spears and made barbed arrows of the kind used only in battle, and practised with them on smaller and smaller targets. When a boy could hit a bamboo cane twenty-five steps away, he was cheered and praised. Tramping into the woods, the boys found some koona shrub, whose leaves they picked to be boiled back at the jujuo. Into the resulting thick, black juice they would dip a cotton thread, and they were shown how that thread, wound around an arrow's barbs, would seep a deadly poison into whatever wound the arrow made.

At the end of the war-training period, the kintango told them more than they had ever known before – and told them more excitingly than they had ever heard it – about that greatest of all Mandinka wars and warriors – the time when the army of the fabled ex-slave general Sundiata, son of Sogolon, the Buffalo Woman, conquered the forces of the Boure Country's King Soumaoro, a king so cruel that he wore human-skin robes and adorned his palace walls with enemy's bleached skulls.

Kunta and his mates held their breaths, hearing how both armies suffered thousands of wounded or dead. But the archers of the Mandinkas closed in on Soumaoro's forces like a giant trap, raining down arrows from both sides and moving in steadily until Soumaoro's terrified army finally fled in rout. For days and nights, said the kintango – and it was the first time the boys ever had seen him smile – the talking drums of every village followed the marching progress of the victorious Mandinka forces, laden with enemy booty and driving thousands of captives before them. In every village, happy crowds jeered and kicked the prisoners, whose shaved heads were bowed and whose hands were tied behind their backs. Finally General Sundiata called a huge meeting of the people, and he brought before them the chiefs of all the villages he had defeated and gave them back their spears of chiefhood's rank, and then he established among those chiefs the bonds of peace, which would last among them for the next one hundred rains. Kunta and his mates went dreamily to their beds, never prouder to be Mandinkas.

As the next moon of training began, drumtalk reached the jujuo telling of new visitors to be expected within the next two days. The excitement with which the news of *any* visitors would have been received, after so long since the fathers and brothers had come to see them, was doubled when the boys learned that the sender of the message was the drummer of Juffure's champion wrestling team, which was coming to conduct special lessons for the trainees.

Late in the afternoon of the next day, the drums announced their arrival even earlier than expected. But the boys' pleasure at seeing all the familiar faces again was forgotten when, without a word, the wrestlers grabbed them and began to flip them onto the ground harder than they had ever been thrown in their lives. And every boy was bruised and hurting when the wrestlers divided them into smaller groups to grapple one another, as the champions supervised. Kunta had never imagined there were so many wrestling holds, nor how effectively they could work if used correctly. And the champions kept drumming into the boys' ears that it was knowledge and expertness and not strength that made the difference between being an ordinary wrestler and a champion. Still, as they demonstrated the holds for their pupils, the boys couldn't help admiring their bulging muscles as much as their skill in using them. Around the fire that night, the drummer from Juffure chanted the names and the feats of great Mandinka wrestling champions of even a hundred rains in the past, and when it was the boys' time for bed, the wrestlers left the jujuo to return to Juffure.

Two days later came news of another visitor. This time the message was brought by a runner from Juffure – a young man of the fourth kafo whom Kunta and his mates knew well, though in his own new manhood, he acted as if he never had seen these third kafo children. Without so much as a glance at them, he ran up to the kintango and announced, between deep breaths, that Kujali N'jai, a griot well known throughout The Gambia, would soon spend one full day at the jujuo.

In three days he arrived, accompanied by several young men of his family. He was much older than any of the griots Kunta had seen before – so old, in fact, that he made the kintango seem young. After gesturing for the boys to squat in a semicircle about him, the old man began to talk of how he became what he was. He told them how, over years of study from young manhood, every griot had buried deep in his mind the records of the ancestors. 'How else could you know of the great deeds of the ancient kings, holy men, hunters, and warriors who came hundreds of rains before us? Have you met them?' asked the old man. 'No! The history of our people is carried to the future in here.' And he tapped his grey head.

The question in the mind of every boy was answered by the old griot: only the sons of griots could become griots. Indeed, it was their solemn *duty* to become griots. Upon finishing their manhood training, these boys – like those grandsons of his own who sat beside him here today – would begin studying and travelling with selected elders, hearing over and again the historical names and stories as they had been passed down. And in due time, each young man would know that special part of the forefathers' history in the finest and fullest detail, just as it had been told to his father and his father's father. And the day would come when that boy would become a man and have sons to whom *he* would tell those stories, so that the events of the distant past would forever live.

When the awed boys had wolfed down their evening meal and rushed back to gather again around the old griot, he thrilled them until late into the night with stories his own father had passed down to him – about the great black empires that had ruled Africa hundreds of rains before.

'Long before toubob ever put his foot in Africa,' the old griot said, there was the Empire of Benin, ruled by an all-powerful king called the Oba, whose every wish was obeyed instantly. But the actual governing of Benin was done by trusted counsellors of the Oba, whose full time was needed just for making the necessary sacrifices to appease the forces of evil and for his proper attentions to a harem of more than a hundred wives. But even before Benin was a yet richer kingdom called Songhai, said the griot. Songhai's capital city was Gao, filled with fine houses for black princes and rich merchants who lavishly entertained travelling tradesmen who brought much gold to buy goods.

'Nor was that the richest kingdom,' said the old man. And he told the boys of ancestral Ghana, in which an entire town was populated with only the King's court. And King Kanissaai had a thousand horses, each of which had three servants and its own urinal made of copper. Kunta could hardly believe his ears. 'And each evening,' said the griot, 'when King Kanissaai would emerge from his palace, a thousand fires would be lit, lighting up all between the heavens and the earth. And the servants of the great King would bring food enough to serve the ten thousand people who gathered there each evening.'

Here he paused, and exclamations of wonder could not be restrained by the boys, who knew well that no sound should be made as a griot talked, but neither he nor even the kintango himself seemed to notice their rudeness. Putting into his mouth half of a kola nut and offering the other half to the kintango, who accepted it with pleasure, the griot drew the skirt of his robe closer about his legs against the chill of the early night and resumed his stories.

'But even Ghana was not the richest black kingdom!' he exclaimed. 'The very richest, the very oldest of them all was the kingdom of ancient Mali!' Like the other empires, Mali had its cities, its farmers, its artisans, its blacksmiths, tanners, dyers, and weavers, said the old griot. But Mali's enormous wealth came from its far-flung trade routes in salt and gold and copper. 'Altogether Mali was four months of travel long and four months of travel wide,' said the griot. 'and the greatest of all its cities was the fabled Timbuktu!' The major centre of learning in all Africa, it was populated by thousands of scholars, made even more numerous by a steady parade of visiting wise men seeking to increase their knowledge – so many that some of the biggest merchants sold nothing but parchments and books. 'There is not a marabout, not a teacher in the smallest village, whose knowledge has not come at least in part from Timbuktu,' said the griot.

When finally the kintango stood up and thanked the griot for the generosity with which he had shared with them the treasures of his mind, Kunta and the others – for the first time since they came to the jujuo – actually dared to voice their displeasure, for the time had come for them to go to bed. The kintango chose to ignore this impertinence, at least for the time being, and sternly commanded them to their huts – but not before they had a chance to beg him to urge the griot to come back and visit them again.

They were still thinking and talking of the wondrous tales the griot had told them when – six days later – word came that a famous moro would soon be visiting the camp. The moro was the highest grade of teacher in The Gambia; indeed, there were only a few of them, and so wise were they – after many rains of study – that their job was to teach not schoolboys but other teachers, such as the arafang of Juffure.

Even the kintango showed unusual concern about this visitor, ordering the entire jujuo to be thoroughly cleaned, with the dirt raked and then brushed with leafy branches to a smoothness that would capture the honour of the fresh footprints of the moro when he arrived. Then the kintango assembled the boys in the compound and told them, 'The advice and the blessings of this man who will be with us is sought not only by ordinary people but also by village chiefs and even by kings.'

When the moro arrived the next morning, five of his students were with him, each carrying headbundles that Kunta knew would contain treasured Arabic books and parchment manuscripts such as those from ancient Timbuktu. As the old man passed through the gate, Kunta and his mates joined the kintango and his assistants on their knees, with their foreheads touching the ground. When the moro had blessed them and their jujuo, they rose and seated themselves respectfully around him as he opened his books and began to read – first from the Koran, then from such unheard-of books as the Taureta La Musa, the Zabora Dawidi and the Lingeeli la Isa, which he said were known to 'Christians' as The Pentateuch of Moses, The Psalms of David and The Book of Isaiah. Each time the moro would open or close a book, roll or unroll a manuscript, he would press it to his forehead and mutter 'Amen!'

When he had finished reading, the old man put his books aside and spoke to them of great events and people from the Christian Koran, which was known as the Holy Bible. He spoke of Adam and Eve, of Joseph and his brethren; of Moses, David, and Solomon; of the death of Abel. And he spoke to them of great men of more recent history, such as Djoulou Kara Naini, known to the toubob as Alexander the Great, a mighty king of gold and silver whose sun had shown over half of the world.

Before the moro finally rose to leave that night, he reviewed what they already knew of the five daily prayers to Allah, and he instructed them thoroughly in how to conduct themselves inside the sacred mosque of their village, which they would enter for their first time when they returned home as men. Then he and his students had to hurry in order to reach the next place on his busy schedule, and the boys honoured him – as the kintango had instructed them – by sing-

103

ing one of the men's songs they had learned from the jalli kea: 'One generation passes on ... Another generation comes and goes ... But Allah abides forever.'

In his hut after the moro had gone that night, Kunta lay awake thinking how so many things – indeed, nearly everything they had learned – all tied together. The past seemed with the present, the present with the future; the dead with the living and those yet to be born; he himself with his family, his mates, his village, his tribe, his Africa; the world of man with the world of animals and growing things – they all lived with Allah. Kunta felt very small, yet very large. Perhaps, he thought, this is what it means to become a man.

25

The time had come for that which made Kunta and every other boy shudder to think of: the kasas boyo operation, which would purify a boy and prepare him to become a father of many sons. They knew it was coming, but when it came it was without warning. One day as the sun reached the noontime position, one of the kintango's assistants gave what seemed to be only a routine order for a kafo to line up in the compound, which the boys did as quickly as usual. But Kunta felt a twinge of fear when the kintango himself came from his hut, as he rarely did at midday, and walked before them.

'Hold out your fotos,' he commanded. They hesitated, not believing – or wanting to believe – what they had heard. 'Now!' he shouted. Slowly and shyly, they obeyed, each keeping his eyes on the ground as he reached inside his loincloth.

Working their way from either end of the line, the kintango's assistants wrapped around the head of each boy's foto a short length of cloth spread with a green paste made of a pounded leaf. 'Soon your fotos will have no feeling,' the kintango said, ordering them back into their huts.

Huddled inside, ashamed and afraid of what would happen next, the boys waited in silence until about mid-afternoon, when again they were ordered outside, where they stood watching as a number of men from Juffure – the fathers, brothers, and uncles who had come before, and others – filed in through the gate. Omoro was among them, but this time Kunta pretended that he didn't see his father. The men formed themselves into a line facing the boys and chanted together: 'This thing to be done ... also has been done to us ... as to the forefathers before us ... so that you also will become ... all of us men together.' Then the kintango ordered the boys back into their huts once again.

Night was falling when they heard many drums suddenly begin to pound just outside the jujuo. Ordered out of their huts, they saw bursting through the gate about a dozen leaping, shouting kankurang dancers. In leafy branch costumes and bark masks, they sprang about brandishing their spears among the terrified boys, and then – just as abruptly as they had appeared – were gone. Almost numb with fear, the boys now heard and followed dumbly the kintango's order to seat themselves close together with their backs against the jujuo's bamboo fence.

The fathers, uncles, and older brothers stood nearby, this time chanting, 'You soon will return to home ... and to your farms ... and in time you will marry ... and life everlasting will spring from your loins.' One of the kintango's assistants called out one boy's name. As he got up, the assistant motioned him behind a long screen of woven bamboo. Kunta couldn't see or hear what happened after that, but a few moments later, the boy reappeared – with a blood-stained cloth between his legs. Staggering slightly, he was half carried by the other assistant back to his place along the bamboo fence. Another boy's name was called; then another, and another, and finally:

'Kunta Kinte!'

Kunta was petrified. But he made himself get up and walk behind the screen. Inside were four men, one of whom ordered him to lie down on his back. He did so; his shaking legs wouldn't have supported him any longer anyway. The men then leaned down, grasped him firmly, and lifted his thighs upward. Just before closing his eyes, Kunta saw the kintango bending over him with something in his hands. Then he felt the cutting pain. It was even worse than he thought it would be, though not as bad as it would have been without the numbing paste. In a moment he was bandaged tightly, and an assistant helped him back outside, where he sat, weak and dazed, alongside the others who had already been behind the screen. They didn't dare to look at one another. But the thing they had feared above all else had now been done.

As the fotos of the kafo began healing, a general air of jubilation rose within the jujuo, for gone forever was the indignity of being mere boys in body as well as in mind. Now they were very nearly men – and they were boundless in their gratitude and reverence for the kintango. And he, in turn, began to see Kunta's kafo with different eyes. The old, wrinkled, grey-haired elder whom they had slowly come to love was sometimes seen even to smile now. And very casually, when talking to the kafo, he or his assistants would say, 'You men—' and to Kunta and his mates, it seemed as unbelievable as it was beautiful to hear.

Soon afterwards the fourth new moon arrived, and two or three members of Kunta's kafo, at the kintango's personal order, began to leave the jujuo each night and trot all the way to the sleeping village of Juffure, where they would slip like shadows into their own mothers' storehouses, steal as much couscous, dried meats, and millet as they could carry, and then race back with it to the jujuo, where it was gleefully cooked the next day – 'to prove yourselves smarter than all women, even your mother', the kintango had told them. But that next day, of course, those boys' mothers would boast to their friends how they had heard their sons prowling and had lain awake listening with pride.

There was a new feeling now in the evenings at the jujuo. Nearly always, Kunta's kafo would squat in a semicircle around the kintango. Most of the time he remained as stern in manner as before, but now he talked to them not as bumbling little boys but as young men of his own village. Sometimes he spoke to them about the qualities of manhood – chief among which, after fearlessness, was total honesty in all things. And sometimes he spoke to them about the forefathers. Worshipful regard was a duty owed by the living to those who dwelled with Allah, he told them. He asked each boy to name the ancestor he remembered best; Kunta named his Grandma Yaisa, and the kintango said that each of the ancestors the boys had named – as was the way of ancestors – was petitioning Allah in the best interests of the living.

Another evening, the kintango told them how in one's village, every person who lived there was equally important to that village; from the newest baby to the oldest elder. As new men, they must therefore learn to treat everyone with the same respect, and – as the foremost of their manhood duties – to protect the welfare of every man, woman, and child in Juffure as they would their own.

'When you return home,' said the kintango, 'you will begin to serve Juffure as its eyes and ears. You will be expected to stand guard over the village – beyond the gates as lookouts for toubob and other savages, and in the fields as sentries to keep the crops safe from scavengers. You will also be charged with the responsibility of inspecting the women's cooking pots – including those of your own mothers – to make sure they are kept clean, and you will be expected to reprimand them most severely if any dirt or insects are found inside.' The boys could hardly wait to begin their duties.

Though all but the oldest of them were still too young to dream of the responsibilities they would assume when they reached the fourth kafo, they knew that some day, as men of fifteen to nineteen rains, they would be appointed to the important job of carrying messages – like the young man who had brought them word of the moro's visit – between Juffure and other villages. It would have been hard for Kunta's kafo to imagine such a thing, but those old enough to be messengers longed for nothing more than to *stop* being messengers; when they reached the fifth kafo at twenty rains, they would graduate to *really* important work – assisting the village elders as emissaries and negotiators in all dealings with other villages. Men of Omoro's age – over thirty – rose gradually in rank and responsibility with each passing rain until they themselves acquired the honoured status of elders. Kunta had often proudly watched Omoro sitting on the edges of the Council of Elders, and looked forward to the day when his father would enter the inner circle of those who would inherit the mantle of office from such revered leaders as the kintango when they were called to Allah.

It was no longer easy for Kunta and the others to pay attention as they should to everything the kintango said. It seemed impossible to them that so much could have happened in the past four moons and that they were really about to become *men*. The past few days seemed to last longer than the moons that preceded them, but finally – with the fourth moon high and full in the heavens – the kintango's assistants ordered the kafo to line up shortly after the evening meal.

Was this the moment for which they had waited? Kunta looked around for their fathers and brothers, who would surely be there for the ceremony. They were nowhere to be seen. And where was the kintango? His eyes searched the compound and found his – standing at the gate of the jujuo – just as he swung it open wide, turned to them, and called out: 'Men of Juffure, return to your village!'

For a moment they stood rooted; then they rushed up whooping and grabbed and hugged their kintango and his assistants, who pretended to be offended by such impertinence. Four moons before, as the hood was being lifted from his head in this very compound, Kunta would have found it difficult to believe that he would be sorry to leave this place, or that he would come to love the stern old man who stood before them on that day; but he felt both emotions now. Then his thoughts turned homewards and he was racing and shouting with the others out the gate and down the path to Juffure. They hadn't gone very far before, as if upon some unspoken signal, their voices were stilled and their pace slowed by the thoughts they all shared, each in his own way – of what they were leaving behind, and of what lay ahead of them. This time they didn't need the stars to find their way.

26

'Aiee! Aiee!' The women's happy shrieks rang out, and the people were rushing from their huts, laughing, dancing, and clapping their hands as Kunta's kafo – and those who had turned fifteen and become fourth kafo while they were away at the jujuo – strode in through the village gate at the break of dawn. The new men walked slowly, with what they hoped was dignity, and they didn't speak or smile – at first. When he saw his mother running towards him, Kunta felt like dashing to meet her, and he couldn't stop his face from lighting up, but he made himself continue walking at the same measured pace. Then Binta was upon him – arms around his neck, hands caressing his cheeks, tears welling in her eyes, murmuring his name. Kunta permitted this only briefly before he drew away. being now a man; but he made it seem as if he did so only to get a better look at the yowling bundle cradled snugly in the sling across her back. Reaching inside, he lifted the baby out with both hands.

'So this is my brother Madi!' he shouted happily, holding him high in the air.

Binta beamed at his side as he walked towards her hut with the baby in his arms – making faces and cooing and squeezing the plump little cheeks. But Kunta wasn't so taken with his little brother that he failed to notice the herd of naked children that followed close behind them with eyes as wide as their mouths. Two or three were at his knees, and others darted in and out among Binta and the other women, who were all exclaiming over how strong and healthy Kunta looked, how manly he'd become. He pretended not to hear, but it was music to his ears.

Kunta wondered where Omoro was, and where Lamin was – remembering abruptly that his little brother would be away grazing the goats. He had sat down inside Binta's hut before he noticed that one of the bigger first-kafo children had followed them inside and now stood staring at him and clinging to Binta's skirt. 'Hello, Kunta,' said the little boy. It was Suwadu! Kunta couldn't believe it. When he had left for manhood training, Suwadu was just something underfoot, too small to take notice of except when he was annoying Kunta with his eternal whining. Now, within the space of four moons, he seemed to have grown taller, and he was beginning to talk; he had become a *person*. Giving the baby back to Binta, he picked up Suwadu and swung him high up to the roof of Binta's hut, until his little brother yelped with delight.

When he finished visiting with Suwadu, who ran outside to see some of the other new men, the hut fell silent. Brimming over with joy and pride, Binta felt no need to speak. Kunta did. He wanted to tell her how much he had missed her and how it gladdened him to be home. But he couldn't find the words. And he knew it wasn't the sort of thing a man should say to a woman – even to his mother.

'Where is my father?' he asked finally.

'He's cutting thatch grass for your hut,' said Binta. In his excitement, Kunta had nearly forgotten that, as a man, he would now have his own private hut. He walked outside and hurried to the place where his father had always told him one could cut the best quality of roofing thatch.

Omoro saw him coming, and Kinta's heart raced as he saw his father begin walking to meet him. They shook hands in the manner of men, each looking deeply into the other's eyes, seeing the other for the first time as man to man. Kunta felt almost weak with emotion, and they were silent for a moment. Then Omoro said, as if he were commenting on the weather, that he had acquired for Kunta a hut whose previous owner had married and built a new house. Would he like to inspect the hut now? Kunta said softly that he would, and they walked along together, with Omoro doing most of the talking, since Kunta was still having trouble finding words.

The hut's mud walls needed as many repairs as the thatching. But Kunta hardly noticed or cared, for this was his own private hut, and it was all the way across the village from his mother's. He didn't allow himself to show his satisfaction, of course, let alone to speak of it. Instead, he told Omoro only that he would make the repairs himself. Kunta could fix the walls, said Omoro, but he would like to finish the roof repairs he had already begun. Without another word, he turned and headed back to the thatch-grass field – leaving Kunta standing there, grateful for the everyday manner with which his father had begun their new relationship as men.

Kunta spent most of the afternoon covering every corner of Juffure, filling his eyes with the sight of all the dearly remembered faces, familiar huts and haunts – the village well, the schoolyard, the baobab and silk-cotton trees. He hadn't realized how homesick he had been until he began to bask in the greetings of everyone he passed. He wished it was time for Lamin to return with the goats, and found himself missing one other very special person, even if she was a woman. Finally – not caring whether it was something a man should properly do – he headed for the small, weathered hut of old Nyo Boto.

'Grandmother!' he called at the door.

'Who is it?' came the reply in a high, cracked, irritable tone.

'Guess, Grandmother!' said Kunta, and he went inside the hut.

It took his eyes a few moments to see her better in the dim light. Squatting beside a bucket and plucking long fibres from a slab of baobab bark that she had been soaking with water from the bucket, she peered sharply at him for a while before speaking. 'Kunta!'

'It's so good to see you, Grandmother!' he exclaimed.

Nyo Boto returned to her plucking of the fibres. 'Is your mother well?' she asked, and Kunta assured her that Binta was.

He was a little taken aback, for her manner was almost as if he hadn't even been away anywhere, as if she hadn't noticed that he had become a man.

'I thought of you often while I was away – each time I touched the saphie charm you put on my arm.'

She only grunted, not even looking up from her work.

He apologized for interrupting her and quickly left, deeply hurt and terribly confused. He wouldn't understand until much later that her rebuff had hurt Nyo Boto even more than it did him; she had acted as she knew a woman must towards one who could no longer seek comfort at her skirts.

Still troubled, Kunta was walking slowly back towards his new hut when he heard a familiar commotion: bleating goats, barking dogs, and shouting boys. It was the second kafo returning from their afternoon's work in the bush. Lamin would be among them. Kunta began to search their faces anxiously as the boys approached. Then Lamin saw him, shouted his name, and came dashing, wreathed in smiles.

But he stopped short a few feet away when he saw his brother's cool expression, and they stood looking at each other. It was finally Kunta who spoke.

'Hello.'

'Hello, Kunta.'

Then they looked at each other some more. Pride shone in Lamin's eyes, but Kunta saw also the same hurt he had just felt in the hut of Nyo Boto, and uncertainty about just what to make of his new big brother. Kunta was thinking that the way they were both acting wasn't as he would have had it be, but it was necessary that a man be regarded with a certain amount of respect, even by his own brother.

Lamin was the first to speak again: 'Your two goats are both big with kids.' Kunta was delighted; that meant he would soon own four, maybe even five goats, if one of those nannies was big with twins. But he didn't smile or act surprised. 'That's good news,' he said, with even less enthusiasm than he wanted to show. Not knowing what else to say, Lamin dashed away without another word, hollering for his wuolo dogs to reassemble his goats, which had begun to wander.

Binta's face kept a set, tight expression as she assisted Kunta in moving to his own hut. His old clothes were all outgrown, she said, and with her tone properly respectful, added that whenever he had time for her to measure him between the important things he had to do, she would sew him some new clothes. Since he owned not much more than his bow and arrows and his slingshot, Binta kept murmuring, 'You'll need this' and 'You'll need that,' until she had provided him with such household essentials as a pallet, some bowls, a stool, and a prayer rug she had woven while he was away. With each new thing, as he had always heard his father do, Kunta would grunt, as if he could think of no objection to having it in his house. When she noticed him scratching his head, she offered to inspect his scalp for ticks, and he bluntly told her 'No!' ignoring the grumbling sounds she made afterwards.

It was nearly midnight when Kunta finally slept, for much was on his mind. And it seemed to him that his eyes had hardly closed before the crowing cocks had waked him, and then came the sing-song call of the alimamo to the mosque, for what would be the first morning prayer that he and his mates would be allowed to attend with the other men of Juffure. Dressing quickly, Kunta took his new prayer rug and fell in among his kafo as, with heads bowed and rolled prayer rugs under their arms – as if they had done it all their lives – they entered the sacred mosque behind the other men of the village. Inside, Kunta and the others watched and copied every act

111

and utterance of the older men, being especially careful to be neither too soft nor too loud in their reciting of the prayers.

After prayers, Binta brought breakfast to her new man's hut. Setting the bowl of steaming couscous before Kunta – who just grunted again, not letting his face say anything – Binta left quickly, and Kunta ate without pleasure, irritated by a suspicion that she had seemed to be suppressing something like mirth.

After breakfast, he joined his mates in undertaking their duties as the eyes and ears of the village with a diligence their elders found equally amusing. The women could hardly turn around without finding one of the new men demanding to inspect their cooking pots for insects. And rummaging around outside peoples' huts and all around the village fence, they found hundreds of spots where the state of repair failed to measure up to their exacting standards. Fully a dozen of them drew up buckets of well water, tasting carefully from the gourd dipper in hopes of detecting a saltiness or a muddiness or something else unhealthy. They were disappointed, but the fish and turtle that were kept in the well to eat insects were removed anyway and replaced with fresh ones.

The new men, in short, were everywhere. 'They are thick as fleas!' old Nyo Boto snorted as Kunta approached a stream where she was pounding laundry on a rock, and he all but sprinted off in another direction. He also took special care to stay clear of any known place where Binta might be, telling himself that although she was his mother, he would show her no special favours; that, indeed, he would deal firmly with her if she ever made it necessary. After all, she was a woman.

27

Juffure was so small, and its kafo of diligent new men so numerous, it soon seemed to Kunta, that nearly every roof, wall, calabash, and cooking pot in the village had been inspected, cleaned, repaired, or replaced moments before he got to it. But he was more pleased than disappointed, for it gave him more time to spend farming the small plot assigned to his use by the Council of Elders. All new men grew their own couscous or groundnuts, some to live on and the rest to trade – with those who grew too little to feed their families – for things they needed more than food. A young man who tended his crops well, made good trades, and managed his goats wisely – perhaps swapping a dozen goats for a female calf that would grow up and have other calves – could move ahead in the world and become a man of substance by the time he reached twenty-five or thirty rains and began to think about taking a wife and raising sons of his own.

Within a few moons after his return, Kunta had grown so much more than he could eat himself, and made such shrewd trades for this or that household possession to adorn his hut, that Binta began to grumble about it within his hearing. He had so many stools, wicker mats, food bowls, gourds, and sundry other objects in his hut, she would mutter, that there was hardly any room left inside for Kunta. But he charitably chose to ignore her impertinence, since he slept now upon a fine bed of woven reeds over a springy bamboo mattress that she had spent half a moon making for him.

In his hut, along with several saphies he had acquired in exchange for crops from his farm plot, he kept a number of other potent spiritual safeguards: the perfumed extracts of certain plants and barks which, like every other Mandinka man, Kunta rubbed onto his forehead, upper arms, and thighs each night before going to bed. It was believed that this magical essence would protect a man from possession by evil spirits while he slept. It would also make him smell good – a thing that, along with his appearance, Kunta had begun to think about.

He and the rest of his kafo were becoming increasingly exasper- ated about a matter that had been rankling their manly pride for many moons. When they went off to manhood training, they had left behind a group of skinny, giggling, silly little girls who played almost as hard as the boys. Then, after only four moons away, they had returned – as new men – to find these same girls, with whom they had grown up, flouncing about wherever one looked, poking out their mango-sized breasts, tossing their heads and arms, showing off their jangly new earrings, beads, and bracelets. What irritated Kunta and the others wasn't so much that the girls were behaving so absurdly, but that they seemed to be doing so exclusively for the benefit of men at least ten rains older than themselves. For new men like Kunta, these maidens of marriageable age – fourteen and fifteen – had scarcely a glance except to sneer or laugh. He and his mates finally grew so disgusted with these airs and antics that they resolved to pay no further attention either to the girls or to the all-too-willing older men they sought to entice with such fluttery coyness.

But Kunta's foto would be as hard as his thumb some mornings when he waked. Of course, it had been hard many times before, even when he was Lamin's age; but now it was much different in the feeling, very deep and strong. And Kunta couldn't help putting his hand down under his bedcover and tightly squeezing it. He also couldn't help thinking about things he and his mates had overheard – about fotos being put into women.

One night dreaming – for ever since he was a small boy, Kunta had dreamed a great deal, even when he was awake, Binta liked to say – he found himself watching a harvest-festival seoruba, when the loveliest, longest-necked, sootiest-black maiden there chose to fling down her headwrap for him to pick up. When he did so, she rushed home shouting, 'Kunta likes me!,' and after careful consideration, her parents gave permission for them to marry. Omoro and Binta also agreed, and both fathers bargained for the bride price. 'She is beautiful,' said Omoro, 'but my concerns are of her true value as my son's wife. Is she a strong, hard worker? Is she of pleasant disposition in the home? Can she cook well and care for children? And above all, is she guaranteed a virgin?' The answers were all yes, so a price was decided and a date set for the wedding.

Kunta built a fine new mud house, and both mothers cooked bountiful delicacies, to give guests the best impression. And on the wedding day, the adults, children, goats, chickens, dogs, parrots, and monkeys all but drowned out the musicians they had hired. When the bride's party arrived, the praise singer shouted of the fine families being joined together. Yet louder shouts rose when the bride's best girlfriends roughly shoved her inside Kunta's new house. Grinning and waving to everyone, Kunta followed her and drew the curtain across the door. When she had seated herself on his bed, he sang to her a famous ancestral song of love: 'Mandumbe, your long neck is very beautiful . . .' Then they lay down on soft cured hides and she kissed him tenderly, and they clung together very tightly. And then the thing happened, as Kunta had come to imagine it from the ways it had been described to him. It was even greater than he had been told, and the feeling grew and grew – until finally he *burst*.

Jerking suddenly awake, Kunta lay very still for a long moment, trying to figure out what had happened. Then, moving his hand down between his legs, he felt the warm wetness on himself – and on his bed. Frightened and alarmed, he leaped up, felt for a cloth, and wiped himself off, and the bed, too. Then, sitting there in the darkness, his fear was slowly overtaken by embarrassment, his embarrassment by shame, his shame by pleasure, and his pleasure, finally, by a kind of pride. Had this ever happened to any of his mates? He wondered. Though he hoped it had, he also hoped it hadn't, for perhaps this is what happens when one really becomes a man, he thought; and he wanted to be the first. But Kunta knew that he would never know, for this experience and even these thoughts weren't the kind he could ever share with anyone. Finally, exhausted and exhilarated, he lay down again and soon fell into a mercifully dreamless sleep.

28

Kunta knew every man, woman, child, dog, and goat in Juffure, he told himself one afternoon while he sat eating lunch beside his plot of groundnuts, and in the course of his new duties, he either saw or spoke with almost all of them nearly every day. Why, then, did he feel so alone? Was he an orphan? Did he not have a father who treated him as one man should another? Did he not have a mother who tended dutifully to his needs? Did he not have brothers to look up to him? As a new man, was he not their idol? Did he not have the friendship of those with whom he had played in the mud as children, herded goats as boys, returned to Juffure as men? Had he not earned the respect of his elders – and the envy of his kafo mates – for husbanding his farm plot into seven goats, three chickens, and a splendidly furnished hut before reaching his sixteenth birthday? He couldn't deny it.

And yet he was lonely. Omoro was too busy to spend even as much time with Kunta as he had when he had only one son and fewer responsibilities in the village. Binta was busy too, taking care of Kunta's younger brothers, but his mother and he had little to say to one another anyway. Even he and Lamin were no longer close; while he had been away at the jujuo, Suwadu had become Lamin's adoring shadow as Lamin had once been Kunta's, and Kunta watched with mixed emotions while Lamin's attitude towards his little brother warmed from irritation to toleration to affection. Soon they were inseparable, and this had left as little room for Kunta as it had for Madi, who was too young yet to join them but old enough to whine because they wouldn't let him. On days when the two older boys couldn't get out of their mother's hut fast enough, of course, Binta would often order them to take Madi along, so that she could get him out from underfoot, and Kunta would have to smile in spite of himself at the sight of his three brothers marching around the village, one behind the other, in the order of their births, with the two in front staring glumly ahead while the little one, smiling happily, brought up the rear, almost running to keep up.

No one walked behind Kunta any longer, and not often did anyone choose to walk beside him either, for his kafo mates were occupied almost every waking hour with their new duties and – perhaps, like him – with their own broodings about what had so far proved to be the dubious rewards of manhood. True, they had been given their own farm plots and were beginning to collect goats and other possessions. But the plots were small, the work hard, and their possessions were embarrassingly few in comparison to those of older men. They had also been made the eyes and ears of the village, but the cooking pots were kept clean without their supervision, and nothing ever trespassed in the fields except occasional baboon families or dense flocks of birds. Their elders, it soon became clear, got to do all the really important jobs, and as if to rub it in, gave the new men only what they felt was the appearance of respect, as they had been given only the appearance of responsibility. Indeed, when they paid any attention at all to the younger men, the elders seemed to have as much difficulty as the young girls of the village in restraining themselves from laughter, even when one of them performed the most challenging task without a mistake. Well, some day he would be one of those older men, Kunta told himself, and he would wear the mantle of manhood not only with more dignity but also with more compassion and understanding towards younger men than he and his mates received now.

Feeling restless – and a little sorry for himself – that evening, Kunta left his hut to take a solitary walk. Though he had no destination in mind, his feet drew him towards the circle of rapt children's faces glowing in the light of the campfire around which the old grandmothers were telling their nightly stories to the first kafo of the village. Stopping close enough to listen – but not close enough to be noticed listening – Kunta squatted down on his haunches and pretended to be inspecting a rock at his feet while one of the wrinkled old women waved her skinny arms and jumped around the clearing in front of the children as she acted out her story of the four thousand brave warriors of the King of Kasoon who had been driven into battle by the thunder of five hundred great war drums and the trumpeting of five hundred elephant-tusk horns. It was a story he had heard many times around the fires as a child, and as he looked at the wide-eyed faces of his brothers Madi in the front row, and Suwadu in the back row, it somehow made him feel sad to hear it again.

With a sigh, he rose and walked slowly away – his departure as unnoticed as his arrival had been. At the fire where Lamin sat with other boys his age chanting their Koranic verses, and the fire where Binta sat with other mothers gossiping about husbands, households, children, cooking, sewing, make-up, and hairdos, he felt equally unwelcome. Passing them by, he found himself finally beneath the spreading branches of the baobab where the men of Juffure sat around the fourth fire discussing village business and other matters of gravity. As he had felt too old to be wanted around the first fire, he felt too young to be wanted around this one. But he had no place else to go, so Kunta seated himself among those in the outer circle – beyond those of Omoro's age, who sat closer to the fire, and those of the kintango's age, who sat closest, among the Council of Elders. As he did so, he heard one of them ask:

'Can anyone say how many of us are getting stolen?'

They were discussing slave taking, which had been the main subject around the men's fire for the more than one hundred rains that toubob had been stealing people and shipping them in chains to the kingdom of white cannibals across the sea.

There was silence for a little while, and then the alimamo said, 'We can only thank Allah that it's less now than it was.'

'There are fewer of us left to steal!' said an angry elder.

'I listen to the drums and count the lost,' said the kintango. 'Fifty to sixty each new moon just from along our part of the bolong would be my guess.' No one said anything to that, and he added, 'There is no way, of course, to count the losses farther inland, and farther up the river.'

'Why do we count only those *taken away* by the toubob?' asked the arafang. 'We must count also the burned baobabs where villages once stood. He has killed more in fires and in fighting him than he has ever taken away!'

The men stared at the fire for a long time, and then another elder broke the silence: 'Toubob could never do this without help from our own people. Mandinkas, Fulas, Wolofs, Jolas – none of The Gambia's tribes is without its slatee traitors. As a child I saw these

117

slatees beating those like themselves to walk faster for the toubob!'

'For toubob money, we turn against our own kind,' said Juffure's senior elder. 'Greed and treason – these are the things toubob has given us in exchange for those he has stolen away.'

No one talked again for a while, and the fire sputtered quietly. Then the kintango spoke again: 'Even worse than toubob's money is that he lies for nothing and he cheats with method, as naturally as he breathes. That's what gives him the advantage over us.'

A few moments passed, and then a young man of the kafo ahead of Kunta's asked, 'Will toubob never change?'

'That will be,' said one of the elders, 'when the river flows backwards!'

Soon the fire was a pile of smoking embers, and the men began to get up, stretch themselves, wish one another goodnight, and head home to their huts. But five young men of the third kafo stayed behind – one to cover with dust the warm ashes of all the fires, and the rest, including Kunta, to take the late shift as village lookouts beyond each corner of Juffure's high bamboo fence. After such alarming talk around the fire, Kunta knew he would have no trouble staying awake, but he didn't look forward to spending this particular night beyond the safety of the village.

Ambling through Juffure and out the gate with what he hoped was nonchalance, Kunta waved to his fellow guards and made his way along the outside of the fence – past the sharp-thorned bushes piled thickly against it, and the pointed stakes concealed beneath them – to a leafy hiding place that afforded him a silvery view of the surrounding countryside on this moonlit night. Getting as comfortable as he could, he slung his spear across his lap, drew up his knees, clasped his arms around them for warmth, and settled in for the night. Scanning the bush with straining eyes for any sign of movement, he listened to the shrilling of crickets, the eerie whistling of night birds, the distant howling of hyenas, and the shrieks of unwary animals taken by surprise, and he thought about the things the men had said around the fire. When dawn came without an incident, he was almost as surprised that he hadn't been set upon by slave stealers as he was to realize that for the first time in a moon, he hadn't spent a moment worrying about his personal problems.

29

Nearly every day, it seemed to Kunta, Binta would irritate him about something. It wasn't anything she would do or say, but in other ways – little looks, certain tones of voice – Kunta could tell she disapproved of something about him. It was worst when Kunta added to his possessions new things that Binta hadn't obtained for him herself. One morning, arriving to serve his breakfast, Binta nearly dropped the steaming couscous upon Kunta when she saw he was wearing his first dundiko not sewn with her own hands. Feeling guilty for having traded a cured hyena hide to get it, Kunta angrily offered her no explanation, though he could feel that his mother was deeply hurt.

From that morning on, he knew that Binta never brought his meals without her eyes raking every item in his hut to see if there was anything else – a stool, a mat, a bucket, a plate, or a pot – that she'd had nothing to do with. If something new had appeared, Binta's sharp eyes would never miss it. Kunta would sit there fuming while she put on that look of not caring and not noticing that he had seen her wear so many times around Omoro, who knew as well as Kunta did that Binta could hardly wait to get to the village well among her women friends so that she could loudly bemoan her troubles – which was what all Mandinka women did when they disagreed with their husbands.

One day, before his mother arrived with the morning meal, Kunta picked up a beautifully woven basket that Jinna M'Baki, one of Juffure's several widows, had given him as a gift, and he set it just inside the door of his hut, where his mother would be sure to all but stumble over it. The widow was actually a little younger than Binta, it occurred to him. While Kunta was still a second-kafo goatherd, her husband had gone away to hunt and never returned. She lived quite near Nyo Boto, whom Kunta often visited, and that was how he and the widow had seen each other and come to speak to each other as Kunta had grown older. It had annoyed Kunta when the widow's gift caused some of Kunta's friends to tease him about her reason for giving him a valuable bamboo basket. When Binta arrived at his hut and saw it – recognizing the widow's style of weaving – she flinched as if the basket were a scorpion before managing to compose herself.

She didn't say a word about it, of course, but Kunta knew he had made his point. He was no longer a boy, and it was time for her to stop acting like his mother. He felt it was his own responsibility to change her in that regard. It wasn't something to speak to Omoro about, for Kunta knew he couldn't put himself into the ridiculous position of asking Omoro's advice on how to make Binta respect her son the same as she did her husband. Kunta thought about discussing his problem with Nyo Boto, but changed his mind when he recalled how peculiarly she had acted towards him upon his return from manhood training.

So Kunta kept his own counsel, and before long he decided not to go any more into Binta's hut, where he had lived most of his life. And when Binta brought his meals, he would sit stiffly silent while she set his food on the mat before him and left without speaking or even looking at him. Kunta finally began thinking seriously of seeking out some new eating arrangement. Most of the other new young men still ate from their mothers' kitchens, but some were cooked for by an older sister or a sister-in-law. If Binta got any worse, Kunta told himself, he was going to find some other woman to cook for him – perhaps the widow who had given him the woven basket. He knew without asking that she would gladly cook for him – and yet Kunta didn't want to let her know that he was even considering such a thing. In the meantime, he and his mother continued to meet at mealtimes – and to act as if they didn't even see each other.

Early one morning, returning from a night of sentry duty out in the groundnut fields, Kunta saw hurrying along the trail some distance ahead of him three young men whom he could tell were about his own age, and whom he knew had to be travellers from somewhere else. Shouting until they turned around, he went running to meet and greet them. They told Kunta they were from the village of Barra, a day and a night of walking from Juffure, and they were on their way to hunt for gold. They were of the Feloop tribe, which was a branch of Mandinka, but he had to listen carefully to understand them, as they did to understand him. It made Kunta remember his visit with his father to his uncle's new village, where he couldn't understand what some people were saying, although they lived only two or three days away from Juffure.

Kunta was intrigued by the trip the young men were taking. He thought it might also interest some of his friends, so he asked the young men to stop in his village for a day of hospitality before they went on. But they graciously refused the invitation, saying that they had to reach the place where the gold could be panned by the third afternoon of travel. 'But why don't you come along with us?' one of the young men asked Kunta.

Never having dreamed of such a thing, Kunta was so taken aback that he found himself saying no, telling them that as much as he appreciated the offer, he had much work to do on his farm, as well as other duties. And the three young men expressed their regret. 'If you should change your mind, please join us,' one said. And they got down on their knees and drew in the dust to show Kunta where the gold-hunting place was located – about two days and nights of travel beyond Juffure. The father of one of the boys, a travelling musician, had told them where it was.

Kunta walked along talking with his newfound friends until they came to where the travellers' trail forked. After the three men took the fork that led on past Juffure – and turned to wave back at him – Kunta walked slowly home. He was thinking hard as he entered his hut and lay down on his bed, and though he had been awake all night, he still couldn't seem to fall asleep. Perhaps he might go to hunt gold after all if he could find a friend to tend his farm plot. And he knew that someone of his mates would take over his sentry duties if they were only asked – as he would gladly do if they asked him.

Kunta's next thought hit him so hard it made him leap right up out of bed: as a man now, he could take Lamin along, as his father had once taken *him*. For the next hour Kunta paced the dirt floor of his hut, his mind wrestling with the questions raised by this exciting thought. First of all, would Omoro permit such a trip for Lamin, who was yet a boy and thus required his father's approval? It galled Kunta enough, as a man, to have to ask permission for anything; but suppose Omoro said *no*? And how would his three new friends feel about it if he showed up with his little brother?

Come to think of it, Kunta wondered why he was pacing the floor, and risking serious embarrassment, just to do a favour for Lamin. After all, ever since he had returned from manhood training, Lamin hadn't even been that close to him any more. But Kunta knew that this wasn't something that either of them wanted. They had really enjoyed each other before Kunta went away. But now Lamin's time was taken up by Suwadu, who was always hanging around his bigger brother in the same way that Lamin used to hang around Kunta, full of pride and admiration. But Kunta felt that Lamin had never quit feeling that way about him. If anything, he felt that Lamin admired his big brother even more than before. It was just that some kind of distance had come between them because of his having become a man. Men simply spent no great deal of time with boys; and even if that wasn't as he and Lamin wanted it, there just seemed no way for either of them to crack through it – until Kunta thought of taking Lamin along on his gold-hunting trip.

'Lamin is a good boy. He displays his home-training well. And he takes good care of my goats,' was Kunta's opening comment to Omoro, for Kunta knew that men almost never began conversations directly with what they meant to discuss. Omoro, of course, knew this, too. He nodded slowly and replied: 'Yes, I would say that is true.' As calmly as he could, Kunta then told his father of meeting his three new friends and of their invitation to join them in hunting for gold. Taking a deep breath, Kunta said finally, 'I've been thinking that Lamin might enjoy the trip.'

Omoro's face showed not a flicker of expression. A long moment passed before he spoke. 'For a boy to travel is good,' he said – and Kunta knew that his father was at least not going to say no absolutely. In some way, Kunta could feel his father's trust in him, but also his concern, which he knew Omoro didn't want to express any more strongly than he had to. 'It has been rains since I've had any travel in that area. I seem not to remember that trail's route very well,' said Omoro, as casually as if they were merely discussing the weather. Kunta knew that his father – whom Kunta had never known to forget anything – was trying to find out if he knew the route to the gold-hunting place.

Dropping onto his knees in the dust, Kunta drew the trail with a stick as if he had known it for years. He drew circles to show the villages that were both near the trail and at some distance from it along the way. Omoro got down onto his knees as well, and when Kunta had finished drawing the trail, said, 'I would go so as to pass close by the most villages. It will take a little longer, but it will be the safest.'

Kunta nodded, hoping that he appeared more confident than he suddenly felt. The thought hit him that though the three friends he had met, travelling together, could catch each other's mistakes – if they made any – he, travelling with a younger brother for whom he would be responsible, would have no one to help if something went wrong.

Then Kunta saw Omoro's finger circling the last third of the trail. 'In this area, few speak Mandinka,' Omoro said. Kunta remembered the lessons of his manhood training and looked into his father's eyes. 'The sun and the stars will tell me the way,' he said.

A long moment passed, and then Omoro spoke again. 'I think I'll go by your mother's house.' Kunta's heart leaped. He knew it was his father's way of saying that his permission was given, and he felt it best that he personally make his decision known to Binta.

Omoro wasn't long in Binta's hut. He had hardly left to return to his own when she burst out her door, hands pressed tightly to her shaking head. 'Madi! Suwadu!' she shrieked, and they came rushing to her from among the other children.

Now other mothers came from their huts, and unmarried girls, all rushing behind Binta as she began hollering and pulling the two boys alongside her towards the well. Once there, all of the women crowded about her as she wept and moaned that now she had only two children left, that her others certainly would soon be lost to toubob.

A second-kafo girl, unable to contain the news of Kunta's trip with Lamin, raced all the way out to where the boys of her kafo were grazing the goats. A short time later, back in the village, heads jerked around with smiles on their faces as a deliriously joyful boy came whooping into the village in a manner fit to wake the ancestors. Catching up with his mother just outside her hut, Lamin – though still a hand's span shorter than her – bearhugged Binta, planted big kisses on her forehead and swept her whirling up off her feet as she shouted to be put down. Once back on the ground, she ran to pick up a nearby piece of wood and struck Lamin with it. She would have done it again, but he dashed away – feeling no pain – towards Kunta's hut. He didn't even knock as he burst inside. It was an unthinkable intrusion into a man's house – but after a glimpse at his brother's face, Kunta had to overlook it. Lamin just stood there, looking up into the face of his big brother. The boy's mouth was trying to say something; indeed, his whole body was trembling, and Kunta had to catch himself to keep from grabbing and hugging Lamin in the rush of love he felt passing between them in that moment.

Kunta heard himself speaking, his tone almost gruff. 'I see you've already heard. We'll leave tomorrow after first prayer.'

Man or not, Kunta took care to walk nowhere near Binta as he made several quick calls to see friends about caring for his farm and filling in for him on sentry duty. Kunta could tell where Binta was from the sound of her wailing as she marched around the village holding Madi and Suwadu by the hand. 'These two only I have left!' she cried, as loudly as she could. But like everyone else in Juffure, she knew that no matter what she felt or said or did, Omoro had spoken.

30

At the travellers' tree, Kunta prayed for their journey to be a safe one. So that it would be a prosperous one as well, he tied the chicken he had brought along to a lower branch by one of its legs, leaving it flapping and squawking there as he and Lamin set forth on the trail. Though he didn't turn back to look, Kunta knew Lamin was trying very hard to keep pace with him, and to keep his headload balanced – and to keep Kunta from noticing either.

After an hour, the trail took them by a low, spreading tree strung thickly with beads. Kunta wanted to explain to Lamin how such a tree meant that living nearby were some of the few Mandinkas who were kafirs, pagan unbelievers who used snuff and smoked tobacco in pipes made of wood with earthen bowls, and also drank a beer they made of mead. But more important than that knowledge was for Lamin to learn the discipline of silent marching. By noontime, Kunta knew that Lamin's feet and legs would be hurting him badly, and also his neck under the heavy headload. But it was only by keeping on despite pain that a boy could toughen his body and his spirit. At the same time, Kunta knew that Lamin must stop for rest before he collapsed, which would hurt his pride.

Taking the bypass trail to miss the first village they passed, they soon shook off the naked little first-kafo children who raced out to inspect them. Kunta still didn't look back, but he knew that Lamin would have quickened his pace and straightened his back for the children's benefit. But as they left the children and the village behind, Kunta's mind drifted off Lamin to other things. He thought again of the drum he was going to make for himself – making it first in his mind, as the men did who carved out masks and figures. For the drum's head, he had a young goat's skin already scraped and curing in his hut, and he knew just the place – only a short trot beyond the women's rice fields – where he could find the tough wood he needed for a strong drum frame. Kunta could almost hear how his drum was going to sound.

As the trail took them into a grove of trees close by the path, Kunta tightened his grip on the spear he carried, as he had been taught to do. Cautiously, he continued walking – then stopped and listened very quietly. Lamin stood wide-eyed behind him, afraid to breathe. A moment later, however, his big brother relaxed and began walking again, towards what Kunta recognized – with relief – as the sound of several men singing a working song. Soon he and Lamin came into a clearing and saw twelve men dragging a dugout canoe with ropes. They had felled a tree and burned and chopped it out, and now they were starting to move it the long way to the river. After each haul on the ropes, they sang the next line of the song, each one ending 'All together!' then again, straining hard, as they moved the dugout about another arm's length. Waving to the men, who waved back, Kunta passed them and made a mental note to tell Lamin later who these men were and why they had made the canoe from a tree that grew here in the forest rather than near the riverbank: they were from the village of Kerewan, where they made the best Mandinka dugouts; and they knew that only forest trees would float.

Kunta thought with a rush of warmth about the three young men from Barra whom they were travelling to meet. It was strange that though they never had seen each other before, they seemed as brothers. Perhaps it was because they too were Mandinkas. They said things differently than he did, but they weren't different *inside*. Like them, he had decided to leave his village to seek his fortune – and a little excitement – before returning to their homes ahead of the next big rains.

When the time neared for the alansaro prayer in mid-afternoon, Kunta stepped off the trail where a small stream ran among trees. Not looking at Lamin, he slipped off his headload, flexed himself, and bent to scoop up handfuls of water in order to splash his face. He drank sparingly, then, in the midst of his prayer, he heard Lamin's headload thud to the earth. Springing up at the end of the prayer intending to rebuke him, he saw how painfully his brother was crawling towards the water. But Kunta still made his voice hard: 'Sip a little at a time!' As Lamin drank, Kunta decided that an hour's resting here would be long enough. After eating a few bites of food, he thought, Lamin should be able to keep walking until time for the fitiro prayer, at about dusk, when a fuller meal and a night's rest would be welcomed by them both.

But Lamin was too tired even to eat. He lay where he had drunk from the stream, face down with his arms flung out, palms up. Kunta stepped over quietly to look at the soles of his feet; they weren't bleeding yet. Then Kunta himself catnapped, and when he got up he took from his headload enough dried meat for two. Shaking Lamin awake, he gave him his meat and ate his own. Soon they were back on the trail, which made all the turns and passed all the landmarks the young men from Barra had drawn for Kunta. Near one village, they saw two old grandmothers and two young girls with some first-kafo children busily catching crabs, darting their hands into a little stream and snatching out their prey.

Near dusk, as Lamin began to grab more and more often at his headload, Kunta saw ahead a flock of large bushfowl circling down to land. Abruptly he stopped, concealing himself, as Lamin sank onto his knees behind a bush nearby. Kunta pursed his lips, making the male bushfowl mating call, and shortly several fat, fine hens came flapping and waddling over. They were cocking their heads and looking around when Kunta's arrow went straight through one. Jerking its head off, he let the blood drain out, and while the bird roasted he built a rough bush shelter, then prayed. He also roasted some ears of wild corn that he had plucked along the way before awakening Lamin, who had fallen asleep again the moment they put their headloads down. Hardly had Lamin wolfed down his meal before he flopped back down onto the soft moss under a slanting roof of leafy boughs and went back to sleep without a murmur.

Kunta sat hugging his knees in the night's still air. Not far away, hyenas began yipping. For some time, he diverted himself by identifying the other sounds of the forest. Then three times he faintly heard a melodious horn. He knew it was the next village's final prayer call, blown by their alimamo through a hollowed elephant's tooth. He wished that Lamin had been awake to hear its haunting cry, which was almost like a human voice, but then he smiled, for his brother was beyond caring what anything sounded like. Then himself praying, Kunta also slept.

Soon after sunrise, they were passing that village and hearing the drumming rhythm of the women's pestles pounding couscous for breakfast porridge. Kunta could almost taste it; but they didn't stop. Not far beyond, down the trail, was another village, and as they went by, the men were leaving their mosque and the women were bustling around their cooking fires. Still farther on, Kunta saw ahead of them an old man sitting beside the trail. He was bent nearly double over a number of cowrie shells, which he was shuffling and reshuffling on a plaited bamboo mat while mumbling to himself. Not to interrupt him, Kunta was about to pass by when the old man looked up and hailed them over to where he sat.

'I come from the village of Kootacunda, which is in the kingdom of Wooli, where the sun rises over the Simbani forest,' he said in a high, cracking voice. 'And where may you be from?' Kunta told him the village of Juffure, and the old man nodded. 'I have heard of it.' He was consulting his cowries, he said, to learn their next message about his journey to the city of Timbuktu, 'which I want to see before I die,' and he wondered if the travellers would care to be of any help to him. 'We are poor, but happy to share whatever we have with you, Grandfather,' said Kunta, easing off his headload, reaching within it and withdrawing some dried meat, which he gave the old man, who thanked him and put the food in his lap.

Peering at them both, he asked, 'You are brothers travelling?'

'We are, Grandfather,' Kunta replied.

'That is good!' the old man said, and picked up two of his cowries. 'Add this to those on your hunting bag, and it will bring you a fine profit,' he said to Kunta, handing him one of the cowries. 'And you, young man,' he said to Lamin, giving him the other, 'keep this for when you become a man with a bag of your own.' They both thanked him, and he wished them Allah's blessings.

They had walked on for quite a while when Kunta decided that the time was ripe to break his silence with Lamin. Without stopping or turning, he began to speak: 'There is a legend, little brother, that it was travelling Mandinkas who named the place where that old man is bound. They found there a kind of insect they had never seen before and named the place "Tumbo Kutu", which means "new insect".' When there was no response from Lamin, Kunta turned his head; Lamin was well behind, bent down over his headload – which had fallen open on the ground – and struggling to tie it back together. As Kunta trotted back, he realized that Lamin's grabbing at his headload had finally caused it to work its bindings loose and that he had somehow eased it off his head without making any noise, not wanting to break the rule of silence by asking Kunta to stop. While Kunta was retying the headload, he saw that Lamin's feet were bleeding; but this was to be expected, so he said nothing of it. The tears shone in Lamin's eyes as he got the load back on his head, and they went on. Kunta upbraided himself that he hadn't missed Lamin's presence and might have left him behind.

They hadn't walked much farther when Lamin let out a choked scream. Thinking he had stepped on a thorn, Kunta turned – and saw his brother staring upwards at a big panther flattened on the limb they would have walked under in another moment. The panther went *sssss*, then seemed to flow almost lazily into the branches of a tree and was gone from sight. Shaken, Kunta resumed walking, alarmed and angry and embarrassed at himself. Why had he not seen that panther? The odds were that it was only wishing to remain unseen and wouldn't have sprung down upon them, for unless the big cats were extremely hungry, they rarely attacked even their animal prey during the daylight, and humans seldom at any time, unless they were cornered, provoked, or wounded. Still, a picture flashed through Kunta's memory of the panther-mangled nanny goat from his goatherding days. He could almost hear the kintango's stern warning: 'The hunter's senses must be fine. He must hear what others cannot, smell what others cannot. He must see through the darkness.' But while he had been walking along with his own thoughts wandering, it was Lamin who had seen the panther. Most of his bad troubles had come from that habit, which he absolutely must correct, he thought. Bending quickly without breaking pace, Kunta picked up a small stone, spat on it three times, and hurled it far back down the trail, the stone having thus carried behind them the spirits of misfortune.

They walked on with the sun burning down upon them as the country gradually changed from green forest to oil palms and muddy, dozing creeks, taking them past hot, dusty villages where – just as in Juffure – first-kafo children ran and screamed around in packs, where men lounged under the baobab and women gossiped beside the well. But Kunta wondered why they let their goats wander around these villages, along with the dogs and chickens, rather than keep them either out grazing or penned up, as in Juffure. He decided that they must be an odd, different kind of people.

They pushed on over grassless, sandy soil sprinkled with the burst dry fruit of weirdly shaped baobabs. When the time came to pray, they rested and ate lightly, and Kunta would check Lamin's head-bundle and his feet, whose bleeding was not so bad any more. And the crossroads kept unfolding like a picture, until finally there was the huge old shell of a baobab that the young men from Barra had described. It must have been hundreds of rains old to be dying at last, he thought, and he told Lamin what one of the young men had told him: 'A griot rests inside there,' adding from his own knowledge that griots were always buried not as other people were but within the shells of ancient baobabs, since both the trees and the histories in the heads of griots were timeless. 'We're close now,' Kunta said, and he wished he had the drum he was going to make, so that he could signal ahead to his friends. With the sinking of the sun, they finally reached the clay pits – and there were the three young men.

'We felt you would come!' they shouted, happy to see him. They merely ignored Lamin as if he were their own second-kafo brother. Amid brisk talk, the three young men proudly showed the tiny grains of gold they had collected. By the next morning's first light, Kunta and Lamin had joined in, chopping up chunks of sticky clay, which they dropped into large calabashes of water. After whirling the calabash, then slowly pouring off most of the muddy water, they carefully felt with their fingers to see if any gold grains had sunk to the bottom. Now and then there was a grain as tiny as a millet seed, or maybe a little larger.

They worked so feverishly that there was no time for talk. Lamin seemed even to forget his aching muscles in the search for gold. And each precious grain went carefully into the hollow of the largest quills from bush pigeons' wings, stoppered with a bit of cotton. Kunta and Lamin had six quills full when the three young men said they'd collected enough. Now, they said, they'd like to go farther up the trail, deeper into the interior of the country, to hunt elephants' teeth. They said they had been told where old elephants sometimes broke off their teeth in trying to uproot small trees and thick brush while feeding. They had heard also that if one could ever find the secret graveyards of the elephants, a fortune in teeth would be there. Would Kunta join them? He was sorely tempted; this sounded even more exciting than hunting for gold. But he couldn't go – not with Lamin. Sadly he thanked them for the invitation and said he must return home with his brother. So warm farewells were exchanged, but not before Kunta had made the young men accept his invitation to stop for hospitality in Juffure on their way home to Barra.

The trip back seemed shorter to Kunta. Lamin's feet bled worse, but he walked faster when Kunta handed him the quills to carry, saying, 'Your mother should enjoy these.' Lamin's happiness was no greater than his own at having taken his brother travelling, just as their father had done for him – just as Lamin would one day take Suwadu, and Suwadu would take Madi. They were approaching Juffure's travellers' tree when Kunta heard Lamin's headload fall off again. Kunta whirled angrily, but then he saw his brother's pleading expression. 'All right, get it later!' he snapped. Without a word, his aching muscles and his bleeding feet forgotten, Lamin bolted past Kunta for the village, his thin legs racing faster than they'd ever taken him.

By the time Kunta entered the village gate, excited women and children were clustered around Binta, who was sticking the six quills of gold into her hair, clearly bursting with relief and happiness. A moment later, Binta's and Kunta's faces exchanged a look of tenderness and warmth far beyond the usual greetings that passed between mother and her grown-up son home from travelling. The women's clacking tongues soon let everyone in Juffure know what the two oldest Kinte sons had brought home with them. 'There's a cow on Binta's head!' shouted an old grandmother – there was enough gold in the quills to buy a cow – and the rest of the women took up that cry.

'You did well,' said Omoro simply when Kunta met him. But the feeling they shared without further words was even greater than with Binta. In the days that followed, elders seeing Kunta around the village began to speak to him and smile in a special way, and he solemnly replied with his respects. Even Suwadu's little second-kafo mates greeted Kunta as a grown-up, saying 'Peace!' and then standing with palms folded over their chests until he passed by. Kunta even chanced to overhear Binta one day gossiping about 'the two men I feed,' and he was filled with pride that his mother had finally realized he was a man.

It was all right with Kunta now not only for Binta to feed him, but even to do such things as searching on Kunta's head for ticks, as she had been resenting not doing. And Kunta felt it all right now also to visit her hut again now and then. As for Binta, she bustled about all smiles, even humming to herself as she cooked. In an offhand manner, Kunta would ask if she needed him to do anything; she would say so if she did, and he did whatever it was as soon as he could. If he but glanced at Lamin or Suwadu, when they were playing too loudly, for example, they were instantly still and quiet. And Kunta liked tossing Madi into the air, catching him as he fell, and Madi liked it even more. As for Lamin, he clearly regarded his manbrother as ranking second only to Allah. He cared for Kunta's seven goats – which were multiplying well – as if they were goats of gold, and he eagerly helped Kunta to raise his small farm plot of couscous and groundnuts.

Whenever Binta needed to get some work done around the hut, Kunta would take all three children off her hands, and she would stand smiling in her doorway as he marched off with Madi on his shoulder, Lamin following – strutting like a rooster – and Suwadu jealously tagging along behind. It was nice, thought Kunta – so nice that he caught himself wishing that he might have a family of his own like this someday. But not until the time comes, of course, he told himself; and that's a long way off.

31

As new men were permitted to do whenever there was no conflict with their duties, Kunta and others of his kafo would sit at the outermost edges of the formal sessions of the Council of Elders, which were held once each moon under Juffure's ancient baobab. Sitting beneath it on cured hides very close together, the six senior elders seemed almost as old as the tree, Kunta thought, and to have been carved from the same wood, except that they were as black as ebony against the white of their long robes and round skullcaps. Seated facing them were those with troubles or disputes to be resolved. Behind the petitioners, in rows, according to their ages, sat junior elders such as Omoro, and behind them sat the new men of Kunta's kafo. And behind *them* the village women could sit, though they rarely attended except when someone in their immediate family was involved in a matter to be heard. Once in a long while, *all* the women would be present – but only if a case held the promise of some juicy gossip.

No women at all attended when the Council met to discuss purely administrative affairs, such as Juffure's relationship with other villages. On the day for matters of the people, however, the audience was large and noisy – but all settled quickly into silence when the most senior of the elders raised his stick, sewn with bright-coloured beads, to strike out on the talking drum before him the name of the first person to be heard. This was done according to their ages, to serve the needs of the oldest first. Whoever it was would stand, stating his case, the senior elders all staring at the ground, listening until he finished and sat down. At this point, any of the elders might ask him questions.

If the matter involved a dispute, the second person now presented his side, followed by more questions, whereupon the elders turned around to present their backs as they huddled to discuss the matter, which could take a long time. One or more might turn with further questions. But all finally turned back around towards the front, one motioning the person or persons being heard to stand again, and the senior elder then spoke their decision, after which the next name was drumtalked.

Even for new men like Kunta, most of these hearings were routine matters. People with babies recently born asked for a bigger farm plot for the husband and an additional rice plot for the wife –

requests that were almost always quickly granted, as were the first farming-land requests of unmarried men like Kunta and his mates. During man-training, the kintango had directed them never to miss any Council of Elders sessions unless they had to, as the witnessing of its decisions would broaden a man's knowledge as his own rains increased until he too would be a senior elder. Attending his first session, Kunta had looked at Omoro seated ahead of him, wondering how many hundreds of decisions his father must have in his head, though he wasn't even a senior elder yet.

At his first session, Kunta witnessed a land matter involving a dispute. Two men both claimed the fruit of some trees originally planted by the first man on land to which the second man now had the farming rights, since the first man's family had decreased. The Council of Elders awarded the fruit to the first man, saying, 'If he hadn't planted the trees, that fruit wouldn't be there.'

At later sessions, Kunta saw people frequently charged with breaking or losing something borrowed from an irate lender who claimed that the articles had been both valuable and brand-new, Unless the borrower had witnesses to disprove that he was usually ordered to pay for or replace the article at the value of a new one. Kunta also saw furious people accusing others of inflicting bad fortune on them through evil magic. One man testified that another had touched him with a cock's spur, making him violently ill. A young wife declared that her new mother-in-law had hidden some bourein shrub in the wife's kitchen, causing whatever was cooked there to turn out badly. And a widow claimed that an old man whose advances she had spurned had sprinkled powdered eggshells in her path, making her walk into a long succession of troubles, which she proceeded to describe. If presented with enough impressive evidence of evil magic's motives and results, the Council would command immediate corrective magic to be done by the nearest travelling magic man, whom a drumtalk message would summon to Juffure at the expense of the evil-doer.

Kunta saw debtors ordered to pay up, even if they had to sell their possessions; or with nothing to sell, to work off the amount as the lender's slave. He saw slaves charging their masters with cruelty, or with providing unsuitable food or lodgings, or with taking more than their half share of what the slaves' work had produced. Masters, in turn, accused slaves of cheating by hiding some of their produce, or of insufficient work, or of deliberately breaking farm tools. Kunta saw the Council weigh carefully the evidence in these cases, along with each person's past record in the village, and it was not uncommon for some slaves' reputations to be better than their masters'!

But sometimes there was no dispute between a master and his slave. Indeed, Kunta saw them coming together asking permission for the slave to marry into the master's family. But any couple intending to marry, first had to obtain the Council's permission. Couples judged by the Council to be too close of kinship were refused out of hand, but for those not thus disqualified, there was a waiting period of one moon between the request and the reply, during which the villagers were expected to pay quiet visits to any senior elder and reveal any private information, either good or bad, about the couple in question. Since childhood, had each of them always demonstrated a good home-training? Had either of them ever caused undue trouble to anyone, including their own families? Had either of them ever displayed any undesirable tendencies of any kind, such as cheating or telling less than the full truth? Was the girl known for being irritable and argumentative? Was the man known for beating goats unmercifully? If so, the marriage was refused, for it was believed that such a person might pass these traits along to his or her children. But as Kunta knew even before he began attending the Council sessions, most couples won approval for marriage, because both sets of parents involved had already learned the answers to these questions, and found them satisfactory, before granting their own permission.

At the Council sessions, however, Kunta learned that sometimes parents hadn't been told things that people did tell the senior elders. Kunta saw one marriage permission flatly refused when a witness came forth to testify that the young man of the planned marriage, as a young goatherd, had once stolen a basket from him, thinking he hadn't been seen. The crime hadn't been reported then, out of compassion for the fact that he was still a boy; if it *had* been reported, the law would have dictated that his right hand be cut off. Kunta sat riveted as the young thief, exposed at last, burst into tears, blurting out his guilt before his horrified parents and the girl he was asking to marry, who began screaming. Soon afterwards, he disappeared from Juffure and was never seen or heard of again.

After attending Council sessions for a number of moons, Kunta guessed that most problems for the senior elders came from married people – especially from men with two, three, or four wives. Adultery was the most frequent charge by such men, and unpleasant things happened to an offending man if a husband's accusation was backed up with convincing outside testimony or other strong evidence. If a wronged husband was poor and the offending man well

133

off, the Council might order the offender to deliver his possessions to the husband, one at a time, until the husband said, 'I have enough,' which might not be until the adulterer had only his bare hut left. But with both men poor, which was usually the case, the Council might order the offender to work as the husband's slave for a period of time considered worth the wrongful use of his wife. And Kunta flinched for one repeated offender when the elders set a date and time for him to receive a public flogging of thirty-nine lashes across his bare back by his most recently wronged husband, according to the ancient Moslem rule of 'forty, save one'.

Kunta's own thoughts about getting married cooled somewhat as he watched and listened to the angry testimony of injured wives and husbands before the Council. Men charged that their wives failed to respect them, were unduly lazy, were unwilling to make love when their turn came, or were just generally impossible to live with. Unless an accused wife presented a strong counter-argument, with some witnesses to bear her out, the senior elders usually told the husband to go that day and set any three possessions of his wife's outside her hut and then utter towards those possessions, three times, with witnesses present, the words, 'I divorce you!'

A wife's most serious charge – certain to bring out every woman in the village if it was suspected in advance – was to claim that her husband was not a man, meaning that he was inadequate with her in bed. The elders would appoint three old persons, one from the family of the defiant wife, another from the family of the husband, and the third from among the elders themselves. A date and time would be set for them to observe the wife and husband together in his bed. If two of the three voted that the wife was right, she won her divorce, and her family kept the dowry goats; but if two observers voted that the husband performed well, he not only got the goats back but also could beat the wife and divorce her if he wished to.

In the rains since Kunta had returned from manhood training, no case that had been considered by the Council filled him and his mates with as much anticipation as the one that began with gossip and whispering about two older members of their own kafo and a pair of Juffure's most eligible widows. On the day the matter finally came before the Council, nearly everyone in the village gathered early to assure themselves of the best possible seats. A number of routine old people's problems were settled first, and then came the case of Dembo Dabo and Kadi Tamba, who had been granted a divorce more than a rain before but now were back before the Council grinning widely and holding hands and asking permission to remarry.

They stopped grinning when the senior elder told them sternly: 'You insisted on divorce; therefore you may not remarry – until each of you has had another wife and husband in between.'

The gasps from those in the rear were hushed by the drumtalk announcement of the next names to be called: 'Tuda Tamba and Kalilu Conteh! Fanta Bedeng and Sefo Kela!' The two members of Kunta's kafo and the two widows stood up. The taller widow, Fanta Bedeng, spoke for all of them, sounding as if she had carefully practised what to say; but nervousness still gripped her. 'Tuda Tamba with her thirty-two rains and I with my thirty-three have small chance of catching more husbands,' she said, and proceeded to ask the Council to approve of teriya friendships for her and Tuda Tamba to cook for and sleep with Sefo Kela and Kalilu Conteh, respectively.

Different elders asked a few questions of all four – the widows responding confidently, Kunta's friends uncertainly, in sharp contrast to their usual boldness of manner. And then the elders turned around, murmuring among themselves. The audience was so tense and quiet that a dropped groundnut could have been heard as the elders finally turned back around. The senior elder spoke: 'Allah would approve! You widows will have a man to use, and you new men will get valuable experience for when you marry later.'

The senior elder rapped his stick twice hard against the edge of the talking drum and glared at the buzzing women in the rear. Only when they fell silent was the next name called: 'Jankeh Jallon!' Having but fifteen rains, she was thus the last to be heard. All of Juffure had danced and feasted when she found her way home after escaping from some toubob who had kidnapped her. Then, a few moons later, she became big with child, although unmarried, which caused much gossip. Young and strong, she might still have found some old man's acceptance as a third or fourth junior wife. But then the child was born: he was a strange pale tan colour like a cured hide, and had very odd hair – and wherever Jankeh Jallon would appear thereafter, people would look at the ground and hurry elsewhere. Her eyes glistening with tears, she stood up now and asked the Council: What was she to do? The elders didn't turn around to confer, the senior elder said they would have to weigh the matter – which was a most serious and difficult one – until the next moon's Council meeting. And with that, he and the five other elders rose and left.

Troubled, and somehow unsatisfied, by the way the session had ended, Kunta remained seated for a few moments after most of his mates and the rest of the audience had got up – chattering among themselves – and headed back towards their huts. His head was still full of thoughts when Binta brought his evening meal, and he said not a word to her as he ate, nor she to him. Later, as he picked up his spear and his bow and arrow and ran with his wuolo dog to his sentry post – for this was his night to stand guard outside the village – Kunta was still thinking: about the tan baby with the strange hair, about his no doubt even stranger father, and about whether this toubob would have eaten Jankah Jallon if she had not escaped from him.

32

In the moonlit expanse of ripening fields of groundnuts, Kunta climbed the notched pole and sat down crosslegged on the lookout platform that was built into its sturdy fork, high above the ground. Placing his weapons beside him – along with the axe with which he planned the next morning, at last, to chop the wood for his drum frame – he watched as his wuolo dog went trotting and sniffing this way and that in the fields below. During Kunta's first few moons on sentry duty, rains ago, he remembered snatching at his spear if so much as a rat went rustling through the grass. Every shadow seemed a monkey, every monkey a panther, and every panther a toubob, until his eyes and ears became seasoned to his task. In time, he found he could tell the difference between the snarl of a lion and that of a leopard. It took longer, however, for him to learn how to remain vigilant through these long nights. When his thoughts began to turn inwards, as they always did, he often forgot where he was and what he was supposed to be doing. But finally he learned to keep alert with half of his mind and yet still explore his private thoughts with the other.

Tonight, he was thinking about the teriya friendships that had been approved for his two friends by the Council of Elders. For several moons, they had been telling Kunta and his mates that they were going to take their case before the Council, but no one had really believed them. And now it was done. Perhaps at this very moment, he thought, they might be performing the teriya act in bed

136

with their two widows. Kunta suddenly sat upright trying to picture what it must be like.

It was chiefly from his kafo's gossip that Kunta knew what little he did know about under women's clothes. In marriage negotiations, he knew, girls' fathers had to guarantee them as virgins to get the best bride price. And a lot of bloodiness was connected with women, he knew that. Every moon they had blood; and whenever they had babies; and the night when they got married. Everyone knew how the next morning, the newlyweds' two mothers went to the hut to put into a woven basket the white pagne cloth the couple had slept on, taking its bloodiness as proof of the girl's virginity to the alimamo, who only then walked around the village drumtalking Allah's blessing on that marriage. If that white cloth wasn't bloodied, Kunta knew, the new husband would angrily leave the hut with the two mothers as his witnesses and shout loudly, 'I divorce you!' three times for all to hear.

But teriya involved none of that – only new men sleeping with a willing widow and eating her cooking. Kunta thought for a little while about how Jinna M'Baki had looked at him, making no secret of her designs, amid the previous day's jostling crowd as the Council session ended. Almost without realizing, he squeezed his hard foto, but he forced back the strong urge to stroke it because that would seem as if he was giving in to what that widow wanted, which was embarrassing even to think about. He didn't really want the stickiness with her, he told himself; but now that he was a man, he had every right, if he pleased, to *think* about teriya, which the senior elders themselves had shown was nothing for a man to be ashamed of.

Kunta's mind returned to the memory of some girls he and Lamin had passed in one village when returning from their gold-hunting trip. There had been about ten of them, he guessed, all beautifully black, in tight dresses, colourful beads, and bracelets, with high breasts and little hair plaits sticking up. They had acted so strangely as he went by that it had taken Kunta a moment to realize that the show they made of looking away whenever he looked at them meant not that they weren't interested in him but that they wanted him to be interested in *them*.

Females were so confusing, he thought. Girls of their age in Juffure never paid enough attention to him even to look away. Was it because they knew what he was really like? Or was it because they knew he was far younger than he looked – too young to be worthy of their interest? Probably the girls in that village believed no travelling man leading a boy could have less than twenty or twenty-five rains, let alone his seventeen. They would have scoffed if they had known. Yet he was being sought after by a widow who knew very well how young he was. Perhaps he was lucky not to be older, Kunta thought. If he was, the girls of Juffure would be carrying on over him the way the girls of that village had, and he knew they all had just one thing on their minds: marriage. At least Jinna M'Baki was too old to be looking for anything more than a teriya friendship. Why would a man want to marry when he could get a woman to cook for him and sleep with him without getting married? There must be some reason. Perhaps it was because it was only through marrying that a man could have sons. That was a good thing. But what would he have to teach those sons until he had lived long enough to learn something about the world – not just from his father, and from the arafang, and from the kintango, but also by exploring it for himself, as his uncles had done?

His uncles weren't married even yet, though they were older than his father, and most men of their rains had already taken second wives by now. Was Omoro considering taking a second wife? Kunta was so startled at the thought that he sat up straight. And how would his mother feel about it? Well, at least Binta, as the senior wife, would be able to tell the second wife her duties, and make certain she worked hard and set her sleeping turns with Omoro. Would there be trouble between the two women? No, he was sure Binta wouldn't be like the kintango's senior wife, who it was commonly known shouted so much abuse at his junior wives, keeping them in such a turmoil, that he rarely got any peace.

Kunta shifted the position of his legs to let them hang for a while over the edge of his small perch, to keep the muscles from cramping. His wuolo dog was curled on the ground below him, its smooth brown fur shining in the moonlight, but he knew that the dog only seemed to be dozing, and that his nose and ears were alertly twitching for the night air's slightest smell or sound of warning to bound up racing and barking after the baboons that had lately been raiding the groundnut fields almost every night. During each long lookout duty, few things pleased Kunta more than when, maybe a dozen times in the course of a night, he would be jerked from his thoughts by sudden distant snarlings as a baboon was sprung upon in the brush by a big cat – especially if the baboon's growling turned into a scream quickly hushed, which meant that it had not escaped.

But it all was quiet now as Kunta sat on the edge of his platform and looked out across the fields. The only sign of life, in fact, beyond the tall grass, was the bobbing yellow light of a Fulani herdsman in the distance as he waved his grass torch to frighten away some animal, probably a hyena, that was roaming too close to his cows. So good were the Fulani at tending cattle that people claimed they could actually talk with their animals. And Omoro had told Kunta that each day, as part of their pay for herding, the Fulani would siphon a little blood from the cows' necks, which they mixed with milk and drank. What a strange people, thought Kunta. Yet though they were not Mandinka, they were from The Gambia, like him. How much stranger must be the people – and the customs – one would find beyond the borders of his land.

Within a moon after he returned from gold hunting with Lamin, Kunta had been restless to get on the road once again – this time for a *real* trip. Other young men of his kafo, he knew, were planning to travel somewhere as soon as the groundnuts and couscous got harvested, but none was going to venture far. Kunta, however, meant to put his eyes and feet upon that distant place called Mali, where, some three or four hundred rains before, according to Omoro and his uncles, the Kinte clan had begun. These forefather Kintes, he remembered, had won fame as blacksmiths, men who had conquered fire to make iron weapons that won wars and iron tools that made farming less hard. And from this original Kinte family, all of their descendants and all of the people who worked for them had taken the Kinte name. And some of that clan had moved to Mauretania, the birthplace of Kunta's holy-man grandfather.

So that no one else, even Omoro, would know about his plan until he wanted it known, Kunta had consulted in the strictest confidence with the arafang about the best route to Mali. Drawing a rough map in the dust, then tracing his finger along it, he had told Kunta that by following the banks of the Kamby Bolongo about six days in the direction of one's prayers to Allah, a traveller would reach Samo Island. Beyond there, the river narrowed and curved sharply to the left and began a serpent's twists and turns, with many confusing bolongs leading off as wide as the river, whose swampy banks couldn't be seen in some areas for the thickness of the mangroves growing sometimes as high as ten men. Where one could see the riverbanks, the schoolmaster told him, they abounded with monkeys, hippopotamus, giant crocodiles and herds of as many as five hundred baboons.

But two to three days of that difficult travelling should bring Kunta to a second large island, where the low, muddy banks would rise into small cliffs matted with shrubs and small trees. The trail, which twisted alongside the river, would take him past villages of Bansang, Karantaba and Diabugu. Soon afterwards he would cross the eastern border of The Gambia and enter the Kingdom of Full-adu, and a half day's walking from there, he would arrive at the village of Fatoto. Out of his bag, Kunta took the scrap of cured hide the arafang had given him. On it was the name of a colleague in Fatoto who he said would give Kunta directions for the next twelve to four-teen days, which would take him across a land called Senegal. Beyond that, said the arafang, lay Mali and Kunta's destination, Ka-ba, that land's main place. To go there and return, the arafang figured, would take about a moon – not counting whatever time Kunta chose to spend in Mali.

So many times had Kunta drawn and studied the route on his hut's dirty floor – erasing it before Binta brought his meals – that he could almost see it before him as he sat on his perch in the groundnut fields. Thinking about the adventures that awaited him along that trail – and in Mali – he could hardly contain his eagerness to be off. He was almost as eager to tell Lamin of his plans, not only because he wanted to share his secret, but also because he had decided to take his little brother along. He knew how much Lamin had boasted about that earlier trip with his brother. Since then, Lamin had also been through manhood training and would be a more experienced and trustworthy travelling companion. But Kunta's deepest reason for deciding to take him, he had to admit, was simply that he wanted company.

For a moment, Kunta sat in the dark smiling to himself, thinking of Lamin's face when the time would come for him to know. Kunta planned, of course, to drop the news in a very offhand way, as if he had just happened to think of it. But before then he must speak about it with Omoro, whom he knew now would feel no undue con-cern. In fact, he was sure that Omoro would be deeply pleased, and that even Binta, though she would worry, would be less upset than before. Kunta wondered what he might bring to Binta from Mali that she would treasure even more than her quills of gold. Perhaps some fine moulded pots, or a bolt of beautiful cloth; Omoro and his uncles had said that the ancient Kinte women in Mali had been famed for the pots they made and for the brilliant patterns of cloth they wove, so maybe the Kinte women there still did those things.

When he returned from Mali, it occurred to Kunta, he might plan still another trip for a later rain. He might even journey to that distant place beyond endless sands where his uncles had told of the long caravans of strange animals with water stored in two humps on their backs. Kalilu Conteh and Sefo Kela could have their old, ugly teriya widows; he, Kunta Kinte, would make a pilgrimage to Mecca itself. Happening at that moment to be staring in the direction of that holy city, Kunta became aware of a tiny, steady yellow light far across the fields. The Fulani herdsman over there, he realized, was cooking his breakfast. Kunta hadn't even noticed the first faint streaks of dawn in the east.

Reaching down to pick up his weapons and head home, he saw his axe and remembered the wood for his drum frame. But he was tired, he thought; maybe he'd chop the wood tomorrow. No, he was already halfway to the forest, and if he didn't do it now, he knew he would probably let it go until his next sentry duty, which was twelve days later. Besides, it wouldn't be manly to give in to his weariness. Moving his legs to test for any cramps and feeling none, he climbed down the notched pole to the ground, where his wuolo dog waited, making happy little barks and wagging his tail. After kneeling for his suba prayer, Kunta got up, stretched, took a deep breath of the cool morning air, and set off towards the bolong at a lope.

33

The familiar perfumes of wild flowers filled Kunta's nostrils as he ran, wetting his legs, through grass glistening with dew in the first rays of sunshine. Hawks circled overhead looking for prey, and the ditches beside the fields were alive with the croaking of frogs. He veered away from a tree to avoid disturbing a flock of blackbirds that filled its branches like shiny black leaves. But he might have saved himself the trouble, for no sooner had he passed by than an angry, raucous cawing made him turn his head in time to see hundreds of crows bullying the blackbirds from their roost.

Breathing deeply as he ran, but still not out of breath, he began to smell the musky aroma of the mangroves as he neared the low, thick underbrush that extended far back from the banks of the bolong. At the first sight of him, a sudden snorting spread among the wild pigs, which in turn set off a barking and snarling among the baboons, whose big males quickly pushed their females and babies behind them. When he was younger, he would have stopped to imitate them, grunting and jumping up and down, since this never failed to annoy the baboons, who would always shake their fists and sometimes throw rocks. But he was no longer a boy, and he had learned to treat all of Allah's creatures as he himself wished to be treated: with respect.

Fluttering white waves of egrets, cranes, storks and pelicans rose from their sleeping places as he picked his way through the tangled mangrove down to the bolong. Kunta's wuolo dog raced ahead chasing watersnakes and big grown turtles down their mudslides into the water, where they left not even a ripple.

As he always did whenever he felt some need to come here after a night's lookout duty, Kunta stood awhile at the edge of the bolong, today watching a grey heron trailing its long, thin legs as it flew at about a spear's height above the pale green water, rippling the surface with each downbeat of its wings. Though the heron was looking for small game, he knew that this was the best spot along the bolong for kujalo, a big, powerful fish that Kunta loved to catch for Binta, who would stew it for him with onions, rice and bitter tomatoes. With his stomach already rumbling for breakfast, it made him hungry just to think of it.

A little farther downstream, Kunta turned away from the water's edge along a path he himself had made to an ancient mangrove tree that he thought must know him, after countless visits, as well as he knew it. Pulling himself up into the lowest branch, he climbed all the way to his favourite perch near the top. From here, in the clear morning, with the sun warm on his back, he could see all the way to the next bend in the bolong, still carpeted with sleeping waterfowl, and beyond them to the women's rice plots, dotted with their bamboo shelters for nursing babies. In which one of them, he wondered, had his mother put him when he was little? This place in the early morning would always fill Kunta with a greater sense of calm, and wonder, than anywhere else he knew of. Even more than in the village mosque, he felt here how totally were everyone and everything in the hands of Allah, and how everything he could see and hear and smell from the top of this tree had been here for longer than men's memories, and would be here long after he and his sons and his sons' sons had joined their ancestors.

Trotting away from the bolong towards the sun for a little while, Kunta finally reached the head-high grass surrounding the grove where he was going to pick out and chop a section of tree trunk just the right size for the body of his drum. If the green wood started drying and curing today, he figured it would be ready to hollow out and work on in a moon and a half, about the time he and Lamin would be returning from their trip to Mali. As he stepped into the grove, Kunta saw a sudden movement out of the corner of his eye. It was a hare, and the wuolo dog was after it in a flash as it raced for cover in the tall grass. He was obviously chasing it for sport rather than for food, since he was barking furiously; Kunta knew that a hunting wuolo never made noise if he was really hungry. The two of them were soon out of earshot, but Kunta knew that his dog would come back when he lost interest in the chase.

Kunta headed forward to the centre of the grove, where he would find more trees from which to choose a trunk of the size, smoothness, and roundness that he wanted. The soft, mossy earth felt good under his feet as he walked deeper into the dark grove, but the air here was damp and cold, he noticed, the sun not being high enough or hot enough yet to penetrate the thick foliage overhead. Leaning his weapons and axe against a warped tree, he wandered here and there, occasionally stooping, his eyes and fingers examining for just the right trunk, one just a little bit larger – to allow for drying shrinkage – than he wanted his drum to be.

He was bending over a likely prospect when he heard the sharp crack of a twig, followed quickly by the squawk of a parrot overhead. It was probably the dog returning, he thought in the back of his mind. But no grown dog ever cracked a twig, he flashed, whirling in the same instant. In a blur, rushing at him, he saw a white face, a club upraised; heard heavy footfalls behind him. *Toubob!* His foot lashed up and caught the man in the belly – it was soft and he heard a grunt – just as something hard and heavy grazed the back of Kunta's head and landed like a tree-trunk on his shoulder. Sagging under the pain, Kunta spun – turning his back on the man who lay doubled over on the ground at his feet – and pounded with his fists on the faces of two black men who were lunging at him with a big sack, and at another toubob swinging a short, thick club, which missed him this time as he sprang aside.

His brain screaming for any weapon, Kunta leaped into them – clawing, butting, kneeing, gouging – hardly feeling the club that was pounding against his back. As three of them went down with him, sinking to the ground under their combined weight, a knee smashed into Kunta's lower back, rocking him with such pain that he gasped. His open mouth meeting flesh, his teeth clamped, cut, tore. His numb fingers finding a face, he clawed deeply into an eye, hearing its owner howl as again the heavy club met Kunta's head.

Dazed, he heard a dog's snarling, a toubob screaming, then a sudden piteous yelp. Scrambling to his feet, wildly twisting, dodging, ducking to escape more clubbing, with blood streaming from his split head, he saw one black cupping his eye, one of the toubob holding a bloody arm, standing over the body of the dog, and the remaining pair circling him with raised clubs. Screaming his rage, Kunta went for the second toubob, his fists meeting and breaking the force of the descending club. Almost choking with the awful toubob stink, he tried desperately to wrench away the club. Why had he not *heard* them, *sensed* them, *smelled* them?

Just then the black's club smashed into Kunta once again, staggering him to his knees, and the toubob sprang loose. His head ready to explode, his body reeling, raging at his own weakness, Kunta reared up and roared, flailing blindly at the air, everything blurred with tears and blood and sweat. He was fighting for more than his life now. Omoro! Binta! Lamin! Suwadu! Madi! The toubob's heavy club crashed against his temple. And all went black.

34

Kunta wondered if he had gone mad. Naked, chained, shackled, he awoke on his back between two other men in a pitch darkness full of steamy heat and sickening stink and a nightmarish bedlam of shrieking, weeping, praying and vomiting. He could feel and smell his own vomit on his chest and belly. His whole body was one spasm of pain from the beatings he had received in the four days since his capture. But the place where the hot iron had been put between his shoulders hurt the worst.

A rat's thick, furry body brushed his cheek, its whiskered nose sniffing at his mouth. Quivering with revulsion, Kunta snapped his teeth together desperately, and the rat ran away. In rage, Kunta snatched and kicked against the shackles that bound his wrists and ankles. Instantly, angry exclamations and jerking came back from whomever he was shackled to. The shock and pain adding to his fury, Kunta lunged upwards, his head bumping hard against wood – right on the spot where he had been clubbed by the toubob back in the woods. Gasping and snarling, he and the unseen man next to him battered their iron cuffs at each other until both slumped back in exhaustion. Kunta felt himself starting to vomit again, and he tried to force it back, but couldn't. His already emptied belly squeezed up a thin, sour fluid that drained from the side of his mouth as he lay wishing that he might die.

He told himself that he mustn't lose control again if he wanted to save his strength and his sanity. After a while, when he felt he could move again, he very slowly and carefully explored his shackled right wrist and ankle with his left hand. They were bleeding. He pulled lightly on the chain; it seemed to be connected to the left ankle and wrist of the man he had fought with. On Kunta's left, chained to him by the ankles, lay some other man, someone who kept up a steady moaning, and they were all so close that their shoulders, arms and legs touched if any of them moved even a little.

Remembering the wood he had bumped into with his head, Kunta drew himself upwards again, just enough for it to bump gently; there wasn't enough space even to sit up. And behind his head was a wooden wall. I'm trapped like a leopard in a snare, he thought. Then he remembered sitting in the darkness of the manhood-training hut after being taken blindfolded to the jujuo so many rains before, and a sob welled up in his throat; but he fought it back. Kunta made himself think about the cries and groans he was hearing all around him. There must be many men here in the blackness, some close, some farther away, some beside him, others in front of him, but all in one room, if that's what this was. Straining his ears, he could hear still more cries, but they were muffled and came from below, beneath the splintery planking he lay on.

Listening more intently, he began to recognize the different tongues of those around him. Over and over, in Arabic, a Fulani was shouting, 'Allah in heaven, help me!' And a man of the Serere tribe was hoarsely wailing what must have been the names of his family. But mostly Kunta heard Mandinkas, the loudest of them babbling wildly in the sira kango secret talk of men, vowing terrible deaths to all toubob. The cries of the others were so slurred with weeping that Kunta could identify neither their words nor their languages, although he knew that some of the strange talk he heard must come from beyond The Gambia.

As Kunta lay listening, he slowly began to realize that he was trying to push from his mind the impulse to relieve the demands of his bowels, which he had been forcing back for days. But he could hold it in no longer, and finally the faeces curled out between his buttocks. Revolted at himself, smelling his own addition to the stench, Kunta began sobbing, and again his belly spasmed, producing this time only a little spittle; but he kept gagging. What sins was he being punished for in such a manner as this? He pleaded to Allah for an answer. It was sin enough that he hadn't prayed once since the morning he went for the wood to make his drum. Though he couldn't get onto his knees, and he knew not even which way was east, he closed his eyes where he lay and prayed, beseeching Allah's forgiveness.

Afterwards, Kunta lay for a long time bathing dully in his pains, and slowly became aware that one of them, in his knotted stomach, was nothing more than hunger. It occurred to him that he hadn't eaten anything since the night before his capture. He was trying to remember if he had *slept* in all that time, when suddenly he saw himself walking along a trail in the forest; behind him walked two blacks, ahead of him a pair of toubob with their strange clothes and their long hair in strange colours. Kunta jerked his eyes open and shook his head; he was soaked in sweat and his heart was pounding. He had been asleep without knowing. It had been a nightmare; or was the nightmare this stinking blackness? No, it was as real as the scene in the forest in his dream had been. Against his will, it all came back to him.

After fighting the black slatees and the toubob so desperately in the grove of trees, he remembered awakening – into a wave of blinding pain – and finding himself gagged, blindfolded and bound with his wrists behind him and his ankles hobbled with knotted rope. Thrashing to break free, he was jabbed savagely with sharp sticks until blood ran down his legs. Yanked onto his feet and prodded with the sticks to begin moving, he stumbled ahead of them as fast as his hobbles would permit.

Somewhere along the banks of the bolong –Kunta could tell by the sounds, and the feel of the soft ground beneath his feet – he was shoved down into a canoe. Still blindfolded, he heard the slatees grunting, rowing swiftly, with the toubob hitting him whenever he struggled. Landing, again they walked, until finally that night they reached a place where they threw Kunta on the ground, tied him with his back to a bamboo fence and, without warning, pulled off his blindfold. It was dark, but he could see the pale face of the toubob standing over him, and the silhouettes of others like him on the ground nearby. The toubob held out some meat for him to bite off a piece. He turned his head aside and clamped his jaws. Hissing with rage, the toubob grabbed him by the throat and tried to force his mouth open. When Kunta kept it shut tight, the toubob drew back his fist and punched him hard in the face.

Kunta was let alone the rest of the night. At dawn, he began to make out – tied to other bamboo trunks – the figures of the other captured people, eleven of them – six men, three girls and two children – all guarded closely by armed slatees and toubob. The girls were naked; Kunta could only avert his eyes; he never had seen a woman naked before. The men, also naked, sat with murderous hatred etched in their faces, grimly silent and crusted with blood from whip cuts. But the girls were crying out, one about dead loved ones in a burned village; another, bitterly weeping, rocked back and forth cooing endearments to an imaginary infant in her cradled arms, and the third shrieked at intervals that she was going to Allah.

In wild fury, Kunta lunged back and forth trying to break his bonds. A heavy blow with a club again knocked him senseless. When he came to, he found that he too was naked, that all of their heads had been shaved and their bodies smeared with red palm oil. At around noonday, two new toubob entered the grove. The slatees, now all grins, quickly untied the captives from the bamboo trunks, shouting to them to stand in a line. Kunta's muscles were knotted with rage and fear. One of the new toubob was short and stout and his hair was white. The other towered over him, tall and huge and scowling, with deep knife scars across his face, but it was the white-haired one before whom the slatees and the other toubob grinned and all but bowed.

Looking at them all, the white-haired one gestured for Kunta to step forward, and lurching backwards in terror, Kunta screamed as a whip seared across his back. A slatee from behind grappled him downwards to his knees, jerking his head backwards. The white-haired toubob calmly spread Kunta's trembling lips and studied his teeth. Kunta attempted to spring up, but after another blow of the whip, he stood as ordered, his body quivering as the toubob's fingers explored his eyes, his chest, his belly. When the fingers grasped his foto, he lunged aside with a choked cry. Two slatees and more lashings were needed to force Kunta to bend over almost double, and in horror he felt his buttocks being spread wide apart. Then the white-haired toubob roughly shoved Kunta aside and, one by one, he similarly inspected the others, even the private parts of the wailing girls. Then whips and shouted commands sent the captives all dashing around within the enclosure, and next springing up and down on their haunches.

After observing them, the white-haired toubob and the huge one with the knife-scarred face stepped a little distance away and spoke briefly in low tones. Stepping back, the white-haired one, beckoning another toubob, jabbed his finger at four men, one of them Kunta, and two of the girls. The toubob looked shocked, pointing at the others in a beseeching manner. But the white-haired one shook his head firmly. Kunta sat straining against his bonds, his head threatening to burst with rage, as the toubob argued heatedly. After a while, the white-haired one disgustedly wrote something on a piece of paper that the other toubob angrily accepted.

Kunta struggled and howled with fury as the slatees grabbed him again, wrestling him to a seated position with his back arched. Eyes wide with terror, he watched as a toubob withdrew from the fire a long, thin iron that the white-haired one had brought with him. Kunta was already thrashing and screaming as the iron exploded pain between his shoulders. The bamboo grove echoed with the screams of the others, one by one. Then red palm oil was rubbed over the peculiar *LL* shape Kunta saw on their backs.

Within the hour, they were hobbling in a line of clanking chains, with the slatees' ready whips flailing down on anyone who baulked or stumbled. Kunta's back and shoulders were ribboned with bleeding cuts when late that night they reached two canoes hidden under thick, overhanging mangroves at the river's banks. Split into two groups, they were rowed through darkness by the slatees, with the toubob lashing out at any sign of struggle.

When Kunta saw a vast dark shape looming up ahead in the night, he sensed that this was his last chance. Springing and lunging amid shouts and screams around him, he almost upset the canoe in his struggle to leap overboard; but he was bound to the others and couldn't make it over the side. He almost didn't feel the blows of the whips and clubs against his ribs, his back, his face, his belly, his head – as the canoe bumped against the side of the great dark thing. Through the pain, he could feel the warm blood pouring down his face, and he heard above him the exclamations of many toubob. Then ropes were being looped around him, and he was helpless to resist. After being half pushed and half pulled up some strange rope ladder, he had enough strength left to twist his body wildly in another break for freedom; again he was lashed with whips, and hands were grabbing him amid an overwhelming toubob smell and the sound of women shrieking and loud toubob cursing.

Through swollen lids, Kunta saw a thicket of legs and feet all around him, and managing an upward glance while trying to shield his bleeding face with his forearm, he saw the short toubob with the white hair standing calmly making marks in a small book with a stubby pencil. Then he felt himself being snatched upright and shoved roughly across a flat space. He caught a glimpse of tall poles with thick wrappings of coarse white cloth. Then he was being guided, stumbling weakly down some kind of narrow steps, into a place of pitch blackness; at the same instant, his nose was assaulted by an unbelievable stink, and his ears by cries of anguish.

Kunta began vomiting as the toubob – holding dim yellowish flames that burned within metal frames carried by a ring – shackled his wrists and ankles, then shoved him backwards, close between two other moaning men. Even in his terror, he sensed that lights bobbing in other directions meant that the toubob were taking those who had come with him to be shackled elsewhere. Then he felt his thoughts slipping; he thought he must be dreaming. And then, mercifully, he was.

35

Only the rasping sound of the deck hatch being opened told Kunta if it was day or night. Hearing the latch click, he would jerk his head up – the only free movement that his chains and shackles would allow – and four shadowy toubob figures would descend, two of them with bobbing lights and whips guarding the other pair as they all moved along the narrow aisleways pushing a tub of food. They would thrust tin pans of the stuff up onto the filth between each two shacklemates. So far, each time the food had come, Kunta had clamped his jaws shut, preferring to starve to death, until the aching of his empty stomach had begun to make his hunger almost as terrible as the pains from his beatings. When those on Kunta's level had been fed, the lights showed the toubob descending farther below with the rest of the food.

Less often than the feeding times, and usually when it was night outside, the toubob would bring down into the hold some new captives, screaming and whimpering in terror as they were shoved and lashed along to wherever they were to be chained into empty spaces along the rows of hard plank shelves.

One day, shortly after a feeding time, Kunta's ears picked up a strange, muted sound that seemed to vibrate through the ceiling over his head. Some of the other men heard it too, and their moaning ended abruptly. Kunta lay listening intently; it sounded as if many feet were dashing about overhead. Then – much nearer to them in the darkness – came a new sound, as of some very heavy object being creaked very slowly upwards.

Kunta's naked back felt an odd vibration from the hard, rough planking he lay on. He felt a tightening, a swelling within his chest, and he lay frozenly. About him he heard thudding sounds that he knew were men lunging upwards, straining against their chains. It felt as if all of his blood had rushed into his pounding head. And then terror went clawing into his vitals as he sensed in some way that this place was moving, taking them away. Men started shouting all around him, screaming to Allah and His spirits, banging their heads against the planking, thrashing wildly against their rattling shackles. 'Allah, I will never pray to you less than five times daily!' Kunta shrieked into the bedlam, 'Hear me! Help me!'

The anguished cries, weeping, and prayers continued, subsiding only as one after another exhausted man went limp and lay gasping for breath in the stinking blackness. Kunta *knew* that he would never see Africa again. He could feel clearly now, through his body against the planks, a slow, rocking motion, sometimes enough that his shoulders or arms or hips would press against the brief warmth of one of the men he was chained between. He had shouted so hard that he had no voice left, so his mind screamed it instead: 'Kill toubob – and their traitor black helpers!'

He was sobbing quietly when the hatch opened and the four toubob came bumping down with their tub of food. Again he clamped his jaws against his spasms of hunger, but then he thought of something the kintango had once said – that warriors and hunters must eat well to have greater strength than other men. Starving himself meant that weakness would prevent him from killing toubob. So this time, when the pan was thrust onto the boards between him and the man next to him, Kunta's fingers also clawed into the thick mush. It tasted like ground maize boiled with palm oil. Each gulping swallow pained his throat in the spot where he had been choked for not eating before, but he swallowed until the pan was empty. He could feel the food like a lump in his belly, and soon it was rising up his throat. He couldn't stop it, and a moment later the gruel was back on the planking. He could hear, over the sound of his own retching, that of others doing the same thing.

As the lights approached the end of the long shelf of planks on which Kunta lay, suddenly he heard chains rattling, a head bumping, and then a man screaming hysterically in a curious mixture of Mandinka and what sounded like some toubob words. An uproarious burst of laughter came from the toubob with the feeding tub, then their whips lashing down, until the man's cries lapsed, into babbling and whimpering. Could it be? Had he heard an African speaking toubob? Was there slatee down there among them? Kunta had heard that toubob would often betray their black traitor helpers and throw them into chains.

After the toubob had gone on down to the level below, scarcely a sound was heard on Kunta's level until they reappeared with their emptied tub and climbed back up outside, closing the hatch behind them. At that instant, an angry buzzing began in different tongues, like bees swarming. Then, down the shelf from where Kunta lay, there was a heavy chain-rattling blow, a howl of pain and bitter cursing in the same hysterical Mandinka. Kunta heard the man shriek, 'You think I am toubob?' There were more violent, rapid blows and desperate screams. Then the blows stopped, and in the blackness of the hold came a high squealing – and then an awful gurgling sound, as of a man whose breath was being choked off. Another rattling of chains, a tattoo of bare heels kicking at the planks, then quiet.

Kunta's head was throbbing, and his heart was pounding, as voices around him began screaming, 'Slatee! Slatees die!' Then Kunta was screaming along with them and joining in a wild rattling of chains – when suddenly with a rasping sound the hatch was opened, admitting its shaft of daylight and a group of toubob with lights and whips. They had obviously heard the commotion below them, and though now almost total silence had fallen in the hold, the toubob rushed among the aisles shouting and lashing left and right with their whips. When they left without finding the dead man, the hold remained silent for a long moment. Then, very quietly, Kunta heard a mirthless laugh from the end of the shelf next to where the traitor lay dead.

The next feeding was a tense one. As if the toubob sensed something amiss, their whips fell even more often than usual. Kunta jerked and cried out as a bolt of pain cut across his legs. He had learned that when anyone didn't cry out from a blow, he would get a severe beating until he did. Then he clawed and gulped down the tasteless mush as his eyes followed the lights moving on down along the shelf.

Every man in the hold was listening when one of the toubob exclaimed something to the others. A jostling of lights could be seen, then more exclamations and cursings, and then one of the toubob rushed down the aisle and up through the hatch, and he soon returned with two more. Kunta could hear the iron cuffs and chains being unlocked. Two of the toubob then half carried, half dragged the body of the dead man along the aisle and up the hatch, while the others continued bumping their food tub along the aisles.

The food team was on the level below when four more toubob climbed down through the hatch and went directly to where the slatee had been chained. By twisting his head, Kunta could see the lights raised high. With violent cursing, two of the toubob sent their whips whistling down against flesh. Whoever was being beaten refused at first to scream; though just listening to the force of the blows was almost paralysing to Kunta, he could hear the beaten man flailing against his chains in the agony of his torture – and of his grim determination not to cry out.

Then the toubob were almost shrieking their curses, and the lights could be seen changing hands as one man spelled the other with the lash. Finally the beaten man began screaming – first a Foulah curse, then things that could not be understood, though they too were in the Foulah tongue. Kunta's mind flashed a thought of the quiet, gentle Foulah tribe who tended Mandinka cattle – as the lashing sounds continued until the beaten man barely whimpered. Then the four toubob left, cursing, gasping and gagging in the stink.

The moans of the Foulah shivered through the black hold. Then, after a while, a clear voice called out in Mandinka, 'Share his pain! We must be in this place as one village!' The voice belonged to an elder. He was right. The Foulah's pains had been as Kunta's own. He felt himself about to burst with rage. He also felt, in some nameless way, a terror greater than he had ever known before, and it seemed to spread from the marrow of his bones. Part of him wanted to die, to escape all of this; but no, he must live to avenge it. He forced himself to lie absolutely still. It took a long while, but finally he felt his strain and confusion, even his body's pains, begin to ebb – except for the place between his shoulders where he had been burned with the hot iron. He found that his mind could focus better now on the only choice that seemed to lie before him and the others: Either they would all die in this nightmare place, or somehow the toubob would have to be overcome and killed.

36

The stinging bites, then the itching of the body lice, steadily grew worse. In the filth, the lice as well as the fleas had multiplied by the thousands until they swarmed all over the hold. They were worst wherever the body crevices held any hair. Kunta's armpits, and around his foto, felt as if they were on fire, and his free hand scratched steadily wherever his shackled hand couldn't reach.

He kept having thoughts of springing up and running away; then, a moment later, his eyes would fill with tears of frustration, anger would rise in him, and he would fight it all back down until he felt again some kind of calm. The worst thing was that he couldn't *move* anywhere; he felt he wanted to *bite* through his chains. He decided that he must keep himself focused upon something, anything to occupy his mind or his hands, or else he would go mad – as some men in the hold seemed to have done already, judging from the things they cried out.

By lying very still and listening to the breathing sounds of the men on either side of him, Kunta had long since learned to tell when either of them was asleep or awake. He concentrated now upon hearing farther away from him. With more and more practice at listening intently to repeated sounds, he discovered that his ears after a while could discern their location almost exactly; it was a peculiar sensation, almost as if his ears were serving for eyes. Now and then, among the groans and curses that filled the darkness, he heard the thump of a man's head against the planks he lay on. And there was another odd and monotonous noise. It would stop at intervals, then resume after a while; it sounded as if two pieces of metal were being rubbed hard together, and after hearing more of it Kunta figured that someone was trying to wear the links of his chains apart. Kunta often heard, too, brief exclamations and janglings of chains as two men furiously fought, jerking their shackles against each other's ankles and wrists.

Kunta had lost track of time. The urine, vomit, and faeces that reeked everywhere around him had spread into a slick paste covering the hard planking of the long shelves on which they lay. Just when he had begun to think he couldn't stand it any more, eight toubob came down the hatchway, cursing loudly. Instead of the routine food container, they carried what seemed to be some kind of long-handled hoes and four large tubs. And Kunta noticed with astonishment that they were not wearing any clothes at all.

The naked toubob almost immediately began vomiting worse than any of the others who had come before. In the glow of their lights, they all but sprang along the aisles in teams of two, swiftly thrusting their hoes up onto the shelves and scraping some of the mess into their tubs. As each tub was filled, the toubob would drag it back along the aisle and go bumping it up the steps through the opened hatchway to empty it outside, and then they would return. The toubob were gagging horribly by now, their faces contorted grotesquely, and their hairy, colourless bodies covered with blobs of the mess they were scraping off the shelves. But when they finished their job and were gone, there was no difference in the hot, awful, choking stench of the hold.

The next time that more than the usual four toubob descended with their food tubs, Kunta guessed that there must be as many as twenty of them clumping down the hatch steps. He lay frozen. Turning his head this way and that, he could see small groups of toubob posting themselves around the hold, some carrying whips and guns, guarding others with lights upraised at the ends of each shelf of chained men. A knot of fear grew in Kunta's belly as he began hearing strange clicking sounds, then heavy rattlings. Then his shackled right ankle began jerking; with flashing terror he realized that the toubob were releasing him. Why? What terrible thing was going to happen now? He lay still, his right ankle no longer feeling the familiar weight of the chain, hearing all around the hold more clicking sounds and the rattling of chains being pulled. Then the toubob started shouting and lashing with their whips. Kunta knew that it meant for them to get down off their shelves. His cry of alarm joined a sudden bedlam of shrieks in different tongues as the men reared their bodies upwards, heads thudding against the ceiling timbers.

The whips lashed down amid screams of pain as one after another pair of men went thumping down into the aisleways. Kunta and his Wolof shacklemate hugged each other on the shelf as the searing blows jerked them convulsively back and forth. Then hands clamped roughly around their ankles and hauled them across the shelf's mushy filth and into the tangle of other men in the aisleway, all of them howling under the toubob whips. Wrenching and twisting in vain to escape the pain, he glimpsed shapes moving against the light of the opened hatchway. The toubob were snatching men onto their feet – one pair after another – then beating and shoving them along, stumbling in the darkness, towards the hatchway's steps. Kunta's legs felt separated from the rest of his body as he went lurching alongside the Wolof, shackled by their wrists, naked, crusted with filth, begging not to be eaten.

The first open daylight in nearly fifteen days hit Kunta with the force of a hammer between his eyes. He reeled under the bursting pain, flinging his free hand up to cover his eyes. His bare feet told him that whatever they were walking on was moving slightly from side to side. Fumbling blindly ahead, with even his cupped hand and clamped eyelids admitting some tormenting light, trying futilely to breathe through nostrils nearly plugged with snot, he gaped open his cracked lips and took a deep breath of sea air – the first of his life. His lungs convulsed from its rich cleanness, and he crumpled to the deck, vomiting alongside his shacklemate. All about him he heard more vomiting, chains clanking, lashes meeting flesh, and shrieks of pain amid toubob shouts and curses and strange flapping sounds overhead.

When another whip ripped across his back, Kunta shrank to one side, hearing his Wolof partner gasp as the lash hit him. It kept tearing at them both until somehow they stumbled to their feet. He slit his eyes to see if he could escape some of the blows; but new pains stabbed into his head as their tormentor shoved them towards where Kunta could see the blurred forms of other toubob passing a length of chain through the shackles around each man's ankles. There had been more of them down there in the darkness than he had ever realized – and far more toubob than had ever gone below. In the bright sunlight, they looked even paler and more horrible, their faces pitted with the holes of disease, their peculiar long hair in colours of yellow or black or red, some of them even with hair around their mouths and under their chins. Some were bony, others fat, some had ugly scars from knives, or a hand, eye, or limb missing, and the backs of many were criss-crossed with deep scars. It flashed through Kunta's mind how his teeth had been counted and inspected, for several of these toubob he saw had but few teeth.

Many of them were spaced along the rails, holding whips, long knives, or some kind of heavy metal stick with a hole in the end, and Kunta could see beyond them an amazing sight – an unbelievable endlessness of rolling blue water. He jerked his head upward towards the slapping sounds above and saw that they came from giant white cloths billowing among huge poles and many ropes. The cloths seemed to be filled up with the wind. Turning about, Kunta saw that a high barricade of bamboo taller than any man extended completely across the width of the huge canoe. Showing through the barricade's centre was the gaping black mouth of a huge, terrible-looking metal thing with a long, thick, hollow shaft, and the tips of more metal sticks like the ones the toubob had been holding at the rail. Both the huge thing and the sticks were pointed towards where he and the other naked men were grouped.

As their ankle shackles were being linked onto the new chain, Kunta got the chance to take a good look at his Wolof shacklemate for the first time. Like himself, the man was crusted from head to foot with filth. He seemed about the rains of Kunta's father Omoro, and the Wolof had that tribe's classic facial features, and he was very black of colour. The Wolof's back was bleeding from where the whippings had cut into him, and pus was oozing from where an LL mark had been burned into his back. Kunta realized, as their eyes searched each other, that the Wolof was staring at him with the same astonishment. Amid the commotion, they had time to stare also at the other naked men, most of them gibbering in their terror. From the different facial features, tribal tattoos, and scarification marks, Kunta could tell that some were Foulah, Jola, Serere and Wolof, like his partner, but most were Mandinkas – and there were some he could not be sure of. With excitement, Kunta saw the one he was sure must have killed the slatee. He was indeed a Foulah; blood from the beating he had received was crusted all over him.

They were all soon being shoved and whipped towards where another chain of ten men was being doused with buckets of seawater drawn up from over the side. Then other toubob with long-handled brushes were scrubbing the screaming men. Kunta screamed, too, as the drenching salt water hit him, stinging like fire in his own bleeding whip cuts and the burned place on his back. He cried even louder as the stiff brush bristles not only loosened and scraped off some of his body's crusted filth but also tore open his scabbed lash cuts. He saw the water frothing and pinkish at their feet. Then they were herded back towards the centre of the deck, where they flopped down in a huddle. Kunta gawked upwards to see toubob springing about on the poles like monkeys, pulling at the many ropes among the great white cloths. Even in Kunta's shock, the heat of the sun felt warm and good, and he felt an incredible sense of relief that his skin was freed of some of its filth.

About twenty women, most of them teen-aged, and four children, came running naked and without chains from behind the barricade, ahead of two grinning toubob with whips. Kunta instantly recognized the girls who had been brought on board with him – as with flooding rage he watched all of the toubob leering at their nakedness, some of them even rubbing their fotos. By sheer force of will, he fought the urge to go lunging after the nearest toubob despite their weapons. Hands clutched into fists, he sucked hard for air to keep breathing, wrenching his eyes away from the terrified women.

Then a toubob near the rail began pulling out and pushing in between his hands some peculiar folding thing that made a wheezing sound. Another joined in, beating on a drum from Africa, as other toubob now moved themselves into a ragged line with the naked men, women and children staring at them. The toubob in the line had a length of rope, and each of them looped one ankle within it, as if that rope was a length of chain such as linked the naked men. Smiling now, they began jumping up and down together in short hops, keeping in time with the drumbeats and the wheezing thing. Then they and the other armed toubob gestured for the men in chains to jump in the same manner. But when the chained men continued to stand as if petrified, the toubobs' grins became scowls, and they began laying about with whips.

'Jump!' shouted the oldest woman suddenly, in Mandinka. She was of about the rains of Kunta's mother Binta. Bounding out, she began jumping herself. 'Jump!' she cried shrilly again, glaring at the girls and children, and they jumped as she did. 'Jump to kill toubob!' she shrieked, her quick eyes flashing at the naked men, her arms and hands darting in the movements of the warrior's dance. And then, as her meaning sank home, one after another shackled pair of men began a weak, stumbling hopping up and down, their chains clanking against the deck. With his head down, Kunta saw the welter of hopping feet and legs, feeling his own legs rubbery under him as his breath came in gasps. Then the singing of the woman was joined by the girls. It was a happy sound, but the words they sang told how these horrible toubob had taken every woman into the dark corners of the canoe each night and used them like dogs. 'Toubob fa!' (Kill toubob) they shrieked with smiles and laughter. The naked, jumping men joined in: 'Toubob fa!' Even the toubob were grinning now, some of them clapping their hands with pleasure.

But Kunta's knees began to buckle beneath him and his throat went tight when he saw, approaching him, the short, stocky toubob with white hair, and with him the huge, scowling one with the knife-scarred face who also had been at that place where Kinta was examined and beaten and choked and burned before he was brought here. In an instant, as the other naked people saw these two, a sudden silence fell, and the only sound to be heard was that of great, slap-

157

ping cloths overhead, for even the rest of the toubob had stiffened at their presence.

Barking out something hoarsely, the huge one cleared the other toubob away from the chained people. From his belt there dangled a large ring of the slender, shiny things that Kunta had glimpsed others using as they had opened the chains. And then the white-haired one went moving among the naked people, peering closely at their bodies. Wherever he saw whip cuts badly festered, or pus draining from rat bites or burned places, he smeared on some grease from a can that the huge one handed to him. Or the huge one himself would sprinkle a yellowish powder from a container on wrists and ankles that became a sickly, moist, greyish colour beneath the iron cuffs. As the two toubob moved nearer to him, Kunta shrank in fear and fury, but then the white-haired one was smearing grease on his festering places and the huge one was sprinkling his ankles and wrists with the yellowish powder, neither of them seeming even to recognize who Kunta was.

Then, suddenly, amid rising shouts among the toubob, one of the girls who had been brought with Kunta was springing wildly between frantic guards. As several of them went clutching and diving for her, she hurled herself screaming over the rail and went plunging downwards. In the great shouting commotion, the white-haired toubob and the huge one snatched up whips and with bitter curses lashed the backs of those who had gone sprawling after, letting her slip from their grasp.

Then the toubob up among the cloths were yelling and pointing towards the water. Turning in that direction, the naked people saw the girl bobbing in the waves – and not far away, a pair of dark fins coursing swiftly towards her. Then came another scream – a blood-chilling one – then a frothing and thrashing, and she was dragged from sight, leaving behind only a redness in the water where she had been. For the first time, no whips fell as the chained people, sick with horror, were herded back into the dark hold and rechained into their places. Kunta's head was reeling. After the fresh air of the ocean, the stench smelled even worse than before, and after the daylight, the hold seemed even darker. When soon a new disturbance arose, seeming somewhat distant, his practised ears told him that the toubob were driving up onto the deck the terrified men from the level below.

After a while, he heard near his right ear a low mutter. *'Jula?'* Kunta's heart leaped. He knew very little of the Wolof tongue, but he did know that Wolof and some others used the word *jula* to mean travellers and traders who were usually Mandinkas. And twisting his head a bit closer to the Wolof's ear, Kunta whispered, '*Jula.* Mandinka.' For moments, as he lay tensely, the Wolof made no return sound. It went flashing through Kunta's head that if he could only speak many languages, as his father's brothers did – but he was ashamed to have brought them to this place, even in his thoughts.

'Wolof. Jebou Manga,' the other man whispered finally, and Kunta knew that was his name.

'Kunta Kinte,' he whispered back.

Exchanging a whisper now and then in their desperation to communicate, they picked at each other's minds to learn a new word here, another there, in their respective tongues. It was much as they had learned their early words as first-kafo children. During one of the intervals of silence between them, Kunta remembered how when he had been a lookout against the baboons in the groundnut fields at night, the distant fire of a Fulani herdsman had given him a sense of comfort and he had wished that there had been some way he could exchange words with this man he had never seen. It was as if that wish were being realized now, except that it was with a Wolof, unseen for the weeks they had been lying there shackled to each other.

Every Wolof expression Kunta had ever heard he now dragged from his memory. He knew that the Wolof was doing the same with Mandinka words, of which he knew more than Kunta knew of Wolof words. In another time of silence between them, Kunta sensed that the man who lay on his other side, who never had made any sound other than moaning in pain, was listening closely to them. Kunta realized from the low murmuring that spread gradually throughout the hold that once the men had actually been able to see each other up in the daylight, he and his own shacklemate weren't the only ones trying now to communicate with one another. The murmuring kept spreading. The hold would fall silent now only when the toubob came with the food tub, or with the brushes to clean the filth from the shelves. And there was a new quality to the quietness that would fall at these times; for the first time since they had been captured and thrown in chains, it was as if there was among the men a sense of being together.

37

The next time the men were taken up onto the deck, Kunta made a point of looking at the man behind him in line, the one who lay beside him to the left when they were below. He was a Serere tribesman, much older than Kunta, and his body front and back was creased with whip cuts, some of them so deep and festering that Kunta felt badly for having wished sometimes that he might strike the man in the darkness for moaning so steadily in his pain. Staring back at Kunta, the Serere's dark eyes were full of fury and defiance. A whip lashed out even as they stood looking at each other – this time at Kunta, spurring him to move ahead. The force of the blow drove him nearly to his knees and triggered an explosion of rage. With his throat ripping out almost an animal's cry, Kunta lunged off balance towards the toubob, only to fall, sprawling, dragging his shacklemate down with him, as the toubob nimbly sprang clear of them both. Men milled around them as the toubob, his eyes narrowing with hatred, brought the whip down over and over on both Kunta and the Wolof, like a slashing knife. Trying to roll away, Kunta was kicked heavily in his ribs. But somehow he and the gasping Wolof managed to stagger back up among the other men from their shelf who were shambling towards their dousing with buckets of seawater.

A moment later, the stinging saltiness of it was burning in Kunta's wounds, and his screams joined those of others over the sound of the drum and the wheezing thing that had again begun marking time for the chained men to jump and dance for the toubob. Kunta and the Wolof were so weak from their new beating that twice they stumbled, but whip blows and kicks sent them hopping clumsily up and down in their chains. So great was his fury that Kunta was barely aware of the women singing 'Toubob fa!' And when he had finally been chained back down in his place in the dark hold, his heart throbbed with a lust to murder toubob.

Every few days the eight naked toubob would again come into the stinking darkness and scrape their tubs full of the excrement that had accumulated on the shelves where the chained men lay. Kunta would lie still with his eyes staring balefully in hatred, following the bobbing orange lights, listening to the toubob cursing and sometimes slipping and falling into the slickness underfoot – so plentiful now, because of the increasing looseness of the men's bowels, that the filth had begun to drop off the edges of the shelves down into the aisleway.

The last time they were on deck, Kunta had noticed a man limping on a badly infected leg. The chief toubob had applied grease to it, but it hadn't helped, and the man had begun to scream horribly in the darkness of the hold. When they next went on deck, he had to be helped up, and Kunta saw that the leg, which had been greyish before, had begun to rot and stink even in the fresh air. This time the man was kept up on deck when the rest were taken back below. A few days later, the women told the other prisoners in their singing that the man's leg had been cut off and that one of the women had been brought to tend him, but that the man had died that night and been thrown over the side. Starting then, when the toubob came to clean the shelves, they also dropped red-hot pieces of metal into pails of strong vinegar. The clouds of acrid steam left the hold smelling better, but soon it would again be overwhelmed by the choking stink. It was a smell that Kunta felt would never leave his lungs and skin.

The steady murmuring that went on in the hold whenever the toubob were gone kept growing in volume and intensity as the men began to communicate better and better with one another. Words not understood were whispered from mouth to ear along the shelves until someone who knew more than one tongue would send back their meanings. In the process, all of the men along each shelf learned new words in tongues they had not spoken before. Sometimes men jerked upwards, bumping their heads, in the double excitement of communicating with each other and the fact that it was being done without the toubob's knowledge. Muttering among themselves for hours, the men developed a deepening sense of intrigue and of brotherhood. Though they were of different villages and tribes, the feeling grew that they were not from different peoples or places.

When the toubob next came to drive them up onto the deck, the chained men marched as if they were on parade. And when they descended again, several of those men who spoke several tongues managed to change their position in line in order to get chained at the ends of shelves, thus permitting more rapid relaying of translations. The toubob never seemed to notice, for they were either unable or unconcerned to distinguish one chained man from another.

Questions, and responses to them, had begun spreading in the hold. 'Where are we being taken?' That brought a babble of bitterness. 'Who ever returned to tell us?' 'Because they were eaten!' The question, 'How long have we been here?' brought a rash of

161

guesses of up to a moon, until the question was translated to a man who had been able to keep a count of daylights through a small air vent near where he was chained; he said that he counted eighteen days since the great canoe had sailed.

Because of intrusions by toubob with their food tub or their scrapers, an entire day might be used up in relaying of responses to a single statement or question. Anxious inquiries were passed along for men who might know each other. 'Is anyone here from Barrakinda village?' someone asked one day, and after a time there came winging back from mouth to ear the joyous response, 'I, Jabon Sallah, am here!' One day, Kunta nearly burst with excitement when the Wolof hastily whispered, 'Is anyone here from Juffure village?' 'Yes, Kunta Kinte!' he sent back breathlessly. He lay almost afraid to breathe for the hour that it took an answer to return: 'Yes, that was the name. I heard the drums of his grieving village.' Kunta dissolved into sobs, his mind streaming with pictures of his family around a flapping white cockerel that died on its back as the village wadanela went to spread that sad news among all of the people who would then come to Omoro, Binta, Lamin, Suwadu and the baby Madi, all of them squatting about and weeping as the village drums beat out the words to inform whoever might hear them far away that a son of the village named Kunta Kinta now was considered gone forever.

Days of talking sought answers to the question: 'How could the toubob of this canoe be attacked and killed?' Did anyone have or know of anything that might be used as weapons? None did. Up on the deck, had anyone noticed any carelessness or weaknesses on the part of the toubob that could be useful to a surprise attack? Again, none had. The most useful information of any sort had come from the women's singing as the men danced in their chains: that about thirty toubob were riding with them on this big canoe. There had seemed to be many more, but the women were in a better position to count them. The women said also that there had been more toubob at the beginning of the voyage, but five had died. They had been sewn inside white cloths and thrown overboard while the white-haired chief toubob read from some kind of book. The women also sang that the toubob often fought and beat each other viciously, usually as a result of arguments over which ones would next use the women.

Thanks to their singing, not much happened up on the deck that wasn't quickly told to the men dancing in their chains, who then lay discussing it down in the hold. Then came the exciting new development that contact had been established with the men who were chained on the level yet below. Silence would fall in the hold where Kunta lay, and a question would be called out from near the hatchway: 'How many are down here?' And after a time the answer would circulate on Kunta's level: 'We believe about sixty of us.'

The relaying of any information from whatever source seemed about the only function that would justify their staying alive. When there was no news, the men would talk of their families, their villages, their professions, their farms, their hunts. And more and more frequently there arose disagreements about how to kill the toubob, and when it should be tried. Some of the men felt that, whatever the consequences, the toubob should be attacked the next time they were taken up on deck. Others felt that it would be wiser to watch and wait for the best moment. Bitter disagreements began to flare up. One debate was suddenly interrupted when the voice of an elder rang out, 'Hear me! Though we are of different tribes and tongues, remember that we are the same people! We must be as one village, together in this place!'

Murmurings of approval spread swiftly within the hold. That voice had been heard before, giving counsel in times of special stress. It was a voice with experience and authority as well as wisdom. Soon the information passed from mouth to ear that the speaker had been the alcala of his village. After some time, he spoke again, saying now that some leader must be found and agreed upon, and some attack plan must be proposed and agreed upon before there could be any hope of overcoming the toubob, who were obviously both well organized and heavily armed. Again, the hold soon filled with mutterings of approval.

The new and comforting sense of closeness with the other men made Kunta feel almost less aware of the stink and filth, and even the lice and rats. Then he heard the new fear that was circulating – that yet another slatee was believed to be somewhere on the level of men below. One of the women had sung of having been among the group of chained people whom this slatee had helped to bring, blindfolded, onto this canoe. She had sung that it was night when her blindfold was removed, but she had seen the toubob give that slatee liquor, which he drank until he stumbled about drunkenly, and then the toubob, all howling with laughter, had knocked him unconscious and dragged him into the hold. The woman sang that though she was not able to tell in any definite way the face of that slatee, he was almost surely somewhere below in chains like the rest, in terror that he would be discovered and killed, as he now knew that one slatee had already. In the hold, the men discussed how probably this slatee, too, was able to speak some toubob words, and in hopes of saving his miserable life, he might try to warn the toubob of any attack plans he learned of.

It occurred to Kunta, as he shook his shackles at a fat rat, why he had known little of slatees until now. It was because none of them would dare to live among people in villages, where even a strong suspicion of who they were would bring about their instant death. He remembered that back in Juffure he often had felt that his own father Omoro and yet older men, when they sat around the night fires, would seem to be needlessly occupied with dark worries and gloomy speculations about dangers to which he and the other younger men privately thought they themselves would never succumb. But now he understood why the older men had worried about the safety of the village; they had known better than he how many slatee slithered about many of them in The Gambia. The despised tan-coloured sasso borro children of toubob fathers were easy to identify; but not all. Kunta thought now about the girl of his village who had been kidnapped by toubob and then escaped, who had gone to the Council of Elders just before he had been taken away, wanting to know what to do about her sasso borro infant, and he wondered what the Council of Elders had decided for her to do.

Some few slatees, he learned now, from the talk in the hold, only supplied toubob canoes with such goods as indigo, gold and elephants' teeth. But there were hundreds of others who helped toubob to burn villages and capture people. Some of the men told how children were enticed with slices of sugar cane; then bags were thrown over their heads. Others said the slatees had beaten them mercilessly during the marches after their capture. One man's wife, big with child, had died on the road. The wounded son of another was left bleeding to die from whip cuts. The more Kunta heard, the more his rage became as great for others as for himself.

He lay there in the darkness hearing the voice of his father sternly warning him and Lamin never to wander off anywhere alone; Kunta desperately wished that he had heeded his father's warnings. His heart sank with the thought that he would never again be able to listen to his father, that for the rest of whatever was going to be his life, he was going to have to think for himself.

'All things are the will of Allah!' That statement – which had begun with the alcala – went from mouth to ear, and when it came to Kunta from the man lying on his left side, he turned his head to whisper the words to his Wolof shacklemate. After a moment, Kunta realized that the Wolof hadn't whispered the words on to the next man, and after wondering for a while why not, he thought that perhaps he hadn't said them clearly, so he started to whisper the message once again. But abruptly the Wolof spat out loudly enough to be heard across the entire hold, 'If your Allah wills this, give me the devil!' From elsewhere in the darkness came several loud exclamations of agreement with the Wolof, and arguments broke out here and there.

Kunta was deeply shaken. The shocked realization that he lay with a pagan burned into his brain, faith in Allah being as precious to him as life itself. Until now he had respected the friendship and the wise opinions of his older shacklemate. But now Kunta knew that there could never be any more companionship between them.

38

Up on the deck now, the women sang of having managed to steal and hide a few knives, and some other things that could be used as weapons. Down in the hold, even more strongly than before, the men separated into two camps of opinion. The leader of the group that felt the toubob should be attacked without delay was a fierce-looking, tattooed Wolof. On the deck, every man had seen him dancing wildly in his chains while baring his sharply filed teeth at the toubob, who clapped for him because they thought he was grinning. Those who believed in the wisdom of further watchful preparation were led by the tawny Foulah who had been beaten for choking the slatee to death.

There were a few followers of the Wolof who exclaimed that the toubob should be attacked when many of them were in the hold, where the chained men could see better than they and the element of surprise would be greatest – but those who urged this plan were dismissed as foolish by the others, who pointed out that the bulk of the toubob would still be up on the deck, and thus able to kill the chained men below like so many rats. Sometimes when the arguments between the Wolof and the Foulah would reach the point of shouting, the alcala would intervene, commanding them to be quieter lest their discussion be overheard by the toubob.

Whichever leader's thinking finally prevailed, Kunta was ready to fight to the death. Dying held no fear for him any more. Once he had decided that he would never see his family and home again, he felt the same as dead already. His only fear now was that he might die without at least one of the toubob also dead by his hand. But the leader towards whom Kunta was most inclined – along with most of the men, he felt – was the cautious, whip-scarred Foulah. Kunta had found out by now that most of the men in the hold were Mandinkas, and every Mandinka knew well that the Foulah people were known for spending years, even their entire lives if need be, to avenge with death any serious wrong ever done to them. If someone killed a Foulah and escaped, the Foulah's sons would never rest until one day they found and killed the murderer.

'We must be as one behind the leader we agree upon,' the alcala counselled. There was angry muttering from those who followed the Wolof, but as it had become clear that most of the men sided with the Foulah, he promptly issued his first order. 'We must examine toubob's every action with the eyes of hawks. And when the time comes, we must be warriors.' He advised them to follow the counsel of the woman who had told them to look happy when they jumped on deck in their chains. That would relax the toubob's guard, which would make them easier to take by surprise. And the Foulah also said that every man should locate with his eyes any weaponlike object that he could swiftly grab and use. Kunta was very pleased with himself, for during his times up on deck, he had already spotted a spike, tied loosely beneath a space of railing, which he intended to snatch and use as a spear to plunge into the nearest toubob belly. His fingers would clutch around the handle he imagined in his hands every time he thought of it.

Whenever the toubob would jerk the hatch cover open and climb down among them, shouting and wielding their whips, Kunta lay as still as a forest animal. He thought of what the kintango had said during manhood training, that the hunter should learn from what Allah himself had taught the animals – how to hide and watch the hunters who sought to kill them. Kunta had lain for hours thinking how the toubob seemed to *enjoy* causing pain. He remembered with loathing the times when toubob would laugh as they lashed the men – particularly those whose bodies were covered with bad sores – and then disgustedly wipe off the ooze that splattered onto them. Kunta lay also bitterly picturing the toubob in his mind as they forced the women into the canoe's dark corners in the nights; he imagined that he could hear the women screaming. Did the toubob have no women of their own? Was that why they went like dogs after others' women? The toubob seemed to respect nothing at all; they seemed to have no gods, not even any spirits to worship.

The only thing that could take Kunta's mind off the toubob – and how to kill them – was the rats, which had become bolder and bolder with each passing day. Their nose whiskers would tickle between Kunta's legs as they went to bite a sore that was bleeding or running with pus. But the lice preferred to bite him on the face, and they would suck at the liquids in the corners of Kunta's eyes, or the snot draining from his nostrils. He would squirm his body, with his fingers darting and pinching to crush any lice that he might trap between his nails. But worse even than the lice and rats was the pain in Kunta's shoulders, elbows and hips, stinging now like fire from the weeks of steady rubbing against the hard, rough boards beneath him. He had seen the raw patches on other men when they were on deck, and his own cries joined theirs whenever the big canoe pitched or rolled somewhat more than usual.

And Kunta had seen that when they were up on the deck, some of the men had begun to act as if they were zombies – their faces wore a look that said that they were no longer afraid, because they no longer cared whether they lived or died. Even when the whips of the toubob lashed them, they would react only slowly. When they had been scrubbed of their filth, some were simply unable even to try jumping in their chains, and the white-haired chief toubob, with a look of worry, would order the others to permit those men to sit, which they did with their foreheads between their knees and the thin, pinkish fluid draining down their raw backs. Then the chief toubob would force their heads backwards and into their upturned mouths pour some stuff that they would usually choke up. And some of them fell limply on their sides, unable to move, and toubob would carry them back into the hold. Even before these men died, which most of them did, Kunta knew that in some way they had willed themselves to die.

But in obedience to the Foulah, Kunta and most of the men tried to keep acting happy as they danced in their chains, although the effort was like a canker in their souls. It was possible to see, though, that when the toubob were thus made more relaxed, fewer whips fell on backs, and the men were allowed to remain on the sunlit deck for longer periods than before. After enduring the buckets of seawater and the torture of the scrubbing brushes, Kunta and the rest of the men sat resting on their haunches and watched the toubob's every move – how they generally spaced themselves along the rails; how they usually kept their weapons too close to be grabbed away. No

167

chained man's eye missed it whenever any toubob leaned his gun briefly against the rails. While they sat on the deck, anticipating the day when they would kill the toubob, Kunta worried about the big metal thing that showed through the barricade. He knew that at whatever cost in lives, that weapon would have to be overwhelmed and taken, for even though he didn't know exactly what it was, he knew that it was capable of some terrible act of destruction, which was of course why the toubob had placed it there.

He worried also about those few toubob who were always turning the wheel of the big canoe, a little this way, a little that way, while staring at a round brownish metal thing before them. Once, when they were down in the hold, the alcala spoke his own thought: 'If those toubob are killed, who will run this canoe?' And the Foulah leader responded that those toubob needed to be taken alive. 'With spears at their throats,' he said, 'they will return us to our land, or they will die.' The very thought that he might actually see his land, his home, his family once again sent a shiver down Kunta's spine. But even if that should happen, he thought he would have to live to very old if he was ever to forget, even a little bit, what the toubob had done to him.

There was yet another fear within Kunta – that the toubob might have the eyes to notice how differently he and the other men danced in their chains on the deck, for now they were really dancing; they couldn't help their movements from showing what was deep in their minds: swift gestures of hurling off shackles and chains, then clubbing, strangling, spearing, killing. While they were dancing, Kunta and the other men would even whoop out hoarsely their anticipation of slaughter. But to his great relief, when the dancing ended and he could again contain himself, he saw that the unsuspecting toubob only grinned with happiness. Then, one day up on the deck, the chained people suddenly stood rooted in astonishment and stared – along with the toubob – at a flight of hundreds of flying fish that filled the air above the water like silvery birds. Kunta was watching, dumbfounded, when suddenly he heard a scream. Whirling, he saw the fierce, tattooed Wolof in the act of snatching a metal stick from a toubob. Swinging it like a club, he sent the toubob's brains spraying onto the deck; as other toubob snapped from their frozen positions of shock, he battered another to the deck. It was done so swiftly that the Wolof, bellowing in rage, was clubbing his fifth toubob when the flash of a long knife lopped off his head cleanly at the shoulders. His head hit the deck before his body had crumpled down, and both spurted blood from their stumps. The eyes in the face were still open, and they looked very surprised.

Amid shoutings of panic, more and more toubob scrambled to the scene, rushing out of doors and sliding like monkeys down from among the billowing white cloths. As the women shrieked, the shackled men huddled together in a circle. The metal sticks barked flame and smoke; then the big black barrel exploded with a thunderous roar and a gushing cloud of heat and smoke just over their heads, and they screamed and sprawled over each other in horror.

From behind the barricade bolted the chief toubob and his scarfaced mate, both of them screaming in rage. The huge one struck the nearest toubob a blow that sent blood spurting from his mouth, then all of the other toubob were a mass of screaming and shouting as with their lashes and knives and firesticks they rushed to herd the shackled men back towards the open hatch. Kunta moved, not feeling the lashes that struck him, still awaiting the Foulah's signal to attack. But almost before he realized it, they were below and chained back in their dark places and the hatch cover had been slammed down.

But they were not alone. In the commotion, a toubob had been trapped down there with them. He dashed this way and that in the darkness, stumbling and bumping into the shelves, screaming in terror, scrambling up when he fell and dashing off again. His howlings sounded like some primeval beast's. *'Toubob fa!'* somebody shouted, and other voices joined him: *'Toubob fa! Toubob fa!'* They shouted, louder and louder, as more and more men joined the chorus. It was as if the toubob knew they meant it for him, and pleading sounds came from him as Kunta lay silent as if frozen, none of his muscles able to move. His head was pounding, his body poured out sweat, he was gasping to breathe. Suddenly the hatch cover was snatched open and a dozen toubob came pounding down the stairs into the dark hold. Some of their whips had slashed down onto the trapped toubob before he could make them realize he was one of them.

Then, under viciously lashing whips, the men were again unchained and beaten, kicked back up onto the deck, where they were made to watch as four toubob with heavy whips beat and cut into a pulpy mess the headless body of the Wolof. The chained men's naked bodies shone with sweat and blood from their cuts and sores, but scarcely a sound came from among them. Every one of the toubob was heavily armed now, and murderous rage was upon their faces as they stood in a surrounding ring, glaring and breathing heavily. Then the whips lashed down again as the naked men were beaten back down into the hold and rechained in their places.

For a long while, no one dared even to whisper. Among the torrent of thoughts and emotions that assailed Kunta when his terror had subsided enough for him to think at all was the feeling that he wasn't alone in admiring the courage of the Wolof, who had died as a warrior was supposed to. He remembered his own tingling anticipation that the Foulah leader would at any instant signal an attack – but that signal hadn't come. Kunta was bitter, for whatever might have happened would have been all over now; and why not die now? What better time was going to come? Was there any reason to keep hanging on to life here in this stinking darkness? He wished desperately that he could communicate as he once did with his shackle-mate, but the Wolof was a pagan.

Mutterings of anger at the Foulah's failure to act were cut short by his dramatic message: The attack, he announced, would come the next time the men on their level of the hold were on deck being washed and jumping in their chains, when the toubob seemed most relaxed. 'Many among us will die,' the Foulah said, 'as our brother has died for us – but our brothers below will avenge us.'

There was grunting approval in the murmurings that circulated now. And Kunta lay in the darkness listening to the raspings of a stolen file rubbing against chains. He knew for weeks that the file marks had been carefully covered with filth so that the toubob wouldn't see. He lay fixing in his mind the faces of those who turned the great wheel of the canoe, since their lives were the only ones to be spared.

But during that long night in the hold, Kunta and the other men began to hear an odd new sound they had never heard before. It seemed to be coming through the deck from over their heads. Silence fell rapidly in the hold and, listening intently, Kunta guessed that stronger winds must be making the great white cloths flap much harder than usual. Soon there was another sound, as if rice was falling onto the deck; he guessed after a while that it must be rain pelting down. Then he was sure that he heard, unmistakably, the muffled crack and rumble of heavy thunder.

Feet could be heard pounding on the deck overhead, and the big canoe began to pitch and shudder. Kunta's screams were joined by others' as each movement up and down, or from side to side, sent the chained men's naked shoulders, elbows, and buttocks – already festered and bleeding – grinding down even harder against the rough boards beneath them, grating away still more of the soft, infected skin until the muscles underneath began rubbing against the boards. The hot, lancing pains that shot from head to foot almost blacked him out, and it was as if from afar that he became dimly aware of the sound of water pouring down into the hold – and of shrieks amid a bedlam of terror.

The water poured more and more rapidly into the hold until Kunta heard the sound of something heavy, like some great coarse cloth, being dragged over the deck above. Moments later, the flood subsided to a trickle – but then Kunta began to sweat and gag. The toubob had covered the holes above them to shut out the water, but in so doing they had cut off all air from the outside, trapping the heat and stench entirely within the hold. It was beyond tolerance, and the men began to choke and vomit, rattling their shackles frantically and screaming in panic. Kunta's nose, throat, and then his lungs felt as if they were being stuffed with blazing cotton. He was gasping for more breath to scream with. Surrounded by the wild frenzy of jerking chains and suffocating cries, he didn't even know it when both his bladder and his bowels released themselves.

Sledgehammer waves crashed on the hull, and the timbers behind their heads strained against the pegs that held them together. The choked screams of the men down in the hold grew louder when the great canoe plunged sickeningly downward, shuddering as tons of ocean poured across her. Then, miraculously, she rose again under the torrential rains that beat down on her like hailstones. As the next mountainous broadside drove her back down again, and up again – heeling, rolling, trembling – the noise in the hold began to abate as more and more of the chained men fainted and went limp.

When Kunta came to, he was up on deck, amazed to find himself still alive. The orange lights, moving about, made him think at first they were still below. Then he took a deep breath and realized it was fresh air. He lay sprawled on his back, which was exploding with pains so terrible that he couldn't stop crying, even in front of the toubob. He saw them far overhead, ghostly in the moonlight, crawling along the crossarms of the tall, thick poles; they seemed to be trying to unroll the great white cloths. Then, turning his pounding head towards a loud noise, Kunta saw still more toubob stumbling up through the open hatchway, staggering as they dragged the limp, shackled forms of naked men up onto the deck of the canoe, dumping them down near Kunta and others already piled up like so many logs.

Kunta's shacklemate was trembling violently and gagging between moans. And Kunta's own gagging wouldn't stop as he watched the white-haired chief toubob and the huge scarred one shouting and cursing at the others, who were slipping and falling in the vomit underfoot, some of it their own as they continued to drag up bodies from below.

The great canoe was still pitching heavily, and drenching spray now and then splashed over the quarterdeck. The chief toubob had difficulty keeping his balance, now moving hurriedly, as another toubob followed him with a light. One or the other of them would turn upwards the face of each limp, naked man, and the light would be held close; the chief toubob would peer closely and sometimes he would put his fingers on one wrist of that shackled man. Sometimes, then, cursing bitterly, he would bark an order and the other toubob would lift and drop the man into the ocean.

Kunta knew these men had died below. He asked himself how Allah, of whom it was said that He was in all places at all times, could possibly be here. Then he thought that even to question such a thing would make him no better than the pagan shuddering and moaning alongside him. And he turned his thoughts to prayer for the souls of the men who had been thrown over the side, joined already with their ancestors. He envied them.

39

By the time the dawn came, the weather had calmed and cleared, but the ship still rolled in heavy swells. Some of the men who still lay on their backs, or on their sides, showed almost no signs of life; others were having dreadful convulsions. But along with most of the other men, Kunta had managed to get himself into a sitting position that relieved somewhat the horrible pains in his back and buttocks. He looked dully at the backs of those nearby; all were bleeding afresh through blood already dried and clotted, and he saw what seemed to be bones showing at the shoulders and elbows. With a vacant look in another direction, he could see a woman lying with her legs wide apart; her private parts, turned in his direction, were smudged with some strange greyish-yellowish paste, and his nose picked up some indescribable smell that he knew must come from her.

Now and then one of the men who were still lying down would try to raise himself up. Some would only fall back, but among those who succeeded in sitting up, Kunta noticed, was the Foulah leader. He was bleeding heavily, and his expression was of one who wasn't part of what was going on around him. Kunta didn't recognize many of the other men he saw. He guessed that they must be from the level below his. These were the men whom the Foulah had said would avenge the dead from the first level after the toubob were attacked. The attack. Kunta didn't have the strength even to think about it any more.

In some of the faces around him, including that of the man he was shackled to, Kunta saw that death was etched. Without knowing why, he was sure they were going to die. The face of the Wolof was greyish in colour, and each time he gasped to breathe there was a bubbling sound in his nose. Even the Wolof's shoulder and elbow bones, which showed through the raw flesh, had a greyish look. Almost as if he knew that Kunta was looking at him, the Wolof's eyes fluttered open and looked back at Kunta – but without a sign of recognition. He was a pagan, but . . . Kunta extended a finger weakly to touch the Wolof on the arm. But there was no sign of any awareness of Kunta's gesture, or of how much it had meant.

Although his pains didn't subside, the warm sun began to make Kunta feel a little better. He glanced down and saw, in a pool around where he sat, the blood that had drained from his back – and a shuddering whine forced itself up his throat. Toubob who were also sick and weak were moving about with brushes and buckets, scrubbing up vomit and faeces, and others were bringing tubs of filth up from below and dumping it over the side. In the daylight, Kunta vacantly noted their pale, hairy skins, and the smallness of their fotos.

After a while he smelled the steam of boiling vinegar and tar through the gratings as the chief toubob began to move among the shackled people applying his salve. He would put a plaster of cloth smeared with powder wherever the bones showed through, but seeping blood soon made the plasters slip and fall off. He also opened some of the men's mouths – including Kunta's – and forced down their throats something from a black bottle.

At sunset, those who were well enough were fed – maize boiled with red palm oil and served in a small tub they dipped into with their hands. Then each of them had a scoopful of water brought by a toubob from a barrel that was kept at the foot of the biggest of the poles on deck. By the time the stars came out, they were back below in chains. The emptied spaces on Kunta's level, where men had died, were filled with the sickest of the men from the level below, and their moans of suffering were even louder than before.

For three days Kunta lay among them in a twilight of pain, vomiting, and fever, his cries mingled with theirs. He was also among those racked with fits of deep, hoarse coughing. His neck was hot and swollen, and his entire body poured with sweat. He came out of his stupor only once, when he felt the whiskers of a rat brush along his hip; almost by reflex his free hand darted out and trapped the rat's head and foreparts in its grasp. He couldn't believe it. All the rage that had been bottled up in him for so long flooded down his arm and into his hand. Tighter and tighter he squeezed – the rat wriggling and squealing frantically – until he could feel the eyes popping out, the skull crunching under his thumb. Only then did the strength ebb from his fingers and the hand open to release the crushed remains.

A day or two later, the chief toubob began to enter the hold himself, discovering each time – and unchaining – at least one more lifeless body. Gagging in the stench, with others holding up lights for him to see by, he applied his salve and powder and forced the neck of his black bottle into the mouths of those still living. Kunta fought not to scream with pain whenever the fingers touched the grease to his back or the bottle to his lips. He also shrank from the touch of those pale hands against his skin; he would rather have felt the lash. And in the light's orange glow, the faces of the toubob had a kind of paleness without features that he knew would never leave his mind any more than the stink in which he lay.

Lying there in filth and fever, Kunta didn't know if they had been down in the belly of this canoe for two moons or six, or even as long as a rain. The man who had been lying near the vent through which they had counted the days was dead now. And there was no longer any communication among those who had survived.

Once when Kunta came jerking awake from a half sleep, he felt a nameless terror and sensed that death was near him. Then, after a while, he realized that he could no longer hear the familiar wheezing of his shacklemate beside him. It was a long time before Kunta could bring himself to reach out a hand and touch the man's arm. He recoiled in horror, for it was cold and rigid. Kunta lay shuddering. Pagan or not, he and the Wolof had talked together, they had lain together. And now he was alone.

When the toubob came down again, bringing the boiled corn,

Kunta cringed as their gagging and muttering came closer and closer. Then he felt one of them shaking the body of the Wolof and cursing. Then Kunta heard food being scraped as usual into his own pan, which was thrust up between him and the still Wolof, and the toubob moved on down the shelf. However starved his belly was, Kunta couldn't think of eating.

After a while two toubob came and unshackled the Wolof's ankle and wrist from Kunta's. Numb with shock, he listened as the body was dragged and bumped down the aisle and up the stairs. He wanted to shove himself away from that vacant space, but the instant he moved, the raking of his exposed muscles against the boards made him scream in agony. As he lay still, letting the pain subside, he could hear in his mind the death wailings of the women of the Wolof's village, mourning his death. '*Toubob fa!*' he screamed into the stinking darkness, his cuffed hand jangling the chain of the Wolof's empty cuff.

The next time he was up on deck, Kunta's glance met the gaze of one of the toubob who had beaten him and the Wolof. For an instant they looked deeply into each other's eyes, and though the toubob's face and eyes tightened with hatred, this time no whip fell upon Kunta's back. As Kunta was recovering from his surprise, he looked across the deck and for the first time since the storm, saw the women. His heart sank. Of the original twenty, only twelve remained. But he felt a pang of relief that all four of the children had survived.

There was no scrubbing this time – the wounds on the men's backs were too bad – and they jumped in their chains only weakly, this time to the beat of the drum alone; the toubob who had squeezed the wheezing thing was gone. As well as they could, in their pain, the women who were left sang that quite a few more toubob had been sewn into white cloths and dropped overboard.

With a great weariness in his face, the white-haired toubob was moving among the naked people with his salve and bottle when a man with the empty shackles of a dead partner dangling from his wrist and ankle bolted from where he stood and raced to the rail. He had scrambled halfway over it when one of the nearby toubob managed to catch up with him and grab the trailing chain just as he leaped. An instant later his body was banging against the side of the great canoe and the deck was ringing with his strangled howls. Suddenly, unmistakably, amid the cries, Kunta heard some toubob words. A hissing rose from the chained men; it was the other slatee, without question. As the man flailed against the hull – screeching '*Toubob fa!*' and then begging for mercy – the chief toubob went over to the rail and looked down. After listening for a moment, he abruptly jerked the chain from the other toubob and let the slatee drop screaming into the sea. Then, without a word, he went back to greasing and powdering wounds as if nothing had happened.

Though their whips fell less often, the guards seemed to act terrified of their prisoners now. Each time the prisoners were brought up on deck, the toubob ringed them closely, with firesticks and knives drawn, as if at any moment the shackled people might attack. But as far as Kunta was concerned, though he despised the toubob with all his being, he didn't care about killing them any more. He was so sick and weak that he didn't even care if he lived or died himself. Up on the deck he would simply lie down on his side and close his eyes. Soon he would feel the chief toubob's hands smearing salve on his back again. And then, for a while, he would feel nothing but the warmth of the sun and smell only the fresh ocean breeze, and the pain would dissolve into a quiet haze of waiting – almost blissfully – to die and join his ancestors.

Occasionally, down in the hold, Kunta would hear a little murmuring here and there, and he wondered what they could find to talk about. And what was the point? His Wolof shacklemate was gone, and death had taken some of those who had translated for the others. Besides, it took too much strength to talk any more. Each day Kunta felt a little worse, and it didn't help to see what was happening to some of the other men. Their bowels had begun to drain out a mixture of clotted blood and thick, greyish-yellow, horribly foul-smelling mucus.

When they first smelled and saw the putrid discharge, the toubob became agitated. One of them went rushing back up through the hatch, and minutes later the chief toubob descended. Gagging, he gestured sharply for the other toubob to unshackle the screaming men and remove them from the hold. More toubob soon returned with lights, hoes, brushes, and buckets. Vomiting and gasping curses, they scraped, scrubbed, and scrubbed again the shelves from which sick men had been taken away. Then they poured boiling vinegar on those places and moved the men lying next to those places to other empty spaces farther away.

But nothing helped, for the bloody contagion – which Kunta heard the toubob call 'the flux' – spread and spread. Soon he too began to writhe with pains in his head and back, then to roast and shiver with fever and chills, and finally to feel his insides clenching and squeezing out the stinking blood and ooze. Feeling as if his entrails were coming out along with the discharge, Kunta nearly fainted from the pain. Between screams, he cried out things he could hardly believe he was uttering: 'Omoro – Omar the Second Caliph, third after Muhammad the Prophet! Kairaba – Kairaba means peace!' Finally his voice was all but gone from shrieking and could hardly be heard amid the sobbing of the others. Within two days, the flux had afflicted nearly every man in the hold.

By now the bloody globs were dripping down off the shelves into the aisleways, and there was no way for the toubob to avoid brushing against it or stepping on it – cursing and vomiting – whenever they went into the hold. Each day now the men would be taken up on deck while the toubob took down buckets of vinegar and tar to boil into steam to clean the hold. Kunta and his mates stumbled up through the hatch and across to where they would flop down on the deck, which would soon be fouled with the blood from their backs and the discharge from their bowels. The smell of the fresh air would seem to go all through Kunta's body, from his feet to his head and then, when they were returned to the hold, the vinegar and tar smell would do the same, although the smell of it never killed the stench of the flux.

In his delirium, Kunta saw flashing glimpses of his Grandma Yaisa lying propped up on one arm on her bed talking to him for the last time, when he was but a small boy; and he thought of old Grandmother Nyo Boto, and the stories she would tell when he was back in the first kafo, about the crocodile who was caught in a trap by the river when the boy came along to set it free. Moaning and babbling, he would claw and kick when the toubob came anywhere near him.

Soon most of the men could no longer walk at all, and toubob had to help them up onto the deck so that the white-haired one could apply his useless salve in the light of day. Every day someone died and was thrown overboard, including a few more of the women and two of the four children – as well as several of the toubob themselves. Many of the surviving toubob were hardly able to drag themselves around any more, and one manned the big canoe's wheel while standing in a tub that would catch his flux mess.

The nights and the days tumbled into one another until one day Kunta and the few others from below who yet could manage to drag themselves up the hatch steps stared over the rail with dull astonishment at a rolling carpet of gold-coloured seaweed floating on the surface of the water as far as they could see. Kunta knew that the water couldn't continue forever, and now it seemed that the big canoe was about to go over the edge of the world – but he didn't really care. Deep within himself, he sensed that he was nearing the end; he was unsure only of by what means he was going to die.

Dimly he noted that the great white sheets were dropping, no longer full of wind as they had been. Up among the poles, the toubob were pulling their maze of ropes to move the sheets this way and that, trying to pick up any little breeze. From the toubob down on the deck, they drew up buckets of water and sloshed them against the great cloths. But still the great canoe remained becalmed, and gently it began to roll back and forth upon the swells.

All the toubob were on the edges of their tempers now, the white-haired one even shouting at his knife-scarred mate, who cursed and beat the lesser toubob more than before, and they in turn fought with each other even more than they had before. But there were no further beatings of the shackled people, except on rare occasions, and they began to spend almost all the daylight hours up on deck, and – to Kunta's amazement – they were given a full pint of water every day.

When they were taken up from the hold one morning, the men saw hundreds of flying fish piled up on the deck. The women sang that the toubob had set lights out on deck the night before to lure them, and they had flown aboard and floundered about in vain trying to escape. That night they were boiled with the maize, and the taste of fresh fish startled Kunta with pleasure. He wolfed the food down, bones and all.

When the stinging yellow powder was sprinkled next against Kunta's back, the chief toubob applied a thick cloth bandage against his right shoulder. Kunta knew that meant his bone had begun showing through, as was the case with so many other men already, especially the thinner ones, who had the least muscle over their bones. The bandaging made Kunta's shoulder hurt even more than before. But he hadn't been back down in the hold for long before the seeping blood made the soaked bandage slip loose. It didn't matter. Sometimes his mind would dwell on the horrors he had been through, or on his deep loathing of all toubob; but mostly he just lay in the stinking darkness, eyes gummy with some yellowish matter, hardly aware that he was still alive.

He heard other men crying out, or beseeching Allah to save them, but he neither knew nor cared who they were. He would drift off into fitful, moaning sleep, with jumbled dreams of working in the fields back in Juffure, of leafy green farms, of fish leaping from the glassy surface of the bolong, of fat antelope haunches roasting over glowing coals, of gourds of steaming tea sweetened with honey. Then, drifting again into wakefulness, he sometimes heard himself mouthing bitter, incoherent threats and begging aloud, against his will, for a last look at his family. Each of them – Omoro, Binta, Lamin, Suwadu, Madi – was a stone in his heart. It tortured him to think that he had caused them grief. Finally he would wrench his mind away to something else, but it wouldn't help. His thoughts would always drift to something like the drum he had been going to make for himself. He'd think about how he would have practised on it at night while guarding the groundnut fields, where no one could hear his mistakes. But then he would remember the day he had gone to chop down the tree trunk for the drum, and it would all come flooding back.

Among the men who were still alive, Kunta was one of the last who were able to climb down unassisted from their shelf and up the steps to the deck. But then his wasting legs began trembling and buckling under him and finally he, too, had to be half carried and half dragged to the deck. Moaning quietly, with his head between his knees, rheumy eyes clamped tight, he sat limply until his turn came to be cleaned. The toubob now used a large soapy sponge lest a hard-bristled brush do further damage to the men's gouged and bleeding backs. But Kunta was still better off than most, who were able only to lie on their sides, seeming almost as if they had stopped breathing.

Among them all, only the remaining women and children were reasonably healthy; they hadn't been shackled and chained down within the darkness, filth, stench, lice, fleas, rats, and contagion. The oldest of the surviving women, one of about Binta's rains – Mbuto was her name, a Mandinka of the village of Kerewan – had such stateliness and dignity that even in her nakedness it was as if she wore a robe. The toubob didn't even stop her from moving with comforting words among the shackled men lying sick on the deck, rubbing fevered chests and foreheads. 'Mother! Mother!' Kunta whispered when he felt her soothing hands, and another man, too weak to speak, just gaped his jaws in an attempt to smile.

Finally, Kunta could no longer even eat without help. The draining shreds of muscle in his shoulders and elbows refused to lift his hands enough for him to claw into the food pan. Often now the feeding was done with the men up on deck, and one day Kunta's fingernails were scrabbling to get up over the edges of the pan when the scar-faced toubob noticed it. He barked an order at one of the lesser toubob, who proceeded to force into Kunta's mouth a hollow tube and pour the gruel through it. Gagging on the tube, Kunta gulped and slobbered the food down, then sprawled out on his belly.

The days were growing hotter, and even up on the deck everyone was sweltering in the still air. But after a few more days, Kunta began to feel a breath of cooling breeze. The big cloths up on the tall poles started to snap again and soon were billowing in the wind. The toubob up above were springing about like monkeys again, and soon the big canoe was cutting through the water with froth curling at her bow.

The next morning, more toubob than usual came thudding down through the hatch, and much earlier than ever before. With great excitement in their words and movements, they rushed along the aisles, unchaining the men and hurriedly helping them upward. Stumbling up through the hatch behind a number who were ahead of him, Kunta blinked in the early-morning light and then saw the other toubob and the women and children standing at the rails. The toubob were all laughing, cheering, and gesturing wildly. Between the scabbed backs of the other men, Kunta squinted and then saw . . .

Though still blurred in the distance, it was unmistakably some piece of Allah's earth. These toubob really did have some place to put their feet upon – the land of toubabo doo – which the ancient forefathers said stretched from the sunrise to the sunset. Kunta's whole body shook. The sweat came popping out and glistened on his forehead. The voyage was over. He had lived through it all. But his tears soon flooded the shoreline into a grey, swimming mist, for Kunta knew that whatever came next was going to be yet worse.

40

Back down in the darkness of the hold, the chained men were too afraid to open their mouths. In the silence, Kunta could hear the ship's timbers creaking, the muted *ssss* of the sea against the hull, and the dull clumpings of toubob feet rushing about on the deck overhead.

Suddenly some Mandinka began shrieking the praises of Allah, and soon all the others had joined him – until there was a bedlam of praise and praying and of chains being rattled with all the strength the men could muster. Amid the noise, Kunta didn't hear the hatch when it scraped open, but the jarring shaft of daylight stilled his tongue and jerked his head in that direction. Blinking his eyes to compress the mucus in them, he watched dimly as the toubob entered with their lanterns and began to herd them – with unusual haste – back onto the deck. Wielding their long-handled brushes once again. the toubob ignored the men's screams as they scrubbed the encrusted filth from their festering bodies, and the chief toubob moved down the line sprinkling his yellow powder. But this time, where the muscles were rubbed through deeply, he signalled for his big assistant to apply a black substance with a wide, flat brush. When it touched Kunta's raw buttocks, the rocketing pain smashed him dizzily to the deck.

As he lay with his whole body feeling as if it were on fire, he heard men howling anew in terror, and snapping his head up, he saw several of the toubob engaged in what could only be preparing the men to be eaten. Several of them, in pairs, were pushing first one chained man and then the next into a kneeling position where he was held while a third toubob brushed onto his head a white frothing stuff and then, with a narrow, gleaming thing, raked the hair off his scalp, leaving blood trickling down across his face.

When they reached Kunta and seized him, he screamed and struggled with all his might until a heavy kick in the ribs left him gasping for breath while the skin of his head numbly felt the frothing and the scraping. Next the chained men's bodies were oiled until they shone, and then they were made to step into some odd loincloth that had two holes the legs went through and that also covered their private parts. Finally, under the close scrutiny of the chief toubob, they were chained prostrate along the rails as the sun reached the centre of the sky.

Kunta lay numbly, in a kind of stupor. It came into his mind that when they finally ate his flesh and sucked the bones, his spirit would already have escaped to Allah. He was praying silently when barking shouts from the chief toubob and his big helper made him open his eyes in time to watch the lesser toubob dashing up the tall poles. Only this time their grunts, as they strained at the ropes, were mixed with excited shouts and laughter. A moment later most of the great white sheets slackened and crumpled downward.

Kunta's nostrils detected a new smell in the air; actually, it was a mingling of many smells, most of them strange and unknown to him. Then he thought he heard new sounds in the distance, from across the water. Lying on the deck, with his crusty eyes half shut, he couldn't tell from where. But soon the sounds grew closer, and as they did, his fearful whimperings joined those of his mates. As the sounds got louder and louder, so did their praying and gibbering – until finally, in the light wind, Kunta could smell the bodies of many unfamiliar toubob. Just then the big canoe bumped hard against something solid and unyielding, and it lurched heavily, rocking back and forth until, for the first time since they left Africa four and a half moons before, it was secured by ropes and fell still.

The chained men sat frozen with terror. Kunta's arms were locked around his knees, and his eyes were clamped shut as if he were paralysed. For as long as he could, he held his breath against the sickening wave of smells, but when something clumped heavily onto the deck, he slit his eyes open and saw two new toubob stepping down from a wide plank holding a white cloth over their noses. Moving briskly, they shook hands with the chief toubob, who was now all grins, clearly anxious to please them. Kunta silently begged Allah's forgiveness and mercy as the toubob began rushing along the rails unchaining the black men and gesturing with shouts for them to stand up. When Kunta and his mates clutched at their chains – not wanting to let go of what had become almost a part of their bodies – the whips began to crack, first over their heads, then against their backs. Instantly, amid screams, they let go of the chains and stumbled to their feet.

Over the side of the big canoe, down on the dock, Kunta could see dozens of toubob stamping, laughing, pointing in their excitement, with dozens more running from all directions to join them. Under the whips, they were driven in a stumbling single file up over the side and down the sloping plank towards the waiting mob. Kunta's knees almost buckled under him as his feet touched the toubob earth, but other toubob with cocked whips kept them moving closely alongside the jeering crowd, their massed smell like the blow of a giant fist in Kunta's face. When one black man fell, crying out to Allah, his chains pulled down the men ahead of and behind him. Whips lashed them all back up again as the toubob crowd screamed in excitement.

The impulse to dash and escape surged wildly in Kunta, but the whips kept his chained line moving. They trudged past toubob riding in extraordinary two-wheeled and four-wheeled vehicles drawn by huge animals that looked a little like donkeys; then past a toubob throng milling around in some kind of market-place stacked with colourful piles of what seemed to be fruits and vegetables. Finely clothed toubob regarded them with expressions of loathing, while more roughly clad toubob pointed and hooted with enjoyment. One of the latter, he noticed, was a she toubob, her stringy hair the colour of straw. After seeing the hungry way the toubob on the great canoe had lusted after black women, he was amazed to see that the toubob had women of their own; but looking at this specimen, he could understand why they preferred Africans.

Kunta darted a glance sideways as they passed a group of toubob screaming crazily around a flurry of two cocks fighting with each other. And hardly had that din faded behind them when they came upon a shouting crowd leaping this way and that to avoid being bowled over by three toubob boys as they raced and dived after a squealing, filthy swine that looked shiny with grease. Kunta couldn't believe his eyes.

As if lightning had struck him, Kunta then glimpsed two black men who were not from the big canoe – a Mandinka and a Serere, there was no doubt. He jerked his head around to stare as they walked quietly behind a toubob. He and his mates weren't alone after all in this terrible land! And if these men had been allowed to live, perhaps they too would be spared from the cooking cauldron. Kunta wanted to rush over and embrace them; but he saw their expressionless faces and the fear in their downcast eyes. And then his nose picked up their smell; there was something wrong with it. His mind reeled; he couldn't comprehend how black men would docilely follow behind a toubob who wasn't watching them or even carrying a weapon, rather than try to run away – or kill him.

He didn't have time to think about it further, for suddenly they found themselves at the open door of a large, square house of baked mud bricks in oblong shapes with iron bars set into a few open spaces along the sides. The chained men were whipped inside the wide door by the toubob guarding it, then into a large room. Kunta's feet felt cool on the floor of hard-packed earth. In the dim light that came through the two iron-barred openings, his blinking eyes picked out the forms of five black men huddled along one wall. They didn't so much as lift their heads as the toubob locked the wrists and ankles of Kunta and his mates in thick iron cuffs attached to short chains that were bolted to the walls.

Along with the others, Kunta then huddled down himself, with his chin against his clasped knees, his mind dazed and reeling with all that he had seen and heard and smelled since they had got off the great canoe. After a little while, another black man entered. Without looking at anyone, he put down some tins of water and food before each man and quickly left. Kunta wasn't hungry, but his throat was so dry that finally he couldn't stop himself from sipping a small amount of the water; it tasted strange. Numbly, he watched through one of the iron-barred spaces as the daylight faded into darkness.

183

The longer they sat there, the deeper Kunta sank into a kind of nameless terror. He felt that he would almost have preferred the dark hold of the big canoe, for at least he had come to know what to expect next there. He shrank away whenever a toubob came into the room during the night; their smell was strange and overpowering But he was used to the other smells – sweat, urine, dirty bodies, the stink as some chained man went through the agony of relieving his bowels amid the others' mingled praying and cursing and moaning and rattling of their chains.

Suddenly all the noises ceased when a toubob came in carrying a light such as those that had been used on the big canoe, and behind him, in the soft yellowish glow, another toubob who was striking with his whip some new black one who was crying out in what sounded like the toubob tongue. That one was soon chained, and the two toubob left. Kunta and his mates remained still, hearing the newcomer's piteous sounds of suffering and pain.

The dawn was near, Kunta sensed, when from somewhere there came into his head as clearly as when he had been in manhood training the high, sharp voice of the kintango: 'A man is wise to study and learn from the animals.' It was so shocking that Kunta sat bolt upright. Was it finally some message from Allah? What could be the meaning of learning from the animals – here, now? He was himself, if anything, like an animal in a trap. His mind pictured animals he had seen in traps. But sometimes the animals escaped before they were killed. Which ones were they?

Finally, the answer came to him. The animals he had known to escape from their traps were those that had not gone raging around within the trap until they were weakened to exhaustion; those that escaped had made themselves wait quietly, conserving their strength until their captors came, and the animal seized upon their carelessness to explode its energies in a desperate attack – or more wisely – a flight towards freedom.

Kunta felt intensely more alert. It was his first positive hope since he had plotted with the others to kill the toubob on the big canoe. His mind fastened upon it now: escape. He must appear to the toubob to be defeated. He must not rage or fight yet; he must seem to have given up any hope.

But even if he managed to escape, where would he run? Where could he hide in this strange land? He knew the country around Juffure as he knew his own hut, but here he knew nothing whatever. He didn't even know if toubob had forests, or if they did, whether he would find in them the signs that a hunter would use. Kunta told

184

himself that these problems would simply have to be met as they came.

As the first streaks of dawn filtered through the barred windows, Kunta dropped fitfully off to sleep. But no sooner had he closed his eyes, it seemed, than he was awakened by the strange black one bringing containers of water and food. Kunta's stomach was clenched with hunger, but the food smelled sickening, and he turned away. His tongue felt foul and swollen. He tried to swallow the slime that was in his mouth, and his throat hurt with the effort.

He looked dully about him at his mates from the big canoe; they all seemed unseeing, unhearing – drawn within themselves. Kunta turned his head to study the five who were in the room when they arrived. They wore ragged toubob clothing. Two of them were of the light brown sasso-borro skin colour that the elders had said resulted from some toubob taking a black woman. Then Kunta looked at the newcomer who had been brought in during the night; he sat slumped forward, with dried blood caked in his hair and staining the toubob garment he wore, and one of his arms hung in an awkward way that told Kunta it had been broken.

More time passed, and finally Kunta fell asleep again – only to be awakened once more, this time much later, by the arrival of another meal. It was some kind of steaming gruel, and it smelled even worse than the last thing they'd set in front of him. He shut his eyes not to see it, but when nearly all of his mates snatched up the containers and began wolfing the stuff down, he figured it might not be so bad after all. If he was ever going to escape from this place, thought Kunta, he would need strength. He would force himself to eat a little bit – but just a little. Seizing the bowl, he brought it to his open mouth and gulped and swallowed until the gruel was gone. Disgusted with himself, he banged the bowl back down and began to gag, but he forced it down again. He had to keep the food inside him if he was going to live.

From that day on, three times a day, Kunta forced himself to eat the hated food. The black one who brought it came once each day with a bucket, hoe, and a shovel to clean up after them. And once each afternoon, two toubob came to paint more of the stinging black liquid over the men's worst open sores, and sprinkled the yellow powder over the smaller sores. Kunta despised himself for the weakness that made him jerk and moan from the pain along with the others.

Through the barred window, Kunta counted finally six daylights and five nights. The first four nights, he had heard faintly from somewhere, not far away, the screams of women whom he recognized from the big canoe. He and his mates had had to sit there, burning with humiliation at being helpless to defend their women, let alone themselves. But it was even worse tonight, for there were no cries from the women. What new horror had been visited upon them?

Nearly every day, one or more of the strange black men in toubob clothes would be shoved stumbling into the room and chained. Slumped against the wall behind them, or curled down on the floor, they always showed signs of recent beatings, seeming not to know where they were or to care what might happen to them next. Then, usually before another day had passed, some important-acting toubob would enter the room holding a rag over his nose, and always one of those recent prisoners would start shrieking with terror – as that toubob kicked and shouted at him; then that black one would be taken away.

Whenever he felt that each bellyful of food had settled, Kunta would try to make his mind stop thinking in an effort to sleep. Even a few minutes of rest would blot out for that long a time this seemingly unending horror, which for whatever reason was the divine will of Allah. When Kunta couldn't sleep, which was most of the time, he would try to force his mind on to things other than his family or his village, for when he thought of them he would soon be sobbing.

41

Just after the seventh morning gruel, two toubob entered the barred room with an armload of clothes. One frightened man after another was unchained and shown how to put them on. One garment covered the waist and legs, a second the upper body. When Kunta put them on, his sores – which had begun to show signs of healing – immediately started itching.

In a little while, he began to hear the sound of voices outside; quickly it grew louder and louder. Many toubob were gathering – talking, laughing – not far beyond the barred window. Kunta and his mates sat in their toubob clothes gripped with terror at what was about to happen – whatever it might be.

When the two toubob returned, they quickly unchained and

marched from the room three of the five black ones who had originally been there. All of them acted somehow as if this had happened to them enough times before that it no longer mattered. Then, within moments, there was a change in the toubob sounds from outside; it grew much quieter, and then one toubob began to shout. Struggling vainly to understand what was being said, Kunta listened uncomprehendingly to the strange cries: 'Fit as a fiddle! Plenty of spirit in this buck!' And at brief intervals other toubob would interrupt with loud exclamations: 'Three hundred and fifty!' 'Four hundred!' 'Five!' And the first toubob would shout: 'Let's hear six! Look at him! Works like a mule!'

Kunta shuddered with fear, his face running with sweat, breath tight in his throat. When four toubob came into the room – the first two plus two others – Kunta felt paralysed. The new pair of toubob stood just within the doorway holding short clubs in one hand and small metal objects in the other. The other two moved along Kunta's side of the wall unlocking the iron cuffs. When anyone cried out or scuffled, he was struck with a short, thick, leather strap. Even so, when Kunta felt himself touched, he came up snarling with rage and terror. A blow against his head made it seem to explode; he felt only dimly a jerking at the chain on his cuffs. When his head began to clear, he was the first of a chained line of six men stumbling through a wide doorway out into the daylight.

'Just picked out of the trees!' The shouting one was standing on a low wooden platform with hundreds of other toubobs massed before him. As they gaped and gestured, Kunta's nose recoiled from the thickness of their stink. He glimpsed a few black ones among the toubob, but their faces seemed to be seeing nothing. Two of them were holding in chains two of the black ones who had just been brought from the barred room. Now the shouting one began striding rapidly down the line of Kunta and his companions, his eyes appraising them from head to foot. Then he walked back up the line, thrusting the butt of his whip against their chests and bellies, all the while making his strange cries: 'Bright as monkeys! Can be trained for anything!' Then back at the end of the line, he prodded Kunta roughly towards the raised platform. But Kunta couldn't move, except to tremble; it was as if his senses had deserted him. The whip's butt seared across the scabbing crust of his ulcerated buttocks; nearly collapsing under the pain, Kunta stumbled forward, and the toubob clicked the free end of his chain into an iron thing.

'Top prime – young and supple!' the toubob shouted. Kunta was already so numb with terror that he hardly noticed as the toubob crowd moved in more closely around him. Then, with short sticks and whip butts, they were pushing apart his compressed lips to expose his clenched teeth, and with their bare hands prodding him all over – under his armpits, on his back, his chest, his genitals. Then some of those who had been inspecting Kunta began to step back and make strange cries.

'Three hundred dollars! ... three fifty!' The shouting toubob laughed scornfully. 'Five hundred! ... six!' He sounded angry. 'This is a choice young nigger! Do I hear seven fifty?'

'Seven fifty!' came a shout.

He repeated the cry several times, then shouted 'Eight!' until someone in the crowd shouted it back. And then, before he had a chance to speak again, someone else shouted, 'Eight fifty!'

No other calls came. The shouting toubob unlocked Kunta's chain and jerked him towards a toubob who came stepping forward. Kunta felt an impulse to make his move right then, but he knew he would never make it – and anyway, he couldn't seem to move his legs.

He saw a black one moving forward behind the toubob to whom the shouter had handed his chain. Kunta's eyes entreated this black one, who had distinctly Wolof features, *My Brother, you come from my country* ... But the black one seemed not even to see Kunta as, jerking hard on the chain so that Kunta came stumbling after him, they began moving through the crowd. Some of the younger toubob laughed, jeered, and poked at Kunta with sticks as they passed, but finally they left them behind and the black one stopped at a large box sitting up off the ground on four wheels behind one of those enormous donkey-like animals he had seen on his way here from the big canoe.

With an angry sound, the black one grasped Kunta around the hips and boosted him up over the side and onto the floor of the box, where he crumpled into a heap, hearing the free end of his chain click again into something beneath a raised seat at the front end of the box behind the animal.

Two large sacks of what smelled like some kind of grain were piled near where Kunta lay. His eyes were shut tight; he felt as if he never wanted to see anything again – especially this hated black slatee.

After what seemed a very long time, Kunta's nose told him that the toubob had returned. The toubob said something, and then he and the black one climbed onto the front seat, which squeaked under their weight. The black one made a quick sound and flicked a leather thong across the animal's back; instantly it began pulling the rolling box ahead.

Kunta was so dazed that for a while he didn't even hear the chain locked to his ankle cuff rattling against the floor of the box. He had no idea how far they had travelled when his next clear thought came, and he slit his eyes open far enough to study the chain at close range. Yes, it was smaller than the one that had bound him on the big canoe; if he collected his strength and sprang, would this one tear loose from the box?

Kunta raised his eyes carefully to see the backs of the pair who sat ahead, the toubob sitting stiffly at one end of the plank seat, the black one slouched at the other end. They both sat staring ahead as if they were unaware that they were sharing the same seat. Beneath it – somewhere in shadow – the chain seemed to be securely fastened; he decided that it was not yet time to jump.

The odour of the grain sacks alongside him was overpowering, but he could also smell the toubob and his black driver – and soon he smelled some other black people, quite nearby. Without making a sound, Kunta inched his aching body upwards against the rough side of the box, but he was afraid to lift his head over the side, and didn't see them.

As he lay back down, the toubob turned his head around, and their eyes met. Kunta felt frozen and weak with fear, but the toubob showed no expression and turned his back again a moment later. Emboldened by the toubob's indifference, he sat up again – this time a little farther – when he heard a singing sound in the distance gradually growing louder. Not far ahead of them he saw a toubob seated on the back of another animal like the one pulling the rolling box. The toubob held a coiled whip, and a chain from the animal was linked to the wrist cuffs of about twenty blacks – or most of them were black, some brown – walking in a line ahead of him.

Kunta blinked and squinted to see better. Except for two fully clothed women, they were all men and all bare from the waist up, and they were singing with deep mournfulness. He listened very carefully to the words, but they made no sense whatever to him. As the rolling box slowly passed them, neither the blacks nor the toubob so much as glanced in their direction, though they were close enough to touch. Most of their backs, Kunta saw, were criss-crossed with whip scars, some of them fresh, and he guessed at some of their tribes: Foulah, Yoruba, Mauretanian, Wolof, Mandinka. Of those he was more certain than of the others, most of whom had had the misfortune to have toubob for fathers.

Beyond the blacks, as far as Kunta's runny eyes would let him see, there stretched vast fields of crops growing in different colours.

Alongside the road was a field planted with what he recognized as maize. Just as it was back in Juffure after the harvest, the stalks were brown and stripped of ears.

Soon afterwards, the toubob leaned over, took some bread and some kind of meat out of a sack beneath the seat, broke off a piece of each, and set them on the seat between him and the black one, who picked it up with a tip of his hat and began to eat. After a few moments the black one turned in his seat, took a long look at Kunta, who was watching intently, and offered him a chunk of bread. He could smell it from where he lay, and the fragrance made his mouth water, but he turned his head away. The black one shrugged and popped it into his own mouth.

Trying not to think about his hunger, Kunta looked out over the side of the box and saw, at the far end of a field, what appeared to be a small cluster of people bent over, seemingly at work. He thought they must be black, but they were too far away to be sure. He sniffed the air, trying to pick up their scent, but couldn't.

As the sun was setting, the box passed another like it, going in the opposite direction, with a toubob at the reins and three first-kafo black children riding behind him. Trudging in chains behind the box were seven adult blacks, four men wearing ragged clothes and three women in coarse gowns. Kunta wondered why these were not also singing; then he saw the deep despair on their faces as they flashed past. He wondered where toubob was taking them.

As the dusk deepened, small black bats began squeaking and darting jerkily here and there, just as they did in Africa. Kunta heard the toubob say something to the black one, and before much longer the box turned off onto a small road. Kunta sat up and soon, in the distance, saw a large white house through the trees. His stomach clutched up: What in the name of Allah was to happen now? Was it here that he was going to be eaten? He slumped back down in the box and lay as if he were lifeless.

42

As the box rolled closer and closer to the house, Kunta began to smell – and then hear – more black people. Raising himself up on his elbows, he could just make out three figures in the early dusk as they approached the wagon. The largest among them was swinging one of those small flames Kunta had become familiar with when the toubob had come down into the dark hold of the big canoe; only this one was enclosed in something clear and shiny rather than in metal. He had never seen anything like it before; it looked hard, but you could see through it as if it weren't there. He didn't have the chance to study it more closely, though, for the three blacks quickly stepped to one side as a new toubob strode past them and up to the box, which promptly stopped beside him. The two toubob greeted one another, and then one of the blacks held up the flame so that the toubob in the box could see better as he climbed down to join the other one. They clasped hands warmly and then walked off together towards the house.

Hope surged in Kunta. Would the black ones free him now? But he no sooner thought of it than the flame lit their faces as they stood looking at him over the sides of the wagon; they were laughing at him. What kind of blacks were these who looked down upon their own kind and worked as goats for the toubob? Where had they come from? They looked as Africans looked, but clearly they were not of Africa.

Then the one who had driven the rolling box clucked at the animal and snapped the thongs and the box moved ahead. The other blacks walked alongside, still laughing, until it stopped again. Climbing down, the driver walked back and in the light of the flame jerked roughly at Kunta's chain, making threatening sounds as he unlocked it under the seat, and then gestured for Kunta to get out.

Kunta fought down the impulse to leap for the throats of the four blacks. The odds were too high; his chance would come later. Every muscle in his body seemed to be screaming as he forced himself onto his knees and began to crab backwards in the box. When he took too long to suit them, two of the blacks grabbed Kunta, hoisted him roughly over the side, and half dropped him onto the ground. A moment later the driver had clicked the free end of Kunta's chain around a thick pole.

As he lay there, flooded with pain, fear, and hatred, one of the blacks set before him two tin containers. In the light of the flame, Kunta could see that one was nearly filled with water, and the other held some strange-looking, strange-smelling food. Even so, the saliva ran in Kunta's mouth and down in his throat; but he didn't permit even his eyes to move. The black ones watching him laughed.

Holding up the flame, the driver went over to the thick pole and lunged heavily against the locked chain, clearly for Kunta to see that it could not be broken. Then he pointed with his foot at the water and the food, making threatening sounds, and the others laughed again as the four of them walked away.

Kunta lay there on the ground in the darkness, waiting for sleep to claim them, wherever they had gone. In his mind, he saw himself rearing up and surging desperately again and again against the chain, with all of the strength that he could muster, until it broke and he could escape to . . . Just then he smelled a dog approaching him, and heard it curiously sniffing. Somehow he sensed that it was not his enemy. But then, as the dog came closer, he heard the sound of chewing and the click of teeth on the tin pan. Though he wouldn't have eaten it himself, Kunta leaped up in rage, snarling like a leopard. The dog raced away, and from a short distance started barking. Within a moment, a door had squeaked open nearby and someone was running towards him with a flame. It was the driver, and Kunta sat staring with cold fury as the driver anxiously examined the chain around the base of the post, and next where the chain was attached to the iron cuff around Kunta's ankle. In the dim yellow light, Kunta saw the driver's expression of satisfaction at the empty food plate. With a hoarse grunt, he walked back to his hut, leaving Kunta in the darkness wishing that he could fasten his hands around the throat of the dog.

After a while, Kunta groped around for the container of water and drank some of the contents, but it didn't make him feel any better; in fact, the strength felt drained from his body; it seemed as if he were only a shell. Abandoning the idea of breaking the chain – for now, anyway – he felt as if Allah had turned His back – but why? What thing so terrible had he ever done? He tried to review everything of any significance that he had ever done – right or wrong – up to the morning when he was cutting a piece of wood to make himself a drum and then, too late, heard a twig snap. It seemed to him that every time in his life when he had been punished, it had been because of carelessness and inattention.

Kunta lay listening to the crickets, the whirr of night birds, and the barking of distant dogs – and once to the sudden squeak of a mouse, then the crunch of its bones breaking in the mouth of an animal that had killed it. Every now and then he would tense up with the urge to run, but he knew that even if he were able to rip loose his chain, its rattling would swiftly awaken someone in the huts nearby.

He lay this way – with no thought of sleeping – until the first streaks of dawn. Struggling as well as his aching limbs would let him into a kneeling position, he began his suba prayer. As he was pressing his forehead against the earth, however, he lost his balance and almost fell over on his side; it made him furious to realize how weak he had become.

As the eastern sky slowly brightened, Kunta reached again for the water container and drank what was left. Hardly had he finished it when approaching footsteps alerted him to the return of the four black men. Hurriedly they hoisted Kunta back into the rolling box, which was driven to the large white house, where the toubob was waiting to get onto the seat again. And before he knew it they were back on the main road, headed in the same direction as before.

For a time in the clearing day, Kunta lay staring vacantly at the chain rattling across the floor of the box to where it was locked under the seat. Then, for a while, he let his eyes bore with hatred at the backs of the toubob and the black ahead. He wished he could kill them. He made himself remember that if he was to survive, having survived so much until now, that he must keep his senses collected, he must keep control of himself, he must make himself wait, he must not expend his energy until he knew that it was the right time.

It was around mid-morning when Kunta heard what he knew instantly was a blacksmith pounding on metal; lifting his head, Kunta strained his eyes to see and finally located the sound somewhere beyond a thick growth of trees they were passing. He saw that much forest had been freshly cut, the stumps grubbed up, and in some places, as the rolling box lurched along, Kunta saw and smelled greyish smoke rising from where dry brush was being burned. He wondered if the toubob were thus fertilizing the earth for the next season's crops, as it was done in Juffure.

Next, in the distance ahead, he saw a small square hut beside the road. It seemed to be made of logs, and in a cleared plot of earth before it, a toubob man was plodding behind a brown bullock. The toubob's hands were pressing down hard against the curving handles of some large thing pulled by the bullock that was tearing through the earth. As they came nearer, Kunta saw two more toubob – pale and thin – squatting on their haunches under a tree; three equally skinny swine were rooting around them, and some chickens were pecking for food. In the hut's doorway stood a she toubob with red hair. Then, dashing past her, came three small toubob shouting and waving towards the rolling box. Catching sight of Kunta, they shrieked with laughter and pointed; he stared at them as if they were hyena cubs. They ran alongside the wagon for a good way before turning back, and Kunta lay realizing that he had seen with his own eyes an actual family of toubob.

Twice more, far from the road, Kunta saw large white toubob houses similar to the one where the wagon had stopped the night before. Each was the height of two houses, as if one were on top of another; each had in front of it a row of three or four huge white poles as big around – and almost as tall – as trees; nearby each was a group of small, dark huts where Kunta guessed the blacks lived; and surrounding each was a vastness of cotton fields, all of them recently harvested, flecked here and there with a tuft of white.

Somewhere between these two great houses, the rolling box overtook a strange pair of people walking along the side of the road. At first Kunta thought they were black, but as the wagon came closer he saw that their skin was reddish-brown, and they had long black hair tied to hang down their backs like a rope, and they walked quickly, lightly in shoes and loincloths that seemed to be made of hide, and they carried bows and arrows. They weren't toubob, yet they weren't of Africa either; they even smelled different. What sort of people were they? Neither one seemed to notice the rolling box as it went by, enveloping them in dust.

As the sun began to set, Kunta turned his face towards the east, and by the time he had finished his silent evening prayer to Allah, dusk was gathering. He was getting so weak, after two days without accepting any of the food he had been offered, that he had to lie down limply in the bottom of the rolling box, hardly caring any more about what was happening around him.

But Kunta managed to raise himself up again and look over the side when the box stopped a little later. Climbing down, the driver hung one of those lights against the side of the box, got back in his seat, and resumed the trip. After a long while the toubob spoke briefly, and the black one replied; it was the first time since they had started out that day that the two of them had exchanged a sound. Again the box stopped, and the driver got out and tossed some kind of coverlet to Kunta, who ignored it. Climbing back up onto the seat, the driver and the toubob pulled coverlets over themselves and set out once again.

Though he was soon shivering, Kunta refused to reach for the coverlet and draw it over him, not wishing to give them that satisfaction. They offer me cover, he thought, yet they keep me in chains; and my own people not only stand by and let it happen but actually do the toubob's dirty business for him. Kunta knew only that he must escape from this dreadful place – or die in the attempt. He dared not dream that he would ever see Juffure again, but if he did, he vowed that all of The Gambia would learn what the land of toubob was really like.

Kunta was nearly numb with cold when the rolling box turned suddenly off the main road and onto a bumpier and smaller one. Again he forced his aching body upwards far enough to squint into the darkness – and there in the distance he saw the ghostly whiteness of another of the big houses. As on the previous night, the fear of what would befall him now coursed through Kunta as they pulled up in front of the house – but he couldn't even smell any signs of the toubob or black ones he expected to greet them.

When the box finally stopped, the toubob on the seat ahead of him dropped to the ground with a grunt, bent and squatted down several times to uncramp his muscles, then spoke briefly to the driver with a gesture back at Kunta, and then walked away towards the big house.

Still no other blacks had appeared, and as the rolling box creaked on ahead towards the nearby huts, Kunta lay in the back feigning indifference. But he was tense in every fibre, his pains forgotten. His nostrils detected the smell of other blacks nearby; yet no one came outside. His hopes rose further. Stopping the box near the huts, the black one climbed heavily and clumsily to the ground and trudged over to the nearest hut, the flame bobbing in his hand. As he pushed the door open, Kunta watched and waited, ready to spring, for him to go inside; but instead he turned and came back to the box. Putting his hands under the seat, he unclicked Kunta's chain and held the loose end in one hand as he walked around to the back of the box. Yet something made Kunta still hold back. The black one jerked the chain sharply and barked something roughly to Kunta. As the black one stood watching carefully, Kunta struggled onto all fours – trying to look even weaker than he felt – and began crawling backwards as slowly and clumsily as possible. As he had hoped, the black one lost patience, leaned close, and with one powerful arm, levered Kunta up and over the end of the wagon, and his upraised knee helped to break Kunta's fall to the ground.

At that instant, Kunta exploded upwards – his hands clamping around the driver's big throat like the bone-cracking jaws of a hyena. The flame dropped to the ground as the black one lurched backwards with a hoarse cry; then he came storming back upright with his big hands pounding, tearing, and clawing at Kunta's face and forearms. But somehow Kunta found the strength to grip the throat even tighter as he twisted his body desperately to avoid the driver's club-like blows with thrashing fists, feet, and knees. Kunta's grip would not be broken until the black one finally stumbled backwards and then down, with a deep gurgling sound, and then went limp.

Springing up, fearing above all another barking dog, Kunta slipped away like a shadow from the fallen driver and the overturned flame. He ran bent low, legs crashing through frosted stalks of cotton. His muscles, so long unused, screamed with pain, but the cold, rushing air felt good upon his skin, and he had to stop himself from whooping out loud with the pleasure of feeling so wildly free.

43

The thorny brambles and vines of the brush at the edge of the forest seemed to reach out and tear at Kunta's legs. Ripping them aside with his hands, he plunged on – stumbling and falling, picking himself up again – deeper and deeper into the forest. Or so he thought, until the trees began to thin and he burst suddenly into more low brush. Ahead of him was another wide cotton field, and beyond it yet another big white house with small dark huts beside it. With shock and panic, Kunta sprang back into the woods, realizing that all he had done was cross a narrow stretch of forest that separated two great toubob farms. Crouching behind a tree, he listened to the pounding of his heart and head, and began to feel a stinging in his hands, arms, and feet. Glancing down in the bright moonlight, he saw that they were cut and bleeding from the thorns. But what alarmed him more was that the moon was already down in the sky; it would soon be dawn. He knew that whatever he was going to do, he had little time to decide.

Stumbling back into motion, Kunta knew after only a little while that his muscles would not carry him much farther. He must retreat into the thickest part of the forest he could find and hide there. So he went clawing his way back, sometimes on all fours, his feet and arms and legs tangling in the vines, until at last he found himself in a dense grove of trees. Though his lungs were threatening to burst, Kunta considered climbing one of them, but the softness of the thick carpeting of leaves under his feet told him that many of the trees' leaves had fallen off, which could make him easily seen, so that his best concealment would be on the ground.

Crawling again, he settled finally – just as the sky began to lighten – in a place of deep undergrowth. Except for the wheeze of his own breath, everything was very still, and it reminded him of his long, lonely vigils guarding the groundnut fields with his faithful wuolo dog. It was just then that he heard in the distance the deep baying of a dog. Perhaps he had heard it only in his mind, he thought, snapping to alertness and straining his ears. But it came again – only now there were two of them. He didn't have much time.

Kneeling towards the east, he prayed to Allah for deliverance, and just as he finished, the deep-throated baying came again, closer this time. Kunta decided it was best to stay hidden where he was, but when he heard the howling once again – closer still – just a few minutes later, it seemed that they knew exactly where he was and his limbs wouldn't let him remain there a moment longer. Into the underbrush he crawled again, hunting for a deeper, even more secreted place. Every inch among the brambles raking at his hands and knees was torture, but with every cry from the dogs he scrambled faster and faster. Yet the barking grew ever louder and closer, and Kunta was sure that he could hear now the shouting of men behind the dogs.

He wasn't moving fast enough; springing up, he began to run – stumbling through the brambles – as quickly and quietly as his exhaustion would permit. Almost immediately he heard an explosion; the shock buckled his knees and sent him sprawling into a tangle of briars.

The dogs were snarling at the very edge of the thicket now. Quivering in terror, Kunta could even smell them. A moment later they were thrashing through the underbrush straight for him. Kunta made it up onto his knees just as the two dogs came crashing through the brush and leaped on him, yowling and slavering and snapping as they knocked him over, then sprang backwards to lunge at him again. Snarling himself, Kunta fought wildly to fend them off, using his hands like claws while he tried to crab backwards away from them. Then he heard the men shouting from the edge of the brush, and again there was an explosion, this time much louder. As the dogs relented somewhat in their attack, Kunta heard the men cursing and slashing through the brush with knives.

Behind the growling dogs, he saw first the black one he had choked. He held a huge knife in one hand, a short club and a rope in the other, and he looked murderous. Kunta lay bleeding on his back, jaws clenched to keep from screaming, expecting to be chopped into bits. Then Kunta saw the toubob who had brought him here appear behind the black one, his face reddish and sweating. Kunta waited for the flash and the explosion that he had learned on the big canoe could come from the firestick that a second toubob – one he hadn't seen before – pointed at him now. But it was the black one who now rushed forward furiously, raising his club, when the chief toubob shouted.

The black one halted, and the toubob shouted at the dogs, who drew farther back. Then the toubob said something to the black one, who now moved forward uncoiling his rope. A heavy blow to Kunta's head sent him into a merciful numbing shock. He was dimly aware of being trussed up so tightly that the rope bit into his already bleeding skin; then of being half lifted from among the brambles and made to walk. Whenever he lost his balance and fell down, a whip seared across his back. When they finally reached the forest's edge, Kunta saw three of the donkey-like animals tied near several trees.

As they approached the animals, he tried to bolt away again, but a vicious yank on the free end of the rope sent him tumbling down – and earned him a kick in the ribs. Now the second toubob, holding the rope, moved ahead of Kunta, jerking him stumbling towards a tree near where the animals were tied. The rope's free end was thrown over a lower limb, and the black one hauled on it until Kunta's feet barely touched the ground.

The chief toubob's whistling whip began to lash against Kunta's back. He writhed under the pain, refusing to make any sound, but each blow felt as if it had torn him in half. Finally he began screaming, but the lashing went on.

Kunta was hardly conscious when at last the whip stopped falling. He sensed vaguely that he was being lowered and crumpling onto the ground; then that he was being lifted and draped across the back of one of the animals; then he was aware of movement.

The next thing Kunta knew – he had no idea how much time had passed – he was lying spread-eagled on his back in some kind of hut. A chain, he noticed, was attached to an iron cuff on each wrist and ankle, and the four chains were fixed to the base of four poles at the corners of the hut. Even the slightest movement brought such excruciating pain that for a long while he lay completely still, his face wet with sweat and his breath coming in quick, shallow gasps.

Without moving, he could see that a small, square, open space above him was admitting daylight. Out of the corner of his eye, he could see a recessed place in the wall, and within it a mostly burned log and some ashes. On the other side of the hut, he saw a wide, flat, lumpy thing of cloth on the floor, with corn shucks showing through its holes; he guessed it might be used as a bed.

As dusk showed through the open space above him, Kunta heard – from very near by – the blowing of a strange-sounding horn. And before much more time had passed, he heard the voices of what he smelled were many black people passing near where he was. Then he smelled food cooking. As his spasms of hunger mingled with the pounding in his head and the stabbing pains in his back and his thorn-cut arms and legs, he berated himself for not having waited for a better time to escape, as a trapped animal would have done. He should have first observed and learned more of this strange place and its pagan people.

Kunta's eyes were closed when the hut's door squeaked open; he could smell the black one he had choked, who had helped to catch him. He lay still and pretended to be asleep – until a vicious kick in the ribs shot his eyes wide open. With a curse, the black one set something down just in front of Kunta's face, dropped a covering over his body, and went back out, slamming the door behind him.

The smell of the food before him hurt Kunta's stomach almost as much as the pain in his back. Finally, he opened his eyes. There was some kind of mush and some kind of meat piled upon a flat, round tin, and a squat, round gourd of water beside it. His spread-eagled wrists made it impossible to pick them up, but both were close enough for him to reach with his mouth. Just as he was about to take a bite, Kunta smelled that the meat was the filthy swine, and the bile from his stomach came spewing up and onto the tin plate.

Through the night, he lay drifting into and out of sleep and wondering about these black ones who looked like Africans but ate pig. It meant that they were all strangers – or traitors – to Allah. Silently he begged Allah's forgiveness in advance if his lips would ever touch any swine without his realizing it, or even if he ever ate from any plate that any swine meat had ever been on.

Soon after the dawn showed again through the square opening, Kunta heard the strange horn blow once more; then came the smell of food cooking, and the voices of the black ones hurrying back and forth. Then the man he despised returned, bringing new food and water. But when he saw that Kunta had vomited over the untouched plate that was already there, he bent down with a string of angry curses and rubbed the contents into Kunta's face. Then he set the new food and water before him, and left.

Kunta told himself that he would choke the food down later; he was too sick even to think about it now. After a little while, he heard the door open again; this time he smelled the stench of toubob. Kunta kept his eyes clamped shut, but when the toubob muttered angrily, he feared another kick and opened them. He found himself staring up at the hated face of the toubob who had brought him here; it was flushed with rage. The toubob made cursing sounds and told him with threatening gestures that if he didn't eat the food, he would get more beating. Then the toubob left.

Kunta managed to move his left hand far enough for the fingers to scratch up a small mound of the hard dirt where the toubob's foot had been. Pulling the dirt closer, Kunta pressed his eyes shut and appealed to the spirits of evil to curse forever the womb of the toubob and his family.

44

Kunta had counted four days and three nights in the hut. And each night he had lain listening to the singing from the huts nearby – and feeling more African than he ever felt in his own village. What kind of black people they must be, he thought, to spend their time *singing* here in the land of the toubob. He wondered how many of these strange black ones there were in all of toubob land, those who didn't seem to know or care who or what they were.

Kunta felt a special closeness to the sun each time it rose. He recalled what an old man who had been an alcala had said down in the darkness of the big canoe: 'Each day's new sun will remind us that it rose in our Africa, which is the navel of the earth.'

Although he was spread-eagled by four chains, he had practised until he had learned a way to inch forward or backward on his back and buttocks to study more closely the small but thick iron rings, like bracelets, that fastened the chains to the four poles at the hut's corners. The poles were about the size of his lower leg, and he knew there was no hope of his ever breaking one, or of pulling one from the hard-packed earth floor, for the upper ends went up through the hut's roof. With his eyes and then his fingers, Kunta carefully examined the small holes in the thick metal rings; he had seen his captors insert a narrow metal thing into these holes and turn them, making a *click* sound. When he shook one of the rings, it made the chain rattle – loud enough for someone to hear – so he gave that up. He tried putting one of the rings in his mouth and biting it as hard as he could; finally one of his teeth cracked, lancing pains through his head.

Seeking some dirt preferable to that of the floor in order to make a fetish to the spirits, Kunta scraped out with his fingers a piece of the reddish, hardened mud chinking between the logs. Seeing short, black bristles within the mud, he inspected one curiously; when he realized that it was a hair from the filthy swine, he flung it away – along with the dirt – and wiped off the hand that had held it.

On the fifth morning, the black one entered shortly after the wake-up horn had blown, and Kunta tautened when he saw that along with his usual short, flat club, the man carried two thick iron cuffs. Bending down, he locked each of Kunta's ankles within the cuffs, which were connected by a heavy chain. Only then did he unlock the four chains, one by one, that had kept Kunta spread-eagled. Free to move at last, Kunta couldn't stop himself from springing upwards – only to be struck down by the black one's waiting fist. As Kunta began pushing himself back upwards, a booted foot dug viciously into his ribs. Stumbling upwards once again in agony and rage, he was knocked down even harder. He hadn't realized how much the days of lying on his back had sapped his strength, and he lay now fighting for breath as the black one stood over him with an expression that told Kunta he would keep knocking him down until he learned who was the master.

Now the black one gestured roughly for Kunta to get up. When he couldn't raise his body even onto his hands and knees, the black one jerked him to his feet with a curse and shoved him forward, the ankle cuffs forcing Kunta to hobble awkwardly.

The full force of daylight in the doorway blinded him at first, but after a moment he began to make out a line of black people walking hastily near by in single file, followed closely by a toubob riding a 'hoss', as he had heard that strange animal called. Kunta knew from his smell that he was the one who had held the rope after Kunta had been trapped by the dogs. There were about ten or twelve blacks –

201

the women with red or white rags tied on their heads, most of the men and children wearing ragged straw hats, but a few were bareheaded, and as far as he could see, none of them wore a single saphie charm around their necks or arms. But some of the men carried what seemed to be long, stout knives, and the line seemed to be heading in the direction of the great fields. He thought that it must have been they whom he had heard at night doing all that singing. He felt nothing but contempt for them. Turning his blinking gaze, Kunta counted the huts they had come from: there were ten, including his own – all very small, like his, and they didn't have the stout look of the mud huts of his village, with their roofs of sweet-smelling thatch. They were arranged in rows of five each – positioned, Kunta noticed, so that whatever went on among the blacks living there could be seen from the big white house.

Abruptly the black one began jabbing at Kunta's chest with his finger, then exclaiming, 'You – you Toby!' Kunta didn't understand, and his face showed it, so the black one kept jabbing him and saying the same thing over and over. Slowly it dawned on Kunta that the black one was attempting to make him understand something he was saying in the strange toubob tongue.

When Kunta continued to stare at him dumbly, the black one began jabbing at his own chest. 'Me Samson!' he exclaimed. 'Samson!' He moved his jabbing finger again to Kunta. 'You To-by! Toby. Massa say you name Toby!'

When what he meant began to sink in, it took all of Kunta's self-control to grip his flooding rage without any facial sign of the slightest understanding. He wanted to shout 'I am Kunta Kinte, first son of Omoro, who is the son of the holy man Kairaba Kunta Kinte!'

Losing patience with Kunta's apparent stupidity, the black one cursed, shrugged his shoulders, and led him hobbling into another hut, where he gestured for Kunta to wash himself in a large, wide tin tub that held some water. The black one threw into the water a rag and a brown chunk of what Kunta's nose told him was something like the soap that Juffure women made of hot melted fat mixed with the lye of water dripped through wood ashes. The black one watched, scowling, as Kunta took advantage of the opportunity to wash himself. When he was through, the black one tossed to him some different toubob garments to cover his chest and legs, then a frayed hat of yellowish straw such as the others wore. How would these pagans fare under the heat of Africa's sun, Kunta wondered.

The black one led him next to still another hut. Inside, an old woman irritably banged down before Kunta a flat tin of food. He gulped down the thick gruel, and a bread resembling munko cake, and washed it down with some hot brown beefy-tasting broth from a gourd cup. Next they went to a narrow, cramped hut whose smell told of its use in advance. Pretending to pull down his lower garment, the black one hunched over a large hole cut into a plank seat and grunted heavily as if he were relieving himself. A small pile of corn-cobs lay in one corner, and Kunta didn't know what to make of them. But he guessed that the black one's purpose was to demon-strate the toubob's ways – of which he wished to learn all that he could, the better to escape.

As the black one led him past the next few huts, they went by an old man seated in some strange chair; it was rocking slowly back and forth as he wove dried cornshucks into what Kunta guessed was a broom. Without looking up, the old man cast towards him a not unkindly glance, but Kunta ignored it coldly.

Picking up one of the long, stout knives that Kunta had seen the others carrying, the black one motioned with his head towards the distant field, grunting and gesturing for Kunta to follow him. Hob-bling along in the iron cuffs – which were chafing his ankles – Kunta could see in the field ahead that the females and the younger blacks were bending up and down, gathering and piling dried cornstalks behind the older men in front of them, who slashed down the stalks with swishing blows of their long knives.

Most of the men's backs were bared and glistening with sweat. His eyes searched for any of the branding-iron marks such as his back bore – but he saw only the scars that had been left by whips. The toubob rode up on his 'hoss', exchanged words briefly with the black one, then fixed a threatening stare on Kunta as the black one ges-tured for his attention.

Slashing down about a dozen cornstalks, the black one turned, bent, and made motions for Kunta to pick them up and pile them as the others were doing. The toubob jerked his horse closer alongside Kunta, his whip cocked and the scowl on his face making his intent clear if Kunta should refuse to obey. Enraged at his helplessness, Kunta bent down and picked up two of the cornstalks. Hesitating, he heard the black one's knife swishing ahead. Bending over again, he picked up two more cornstalks, and two more. He could feel the stares of other black ones upon him from adjacent rows, and could see the feet of the toubob's horse. He could feel the relief of the other blacks, and at last the horse's feet moved away.

Without raising his head, Kunta saw that the toubob rode this way or that to wherever he saw someone who wasn't working swiftly enough to please him, and then with an angry shout, his lash would go cracking down across a back.

Off in the distance, Kunta saw that there was a road. On it, a few times during the hot afternoon, through the sweat pouring down his forehead and stinging his eyes, he caught glances of a lone rider on a horse, and twice he saw a wagon being drawn. Turning his head the other way, he could see the edge of the forest into which he had tried to escape. And from where he was piling the cornstalks now, he could see the forest's narrowness, which had helped him to get caught, because he had not realized that narrowness before. After a while, Kunta had to stop glancing in that direction, for the urge to spring up and bound towards those trees was almost irresistible. Each step he took, in any case, reminded him that he would never get five steps across the field wearing those iron hobbles. As he worked through the afternoon, Kunta decided that before he tried his next escape, he must find some kind of weapon to fight dogs and men with. No servant of Allah should ever fail to fight if he is attacked, he reminded himself. If it was dogs or men, wounded buffalo or hungry lions, no son of Omoro Kinte would ever entertain the thought of giving up.

It was after sundown when the horn sounded once again – this time in the distance. As Kunta watched the other blacks hurrying into a line, he wished he could stop thinking of them as belonging to the tribes they resembled, for they were but unworthy pagans not fit to mingle with those who had come with him on the big canoe.

But how stupid the toubob must be to have those of Fulani blood – even such poor specimens as these – picking up cornstalks instead of tending cattle; anyone knew that the Fulani were born to tend cattle, that indeed Fulani and cattle *talked* together. This thought was interrupted as the toubob on his 'hoss' cracked the whip to direct Kunta to the end of the line. As he obeyed, the squat, heavy woman at the end of the line took several quick forward steps, trying to get as far as possible from Kunta. He felt like spitting on her.

As they began to march – each hobbling step chafing at his ankles, which had been rubbed raw and were beginning to seep blood – Kunta heard some hounds barking far away. He shivered, remembering those that had tracked him and attacked him. Then his mind flashed a memory of how his own wuolo had died fighting the men who had captured him in Africa.

Back in his hut, Kunta kneeled and touched his forehead to the hard dirt floor in the direction in which he knew the next sun would rise. He prayed for a long time to make up for the two prayers he had been unable to perform out in the field, which would certainly have been interrupted by a lash across his back from the toubob who rode the 'hoss'.

After finishing his prayer, Kunta sat bolt upright and spoke softly for a while in the secret sira kango tongue, asking his ancestors to help him endure. Then – pressing between his fingers a pair of cock's feathers he had managed to pick up without being noticed while 'Samson' had led him around that morning – he wondered when he would get the chance to steal a fresh egg. With the feathers of the cock and some finely crushed fresh eggshell, he would be able to prepare a powerful fetish to the spirits, whom he would ask to bless the dust where his last footsteps had touched in his village. If that dust was blessed, his footprints would one day reappear in Juffure, where every man's footprints were recognizable to his neighbours, and they would rejoice at this sign that Kunta Kinte was still alive and that he would return safely to his village. Some day.

For the thousandth time, he relived the nightmare of his capture. If only the cracking twig that alerted him had snapped a single footstep earlier, he could have leaped and snatched up his spear. Tears of rage came welling up into Kunta's eyes. It seemed to him that for moons without end, all that he had known was being tracked and attacked and captured and chained.

No! He would not allow himself to act this way. After all, he was a man now, seventeen rains of age, too old to weep and wallow in self-pity. Wiping away the tears, he crawled onto his thin, lumpy mattress of dried cornshucks and tried to go to sleep – but all he could think of was the name 'To-by' he had been given, and rage rose in him once more. Furiously, he kicked his legs in frustration – but the movement only gouged the iron cuffs deeper into his ankles, which made him cry again.

Would he ever grow up to be a man like Omoro? He wondered if his father still thought of him; and if his mother had given to Lamin, Suwadu, and Madi the love that had been taken away from her when he was stolen. He thought of all of Juffure, and of how he had never realized more than now how very deeply he loved his village. As it had often been on the big canoe, Kunta lay for half the night with scenes of Juffure flashing through his mind, until he made himself shut his eyes and finally sleep came.

45

With each passing day, the hobbles on his ankles made it more and more difficult and painful for Kunta to get around. But he kept on telling himself that the chances of gaining freedom depended upon continuing to force himself to do whatever was wanted of him, all behind a mask of complete blankness and stupidity. As he did so, his eyes, ears, and nose would miss nothing – no weapon he might use – no toubob weakness he might exploit – until finally his captors were lulled into removing the cuffs. Then he would run away again.

Soon after the conch horn blew each morning, Kunta would limp outside to watch as the strange black ones emerged from their huts, the sleepiness still in their faces, and splashed themselves with water from buckets drawn up in the well near by. Missing the sound of the village women's pestles thumping the couscous for their families' morning meals, he would enter the hut of the old cooking woman and bolt down whatever she gave him – except for any filthy pork.

As he ate each morning, his eyes would search the hut for a possible weapon he might take without being detected. But apart from the black utensils that hung on hooks above her fireplace, there were only the round, flat tin things upon which she gave him what he ate with his fingers. He had seen her eating with a slender metal object that had three or four closely spaced points to stab the food with. He wondered what it was, and thought that although it was small it might be useful – if he could ever catch her eyes averted for a moment when the shiny object was within reach.

One morning, as he was eating his gruel, watching as the cooking woman cut a piece of meat with a knife he hadn't seen before and plotting what he would do with it if it were in his hands instead of hers, he heard a piercing squeal of agony from outside the hut. It was so close to his thoughts that he nearly jumped from his seat. Hobbling outside, he found the others already lined up for work – many of them still chewing the last bites of 'breakfast', lest they get a lashing for being late – while there on the ground beside them lay a swine thrashing about with blood pulsing from its cut throat as two black men lifted it into a steaming pot of water, then withdrew it and scraped off the hair. The swine's skin was the colour of a toubob, he noticed, as they suspended it by the heels, slit open its belly, and pulled out its insides. Kunta's nose stifled at the spreading smell of guts, and as he marched off with the others towards the fields, he had to suppress a shudder of revulsion at the thought of having to live among these pagan eaters of such a filthy animal.

There was frost on the cornstalks every morning now, and a haziness hung low over the fields until the heat of the climbing sun would burn it away. Allah's powers never ceased to amaze Kunta – that even in a place as distant as this toubob land was across the big water, Allah's sun and moon still rose and crossed the sky; though the sun was not so hot nor the moon so beautiful as in Juffure. It was only the people in this accursed place who seemed not of Allah's doing. The toubob were inhuman, and as for the blacks, it was simply senseless to try to understand them.

When the sun reached the middle of the sky, again the conch horn blew, signalling another line-up for the arrival of a wooden sled pulled by an animal similar to a horse, but more resembling a huge donkey, which Kunta had overheard being spoken of as a 'mule'. Walking beside the sled was the old cooking woman, who proceeded to pass out flat cakes of bread and a gourdful of some kind of stew to each person in the line, who either stood or sat and gulped it down, then drank some water dipped from a barrel that was also on the sled. Every day, Kunta warily smelled the stew before tasting it, to make sure he didn't put any swine meat into his mouth, but it usually contained only vegetables and no meat that he could see or smell at all. He felt better about eating the bread, for he had seen some of the black women making corn into meal by beating it in a mortar with a pestle of stone, about as it was done in Africa, although Binta's pestle was made of wood.

Some days they served foods Kunta knew of from his home, such as groundnuts, and kanjo – which was called 'okra' – and so-so, which was called 'black-eyed peas'. And he saw how much these black ones loved the large fruit that he heard here being called 'watermelon'. But he saw that Allah appeared to have denied these people the mangoes, the hearts of palm, the breadfruits, and so many of the other delicacies that grew almost anywhere one cared to look on the vines and trees and bushes in Africa.

Every now and then the toubob who had brought Kunta to this place – the one they called 'massa' – rode out into the fields when they were working. In his whitish straw hat, as he spoke to the toubob field boss, he gestured with a long, slender, plaited leather switch, and Kunta noticed that the toubob 'oberseer' grinned and shuffled almost as much as the blacks whenever he was around.

Many such strange things happened each day, and Kunta would sit thinking about them back in his hut while he waited to find sleep.

These black ones seemed to have no concern in their lives beyond pleasing the toubob with his lashing whip. It sickened him to think how these black ones jumped about their work whenever they saw a toubob, and how, if that toubob spoke a word to them, they rushed to do whatever he told them to. Kunta couldn't fathom what had happened to so destroy their minds that they acted like goats and monkeys. Perhaps it was because they had been born in this place rather than in Africa, because the only homes they had ever known were the toubob's huts of logs glued together with mud and swine bristles. These black ones had never known what it meant to sweat under the sun not for toubob masters but for themselves and their own people.

But no matter how long he stayed among them, Kunta vowed never to become *like* them, and each night his mind would go exploring again into ways to escape from this despised land. He couldn't keep from reviling himself almost nightly for his previous failure to get away. Playing back in his mind what it had been like among the thorn bushes and the slavering dogs, he knew that he must have a better plan for the next time. First he had to make himself a saphie charm to insure safety and success. Then he must either find or make some kind of weapon. Even a sharpened stick could have speared through those dogs' bellies, he thought, and he could have been away again before the black one and the toubob had been able to cut their way through the underbrush to where they had found him fighting off the dogs. Finally, he must acquaint himself with the surrounding countryside so that when he escaped again, he would know where to look for better hiding places.

Though he often lay awake half the night, restless with such thoughts, Kunta always awoke before the first crowing of the cocks, which always aroused the other fowl. The birds in this place, he noticed, merely twittered and sang – nothing like the deafening squawks of great flocks of green parrots that had opened the mornings in Juffure. There didn't seem to be any parrots here, or monkeys either, which always began the day at home by chattering angrily in the trees overhead, breaking off sticks and hurling them to the ground at the people underneath. Nor had Kunta seen any goats here – a fact he found no less incredible than that these people kept swine in pens – 'pigs' or 'hogs', they called them – and even *fed* the filthy things.

But the squealing of the swine, it seemed to Kunta, was no uglier than the language of the toubob who so closely resembled them. He would have given anything to hear even a sentence of Mandinka, or any other African tongue. He missed his chain-mates from the big canoe – even those who weren't Moslem – and he wondered what had happened to them. Where had they been taken? To other toubob farms such as this one? Wherever they were, were they longing as he was to hear once again the sweetness of their own tongues – and yet feeling shut out and alone, as he did, because they knew nothing of the toubob language?

Kunta realized that he would have to learn something of this strange speech if he was ever to understand enough about the toubob or his ways to escape from him. Without letting anyone know, he already recognized some words: 'pig', 'hog', 'watermelon', 'black-eyed peas', 'oberseer', 'massa', and especially 'yes-suh, massa', which was about the only thing he ever heard the black ones say to them. He had also heard the black ones describe the she toubob who lived with 'massa' in the big white house as 'the missus'. Once, from a distance, Kunta had glimpsed her, a bony creature the colour of a toad's underbelly, as she walked around cutting off some flowers among the vines and bushes that grew alongside the big house.

Most of the other toubob words that Kunta heard still confused him. But behind his expressionless mask, he tried hard to make sense of them, and slowly he began to associate various sounds with certain objects and actions. But one sound in particular was extremely puzzling to him, though he heard it exclaimed over and over nearly every day by toubob and blacks alike. What, he wondered, was a 'nigger'?

46

With the cutting and piling of the cornstalks at last completed, the 'oberseer' began assigning different blacks to a variety of tasks after the conch horn blew each dawn. One morning Kunta was given the job of snapping loose from their thick vines and piling onto a 'wagon', as he'd learned they called the rolling boxes, a load of large, heavy vegetables the colour of over-ripe mangoes and somewhat resembling the big gourds that women in Juffure dried out and cut in half to make household bowls. The blacks here called them 'punkins'.

Riding with the 'punkins' on the wagon to unload them at a large building called the 'barn', Kunta was able to see that some of the black men were sawing a big tree into thick sections and splitting them with axes and wedges into firewood that children were stacking into long rows as high as their heads. In another place, two men were hanging over thin poles the large leaves of what his nose told him was the filthy pagan tobacco; he had smelled it once before on one of the trips he had taken with his father.

As he rode back and forth to the 'barn', he saw that just as it was done in his own village, many things were being dried for later use. Some women were collecting a thick brown 'sagegrass', he heard them call it, and tying it into bundles. And some of the garden's vegetables were being spread out on cloths to dry. Even moss – which had been gathered by groups of children and plunged into boiling water – was being dried as well; he had no idea why.

It turned his stomach to watch – and listen – as he passed a pen where still more swine were being butchered. Their hair, too, he noticed, was being dried and saved – probably for mortar – but the thing that really sickened him was to see the swines' bladders being removed, blown up, tied at the ends, and hung up to dry along a fence; Allah only knew for what unholy purpose.

When he had finished harvesting and storing the 'punkins', Kunta was sent with several others to a grove of trees, the limbs of which they were told to shake vigorously so that the nuts growing in them would fall to the ground, where they were picked up by first-kafo children carrying baskets. Kunta picked up one of the nuts and hid it in his clothes to try later when he was alone; it wasn't bad.

When the last of these tasks was done, the men were put to work repairing things that needed it. Kunta helped another man fix a fence. And the women seemed to be busy in a general cleaning of the big white house and their own huts. He saw some of them washing things, first boiling them in a large black tub, then rubbing them up and down against a wrinkled piece of tin in soapy water; he wondered why none of them knew how to wash clothing properly by beating it against rocks.

Kunta noticed that the whip of the 'oberseer' seemed to strike down upon someone's back much less often than before. He felt in the atmosphere something similar to the time in Juffure when the harvest had all been put safely into the storehouses. Even before the evening's conch horn would blow to announce the end of the day's work, some of the black men would begin cavorting and prancing and singing among themselves. The 'oberseer' would wheel his horse around and brandish his whip, but Kunta could tell he didn't really mean it. And soon the other men would join in, and then the women – singing words that made no sense at all to Kunta. He was so filled with disgust for all of them that he was glad when the conch horn finally signalled for them to return to their huts.

In the evenings, Kunta would sit down sideways just inside the doorway of his hut, heels flat against the packed dirt floor to minimize the iron cuffs' contact with his festering ankles. If there was any light breeze, he enjoyed feeling it blowing against him, and thinking about the fresh carpet of gold and crimson leaves he would find under the trees the next morning. At such times, his mind would wander back to harvest-season evenings in Juffure, with the mosquitoes and other insects tormenting the people as they sat around the smoky night fires and settled into long conversations that would be punctuated now and then by the distant snarling of leopards and the screaming of hyenas.

One thing he didn't hear, it occurred to him, and hadn't heard since he left Africa, was the sound of drums. The toubob probably didn't allow these black people to have any drums; that had to be the reason. But why? Was it because the toubob knew and feared how the sound of the drums could quicken the blood of everyone in a village, until even the little children and the toothless old ones would dance wildly? Or how the rhythm of the drums would drive wrestlers to their greatest feats of strength? Or how the hypnotic beat could send warriors into a frenzy against their enemies? Or perhaps the toubob were simply afraid to allow a form of communication they couldn't understand that could travel the distance between one farm and another.

But these heathen blacks wouldn't understand drumtalk any better than the toubob. Kunta was forced to concede, though – if only with great reluctance – that these pagan blacks might not be totally irredeemable. Ignorant as they were, some of the things they did were purely African, and he could tell that they were totally unaware of it themselves. For one thing, he had heard all his life the very same sounds of exclamation, accompanied by the very same hand gestures and facial expressions. And the way these blacks moved their bodies was also identical. No less so was the way these blacks laughed when they were among themselves – with their whole bodies, just like the people of Juffure.

And Kunta had been reminded of Africa in the way that black women here wore their hair tied up with strings into very tight plaits – although African women often decorated their plaits with colourful beads. And the women of this place knotted cloth pieces over their heads, although they didn't tie them correctly. Kunta saw that even some of these black men wore their hair in short plaits, too, as some men did in Africa.

Kunta also saw Africa in the way that black children here were trained to treat their elders with politeness and respect. He saw it in the way that mothers carried their babies with their plump little legs straddling the mothers' bodies. He noticed even such small customs as how the older ones among these blacks would sit in the evenings rubbing their gums and teeth with the finely crushed end of a twig, which would have been lemongrass root in Juffure. And though he found it difficult to understand how they could do it here in toubob land, Kunta had to admit that these blacks' great love of singing and dancing was unmistakably African.

But what really began to soften his heart somewhat towards these strange people was the fact that over the past moon, their great showing of distaste for him had continued only when the 'oberseer' or the 'massa' was around. When Kunta came by anywhere the blacks were among themselves, most of them by now would quickly nod, and he would notice their expressions of concern for the worsening condition of his left ankle. Though he always coldly ignored them and hobbled on, he would sometimes find himself later almost wishing that he had returned their nods.

One night, when Kunta had fallen asleep but drifted again into wakefulness, as he often did, he lay staring up into the darkness and feeling that Allah had somehow, for some reason, *willed* him to be here in this place amid the lost tribe of a great black family that reached its roots back among the ancient forefathers; but unlike himself, these black ones in this place had no knowledge whatsoever of who they were and where they'd come from.

Feeling around him, in some strange way, the presence of his holyman grandfather, Kunta reached out into the darkness. There was nothing to be felt, but he began speaking aloud to the Alquaran Kairaba Kunta Kinte, imploring him to make known the purpose of his mission here, if there be any. He was startled to hear the sound of his own voice. Up to this moment in the toubob's land, he had never uttered a sound addressed to anyone but Allah, except for those cries that had been torn from him by a lash.

The next morning, as he joined the others in line for the march to work, Kunta almost caught himself saying, 'Mornin',' as he had heard them greet each other every day. But though he knew enough toubob words by now not only to understand a good deal of what was said to him but also to make himself somewhat understood as well, something made him decide to continue keeping that knowledge to himself.

It occurred to Kunta that these blacks masked their true feelings for the toubob as carefully as he did his changing attitude towards *them*. He had by now many times witnessed the blacks' grinning faces turn to bitterness the instant a toubob turned his head away. He had seen them break their working tools on purpose, and then act totally unaware of how it happened as the 'oberseer' bitterly cursed them for their clumsiness. And he had seen how blacks in the field, for all their show of rushing about whenever the toubob was nearby, were really taking twice as much time as they needed to do whatever they were doing.

He was beginning to realize, too, that like the Mandinkas' own secret sira kango language, these blacks shared some kind of communication known only among themselves. Sometimes when they were working out in the field, Kunta's glance would catch a small, quick gesture or movement of the head. Or one of them would utter some strange, brief exclamation; at unpredictable intervals another, and then another, would repeat it, always just beyond the hearing of the 'oberseer' as he rode about on his horse. And sometimes with him right there among them, they would begin singing something that told Kunta – even though he couldn't understand it – that some message was being passed, just as the women had done for the men on the big canoe.

When darkness had fallen among the huts and the lamp lights no longer glowed from the windows in the big house, Kunta's sharp ears would detect the swift rustling of one or two blacks slipping away from 'slave row' – and a few hours later, slipping back again. He wondered where they were going and for what – and why they were crazy enough to come back. And the next morning in the fields, he would try to guess which of them had done it. Whoever it was, he thought he just might possibly learn to trust them.

Two huts away from Kunta, the blacks would seat themselves around the small fire of the old cooking woman every evening after 'supper', and the sight would fill Kunta with a melancholy memory of Juffure, except that the women here sat with the men, and some of both sexes were puffing away on pagan tobacco pipes that now and then glowed dully in the gathering darkness. Listening intently from

213

where he sat just inside his doorway, Kunta could hear them talking over the rasping of the crickets and the distant hooting of owls in the forest. Though he couldn't understand the words, he felt the bitterness in their tone.

Even in the dark, Kunta by now could picture in his mind the face of whichever black was talking. His mind had filed away the voices of each of the dozen adults, along with the name of the tribe he felt that particular one most resembled. He knew which ones among them generally acted more carefree, and which seldom even smiled, a few of them not even around the toubob.

These evening meetings had a general pattern that Kunta had learned. The first talker was usually the woman who cooked in the big house. She mimicked things said by both the 'massa' and the 'missus'. Then he heard the big black one who had captured him imitating the 'oberseer', and he listened with astonishment as the others all but choked trying to stifle their laughter, lest they be heard in the big white house.

But then the laughter would subside and they would sit around talking among themselves. Kunta heard the helpless, haunted tone of some, and the anger of others, even though he grasped only a little of what they discussed. He had the feeling that they were recalling things that had happened to them earlier in their lives. Some of the women in particular would be talking and then suddenly break into tears. Finally the talking would grow quiet as one of the women began to sing, and the others joined in. Kunta couldn't understand the words – 'No-body knows de troubles I'se seed' – but he felt the sadness in the singing.

At last there came a voice that Kunta knew was the oldest man among them, the one who sat in the rocking chair and wove things of cornshucks, and who blew the conch horn. The others would bow their heads, and he would begin speaking slowly what Kunta guessed was some kind of prayer, though it was certainly not to Allah. But Kunta remembered what was said by the old alcala down in the big canoe: 'Allah knows every language.' While the prayer continued, Kunta kept hearing the same odd sound exclaimed sharply by both the old man and others who kept interrupting him with it: 'Oh Lawd!' He wondered if this 'Oh Lawd' was their Allah.

A few days later, the night winds began to blow with a coldness beyond any that Kunta had ever felt, and he woke up to find the last leaves stripped from the trees. As he stood shivering in line to go out to the fields, he was bewildered when the 'oberseer' directed everyone into the barn instead. Even the massa and the missus were there,

214

and with them four other finely dressed toubob who watched and cheered as the blacks were separated into two groups and made to race each other at ripping off and flinging aside the whitened, dried outside shucks from the piled harvest of corn.

Then the toubob and the blacks – in two groups – ate and drank their fill. The old black man who prayed at night then took up some kind of musical instrument with strings running down its length – it reminded Kunta of the ancient kora from his own homeland – and began to make some very odd music on it by jerking some kind of wand back and forth across the strings. The other blacks got up and began to dance – wildly – as the watching toubob, even the 'oberseer', gleefully clapped and shouted from the sidelines. Their faces reddened with excitement, all the toubob suddenly stood up, and as the blacks shrank to the side, they clapped their way out into the middle of the floor and began to dance in an awkward way while the old man played as if he had gone mad and the other blacks jumped up and down and clapped and screamed as if they were seeing the greatest performance of their lives.

It made Kunta think of a story he had been told by his beloved old Grandmother Nyo Boto when he was in the first kafo. She had told how the king of a village had called together all of the musicians and commanded them to play their very best for him to dance for the people, including even the slaves. And the people were all delighted and they left all singing loudly to the skies and there had never been another king like him.

Back in his hut later that night reflecting upon what he had seen, it occurred to Kunta that in some strong, strange and very deep way, the blacks and the toubob had some need for each other. Not only during the dancing in the barn, but also on many other occasions, it had seemed to him that the toubob were at their happiest when they were close around the black ones – even when they were beating them.

47

Kunta's left ankle had become so infected that pus draining from the wound all but covered the iron cuff with a sickly yellow slickness, and his crippled limping finally caused the 'oberseer' to take a close look. Turning his head away, he told Samson to remove the cuffs.

It was still painful to raise his foot, but Kunta was so thrilled to be unfettered that he hardly felt it. And that night, after the others had gone to bed and all had become still, Kunta limped outside and stole away once again. Crossing a field in the opposite direction from the one he had fled across the last time, he headed towards what he knew was a wider, deeper forest on the other side. He had reached a ravine and was clambering up the far side on his belly when he heard the first sound of a movement in the distance. He lay still with his heart pounding as he heard heavy footfalls approaching and finally the hoarse voice of Samson cursing and shouting, 'Toby! Toby!' Gripping a stout stick he had sharpened into a crude spear, Kunta felt strangely calm, almost numb, as his eyes coldly watched the bulky silhouette moving quickly this way and that in the brush at the top of the ravine. Something made him sense that Samson feared for himself if Kunta succeeded in getting away. Closer and closer he stalked – Kunta coiled tight but motionless as a stone – and then the moment came. Hurling the spear with all his might, he grunted slightly with the pain it caused and Samson, hearing him, sprang instantly to one side; it missed him by a hair.

Kunta tried to run, but the weakness of his ankles made him hardly able to keep upright, and when he whirled to fight, Samson was upon him, slamming with his greater weight behind each blow, until Kunta was driven to the earth. Hauling him back upwards Samson kept pounding, aiming only at his chest and belly, as Kunta tried to keep his body twisting as he gouged and bit and clawed. Then one massive blow sent him crashing down again, this time to stay. He couldn't even move to defend himself any further.

Gasping for breath, Samson tied Kunta's wrists tightly together with a rope, and then began jerking Kunta along by its free end, back towards the farm, kicking him savagely whenever he stumbled or faltered, and cursing him every step of the way.

It was all Kunta could do to keep staggering and lurching behind Samson. Dizzy from pain and exhaustion – and disgust with himself – he grimly anticipated the beatings he would receive when they reached his hut. But when they finally arrived – shortly before dawn – Samson only gave him another kick or two and then left him alone lying in a heap.

Kunta was so used up that he trembled. But with his teeth he began to gnash and tear at the fibres of the rope binding his wrists together, until his teeth hurt like flashes of fire. But the rope finally came apart just as the conch horn blew. Kunta lay weeping. He had failed again, and he prayed to Allah.

Through the days that followed, it was as if he and Samson shared some secret pact of hatred. Kunta knew how closely he was being watched; he knew that Samson was waiting for any excuse to hurt him in a manner the toubob would approve. Kunta responded by going through the motions of doing whatever work he was given to do as if nothing had happened – but even faster and more efficiently than before. He had noticed how the 'oberseer' paid less attention to those who worked the hardest or did the most grinning. Kunta couldn't bring himself to grin, but with grim satisfaction he noted that the more he sweated, the less often the lash fell across his back.

One evening after work, Kunta was passing near the barn when he spotted a thick iron wedge lying half concealed among some of the sawed sections of trees where the 'oberseer' had two men splitting firewood. Glancing around quickly in all directions, and seeing no one watching, Kunta snatched up the wedge and, concealing it in his shirt, hurried to his hut. Using it to dig a hole in the hard dirt floor, he placed the wedge in the hole, packed the loose dirt back over it, then beat it down carefully with a rock until the floor looked completely undisturbed.

He spent a sleepless night worrying that a wedge discovered missing might cause all of the cabins to be searched. He felt better when there was no outcry the following day, but he still wasn't sure just how he might employ the wedge to help himself escape, when that time came again.

What he really wanted to get his hands on was one of those long knives that the 'oberseer' would issue to a few of the men each morning. But each evening he would see the 'oberseer' demanding the knives back and counting them carefully. With one of those knives, he could cut brush to move more quickly within a forest, and if he had to, he could kill a dog – or a man.

One cold afternoon almost a moon later – the sky bleak and slaty – Kunta was on his way across one of the fields to help another man repair a fence when, to his astonishment, what looked like salt began to fall from the sky, at first lightly, then more rapidly and thickly. As

217

the salt became a flaky whiteness, he heard the blacks nearby exclaiming, 'Snow!' and guessed that was what they called it. When he bent down to pick some of it up, it was cold to his touch – and even colder when he licked it off a finger with his tongue. It stung, and it had no taste whatever. He tried to smell it, but not only did there seem to be no odour either, it also disappeared into watery nothingness. And wherever he looked on the ground was a whitish film.

But by the time he reached the other side of the field, the 'snow' had stopped and even begun to melt away. Hiding his amazement, Kunta composed himself and nodded silently to his black partner, who was waiting by the broken fence. They set to work – Kunta helping the other man to string a kind of metal twine that he called 'wire'. After a while they reached a place almost hidden by tall grass, and as the other man hacked some of it down with the long knife he carried, Kunta's eyes were gauging the distance between where he stood and the nearest woods. He knew that Samson was nowhere near and the 'oberseer' was keeping watch in another field that day. Kunta worked busily, to give the other man no suspicion of what was in his mind. But his breath came tensely as he stood holding the wire tight and looking down on the head of the man bent over his work. The knife had been left a few steps behind them, where the chopping of the brush had stopped.

With a silent prayer to Allah, Kunta clasped his hands together, lifted them high, and brought them down across the back of the man's neck with all the violence of which his slight body was capable. The man crumpled without a sound, as if he had been pole-axed. Within a moment, Kunta had bound the man's ankles and wrists with the wire. Snatching up the long knife, Kunta suppressed the impulse to stab him – this was not the hated Samson – and went running towards the wood, bent over almost double. He felt a lightness, as if he were running in a dream, as if this weren't really happening at all.

He came out of it a few moments later – when he heard the man he had left alive yelling at the top of his lungs. He should have killed him, Kunta thought, furious with himself, as he tried to run yet faster. Instead of fighting his way deeply into the underbrush when he reached the woods, he skirted it this time. He knew that he had to achieve distance first, then concealment. If he got far enough fast enough, he would have time to find a good place to hide and rest before moving on under cover of the night.

Kunta was prepared to live in the woods as the animals did. He had learned many things about this toubob land by now, together with what he already knew from Africa. He would capture rabbits and other rodents with snare traps and cook them over a fire that wouldn't smoke. As he ran, he stayed in the area where the brush would conceal him but wasn't thick enough to slow him down.

By nightfall, Kunta knew that he had run a good distance. Yet he kept going, crossing gullies and ravines, and for quite a way down the bed of a shallow stream. Only when it was completely dark did he allow himself to stop, hiding himself in a spot where the brush was dense but from which he could easily run if he had to. As he lay there in the darkness, he listened carefully for the sound of dogs. But there was nothing but stillness all around him. Was it possible? Was he really going to make it this time?

Just then he felt a cold fluttering on his face, and reached up with his hand. 'Snow' was falling again! Soon he was covered – and surrounded – by whiteness as far as he could see. Silently it fell, deeper and deeper, until Kunta began to fear he was going to be buried in it; he was already freezing. Finally he couldn't stop himself from leaping up and running to look for better cover.

He had run a good way when he stumbled and fell; he wasn't hurt, but when he looked back, he saw with horror that his feet had left a trail in the snow so deep that a blind man could follow him. He knew that there was no way he could erase the tracks, and he knew that the morning was now not far away. The only possible answer was more distance. He tried to increase his speed, but he had been running most of the night, and his breath was coming in laboured gasps. The long knife had begun to feel heavy; it would cut brush, but it wouldn't melt 'snow'. The sky was beginning to lighten in the east when he heard, far ahead of him, the faint sound of conch horns. He changed course in the next stride. But he had the sinking feeling that there was nowhere he could find to rest safely amid this blanketing whiteness.

When he heard the distant baying of the dogs, a rage flooded up in him such as he had never felt before. He ran like a hunted leopard, but the barking grew louder and louder, and finally, when he glanced back over his shoulder for the tenth time, he saw them gaining on him. The men couldn't be far behind. Then he heard a gun fire, and somehow it propelled him forward even faster than before. But the dogs caught up with him anyway. When they were but strides away, Kunta whirled and crouched down, snarling back at them. As they came lunging forward with their fangs bared, he too lunged at them, slashing open the first dog's belly with a single sideways swipe of the knife; with another blur of his arm, he hacked the blade between the eyes of the next one.

Springing away, Kunta began running again. But soon he heard the men on horses crashing through the brush behind him, and he all but dived for the deeper brush where the horses couldn't go. Then there was another shot, and another – and he felt a flashing pain in his leg. Knocked down in a heap, he had staggered upright again when the toubob shouted and fired again, and he heard the bullets thud into trees by his head. Let them kill me, thought Kunta; I will die as a man should. Then another shot hit the same leg, and it smashed him down like a giant fist. He was snarling on the ground when he saw the 'oberseer' and another toubob coming towards him with their guns levelled and he was about to leap up and force them to shoot him again and be done with it, but the wounds in his leg wouldn't let him rise.

The other toubob held his gun at Kunta's head as the 'oberseer' jerked off Kunta's clothing until he stood naked in the snow, the blood trickling down his leg and staining the whiteness at his feet. Cursing with each breath, the 'oberseer' knocked Kunta all but senseless with his fist; then both of them tied him facing a large tree, with his wrists bound on the other side.

The lash began cutting into the flesh across Kunta's shoulders and back, with the 'oberseer' grunting and Kunta shuddering under the force of each blow. After a while Kunta couldn't stop himself from screaming with the pain, but the beating went on until his sagging body pressed against the tree. His shoulders and back were covered with long, half-opened bleeding welts that in some places exposed the muscles beneath. He couldn't be sure, but the next thing Kunta knew he had the feeling he was falling. Then he felt the coldness of the snow against him and everything went black.

He came to in his hut, and along with his senses, pain returned – excruciating and enveloping. The slightest movement made him cry out in agony; and he was back in chains. But even worse, his nose informed him that his body was wrapped from feet to chin in a large cloth soaked with grease of the swine. When the old cooking woman came in with food, he tried to spit at her, but succeeded only in throwing up. He thought he saw compassion in her eyes.

Two days later, he was awakened early in the morning by the sounds of festivities. He heard black people outside the big house shouting 'Christmas gif', Massa!' and he wondered what they could possibly have to celebrate. He wanted to die, so that his soul could join the ancestors; he wanted to be done forever with misery unending in this toubob land, so stifling and stinking that he couldn't draw a clean breath in it. He boiled with fury that instead of beating him like a man, the toubob had stripped him naked. When he became well, he would take revenge – and he would escape again. Or he would die.

48

When Kunta finally emerged from his hut, again with both of his ankles shackled, most of the other blacks avoided him, rolling their eyes in fear of being near him, and moving quickly elsewhere, as if he were a wild animal of some kind. Only the old cooking woman and the old man who blew the conch horn would look at him directly.

Samson was nowhere to be seen. Kunta had no idea where he had gone, but Kunta was glad. Then, a few days later, he saw the hated black one bearing the unhealed marks of a lash; he was gladder still. But at the slightest excuse, the lash of the toubob 'oberseer' fell once again on Kunta's back as well.

He knew every day that he was being watched as he went through the motions of his work, like the others moving more quickly when the toubob came anywhere near, then slowing down as they left. Unspeaking, Kunta did whatever he was ordered to do. And when the day was over, he carried his melancholy – deep within himself – from the fields back to the dingy little hut where he slept.

In his loneliness, Kunta began talking to himself, most often in imaginary conversations with his family. He would talk to them mostly in his mind, but sometimes aloud. 'Fa,' he would say, 'these black ones are not like us. Their bones, their blood, their sinews, their hands, their feet are not their own. They live and breathe not for themselves but for the toubob. Nor do they own anything at all, not even their own children. They are fed and nursed and bred for others.'

'Mother,' he would say, 'these women wear cloths upon their heads, but they do not know how to tie them; there is little that they cook that does not contain the meat or the greases of the filthy swine,

221

and many of them have lain down with the toubob, for I see their children who are cursed with the sasso-borro half colour.'

And he would talk with his brothers Lamin, Suwadu and Madi, telling them that even the wisest of the elders could never really adequately impress upon them the importance of realizing that the most vicious of the forest animals was not half as dangerous as the toubob.

And so the moons passed in this way, and soon the spikes of 'ice' had fallen and melted into water. And before long after that, green grass came peeping through the dark-reddish earth, the trees began to show their buds, and the birds were singing once again. And then came the ploughing of the fields and the planting of the endless rows. Finally the sun's rays upon the soil made it so hot that Kunta was obliged to step quickly, and if he had to stop, to keep his feet moving to prevent them from blistering.

Kunta had bided his time and minded his own business, waiting for his keepers to grow careless and take their eyes off him once again. But he had the feeling that even the other blacks were still keeping an eye on him, even when the 'oberseer' and the other toubob weren't around. He had to find some way not to be so closely watched. Perhaps he could take advantage of the fact that the toubob didn't look at blacks as people but as things. Since the toubob's reactions to these black things seemed to depend on how those things acted, he decided to act as inconspicuous as possible.

Though it made him despise himself, Kunta forced himself to start behaving the way the other blacks did whenever the toubob came anywhere near. Hard as he tried, he couldn't bring himself to grin and shuffle, but he made an effort to appear co-operative, if not friendly; and he made a great show of looking busy. He had also learned a good many more toubob words by now, always keenly listening to everything that was said around him, either out in the fields or around the huts at night, and though he still chose not to speak himself, he began to make it clear that he could understand.

Cotton – one of the main crops on the farm – grew quickly here in the toubob's land. Soon its flowers had turned into hard green bolls and split open, each filled with fluffy balls, until the fields as far as Kunta could see were vast seas of whiteness, dwarfing the fields he had seen around Juffure. It was time to harvest, and the wake-up horn began blowing earlier in the morning, it seemed to Kunta, and the whip of the 'oberseer' was cracking in warning even before the 'slaves', as they were called, could tumble from their beds.

By watching others out in the field, Kunta soon learned that a hunched position made his long canvas sack seem to drag less heavily behind him as the endlessly repeated handful of cotton from the bolls slowly filled his sack. Then he would drag it to be emptied in the wagon that waited at the end of the rows. Kunta filled his sack twice a day, which was about average, although there were some – hated and envied by the others for bending their backs so hard to please the toubob, and succeeding at it – who could pick cotton so fast that their hands seemed a blur; by the time the horn blew at dusk, their sacks would have been filled and emptied into the wagon at least three times.

When each cotton wagon was filled, it was taken to a storehouse on the farm, but Kunta noticed that the overflowing wagons of tobacco harvested in the larger fields adjoining his were driven away somewhere down the road. Four days passed before it returned empty – just in time to pass another loaded wagon on its way out. Kunta also began seeing other loaded tobacco wagons, doubtless from other farms, rolling along the main road in the distance, drawn sometimes by as many as four mules. Kunta didn't know where the wagons were going, but he knew they went a long way, for he had seen the utter exhaustion of Samson and other drivers when they had returned from one of their trips.

Perhaps they would go far enough to take him to freedom. Kunta found it hard to get through the next several days in his excitement with this tremendous idea. He ruled out quickly any effort to hide on one of this farm's wagons; there would be no time without someone's eyes too near for him to slip unnoticed into a load of tobacco. It must be a wagon moving along the big road from some other farm. Using the pretext of going to the outhouse late that night, Kunta made sure that no one was about, then went to a place where he could see the road in the moonlight. Sure enough – the tobacco wagons were travelling at night. He could see the flickering lights each wagon carried, until finally those small specks of brightness would disappear in the distance.

He planned and schemed every minute, no details of the local tobacco wagons escaping his notice. Picking in the fields, his hands fairly flew; he even made himself grin if the 'oberseer' rode anywhere near. And all the time he was thinking how he would be able to leap onto the rear end of a loaded, rolling wagon at night and burrow under the tobacco without being heard by the drivers up front because of the bumping wagon's noise, and unseen not only because of the darkness but also because of the tall mound of leaves between the drivers and the rear of the wagon. It filled him with revulsion even to

223

think of having to touch and smell the pagan plant he had managed to stay away from all his life, but if that was the only way to get away, he felt sure that Allah would forgive him.

49

Waiting one evening soon afterwards behind the 'outhouse', as the slaves called the hut where they went to relieve themselves, Kunta killed with a rock one of the rabbits that abounded in the woods nearby. Carefully he sliced it thinly and dried it as he had learned in manhood training, for he would need to take some nourishment along with him. Then, with a smooth rock, he honed the rusted and bent knife blade he had found and straightened, and wired it into a wooden handle that he had carved. But even more important than the food and the knife was the saphie he had made – a cock's feather to attract the spirits, a horse's hair for strength, a bird's wishbone for success – all tightly wrapped and sewn within a small square of gunny-sacking with a needle he had made from a thorn. He realized the foolishness of wishing that his saphie might be blessed by a holy man, but any saphie was better than no saphie at all.

He hadn't slept all night, but far from being tired, it was all Kunta could do not to burst with excitement – to keep from showing any emotion at all – throughout the next day's working in the fields. For tonight would be the night. Back in his hut after the evening meal, his hands trembled as he pushed into his pocket the knife and the dried slices of rabbit, then tied his saphie tightly around his upper right arm. He could hardly stand hearing the familiar early-night routine of the other blacks; for each moment, which seemed to be taking forever to pass, might bring some unexpected occurrence that could ruin his plan. But the bone-weary field hands' mournful singing and praying soon ended. To let them get safely asleep, Kunta waited as much longer as he dared.

Then, grasping his homemade knife, he eased out into the dark night. Sensing no one about, he bent low and ran as fast as he could go, plunging after a while into a small, thick growth of brush just below where the big road curved. He huddled down, breathing hard.

Suppose no more wagons were coming tonight? The thought lanced through him. And then a nearly paralysing, worse fear: suppose the driver's helper sits as a rear lookout? But he had to take the chance.

He heard a wagon coming minutes before he saw its flickering light. Teeth clenched, muscles quivering, Kunta felt ready to collapse. The wagon seemed barely crawling. But finally, it was directly across from him and slowly passing. Two dim figures sat on its front seat. Feeling like screaming, he lunged from the growth of brush. Trotting low behind the squeaking, lurching wagon, Kunta awaited the road's next rough spot; then his outstretched hand clawed over the tailboard, and he was vaulting upwards, over the top, and into the mountain of tobacco. He was on board!

Frantically he went burrowing in. The leaves were packed together far more tightly than he had expected, but at last his body was concealed. Even after pawing open an air space to breathe more freely – the stench of the filthy weed almost made him sick – he had to keep moving his back and shoulders a bit this way or that, trying to get comfortable under the pressing weight. But finally he found the right position, and the rocking motion of the wagon, cushioned by the leaves, which were very warm around him, soon made him drowsy.

A loud bump brought him awake with a sickening start, and he began to think about being discovered. Where was the wagon going, and how long would it take to get there? And when it arrived, would he be able to slip away unseen? Or would he find himself trailed and trapped again? Why had he not thought of this before? A picture flashed into his mind of the dogs, and Samson, and the toubob with their guns, and Kunta shuddered. Considering what they did to him last time, he knew that this time his *life* would depend upon not getting caught.

But the more he thought of it, the stronger his urge grew to leave the wagon now. With his hands, he parted the leaves enough to poke his head out. Out in the moonlight were endless fields and countryside. He couldn't jump out now. The moon was bright enough to help his pursuers as much as it could help him. And the longer he rode, the less likely it was that the dogs could ever track him. He covered up the hole and tried to calm himself; but every time the wagon lurched, he feared that it was going to stop, and his heart would nearly leap from his chest.

Much later, when he opened the hole again and saw that it was nearing dawn, Kunta made up his mind. He had to leave the wagon right now, before he came any closer to the enemy of open daylight. Praying to Allah, he grasped the handle of his knife and began to wriggle out of his hole. When his entire body was free, he waited again for the wagon to lurch. It seemed to take an eternity, but when it finally did he made a light leap – and was on the road. A moment later he was out of sight in the bushes.

Kunta swung in a wide arc to avoid two toubob farms where he could see the familiar big house with the small, dark huts nearby. The sounds of their wake-up horns floated across the still air to his ears, and as the dawn brightened, he was slashing through underbrush deeper and deeper into what he knew was a wide expanse of forest. It was cool in the dense woods, and the dew that sprinkled onto him felt good, and he swung his knife as if it were weightless, grunting in his pleasure with each swing. During the early afternoon, he happened upon a small stream of clear water tippling over mossy rocks, and frogs jumped in alarm as he stopped to drink from it with his cupped hands. Looking around and feeling safe enough to rest for a while, he sat down on the bank and reached into his pocket. Taking out a piece of the dried rabbit and swashing it around in the stream, he put it in his mouth and chewed. The earth was springy and soft beneath him, and the only sounds he could hear were made by the toads and the insects and the birds. He listened to them as he ate, and watched sunlight stippling the leafy boughs above him with splashes of gold among the green; and he told himself that he was glad he didn't have to run as hard or as steadily as he had before, for exhaustion had made him an easy prey.

On and on he ran, for the rest of the afternoon, and after pausing for his sundown prayer, he went on still farther until darkness – and weariness – forced him to stop for the night. Lying on his bed of leaves and grass, he decided that later he would build himself a shelter of forked sticks with a roof of grass, as he had learned in manhood training. Sleep claimed him quickly, but several times during the night he was awakened by mosquitoes, and he heard the snarlings of wild animals in the distance as they made their kills.

Up with the first rays of the sun, Kunta quickly sharpened his knife and then was off again. A while later he came upon what was clearly a trail where a number of men had walked; although he could see that it had not been used in a long time, he ran back into the woods as fast as he could go.

Deeper and deeper into the forest, his knife kept slashing. Several times he saw snakes, but on the toubob farm he had learned that they would not attack unless they were frightened or cornered, so he let them slither away. Now and then he would imagine that he heard a dog barking somewhere, and he would shiver, for more than men, he feared dogs' noses.

Several times during the day, Kunta got into foliage so dense that in some places even his knife wasn't stout enough to clear a path, and he had to return and find another way. Twice he stopped to sharpen his knife, which seemed to be getting dull more and more often, but when it didn't work any better afterwards, he suspected that the constant slashing at briars, bushes and vines had begun to sap his strength. So he paused to rest again, ate some more rabbit – and some wild blackberries – and drank water that he found in cupped leaves of plants at the bases of trees. That night he rested by another stream, plunging into sleep the moment he lay down, deaf to the cries of animals and night birds, insensible even to the buzzing and biting of the insects that were drawn to his sweaty body.

It wasn't until the next morning that Kunta began to think about where he was going. He hadn't let himself think of it before. Since he couldn't know where he was going because he didn't have any idea where he was, he decided that his only course was to avoid nearness to any other human beings, black or toubob, and to keep running towards the sunrise. The maps of Africa he'd seen as a boy showed the big water to the west, so he knew that eventually he'd reach it if he kept moving east. But when he thought about what might happen then, even if he wasn't caught; of how he would ever be able to cross the water, even if he had a boat; of how he would ever get safely to the other side, even if he knew the way – he began to get deeply frightened. Between prayers, he fingered the saphie charm on his arm even as he ran.

That night, as he lay hidden beneath a bush, he found himself thinking of the Mandinkas' greatest hero, the warrior Sundiata, who had been a crippled slave so meanly treated by his African master that he had escaped and gone hiding in the swamps, where he found and organized other escaped ones into a conquering army that carved out the vast Mandinka Empire. Maybe, Kunta thought as he set out again on this fourth day, he could find other escaped Africans somehow here in the land of toubob, and maybe they would be as desperate as he was to feel their toes once again in the dust of their native land. Maybe enough of them together could build or steal a big canoe. And then ...

Kunta's reverie was interrupted by a terrible sound. He stopped in his tracks. No, it was impossible! But there was no mistake; it was the baying of hounds. Wildly he went hacking at the brush, stumbling and falling and scrambling up again. Soon he was so tired that when he fell again, he just sat there, very still, clutching the handle of his knife and listening. But he heard nothing now – nothing but the sounds of the birds and the insects.

Had he really heard the dogs? The thought tormented him. He didn't know which was his worst enemy: the toubob or his own imagination. He couldn't afford to assume that he hadn't really heard them, so he started running again; the only safety was to keep moving. But soon – exhausted not only by having to race so far and so fast, but also by fear itself – he had to rest again. He would close his eyes for just a moment, and then get going again.

He awoke in a sweat, sitting bolt upright. It was pitch dark! He had slept the day away! Shaking his head, he was trying to figure out what had wakened him when suddenly he heard it again: the baying of dogs, this time much closer than before. He sprang up and away so frantically that it was several moments before it flashed upon his mind that he had forgotten his long knife. He dashed back where he had lain, but the springy vines were a maze, and though he knew – maddeningly – that he had to be within arm's length of it, no amount of groping and scrabbling enabled him to lay his hand on it.

As the baying grew steadily louder, his stomach began to churn. If he didn't find it, he knew he would get captured again – or worse. With his hands jerking around everywhere underfoot, he finally grabbed hold of a rock about the size of his fist. With a desperate cry, he snatched it up and bolted into the deep brush.

All that night, like one possessed, he ran deeper and deeper into the forest – tripping, falling, tangling his feet in vines, stopping only for moments to catch his breath. But the hounds kept gaining on him, closer and closer, and finally, soon after dawn, he could see them over his shoulder. It was like a nightmare repeating itself. He couldn't run any farther. Turning and crouching in a little clearing with his back against a tree, he was ready for them – right hand clutching a stout limb he had snapped off another tree while he was running at top speed, left hand holding the rock in a grip of death.

The dogs began to lunge towards Kunta, but with a hideous cry he lashed the club at them so ferociously that they retreated and cowered just beyond its range, barking and slavering, until the two toubob appeared on their horses.

Kunta had never seen these men before. The younger one drew a gun, but the older one waved him back as he got down off his horse and walked towards Kunta. He was calmly uncoiling a long black whip.

Kunta stood there wild-eyed, his body shaking, his brain flashing a memory of toubob faces in the wood grove, on the big canoe, in the prison, in the place where he had been sold, on the heathen farm, in the woods where he had been caught, beaten, lashed and shot three times before. As the toubob's arm reared backwards with the lash, Kunta's arm whipped forwards with a viciousness that sent him falling sideways as his fingers released the rock.

He heard the toubob shout; then a bullet cracked past his ear, and the dogs were upon him. As he rolled over and over on the ground ripping at the dogs, Kunta glimpsed one toubob's face with blood running down it. Kunta was snarling like a wild animal when they called off the dogs and approached him with their guns drawn. He knew from their faces that he would die now, and he didn't care. One lunged forward and grabbed him while the old clubbed with the gun, but it still took all of their strength to hold him, for he was writhing, fighting, moaning, shrieking in both Arabic and Mandinka – until they clubbed him again. Wrestling him violently towards a tree, they tore the clothes off him and tied him tightly to it around the middle of his body. He steeled himself to be beaten to death.

But then the bleeding toubob halted abruptly, and a strange look came onto his face, almost a smile, and he spoke briefly, hoarsely to the younger one. The younger one grinned and nodded, then went back to his horse and unlashed a short-handled hunting axe that had been stowed against the saddle. He chopped a rotting tree trunk away from its roots and pulled it over next to Kunta.

Standing before him, the bleeding one began making gestures. He pointed to Kunta's genitals, then to the hunting knife in his belt. Then he pointed to Kunta's foot, and then to the axe in his hand. When Kunta understood, he howled and kicked – and was clubbed again. Deep in his marrow, a voice shouted that a man, to be a man, must have sons. And Kunta's hands flew down to cover his foto. The two toubob were wickedly grinning.

One pushed the trunk under Kunta's right foot as the other tied the foot to the trunk so tightly that all of Kunta's raging couldn't free it. The bleeding toubob picked up the axe. Kunta was screaming and thrashing as the axe flashed up, then down so fast – severing skin, tendons, muscles, bone – that Kunta heard the axe thud into the trunk as the shock of it sent the agony deep into his brain. As the explosion of pain bolted through him, Kunta's upper body spasmed forward and his hands went flailing downwards as if to save the front half of his foot, which was falling forwards, as bright red blood jetted from the stump as he plunged into blackness.

50

For the better part of a day, Kunta lapsed into and out of consciousness, his eyes closed, the muscles of his face seeming to sag, with spittle dribbling from a corner of his open mouth. As he gradually grew aware that he was alive, the terrible pain seemed to split into parts – pounding within his head, lancing throughout his body, and searing in his right leg. When his eyes required too much effort to open, he tried to remember what had happened. Then it came to him – the flushed, contorted toubob face behind the axe flashing upwards, the *thunk* against the stump, the front of his foot toppling off. Then the throbbing in Kunta's head surged so violently that he lapsed mercifully back into blackness.

The next time he opened his eyes, he found himself staring at a spider web on the ceiling. After a while, he managed to stir just enough to realize that his chest, wrists and ankles were tied down, but his right foot and the back of his head were propped against something soft, and he was wearing some kind of gown. And mingled with his agony was the smell of something like tar. He had thought he knew all about suffering before, but this was worse.

He was mumbling to Allah when the door of the hut was pushed open; he stopped instantly. A tall toubob he had never seen came in carrying a small black bag. His face was set in an angry way, though the anger seemed not to be directed at Kunta. Waving away the buzzing flies, the toubob bent down alongside him. Kunta could see only his back; then something the toubob did to his foot brought such a shock that Kunta shrieked like a woman, rearing upwards against the chest rope. Finally turning around to face him, the toubob placed his palm against Kunta's forehead and then grasped his wrist lightly and held it for a long moment. Then he stood up, and while he watched the grimaces on Kunta's drawn face, called out sharply, 'Bell!'

A black-skinned woman, short and powerfully built, with a stern but not forbidding face, soon came inside bringing water in a tin container. In some peculiar way, Kunta felt that he recognized her, that in some dream she had been already there looking down at him and bending beside him with sips of water. The toubob spoke to her in a gentle way as he took something from his black bag and stirred it into a cup of the water. Again the toubob spoke, and now the black woman kneeled and one of her hands raised the back of Kunta's head as the other tilted the cup for him to drink, which he did being too sick and weak to resist.

His fleeting downward glance enabled him to catch a glimpse of the tip of the huge bandaging over his right foot; it was rust-coloured with dried blood. He shuddered, wanting to spring up, but his muscles felt as useless as the vile-tasting stuff that he was permitting to go down his throat. The black woman then eased his head back down, the toubob said something to her again, and she replied, and the two of them went out.

Almost before they were gone, Kunta floated off into deep sleep. When next he opened his eyes late that night, he couldn't remember where he was. His right foot felt as if it were afire; he started to jerk it upwards, but the movement made him cry out. His mind lapsed off into a shadowy blur of images and thoughts, each of them drifting beyond his grasp as quickly as they came. Glimpsing Binta, he told her that he was hurt, but not to worry, for he would be home again as soon as he was able. Then he saw a family of birds flying high in the sky and a spear piercing one of them. He felt himself falling, crying out, desperately clutching out at nothingness.

When he woke up again, Kunta felt sure that something terrible had happened to his foot; or had it been a nightmare? He only knew that he was very sick. His whole right side felt numb; his throat was dry; his parched lips were starting to split from fever; he was soaked in sweat, and it had a sickly smell. Was it possible that anyone would really chop off another's foot? Then he remembered that toubob pointing to his foot and to his genitals, and the horrible expression on his face. Again the rage flooded up; and Kunta made an effort to flex his toes. It brought a blinding sheet of pain. He lay there waiting for it to subside, but it wouldn't. And it was unbearable – except that somehow he was bearing it. He hated himself for wanting that toubob to come back with more of whatever it was he put in the water that had given him some ease.

Time and again he tried to pull his hands free of the loose binding at his sides, but to no avail. He lay there writhing and groaning in anguish when the door opened again. It was the black woman, the yellowish light from the flame flickering on her black face. Smiling, she began making sounds, facial expressions, and motions that Kunta knew was an effort to make him understand something. Pointing towards the hut's door, she pantomimed a tall man walking in, then giving something to drink to a moaning person, who then broadly smiled as if feeling much better. Kunta made no sign that he understood her meaning that the tall toubob was a man of medicine.

Shrugging, she squatted down and began pressing a damp, cooling cloth against Kunta's forehead. He hated her no less for it. Then she motioned that she was going to raise his head for him to sip some of the soup she had brought. Swallowing it, he felt flashing anger at her pleased look. Then she made a small hole in the dirt floor into which she set a round, long, waxy thing and lighted a flame at the top of it. With gesture and expression, she asked finally if there was anything else he wanted. He just glowered at her, and finally she left.

Kunta stared at the flame, trying to think, until it guttered out against the dirt. In the darkness, the kill-toubob plotting in the big canoe came into his mind; he longed to be a warrior in a great black army slaughtering toubob as fast as his arms could swing. But then Kunta was shuddering, fearful that he was dying himself, even though that would mean he would be forevermore with Allah. After all, none had ever returned from Allah to tell what it was like with Him; nor had any ever returned to their villages to tell what it was like with the toubob.

On Bell's next visit, she looked down with deep concern into Kunta's bloodshot and yellowing eyes, which had sunken farther into his fevered face. He lay steadily shuddering, groaning, even thinner than when he had been brought here the week before. She went back outside, but within an hour was back with thick cloths, two steaming pots, and a pair of folded quilts. Moving quickly and – for some reason – furtively, she covered Kunta's bared chest with a thick, steaming poultice of boiled leaves mixed and mashed with something acrid. The poultice was so blistering hot that Kunta moaned and tried to shake it off, but Bell firmly shoved him back. Dipping cloths into her other steaming pot, she wrung them out and packed them over the poultice, then covered Kunta with the two quilts.

She sat and watched the sweat pour from him onto the dirt floor in rivulets. With a corner of her apron, Bell dabbed at the sweat that trickled into his closed eyes, and finally he lay entirely limp. Only when she felt the chest cloths and found them barely warm did she remove them. Then, wiping his chest clean of all traces of the poultice, she covered him with the quilts and left.

When he next awakened, Kunta was too weak even to move his body, which felt about to suffocate under the heavy quilts. But – without any gratitude – he knew that his fever was broken.

He lay wondering where that woman had learned to do what she had done. It was like Binta's medicines from his childhood, the herbs of Allah's earth passed down from the ancestors. And Kunta's mind played back to him, as well, the black woman's secretive manner, making him realize that it had not been toubob medicine. Not only was he sure that the toubob were unaware of it, he knew that the toubob should never know of it. And Kunta found himself studying the black woman's face in his mind. What was it the toubob had called her? 'Bell.'

With reluctance, after a while, Kunta decided that more than any other tribe, the woman resembled his own. He tried to picture her in Juffure, pounding her breakfast couscous, paddling her dugout canoe through the bolong, bringing in the sheaves of the rice harvest balanced on her head. But then Kunta reviled himself for the ridiculousness of thinking of his village in any connection with these pagan, heathen black ones here in the toubob's land.

Kunta's pains had become less constant now, and less intense; it hurt now mostly when he tried to strain against the bonds in his desperate achings to move around. But the flies tormented him badly, buzzing around his bandaged foot, or what was left of it, and now and then he would jerk that leg a little to make the flies swarm up awhile before returning.

Kunta began to wonder where he was. Not only was this not his own hut, but he could also tell from the sounds outside, and the voices of black people walking by, that he had been taken to some new farm. Lying there, he could smell their cooking and hear their early-night talking and singing and praying, and the horn blowing in the morning.

And each day the tall toubob came into the hut, always making Kunta's foot hurt as he changed the bandage. But when Bell came three times daily – she brought food and water, along with a smile and a warm hand on his forehead. He had to remind himself that these blacks were no better than the toubob. This black and this toubob may not mean him any harm – though it was too soon to be sure – but it was the black Samson who had beaten him almost to death, and it was toubob who had lashed him and shot him and cut his foot off. The more he gained in strength, the deeper grew his rage at having to lie there helpless, unable even to move anywhere, when for all of his seventeen rains he had been able to run, bound, and climb anywhere he wanted to. It was monstrous beyond understanding or endurance.

When the tall toubob untied Kunta's wrists from the short stakes that had held them at his sides, Kunta spent the next few hours trying futilely to raise his arms; they were too heavy. Grimly, bitterly, relentlessly, he began forcing usefulness back into his arms by flexing his fingers over and over, then making fists – until finally he could raise his arms. Next he began struggling to pull himself up on his elbows, and once he succeeded, he spent hours braced thus staring down at the bandaging over his stump. It seemed as big as a 'punkin', though it was less bloody than the previous bandagings he had glimpsed as the toubob took them off. But when he tried now to raise the knee of that same leg, he found that he couldn't yet bear the pain.

He took out his fury and his humiliation on Bell when she came to visit him the next time, snarling at her in Mandinka and banging down the tin cup after he drank. Only later did he realize that it was the first time since he arrived in toubob's land that he had spoken to anyone else aloud. It made him even more furious to recall that her eyes had seemed warm despite his show of anger.

One day, after Kunta had been there for nearly three weeks, the toubob motioned for him to sit up as he began to unwrap the bandaging. As it came nearer to the foot, Kunta saw the cloth stickily discoloured with a thick, yellowish matter. Then he had to clamp his jaws as the toubob removed the final cloth – and Kunta's senses reeled when he saw the swollen heel half of his foot covered with a hideous thick, brownish scab. Kunta almost screamed. Sprinkling something over the wound, the toubob applied only a light, loose bandaging over it, then picked up his black bag and hurriedly left.

For the next two days, Bell repeated what the toubob had done, speaking softly as Kunta cringed and turned away. When the toubob returned on the third day, Kunta's heart leaped when he saw him carrying two stout straight sticks with forked tops; Kunta had seen hurt people walk with them in Juffure. Bracing the stout forks under his arms, the toubob showed him how to hobble about swinging his right foot clear of the ground.

Kunta refused to move until they both left. Then he struggled to pull himself upright, leaning against the wall of the hut until he could endure the throbbing of his leg without falling down. Sweat was coursing down his face before he had manoeuvred the forks of the sticks underneath his armpits. Giddy, wavering, never moving far from the wall for support, he managed a few awkward, hopping forward swings of his body, the bandaged stump threatening his balance with every movement.

When Bell brought his breakfast the next morning, Kunta's glance caught the quick pleasure on her face at the marks made by the ends of the forked sticks in the hard dirt floor. Kunta frowned at her, angry at himself for not remembering to wipe away those marks. He refused to touch the food until the woman left, but then he ate it quickly, knowing that he wanted its strength now. Within a few days, he was hobbling freely about within the hut.

51

In many ways, this toubob farm was very different from the last one, Kunta began to discover the first time he was able to get to the hut's doorway on his crutches and stand looking around outside. The black people's low cabins were all neatly whitewashed, and they seemed to be in far better condition, as was the one that he was in. It contained a small, bare table, a wall shelf on which were a tin plate, a drinking gourd, a 'spoon', and those toubob eating utensils for which Kunta had finally learned the names: a 'fork' and a 'knife'; he thought it stupid for them to let him have such things within his reach. And his sleeping mat on the floor had a thicker stuffing of cornshucks. Some of the huts he saw near by even had small garden plots behind them, and the one closest to the toubob's big house had a colourful, circular flower patch growing in front of it. From where he stood in the doorway, Kunta could see anyone walking in any direction, and whenever he did, he would quickly crouch back inside and remain there for some time before venturing back to the doorway.

Kunta's nose located the outhouse. Each day, he held back his urges until he knew that most of them were out at their tasks in the fields, and then – carefully making sure that no one was near by – he would go crutching quickly across the short distance to make use of the place, and then get safely back.

It was a couple of weeks before Kunta began to make brief ventures beyond that nearby hut, and the hut of slave row's cooking woman, who wasn't Bell, he was surprised to discover. As soon as he was well enough to get around, Bell had stopped bringing him his meals – or even visiting. He wondered what had become of her – until one day, as he was standing in his doorway, he caught sight of her coming out the back door of the big house. But either she didn't see him or she pretended not to, as she walked right past him on her way to the outhouse. So she was just like the others after all; he had known it all along. Less often, Kunta caught glimpses of the tall toubob, who was usually getting into a black-covered buggy that would then go hurrying away, with its two horses being driven by a black who sat on a seat up front.

After a few more days, Kunta began to stay outside his hut even when the field workers returned in the evening, shambling along in a tired group. Remembering the other farm he had been on, he wondered why these black ones weren't being followed by some toubob with a whip on a horse. They passed close by Kunta – without seeming to pay him any attention at all – and disappeared into their huts. But within a few moments most of them were back outside again going about their chores. The men did things around the barn, the women milked cows and fed chickens. And the children lugged buckets of water and as much firewood as their arms could carry; they were obviously unaware that twice as much could be carried if they would bundle the wood and balance it, or the water buckets, on their heads.

As the days passed, he began to see that although these black ones lived better than those on the previous toubob farm, they seemed to have no more realization than the others that they were a lost tribe, that any kind of respect or appreciation for themselves had been squeezed out of them so thoroughly that they seemed to feel that their lives were as they should be. All they seemed to be concerned about was not getting beaten, having enough to eat and somewhere to sleep. There weren't many nights that Kunta finally managed to fall asleep before lying awake burning with fury at the misery of his people. But they didn't even seem to know that they were miserable. So what business was it of his if these people seemed to be satisfied with their pathetic lot? He lay feeling as if a little more of him was dying every day, that while any will to live was left to him, he should try to escape yet again, whatever the odds or the consequences. What good was he anymore – alive or dead? In the twelve moons since he was snatched from Juffure – how much older than his rains he had become.

It didn't help matters any that no one seemed to have found any kind of useful work for Kunta to do, though he was getting around ably enough on his crutches. He managed to convey the impression that he was occupied sufficiently by himself and that he had no need or desire to associate with anybody. But Kunta sensed that the other blacks didn't trust him any more than he trusted them. Alone in the nights, though, he was so lonely and depressed, spending hours staring up into the darkness, that he felt as if he were falling in upon himself. It was like a sickness spreading within him. He was amazed and ashamed to realize that he felt the need for love.

Kunta happened to be outside one day when the toubob's buggy rolled into the yard with the black driver's seat shared by a man of sasso-borro colour. When the toubob got out and went into the big house, the buggy came on nearer the huts and stopped again. Kunta saw the driver grasp the brown one under his arms to help him descend, for one of his hands seemed to be encased in what looked like hardened white mud. Kunta had no idea what it was, but it seemed likely that the hand was injured in some way. Reaching back into the buggy with his good hand, the brown one took out an oddly shaped dark box and then followed the driver down the row of huts to the one at the end that Kunta knew was empty.

Kunta was so filled with curiosity that in the morning he made it his business to hobble down to that hut. He hadn't expected to find the brown one seated just inside his doorway. They simply looked at each other. The man's face and eyes were expressionless. And so was his voice when he said 'What you want?' Kunta had no idea what he was saying. 'You one a dem African niggers.' Kunta recognized that word he'd heard so often, but not the rest. He just stood there. 'Well, git on, den!' Kunta heard the sharpness, sensed the dismissal. He all but stumbled, wheeling around, and went crutching in angry embarrassment back on up to his own hut.

He grew so furious every time he thought about that brown one that he wished he knew enough of the toubob tongue to go and shout, 'At least I'm black, not brown like you!' From that day on, Kunta wouldn't look in the direction of that hut whenever he was outside. But he couldn't quell his curiosity about the fact that after each evening's meal, most of the other blacks hastened to gather at that last hut. And, listening intently from within his own doorway, Kunta could hear the voice of the brown one talking almost steadily. Sometimes the others burst into laughter, and at intervals he could hear them barraging him with questions. Who or what was he, Kunta ached to know.

In mid-afternoon about two weeks later, the brown one chanced to be emerging from the privy at the very moment Kunta was approaching it. The brown one's bulky white arm covering was gone, and his hands were plaiting two cornshucks as the furious Kunta rapidly crutched on past. Sitting inside, Kunta's head whirled with the insults he wished he could have expressed. When he came back outside, the brown one was calmly standing there, his matter-of-fact expression as if nothing had ever happened between them. Still twisting and plaiting cornshucks between his fingers, he beckoned with his head for Kunta to follow him.

It was so totally unexpected – and disarming – that Kunta found himself following the brown one back to his cabin without a word. Obediently, Kunta sat down on the stool the brown one pointed to and watched as his host seated himself on the other stool, still plaiting. Kunta wondered if he knew that he was plaiting much the same as Africans did.

After a while more of reflective silence, the brown one began speaking: 'I been hearin' 'bout you so mad. You lucky dey ain't kilt you. Dey could of, an' been inside de law. Jes' like when dat white man broke my hand 'cause I got tired of fiddlin'. Law say anybody catch you 'scapin' can kill you and no punishment for him. Dat law gits read out again eve'y six months in white folks' churches. Looka here, don't start me on white folks' laws. Startin' up a new settlement, dey firs' builds a courthouse, fo' passin' more laws; nex' buildin's a church to prove dey's Christians. I b'lieve all dat Virginia's House of Burgess do is pass more laws 'gainst niggers. It's a law niggers can't carry no gun, even no stick that look like a club. Law say twenty lashes you get caught widdout a travellin' pass, ten lashes if'n you looks white folks in dey eyes, thirty lashes if'n you raises your hand 'gainst a white Christian. Law say no nigger preachin' less'n a white man dere to listen; law say can't be no nigger funeral if dey think it's a meetin'. Law say cut your ear off if'n white folks swear you lied, both ears if dey claim you lied twice. Law say you *kill* anybody white, you hang; kill 'nother nigger, you jes' gits whipped. Law say reward a Indian catchin' a 'scaped nigger wid all de tobacco dat Indian can carry. Law 'gainst teachin' any nigger to read or write, or givin' any nigger any book. Dey's even a law 'gainst niggers beatin' any drums – any dat African stuff.'

Kunta sensed that the brown one knew he couldn't understand, but that he both liked to talk and feel that Kunta's listening might somehow bring him at least closer to comprehension. Looking at the brown one's face as he spoke, and listening to his tone, Kunta felt he almost *could* understand. And it made him want to both laugh and cry that someone was actually talking to him as one human being to another.

' 'Bout your foot, looka here, it ain't jes 'foots and arms but dicks an' nuts gits cut off. I seen plenty ruined niggers like dat still workin'. Seen niggers beat till meat cut off dey bones. Nigger women's full of baby gits beat layin' face down over a hole dug for dey bellies. Niggers gits scraped raw, den covered with turpentine or salt, den rubbed wid straw. Niggers caught talkin' 'bout revolt made to dance on hot embers 'til dey falls. Ain't hardly nothin' ain't done to niggers, an' if dey die 'cause of it, ain't no crime long as dey's owned by whoever done it, or had it done. Dat's de law. An' if you thinks dat's bad, you ought to hear what folks tell gits did to dem niggers dat some slave boats sells crost the water on dem West Indies sugar plantations.'

Kunta was still there listening – and trying to understand – when a first-kafo-sized boy came in with the brown one's evening meal. When he saw Kunta there, he dashed out and soon returned with a covered plate for him, too. Kunta and the brown one wordlessly ate together, and then Kunta abruptly rose to leave, knowing that the others would soon be coming to the hut, but the brown one's gesture signalled Kunta to stay.

As the others began arriving a few minutes later, none were able to mask their surprise at seeing Kunta there – particularly Bell, who was one of the last to show up. Like most of the rest, she simply nodded – but with the trace of a smile, it seemed to Kunta. In the gathering darkness, the brown one proceeded to hold forth for the group as he had done for Kunta, who guessed that he was telling them some kind of stories. Kunta could tell when a story ended, for abruptly they would all laugh – or ask questions. Now and then Kunta recognized some of the words that had become familiar to his ears.

When he went back to his own hut, Kunta was in a turmoil of emotion about mingling with these black ones. Sleepless late that night, his mind still tumbling with conflicts, he recalled something Omoro had said once when Kunta had refused to let go of a choice mango after Lamin begged for a bite: 'When you clench your fist, no one can put anything in your hand, nor can your hand pick up anything.'

But he also knew that his father would be in the fullest of agreement with him that, no matter what, he must never become anything like these black people. Yet each night, he felt strangely drawn to go among them at the hut of the brown one. He resisted the temptation, but almost every afternoon now, Kunta would hobble over to visit with the brown one when he was alone. 'Git my fingers back to workin' right to fiddle again,' he said while weaving his cornshucks one day. 'Any kin' of luck, dis massa here go 'head an' buy me an' hire me out. I done fiddled all over Virginia, make good money for him an' me both. Ain't much I ain't seen an' done, even if'n you don't know what I'm talkin' 'bout. White folks says all Africans knows is livin' in grass huts an' runnin' 'roun' killin' an' eatin' one 'nother.'

He paused in his monologue, as if expecting some kind of reaction, but Kunta just sat there watching and listening impassively and fingering his saphie charm.

'See what I means? You got to put away all dat stuff,' said the brown one, pointing to the charm. 'Give it up. You ain't goin' nowheres, so you might's well face facks an' start fittin' in, Toby, you hear?'

Kunta's face flashed with anger. 'Kunta Kinte!' he blurted, astonished at himself.

The brown one was equally amazed. 'Looka here, he can talk! But I'm tellin' you, boy, you got to forgit all dat African talk. Make white folks mad an' scare niggers. Yo' name Toby. Dey calls me Fiddler.' He pointed to himself. 'Say dat. Fiddler!' Kunta looked at him blankly, though he understood exactly what he meant. 'Fiddler! It's a fiddler. Understan' – fiddler?' He made a sawing motion across his left arm with the other hand. This time Kunta wasn't pretending when he looked blank.

Exasperated, the brown one got up and brought from a corner the oddly shaped box that Kunta had seen him arrive with. Opening it, he lifted out an even more oddly shaped light brown wooden thing with a slender black neck and four taut, thin strings running almost its length. It was the same musical instrument he had heard the old man play at the other farm.

'Fiddle!' exclaimed the brown one.

Since they were alone, Kunta decided to say it. He repeated the sound: 'Fiddle.'

Looking pleased, the brown one put the fiddle away and closed the case. Then, glancing around, he pointed. 'Bucket!' Kunta repeated it, fixing in his head what that thing was. 'Now, water!' Kunta repeated it.

After they had gone through a score or more of new words, the brown one pointed silently at the fiddle, the bucket, water, chair, cornshucks and other objects, his face a question mark for Kunta to repeat the right word for all of them. A few of the names he promptly repeated; he fumbled with a few others and was corrected; and some sounds he was unable to say at all. The brown one refreshed him on those, then reviewed him on them all. 'You ain't dumb as you looks,' he grunted by suppertime.

The lessons continued through the following days and stretched into weeks. To Kunta's astonishment, he began to discover that he was becoming able not only to understand but also to make himself understood to the brown one in a rudimentary way. And the main thing he wanted him to understand was why he refused to surrender his name or his heritage, and why he would rather die a free man on the run than live out his life as a slave. He didn't have the words to tell it as he wished, but he knew the brown one understood, for he frowned and shook his head. One afternoon not long afterwards, arriving at the brown one's hut, Kunta found another visitor already there. It was the old man he'd seen now and then hoeing in the flower garden near the big house. With a glance at the brown one's affirming nod, Kunta sat down.

The old man began to speak. 'Fiddler here tell me you run away four times. You see what it got you. Jes' hopes you done learned your lesson like I done. 'Cause you ain't done nothin' new. My young days, I run off so much dey near 'bout tore my hide off 'fore I got it in my head ain't nowhere to run to. Run two states away, dey jes' tell about it in dey papers an' sooner later you gits cotched an' nearly kilt, an' win' up right back where you come from. Ain't hardly nobody ain't thought about runnin'. De grinnin'est niggers thinks about it. But ain't nobody I ever knowed ever got away. Time you settled down and made de best of things de way dey is, 'stead of wastin' yo' young years, like I did, plottin' what cain't be done. I done got ol' an' wore out now. Reckon since you been born I been actin' like de no-good, lazy, shiftless, head-scratchin' nigger white folks says us is. Only reason massa keep me here, he know I ain't got no good auction value, an' he git more out of me jes' halfway doin' de gardenin'. But I hears tell from Bell massa gwine put you to workin' wid me tomorrow.'

Knowing that Kunta had understood hardly any of what the gardener had said, the fiddler spent the next half hour explaining what the old man had told him – only slowly and more simply, in words Kunta was familiar with. He had mixed feelings about nearly everything the gardener had said. He understood that the old man meant well by his advice – and he was beginning to believe that escape was indeed impossible – but even if he never got away, he could never pay the price of giving up who and what he had been born in order to live out his years without another beating. And the thought of spending them as a crippled gardener filled him with rage and humiliation. But perhaps just for a while, until he got his strength back. And it might be good to get his mind off himself and his hands in the soil again – even if it wasn't his own.

The next day, the old gardener showed Kunta what to do. As he chopped away at the weeds that seemed to spring up daily among the vegetables, so did Kunta. As he plucked tomato worms and potato bugs from the plants and squashed them underfoot, so did Kunta. They got along well, but apart from working side by side, they didn't communicate much, either. Usually the old man would only make grunts and gestures whenever Kunta needed to be shown how to do some new task, and Kunta, without responding, simply did as he was told. He didn't mind the silence; as a matter of fact, his ears needed a few hours' rest each day between conversations with the fiddler, who ran his mouth every minute they were together.

That night after the evening meal, Kunta was sitting in the doorway of his hut when the man called Gildon – who made the horse and mule collars and also shod the black people – walked up to him and held out a pair of shoes. At the orders of the 'massa', he said he had made them especially for Kunta. Taking them and nodding his thanks, Kunta turned them over and over in his hands before deciding to try them on. It felt strange to have such things on his feet, but they fitted perfectly – even though the front half of the right shoe was stuffed with cotton. The shoemaker bent down to tie the lacings, then suggested that Kunta get up and walk around in them to see how they felt. The left shoe was fine, but he felt tiny stinging sensations in his right foot as he walked awkwardly and gingerly around outside his hut without the crutches. Seeing his discomfort, the shoemaker said that was because of the stump, not the shoe, and he would get used to it.

Later that day, Kunta walked a bit farther, testing, but the right foot was still uncomfortable, so he removed a little of the cotton stuffing and put it back on. It felt better, and finally he dared to put his full weight on that foot, and there wasn't any undue pain. Every now and then he would continue to experience the phantom pain of his right toes aching, as he had nearly every day since he started walking around, and he would glance downwards – always with surprise – to find that he didn't have any. But he kept practising walking around, and feeling better than he let his face show; he had been afraid that he would always have to walk with crutches.

That same week the massa's buggy returned from a trip, and the black driver, Luther, hurried to Kunta's hut, beckoning him down to the fiddler's, where Kunta watched him say something, grinning broadly. Then with gestures towards the big house and with selected key words, the fiddler made Kunta nod in understanding that Massa William Waller, the toubob who lived in the big house, now owned Kunta. 'Luther say he just got a deed to you from his brother who had you at first, so you his now.' As usual, Kunta did not let his face show his feelings. He was angry and ashamed that anyone could 'own' him; but he was also deeply relieved, for he had feared that one day he would be taken back to that other 'plantation', as he now knew the toubob farms were called. The fiddler waited until Luther had left before he spoke again – partly to Kunta and partly to himself. 'Niggers here say Massa William a good master, an' I seen worse. But ain't none of 'em no good. Dey all lives off us niggers. Niggers is the biggest thing dey got.'

52

Almost every day now, when work was done, Kunta would return to his hut and after his evening prayer would scratch up the dirt in a little square on his floor and draw Arabic characters in it with a stick, then sit looking for a long time at what he had written, often until supper. Then he would rub out what he had written, and it would be time to go down and sit among the others as the fiddler talked. Somehow his praying and his studying made it all right to mix with them. That way, it seemed to him he could remain himself without having to remain *by* himself. Anyway, if they had been in Africa, there would have been someone like the fiddler to go to, only he would have been a wandering musician and griot travelling from one village to the next and singing as he played his kora or his balafon in between the telling of fascinating stories drawn from his adventures.

Just as it had been done in Africa, Kunta had also begun to keep track of the passing of time by dropping a small pebble into a gourd on the morning after each new moon. First he had dropped into the gourd twelve rounded, multicoloured stones for the twelve moons he

243

guessed he'd spent on the first toubob farm; then he dropped in six more for the time he'd been here on this new farm; and then he had carefully counted out 204 stones for the seventeen rains he'd reached when he was taken from Juffure, and dropped them into the gourd. Adding them all up, he figured that he was now into his nineteenth rain.

So as old as he felt, he was still a young man. Would he spend the rest of his life here, as the gardener had, watching hope and pride slip away along with the years, until there was nothing left to live for and time had finally run out? The thought filled him with dread – and determination not to end up the way the old man had, doddering around in his plot, uncertain which foot to put before the other. The poor man was worn out long before the midday meal, and through the afternoons he was only able to pretend that he was working at all, and Kunta had to shoulder almost all the load.

Every morning, as Kunta bent over his rows, Bell would come with her basket – Kunta had learned that she was the cook in the big house – to pick the vegetables she wanted to fix for the massa that day. But the whole time she was there, she never so much as looked at Kunta, even when she walked right past him. It puzzled and irritated him, remembering how she had attended him daily when he lay fighting to survive, and how she would nod at him during the evenings at the fiddler's. He decided that he hated her, that the only reason she had acted as his nurse back then was because the massa had ordered her to do it. Kunta wished that he could hear whatever the fiddler might have to say about this matter, but he knew that his limited command of words wouldn't allow him to express it right – apart from the fact that even asking would be too embarrassing.

One morning not long afterwards, the old man didn't come to the garden, and Kunta guessed that he must be sick. He had seemed even more feeble than usual for the past few days. Rather than going right away to the old man's hut to check on him, Kunta went straight to work watering and weeding, for he knew that Bell was due at any moment, and he didn't think it would be fitting for her to find no one there when she arrived.

A few minutes later she showed up and, still without looking at Kunta, went about her business, filling her basket with vegetables as Kunta stood holding his hoe and watching her. Then, as she started to leave, Bell hesitated, looked around, set the basket on the ground, and – throwing a quick, hard glance at Kunta – marched off. Her message was clear that he should bring her basket to the back door of the big house, as the old man had always done. Kunta all but exploded with rage, his mind flashing an image of dozens of Juffure women bearing their headloads in a line past the bantaba tree where Juffure's men always rested. Slamming down his hoe, he was about to stamp away when he remembered how close she was to the massa. Gritting his teeth, he bent over, seized the basket, and followed silently after Bell. At the door, she turned around and took the basket as if she didn't even see him. He returned to the garden seething.

From that day on, Kunta more or less became the gardener. The old man, who was very sick, came only now and then, whenever he was strong enough to walk. He would do a little something for as long as he felt able, which wasn't very long, and then hobble back to his hut. He reminded Kunta of the old people back in Juffure who, ashamed of their weakness, continued to totter about making the motions of working until they were forced to retreat to their pallets, and finally were rarely seen out any more at all.

The only new duty Kunta really hated was having to carry that basket for Bell every day. Muttering under his breath, he would follow her to the door, thrust it into her hands as rudely as he dared, then turn on his heel and march back to work, as fast as he could go. As much as he detested her, though, his mouth would water when now and then the air would waft to the garden the tantalizing smells of the things that Bell was cooking.

He had dropped the twenty-second pebble into his calendar gourd when – without any outward sign of change – Bell beckoned him on into the house one morning. After a moment's hesitation, he followed her inside and set the basket on a table there. Trying not to look amazed at the strange things he saw everywhere around him in this room, which they called the 'kitchen', he was turning to leave when she touched him on the arm and handed him a biscuit with what looked like a piece of cold beef between the slices. As he stared at it in puzzlement, she said, 'Ain't you never seed a san'wich befo'? It ain't gonna bite you. You s'posed to bite *it*. Now git on outa here.'

As time went on, Bell began to give him more than he could carry in his hand – usually a tin plate piled with something called 'corn-pone', a kind of bread he had never tasted before, along with boiled fresh mustard greens in their own delicious potliquor. He had sown the mustard's tiny seeds himself – in garden soil mixed with rich black dirt dug from the cow pasture – and the tender greens had swiftly, luxuriously sprung up. He loved no less the way she cooked the long, slender field peas that grew on the vines coiling around the sweet corn's stalks. She never gave him any obvious meat of the pig, though he wasn't sure how she knew that. But whatever she gave him, he would always wipe off the plate carefully with a rag before returning it. Most often he would find her at her 'stove' – a thing of iron that contained fire – but sometimes she would be on her knees scrubbing the kitchen floor with oak ashes and a hard-bristled brush. Though at times he wanted to say something to her, he could never muster a better expression of his appreciation than a grunt – which now she returned.

One Sunday after supper, Kunta had got up to stretch his legs and was walking around the fiddler's hut idly patting himself on the belly when the brown one, who had been talking steadily all through the meal, interrupted his monologue to exclaim, 'Looka here, you startin' to fill out!' He was right. Kunta hadn't looked – or felt – better since he left Juffure.

After months of incessant plaiting to strengthen his fingers, the fiddler, too, felt better than he had in a long time – since his hand was broken – and in the evenings he had begun to play his instrument again. Holding the peculiar thing in his cupped hand and under his chin, the fiddler raked its strings with his wand – which seemed to be made of long, fine hairs – and the usual evening audience would shout and break into applause when each song had finished. 'Dat ain't nothin'!' he would say disgustedly. 'Fingers ain't nimble yet.'

Later, when they were alone, Kunta asked haltingly, 'What is nimble?'

The fiddler flexed and wiggled his fingers. 'Nimble! Nimble. Get it?' Kunta nodded.

'You a lucky nigger, what you is,' the fiddler went on. 'Jes' piddlin' 'rou' eve'yday in dat garden. Ain't hardly nobody got a job dat sof' 'cept on plantations whole lot bigger'n dis.'

Kunta thought he understood, and he didn't like it. 'Work *hard*,' he said. And nodding at the fiddler on his chair, he added, 'Harder dan *dat*.'

The fiddler grinned. 'You awright, African!'

53

The 'months', as they called moons here, were passing more quickly now, and before long the hot season known as 'summer' was over and harvest time had begun along with a great many more duties for Kunta and the others. While the rest of the blacks – even Bell – were busy with the heavy work out in the fields, he was expected to tend the chickens, the livestock, and the pigs in addition to his garden. And at the height of the cotton picking, he was called upon to drive the wagon along the rows. Except for having to feed the filthy swine, which almost made him ill, Kunta didn't mind the extra work, for it made him feel less of a cripple. But it was seldom that he got back to his hut before dark – so tired out that he sometimes even forgot to eat his supper. Taking off nothing but his frayed straw hat and his shoes – to relieve the aching of his half foot – he would flop down on his cornshuck mattress, pulling his quilt of cotton-stuffed burlap up over him, and within moments he would be sound asleep, in clothes still wet with sweat.

Soon the wagons were piled high with cotton, then with plump ears of corn, and the golden tobacco leaves were hanging up to dry. The hogs had been killed, cut into pieces, and hung over slowly burning hickory, and the smoky air was turning cold when everyone on the plantation began preparing for the 'harvest dance', an occasion so important that even the massa would be there. Such was their excitement that when Kunta found out that the black people's Allah didn't seem to be involved, he decided to attend himself – but just to watch.

By the time he got up the courage to join the party, it was well under way. The fiddler, whose fingers were finally nimble again, was sawing away at his strings, and another man was clacking two beef bones together to keep time as someone shouted, 'Cakewalk!' Dancers coupled off and hurried out before the fiddler. Each woman put her foot on the man's knee while he tied her shoestring; then the fiddler sang out, 'Change partners!' and when they did, he began to play madly, and Kunta saw that the dancers' footsteps and body motions were imitating their planting of the crops, the chopping of wood, the picking of cotton, the swinging of scythes, the pulling of corn, the pitchforking of hay into wagons. It was all so much like the harvest dancing back in Juffure that Kunta's good foot was soon tapping away on the ground – until he realized what he was doing and looked around, embarrassed, to see if anyone had noticed.

But no one had. At that moment, in fact, almost everyone had begun to watch a slender fourth-kafo girl who was dipping and whirling around as light as a feather, her head tossing, her eyes rolling, her arms describing graceful patterns. Soon the other dancers, exhausted, were moving to the sides to catch their breaths and stare; even her partner was hard put to keep up.

When he quit, gasping, a shout went up, and when finally even she went stumbling towards the sidelines, a whooping and hollering engulfed her. The cheering got even louder when Massa Waller awarded that girl a half-dollar prize. And smiling broadly at the fiddler, who grinned and bowed in return, the massa left them amid more shouting. But the cakewalk was far from over, and the other couples, rested by now, rushed back out and went on as before, seemingly ready to dance all night.

Kunta was lying on his mattress thinking about what he had heard and seen when suddenly there came a rapping at his door.

'Who dat?' he demanded, astonished, for only twice had anyone ever come to his hut in all the time he'd lived there.

'Kick dis do' in, nigger!'

Kunta opened the door, for it was the voice of the fiddler; instantly he smelled the liquor on his breath. Though he was repelled, Kunta said nothing, for the fiddler was bursting to talk, and it would have been unkind to turn him away just because he was drunk.

'You seen massa!' said the fiddler. 'He ain't knowed I could play dat good! Now you watch an' see if'n he don't 'range for me to play for white folks to hear me, an' den hire me out!' Beside himself with happiness, the fiddler sat on Kunta's three-legged stool, fiddle across his lap, and went on babbling.

'Looka here, I second fiddled with the best! You ever hear of Sy Gilliat from Richmond?' He hesitated. 'Naw, 'course you ain't! Well, dat's de fiddlin'est slave nigger in de worl', and I fiddled wid him. Looka here, he play for nothin' but big white folks' balls an' dances, I mean like the Hoss Racin' Ball every year, and like dat. You oughta see him wid dat gold-painted fiddle of his an' him wearin' court dress wid his brown wig an' Lawd, dem manners! Nigger name London Briggs behin' us playin' flute an' clarinet! De minuets, de reels, de congos, hornpipes, jigs, even jes' caperin' 'bout – don't care what it was, we'd have dem white folks dancin' up a storm!'

The fiddler carried on like this for the next hour – until the alcohol wore off – telling Kunta of the famous singing slaves who worked in Richmond's tobacco factories; of other widely known slave musicians who played the 'harpsichord', the 'pianoforte', and the 'violin' – whatever they were – who had learned to play by listening to toubob musicians from someplace called 'Europe', who had been hired to come to plantations to teach the massas' children.

The following crispy cold morning saw the starting of new tasks. Kunta watched as the women mixed hot melted tallow with wood-ash lye and water, boiling and stirring, then cooling the thick brown mixture in wooden trays to let it set for four nights and three days before they cut it into oblong cakes of hard brown soap. To his complete distaste, he saw men fermenting apples, peaches and persimmons into something foul-smelling that they called 'brandy', which they put into bottles and barrels. Others mixed gluey red clay, water and dried hog hair to press into cracks that had appeared in their huts. Women stuffed some mattresses with cornshucks like Kunta's, and some others with the moss he had seen drying; and a new mattress for the massa was filled with goose feathers.

The slave who built things from wood was making new tubs in which clothes would be soaked in soapy water before being boiled and lumped onto a wooden block to be beaten with a stick. The man who made things with leather – horse collars, harnesses, and shoes – was now busily tanning cows' hides. And women were dyeing into different colours the white cotton cloth the massa had bought to make clothes with. And just as it was in Juffure, all of the nearby vines, bushes and fences were draped with drying cloths of red, yellow and blue.

With each passing day, the air became colder and colder, the sky greyer and greyer, until soon the ground was covered once again with snow and ice that Kunta found as unpleasant as it was extraordinary. And before long the other blacks were beginning to talk with great excitement about 'Christmas', which he had heard of before. It seemed to have to do with singing, dancing, eating and giving of gifts, which sounded fine – but it also seemed to involve their Allah, so even though Kunta really enjoyed by now the gatherings at the fiddler's, he decided it would be best to stay to himself until the pagan festivities were safely over. He didn't even visit the fiddler, who looked curiously at Kunta the next time he saw him, but said nothing about it.

Thence swiftly came another springtime season, and as he knelt planting among his rows, Kunta remembered how lush the fields around Juffure always looked at this time of year. And he recalled as a second-kafo boy how happily he had gone prancing out behind the hungry goats in this green season. Here in this place the black 'young'uns' were helping to chase and catch the *baaaing*, bounding 'sheep', as the animals were called, and then fighting out whose turn was next to sit on the head of a desperately struggling sheep while a man snipped off the thick, dirty wool with a pair of shears. The fiddler explained to Kunta that the wool would be taken off somewhere to be cleaned and 'carded into bats', which then would be returned for the women to spin woollen thread from which they would weave cloth for the making of winter clothes.

The garden's ploughing, planting, and cultivating went by for Kunta in a sweating blur of dawns to darks. Early in the midsummer month they called 'July', those who worked out in the fields would return exhausted to their huts every night as they pressed to complete the last hoeing of grass from around the waist-high cotton and corn that was heavy with tasselled heads. It was hard work, but at least there was plenty to eat in the storehouses that had been filled to overflowing the past fall. At this time in Juffure, Kunta thought, the people's stomachs would be aching as they made soup from roots, grubworms, grass and anything else they could find, because the crops and fruits so lushly green were not yet ripe.

The 'laying by' had to be finished before the second 'Sunday' in July, Kunta learned, when the blacks from most of the plantations in this area – which was called 'Spotsylvania County' – would be permitted to travel someplace to join in some kind of 'camp meetin'.' Since, whatever it was, it had to do with their Allah, no one even suggested that Kunta go along with the more than twenty of them who left very early that Sunday morning, packed into a wagon whose use Massa Waller had approved.

Nearly everyone was gone for the next few days – so many that few would have been there to notice if Kunta had tried to run away again – but he knew that even though he had learned to get around all right and make himself fairly useful, he would never be able to get very far before some slave catcher caught up with him again. Though it shamed him to admit it, he had begun to prefer life as he was allowed to live it here on this plantation to the certainty of being captured and probably killed if he tried to escape again. Deep in his heart, he knew he would never see his home again, and he could feel something precious and irretrievable dying inside of him forever. But hope remained alive; though he might never see his family again, perhaps someday he might be able to have one of his own.

54

Another year had passed – so fast that Kunta could hardly believe it – and the stones in his gourd told him that he had reached his twentieth rain. It was cold again, and 'Christmas' was once more in the air. Though he felt the same as he always had about the black ones' Allah, they were having such a good time that he began to feel his own Allah would have no objection to his merely observing the activities that went on during this festive season.

Two of the men, having received week-long travelling passes from Massa Waller, were packing to go and visit their mates living on other plantations; one of the men was going to see a new baby for the first time. But every hut except theirs – and Kunta's – was busy with some kind of preparations, chiefly the fixing up of party clothes with lace and beads, and the taking of nuts and apples from their storage places.

And up in the big house, all of Bell's pots and pans were bubbling with yams and rabbits and roast pig – and many dishes made from animals Kunta had never seen or heard of until he came to this country: turkey, 'coons, 'possums and the like. Though he was hesitant at first, the succulent smells from her kitchen soon persuaded Kunta to try everything – except for pig, of course. Nor was he interested in sampling the liquor Massa Waller had promised for the black ones: two barrels of hard cider, one of wine, and a keg of whisky he had brought in his buggy from somewhere else.

Kunta could tell that some of the liquor was being quietly consumed in advance, no little of it by the fiddler. And along with the drinkers' antics, the black children were running around holding dried hog bladders on sticks closer and closer to fires until each one burst with a loud bang amid general laughing and shouting. He thought it was all unbelievably stupid and disgusting.

When the day finally came, the drinking and eating began in earnest. From the door of his hut, Kunta watched as guests of Massa Waller's arrived for the midday feast, and afterwards as the slaves assembled close by the big house and began to sing, led by Bell, he saw the massa raise the window, smiling; then he and the other white folks came outside and stood listening, seeming to be enthralled. After that the massa sent Bell to tell the fiddler to come and play for them, which he did.

Kunta could understand their having to do what they were told, but why did they seem to *enjoy* it so much? And if the whites were so fond of their slaves that they gave them presents, why didn't they make them really happy and set them free? But he wondered if some of these blacks, like pets, would be able to survive, as he could, unless they were taken care of.

But was he any better than they were? Was he all that different? Slowly but surely, he couldn't deny that he was easing into acceptance of their ways. He was most troubled about his deepening friendship with the fiddler. His drinking of liquor deeply offended Kunta, and yet had not a pagan the right to be a pagan? The fiddler's boastfulness also bothered Kunta, yet he believed that all the fiddler had boasted of was true. But the fiddler's crude and irreverent sense of humour was distasteful to him; and Kunta had come to dislike intensely hearing the fiddler call him 'nigger', since he had learned that it was the white man's name for blacks. But had it not been the fiddler who had taken it upon himself to teach him to talk? Was it not he whose friendship had made it easier for him to feel less of a stranger with the other blacks? Kunta decided that he wanted to know the fiddler better.

Whenever the proper time came, in the best roundabout way he could, he would ask the fiddler about some of the questions that were in his mind. But two more pebbles had been dropped into his gourd before one quiet Sunday afternoon, when no one was working, he went down to the familiar last hut on slave row, and found the fiddler in a rare quiet mood.

After exchanging greetings, they were both silent for a time. Then, just to make conversation, Kunta said he had overheard the massa's driver, Luther, say that white folks were talking about 'taxes' wherever he drove the massa. What were taxes, anyway, he wanted to know.

'Taxes is money got to be paid extry on near 'bout anything white folks buys,' replied the fiddler. 'Dat king 'crost de water puts on de taxes to keep him rich.'

It was so unlike the fiddler to be so brief that Kunta figured he must be in a bad mood. Discouraged, he sat there for a while in silence, but finally he decided to spit out what was really on his mind: 'Where you was fo' here?'

The fiddler stared at him for a long, tense moment. Then he spoke, his voice cutting. 'I know every nigger here figgerin' 'bout me! Wouldn't tell nobody else nothin'! But you diff'rent.'

He glared at Kunta. 'You know how come you diff'rent? 'Cause you don't know nothin'! You done got snatched over here, an' got your foot cut, you thinks you been through all dey is! Well, you ain't de only one had it bad.' His voice was angry. 'You ever tells what I'm gonna tell you, I'll catch you upside de head!'

'I ain't!' Kunta declared.

The fiddler leaned forward and spoke softly so as not to be overheard. 'Massa I had in No'th Ca'lina got drowned. Ain't nobody's bidness how. Anyway, same night I lit out, an' he ain't had no wife or young'uns to claim me. I hid out with Injuns 'til I figured it was safe to leave an' git here to Virginia an' keep on fiddlin'.'

'What "Virginia"?' asked Kunta.

'Man, you really *don't* know nothin', does you? Virginia's the colony you livin' in, if you want to call dis livin'.'

'What's a colony?'

'You even dumber'n you *look*. Dey's thirteen colonies that go to make up this country. Down south of here there's the Ca'linas, and up north they's Maryland, Pennsylvania, New York, and a bunch of others. I ain't never been up dere, an' neither has most niggers. I hear tell lotta white folks up dere don't hold with slavery and sets us folk free. Myself, I'm kind of a half-free nigger. I have to be roun' some massa 'case pattyrollers ever catches me.' Kunta didn't understand, but he acted as if he did, since he didn't feel like getting insulted again.

'You ever seen Injuns?' the fiddler demanded.

Kunta hesitated. 'I seen some.'

'Dey was here 'fo' white folks. White folks tell you one of dem name Columbus discover dis place. But if he foun' Injuns here, he ain't discover it, is he?' The fiddler was warming to his subject. 'White man figger whoever somewhere 'fore him don't count. He call dem savages.'

The fiddler paused to appreciate his wit, and then went on. 'You ever seen Injuns' teepees?' Kunta shook his head no. The fiddler enclosed three of his spread fingers within a small rag. 'De fingers is poles an' de rag is hides. Dey lives inside dat.'

He smiled. 'Bein' from Africa, you prob'ly thinks you knows all dey is 'bout huntin' and like that, but ain't nobody hunts or travels good as Injuns. Once one go somewhere it's a map in his head how he went. But Injun mammies – dey calls 'em squaws – carries dey young'uns on dey backs, like I hears y'all's mammies does in Africa.'

Kunta was surprised that the fiddler knew that, and couldn't help showing it. The fiddler smiled again and continued the lesson. 'Some Injuns hates niggers, an' some likes us. Niggers an' lan' is Injuns' big troubles with white folks. White folks wants all the Injuns' land and hates Injuns what hides niggers!' The fiddler's eyes searched Kunta's face. 'Y'all Africans and Injuns made de same mistake – lettin' white folks into where you live. You offered him to eat and sleep, then first thing you know he kickin' you out or lockin' you up!'

The fiddler paused again. Then suddenly he burst out: 'What put me out with you African niggers, looka here! I knowed five or six ack like you! Don't know how come I took up wid you in de firs' place! You git over here figgerin' niggers here ought to be like you is! How you 'spec we gon' know 'bout Africa? We ain't never been dere, an' ain't goin' neither!' Glaring at Kunta, he lapsed into silence.

And fearful of provoking another outburst, Kunta soon left without another word, rocked onto his heels by what the fiddler had said to him. But the more he thought about it back in his hut, the better he felt about it. The fiddler had taken off his mask; that meant he was beginning to *trust* Kunta. For the first time in his acquaintance with anyone in the three rains since he had been stolen from his homeland, Kunta was actually beginning to *know* someone.

55

Over the next several days, as he worked in the garden, Kunta thought a great deal about how long it had taken him to realize how little he really knew about the fiddler, and about how much more there was to know about him. Almost certainly he reflected no less of a mask was still being worn for him by the old gardener, whom Kunta had been going to visit now and then. And he didn't know Bell much better, though he and she had some daily exchange of talk – or rather Kunta mostly listened while he ate whatever food she gave him; but it was always about small and impersonal matters. It occurred to him how both Bell and the gardener had sometimes started to say something, or hinted at something, but then never finished. They were both cautious people in general, but it seemed they were especially so with him. He decided to get to know them both better. On his next visit to the old gardener, Kunta began in his indirect Mandinka way by asking about something the fiddler had told him. Kunta said he had heard about 'pattyrollers', but he was uncertain who or what they were.

'Dey's low-down po' white trash dat ain't never owned a nigger in dey lives!' the old gardener said heatedly. 'It's a ol' Virginia law to patrol de roads, or anywhere else niggers is, an' whip an' jail any of 'em gits cotched widdout a writ-out pass from dey massa. An' who gits hired to do it is dem po' whites what jes' loves cotchin' an' beatin' somebody else's niggers 'cause *dey* ain't got none. What's behind it, y'understan', all white folks scared to death dat any loose nigger is plannin' a re-volt. Fact, ain't nothin' pattyrollers loves more'n claimin' to suspicion some nigger, an' bustin' in an' strippin' him buck naked right before his wife an young'uns an' beatin' him bloody.'

Seeing Kunta's interest, and pleased by his visit, the old gardener went on: 'Massa we got don't 'prove a dat. It's how come he don't have no oberseer. He say he don't want nobody beatin' his niggers. He tell his niggers to obersee deyselves, jes' do de work like dey know to, an' don't never break none a his rules. He swear sun won't set here on no nigger break his rules.'

Kunta wondered what the rules were, but the gardener kept on talking. 'Reason massa like he is 'cause he of a family was rich even 'fore dey come here from dat England 'crost de water. Dem Wallers always been what most massas jes' tries to act like dey is. 'Cause most of dese massas ain't nothin' but coonhunters what got hole of a piece of lan' an' one or two niggers dey worked half to death, an' jes' kep' on growin' from dat.

'Ain't many plantations got a whole lot of slaves. Mos' of 'em jes' maybe anywhere from one to five or six niggers. Us twenty here make dis one pretty big. Two out of every three white folks ain't got no slaves at all, dat's what I heared. Real big plantations with fifty or a hunnud slaves is mostly where de black dirt is; dem river bottoms like in Lousiana, Miss'ippi, an' Alabama got some, too; an' dem coasts a Geo'gia an' South Ca'lina where dey grows rice.'

'How ol' you?' Kunta asked abruptly.

The gardener looked at him. 'Older'n you or anybody else thinks I is.' He sat as if musing for a moment. 'I heared the Indians' war whoopin' when I was a chile.'

After a silent moment with his head down, he glanced up at Kunta and began singing, '*Ah yah, tair umbam, boowah—*' Kunta sat astounded. '*Kee lay zee day nic olay, man lun dee nic o lay ah wah nee—*' Stopping, the old man said, 'My mammy used to sing dat. Say

255

she got it from her mammy, who come from Africa, same as you did. You know by dem sounds where she come from?'

'Soun' like Serere tribe,' said Kunta. 'But I don't know dem words. I heared Serere spoke on the boat what brung me.'

The old gardener looked furtively around. 'Gon' shut up wid dat singin'. Some nigger hear it an' tell massa. White folks don't want no niggers talkin' no African.'

Kunta had been about to say that there was no question the old man was a fellow Gambian, of Jolof blood, with their high noses and flat lips and skins even deeper black than most other Gambian tribes. But when the gardener said what he said, he decided it was better not to speak of such things. So he changed the subject, asking where the old man was from and how he had ended up on this plantation. The gardener didn't answer right away. But finally, he said, 'Nigger suffered a lot like I is learn a lot,' and he looked carefully at Kunta, appearing to be deciding whether or not to go on. 'I were a good man once. I could ben' a crowbar over my leg. I could lif' a sack of meal dat would fell a mule. Or I could lif' a grown man by he belt wif my arm straight out. But I got worked an' beat near 'bout to death 'fo' my massa what done it sign me over to dis massa to pay a bill.' He paused. 'Now I done got enfeebled, I jes' wants to res' out whatever time I got lef'.'

His eyes searched Kunta. 'Sho' don' know how come I'm tellin' you dis. I ain't really bad off as I ack. But massa won't sell me long as he *think* I'm bad off. I seen you caught on how to garden some, though.' He hesitated. 'I could git back out dere an he'p if'n you wants me to – but not too much. I jes' ain't much good no mo',' he said sadly.

Kunta thanked the old man for offering, but reassured him that he'd be able to get along fine. A few minutes later he excused himself, and on his way back to his hut, got angry with himself for not feeling more compassion towards the old man. He was sorry he had been through so much, but he couldn't help turning a cold ear towards anyone who just rolled over and gave up.

The very next day, Kunta decided to see if he could get Bell talking too. Since he knew that Massa Waller was her favourite subject, he began by asking why he wasn't married. 'Him sho' was married – him an' Miss Priscilla, same year I come here. She was pretty as a hummin'bird. Wasn't hardly no bigger'n one, neither. Dat's how come she died birthin' dey first baby. Was a little gal; it died too. Terriblest time I guess anybody ever seen 'roun' here. An' massa ain't never been the same man since. Jes' work, work, work, seem like sometime he tryin' to kill hisself. He cain't bear to think a nobody sick or hurt he can he'p. Massa would doctor a sick cat quick as he would some hurt nigger he hear 'bout, like dat fiddler you always talkin' to – or like when you was brung here. He got so mad 'bout how dey done your foot, he even bought you away from his own brother John. 'Co'se wunt his doin', it was dem po'cracker nigger catchers he hired, who say you tried to kill 'em.'

Kunta listened, realizing that just as he was only beginning to appreciate the individual depths and dimensions of the black ones, it had never occurred to him that even white folks could also have human sufferings, though their ways in general could never be forgiven. He found himself wishing that he could speak the white folks' tongue well enough to say all this to Bell – and to tell her the story his old grandmother Nyo Boto had told him about the boy who tried to help the trapped crocodile, the story Nyo Boto always ended with, 'In the world, the payment for good is often bad.'

Thinking of home reminded Kunta of something he'd been wanting to tell Bell for a long time, and this seemed like a good moment. Except for her brown colour, he told her proudly, she looked almost like a handsome Mandinka woman.

He didn't have long to wait for her response to this great compliment. 'What fool stuff you talkin' 'bout?' she said irately. 'Don' know how come white folks keep on emptyin' out boatloads a you Africa niggers!'

56

For the next month, Bell wouldn't speak to Kunta – and even carried her own basket back to the big house after she had come for the vegetables. Then, early one Monday morning, she came rushing out to the garden, eyes wide with excitement, and blurted, 'Sheriff jes' rid off! He tol' massa been some big fightin' up Nawth somewhere call Boston! It's dem white folks so mad 'bout dem king's taxes from 'crost de big water. Massa got Luther hitchin' de buggy to git to de county seat. He sho' upset!'

Suppertime found everyone clustered around the fiddler's hut for his and the gardener's opinions, the gardener being slave row's oldest person, the fiddler its best travelled and most worldly.

'When it was?' somebody asked, and the gardener said, 'Well, anything we hears from up Nawth got to of happened a while back.'

The fiddler added, 'I heared dat from up roun' where dat Boston is, ten days is de quickest dat fast hosses can git word here to Virginia.'

In the deepening dusk, the massa's buggy returned. Luther hurried to slave row with further details he had picked up: 'Dey's tellin' it dat one night some a dem Boston peoples got so mad 'bout dem king's taxes dey marched on dat king's soldiers. Dem soldiers commence to shootin', an' firs' one kilt was a nigger name a Crispus Attucks. Dey callin' it "De Boston Massacree"!'

Little else was talked of for the next few days, as Kunta listened, unsure what it was all about and why white folks – and even the blacks – were so agog about whatever was happening so far away. Hardly a day passed without two or three passing slaves 'Yooo-hooo-ah-hoooing' from the big road with a new rumour. And Luther kept bringing regular reports from house slaves, stablehands, and other drivers he talked with on every journey the massa made to attend sick people or to discuss what was going on in New England with other massas in their big houses, or the county seat or nearby towns.

'White folks ain't got no secrets,' the fiddler said to Kunta. 'Dey's swamped deyselves wid niggers. Ain't much dey do, hardly nowheres dey go, it ain't niggers listenin'. If dey eatin' an' talkin', nigger gal servin' 'em actin' dumber'n she is, 'memberin' eve'y word she hear. Even when white folks gits so scared dey starts spellin' out words, if any niggers roun', well, plenty house niggers ain't long repeatin' it letter for letter to de nearest nigger what can spell an' piece together what was said. I mean dem niggers don' sleep 'fore dey knows what dem white folks was talkin' 'bout.'

What was happening 'up Nawth' continued to arrive piece by piece through the summer and into the fall. Then, as time passed, Luther began to report that as exercised as white folks were about the taxes, that wasn't their only worry. 'Dey's sayin' it's some counties got twice many niggers as white folks. Dey's worryin' dat king 'crost the water might start offerin' us niggers freedom to fight 'gainst dese white folks.' Luther waited for the gasps of his audience to subside. 'Fact,' he said, 'done heared some white folks so scared, done took to lockin' dey doors at night, done even quit talkin' roun' dey house niggers.'

258

Kunta lay on his mattress at night for weeks afterwards thinking about 'freedom'. As far as he could tell, it meant having no massa at all, doing as one wanted, going wherever one pleased. But it was ridiculous, he decided finally, to think that white folks would bring blacks all the way across the big water to work as slaves – and then set them free. It would never happen.

Shortly before Christmas, some of Massa Waller's relatives arrived for a visit, and their black buggy driver was eating his fill in Bell's kitchen while regaling her with the latest news .'Done heared dat over in Geo'gia,' he said, 'nigger name a George Leile, de Baptis' white folks done give 'im a licence to preach to niggers up an' down de Savannah River. Hear de claim he gon' start a African Baptis' church in Savannah. First time I heard 'bout any nigger church . . .'

Bell said, 'I heard 'bout one 'fo' now in Petersburg, right here in Virginia. But tell me, you heared anythin' about de white folks' troubles up Nawth?'

'Well, I hear tell while back whole lotta impo'tant white folks had a big meetin' in dat Philadelphia. Dey call it de First Continental Congress.'

Bell said she had heard that. In fact, she had painstakingly read it in Massa Waller's Virginia *Gazette*, and then she had shared the information with the old gardener and the fiddler. They were the only ones who knew she could read a little. When they had spoken about it recently, the gardener and the fiddler had agreed that Kunta shouldn't be told of her ability. True, he knew how to keep his mouth shut, and he had come to understand and express things unexpectedly well for anyone from Africa, but they felt that he couldn't yet fully appreciate how serious the consequences would be if the massa got the slightest hint that she could read: he would sell her away that same day.

By early the next year – 1775 – almost no news from any source was without some further development in Philadelphia. Even from what Kunta heard and could understand, it was clear that the white folks were moving towards a crisis with the king across the big water in the place called England. And there was a lot of exclaiming about some Massa Patrick Henry having cried out, 'Give me liberty or give me death!' Kunta liked that, but he couldn't understand how somebody *white* could say it; white folks looked pretty free to him.

Within a month came news that two whites named William Dawes and Paul Revere had raced on horses to warn somebody of hundreds of king's soldiers heading for somewhere called 'Concord' to destroy rifles and bullets that were stored there. And soon afterwards they

259

heard that in a furious battle at 'Lexington', some 'minutemen' had lost only a handful while killing over two hundred king's soldiers. Scarcely two days later came word that yet another thousand of them had fallen in a bloody battle at a place called 'Bunker Hill'. 'White folks at the county seat is laughin', sayin' dem king's soldiers wears red coats not to show de blood,' said Luther. 'Heared some a dat blood gettin' spilt by niggers fightin' 'longside white folks.' Wherever he went now, he said he kept on hearing that Virginia massas were showing greater than usual signs of mistrust towards their slaves – 'even dey oldest house niggers!'

Relishing his new importance along slave row, Luther arrived home from a trip in June to find an anxious audience awaiting his latest news. 'It's some Massa George Washington got picked to run a army. Nigger tol' me he's heared he got a big plantation wid plenty a slaves.' He said he had also heard that some New England slaves had been set free to help fight the king's redcoats.

'I knowed it!' the fiddler exclaimed. 'Niggers gon' git dragged in it an' kilt, jes' like dat French an' Indian War. Den soon's it's over, white folks be right back whippin' niggers!'

'Maybe not,' said Luther. 'Heared some white folks call themselves Quakers done put together a Anti-Slavery Society, up in dat Philadelphia. Reckon dey's some white folks jes' don't believe in niggers bein' slaves.'

'Me neither,' put in the fiddler.

The frequent bits of news that Bell contributed would sound as if she had been discussing them with the massa himself, but she finally admitted that she had been listening at the keyhole of the dining room whenever the massa had guests, for not long ago he had curtly told her to serve them and leave immediately, closing the door behind her; then she had heard him lock it. 'An' I knows dat man better'n his mammy!' she muttered indignantly.

'What he say in dere after he lock de do'?' asked the fiddler impatiently.

'Well, tonight he say don't seem no way not to fight dem English folks. He speck dey gon' send big boatloads a soldiers over here. He say it's over two hunnud thousand slaves just in Virginia, an' de biggest worry is if dem Englishmans ever riles up us niggers 'gainst white folks. Massa say he feel loyal to de king as any man, but ain't nobody can stan' dem taxes.'

'Gen'l Washington done stopped 'em taking any more niggers in the Army,' said Luther, 'but some free niggers up Nawth is arguin' dey's part of dis country an' wants to fight.'

'Dey sho' gon' git dey chance, jes' let 'nough white folks git kilt,' said the fiddler. 'Dem free niggers is *crazy*.'

But the news that followed two weeks later was even bigger. Lord Dunmore, the royal governor of Virginia, had proclaimed freedom for slaves who would leave their plantations to serve on his English fleet of fishing boats and frigates.

'Massa fit to be tied,' reported Bell. 'Man come to dinner say lotta talk 'bout chainin' or jailin' slaves suspicioned a joinin' up – or even thinkin' 'bout it – an' maybe kidnappin' an' hangin' dat Lord Dunmore.'

Kunta had been given the job of watering and feeding the horses of the flushed, agitated massas who visited the grim-jawed Massa Waller. And Kunta told how some of the horses had sweat-soaked flanks from long, hard riding, and how some of the massas were even driving their own buggies. One of them, he told the others, was John Waller, the massa's brother, the man who had bought Kunta when they took him off the boat eight years before. After all that time, he had known that hated face at first glance, but the man had tossed the reins to Kunta with no apparent recognition.

'Don' ack so surprised,' said the fiddler. 'Massa like him ain't gone say howdy to no nigger. 'Specially if'n he 'members who you is.'

Over the next few weeks, Bell learned at the keyhole of the massa's and his visitors' alarm and fury that thousands of Georgia, South Carolina, and Virginia slaves were said to be boldly fleeing their plantations to join Lord Dunmore. Some said they had heard that most of the fleeing slaves were simply heading for the North. But all the whites agreed on the need to start breeding more bloodhounds.

Then one day Massa Waller called Bell into the living room and twice read slowly aloud a marked item in his Virginia *Gazette*. He ordered Bell to show it to the slaves, and handed the paper to her. She did as she was told, and they reacted just as she had – less with fear than anger. 'Be not, ye Negroes, tempted to ruin yourselves ... whether we suffer or not, if you desert us, you most certainly will.'

Before returning the *Gazette*, Bell spelled out for her own information several other news items in the privacy of her cabin, and among them were reports of actual or predicted slave revolts. Later the massa shouted at her for not returning the paper before supper, and Bell apologized in tears. But soon she was sent out again with another message – this time the news that Virginia's House of Burgesses had decreed 'death without benefit of clergy for all Negro or other slaves conspiring to rebel or make insurrections.'

'What do it mean?' a field hand asked, and the fiddler replied,

'Uprise, an' white folks won't call no preacher when dey kills you!'

Luther heard that some white folks called 'Tories', and some other kind called 'Scotchmen', were joining with the English. 'An' sheriff's nigger tol' me dat Lord Dunmore's ruinin' river plantations, burnin' big houses, an' tellin' de niggers he free 'em if'n dey come on an' jine 'im.' Luther told how in Yorktown and other towns, any blacks caught out at night were being whipped and jailed.

Christmas that year was but a word. Lord Dunmore was reported to have barely outraced a mob onto the safety of his flagship. And a week later came incredible news that Dunmore, with his fleet off Norfolk, had ordered the city emptied within one hour. Then his guns began a bombardment that set raging fires, and much of Norfolk had been reduced to ashes. In what was left, Bell reported, water and food were scarce, and fever had broken out, killing so many that Hampton Roads' waters were dotted with bloated bodies drifting ashore with the tides. 'Say dey's buryin' 'em in san' an' mud,' said Luther. 'An' lotta niggers near 'bout starvin' an' scared to death on dem English boats.'

Mulling over all these terrible events, Kunta felt that in some unfathomable way, all of this suffering must have some meaning, some reason, that Allah must have willed it. Whatever was going to happen next, both to black and white, must be His design.

It was early in 1776 when Kunta and the others heard that a General Cornwallis had come from England with boatfuls of sailors and soldiers trying to cross a big 'York River', but a great storm had scattered the boats. They heard next that another Continental Congress had met, with a group of massas from Virginia moving for complete separation from the English. Then two months of minor news passed before Luther returned from the county seat with the news that after another meeting on 4 July, 'All the white folks I seen is jes' carryin' on! Somethin' 'bout some Decoration a Ind'pen'ence. Heared 'em say Massa John Hancock done writ his name real big so the king wouldn't have to strain none to see it.'

On his next trips to the county seat, Luther returned with accounts he had heard that in Baltimore, a life-sized rag doll 'king' had been carted through the streets, then thrown into a bonfire surrounded by white people shouting 'Tyrant! Tyrant!' And in Richmond, rifles had been fired in volleys as shouting white people waved their torches and drank toasts to each other. Along the subdued slave row, the old gardener said, 'Ain't nothin' neither way for niggers to holler 'bout. England or here, dey's all white folks.'

Later that summer, Bell bustled over to slave row with news from a dinner guest that the House of Burgesses had just recently passed an act that 'say dey gon' take niggers in the Army as drummers, fifers, or pioneers.'

'What's pioneers?' asked a field hand.

'It mean git stuck up front an' git kilt!' said the fiddler.

Luther soon brought home an exciting account of a big battle right there in Virginia that had slaves fighting on both sides. Amid a hail of musket balls from hundreds of redcoats and Tories, along with a group of convicts and blacks, a smaller force of white 'Colonials' and their blacks was driven across a bridge, but in the rear a slave soldier named Billy Flora had ripped up and hurled away enough planks from the bridge that the English forces had to stop and withdraw, saving the day for the Colonial forces.

'Rip up a bridge! Dat musta been some strong nigger!' the gardener exclaimed.

When the French entered the war on the Colonial side in 1778, Bell relayed reports that one state after another was authorizing the enlisting of slaves with the promise of freedom when the war was won. 'Now ain't but two states lef' dat say dey ain't gon' never let niggers fight, dat's South Ca'lina an' Geo'gia.'

'Dat de only thing good I ever heared 'bout neither one a dem!' said the fiddler.

As much as he hated slavery, it seemed to Kunta that no good could come of the white folks giving guns to blacks. First of all, the whites would always have more guns than the blacks, so any attempt to revolt would end in defeat. And he thought about how in his own homeland, guns and bullets had been given by the toubob to evil chiefs and kings, until blacks were fighting blacks, village against village, and selling those they conquered – their own people – into chains.

Once Bell heard the massa say that as many as five thousand blacks, both free and slave, were in the fighting that was going on, and Luther regularly brought stories of blacks fighting and dying alongside their massas. Luther also told of some all-black companies from 'up Nawth', even one all-black battalion called 'The Bucks of America'. 'Even dey colonel is a nigger,' said Luther. 'His name Middleton.' He looked archly at the fiddler. 'You won't never guess what he is!'

'What you mean?' said the fiddler.

'He a fiddler, too! An' it's time to do some fiddlin'!'

Then Luther hummed and sang a new song he had heard in the county seat. The catchiness of it was easy to pick up, and soon others were singing it, and still others beating time with sticks. 'Yankee Doodle came to town, ridin' on a pony ...' And when the fiddler started playing, the slave row young'uns began to dance and clap their hands.

With May of 1781 came the astounding story that redcoats on horses had ruined Massa Thomas Jefferson's plantation called Monticello. The crops had been destroyed, the barn burned, the live-stock run off, and all the horses and thirty slaves had been taken. 'White folks sayin' Virginia got to be saved,' Luther reported, and soon after he told of white joy because General Washington's army was headed there. 'An' niggers a plenty is in it!' October brought reports that the combined forces of Washington and Lafayette had poured shot and shell into Yorktown, attacking England's Cornwallis. And they soon learned of other battles raging in Virginia, New York, North Carolina, Maryland, and other states. Then in the third week of the month came the news that set even slave row shouting: 'Cornwallis done surrendered! War am ober! Freedom am won!'

Luther barely had time to sleep between buggy journeys now, and the massa was even smiling again – for the first time in years, said Bell.

'Ev'ywhere I's been, de niggers is hollerin' loud as white folks,' said Luther.

But he said that slaves everywhere had rejoiced most over their special hero, 'Ol' Billy' Flora, who had recently been discharged and carried his faithful musket back to Norfolk.

'Y'all come here!' Bell shouted, summoning the others on slave row not long after. 'Massa jes' tol' me dey done named that Philadelphia firs' capital of Newnited States!' But it was Luther who told them later, 'Massa Jefferson done put up some kin' of Manumission Ack. It say massas got de right to free niggers, but tell me dem Quakers an' antislavery folks an' free niggers up Nawth is hollerin' an' goin' on 'cause the Ack say massas don't have to, not less'n dey want to.'

When General Washington disbanded the army early in November of 1783, formally ending what most people had begun calling 'The Seven Years' War', Bell told everyone in slave row, 'Massa say gon' be peace now.'

'Ain't gon' be no peace, not long as it's white folks,' said the fiddler sourly, ' 'cause ain't nothin' dey loves better'n killin'. His glance flicked among the faces around him. 'Jes' watch what I tell you – it's gon' be worse'n it was for us niggers.'

Kunta and the old gardener sat later talking quietly. 'You seen aplenty since you been here. How long it's been, anyhow?' Kunta didn't know, and that troubled him.

That night, when he was alone, Kunta spent hours carefully arranging into piles of twelve all of the multicoloured pebbles that he had dropped faithfully into his gourd with each new moon. He was so stunned by what the stones finally told him that the gardener never learned the answer to his question. Surrounding him there on the dirt floor of his hut were seventeen piles of stones. He was thirty-four rains old! What in the name of Allah had happened to his life? He had been in the white mans' land as long as he had lived in Juffure. Was he still an African, or had he become a 'nigger', as the others called themselves? Was he even a man? He was the same age as his father when he had seen him last, yet he had no sons of his own, no wife, no family, no village, no people, no homeland; almost no past at all that seemed real to him any more – and no future he could see. It was as if The Gambia had been a dream he'd had once long ago. Or was he still asleep? And if he was, would he ever waken?

57

Kunta didn't have long to brood about the future, for a few days later came news that took the plantation by storm. A captured runaway housegirl, reported Bell breathlessly after the sheriff arrived for a hushed meeting with the massa behind closed doors, had admitted under a lashing that her crude escape route had been drawn for her by none other than the massa's driver, Luther.

Storming out to slave row before Luther could run away, Massa Waller confronted him with the sheriff and demanded angrily to know if it was true. Terrified, Luther admitted that it was. Red-faced with rage, the massa lifted his arm to strike, but when Luther begged for mercy, he lowered it again and stood there staring silently at Luther for a long moment, tears of fury welling in his eyes.

At last he spoke, very quietly: 'Sheriff, put this man under arrest and take him to jail. He is to be sold at the next slave auction.' And without another word he turned and walked back to the house, ignoring Luther's anguished sobs.

Speculation had hardly begun about who would be assigned to replace him as the massa's driver when Bell came out one night and told Kunta that the massa wanted to see him right away. Everyone watched – but no one was surprised – as he went cripping into the house behind Bell. Though he suspected why he had been called, Kunta felt a little scared, for he had never spoken to the massa or even been beyond Bell's kitchen in the big house during all his sixteen years on the plantation.

As Bell led him through the kitchen into a hallway, his eyes goggled at the shining floor and the high, papered walls. She knocked at a huge carved door. He heard the massa say, 'Come in!' and Bell went on inside, turning to beckon expressionlessly to Kunta. He couldn't believe the size of the room, it seemed as big as the inside of the barn. The polished oaken floor was covered with rugs, and the walls were hung with paintings and tapestries. The richly dark, matched furniture was waxed, and long rows of books sat on recessed shelves. Massa Waller sat at a desk reading under an oil lamp with a circular shade of greenish glass, and his finger held his place in his book when, after a moment, he turned around to face Kunta.

'Toby, I need a buggy driver. You've grown into a man on this place, and I believe you're loyal.' His widely set blue eyes seemed to pierce Kunta. 'Bell tells me that you never drink. I like that, and I've noticed how you conduct yourself.' Massa Waller paused. Bell shot a look at Kunta. 'Yassuh, Massa,' he said quickly.

'You know what happened to Luther?' the massa asked. 'Yassuh,' said Kunta. The massa's eyes narrowed, and his voice turned cold and hard. 'I'd sell you in a minute,' he said. 'I'd sell Bell if you two had no better sense.'

As they stood there silently, the massa reopened his book. 'All right, start driving me tomorrow. I'm going to Newport. I'll show you the way until you learn.' The massa glanced at Bell. 'Get him the proper clothes. And tell the fiddler that he'll be replacing Toby in the garden.'

'Yassuh, Massa,' Bell said, as she and Kunta left.

Bell brought him the clothing, but it was the fiddler and the old gardener who supervised Kunta's dressing early the next morning in the starched and pressed canvas trousers and cotton hemp shirt. They didn't look too bad, but that black string tie they helped him put on next, he felt, made him look ridiculous.

'Newport ain't nowhere to drive, jes' right up next to Spotsylvania Courthouse,' said the old gardener. 'It's one a de ol' Waller family big houses.'

The fiddler – who by this time had been told of his own new duties as well as Kunta's – was walking around inspecting him with an expression that revealed transparently both his pleasure and his jealousy. 'You a sho' nuff special nigger now, no two ways 'bout it. Jes' don't let it git to yo' head.'

It was unnecessary advice for one who – even after all this time – found no dignity in anything he was made to do for the white man. But whatever small excitement Kunta felt at the prospect of being able to leave his garden behind and widen his horizons – as his uncles Janneh and Saloum had done – was soon forgotten in the heat of his new duties.

Summoned by his patients at any hour of the day or night, Massa Waller would call Kunta rushing from his hut to hitch the horses for breakneck rides to homes sometimes many miles from the plantation down narrow, twisting roads that were hardly smoother than the countryside around them. Lurching and careening over ruts and potholes, laying on the whip until the horses heaved for breath, Massa Waller clinging to his canopied rear seat, Kunta showed a knack for the reins that somehow saw them safely to their destination even in the spring thaw, when the red-clay roads turned into treacherous rivers of mud.

Early one morning, the massa's brother John came galloping in, frantically reporting that his wife's labour pains had begun, although it was two months before the birth had been expected. Massa John's horse was too exhausted to return without rest, and Kunta had driven both of them back to Massa John's barely in the nick of time. Kunta's own overheated horses hadn't cooled down enough for him to give them water when he heard the shrill cries of a newborn baby. It was a five-pound girl, the massa told him on their way home, and they were going to call her Anne.

And so it went. During that same frantic summer and fall, there was a plague of black vomiting that claimed victims all over the county – so many that Massa Waller and Kunta couldn't keep up with them, and soon drove themselves into fever. Downing copious dosages of quinine to keep them going, they saved more lives than they lost. But Kunta's own life became a blur of countless big house kitchens, catnaps on pallets in strange huts or in haymows, and endless hours of sitting in the buggy outside shanties and grand homes listening to the same cries of pain while he waited for the massa to reappear so that they could return home – or more often drive on to the next patient.

But Massa Waller didn't travel always in the midst of crisis. Sometimes entire weeks would pass without anything more urgent than routine house calls or visits to one of a seemingly inexhaustible assortment of relatives and friends whose plantations were located somewhere within driving distance. On such occasions – particularly in the spring and summer, when the meadows were thick with flowers, wild strawberries, and blackberry thickets, and the fences were trellised with lushly growing vines – the buggy would roll along leisurely behind its finely matched pair of bay horses, Massa Waller sometimes nodding off under the black canopy that shielded him from the sun. Everywhere were quail whirring up, brilliant red cardinals hopping about, meadow larks and whippoorwills calling out. Now and then a bullsnake sunning on the road, disturbed by the oncoming buggy, would go slithering for safety, or a buzzard would go flapping heavily away from its dead rabbit. But Kunta's favourite sight was a lonely old oak or cedar in the middle of a field; it would send his mind back to the baobabs of Africa, and to the elders' saying that wherever one stood alone, there had once been a village. At such times he would think of Juffure.

On his social calls, the massa went most often to visit his parents at Enfield, their plantation on the borderline between King William County and King and Queen County. Approaching it – like all the Waller family big houses – the buggy would roll down a long double avenue of huge old trees and stop beneath a massive black walnut tree on the wide front lawn. The house, which was much bigger and richer looking than the massa's, sat on a slight rise overlooking a narrow, slow-moving river.

During his first few months of driving, the cooks at the various plantations in whose kitchens Kunta was fed – but most especially Hattie Mae, the fat, haughty, shiny-black cook at Enfield – had eyed him critically, as fiercely possessive of their domains as Bell was at Massa Waller's. Confronted with Kunta's stiff dignity and reserve, though, none quite ventured to challenge him in any way directly, and he would silently clean his plate of whatever they served him, excepting any pork. Eventually, however, they began to get used to his quiet ways, and after his sixth or seventh visit, even the cook at Enfield apparently decided that he was fit for her to talk to and deigned to speak to him.

'You know where you at?' she asked him suddenly one day in the middle of his meal. He didn't answer, and she didn't wait for one.

'Dis here's de first Newnited States house of de Wallers. Nobody but Wallers lived here for a hunerd an' fifty years!' She said that when Enfield had been built it was only half its present size, but that later another house had been brought up from near the river and added on. 'Our fireplace is bricks brought in boats from England,' she said proudly. Kunta nodded politely as she droned on, but he was unimpressed.

Once in a while, Massa Waller would pay a visit to Newport, Kunta's first destination as a driver; it seemed impossible to believe that an entire year had passed since then. An old uncle and aunt of the massa's lived there in a house that looked to Kunta very much like Enfield. While the white folks ate in the dining room, the cook at Newport would feed Kunta in the kitchen, strutting around with a large ring of keys on a thin leather belt around the top of her apron. He had noticed by now that every senior housemaid wore such a key ring. On it, he had learned, in addition to her keys for the pantry, the smokehouse, the cooling cellar, and other food-storage places, were the keys to all the rooms and closets in the big house. Every cook he'd met would walk in a way to make those keys jangle as a badge of how important and trusted she was, but none jangled them louder than this one.

On a recent visit, having decided – like the cook at Enfield – that he might be all right after all, she pressed a finger to her lips and led Kunta on tiptoe to a small room farther within the big house. Making a great show of unlocking the door with one of the keys at her waist, she led him inside and pointed to one wall. On it was a mounted display of what she explained were the Wallers' coat of arms, their silver seal, a suit of armour, silver pistols, a silver sword, and the prayer book of the original Colonel Waller.

Pleased at the ill-concealed amazement on Kunta's face, she exclaimed, 'Ol' colonel built dat Enfield, but he buried right here.' And walking outside, she showed him the grave and its lettered tombstone. After a minute, as Kunta stared at it, she asked with a rehearsed casualness, 'You wanna know what it say?' Kunta nodded his head, and rapidly she 'read' the long since memorized inscription: 'Sacred to Memory of Colonel John Waller, Gentleman, third son of John Waller and Mary Key, who settled in Virginia in 1635, from Newport Paganel, Buckinghamshire.'

Several cousins of massa's, Kunta soon discovered, lived at Prospect Hill, also in Spotsylvania County. Like Enfield, the big house here was one and a half stories high, as were nearly all very old big houses, the cook at Prospect Hill told him, because the king had put an extra tax on two-story houses. Unlike Enfield, Prospect Hill was rather small – smaller than the other Waller family houses – but none, she informed him, whether or not he cared to listen, had as wide an entrance hall or as steep a circular stairway.

'You ain't gwine upstairs, but no reason you cain't know us got four-poster canopy beds up dere so tall dey has to use stepladders, an' under dem is chillun's trundle beds. An' lemme tell you sump'n. Dem beds, de chimney bricks, house beams, hinges on de do's, ev'ything usn's got in here was made or did by slave niggers.'

In the backyard, she showed Kunta the first weaving house he had ever seen, and nearby were the slave quarters – which were about the same as theirs – and below them was a pond, and farther beyond was a slaves' graveyard. 'I knows you ain't want to see dat,' she said, reading his thoughts. He wondered if she also knew how strange and sad he found it to hear her talking – as so many others did – about 'usn's', and acting as if she owned the plantation she lived on instead of the other way around.

58

'How come massa been seein' so much a dat no-good brother a his las' few months?' asked Bell one evening after Kunta trudged in after arriving home from a visit to Massa John's plantation. 'I thought they was no love los' 'tween dem two.'

'Look to me like massa jes' gone crazy 'bout dat li'l ol' gal baby dey got,' said Kunta wearily.

'She sho is a cute li'l thin',' said Bell. After a thoughtful pause, she added, 'Reckon Missy Anne seem to massa like dat li'l gal of his own he los'.'

That hadn't occurred to Kunta, who still found it difficult to think of toubob as actual human beings.

'She gon' be a whole year ol' dis November, ain't she?' asked Bell.

Kunta shrugged. All he knew was that all this running back and forth between the two plantations was wearing ruts in the road – and in his rump. Even though he had no use for Massa John's sour-faced buggy driver Roosby, he told Bell he was grateful for the rest when the massa invited his brother to visit him for a change the week before.

As they were leaving that day, Bell recalled, the massa had looked as happy as his little niece when he tossed her in the air and caught her, squealing and laughing, before handing her up to her mother in the buggy. Kunta hadn't noticed and he didn't care – and he couldn't understand why Bell *did*.

One afternoon a few days later, on their way home from a house call on one of Massa Waller's patients at a plantation not far from Newport, the massa called out sharply to Kunta that he had just passed a turn they should have taken. Kunta had been driving without seeing, so shocked was he by what he had just seen at the patient's big house. Even as he muttered an apology and turned the buggy hastily around, he couldn't rid his mind of the sight of the heavy, very black, Wolof-looking woman he had seen in the backyard. She had been sitting on a stump, both of her large breasts hanging out, matter-of-factly suckling a white infant at one and a black infant at the other. It was a revolting sight to Kunta, and an astonishing one, but when he told the gardener about it later, the old man said, 'Ain' hardly a massa in Virginia ain't sucked a black mammy, or leas' was raised up by one.'

Almost as repulsive to Kunta was something he'd seen all too much of – the kind of demeaning 'games' that went on at the plantations he visited between white and black 'young'uns' of about the same age. The white children seemed to love nothing more than playing 'massa' and pretending to beat the black ones, or playing 'hosses' by climbing onto their backs and making them scramble about on all fours. Playing 'school', the white children would 'teach' the black to read and write, with many cuffings and shriekings about their 'dumbness'. Yet after lunch – which the black children would spend fanning the massa and his family with leafy branches to keep flies away – the white and black children would lie down together and take naps on pallets.

After seeing such things, Kunta would always tell Bell, the fiddler, and the gardener that he'd never understand the toubob if he lived to a hundred rains. And they would always laugh and tell him that they'd seen this sort of thing – and more – all of their lives.

Sometimes, they told him, as the white and black 'young'uns' grew up together, they became very attached to one another. Bell recalled two occasions when the massa had been called to attend white girls who had fallen ill when their lifelong black playmates had been sold away for some reason. Their massas and mistresses had been advised that their daughters' hysterical grief was such that they might well grow weaker and weaker until they died, unless their little girlfriends were quickly found and bought back.

The fiddler said that a lot of black young'uns had learned to play the violin, the harpsichord, or other instruments by listening and observing as their white playmates were taught by music masters whom their rich massas had hired from across the big water. The old gardener said that on his second plantation a white and black boy grew up together until finally the young massa took the black one off with him to William and Mary College. 'Ol' Massa ain't like it a'tall, but Ol' Missy say "It's his nigger if he want to!" An' when dis nigger git back later on, he tol' us in slave row dat dey was heap more young massas dere wid dey niggers as valets, sleepin' right in de room wid 'em. He say heap of times dey take dey niggers wid 'em to classes, den dey argue later on whose nigger learnt de mos'. Dat nigger from my plantation couldn't jes' read an' write, he could figger, too, an' 'cite dem poems an' stuff dey has at colleges. I got sol' away roun' den. Wonder whatever become a him?'

'Lucky if he ain't dead,' the fiddler said. ''Cause white folks is quick to 'spicion a nigger like dat be de first to hatch a uprisin' or a re-volt somewhere. Don't pay to know too much, jes' like I tol' dis African here when he started drivin' massa. Mouf shut an' ears open, dat's de way you learns de mos'—'

Kunta found out how true that was soon afterwards, when Massa Waller offered a ride to a friend of his from one plantation to another. Talking as if he wasn't there – and saying things that Kunta would have found extraordinary even if they hadn't known there was a black sitting right in front of them – they spoke about the frustrating slowness of their slaves' separation of cotton fibres from the seeds by hand when demands for cotton cloth were rapidly increasing. They discussed how more and more, only the largest planters could afford to buy slaves at the robbery prices being demanded by slave traders and slave-ship agents.

'But even if you can afford it, bigness can create more problems than it solves,' said the massa. 'The more slaves you've got, the likelier it is that some kind of revolt could be fomented.'

'We should never have let them bear arms against white men during the war,' said his companion. 'Now we witness the result!' He went on to tell how, at a large plantation near Fredericksburg, some former slave soldiers had been caught just before a planned revolt, but only because a housemaid had got some wind of it and told her mistress in tears. 'They had muskets, scythe blades, pitchforks, they had even made spears,' said the massa's friend. 'It's said their plot was to kill and burn by night and hide by day and keep moving. One of their ringleaders said they expected to die, but not before they had done what the war had showed them they could do to white people.'

'They could have cost many innocent lives,' he heard the massa reply gravely. Massa Waller went on to say that he had read somewhere that over two hundred slave outbreaks had occurred since the first slave ships came. 'I've been saying for years that our greatest danger is that slaves are coming to outnumber whites.'

'You're right!' his friend exclaimed. 'You don't know who's shuffling and grinning and planning to cut your throat. Even the ones right in your house. You simply can't trust any of them. It's in their very nature.'

His back as rigid as a board, Kunta heard the massa say, 'As a doctor, more than once I've seen white deaths that – well, I'll not go into details, but let's just say I've thought some of them suspicious.'

Hardly feeling the reins in his hands, Kunta was unable to comprehend that they could seem so incredibly unaware of him. His mind tumbled with things that he too had heard during the nearly two years now that he had been driving the buggy for the massa. He had heard many a whispering of cooks and maids grinning and bowing as they served food containing some of their own bodily wastes. And he had been told of white folks' meals containing bits of ground glass, or arsenic, or other poisons. He had even heard stories about white babies going into mysterious fatal comas without any trace of the darning needle that had been thrust by housemaids into their soft heads where the hair was thickest. And a big-house cook had pointed out to him the former hut of an old mammy nurse who had been beaten badly and then sold away after severely injuring a young massa who had hit her.

It seemed to Kunta that black women here were even more defiant and rebellious than the men. But perhaps it only appeared that way because the women were more direct and personal about it; they would usually take revenge against white folks who had wronged them. The men tended to be more secretive and less vengeful. The fiddler had told Kunta about a white overseer who had been hanged from a tree by the father of a black girl he had been caught raping; but violence against whites by black men was most often ignited by news of white atrocities or slave rebellions and the like.

There had never been any uprisings, or even any incidents, at the Waller place, but right there in Spotsylvania County, Kunta had heard about some blacks who had hidden muskets and other weapons and vowed to kill their massas or mistresses, or both, and put their plantations to the torch. And there were some men among those he worked with who would meet in secret to discuss anything good or bad that happened to slaves elsewhere and to consider any action they might take to help; but so far they had only talked.

Kunta had never been invited to join them – probably, he thought, because they felt that his foot would make him useless to them in an actual revolt. Whatever their reasons for leaving him out, he felt it was just as well. Though he wished them luck in whatever they might decide to do, Kunta didn't believe that a rebellion could ever succeed against such overwhelming odds. Perhaps, as Massa Waller had said, blacks might soon outnumber whites, but they could never over-power them – not with pitchforks, kitchen knives, and stolen muskets against the massed armies of the white nation and its cannons.

But their worst enemy, it seemed to Kunta, was themselves. There were a few young rebels among them, but the vast majority of slaves were the kind that did exactly what was expected of them, usually without even having to be told; the kind white folks could – and did – trust with the lives of their own children; the kind that looked the other way when the white man took their women into haymows. Why, there were some right there on the plantation he was sure the massa could leave unguarded for a year and find them there – still working – when he returned. It certainly wasn't because they were content; they complained constantly among themselves. But never did more than a handful so much as protest, let alone resist.

Perhaps he was becoming like them, Kunta thought. Or perhaps he was simply growing up. Or was he just growing old? He didn't know; but he knew that he had lost his taste for fighting and running, and he wanted to be left alone; he wanted to mind his own business. Those who didn't had a way of winding up dead.

59

Dozing off in the shade of an oak tree in the backyard of a plantation where the massa was visiting to treat an entire family that had come down with a fever, Kunta woke up with a start when the evening conch horn blew to call the slaves in from the fields. He was still rubbing the sleep from his eyes when they reached the yard. Glancing up as they passed by on their way to wash up for supper, he noticed that there were about twenty or thirty of them. He looked again. Maybe he was still sleeping, but four of them – a man, a woman, and two teenage boys – were *white*.

'Dey's what you call indentured white folks,' his friend the cook explained when he expressed his amazement to her a few minutes later. 'Been here 'bout two months now. Dey's a fambly from someplace 'crost de big water. Massa pay dere way here on de boat, so dey gotta pay him back by workin' seben years as slaves. Den dey free jus' like any other white folks.'

'Dey live in slave row?' asked Kunta.

'Dey got dey own cabin off a ways from our'n, but it jus' as tumbledown as de res'. And dey eats de same mess we does. An' don't get treated no different out in de fiel'.'

'What dey like?' asked Kunta.

'Dey sticks pretty much to deyselves, but dey awright. Ain't like us'ns, but does dey job and don't make no trouble for nobody.'

It seemed to Kunta that these white slaves were better off than most of the free whites he'd seen on the massa's rounds. With often as many as a dozen grown-ups and children packed on top of each other in one-room hovels on tiny patches of red clay or swampland, they scratched out a living so meagre that the blacks laughingly sang a song about them: 'Not po' white, please, O Lawd, fer I'd ruther be a nigger.' Though he had never seen it for himself, Kunta had heard that some of these whites were so poor that they even had to eat dirt. They were certainly skinny enough, and few of them – even the 'chilluns' – had any teeth left. And they smelled like they slept with their flea-bitten hounds, which many of them did. Trying to breathe through his mouth as he waited in the buggy outside their shacks while the massa treated one of them for scurvy or pellagra, watching the women and the children ploughing and chopping while the menfolk lay under a tree with a brown jug of liquor and their dogs, all scratching, it was easy for Kunta to understand why plantation-owning massas and even their slaves scorned and sneered at them as 'lazy, shiftless, no-count white trash'.

In fact, as far as he was concerned, that was a charitable description of heathens so shameless that they managed to commit every conceivable offence against the standards of decency upheld by the most sacrilegious Moslem. On his trips with the massa to neighbouring towns, there would always be packs of them idling around the courthouse or the saloon even in the morning – dressed in their sweat-stained, greasy, threadbare cast-offs, reeking of the filthy tobacco weed, which they puffed incessantly, swigging 'white lightning' from bottles they carried in their pockets, laughing and yelling raucously at one another as they knelt on the ground in alleys playing cards and dice for money.

By mid-afternoon, they would be making complete fools of themselves: bursting drunkenly into song, cavorting wildly up and down the street, whistling and calling out indecently to women who passed by, arguing and cursing loudly among themselves, and finally starting fights that would begin with a shove or a punch – while huge crowds of others like them would gather 'round to cheer them on – and end with ear-biting, eye-gouging, kicking of private parts, and bloody wounds that would almost always call for the massa's urgent attention. Even the wild animals of his homeland, it seemed to Kunta, had more dignity than these creatures.

Bell was always telling stories about poor whites getting flogged for beating their wives and being sentenced to a year's imprisonment for rape. Almost as often, she told about one of them stabbing or shooting another one to death; for that they might be forced to serve six months as a slave. But as much as they loved violence among themselves, Kunta knew from personal experience that they loved violence against black people even more. It was a crowd of poor whites – male and female – that had hooted and jeered and jabbed with sticks at him and his chain mates when they were taken from the big canoe. It was a poor-white overseer who had applied the lash so freely to his back at Massa John's plantation. It was 'cracker white trash' slave catchers who had taken such glee in chopping off his foot. And he had heard about runaways captured by 'pattyrollers' who hadn't given them the choice he'd got and sent them back to their plantations torn and broken almost beyond recognition – and divested of their manhood. He had never been able to figure out why poor whites hated blacks so much. Perhaps, as the fiddler had told him, it was because of *rich* whites, who had everything they didn't: wealth, power, and property, including slaves who were fed, clothed, and housed while they struggled to stay alive. But he could feel no pity for them, only a deep loathing that had turned icy cold with the passing of the years since the swing of an axe held by one of them had ended forever something more precious to him than his own life: the hope of freedom.

Later that summer of 1786, Kunta was returning to the plantation from the county seat with news that filled him with mixed feelings. White folks had been gathering at every corner waving copies of the *Gazette* and talking heatedly about a story in it that told of increasing numbers of Quakers who were not only encouraging slaves to escape, as they had been doing for several years, but had now also begun aiding, hiding, and guiding them to safety in the North. Poor whites and massas alike were calling furiously for the tarring and feathering, even hanging, of any known Quakers who might be even suspected of such seditious acts. Kunta didn't believe the Quakers or anybody else would be able to help more than a few of them escape, and sooner or later they'd get caught themselves. But it couldn't hurt to have white allies – they'd need them – and anything that got their owners so frightened couldn't be all bad.

Later that night, after Kunta told everyone in slave row what he had seen and heard, the fiddler said that when he had been playing for a dance across the county the week before, he'd seen 'dey moufs fallin' open' when he cocked an ear close enough to overhear a lawyer there confiding to a group of big plantation owners that the will of a wealthy Quaker named John Pleasant had bequeathed freedom to his more than two hundred slaves. Bell, who arrived late, said that she had just overheard Massa Waller and some dinner guests bitterly discussing the fact that slavery had recently been abolished in a northern state called 'Massachusetts', and reports claimed that other states near there would do the same.

'What 'bolished mean?' asked Kunta.

The old gardener replied, 'It mean one dese days all us niggers gon' be *free!*'

60

Even when he didn't have anything he'd seen or heard in town to tell the others, Kunta had learned to enjoy sitting around the fire with them in front of the fiddler's hut. But lately he'd found that he was spending less time talking with the fiddler – who had once been his only reason for being there – than with Bell and the old gardener. They hadn't exactly cooled towards one another, but things just weren't the same any more, and that saddened him. It hadn't brought them closer for the fiddler to get saddled with Kunta's gardening duties, though he'd finally managed to get over it. But what he couldn't seem to get used to was the fact that Kunta soon began to replace *him* as the plantation's best-informed source of news and gossip from the outside.

No one could have accused the fiddler of becoming tight-lipped, but as time went on, his famous monologues became shorter and shorter and more and more infrequent; and he hardly ever played fiddle for them any more. After he had acted unusually subdued one evening, Kunta mentioned it to Bell, wondering if he had done or said anything that might have hurt his feelings.

'Don' flatter yourself,' she told him. 'Day an' night fo' months now, fiddler been runnin' back an' fo'th 'crost de county playin' fo' de white folks. He jes' too wo' out to run his mouf like he use to, which is fine wid me. An' he gittin' dollar an' a half a night now eve'y time he play at one a dem fancy white folks' parties he go to. Even when de massa take his half, fiddler get to keep a sebenty-five cents fo' hisself, so how come he bother playin' fo' niggers no mo' – less'n you wants to take up a c'llection an' see if'n he play fo' a nickel.'

She glanced up from the stove to see if Kunta was smiling. He wasn't. But she would have fallen into her soup if he had been. She had seen him smile just once – when he heard about a slave he knew from a nearby plantation who had escaped safely to the North.

'I hears fiddler plannin' to save up what he earn an' buy his freedom from de massa,' she went on.

'Time he got enough to do dat,' said Kunta gravely, 'he gonna be too ol' to leave his hut.'

Bell laughed so hard she almost *did* fall into her soup.

If the fiddler never earned his freedom, it wouldn't be for lack of trying, Kunta decided, after hearing him play at a party one night not long afterwards. He had dropped off the massa and was talking with the other drivers under a tree out on the darkened lawn when the band – led by the fiddler, obviously in rare form tonight – began to play a Virginia reel so lively that even the white folks couldn't keep their feet still.

From where he sat, Kunta could see the silhouettes of young couples whirling from the great hall out onto the veranda through one door and back in again through another. When the dancing was over, everybody lined up at a long table glowing with candles and loaded with more food than slave row got to see in a year. And when they'd had their fill – the host's fat daughter came back three times for more – the cook sent out a trayful of leftovers and a pitcher of lemonade for the drivers. Thinking that the massa might be getting ready to leave, Kunta wolfed down a chicken leg and a delicious sticky sweet creamy something or other that one of the other drivers called 'a ay-clair'. But the massas, in their white suits, stood around talking quietly for hours, gesturing with hands that held long cigars and sipping now and then from glasses of wine that glinted in the light from the chandelier that hung above them, while their wives, in fine gowns, fluttered their handkerchiefs and simpered behind their fans.

The first time he had taken the massa to one of these 'high-falutin' to-dos', as Bell called them, Kunta had been all but overwhelmed by conflicting emotions: awe, indignation, envy, contempt, fascination, revulsion – but most of all a deep loneliness and melancholy from which it took him almost a week to recover. He couldn't believe that such incredible wealth actually existed, that people really lived that way. It took him a long time, and a great many more parties, to realize that they *didn't* live that way, that it was all strangely unreal, a kind of beautiful dream the white folks were having, a lie they were telling themselves: that goodness can come from badness, that it's possible to be civilized with one another without treating as human beings those whose blood, sweat, and mother's milk made possible the life of privilege they led.

Kunta had considered sharing these thoughts with Bell or the old gardener, but he knew he wouldn't be able to find the right words in the toubob tongue. Anyway, both of them had lived here all their lives and couldn't be expected to see it as he did, with the eyes of an outsider – one who had been born free. So, as it had always been when he thought about such things, he kept it to himself – and found himself wishing that, even after all these years, he didn't still feel so alone.

About three months later Massa Waller – ' 'long wid jes' 'bout ev'eybody who's anybody in de state a Virginia,' according to the fiddler – was invited to attend the Thanksgiving Ball his parents held each year at Enfield. Arriving late because the massa, as usual, had to stop off and see a patient on the way, Kunta could hear that the party was well under way as they clip-clopped up the tree-lined driveway towards the big house, which was lit up from top to bottom. Pulling up at the front door, he leaped down to stand at attention while the doorman helped the massa out of the buggy. That's when he heard it. Somewhere very near by, the edges and heels of someone's hands were beating on a drumlike gourd instrument called a qua-qua, and doing it with a sharpness and power that made Kunta know the musician was an African.

It was all he could do to stand still until the door closed behind the massa. Then Kunta tossed the reins to the waiting stableboy and raced as fast as his half foot would let him around the side of the house and across the backyard. The sound, which was getting louder and louder, seemed to be coming from the middle of a crowd of blacks stomping and clapping beneath a string of lanterns that the Wallers had allowed the slaves to put up for their own Thanksgiving celebration. Ignoring their indignant exclamations as he pushed his way through them, Kunta burst into the open circle, and there he was: a lean, grey-haired, very black man squatted on the ground pounding on his qua-qua between a mandolin player and two beef-bone clackers. As they flicked glances up at the sudden commotion, Kunta's eyes met his – and a moment later they all but sprang towards each other, the other blacks gawking, then snickering, as they embraced.

'*Ah-salakium-salaam!*'

'*Malakium-salaam!*'

The words came as if neither of them had ever left Africa. Kunta shoved the older man away to arm's length. 'I ain't seed you here befo',' he exclaimed.

'Jes' sol' here from 'nother plantation,' the other said.

'My massa yo' massa's young'un,' said Kunta. 'I drives his buggy.'

The men around them had begun muttering with impatience for the music to start again, and they were obviously uncomfortable at this open display of Africanness. Both Kunta and the qua-qua player knew they mustn't aggravate the others any further, or one of them might report to the white folks.

'I be back!' said Kunta.

280

'*Salakium-salaam!*' said the qua-qua player, squatting back down.

Kunta stood there for a moment as the music began again, then turned abruptly, through the crowd with his head down – frustrated and embarrassed – and went to wait in the buggy for Massa Waller.

Over the weeks that followed, Kunta's mind tumbled with questions about the qua-qua player. What was his tribe? Clearly he was not Mandinka, nor of any of the other tribes Kunta had ever seen or heard about either in The Gambia or on the big canoe. His grey hair said that he was much older; Kunta wondered if he had as many rains as Omoro would by now. And how had each of them sensed that the other was a servant of Allah? The qua-qua player's ease with toubob speech as well as with Islam said that he had been a long time in the white folks' land, probably for more rains than Kunta had. The qua-qua player said that he had recently been sold to Massa Waller's father; where in toubob land had he been for all those rains before now?

Kunta reviewed in his mind the other Africans he had chanced to see – most of them, unfortunately, when he was with the massa and couldn't afford even to nod at them, let alone meet them – in his three rains of driving the massa's buggy. Among them had even been one or two who were unquestionably Mandinkas. Most of the Africans he had glimpsed as they drove past the Saturday morning slave auctions. But after what had happened one morning about six months before, he had decided never to drive the buggy anywhere near the auctions if he could possibly avoid it without massa suspecting his reason. As they drove by that day, a chained young Jola woman had begun shrieking piteously. Turning to see what was the matter, he saw the wide eyes of the Jola woman fixed on him on the high seat of the buggy, her mouth open in a scream, beseeching him to help her. In bitter, flooding shame, Kunta had lashed his whip down across both horses' rumps and they all but bucked ahead, jolting the massa backwards, terrifying Kunta at what he had done, but the massa had said nothing.

Once Kunta had met an African slave in the county seat while he was waiting for the massa one afternoon, but neither one of them could understand the other's tribal language, and the other man hadn't yet learned to speak the toubob tongue. It seemed unbelievable to Kunta that it was only after twenty rains in the white folks' land that he had met another African with whom he could communicate.

But for the next two months, into the spring of 1788, it seemed to Kunta that the massa visited every patient, relative, and friend within five counties – except for his own parents at Enfield. Once he considered asking him for a travelling pass, which he had never done before, but he knew that would involve questions about where he intended to go and why. He could say he was going to see Liza, the cook at Enfield, but that would let the massa think there was something between them; and he might mention it to his parents, and they might mention it to Liza, and then he'd never hear the end of it, because he knew she had her eye on him and the feeling was definitely not mutual, so Kunta dropped the idea.

In his impatience to get back to Enfield, he had begun to grow irritable with Bell – the more so because he couldn't talk with her about it – or so he told himself, knowing all too well her aversion towards anything African. Thinking about confiding in the fiddler and the old gardener, he had finally decided that although they wouldn't tell anyone else, they wouldn't be able to appreciate the magnitude of meeting someone to talk to from one's native land after twenty rains.

Then one Sunday after lunch, without any notice at all, the massa sent out to have him hitch up the team: he was going to Enfield. Kunta almost leaped from his seat and out the door, Bell staring after him in amazement.

Liza was busy among her pots when he entered the kitchen at Enfield. He asked how she was, adding quickly that he wasn't hungry. She looked warmly at him. 'Ain't seen you in a time,' she said, her voice soft. Then her face became sombre. 'Heared 'bout you an' dat African we done got. Massa heared, too. Some dem niggers tol' 'im, but he ain't said nothin', so I wouldn' worry 'bout it.' She grasped and squeezed Kunta's hand. 'You jes' wait a minute.'

Kunta felt ready to explode with impatience, but Liza was deftly making and wrapping two thick beef sandwiches. She gave them to him, again pressing his hand within hers. Then she walked him towards the kitchen door, where she hesitated. 'Sump'n you ain't never ax me, so I ain't tol' you – my mammy was an African nigger. Reckon dat's how come I likes you so much.'

Seeing Kunta's anxiety to leave, she turned abruptly and pointed, 'Dat hut wid de broke chimney his'n. Most de niggers massa's let go off today. Dey won't git back fo' dark. You jes' be sho' you at yo' buggy fo' your massa come out!'

Limping quickly down slave row, Kunta knocked at the door of the ramshackle one-room hut.

'Who dat?' said the voice he remembered.

'*Ah-salakium-salaam!*' said Kunta. He heard a quick muffled movement within, and the door swung open wide.

61

Since they were Africans, neither man showed how much this moment had been awaited by both of them. The older man offered Kunta his only chair, but when he saw that his guest preferred to squat on the dirt floor as he would have done in a village back home, the qua-qua player grunted with satisfaction, lighted the candle on his leaning table, and squatted down himself.

'I comes from Ghana, an' mine is de Akan peoples. De white folks gimme de name Pompey, but my real one's Boteng Bediako. I's been a long time here. Six white folks' plantations, an' I hopes dis de las' one. How 'bout you?'

Trying to copy the Ghanaian's terse way of speaking, Kunta told him of The Gambia, of Juffure, of being Mandinka, of his family; of his capture and escapes, his foot, doing gardening, and now driving the buggy.

The Ghanaian listened intently, and when Kunta finished, the Ghanaian sat thinking awhile before he spoke again. 'We's all sufferin'. A man wise, he try to learn from it.' He paused and looked appraisingly at Kunta. 'How ol' you is?' Kunta said thirty-seven rains.

'You ain't look it. I's sixty-six.'

'You ain't look dat neither,' said Kunta.

'Well, I's been here longer'n you been born. Wishes back den I could'a knowed sump'n dat I's learned now. But you still young, so I tell it to you. Ol' gran'mammas in you country, dey tell young'uns de stories?' Kunta said that they did. 'Den I tell you one. It's 'bout growin' up where I come from.

'I 'members how de chief a our Akan peoples use to set in this big chair made outa elephants' teeth, an' it was a man always held a umbrella over his head. Den 'longside was de man de chief spoke through. Only way he ever talked, or anybody could talk to him, was

283

through dis man. An' den a boy set at de chief's feet. Dis boy stood for de chief's soul, an' he run de chief's messages to de people. Dis boy run wid a thick-bladed sword, so whoever seed 'im comin' knowed 'zactly who he was. I growed up bein' dat boy, runnin' messages 'mongst de peoples. Dat's how de white mens cotched me.'

Kunta was about to speak when the Ghanaian held up his hand.

'Dat ain't de end a de story. What I's gittin' to, on top of de chief's umbrella was dis carvin' of a hand holdin' a egg. Dat stood for de care a chief used his powers wid. An' dat man de chief talked through, he always held a staff. An' on dat staff a turtle was carved. Turtle stood for dat de key to livin' is patience.' The Ghanaian paused. 'An' it was a bee carved on de shell a dat turtle. Bee stood for dat nothin' can't sting through de turtle's hard shell.'

In the flickering candlelight of the hut, the Ghanaian paused. 'Dis is what I wants to pass on to you, dat I's learned in de white folks' land. What you needs most to live here is patience – wid a hard shell.'

In Africa, Kunta was sure, this man would have been a kintango, or an alcala, if not a chief himself. But he didn't know how to say what he felt, and just sat there without saying anything.

'Look like you got both,' said the Ghanaian finally with a smile. Kunta began to stammer an apology, but his tongue still seemed to be tied. The Ghanaian smiled again, fell silent for a moment himself, then spoke again.

'You Mandinkas spoke of in my country as great travellers an' traders.' He left the statement in midair, clearly waiting for Kunta to say something.

At last Kunta found his voice. 'You heard right. My uncles is travellers. Listenin' to stories dey used to tell, seem like dey been jus' 'bout ev'eywhere. Me and my father once, we went to a new village dey done started a long ways from Juffure. I was plannin' to go to Mecca an' Timbuktu an' Mali an' all like dey done, but I got stole 'fore I had de chance.'

'I knows some 'bout Africa,' said the Ghanaian. 'De chief had me teached by de wise men. I ain't forgot what dey said. An' I's tried to put it together wid things I's heared an' seed since I been here, an' I knows dat most of us dats brought here is stole from West Africa – from up roun' your Gambia all de way down de coast to my Guinea. Is you heared of what white folks calls de "Gold Coast"?'

Kunta said that he hadn't. 'Dey named it dat 'count of de gold dere. Dat coast go clear up to de Volta. It's dat coast where de white folks cotches de Fanti an' de Ashanti peoples. It's dem Ashantis dats said to lead most of de uprisins' an' revolts when dey's brought here.

'Spite dat, de white folks pays some of dey biggest prices for dem, 'cause dey's smart an' strong an' dey's got spirit.

'Den what dey calls de "Slave Coast" is where dey gits de Yorubas an' Dahomans, an' roun' de tip of de Niger dey gits de Ibo.' Kunta said that he had heard the Ibo were a gentle people.

The Ghanaian nodded. 'I's heared of thirty Ibos joined hands an' walked into a river, all singin', an' drowned together. Dat was in Lou'siana.'

Kunta was starting to get worried that the massa might be ready to leave and he might keep him waiting, and a moment of silence passed between them. As Kunta's mind cast about for some topic appropriate to leave on, the Ghanaian said, 'Sho ain't nobody here to set an' talk wid like us is. Heap a times qua-qua got to say what I got on my mind. Reckon maybe I was talkin' to you widout knowin' you was dere.'

Deeply moved, Kunta looked the Ghanaian in the eye for a long moment, and then they both got up. In the candlelight, Kunta noticed on the table the forgotten two sandwiches that Liza had given him. He pointed to them and smiled. 'We can eat anytime. Now I knows you got to go,' said the Ghanaian. 'In my country, whilst we was talkin', I'd a been carvin' somethin' out of a thorn to give you.'

Kunta said that in The Gambia, he would have been carving something from a large dried mango seed. 'Whole heap of times I done wished I had a mango seed to plant an' grow up to remin' me a home,' he said.

The Ghanaian looked solemnly at Kunta. Then he smiled. 'You's young. Seeds you's got a-plenty, you jes' needs de wife to plant 'em in.'

Kunta was so embarrassed that he didn't know how to reply. The Ghanaian thrust out his left arm, and they shook their left hands in the African manner, meaning that they would soon meet again.

'*Ah-salakium-salaam.*'

'*Malaika-salaam.*'

And Kunta cripped hurriedly out into the deepening dusk, past the other small huts, and up towards the big house, wondering if the massa had already come out looking for him. But it was another half hour before the massa appeared, and as Kunta drove the buggy homewards – scarcely feeling the reins in his hands or hearing the horses' hooves on the road – he felt as if he had been talking with his dear father Omoro. No evening of his life had ever meant more to him.

62

'Seen Toby passin' yestiday, hollered at 'im, "Hey, drop by an' set awhile, nigger!" You oughta seen de look he give me, an' ain't even spoke! What you reckon it is?' the fiddler asked the gardener. The gardener had no idea, and they both asked Bell. 'Cain't tell. If he sick or sump'n, he oughta say so. I'm jes' leavin' him 'lone, he actin' so funny!' she declared.

Even Massa Waller noticed that his commendably reserved and reliable driver seemed not to be his usual self. He hoped it wasn't an incubating stage of a current local contagion to which they both had been exposed, so one day he asked Kunta if he felt badly. 'Nawsuh,' Kunta quickly replied, so Massa Waller put further concern out of his mind, so long as his driver got him where he was going.

Kunta had been rocked to the core by his encounter with the Ghanaian, and that very fact made it clear to him how lost he had become. Day by day, year by year, he had become less resisting, more accepting, until finally, without even realizing it, he had forgotten who he was. It was true that he had come to know better and learned to get along with the fiddler, the gardener, Bell, and the other blacks, but he knew now that he could never really be one of them, any more than they could be like him. Alongside the Ghanaian, in fact, the fiddler and the gardener and Bell now seemed to Kunta only irritating. He was glad that they were keeping their distance. Lying on his pallet at night, he was torn with guilt and shame about what he had let happen to himself. He had still been an African when he used to awaken suddenly here in his cabin, jerking upright, shocked to discover that he wasn't in Juffure; but the last time that happened had been many years ago. He had still been an African when his memories of The Gambia and its people had been the only thing that sustained him, but months might pass now without his having a single thought about Juffure. He had still been an African back in those early years when each new outrage had sent him onto his knees imploring Allah to give him strength and understanding; how long had it been since he had even properly prayed to Allah?

His learning to speak the toubob tongue, he realized, had played a big part in it. In this everyday talking, he seldom even thought of Mandinka words any more, excepting those few that for some reason his mind still clung to. Indeed, by now – Kunta grimly faced it – he even *thought* in the toubob tongue. In countless things he did as well

286

as said and thought, his Mandinka ways had slowly been replaced by those of the blacks he had been among. The only thing in which he felt he could take some small pride was that in twenty rains he had never touched the meat of the swine.

Kunta searched his mind; there must have been something else of his original self that he could find someplace. And there was: he had kept his dignity. Through everything, he had worn his dignity as once in Juffure he had worn his saphie charms to keep away the evil spirits. He vowed to himself that now more than ever, his dignity must become as a shield between him and all of those who called themselves 'niggers'. How ignorant of themselves they were; they knew nothing of their ancestors, as he had been taught from boyhood. Kunta reviewed in his mind the names of the Kintes from the ancient clan in old Mali down across the generations in Mauretania, then in The Gambia all the way to his brothers and himself; and he thought of how the same ancestral knowledge was possessed by every member of his kafo.

It set Kunta to reminiscing about those boyhood friends. At first he was only surprised, but then he grew shocked when he found that he couldn't remember their names. Their faces came back to him – along with memories of them racing out beyond the village gate like blackbirds to serve as chattering escorts in Juffure for every traveller who passed by; hurling sticks at the scolding monkeys overhead, who promptly hurled them back; of contests they'd held to see who could eat six mangoes the fastest. But try as Kunta might, he couldn't recall their names, not one of them. He could see his kafo gathered, frowning at him.

In his hut, and driving the massa, Kunta racked his brain. And finally the names did begin to come; one by one: yes, Sitafa Silla – he and Kunta had been best friends! And Kalilu Conteh – he had stalked and caught the parrot at the kintango's command. Sefo Kela – he had asked the Council of Elders for permission to have a teriya sexual friendship with that widow.

The faces of some of the elders began to come back now, and with them the names he thought he had long since forgotten. The kintango was Silla Ba Bibba! The alimamo was Kujali Demba! The wadanela was Karamo Tamba! Kunta remembered his third-kafo graduating ceremony, where he had read his Koranic verses so well that Omoro and Binta gave a fat goat to the arafang, whose name was Brima Cesay. Remembering them all filled Kunta with joy – until it occurred to him that those elders would have died by now, and his kafo mates whom he remembered as little boys would be his age back in Juffure – and he would never see them again. For the first time in many years, he cried himself to sleep.

In the county seat a few days later, another buggy driver told Kunta that some free blacks up North who called themselves 'The Negro Union' had proposed a mass return to Africa of all blacks – both free and slaves. The very thought of it excited Kunta, even as he scoffed that it couldn't ever happen, with massas not only competing to buy blacks but also paying higher prices than ever. Though he knew the fiddler would almost rather stay a slave in Virginia than go to Africa a free man, Kunta wished he could discuss it with him, for the fiddler always seemed to know all there was to know about what was going on anywhere if it had anything to do with freedom.

But for almost two months now Kunta hadn't done more than scowl at the fiddler or at Bell and the gardener either. Not that he needed them or even liked them that much, of course – but the feeling of being stranded kept growing within him. By the time the next new moon rose, and he miserably dropped another pebble into his gourd, he was feeling inexpressibly lonely, as if he had cut himself off from the world.

The next time Kunta saw the fiddler pass by, he nodded at him uncertainly, but the fiddler kept walking as if he hadn't even seen anyone. Kunta was furiously embarrassed. The very next day he and the old gardener saw each other at the same moment, and without missing a step, the gardener turned in another direction. Both hurt and bitter – and with a mounting sense of guilt – Kunta paced back and forth in his hut for more hours that night. The next morning, braving himself, he cripped outside and down slave row to the door of the once-familiar last hut. He knocked.

The door opened. 'What you want?' the fiddler asked coldly.

Swallowing with embarrassment, Kunta said, 'Jes' figgered I'd come by.'

The fiddler spat on the ground. 'Look here, nigger, now hear what I tells you. Me an' Bell an' de ol' man been 'scussin' you. An' we all 'grees if it's anythin' we can't stan', it's a sometimey nigger!' He glared at Kunta. 'Dat's all been wrong wid you! You ain't sick or nothin'.'

Kunta stood looking at his shoes. After a moment, the fiddler's glare softened and he stepped aside. 'Since you'd already here, c'mon in. But I'm gon' tell you – show yo' ass one mo' time, an' you won't git spoke to again 'til you's ol' as Methuselah!'

Choking down his rage and humiliation, Kunta went on inside and sat down, and after a seemingly endless silence between them – which the fiddler obviously had no intention of ending – Kunta forced himself to tell about the back-to-Africa proposal. The fiddler said coolly that he had long known about that, and that there wasn't a snowball's chance in hell that it would ever happen.

Seeing Kunta's hurt expression, the fiddler seemed to relent a little. 'Lemme tell you sump'n I bets *you* ain't heared. Up Nawth in New York, dey's what you call a Manumission Society dat done open a school for free niggers what wants to get learned readin' an' writin' an' all kin's a trades.'

Kunta was so happy and relieved to have the fiddler talking to him again that he hardly heard what his old friend was saying to him. A few minutes later, the fiddler stopped talking for a moment and sat looking at Kunta inquiringly.

'Is I keepin' you up?' he asked finally.

'Hmm?' said Kunta, who had been lost in thought.

'I ax you a question 'bout five minutes ago.'

'Sorry, I was thinkin' 'bout sump'n.'

'Well, since you don' know how to listen, I show ya how it's done.' He sat back and crossed his arms.

'Ain't you gonna go on wid what you was sayin'?' asked Kunta.

'By now I forgits what I was sayin'. Is you forgit what you was thinkin'?'

'It ain't impo'tant. Jes' sump'n been on my mind.'

'Better get if off dere fo' you gits a headache – or gives me one.'

'I cain't 'scuss it.'

'Huh!' said the fiddler, acting insulted. 'If'n *dat* de way you feel . . .'

'Ain't you. It's jes' too *personal*.'

A light began to dawn in the fiddler's eye. 'Don' tell me! It's 'bout a woman, right?'

'Ain't nothin' a de kin'!' said Kunta, flushing with embarrassment. He sat speechless for a moment, then got up and said, 'Well, I be late fo' work, so I see ya later. Thanks fo' talkin' wid me.'

'Sho thing. Jes' lemme know when *you* wants to do some talkin'.'

How had he known? Kunta asked himself on his way to the stable. And why had he insisted on making him talk about it? It was only with the greatest reluctance that Kunta had even let himself *think* about it. But lately he could hardly seem to think about anything else. It had to do with the Ghanaian's advice about planting his seeds.

63

Long before he met the Ghanaian, Kunta had often had a hollow feeling whenever he thought about the fact that if he had been in Juffure, he would have had three or four sons by now – along with the wife who had given birth to them. What usually occasioned these thoughts was when about once each moon, Kunta had a dream from which he always awakened abruptly in the darkness, acutely embarrassed at the hot stickiness that had just burst from his still rigid foto. Lying awake afterwards, he thought not so much of a wife as he did about how he knew that there was hardly a slave row where some man and woman who cared for one another had not simply begun living together in whichever's hut was the better one.

There were many reasons why Kunta didn't want to think about getting married. For one thing, it seemed to involve the couple's 'jumpin' de broomstick' before witnesses from slave row, which seemed ridiculous to Kunta for such a solemn occasion. In a few cases he had heard of, certain favoured house servants might repeat their vows before some white preacher with the massa and mistress looking on, but that was a pagan ceremony. If marrying someone in whatever manner was even to be thought about, the proper bride's age for a Mandinka was fourteen to sixteen rains, with the man about thirty. And in his years in the white folks' land, Kunta hadn't seen one black female of fourteen to sixteen – or even twenty to twenty-five – whom he had not considered preposterously giggling and silly; especially when on Sundays, or for festivities, they painted and powdered their faces until they looked to him more like the death dancers in Juffure who covered themselves with ashes.

As for the twenty or so older women whom Kunta had come to know, they were mostly senior cooks at the big houses where he had driven Massa Waller, such as Liza at Enfield. In fact, Liza was the only one among them all whom he had come to look forward to seeing. She had no mate, and she had given Kunta clear signs of her willingness, if not her anxiety, to get him into much closer quarters than he had ever responded to, although he had thought about it privately. He would have died of shame if there had been any way for her to suspect even remotely that more than once it had been she about whom he had had the sticky dream.

Suppose – just suppose – he were to take Liza for a wife, Kunta thought. It would mean that they would be like so many couples he

290

knew, living separately, each of them on the plantation of their own massa. Usually the man was permitted Saturday afternoon travelling passes to visit his wife, so long as he faithfully returned before dark on Sunday in order to rest up from his often long trip before work resumed at dawn on Monday. Kunta told himself that he would want no part of a wife living not where he was. And he told himself that settled the matter.

But his mind, as if on its own, kept on thinking about it. Considering how talkative and smothery Liza was, and how he liked to spend a lot of time alone, maybe their being able to see each other just on weekends would be a blessing in disguise. And if he were to marry Liza, it was unlikely that they would have to live as so many black couples did, in fear that one of them, or both, might get sold away. For the massa seemed to be happy with him, and Liza was owned by the massa's parents, who apparently liked her. The family connections would also make unlikely the kind of frictions that sometimes arose when two massas were involved, sometimes even causing one or both of them to forbid the marriage.

On the other hand, Kunta thought . . . over and over he turned it in his mind. But no matter how many perfectly sound reasons he could think of for marrying Liza, something held him back. Then one night, while he was lying in bed trying to fall asleep, it struck him like a lightning bolt! – there was another woman he might consider.

Bell.

He thought he must be crazy. She was nearly three times too old – probably beyond forty rains. It was absurd to think about it.

Bell.

Kunta tried to hurl her from his mind. She had entered it only because he had known her for so long, he told himself. He had never even dreamed of her. Grimly, he remembered a parade of indignities and irritations she had inflicted on him. He remembered how she used to all but slam the screen door in his face when he carried her vegetable basket to the kitchen. Even more keenly, he remembered her indignation when he told her she looked Mandinka; she was a heathen. Furthermore, she was just generally argumentative and bossy. And she talked too much.

But he couldn't help remembering how, when he had lain wanting to die, she had visited him five and six times daily; how she had nursed and fed him, even cleaned his soiling of himself, and how her hot poultice of mashed leaves had broken his fever. She was also strong and healthy. And she did cook endless good things in her black pots.

The better she began to look to him, the ruder he was to her whenever he had to go to the kitchen, and the sooner he would leave when he had told her or found out from her whatever he had come for. She began to stare at his retreating back even more coldly than before.

One day after he had been talking for some time with the gardener and the fiddler and worked the conversation very slowly around to Bell, it seemed to Kunta that he had just the right tone of casualness in his voice when he asked, 'Where she was fo' she come here?' But his heart sank when they instantly sat up straighter and looked at him, sensing something in the air.

'Well,' the gardener said after a minute, 'I 'members she come here 'bout two years fo' you. But she ain't never done much talkin' 'bout herself. So ain't much I knows more'n you does—'

The fiddler said Bell had never spoken of her past to him either.

Kunta couldn't put his finger on what it was about their expressions that irritated him. Yes, he could: it was smugness.

The fiddler scratched his right ear. 'Sho' is funny you ax 'bout Bell,' he said, nodding in the gardener's direction, ' 'cause me'n him ain't been long back 'scussin' y'all.' He looked carefully at Kunta.

'We was sayin' seem like y'all both might be jes' what de other'n needs,' said the gardener.

Outraged, Kunta sat with his mouth open, only nothing came out.

Still scratching his ear, the fiddler wore a sly look. 'Yeah, her big behin' be too much to handle for most mens.'

Kunta angrily started to speak, but the gardener cut him off, demanding sharply, 'Listen here, how long you ain't touched no woman?'

Kunta glared daggers. 'Twenty years anyhow!' exclaimed the fiddler.

'Lawd, Gawd!' said the gardener. 'You better git you some 'fo' you dries up!'

'If he ain't a-reddy!' the fiddler shot in. Unable to speak but able to contain himself a moment longer, Kunta leaped up and stamped out. 'Don' you worry!' the fiddler shouted after him. 'You ain't gon' stay dry long wid *her!*'

64

For the next few days, whenever Kunta wasn't off driving the massa somewhere, he spent both his mornings and afternoons oiling and polishing the buggy. Since he was right outside the barn in anyone's view, it couldn't be said that he was isolating himself again, but at the same time it said that his work was keeping him too busy to spend time talking with the fiddler and the gardener – at whom he was still furious for what they had said about him and Bell.

Being off by himself also gave him more time to sort out his feelings for her. Whenever he was thinking of something he didn't like about her, his polishing rag would become a furious blur against the leather; and whenever he was feeling better about her, it would move slowly and sensuously across the seats, sometimes almost stopping as his mind lingered on some disarming quality of hers. Whatever her shortcomings, he had to admit that she had done a great deal in his best interests over the years. He felt certain that Bell had even played a quiet role in the massa's having selected him as his buggy driver. There was no question that in her own subtle ways, Bell had more influence on the massa than anyone else on the plantation, or probably all of them put together. And a parade of smaller things came and went through Kunta's mind. He remembered a time back when he was gardening and Bell had noticed that he was often rubbing at his eyes, which had been itching him in a maddening way. Without a word, she had come out to the garden one morning with some wide leaves still wet with dewdrops, which she shook into his eyes, whereupon the itching had soon stopped.

Not that he felt any less strongly about the things he disapproved of in Bell, Kunta reminded himself as the rag picked up speed – most particularly her disgusting habit of smoking tobacco in a pipe. Even more objectionable was her way of dancing whenever there was some festivity among the blacks. He didn't feel that women shouldn't dance, or do so less than enthusiastically. What bothered him was that Bell seemed to go out of her way to make her behind shake in a certain manner, which he figured was the reason the fiddler and the gardener had said what they did about her. Bell's behind, of course, wasn't any of his business; he just wished she would show a little more respect for herself – and while she was at it, a little more towards him and other men. Her tongue, it seemed to him, was even worse than old Nyo Boto's. He wouldn't mind her being critical if she'd only keep it to herself, or do her criticizing in the company of other women, as it was done in Juffure.

When Kunta had finished with the buggy, he began cleaning and oiling the leather harnesses, and for some reason as he did so, his mind went back to the old men in Juffure who carved things from wood such as the knee-high slab of hickory on which he was sitting. He thought how carefully they would first select and then study some thoroughly seasoned piece of wood before they would ever touch it with their adzes and their knives.

Kunta got up and toppled the hickory block over on its side, sending the beetles that lived beneath it scurrying away. After closely examining both ends of the block, he rolled it back and forth, tapping it with the piece of iron at different places, and always hearing the same solid, seasoned sound. It seemed to him that this excellent piece of wood was serving no real purpose just sitting here. It was there apparently only because someone had put it there long before and no one had ever bothered to move it. Looking around to make sure no one was watching, Kunta rolled the block rapidly to his hut, where he stood it upright in a corner, closed the door, and went back to work.

That night, after bringing the massa back from a trip to the county seat that seemed to take forever, Kunta couldn't sit through supper before getting another look at the hickory block, so he took the food along with him to his cabin. Not even noticing what he was eating, Kunta sat on the floor in front of it and studied it in the light from the flickering candle on his table. In his mind, he was seeing the mortar and pestle that Omoro had carved for Binta, who had worn it slick with many grindings of her corn.

Merely to pass away some of his free time, Kunta told himself, when Massa Waller didn't want to go anywhere, Kunta began to chop away at the block with a sharp hatchet, making a rough shape of the outside rim of a mortar for grinding corn. By the third day, with a hammer and a wood chisel, he dug out the mortar's inside, also roughly, and then he began to carve with a knife. After a week, Kunta's fingers surprised him at how nimbly they flew, considering that he hadn't watched the old men in his village carving things for more than twenty rains.

When he had finished the inside and the outside of the mortar, he found a seasoned hickory limb, perfectly straight and of the thickness of his arm, from which he soon made a pestle. Then he set about smoothing the upper part of the handle, scraping it first with a file, next with a knife, and finally with a piece of glass.

Finished, they both sat in a corner of Kunta's hut for two more weeks. He would look at them now and then, reflecting that they wouldn't look out of place in his mother's kitchen. But now that he had made them, he was unsure what to do with them; at least that's what he told himself. Then one morning, without really thinking about why he was doing it, Kunta picked them up and took them along when he went to check with Bell to see if the massa was going to need the buggy. When she gave him her brief, cold report from behind the screen door, saying that the massa had no travel plans that morning, Kunta waited until her back was turned and found himself setting the mortar and pestle down on the steps and turning to leave as fast as he could go. When Bell's ears caught the gentle thumping sound, which made her turn around, she first saw Kunta cripping away even more hurriedly than usual; then she saw the mortar and pestle on the steps.

Walking to the door, she peered out at Kunta until he had disappeared, then eased the screen door open and looked down at them; she was flabbergasted. Picking them up and bringing them inside, she examined its painstaking carving with astonishment; and then she began to cry.

It was the first time in her twenty-two years on the Waller plantation that any man had made something for her with his own hands. She felt flooding guilt for the way she had been acting towards Kunta, and she remembered how peculiar the fiddler and the gardener had acted recently when she complained to them about him. They must have known of this – but she couldn't be certain, knowing how close-mouthed and reserved Kunta could be in his African way.

Bell was confused about how she should feel – or how she should act the next time he came to check on the massa again after lunch. She was glad she would have at least the rest of the morning to get her mind made up about that. Kunta, meanwhile, sat in his cabin feeling as if he were two people, one of them completely humiliated by the foolish and ridiculous thing the other one had just done – and felt almost deliriously happy and excited about it. What made him do it? What would she think? He dreaded having to return to the kitchen after lunch.

Finally the hour came, and Kunta trudged up the walk as if he were going to his execution. When he saw that the mortar and pestle were gone from the back steps, his heart leaped and sank at the same time. Reaching the screen door, he saw that she had put them on the floor just inside, as if she were uncertain why Kunta had left them there. Turning when he knocked – as if she hadn't heard him coming

– she tried to look calm as she unlatched the door and opened it for him to come on in. That was a bad sign, thought Kunta; she hadn't opened the door to him in months. But he wanted to come in; yet he couldn't seem to take that first step. Rooted where he stood, he asked matter-of-factly about the massa, and Bell, concealing her hurt feelings and her confusion, managed to reply just as matter-of-factly that the massa said he had no afternoon plans for the buggy either. As Kunta turned to go, she added hopefully, 'He been writin' letters all day.' All of the possible things that Bell had thought of that she might say had fled her head, and as he turned again to go, she heard herself blurting 'What dat?' with a gesture towards the mortar and pestle.

Kunta wished that he were anywhere else on earth. But finally he replied, almost angrily, 'For you to grin' cawn wid.' Bell looked at him with her mingled emotions now clearly showing on her face. Seizing the silence between them as an excuse to leave, Kunta turned and hurried away without another word. Bell stood there feeling like a fool.

For the next two weeks, beyond exchanging greetings, neither of them said anything to each other. Then one day, at the kitchen door, Bell gave Kunta a round cake of cornbread. Mumbling his thanks, he took it back to his hut and ate it still hot from the pan and soaked with butter. He was deeply moved. Almost certainly she had made it with meal ground in the mortar he had given her. But even before this he had decided that he was going to have a talk with Bell. When he checked in with her after lunch, he forced himself to say, as he had carefully rehearsed and memorized it, 'I wants a word wid you after supper.' Bell didn't delay her reponse overlong. 'Don't make me no difference,' she said too quickly, regretting it.

By suppertime, Kunta had worked himself into a state. Why had she said what she did? Was she really as indifferent as she seemed? And if she was, why did she make the cornbread for him? He would have it out with her. But neither he nor Bell had remembered to say exactly when or where they would meet. She must have intended for him to meet her at her cabin, he decided finally. But he hoped desperately that some emergency medical call would come for Massa Waller. When none did, and he knew he couldn't put it off any longer, he took a deep breath, opened his cabin door, and strolled casually over to the barn. Coming back outside swinging in his hand a set of harnesses that he figured would satisfy the curiosity of anyone who might happen to see him and wonder why he was out and around, he ambled on down to slave row to Bell's cabin and –

looking around to make sure no one was around – knocked very quietly on the door.

It opened almost before his knuckles touched the wood, and Bell stepped immediately outside. Glancing down at the harness, and then at Kunta, she said nothing – and when he didn't either, she began to walk slowly down towards the back fencerow; he fell into step beside her. The half moon had begun to rise, and in its pale light they moved along without a word. When a groundvine entangled the shoe on his left foot, Kunta stumbled – his shoulder brushing against Bell – and he all but sprang away. Ransacking his brain for something – anything – to say, he wished wildly that he was walking with the gardener or the fiddler, or practically anyone except Bell.

Finally it was she who broke the silence. She said abruptly, 'De white folks done swore in dat Gen'l Washington for de Pres'dent.' Kunta wanted to ask her what that was, but he didn't, hoping that she'd keep on talking. 'An' it's annuder massa name of John Adams is Vice Pres'dent,' she went on.

Floundering, he felt that he must say something to keep the talk going. He said finally, 'Rode massa over to see his brother's young'un yestiddy,' instantly feeling foolish, as he knew full well that Bell already knew that.

'Lawd, he do love dat chile!' Bell said, feeling foolish, since that's about all she ever said about little Missy Anne whenever the subject came up. The silence had built up a little bit again when she went on. 'Don't know how much you knows 'bout massa's brother. He de Spotsylvania County clerk, but he ain't never had our massa's head fo' binness.' Bell was quiet for a few more steps. 'I keeps my ears sharp on little things gits dropped. I knows whole lot more'n anybody thinks I knows.'

She glanced over at Kunta. 'I ain't never had no use for dat Massa John – an' I's sure you ain't neither – but dere's sump'n you ought to know 'bout him dat I ain't never tol' you. It weren't him had your foot cut off. Fact, he pitched a fit wid dem low-down po' white trash what done it. He'd hired 'em to track you wid dey nigger dogs, an' dey claim how come dey done it was you tried to kill one of 'em wid a rock.' Bell paused. 'I 'members it like yestiddy when Sheriff Brock come a-rushin' you to our massa.' Under the moonlight, Bell looked at Kunta. 'You near 'bout dead, massa said. He got so mad when Massa John say he ain't got no use for you no more wid your foot gone, he swore he gon' buy you from him, an' he done it, too. I seen de very deed he bought you wid. He took over a good-sized farm long wid you in de place of money his brother owed him. It's

297

dat big farm wid de pond right where de big road curve, you passes it all de time.'

Kunta knew the farm instantly. He could see the pond in his mind, and the surrounding fields. 'But dey business dealin's don't make no difference, 'cause all dem Wallers is very close,' Bell continued. 'Dey's 'mongst de oldes' families in Virginia. Fact, dey was ol' family in dat England even fo' dey come crost de water to here. Was all kinds of "Sirs" an' stuff, all b'longin' to de Church of England. Was one of dem what writ poems, name of Massa Edmund Waller. His younger brother Massa John Waller was de one what comes here first. He weren't but eighteen, I's heared massa say, when some King Charles de Secon' give him a big lan' grant over where Kent County is now.'

Their pace had become much slower as Bell talked, and Kunta couldn't have been more pleased with Bell's steady talking, although he had already heard from some other Waller family cooks at least some of the things she was saying, though he never would have told her that.

'Anyhow, dis John Waller married a Miss Mary Key, an' dey built de Enfield big house where you takes massa to see his folks. An' dey had three boys, 'specially John de Secon', de younges', who come to be a whole heap of things – read de law while he was a sheriff, den was in de House of Burgesses, an' he helped to found Fredericksburg an' to put together Spotsylvania County. It was him an' his Missis Dorothy what built Newport, an' dey had six young'uns. An' co'se out of all dem, it commence to be Waller chilluns spreadin' all over, an' growin' on up, an' havin' young'uns of dey own. Our massa an' de other Wallers what lives roun' here ain't but a hand'ful of 'em all. Dey's all pretty much high-respected peoples, too, sheriffs an' preachers, county clerks, House of Burgesses, doctors like massa; whole heap of 'em fought in de Revolution, an' I don't know what all.'

Kunta had become so absorbed in what Bell was saying that he was startled when she stopped walking. 'We better git on back,' she said. 'Traipsin' out here till all hours 'mongst dese weeds, be over-sleepin' in de mornin'.' They turned around, and when Bell was quiet for a minute, and Kunta didn't say anything, she realized that he wasn't going to tell her whatever he had on his mind, so she went on chattering about whatever came into her mind until they got back to her cabin, where she turned to face him and fell silent. He stood there looking at her for a long, agonizing moment, and then finally he spoke: 'Well, it gettin' late like you said. So I see you tomorra.' As he

298

walked away, still carrying the harnesses, Bell realized that he hadn't told her whatever it was that he wanted to talk to her about. Well, she told herself – afraid to think that it might be what she thought it was – he'll get around to it in his own time.

It was just as well that she wasn't in a hurry, for though Kunta began to spend a lot of time in Bell's kitchen as she went about her work, she found herself, as usual, doing most of the talking. But she liked having him there to listen. 'I foun' out,' she told him one day, 'dat massa done writ out a will that if he die an' ain't got married, his slaves gon' go to little Missy Anne. But de will say if he do marry, den he wife would git us slaves when he die.' Even so, Bell didn't seem to be unduly disturbed. 'Sho' is a plenty of 'em roun' here would love to grab de massa, but he ain't never married no mo'.' She paused. 'Jes' de same as I ain't.'

Kunta almost dropped the fork from his hand. He was positive that he had heard Bell correctly, and he was jolted to know that Bell had been married before, for it was unthinkable that a desirable wife should not be a virgin. Kunta soon was out of the kitchen and gone into his own cabin. He knew that he must think hard upon this matter.

Two weeks of silence had passed before Bell casually invited Kunta to eat supper with her in her cabin that night. He was so astounded that he didn't know what to say. He had never been alone in a hut with a woman other than his own mother or grandmother. It wouldn't be right. But when he couldn't find the words to speak, she told him what time to show up, and that was that.

He scrubbed himself in a tin tub from head to foot, using a rough cloth and a bar of brown lye soap. Then he scrubbed himself again, and yet a third time. Then he dried himself, and while he was putting on his clothes, he found himself singing softly a song from his village, '*Mandumbe, your long neck is very beautiful—*' Bell didn't have a long neck, nor was she beautiful, but he had to admit to himself that when he was around her, he had a good feeling. And he knew that she felt the same.

Bell's cabin was the biggest one on the plantation, and the one nearest to the big house, with a small bed of flowers growing before it. Knowing her kitchen, her cabin's immaculate neatness was no more than Kunta would expect. The room he entered when she opened the door had a feeling of cosy comfort, with its wall of mud-chinked logs and a chimney of homemade bricks that widened down from the roof to her large fireplace, alongside which hung her shining cooking utensils. And Kunta noticed that instead of the usual one room with one window, such as he had, Bell's cabin had two rooms and two windows, both covered with shutters that she could pull down in case of rain, or when it grew cold. The curtained rear room was obviously where she slept, and Kunta kept his eyes averted from that doorway. On her oblong table in the centre of the room he was in, there were knives and forks and spoons standing in a jar, and some flowers from her garden in another, and two lighted candles were sitting in squat clay holders, and at either end of the table was a high-backed, cane-bottomed chair.

Bell asked him to sit in a rocking chair that was nearer the fireplace. He did, sitting down carefully, for he had never been in one of these contraptions before, but trying hard to act casual about the whole visit as Bell seemed to be.

'I been so busy I ain't even lit de fire,' she said, and Kunta all but leaped up out of the chair, glad to have something he could do with his hands. Striking the flint sharply against the piece of iron, he lit the fluffy cotton that Bell had already placed under fat pinesticks beneath the oak logs, and quickly they caught fire.

'Don't know how come I ax you to come here nohow, place in a mess, an' I ain't got nothin' ready,' Bell said, bustling about her pots.

'Ain't no hurry wid me,' Kunta made himself respond. But her already cooked chicken with dumplings, which she well knew that Kunta loved, was soon bubbling. And when she had served him, she chided him for gobbling so. But Kunta didn't quit until the third helping, with Bell insisting that there was still a little more in the pot.

'Naw, I's fit to bus',' said Kunta truthfully. And after a few more minutes of small talk, he got up and said he had to get on home. Pausing in the doorway, he looked at Bell, and Bell looked at him, and neither of them said anything, and then Bell turned her eyes away, and Kunta cripped on down along slave row to his own cabin.

He awakened more lighthearted than he had felt since leaving Africa – but he told no one why he was acting so uncharacteristically cheerful and outgoing. But he hardly needed to. Word began to get around that Kunta had actually been seen smiling and even laughing in Bell's kitchen. And at first every week or so, then twice a week, Bell would invite Kunta home for supper. Though he thought that once in a while he should make some excuse, he could never bring himself to say no. And always Bell cooked things Kunta had let her know were also grown in The Gambia, such as black-eyed peas, okra, a stew made of peanuts, or yams baked with butter.

Most of their conversations were still one-sided, but neither one seemed to mind. Her favourite topic, of course, was Massa Waller, and it never ceased to amaze Kunta how much Bell knew that he didn't about the man he spent so much more time with than she did.

'Massa funny 'bout different things,' Bell said. 'Like he believe in banks, all right enough, but he keep money hid, too; nobody else don't know where but me. He funny 'bout his niggers, too. He do 'bout anything for 'em, but if one mess up, he'll sell 'im jes' like he done Luther.

' 'Nother thing massa funny 'bout,' Bell went on. 'He won't have a yaller nigger on his place. You ever notice, ceptin' fo' de fiddler, ain't nothin' here but black niggers? Massa tell anybody jes' what he think 'bout it, too. I done heared 'im tellin' some of de biggest mens in dis county, I mean ones dat got plenty yaller niggers deyselves, dat too many white mens is havin' slave chilluns, so dey ain't doin' nothin' but buyin' an' sellin' dey own blood, an' it need to be stopped.'

Though he never showed it, and he kept up a steady drone of 'uh-huh's' when Bell was talking, Kunta would sometimes listen with one ear while he thought about something else. Once when she cooked him a hoe cake, using meal she had made in the mortar and pestle he had carved for her, Kunta was watching her in his mind's eye beating the couscous for breakfast in some African village while she stood at the stove telling him that hoe cakes got their name from slaves cooking them on the flat edge of a hoe when they were working out in the fields.

Now and then Bell even gave Kunta some special dish to take to the fiddler and the gardener. He wasn't seeing as much of them as he had, but they seemed to understand, and the time they spent apart even seemed to increase the pleasure of conversation with them whenever they got together. Though he never discussed Bell with them – and they never brought her up – it was clear from their expressions that they knew she and he were courtin' as well as if their meetings took place on the front lawn. Kunta found this vaguely embarrassing, but there seemed to be nothing he could do about it – not that he particularly cared to.

He was more concerned that there remained some serious matters he wanted to take up with Bell, but he never could quite seem to get around to them. Among them was the fact that she kept on her front-room wall a large, framed picture of the yellow-haired 'Jesus', who seemed to be a relative of their heathen 'Lawd'. But finally he did manage to mention it, and Bell promptly said, 'Ain't but two places everybody's headin' for, heab'n or hell, and where you goin', dat's yo' business!' And she would say no more about it. Her reply discomfited him every time he thought of it, but finally he decided that she had a right to her beliefs, however misguided, just as he had a right to his. Unshaken, he had been born with Allah and he was going to die with Allah – although he hadn't been praying to Him regularly again ever since he started seeing a lot of Bell. He resolved to correct that and hoped that Allah would forgive him.

Anyway, he couldn't feel too harshly about someone, even a pagan Christian, who was so good to one of another faith, even someone as worthy as he was. She was so nice to him, in fact, that Kunta wanted to do something special for her – something at least as special as the mortar and pestle. So one day when he was on his way over to Massa John's to pick up Missy Anne for a weekend visit with Massa Waller, Kunta stopped off by a fine patch of bulrushes he had often noticed, and picked some of the best he could find. With the rushes split into fine pieces, and with some selected, soft inner white cornshucks, over the next several days he plaited an intricate mat with a bold Mandinka design in its centre. It came out even better than he had expected, and he presented it to Bell the next time she had him over for supper. She looked upwards from the mat to Kunta. 'Ain't *nobody* gon' put dey feets on dat!' she exclaimed, turning and disappearing into her bedroom. Back a few moments later with a hand behind her, she said, 'Dis was gonna be for yo' Christmas, but I make you somethin' else.'

She held out her hand. It was a pair of finely knitted woollen socks – one of them with a half foot, the front part filled with soft woollen cushion. Neither he nor Bell seemed to know what to say.

He could smell the aroma of the food she had been simmering, ready to be served, but a strange feeling was sweeping over him as they kept on looking at each other. Bell's hand suddenly grasped his, and with a single motion she blew out both of the candles and swiftly with Kunta feeling as if he were a leaf being borne by a rushing stream, they went together through the curtained doorway into the other room and lay down facing one another on the bed. Looking deeply into his eyes, she reached out to him, they drew together, and for the first time in the thirty-nine rains of his life, he held a woman in his arms.

65

'Massa ain't want to believe me when I tol' 'im,' Bell said to Kunta.
'But he finally say he feel us ought to think on it for a spell yet, 'cause
peoples gittin' married is sacred in de eyes of Jesus.' To Kunta, however, Massa Waller said not a word about it during the next few
weeks. Then one night Bell came running out to Kunta's cabin and
reported breathlessly, 'I done tol' 'im we still wants to marry, an' he
say, well, den, he reckon it's awright!'

The news coursed swiftly through slave row. Kunta was embarrassed as different ones offered their congratulations. He could have
choked Bell for telling even Missy Anne when she came next to visit
her uncle, for the first thing she did after finding out was race about
screaming, 'Bell gon' git married! Bell gon' git married!' Yet at the
same time, deep inside himself, Kunta felt that it was improper for
him to feel any displeasure at such an announcement, since the Mandinka people considered marriage to be the most important thing
after birth itself.

Bell somehow managed to get the massa's promise not to use the
buggy – or Kunta – for the entire Sunday before Christmas, when
everyone would be off work and therefore available to attend the
wedding. 'I knows you don't want no marriage in de big house,' she
told Kunta, 'like we could of had if I'd of asked Massa. And I knows
he don't really want dat neither, so at leas' y'all togedder on dat.' She
arranged for it to be held in the front yard alongside the oval flower
garden.

Everybody on slave row was there in their Sunday best, and standing together on across from them were Massa Waller with little
Missy Anne and her parents. But as far as Kunta was concerned, the
guest of honour – and, in a very real sense, the one responsible for
the whole thing – was his friend the Ghanaian, who had hitched a
ride all the way from Enfield just to be there. As Kunta walked with
Bell out into the centre of the yard, he turned his head towards the
qua-qua player, and they exchanged a long look before Bell's main
praying and singing friend, Aunt Sukey, the plantation's laundress,
stepped forward to conduct the ceremony. After calling for all present to stand closer together, she said, 'Now, I ax everybody here to
pray for dis union dat God 'bout to make. I wants y'all to pray dat
dis here couple is gwine a stay togedder—' she hesitated '—an' dat
nothin' don't happen to cause 'em to git sol' away from one 'nother.

And pray dat dey has good, healthy young'uns.' And then very solemnly, Aunt Sukey placed a broomstick on the close-cropped grass just in front of Kunta and Bell, whom she now motioned to link their arms.

Kunta felt as if he were suffocating. In his mind was flashing how marriages were conducted in his Juffure. He could see the dancers, hear the praise singers and the prayers, and the talking drums relaying the glad tidings to other villages. He hoped that he would be forgiven for what he was doing, that whatever words were spoken to their pagan God, Allah would understand that Kunta still believed in Him and only Him. And then, as if from afar, he heard Aunt Sukey asking, 'Now, y'all two is sho' you wants to git married?' Softly, alongside Kunta, Bell said, 'I does.' And Aunt Sukey turned her gaze to Kunta; he felt her eyes boring into him. And then Bell was squeezing his arm very hard. He forced the words from his mouth: 'I does.' And then Aunt Sukey said, 'Den, in de eyes of Jesus, y'all jump into de holy lan' of matrimony.'

Kunta and Bell jumped high over the broomstick together, as Bell had forced him to practice over and over the day before. He felt ridiculous doing it, but she had warned that a marriage would meet the very worst kind of bad luck if the feet of either person should touch the broomstick, and whoever did it would be the first to die. As they landed safely together on the other side of the broom, all the observers applauded and cheered, and when they had quieted, Aunt Sukey spoke again: 'What God done j'ined, let no man pull asunder. Now y'all be faithful to one 'nother.' She looked at Kunta directly. 'An' be good Christians.' Aunt Sukey turned next to look at Massa Waller. 'Massa, is it anything you cares to say for dis here occasion?'

The massa clearly looked as if he would prefer not to, but he stepped forward and spoke softly. 'He's got a good woman in Bell. And she's got a good boy. And my family here, along with myself, wish them the rest of their lives of good luck.' The loud cheering that followed from all of the slave-row people was punctuated with the happy squeals of little Missy Anne, who was jumping up and down, until her mother pulled her away, and all the Wallers went into the big house to let the blacks continue the celebration in their own way.

Aunt Sukey and other friends of Bell's had helped her cook enough pots of food that they all but hid the top of a long table. And amid the feasting and good cheer, everyone there but Kunta and the Ghanaian partook of the brandy and wines that the massa had sent up from the big-house cellar as his gift. With the fiddler playing steadily and loudly on his instrument ever since the party began,

304

Kunta didn't know how he'd managed to sneak a drink, but from the way he swayed as he played, it was clear that he'd managed to get hold of more than one. He had endured the fiddler's drinking so often that he was resigned to it, but when he saw *Bell* busy filling and refilling her wine glass, he began to get increasingly concerned and embarrassed. He was shocked to overhear her exclaiming to Sister Mandy, another of her friends, 'Been had my eye on him for ten years!' And not long after that, she wobbled over, threw her arms around him, and kissed him full on the mouth right there in front of everyone, amid crude jokes, elbows in the ribs, and uproarious laughter. Kunta was taut as a bowstring by the time the rest of the guests finally began to take their leave. Finally, they were all alone there in the yard, and as Bell wove unsteadily towards him, she said softly in a slurred voice, 'Now you done bought de cow, you gits all de milk you wants!' He was horrified to hear her talk so.

But it wasn't long before he got over it. In fact, before many weeks had passed, he had gained considerably more knowledge of what a big, strong, healthy woman was really like. His hands had explored in the darkness until now he knew for a certainty that Bell's big behind was entirely her own, and none of it was one of those padded bustles that he had heard many women were wearing to make their behinds look big. Though he hadn't seen her naked – she always blew out the candles before he got the chance – he had been permitted to see her breasts, whose largeness he noted with satisfaction were the kind that would supply much milk for a manchild, and that was very good. But it had been with horror that Kunta first saw the deep lash marks on Bell's back. 'I's carryin' scars to my grave jes' like my mammy did,' Bell said, 'but my back sure ain't as bad as your'n,' and Kunta was taken with surprise, for he hadn't seen his own back. He had all but forgotten all those lashings, over twenty years ago.

With her warmth always beside him, Kunta greatly enjoyed sleeping in Bell's tall bed on its soft mattress, filled as it was with cotton instead of straw or cornshucks. Her handmade quilts, too, were comfortable and warm, and it was a completely new and luxurious experience for him to sleep between a pair of sheets. Almost as pleasurable for him were the nicely fitted shirts she made for him, then washed, starched, and ironed freshly every day. Bell even softened the leather of his stiff, high-topped shoes by greasing them with tallow, and she knitted him more socks that were thickly cushioned to fit his half foot.

After years of driving the massa all day and returning at night to a cold supper before crawling onto his solitary pallet, now Bell saw to it that the same supper she fed the massa – unless it was pork, of course – was simmering over the fireplace in their cabin when he got home. And he liked eating on her white crockery dishes with the knives, spoons and forks she had obviously supplied for herself from the big house. Bell had even whitewashed her cabin – he often had to remind himself that now it was *their* cabin – on the outside as well as the inside. All in all, he was amazed to find that he liked almost everything about her, and he would have rebuked himself for not having come to his senses sooner if he hadn't been feeling too good to spend much time thinking about all the years he'd wasted. He just couldn't believe how different things were, how much better life was, than it had been just a few months before and a few yards away.

66

As close as they'd become since they 'jumped de broom', there were times when Kunta would sense that Bell still didn't totally trust him. Sometimes when she was talking to him in the kitchen or the cabin, she would nearly say something, then abruptly veer off onto another subject, filling Kunta with a rush of anger that only his pride enabled him to conceal. And on more than one occasion, he had learned things from the fiddler or the gardener that had to have been picked up at the massa's keyhole. It didn't matter to him what it was she was telling them; what hurt was that she wasn't telling *him*, that she was keeping secrets from her own husband. What hurt him even more was that he had always been so open in sharing with her and them – news they might never have learned otherwise, or at least not for a long time. Kunta began to let weeks go by without telling even Bell about whatever he had overheard in town. When she finally said something to him about it, he said he guessed things had just been kind of quiet lately, and maybe it's just as well because the news never seemed to be any good. But the next time he came back from town, he figured she'd learned her lesson, and he told her that he'd overheard the massa telling one of his friends that he'd just read that in New Orleans a white doctor named Benjamin Rush had written recently that when his longtime black assistant, a slave named James

Derham, had learned as much medicine from him as he felt he knew himself, he had set him free.

'Ain't he de one what become a doctor hisself and got even mo' famous dan de man what learned him?' asked Bell.

'How you know dat? Massa say he jes' read 'bout it hisself, an ain't nobody been here fo' you to hear him tell about it,' said Kunta, as irritated as he was perplexed.

'Oh, I got my ways,' Bell replied mysteriously, changing the subject.

As far as Kunta was concerned, that was the last time she'd ever hear any news from him, and he didn't say another word about it – or almost anything else – for the next week or so. Finally Bell got the hint, and after a good dinner by candlelight there in the cabin one Sunday night, she put her hand on his shoulder and said quietly, 'Something been hard on my mind to tell you.' Going into their bedroom, she returned in a moment with one of the Virginia *Gazettes* that Kunta knew she kept in a stack beneath their bed. He had always assumed that she simply enjoyed turning the pages, as he knew so many blacks did, as well as those poor whites who walked around on Saturdays in the county seat with newspapers opened before their faces, though Kunta and everyone else who saw them knew perfectly well that they couldn't read a word. But in some way now, as he saw the secretive look on Bell's face, he sensed with astonishment what she was about to say.

'I can read some,' Bell hesitated. 'Massa sell me fo' sunup if'n he knowed dat.'

Kunta made no response, for he had learned that Bell would do more talking on her own than if she was asked questions. 'I's knowed some a de words ever since I was a young'un,' she continued. 'It were de chilluns of my massa back den what teached me. Dey liked to play teacher, 'cause dey was going to school, an' de massa and missis didn't pay it no 'tention on count of how de white folks tells deyselves dat niggers is too dumb to learn anythin'.'

Kunta thought about the old black he saw regularly at the Spotsylvania County courthouse, who had swept and mopped there for years, with none of the whites ever dreaming that he had copied the handwriting they left lying around on papers until he had got good enough at it to forge and sign travelling passes, which he sold to blacks.

Peering hard at the tip of her forefinger as it moved across the paper's front page, Bell said finally, 'Here where de House of Burgesses done met again.' She studied the print closely. 'Done passed a new law 'bout taxes.' Kunta was simply amazed. Bell moved to a place farther down the page. 'Right here it's somethin' 'nother 'bout dat England done sent some niggers from dere back to Africa.' Bell glanced upwards at Kunta. 'You want me to pick out mo' what dey say 'bout dat?' Kunta nodded. Bell needed several minutes of staring at her finger, with her lips silently forming letters and words. Then she spoke again. 'Well, ain't sho' 'bout it all, but fo' hunnud niggers done been sent somewheres called, look like, Sierra Leone, on land de England bought from a king dat's dere, an' de niggers is been give some land apiece 'long wid some money for a 'lowance.'

When it seemed as if the very effort of reading had fatigued her, she went thumbing through the inside pages, pointing out to Kunta one after another identical small figures that were recognizable as men carrying a bundle at the end of a stick over their shoulders, and with her finger on the block of print under one of these figures, she said, 'Dat's always 'scribin' dese runaway niggers – like it was one 'bout you de las' time you run off. It tell what colour dey is, what marks dey got on dey faces or arms or legs or backs from bein' beat or branded. An' it tell what dey was wearin' when dey run off, an' sich as dat. An' den it tell who dey belongst to, and what reward bein' offered to whoever catch dem and bring dem back. I seen it be much as five hunnud, an' I seen it be where de nigger done run so much dat he massa so mad he advertise ten dollars fo' de live nigger back an' fi'teen fo' jes' his head.'

Finally she set the paper down with a sigh, seemingly fatigued by the effort of reading. 'Now you knows how I foun' out 'bout dat nigger doctor. Same way de massa did.'

Kunta asked if she didn't think she might be taking chances reading the massa's paper like that.

'T'se real careful,' she said. 'But I tell you one time I got scared to death wid massa,' Bell added. 'One day he jes' walked in on me when I s'posed to be dustin' in de livin' room, but what I *was* doin' was looking in one a dem books a his'n. Lawd, I like to froze. Massa jes' stood dere a minute lookin' at me. But he never said nothin.' He jes' walked out, an' from de next day to dis day it's been a lock on his bookcase.'

When Bell put away the newspaper back under the bed, she was quiet for a while, and Kunta knew her well enough by now to know that she still had something on her mind. They were about ready to go to bed when she abruptly seated herself at the table, as if she had just made up her mind about something, and with an expression both furtive and proud on her face, drew from her apron pocket a pencil and a folded piece of paper. Smoothing out the paper, she began to print some letters very carefully.

'You know what dat is?' she asked, and before Kunta could say no, answered, 'Well, dat's my name. B-e-l-l.' Kunta stared at the pencilled characters, remembering of how for years he had shrunk away from any closeness to toubob writing, thinking it contained some toubob greegrees that might bring him harm – but he still wasn't too sure that was so far-fetched. Bell now printed some more letters. 'Dat's your name, K-u-n-t-a.' She beamed up at him. Despite himself, Kunta couldn't resist bending a little closer to study the strange markings. But then Bell got up, crumpled the paper, and threw it onto the dying embers in the fireplace. 'Ain't never gone git caught wid no writin'.'

Several weeks had passed before Kunta finally decided to do something about an irritation that had been eating at him ever since Bell showed him so proudly that she could read and write. Like their white massas, these plantation-born blacks seemed to take it for granted that those who had come from Africa had just climbed down from the trees, let alone had any experience whatever with education.

So very casually one evening after supper, he knelt down before the cabin's fireplace and raked a pile of ashes out onto the hearth, then used his hands to flatten and smooth them out. With Bell watching curiously, he then took a slender whittled stick from his pocket and proceeded to scratch into the ashes his name in Arabic characters.

Bell wouldn't let him finish, demanding, 'What dat?' Kunta told her. Then, having made his point, he swept the ashes back into the fireplace, sat down in the rocking chair, and waited for her to ask him how he'd learned to write. He didn't have long to wait, and for the rest of the evening he talked, and Bell listened for a change. In his halting speech, Kunta told her how all the children in his village were taught to write, with pens made of hollowed dried grass stalks, and ink of water mixed with crushed potblack. He told her about the arafang, and how his lessons were conducted both mornings and evenings. Warming to his subject, and enjoying the novelty of seeing Bell with her mouth shut for a while, Kunta told her how the students in Juffure had to be able to read well from the Koran before they could graduate, and he even recited for her some Koranic verses. He could tell she was intrigued, but it seemed amazing to him that this was the very first time in all the years he'd known her that she had ever shown the slightest interest in anything about Africa.

Bell tapped the top of the table between them. 'How y'all Africans say "table"?' she asked.

Although he hadn't spoken in Mandinka since he left Africa, the word '*meso*' popped from Kunta's mouth almost before he realized it, and he felt a surge of pride.

'How 'bout *dat?* asked Bell, pointing at her chair. '*Sirango*,' said Kunta. He was so pleased with himself that he got up and began to walk around in the cabin, pointing at things.

Tapping Bell's black iron pot over the fireplace, he said '*kalero*', and then a candle on the table: '*kandio*'. Astonished, Bell had risen from her chair and was following him around. Kunta nudged a burlap bag with his shoe and said '*boto*', touched a dried gourd and said '*mirango*', then a basket that the old gardener had woven: '*sinsingo*'. He led Bell on into their bedroom. '*Larango*,' he said, pointing to their bed, and then a pillow: '*kunglarang*.' Then at the window: '*janerango*', and at the roof: '*kankarango*'.

'Lawd have mercy!' exclaimed Bell. That was far more respect for his homeland than he had ever expected to arouse in Bell.

'Now it time to put our head on de *kunglarang*,' said Kunta, sitting down on the edge of the bed and starting to undress. Bell knitted her brow, then laughed and put her arms around him. He hadn't felt so good in a long time.

67

Though Kunta still liked to visit and swap stories with the fiddler and the gardener, it didn't happen nearly as often as it used to when he was single. This was hardly surprising, since he spent most of his free time with Bell now. But even when they did get together lately, they seemed to feel differently towards him than before – certainly not unfriendly, but undeniably less companionable. It had been they who practically pushed Kunta into Bell's arms, yet now that he was married, they acted a little as if they were afraid it might be catching – or that it might never be; his obvious contentment with hearth and home didn't make them feel any warmer on cold winter nights. But if he didn't feel as close to them as before – in the comradeship they had shared as single men, despite their different origins – he felt somehow more accepted now, as if by marrying Bell he had become one of them. Though their conversations with their married friend weren't as earthy as they had sometimes been before – not that Kunta would admit even to himself that he had ever enjoyed the fiddler's crudities – they had become, with the building of trust and the passage of years, even deeper and more serious.

'Scairt!' declared the fiddler one night. 'Dat's how come white folks so busy countin' everybody in dat census! Dey scairt dey's done brung mo' niggers 'mongst 'em dan dey is white folks!' declared the fiddler.

Kunta said that Bell had told him she'd read in the *Gazette* that in Virginia, the census had recorded only a few more thousand whites than blacks.

'White folks scairder of free niggers dan dey is of us'ns!' the old gardener put in.

'I's heared it's near 'bout sixty thousand free niggers jes' in Virginia,' the fiddler said. 'So it ain't no tellin' how many slave niggers. But even dis state ain't where de mos' is. Dat's down in dem states where de richest lan' make de bes' crops, an' dey got water for boats to take dey crops to de markets, an' . . .'

'Yeah, dem places it be's two niggers for every white folks!' the old gardener interrupted. 'All down in dat Lou'siana Delta, an' de Yazoo Miss'ippi where dey grows sugar cane, an' all down in dat black belt of Alabama, South Ca'lina and Geo'gia where dey grows all dat rice an' indigo, let me tell you dat down on dem great big 'way-back plantations, dey's got all kinds of niggers ain't never been counted.'

'Some o' dem plantations so big dey's split up into littler ones wid oberseers in charge,' the fiddler said. 'An' de massas dat owns dem big plantations is mostly dem big lawyers an' politicians an' businessmen what lives in de cities, an' dey wimminfolks don't want no parts of no plantations 'ceptin' maybe to bring out fancy carriages full of dey friends maybe for Thanksgivin' or Christmas, or summertime picnics.'

'But you know what,' the old gardener exclaimed, 'dem rich city white folks is de very kin' 'mongst which it's dem dat speaks 'gainst slavery.'

The fiddler cut him off. 'Humph! Dat don' mean nothin'! Always been some big white folks dat wants de slavery 'bolished. Shoot,

311

slavery been outlawed here in Virginia ten years now but law or no you notice we still slaves, an' dey still bringin' in more shiploads of niggers.'

'Where dey all bein' taken?' asked Kunta. 'Some buggy drivers I knows say dey massas go on long trips where dey don' hardly see another black face for days at a time.'

'It's a plenty whole counties dat ain't even got one big plantation on 'em, an' hardly no niggers atall,' said the gardener. 'Jes' nothin' but dem little rocky farms dat's sol' for fifty cents a acre to dem white folks so po' dey eats dirt. An' not a whole lot better off dan dem is de ones dat got not much better land an' jes' a handful of slaves.'

'One place I heared 'bout ain't got no handful o' niggers, it's dem West Indies, whatever dem is,' said the fiddler, turning to Kunta. 'You know where? It's 'crost de water like you come from.' Kunta shook his head.

'Anyway,' the fiddler went on, 'I hears it's many as a thousan' niggers b'longin' to one massa dere, raisin' and cuttin' dat cane dat dey makes sugar an 'lasses an' rum out of. Dey tells me a whole lots of dem ships like brung you over here stops off African niggers in dem West Indies to keep 'em awhile jes' to fatten 'em up from dem long trips dat gits 'em so sick an' starved dey's near 'bout dead. Fattens 'em up, den brings 'em on here to git de better prices for niggers dat's fit to work. Leas'ways, dat's what I'se heared.'

It had never failed to amaze Kunta how the fiddler and the gardener seemed to know so much about things they'd never seen and places they'd never been to, for he distinctly recalled having heard both of them say they had never been outside of Virginia and North Carolina. He had travelled far more widely than they had – not only all the way from Africa but also back and forth across the state in the massa's buggy – but they still knew so much more than he did that even after all these years of talking to them, he was finding out things he hadn't known before.

It didn't really bother Kunta to find out how ignorant he was, since they were helping him become less so; but it troubled him deeply to learn over the years that even he was better informed than the average slave. From what he'd been able to observe, most blacks literally didn't even know where they were, let alone who they were.

'I bet you half de niggers in Virginia ain't never been off dey massa's plantations,' said Bell when he raised the subject with her. 'An' ain't never heard of nowhere else 'ceptin' maybe Richmond an' Fredericksburg an' up Nawth, an' don' have no idea where none of dem is. De white folks keeps niggers ign'ant o' where dey is 'cause dey so worried 'bout niggers uprisin' or 'scapin'.'

Before Kunta had the chance to recover from his surprise at hearing an insight like this one coming from Bell rather than the fiddler or the gardener, she spoke again. 'You reckon you still would run again if'n you had de chance?'

Kunta was stunned by the question, and for a long time he didn't answer. Then finally he said, 'Well, long time I ain't done no thinkin' 'bout dat.'

'Whole lots of times I be's thinkin' a heap o' things nobody wouldn't figger I does,' said Bell. 'Like sometime I gits to thinkin' 'bout bein' free, like I hears 'bout dem dat gits away up to de Nawth.' She looked closely at Kunta. 'Don' care how good de massa is, I gits to feelin' like if you an' me was younger'n we is, I believes I'd be ready to leave 'way from here tonight.' As Kunta sat there astonished, she said quietly, 'Reckon I'se got to be too old and scairt now.'

Bell could have been reading the thought he was having at that moment about himself, and it hit him like a fist. He *was* too old to run away again and too beat up. And scared. All the pain and terror of those terrible days and nights of running came back: the blistered feet, the bursting lungs, the bleeding hands, the tearing thorns, the baying of the hounds, the snarling jaws, the gunshots, the sting of the lash, the falling axe. Without even realizing it, Kunta had plunged into a black depression. Knowing that she had aroused it without meaning to, but knowing also that she'd only make it worse by talking about it any further, even to apologize, Bell simply got up and went to bed.

When he finally realized that she was gone, Kunta felt badly that he had cut her out of his thoughts. And it pained him to think how grievously he had underestimated her and the other blacks.

Though they never showed it except to those they loved, and sometimes not even then, he realized at last that they felt – and hated – no less than he the oppressiveness under which they all lived. He wished he could find a way to tell her how sorry he was, how he felt her pain, how grateful he was to feel her love, how strong he felt the bond between them growing deep within himself. Quietly he got up, went into the bedroom, took off his clothes, got into bed, took her in his arms, and made love to her – and she to him – with a kind of desperate intensity.

68

For several weeks, it seemed to Kunta that Bell had been acting very oddly. For one thing, she was hardly talking; but she wasn't even in a bad mood. And she was casting what he felt were peculiar looks at him, then sighing loudly when he stared back. And she had begun smiling mysteriously to herself while rocking in her chair, sometimes even humming tunes. Then one night, just after they'd blown out the candle and climbed into bed, she grasped Kunta's hand and placed it tenderly on her stomach. Something inside her moved beneath his hand. Kunta sprang up fit to split with joy.

Over the next days, he hardly noticed where he was driving. For all he knew, the massa could have been pulling the buggy and the horses sitting on the seat behind him, so filled was his mind's eye with visions of Bell paddling down the bolong to the rice fields with his manchild bundled snugly on her back. He thought of little else but the myriad significances of this coming first-born, even as for Binta and Omoro he had been the first-born. He vowed that just as they and others had done for him in Juffure, he was going to teach this manchild to be a true man, no matter what trials and hazards that might involve here in the land of the toubob. For it was the job of a father to be as a giant tree to his manchild. For where girl-children simply ate food until they grew big enough to marry and go away – and girl-children were their mothers' concerns, in any case – it was the manchild who carried on his family's name and reputation, and when the time came that his parents were old and tottering, it would be the well-reared manchild who put nothing before taking care of them.

Bell's pregnancy took Kunta's mind even farther back to Africa than his encounter with the Ghanaian had done. One night, in fact, he completely forgot Bell was in the cabin while he patiently counted out all the pebbles in his gourd, discovering with astonishment that he hadn't seen his homeland now for exactly 22½ rains. But most evenings she would be talking almost steadily while he sat there hearing less than usual and gazing off at nothing. 'He jes' go off into his Africanisms,' Bell would tell Aunt Sukey, and after a while Bell would rise unnoticed from her chair, quietly leave the room – muttering to herself – and go to sleep alone.

It had been one such night when, about an hour after she'd gone to bed, Kunta was snapped back to the cabin by moans from the bedroom. Was it time? Rushing in, he found her still asleep, but rolling back and forth on the verge of screaming. When he leaned over to touch her cheek, she sat bolt upright there in the darkness, soaked with sweat and breathing hard.

'Lawd, I'm scairt to death for dis baby in my belly!' she said as she put her arms around him. Kunta didn't understand until she composed herself enough to tell how she had dreamed that at a white folks' party game, they had announced that the first prize would be the next black baby to be born on that massa's plantation. Bell was so distraught that Kunta found himself in the unaccustomed role of calming her with assurances that she knew Massa Waller never would do such a thing. He made her agree with that, then climbed into bed alongside her, and finally she went back to sleep.

But Kunta didn't; he lay thinking for quite some time of how he had heard of such things being done – of unborn black babies being given as presents, wagered as gambling bets at card tables and cockfights. The fiddler had told him how the dying massa of a pregnant fifteen-year-old black girl named Mary had willed as slaves to each of his five daughters one apiece of her first five babies. He had heard of black children being security for loans, of creditors claiming them while they were yet in their mother's belly, of debtors selling them in advance to raise cash. At that time in the Spotsylvania County seat slave auctions, he knew the average price that was being asked and paid for a healthy black baby past six months of age – when it was assumed then that it would live – was around two hundred dollars.

None of this was very far from his mind when Bell laughingly told him one evening in the cabin about three months later that during the day the inquisitive Missy Anne had demanded to know why Bell's belly was growing so big. 'I tol' Missy Anne, "I got a li'l biscuit in de oven, honey." ' Kunta was hardly able to keep Bell from seeing his anger at the attention and affection she lavished on that pampered, doll-like child, who was to him but another in the seemingly endless parade of 'li'l missies' and 'li'l massas' he had seen at so many big houses. Now with Bell about to have a child of her own – and his own – it incensed him to think about the first-born son of Kunta and Bell Kinte romping in 'play' with toubob children who would grow up to become their massas – and sometimes even the fathers of their own children. And Kunta had been to more than a few plantations where one of the slave children was almost the same colour as his massa's – in fact, they often looked like twins – because both of them had the same white father. Before Kunta let anything like that happen to Bell, he vowed that he would kill the massa rather than become one of those men he had seen holding their wife's 'high-yaller' baby and living somehow with the knowledge that if he uttered publicly so much as a complaining word, he would certainly get beaten, if not worse.

Kunta thought about how 'high-yaller' slave girls brought high prices at the county seat slave auctions. He had seen them being sold, and he had heard many times about the purposes for which they were bought. And he thought of the many stories he had heard about 'high-yaller' manchildren – about how they were likely to get mysteriously taken away as babies never to be seen again, because of the white fear that otherwise they might grow up into white-looking men and escape to where they weren't known and mix the blackness in their blood with that of white women. Every time Kunta thought about any aspect of blood mixing, he would thank Allah that he and Bell could share the comfort of knowing that whatever otherwise might prove to be His will, their manchild was going to be black.

It was early one night in September of 1790 when the labour pains began to take hold of Bell. But she wouldn't yet let Kunta go for the massa, who had said that he would personally attend her, with Sister Mandy to be in readiness as his assistant if he should need her. Each time the pains came, Bell lay on the bed gritting her teeth to keep from crying out, and she would tighten her grip on Kunta's hand with the strength of a man.

It was during one of the brief intervals between the pains that Bell turned her sweating face to Kunta and said, 'It's something I oughta tol' you 'fore now. I's already done had two chilluns, long time ago, 'fore I ever come here, 'fore I was sixteen years ol'.' Kunta stood looking down at the anguished Bell, astounded. Had he known this – no, he would have married her anyway – but he felt betrayed that she hadn't told him before. Making herself gasp out the words between contractions, Bell told him about the two daughters from whom she had been sold away. 'Jes' nothin' but babies is all dey was.' She began to weep. 'One was jes' startin' to walk good, an' de other'n weren't a year old hardly—' She started to go on, but a spasm of pain clamped her mouth shut and tightened her grip on his hand. When it finally subsided, her grip didn't loosen; she looked up at him through her tears and – reading his racing thoughts – said, 'Case you wond'rin', dere daddy weren't no massa or no oberseer. Was a field nigger 'bout my age. We didn't know no better.'

The pains came again, much sooner than before, and her nails dug into his palm as her mouth opened wide in a soundless scream.

Kunta rushed from the cabin down to Sister Mandy's hut, where he banged the door and called to her hoarsely, then ran on as fast as he could go to the big house. His knocking and calling finally brought Massa Waller, who needed but one glance at Kunta to say, 'I'll be right there!'

Hearing Bell's anguished moans rise into shrieks that went ripping through the quiet of slave row pushed from Kunta's mind any thought of what Bell had revealed to him. As much as he wanted to be by Bell's side, he was glad Sister Mandy had ordered him outside, where he squatted at the door trying to imagine what must be going on inside. He had never learned much about childbirth in Africa, since that was considered women's affair, but he had heard that a woman birthed a child while kneeling over cloths spread on the floor, then sat in a pan of water to clean away the blood, and he wondered if that's what was happening now.

It occurred to Kunta that far away in Juffure, Binta and Omoro were becoming grandparents, and it saddened him to know not only that they would never see his manchild – or he them – but also that they would never know he'd had one.

Hearing the first sharp cries of another voice, Kunta sprang upright. A few minutes later, the massa emerged looking haggard. 'She had a hard time. She's forty-three years old,' he said to Kunta. 'But she'll be fine in a couple of days.' The massa gestured towards the cabin door. 'Give Mandy a little while to clean up, then you go on in there and see your baby girl.'

A girlchild! Kunta was still struggling to compose himself when Sister Mandy appeared at the doorway, smiling and beckoning him inside. Cripping through the front room, he pushed aside the curtain at the bedroom door and there they were. As he moved quietly to her side, a floorboard squeaked and Bell opened her eyes, managing a weak smile. Absently, he found her hand and squeezed, but he scarcely felt it, for he couldn't stop staring at the face of the infant who lay beside her. It was almost as black as his, and the features were unmistakably Mandinka. Though it was a girlchild – which must be the will of Allah – it was nonetheless a child, and he felt a deep pride and serenity in the knowledge that the blood of the Kintes, which had coursed down through the centuries like a mighty river, would continue to flow for still another generation.

Kunta's next thoughts, standing there at the bedside, were of a fitting name for his child. Though he knew enough not to ask the massa for eight days off from work to spend deciding on it, as a new father would in Africa, he knew that the matter would require long and serious reflection, for he knew that what a child was called would really influence the kind of person he or she became. Then it flashed into his mind that whatever name he gave her, she would be also called by the last name of the massa; the thought was so infuriating that Kunta vowed before Allah that this girlchild would grow up knowing her own true name.

Abruptly, without a word, he turned and left. With the sky just beginning to show the traces of early dawn, he went outside and started walking down along the fence row where he and Bell had shared their courtship. He had to think. Remembering what she had told him about her life's greatest grief – having been sold away from her two infant girlchildren – he searched his mind for a name, some Mandinka word, that would have as its meaning Bell's deepest wish never to suffer such a loss again, a name that would protect its owner from ever losing her. Suddenly he had it! Turning the word over and over in his mind, he resisted the temptation to speak it aloud, even just for himself, for that would have been improper. Yes, that had to be it! Exhilarated with his good luck in such a short while, Kunta hurried back along the fencerow to the cabin.

But when he told Bell that he was prepared for his child to be named, she protested far more strongly than he would have thought her capable of in her condition. 'What's sich a rush to name 'er? Name 'er what? We ain't talked 'bout no name nohow!' Kunta knew well how stubborn Bell could be once she got her back up, so there was anguish as well as anger in his voice as he searched for the right words to explain that there were certain traditions that must be honoured, certain procedures that must be followed in the naming of a child; chief among them was the selection of that name by the father alone, who was permitted to tell no one what it was until he had revealed it to the child, and that this was only right. He went on to say that haste was essential lest their child hear first some name that the massa might decide upon for her.

'Now I sees!' said Bell. 'Dese Africanisms you so full of ain't gon' do nothin' but make trouble. An' dey ain't gon' be none of dem heathen ways an' names, neither, for dis chile!'

In a fury, Kunta stormed out of the cabin – and nearly bumped into Aunt Sukey and Sister Mandy on their way in with armloads of towels and steaming pots of water.

' 'Gratulations, Br'er Toby, we comin' to look in on Bell.'

But Kunta scarcely grunted at them as he passed. A field hand named Cato was headed out to ring the first bell of the morning, signalling the others out of their cabins for buckets of water from the well to wash up with before breakfast. Kunta quickly turned off slave row to take the back path that led to the barn, wanting as much distance as he could get between him and those heathen blacks whom the toubob had trained to shrink away in fear from anything smacking of the Africa that had been their very source-place.

In the sanctuary of the barn, Kunta angrily fed, watered and then rubbed down the horses. When he knew that it was time for the massa to have his breakfast, he took the long way around again on his way to the big-house kitchen door, where he asked Aunt Sukey, who was filling in for Bell, if the massa was going to need the buggy. Refusing to speak or even turn around, she shook her head and left the room without even offering him any food. Limping back to the barn, Kunta wondered what Bell had told Aunt Sukey and Sister Mandy for them to go gossiping through slave row; then he told himself that he couldn't care less.

He had to do something with himself; he couldn't just idle away more hours around the barn. Moving outside with the buggy harnesses, he set about his familiar task of killing time by oiling them unnecessarily, as he had just done only two weeks before. He wanted to go back to the cabin to see the baby – and even Bell – but anger rose every time he thought of what a disgrace it was that the wife of a Kinte could want her child to bear some toubob name, which would be nothing but the first step towards a lifetime of self-contempt.

About noontime, Kunta saw Aunt Sukey taking in to Bell a pot of some food – some kind of soup, probably. It made him hungry to think about it; a few minutes later he went out behind the barn where some recently harvested sweet potatoes had been mounded under straw for curing, picked out four of the smaller ones, and – feeling very sorry for himself – ate them raw to appease his stomach.

Dusk was descending before he could bring himself to go home. When he opened the front door and walked in, there was no sound of response from Bell in the bedroom. She could be asleep, he thought, leaning over to light a candle on the table.

'Dat you?'

He could detect no special harshness in Bell's tone. Grunting non-committally, he picked up the candle, pushed aside the curtain, and went into the bedroom. In the ruddy glow, he could see that the expression on her face was as adamant as his own.

'Looka here, Kunta,' she said, wasting no time getting to the point, 'it's some things I knows 'bout our massa better'n you does. You git him mad wid dat African stuff, he sell us all three at de next county seat auction jes' sho's we born!'

Containing the anger within him as well as he could, Kunta stumbled for the words that could make Bell understand the absoluteness of his determination that whatever the risks, his child would bear no toubob name, and that moreover she would be given her name in the proper manner.

As deeply as Bell disapproved, she was even more apprehensive of what Kunta might do if she refused. So with deep misgivings, she finally acquiesced. 'What kin' o' voodoo you got to do?' she asked dubiously. When he said he was simply going to take the baby outdoors for a while, she insisted that he wait until the child awakened and she had nursed her so that she wouldn't be hungry and crying, and Kunta immediately agreed. Bell reckoned that the baby wouldn't wake up for at least another two hours, by which time it would be most unlikely that anyone in slave row would still be up to see whatever mumbo jumbo Kunta was going to perform. Though she didn't show it, Bell was still angry that Kunta prevented her from helping him pick a name for the daughter she had just brought into the world amid such agony; and she dreaded finding out what African-sounding, forbidden name Kunta had come up with, but she was sure that she could deal with the baby's name later in her own way.

It was near midnight when Kunta emerged from the cabin, carrying his first-born wrapped snugly in a blanket. He walked until he felt they were far enough from slave row that it couldn't cast a pall over what was about to take place.

Then, under the moon and the stars, Kunta raised the baby upwards, turning the blanketed bundle in his hands so that the baby's right ear touched against his lips. And then slowly and distinctly, in Mandinka, he whispered three times into the tiny ear, 'Your name is Kizzy. Your name is Kizzy. Your name is Kizzy.' It was done, as it had been done with all of the Kinte ancestors, as it had been done with himself, as it would have been done with this infant had she been born in her ancestral homeland. She had become the first person to know who she was.

Kunta felt Africa pumping in his veins – and flowing from him into the child, the flesh of him and Bell – as he walked on a little farther. Then again he stopped, and lifting a small corner of the blanket he bared the infant's small black face to the heavens, and this time he spoke aloud to her in Mandinka: 'Behold, the only thing greater than yourself!'

When Kunta returned with the baby to the cabin, Bell all but snatched her away, her face tight with fear and resentment as she opened the blanket and examined her from head to toe, not knowing what she was looking for and hoping she wouldn't find it. Satisfied that he hadn't done anything unspeakable – at least nothing that showed – she put the baby to bed, came back into the front room, sat down in the chair across from him, folded her hands carefully in her lap, and asked.

'Awright, lemme have it.'

'Have what?'

'De name, African, what you call her?'

'Kizzy.'

'Kizzy! Ain't nobody never heared no name like dat!'

Kunta explained that in Mandinka 'Kizzy' meant 'you sit down', or 'you stay put', which, in turn, meant that unlike Bell's previous two babies, this child would never get sold away.

She refused to be placated. 'Jes' start troubles!' she insisted. But when she felt Kunta's anger starting to rise again she thought it would be wise to relent. She said she seemed to recall her mother speaking of a grandmother whose name was 'Kibby', which sounded very much the same; at least that's what they could tell the massa if he got suspicious.

The next morning, Bell did her best to hide her nervousness when the massa came to look in on her – even forcing herself to laugh good-naturedly as she told him the baby's name. He only commented that it was an odd name, but he said nothing against it, and Bell breathed a heavy sigh of relief the moment he stepped out the door. Back in the big house, before leaving for a day of visiting his patients with Kunta driving him, Massa Waller opened the large black Bible that he kept locked in a case in the drawing-room, turned to a page devoted to plantation records, dipped his pen in the inkwell, and wrote in fine black script: 'Kizzy Waller, born 12 September 1790.'

69

'She jes' like a li'l nigger doll!' squealed Missy Anne, hopping ecstatically up and down, clapping her hands with delight, as she saw Kizzy for the first time three days later in Bell's kitchen. 'Cain't she be mine?'

Bell smiled widely with pleasure. 'Well, she belongst to me an' her daddy, honey, but jes' soon's she big enough, you sho' can play wid her all you wants!'

And so she did. As often as not, whenever Kunta went to the kitchen now to find out if the buggy would be needed, or simply to visit Bell, he would find the massa's flaxen-haired little niece – four years old now – bent over the edge of Kizzy's basket cooing down at her. 'Jes' pretty as you can be. We gonna have plenty fun soon's you get some size, you hear me? You jes' hurry up an' grow, now!' Kunta never said anything about it, but it galled him to think how that toubob child acted as if Kizzy had entered the world to serve as her plaything, like some extraordinary doll. Bell hadn't even respected his manhood and fatherhood enough to ask his feelings about his daughter playing with the daughter of the man who bought him, he thought bitterly.

It seemed to him sometimes that Bell was less concerned about his feelings than she was about the massa's. He'd lost count of the evening she'd spent talking about what a blessing it was that little Missy Anne had come along to replace Massa Waller's real daughter, who had died at birth along with her mother.

'Oh, Lawd, I jes' even hates to think back on it,' she told him sniffing one night. 'Po' li'l pretty Missis Priscilla weren't hardly no bigger'n a bird. Walkin' roun' here every day singin' to herself an' smilin' at me an' pattin' herself, jes' waitin' for her baby's time. An' den dat mornin' jes' a-screamin' and finally dyin', her an' de li'l baby gal, too! Look like I ain't hardly seen po' massa do no smilin' since – leastways not 'til dis here li'l Missy Anne.'

Kunta felt no pity for the massa's loneliness, but it seemed to him that getting married again would keep the massa too busy to spend so much time doting on his niece, and that way would almost certainly cut down on Missy Anne's visits to the plantation – and therefore to play with Kizzy.

'Ever since then I been watchin' how massa git dat li'l gal in his lap, hol' her close, talk to her, sing her to sleep, an' den jes' set on dere holdin' her ruther'n put her to bed. Jes' act like he don't never want his eyes to leave her all de time she be roun' here. An' I know it's 'cause he's her daddy in his heart.'

It could only dispose the massa even more kindly towards both of them, not to mention towards Kizzy, Bell would tell him, for Missy Anne to strike up a friendship that would bring her over to the massa's house even more often than before. Nor could it hurt Massa John and his sickly wife, she reasoned slyly, that their daughter was developing a special closeness to her uncle, ' 'cause den de closer dey figgers dey is to massa's money.' However important the massa's brother acted, she said she knew for a fact that he borrowed from the massa now and then, and Kunta knew enough not to disbelieve her – not that he really cared which toubob was richer than which, since they were all alike to him.

Oftentimes now, since Kizzy's arrival, as Kunta drove the massa around to see his patients and his friends, he would find imself sharing the wish Bell had often expressed that the massa would marry again – although Kunta's reasons were entirely different from Bell's. 'He jes' be's so pitiful to me livin' all by hisself in dis big house. Fact, I believes dat's how come he jes' want to keep hisself movin', ruther'n settin' roun' here by hisself. Lawd, even li'l ol' Missy Anne sees it! Las' time she was here, I was servin' dem lunch an' all of a sudden she say, "Uncle William, how come you ain't got no wife like everybody else?" An' po' thing, he didn't know what to say to her.'

Though he had never told Bell about it because he knew how much she loved prying into toubob affairs, Kunta knew of several women who would run almost on their tiptoes out to meet the massa's buggy whenever Kunta turned into their driveway. The fat black cook of one of massa's more incurable patients had told Kunta scornfully, 'Dat hateful huzzy ain't got nothin' wrong dat catchin' yo' massa wouldn't cure mighty fast. She done already drive one man to de grave wid her ornery, evil ways, an' now she jes' claimin' sickness to keep yo' massa comin' back here. I sho' wish he could see her soon's y'all leave, a-hollerin' an' carryin' on at us niggers like we was mules or somethin', an' she don't never touch dem medicines he give 'er!' There was another woman patient who would always come onto her front porch with the massa as he left, clinging to one of his arms as if she might fall, and looking up into his face while fluttering her fan weakly. But with both of these women, the massa always acted very stiff and formal, and his visits always seemed to be shorter than with his other patients.

So the months kept on rolling past, with Missy Anne being

323

brought to visit Massa Waller about twice a week, and each time she came she'd spend hours playing with Kizzy. Though he was helpless to do anything about it, Kunta tried at least to avoid seeing them together, but they seemed to be everywhere he turned, and he couldn't escape the sight of his little girl being patted, kissed, or fondled by the massa's niece. It filled him with revulsion – and reminded him of an African saying so old that it had come down from the forefathers: 'In the end, the cat always eats the mouse it's played with.'

The only thing that made it bearable for Kunta was the days and nights in between her visits. It was summer by the time Kizzy began to crawl, and Bell and Kunta would spend the evenings in their cabin watching with delight as she scuttled about the floor with her little diapered behind upraised. But then Missy Anne would show up again and off they'd go, with the older girl frisking in circles around her shouting, 'C'mon, Kizzy, c'mon!' and Kizzy crawling in pursuit as quickly as she could, gurgling with pleasure at the game and the attention. Bell would beam with pleasure, but she'd know that even if Kunta was away driving the massa, he only needed to find out that Missy Anne had been there to return to the cabin that night with his face set and his lips compressed, and for the rest of the night he would be totally withdrawn, which Bell found extremely irritating. But when she considered what might happen if Kunta should ever exhibit his feelings even vaguely in any manner that might reach the massa, she was also a little frightened when he acted that way.

So Bell tried to convince Kunta that no harm could come of the relationship if only he could bring himself to accept it. Oftentimes, she told him, white girls grew up into lifetimes of true devotion and even deep loyalties to black childhood playmates. ' 'Fo' you commence to drivin' de buggy,' she said, 'dey was a white missis died havin' a chile – jes' like his own missis did – only dis time de baby girl lived an' got suckled by a nigger woman what jes' had a baby girl o' her own. Dem li'l gals had growed up near 'bout like sisters when dat massa married again. But dat new missis was so strong 'gainst dem gals bein' close, she finally 'suaded dat massa to sell away de black gal an' her mammy both.' But the moment they were gone, she went on, the white girl went into such continuing hysterics that time and again Massa Waller was sent for, until finally he told the father that further weakness and grief would kill his daughter unless the black girl was returned. 'Dat massa was 'bout ready to whip dat new wife of his'n. He lef' on his ridin' hoss an' ain't no tellin' how much he must o' spent trackin' down de nigger trader dat took de gal an' her mammy away, an' den buyin' dem back from de new massa de nigger trader had sol' dem to. But he brung back dat black gal an' got a lawyer an' deeded her over to be de property o' his own gal.' And Bell said that even now, years later, though that white girl had grown to womanhood, she had never entirely regained her health. 'De black one still livin' right wid her an' takin' care of her, an' neither one ain't never even married!'

As far as Kunta was concerned, if Bell had intended her story as an argument *against* friendship between black and whites rather than in favour of it, she could hardly have made a more eloquent case.

70

From about the time Kizzy had been born, both Kunta and the fiddler had returned to the plantation now and then with news about some island across the big water called 'Haiti', where it was said that around thirty-six thousand mostly French whites were outnumbered by about half a million blacks who had been brought there on ships from Africa to slave on huge plantations growing sugar cane, coffee, indigo and cocoa. One night Bell said she had heard Massa Waller telling his dinner guests that reportedly Haiti's rich class of whites lived like kings while snubbing the many poorer whites who couldn't afford slaves of their own.

' 'Magin' dat! Who ever heared o' such a thing?' said the fiddler sarcastically.

'Hush!' said Bell, laughing, and went on to say that the massa then told his horrified guests that for several generations in Haiti, so much breeding had gone on between white men and slave women that there were now almost twenty-eight thousand mulattoes and high-yallers, commonly called 'coloured people', of whom nearly all had been given freedom by their French owners and fathers. According to one of the other guests, said Bell, these 'coloured people' invariably sought yet lighter-complexioned mates, with their goal being children of entirely white appearance, and those who remained visibly mulatto would bribe officials for documents declaring that their forefathers had been Indians or Spanish or anything but Africans. As astonishing as he found it to believe, and as deeply as he deplored it, Massa Waller had said that through the gift deeds or the last wills of many whites, quite a sizeable number of these 'coloured' had come to own at least one fifth of all the Haitian land – and its slaves – that they vacationed in France and schooled their children there just as the rich whites did, and even snubbed poor whites. Bell's audience was as delighted to hear that as the massa's had been scandalized.

'You gon' laugh out o' de other sides you' moufs,' the fiddler interrupted, 'when you hears what I heared some o' dem rich massas talkin' 'bout at one o' dem so-ciety co-tillyums I played at a while back.' The massas, he said, were nodding their heads as they discussed how those poor whites down in Haiti hated those mulattoes and high-yallers so much that they'd signed petitions until France finally passed laws prohibiting 'coloureds' from walking about at night, from sitting alongside whites in churches, or even from wearing the same kind of fabrics in their clothes. In the meantime, said the fiddler, both whites and 'coloureds' would take out their bitterness towards each other on Haiti's half-million black slaves. Kunta said he had overheard talk in town among laughing whites that made it sound as if Haitian slaves were suffering worse than here. He said he'd heard that blacks getting beaten to death or buried alive as punishment was commonplace, and that pregnant black women were often driven at work until they miscarried. Since he felt it wouldn't have served any purpose other than to terrify them, he didn't tell them that he had heard about even more inhuman bestialities, such as a black man's hands being nailed to a wall until he was forced to eat his own cut-off ears; a toubob woman having all her slaves' tongues cut out; another gagging a black child's mouth until he starved.

In the wake of such horror stories over the past nine or ten months, it didn't surprise Kunta, on one of his trips to town during this summer of 1791, to learn that Haiti's black slaves had risen in a wild, bloody revolt. Thousands of them had swept forth slaughtering, clubbing and beheading white men, gutting children, raping women and burning every plantation building until northern Haiti lay in smoking ruins and the terrorized escaped white population was fighting to stay alive and lashing back – torturing, killing, even skinning every black they could catch. But they had been only a handful of survivors steadily dwindling before the wildly spreading black revolt, until by the end of August the few remaining thousands of whites still alive were in hiding places or trying to flee the island.

Kunta said he had never seen Spotsylvania County's toubob so angry and afraid. 'Seem like dey's even scairder dan de las' uprisin' right here in Virginia,' said the fiddler. 'Was maybe two, three years after you come, but you still weren't hardly talkin' to nobody, so don' reckon you even knowed it. Was right over yonder in New Wales, in Hanover County, during one Christmastime. A oberseer beat some young nigger to de groun', an' dat nigger sprung up an' went at him wid a axe. But he missed 'im, an' de other niggers jumped de oberseer an' beat 'im so bad dat de first nigger come an' saved his life. Dat oberseer went runnin' for help, all bloody, an' meanwhile dem mad niggers caught two more white mens an' tied 'em up and was beatin' on 'em when a great big bunch a' whites come a-runnin' wid guns. Dem niggers took cover in a barn, an' de white folks tried to sweet-talk 'em to come on out, but dem niggers come a-rushin' wid barrel staves an' clubs, an' it woun' up wid two niggers shot dead an' a lot of both white mens an' niggers hurt. Dey put out militia patrols, an' some mo' laws was passed, an' sich as dat, till it simmered down. Dis here Haiti thing done freshened white folks' minds, 'cause dey knows jes' good as me it's a whole heap o' niggers right under dey noses wouldn't need nothin' but de right spark to rise up right now, an' once dat ever get to spreadin', yessuh, it be de same as Haiti right here in Virginia.' The fiddler clearly relished the thought.

Kunta was soon to see the whites' fright for himself whenever he drove in the towns, or near the crossroads stores, taverns, church meetinghouses, or wherever else they gathered in small, agitated clusters, their faces red and scowling whenever he or any other black passed near by. Even the massa, who rarely spoke to Kunta other than to tell him where he wanted to be driven, made even those words noticeably colder and more clipped. Within a week, the Spotsylvania County militia was patrolling the roads, demanding to know the destination and to inspect the travelling permit of any passing blacks, and beating and jailing any they thought acted or even looked suspicious. At a meeting of the area's massas, the soon approaching big annual harvest frolic for slaves was cancelled, along with all other black gatherings beyond home plantations; and even any home slave-row dancing or prayer meetings were to be watched by an overseer or some other white. 'When massa tol' me dat, I tol' him me an' Aunt Sukey an' Sister Mandy gits on our knees an' prays to Jesus togedder every Sunday an' any other chance we gits, but he ain't say nothin' 'bout watchin' us, so we gon' keep right on prayin'!' Bell told the others on slave row.

Alone at home with Kunta and Kizzy for the next several nights in search of the latest news, Bell spelled her way through several newspapers the massa thought he had discarded. It took her the better part of an hour on one big story before she could tell him that 'some kin' o' Bill o' Rights done got . . .' Bell hesitated and drew a deep breath, 'well, it done got rat-ti-fied, or somethin' 'nother.' But there were far more reports about recent events in Haiti – most of which they'd already heard through the slave grapevine. The gist of most of them, she said, was that the Haitian slave revolt could easily spread foolhardy notions among black malcontents in this country, that extreme restrictions and harsh punishments should be imposed. As she folded up the papers and put them away, Bell said, 'Look like to me ain't much more dey can do 'gainst us, less'n it's jes' chain us all up, I reckon.'

Over the next month or two, however, news of further developments in Haiti slowly ebbed, and with it came a gradual easing of tensions – and a lightening of restrictions – throughout the South. The harvest season had begun, and whites were congratulating one another on the bumper cotton crop – and the record prices they were getting for it. The fiddler was being sent for to play at so many big-house balls and parties that during the daytime when he was back home, he did little more than sleep. 'Look like dem massas makin' so much cotton money dey jes' gwine dance deyselves to death!' he told Kunta.

It wasn't long, however, until the white folks had something to be unhappy about again. On his visits to the county seat with the massa, Kunta began to hear angry talk of increasing numbers of 'antislavery societies' organized by 'traitors to the white race' not only in the North but also in the South. Highly dubious, he told Bell what he had heard, and she said she'd been reading the same thing in the massa's newspapers, which attributed their recent and rapid growth to Haiti's black revolt.

'Keeps tryin' tell you it's some good white folks!' she exclaimed. 'Fact of de matter, I'se heared a whole heap of 'em was 'gainst de firs' ships ever bringin' any y'all African niggers here!' Kunta wondered where on earth Bell thought her own grandparents had come from, but she was so wound up that he let it pass. ' 'Cose, anytime somethin' like dat be's in de paper,' she went on, 'de massas gits riled up, rantin' an' hollerin' 'bout enemies of de country an' sich as dat, but what's 'portant is de mo' white folks 'gainst slavery says what dey thinks, den de mo' of dem massas git to wonderin' in dey secret heart is dey right or not.' She stared at Kunta. ' 'Specially dem callin' deyselves Christians.'

She looked at him again, a slyness in her eyes. 'What you think me an' Aunt Sukey an' Sister Mandy be's talkin' 'bout dese Sundays massa think we jes' singin' an' prayin'? I follows white folks close. Take dem Quakers. Dey was 'gainst slavin' even fo' dat Rebolution, I means right here in Virginia,' she went on. 'An' plenty o' dem was massas ownin' a heap o' niggers. But den preachers commence to sayin' niggers was human bein's, wid rights to be free like anybody else, an' you 'members some Quaker massas started to lettin' dey niggers loose, an' even helpin' 'em git up Nawth. By now it done got to where de Quakers dat's still keepin' dey niggers is bein' talked 'bout by de res', an' I'se heared if dey still don't let dem niggers go, dey gwine git disowned by dey church. Gwine on right today, sho' is!' Bell exclaimed.

'An' dem Methodists is de nex' bes'. I 'members readin' ten, leben years back, Methodists called a great big meetin' in Baltimore, an' finally dey 'greed slavin' was 'gainst Gawd's laws an' dat anybody callin' hisself Christian wouldn't have it did to deyselves. So it's mostly de Methodists an' Quakers makin' church fuss to git laws to free niggers. Dem Baptist an' Presbyterian white folks – dat's what massa an' all de Wallers is – well, dey seems like to me jes' half-hearted. Dey's mostly worried 'bout dey own freedom to worship like dey pleases, an' den how dey can keep a clear conscience an' dey niggers bofe.'

For all of Bell's talk of whites who were against slavery – even though she had read some of it in the massa's own newspaper – Kunta had never once heard a toubob opinion expressed that was not absolutely the opposite. And during that spring and summer of 1792, the massa shared his buggy with some of the biggest and richest massas, politicians, lawyers, and merchants in the state. Unless something else was more pressing, their ever-ready topic of conversation was the problems created for them by blacks.

Whoever would successfully manage slaves, someone would always say, must first understand that their African pasts of living in jungles with animals gave them a natural inheritance of stupidity, laziness, and unclean habits, and that the Christian duty of those God had blessed with superiority was to teach these creatures some sense of discipline, morality and respect for work – through example, of course, but also with laws and punishment as needed, although encouragement and rewards should certainly be given to those who proved deserving.

Any laxity on the part of whites, the conversation always continued, would simply invite the kind of dishonesty, tricks and cunning that came naturally to a lower species, and the bleatings of anti-slavery societies and others like them could come only from those, particularly in the North, who had never owned any black ones themselves or tried to run a plantation with them; such people couldn't be expected to realize how one's patience, heart, spirit and very soul could be strained to the breaking point by the trials and burdens of owning slaves.

Kunta had been listening to the same outrageous nonsense for so long that it had become like a litany to him, and he hardly paid any attention to it anymore. But sometimes, while he drove along, he couldn't help asking himself why it was that his countrymen didn't simply kill every toubob who set foot on African soil. He was never able to give himself an answer that he was able to accept.

71

It was about the noon hour on a sultry day late in August when Aunt Sukey came waddling as fast as she could out to the fiddler among his tomato plants and – between gasps – told him that she was worried to death about the old gardener. When he didn't come to her cabin for breakfast, she hadn't thought anything about it, she said breathlessly, but when he didn't appear for lunch either, she became concerned, went to his cabin door, knocked and called as loudly as she could, but got no answer, became alarmed, and thought she'd better come to find out if the fiddler had seen him anywhere. He hadn't.

'Knowed it somehow or 'nother even 'fore I went in there,' the fiddler told Kunta that night. And Kunta said that he had been unable to explain an eerie feeling he had himself as he had driven the massa homewards that afternoon. 'He was jes' lyin' dere in bed real peaceful like,' said the fiddler, 'wid a li'l smile on 'is face. Look like he sleepin'. But Aunt Sukey say he awready waked up in heab'm.' He said he had gone to take the sad news out to those working in the fields, and the boss field hand Cato returned with him to help wash the body and place it on a cooling board. Then they had hung the old gardener's sweat-browned straw hat on the outside of his door in the

330

traditional sign of mourning before the field workers returned and gathered in front of the cabin to pay their last respects, and then Cato and another field hand went to dig a grave.

Kunta returned to his cabin feeling doubly grieved – not only because the gardener was dead, but also because he hadn't been visiting him as much as he could have ever since Kizzy was born. It had just seemed that there was hardly ever enough time anymore; and now it was too late. He arrived to find Bell in tears, which he expected, but he was taken aback at the reason she gave for crying. 'Jes' always seem like to me he was de daddy I ain't never seed,' she sobbed. 'Don't know how come I didn't never let him know, but it ain't gon' never seem de same widout him bein' roun' here.' She and Kunta ate their supper in silence before taking Kizzy with them – bundled against the cool autumn night – to join the others 'settin' wid de dead' until late into the night.

Kunta sat a little apart from the others, with the re. 'less Kizzy on his lap during the first hour of prayers and soft singing, and then some hushed conversation was begun by Sister Mandy, asking if anyone there could recall the old man ever having mentioned any living relatives. The fiddler said, 'One time 'way back I 'members he said he never knowed his mammy. Dat's all I ever heared him say of family.' Since the fiddler had been the closest among them to the old man, and he would know if anyone did, it was decided that there was probably no one to whom word should be sent.

Another prayer was said, another song was sung, then Aunt Sukey said, 'Seem like he done always belonged to some a' de Wallers. I'se heared him talk 'bout de massa ridin' on his shoulders as a boy, so I reckon dat's why massa bring him here later on when he got his own big house.'

'Massa real sorry, too,' said Bell. 'He say for me to tell y'all won't be no workin' for half a day tomorra.'

'Well, leas' he gwine git buried right,' said Ada, the field-hand mother of the boy Noah, who sat impassively beside her. It's a-plenty o'massas jes' 'lows you to quit workin' long enough to come look at de dead nigger' fore he git stuck in de ground still warm.'

'Well, all dese Wallers is quality white folks, so wouldn't none us here have to worry 'bout dat,' said Bell.

Others started talking then about how rich plantation owners sometimes staged very elaborate funerals for usually either long-time big-house cooks or for the old mammies who had suckled and helped to raise two or even three broods of the family's children. 'Dey even gits buried in de white folks' graveyards, wid flat rocks to mark where dey is.'

What a heartwarming – if somewhat belated – reward for a lifetime of toil, thought Kunta bitterly. He remembered the gardener telling him that he had come to the massa's big house as a strong young stablehand, which he had remained for many years until he was kicked badly by a horse. He stayed on the job, but gradually he had become more and more disabled, and finally Massa Waller had told him to spend his remaining years doing whatever he felt able to do. With Kunta as his assistant, he had tended the vegetable garden until he was too feeble to do even that, and from then on had spent most of his time weaving cornshucks into hats and straw into chairbottoms and fans, until advancing arthritis had crippled even his fingers. Kunta recalled another old man he had seen now and then at a rich big house across the county. Though he had long since been allowed to retire, he demanded every morning that some younger blacks carry him out to the garden, where he would lie on his side plucking weeds with gnarled hands among the flowerbeds of his equally old and crippled beloved lifetime missis. And these were the lucky ones, Kunta knew. Many old folks began to get beaten when they were no longer able to perform their previous quota of work, and finally they got sold away for perhaps twenty or thirty dollars to some 'po' white trash' farmer – with aspirations of rising into the planter class – who worked them literally to death.

Kunta was snapped out of those thoughts as everyone rose from their seats all around him, said a final prayer, and headed wearily home for a few hours of sleep that were left before daybreak.

Right after breakfast, the fiddler dressed the old man in the worn dark suit the old man had been given many years before by Massa Waller's daddy. His few other clothes had been burned, since whoever might wear a dead person's clothes would soon die too, Bell told Kunta. Then Cato tied the body on a wide board that he had shaped to a point at both ends with an axe.

A little while later, Massa Waller came out of the big house carrying his big black Bible and fell in behind the slave-row people as they walked with a peculiar pausing, hitching step behind the body being drawn on a mule cart. They were softly chanting a song Kunta had never heard before: 'In de mawnin', when I gits dere, gwine tell my Jesus hi'dy! Hi'dy! . . . In de mawnin', gwine to rise up, tell my Jesus hi'dy! Hi'dy! . . .' They kept on singing all the way to the slave graveyard, which Kunta had noticed everyone avoided in a deep fear of what they called 'ghoses' and 'haints', which he felt must bear some resemblance to his Africa's evil spirits. His people also avoided the burial ground, but out of consideration for the dead whom they didn't wish to disturb, rather than out of fear.

When Massa Waller stopped on one side of the grave, his slaves on the other, old Aunt Sukey began to pray. Then a young field-hand woman named Pearl sang a sad song, 'Hurry home, my weary soul . . . I heared from heab'm today . . . Hurry 'long, my weary soul . . . my sin's forgived, an' my soul's set free . . .' And then Massa Waller spoke with his head bowed, 'Josephus, you have been a good and faithful servant. May God rest and bless your soul. Amen.' Through his sorrow, Kunta was surprised to hear that the old gardener had been called 'Josephus'. He wondered what the gardener's true name had been – the name of his African forefathers – and to what tribe they had belonged. He wondered if the gardener himself had known. More likely he had died as he had lived – without ever learning who he really was. Through misted eyes, Kunta and the others watched as Cato and his helper lowered the old man into the earth he had spent so many years making things grow in. When the shovelfuls of dirt began to thud down onto his face and chest, Kunta gulped and blinked back the tears as the women around him began to weep and the men to clear their throats and blow their noses.

As they trudged silently back from the graveyard, Kunta thought how the family and close friends of one who had died in Juffure would wail and roll in ashes and dust within their huts while the other villagers danced outside, for most African people believed that there could be no sorrow without happiness, no death without life, in that cycle that his own father had explained to him when his beloved Grandma Yaisa had died. He remembered that Omoro had told him, 'Stop weeping now, Kunta,' and explained that Grandma had only joined another of the three peoples in every village – those who had gone to be with Allah, those who were still living, and those who were yet to be born. For a moment, Kunta thought he must try to explain that to Bell, but he knew she wouldn't understand. His heart sank – until he decided a moment later that this would become another of the many things he would one day tell Kizzy about the homeland she would never see.

72

The death of the gardener continued to weigh so heavily on Kunta's mind that Bell finally said something about it one evening after Kizzy went to bed.

'Looka here, Kunta, I knows how you felt 'bout dat gardener, but ain't it 'bout time you snap out of it an' jine de livin'?' He just glared at her. 'Suit yo'se'f. But ain't gwine be much of a secon' birfday fo' Kizzy nex' Sunday wid you mopin' roun' like dis.'

'I be fine,' said Kunta stiffly, hoping Bell couldn't tell that he'd forgotten all about it.

He had five days to make Kizzy a present. By Thursday afternoon he had carved a beautiful Mandinka doll out of pine wood, rubbed it with linseed oil and lampblack, then polished it until it shone like the ebony carvings of his homeland. And Bell, who had long since finished making her a dress, was in the kitchen – dipping two tiny pink candles to put on the chocolate cake Aunt Sukey and Sister Mandy were going to help them eat on Sunday evening – when Massa John's driver Roosby arrived in the buggy.

Bell had to bite her tongue when the massa, beaming, called her in to announce that Missy Anne had persuaded her parents to let her spend an entire weekend with her uncle; she'd be arriving tomorrow evening. 'Make sure you have a guest room ready,' said the massa. 'And why don't you bake a cake or something for Sunday? My niece tells me your little girl is celebrating a birthday, and she'd like to have a party – just the two of them – up in her room. Anne also asked if she could spend the night with her up here in the house, and I said that would be all right, so be sure to prepare a pallet for the floor at the foot of the bed.'

When Bell broke the news to Kunta – adding that the cake she was going to make would have to be served in the big house instead of their cabin, and that Kizzy was going to be so busy partying with Missy Anne that they wouldn't be able to have a party of their own – Kunta was so angry that he couldn't speak or even look at her. Stomping outside, he went straight to the barn, where he'd hidden the doll under a pile of straw, and pulled it out.

He had vowed to Allah that this kind of thing would never happen to his Kizzy – but what could he do? He felt such a sickening sense of frustration that he could almost begin to understand why these blacks finally came to believe that resisting the toubob was as useless as a flower trying to keep its head above the falling snow. But then, staring at the doll, he thought of the black mother he'd heard about who had bashed out her infant's brains against the auction block, screaming, 'Ain't gon' do to her what you done to me!' And he raised the doll over his head to dash it against the wall; then lowered it. No, he could never do that to her. But what about escape? Bell herself had mentioned it once. Would she really go? And if she would, could they ever make it – at their age, with his half foot, with a child barely old enough to walk? He hadn't seriously considered the idea for many years, but he did know the region by now as well as he did the plantation itself. Maybe . . .

Dropping the doll, he got up and walked back to the cabin. But Bell started talking before he got the chance to. 'Kunta, I feels de same as you, but listen to me! I ruther dis dan her growin' up a fiel'-han' young'un like dat li'l ol' Noah. He ain't but two years older'n Kizzy, an' awready dey done started takin' him out dere to pullin' weeds an' totin' water. Don' care how else you feels, seem like you got to 'gree wid dat.' As usual, Kunta said nothing, but he had seen and done enough during his quarter-century years as a slave to know that the life of a field hand was the life of a farm animal, and he would rather die than be responsible for sentencing his daughter to such a fate.

Then one evening a few weeks later, he arrived home to find Bell waiting at the door with the cup of cold milk he always looked forward to after a long drive. When he sat down in his rocking chair to wait for supper, she came up behind him and – without even being asked – rubbed his back in just the spot where she knew it always hurt after a day at the reins. When she set a plate of his favourite African stew in front of him, he knew she must be trying to soften him up for something, but he knew enough not to ask her what. All the way through supper she chattered even more than usual about things that mattered even less than usual, and he was beginning to wonder if she'd ever get around to it when, about an hour after supper, as they were getting ready to go to bed, she stopped talking for a long moment, took a deep breath, and put her hand on his arm. He knew this was it.

'Kunta, I don' know how to tell you this, so I'll jes' spit it out. Massa done tol' me he promise Missy Anne to drop Kizzy off at Massa John's to spen' de day wid her when he pass by dere on his roun's tomorra.'

This was too much. It was outrageous enough to have to sit by and watch while Kizzy was turned slowly into a well-mannered lap dog, but now that she'd been housebroken, they wanted him to deliver the animal to its new keeper. Kunta shut his eyes, struggling to contain his rage, then leaped up from his chair – pulling his arm viciously away from Bell – and bolted out the door. While she lay sleepless in their bed that night, he sat sleepless in the stable beneath his harnesses. Both of them were weeping.

When they pulled up in front of Massa John's house the next morning, Missy Anne ran out to meet them before Kunta even had the chance to lift Kizzy to the ground. She didn't even say goodbye, he thought bitterly, hearing behind them the pealings of girlish laughter as he swerved the horses back down the driveway towards the main road.

It was late afternoon and he had been waiting several hours for the massa outside a big house about twenty miles down the road when a slave came out and told him that Massa Waller might have to sit up all night with their sick missy, and for Kunta to come back for him the next day. Morosely, Kunta obeyed, arriving to find that Missy Anne had begged her sickly mother to let Kizzy stay overnight. Deeply relieved when the reply came that their noise had given her a headache, Kunta was soon rolling back homewards again with Kizzy holding on and bouncing beside him on the narrow driver's seat.

As they rode along, it dawned on Kunta that this was the first time he had been absolutely alone with her since the night he had told her what her name was. He felt a strange and mounting exhilaration as they drove on into the gathering dusk. But he also felt rather foolish. As much thought as he had given to his plans for and his responsibilities to this firstborn, he found himself uncertain how to act. Abruptly he lifted Kizzy up onto his lap. Awkwardly he felt her arms, her legs, her head, as she squirmed and stared at him curiously. He lifted her again, testing how much she weighed. Then, very gravely, he placed the reins within her warm, small palms – and soon Kizzy's happy laughter seemed the most delightful sound he had ever heard.

'You pretty li'l gal,' he said to her finally. She just looked at him. 'You look jes' like my little brudder Madi.'

She just kept looking at him. 'Fa!' he said, pointing to himself. She looked at his finger. Tapping his chest, he repeated, 'Fa.' But she had turned her attention back to the horses. Flicking the reins, she squealed, 'Giddup!' imitating something else she'd heard him say. She smiled proudly up at him, but he looked so hurt that it faded quickly, and they rode on the rest of the way in silence.

It was weeks later, while they were riding home from a second visit

336

with Missy Anne, that Kizzy leaned over towards Kunta, stuck her chubby little finger against his chest, and with a twinkle in her eye, said 'Fa!'

He was thrilled. *'Ee to mu Kizzy leh!'* he said, taking her finger and pointing it back at her. 'Yo' name Kizzy.' He paused. 'Kizzy!' She began to smile, recognizing her own name. He pointed towards himself. 'Kunta Kinte.'

But Kizzy seemed perplexed. She pointed at him: 'Fa!' This time they both smiled wide.

By midsummer Kunta was delighted with how fast Kizzy was learning the words he was teaching her – and how much she seemed to be enjoying their rides together. He began to think there might be hope for her yet. Then one day she happened to repeat a word or two of Mandinka when she was alone with Bell, who later had sent Kizzy over to Aunt Sukey's for supper and was waiting for Kunta when he got home that night.

'Ain't you got no sense atall, man?' she shouted. 'Don't you know you better pay me 'tention – git dat chile an' all us in bad trouble wid dat mess! You better git in yo' hard head she ain't no African!' Kunta never had come so close to striking Bell. Not only had she committed the unthinkable offence of raising her voice to her husband; but even worse, she had disowned his blood and his seed. Could not one breathe a word of one's true heritage without fearing punishment from some toubob? Yet something warned him not to vent the wrath he felt, for any head-on collison with Bell might somehow end his buggy trips with Kizzy. But then he thought she couldn't do that without telling the massa why, and she would never dare to tell. Even so, he couldn't comprehend what had ever possessed him to marry any woman born in toubob land.

While he was waiting for the massa to finish a house call at a nearby plantation the next day, another buggy driver told Kunta the latest story he'd heard about Toussaint, a former slave who had organized a large army of black rebels in Haiti and was leading them successfully against not only the French but also the Spanish and the English. Toussaint, the driver said, had learned about war from reading books about famous ancient fighters named 'Alexander the Great' and 'Julius Caesar', and that these books had been given to him by his former massa, whom he later helped escape from Haiti to the 'Newnited States'. Over the past few months, Toussaint had become for Kunta a hero, ranking second in stature only to the legendary Mandinka warrior Sundiata, and Kunta could hardly wait to get back home and pass this fascinating story along to the others.

337

He forgot to tell them. Bell met him at the stable with the news that Kizzy had come down with a fever and broken out in bumps. The massa called it 'mumps', and Kunta was worried until Bell told him it was only normal in young'uns. When he learned later that Missy Anne had been ordered to stay away until Kizzy recovered – for at least two weeks – he was even a little bit happy about it. But Kizzy had been sick only a few days when Massa John's driver Roosby showed up with a fully dressed toubob doll from Missy Anne. Kizzy fell in love with it. She sat in bed hugging the doll close, rocking it back and forth, exclaiming with her eyes half shut, 'Jes' so pretty!' Kunta left without a word and stormed across the yard to the barn. The doll was still in the loft where he'd dropped it and forgotten it months before. Wiping it off on his sleeve, he carried it back to the cabin and almost shoved it at Kizzy. She laughed with pleasure when she saw it, and even Bell admired it. But Kunta could see, after a few minutes, that Kizzy liked the toubob doll better, and for the first time in his life, he was furious with his daughter.

It didn't make him any happier to notice how eagerly the two girls made up for the weeks of being together they had missed. Although sometimes Kunta was told to take Kizzy to play at Missy Anne's house, it was no secret that Missy Anne preferred to visit at her uncle's, since her mother was quick to complain of headaches because of the noise they made, and would even resort to fainting spells as a final weapon, according to their cook, Omega. But she said, 'ol' missy' had her match in her quick-tongued daughter. Roosby told Bell one day that his missis had yelled at the girls, 'You're actin' just like niggers!' and Missy Anne had shot back, 'Well, niggers has more fun than us, 'cause they ain't got nothin' to worry about!' But the two girls made all the noise they pleased at Massa Waller's. Kunta seldom drove the buggy either way along the flowered drive without hearing the girls shrieking somewhere as they romped in the house, the yards, the garden, and – despite Bell's best efforts to prevent it – even in the chicken coops, the hog pen, and the barn, as well as the unlocked slave-row cabins.

One afternoon, while Kunta was off with the massa, Kizzy took Missy Anne into her cabin to show her Kunta's gourd of pebbles, which she had discovered and become fascinated with while she was home with the mumps. Bell, who happened to walk in just as Kizzy was reaching into the mouth of the gourd, took one look and yelled, 'Git 'way from yo' daddy's rocks! Dey's how he tell how ol' he is!' The next day Roosby arrived with a letter for the massa from his brother, and five minutes later Massa Waller called Bell into the drawing room, the sharpness of his tone frightening her before she left the kitchen. 'Missy Anne told her parents about something she saw in your cabin. What is this African voodoo about rocks being put into a gourd every full moon?' he demanded.

Her mind racing, Bell blurted, 'Rocks? Rocks, Massa?'

'You know very well what I mean!' said the massa.

Bell forced a nervous giggle. 'Oh, I knows what you's talkin' 'bout. Nawsuh, Massa, ain't no voodoo. Ol' African nigger I got jes' cain't count, dat's all, Massa. So every new moon, he drops li'l rock in de gourd so all dem rocks say how ol' he is!'

Massa Waller, still frowning, gestured for Bell to return to the kitchen. Ten minutes after she charged into the cabin, snatched Kizzy from Kunta's lap, and laid into her rear end with an open hand – almost screaming, 'Don't you never bring dat gal in here no mo', I'll wring yo' neck, you hear me!'

After sending the weeping Kizzy fleeing to bed, Bell managed to calm herself enough to explain to Kunta. 'I knows dem gourd an' rocks ain't no harm,' she said, 'but it jes' go to show you what I tol' you 'bout dem African things brings troubles! An' massa don't never forget nothin'!'

Kunta felt such an impotent fury that he couldn't eat supper. After driving the massa nearly every day for over twenty rains, Kunta was amazed and enraged that it could still be a matter of suspicion that he simply recorded his age by dropping stones into a gourd.

It was another two weeks before the tension subsided enough for Missy Anne's visits to resume, but once they did it was as if the incident had never happened; Kunta was almost sorry. With the berry season in full bloom, the girls ranged up and down the vine-covered fencerows finding the dark green wild strawberry patches and coming home with full pails, their hands – and mouths – tinted crimson. Other days they would return with such treasures as snail shells, a wren's nest, or a crusted old arrowhead, all of which they would exhibit gleefully to Bell before hiding them somewhere with great secrecy, whereafter they might make mud pies. By the mid-afternoons, after trooping into the kitchen covered to the elbows with mud-pie batter and being ordered straight outside again to wash up at the well, the joyfully exhausted pair would eat snacks that Bell had ready for them and then lie down together on a quilt pallet for a nap. If Missy Anne was staying overnight, after her supper with the massa, she would keep him company until her bedtime, when he would send her out to tell Bell that it was time for her story. And Bell would bring in an equally worn-out Kizzy and tell them both about the further adventures of Br'er Rabbit getting tricked by Br'er Fox, who finally got tricked himself.

Kunta resented this deepening intimacy between the two girls even more intensely than when he saw it coming in Kizzy's crib. Part of him, he had to admit, was pleased that Kizzy was enjoying her girlhood so much, and he had come to agree with Bell that even being a toubob's pet was better than having to spend her life in the fields. But he was sure that every now and then he could sense even in Bell a certain uneasiness when she was watching the girls romping and playing so closely together. He would dare to think that at least some of those times, Bell must have felt and feared the same things he did. Some nights in their cabin, as he watched her caressing Kizzy in her lap and humming one of her 'Jesus' songs, he would have the feeling, as she looked down at the sleepy face, that she was afraid for her, that she wanted to warn her child about caring too much for any toubob, no matter how mutual the affection seemed. Kizzy was too young to understand such things, but Bell knew all too well what wrenching anguish could result from trusting toubob; had they not sold her away from her first two babies? There was no way even to guess at what might lie ahead for Kizzy, but also for him and Bell. But he knew one thing: Allah would wreak terrible vengeance on any toubob who ever harmed their Kizzy.

73

Two Sundays every month, Kunta drove the massa to church at the Waller meetinghouse about five miles from the plantation. The fiddler had told him that not only the Wallers but also several other important white families had built their own meetinghouses around the county. Kunta had been surprised to discover that the services also were attended by some of the neighbouring lesser white families and even some of the area's 'po' crackers', whom the buggy had often passed as they came and went on foot, carrying their shoes by the strings over their shoulders. Neither the massa nor any of the other 'quality folk', as Bell called them, ever stopped to offer 'po' crackers' a ride; and Kunta was glad of it.

There would always be a long, droning sermon between a lot of equally listless singing and praying, and when it was finally over, everybody would come trailing outside one by one and shake hands with the preacher, and Kunta would notice with amusement how both the 'po' crackers' and those of the massa's class would smile and tip their hats at one another, acting as if their both being white made them both the same. But then when they would spread their picnic lunches under the trees, it was always with the two classes on opposite sides of the churchyard – as if they had just happened to sit apart.

While he was waiting and watching this solemn rite with the other drivers one Sunday, Roosby said under his breath, just loud enough for the others to hear, 'Seem like white folks don' 'joy dey eatin' no more'n dey worshipin'.' Kunta thought to himself that in all the years he had known Bell, he had always managed to claim some urgent chore whenever the time came for one of her 'Jesus' meetings in slave row, but all the way from the barn he had heard enough of the black ones' caterwauling and carrying on to convince him that one of the few things about the toubob that he found worthy of admiration was their preference for quieter worship.

It was only a week or so later that Bell reminded Kunta about the 'big camp meetin' ' she planned to go to in late July. It had been the blacks' big summer event every year since he'd come to the plantation, and since every previous year he had found an excuse not to go along, he was amazed that she would still have the nerve to ask him. He knew little about what went on at these huge gatherings, beyond that they had to do with Bell's heathen religion, and he wanted no part of it. But Bell once more insisted. 'I knows how bad you always wants to go,' she said in her voice heavy with sarcasm. 'Jes' thought I'd tell you far 'nough ahead so's you can work it into yo' plans.'

Kunta couldn't think of a smart answer, and he didn't want to start an argument anyway, so he just said, 'I think about it,' though he had no intention of going.

By the day before the meeting, when he pulled up at the big-house front door after a trip to the county seat, the massa said, 'I won't be needing the buggy tomorrow, Toby. But I've given Bell and the other women permission to go to that camp meeting tomorrow, and I said it would be all right for you to drive them over in the wagon.'

Churning with anger, positive that Bell had plotted this, Kunta tied up the horses behind the barn and without taking the time to unhitch them, headed straight for the cabin. Bell took one look at him standing in the doorway and said, 'Couldn't think up no other

341

way to git you dere when Kizzy git christened.'

'Git what?'

'Christened. Dat mean she jine de church.'

'What church? Dat "O Lawd" religion o' your'n?'

'Don't let's start dat again. Ain't nothin' to do wid me. Missy Anne done ax her folks to take Kizzy to dey meetin'house on Sundays an' set in de back whilst dey prays up front. But she can't go to no white folks' church less'n she christened.'

'Den she ain't gwine no church!'

'You still don' unnerstan', does you, African? It a *priv'lege* to be axed to dey church. You say no, de nex' thing you an' me both out pickin' cotton.'

As they set out the next morning, Kunta sat rigidly staring straight ahead from his high driver's seat, refusing to look back even at his laughing, excited daughter as she sat on her mother's lap, between the other women and their picnic baskets. For a while, they simply chattered among themselves, then they began singing: 'We-uh climbin' Jacob's ladder ... We-uh climbin' Jacob's ladder ... We-uh climbin' Jacob's ladder ... soldiers of de Cross ...' Kunta was so disgusted that he began slapping the reins across the mules' rumps, making the buggy lurch forward and jostling his passengers – but he couldn't seem to do it hard enough or often enough to shut them up. He could even hear Kizzy's piping little voice among the others. The toubob didn't need to steal his child, he thought bitterly, if his own wife was willing to give her away.

Similarly crowded wagons were coming out of other plantations' side roads, and with every happy wave and greeting as they rode along, Kunta became more and more indignant. By the time they reached the camp ground – in a flowered, rolling meadow – he had worked himself into such a state that he hardly noticed the dozen or more wagons that were already there and the others that were arriving from all directions. As each wagon pulled to a halt, the occupants would pile noisily out, hooting and hallooing, soon joining Bell and the others who were kissing and hugging each other in the smiling crowd. Slowly it dawned on Kunta that he had never seen so many black people together in one place in toubob land, and he began to pay attention.

While the women assembled their baskets of food in a grove of trees, the men began to drift towards a small knoll in the middle of a meadow. Kunta tethered the mules to a stake that he drove into the ground, and then sat down behind the wagon – but in such a way that he could see everything that went on. After a while, all of the men had taken seats close to one another on the ground near the top of the knoll – all excepting four who appeared to be the oldest among them; they remained standing. And then, as if by some prearranged signal, the man who seemed to be the oldest of the four – he was very black and stooped and thin, with a white beard – suddenly reared back his head and shouted loudly towards where the women were, 'I say, chilluns of JESUS!'

Unable to believe his eyes or ears, Kunta watched as the women swiftly turned and shouted as one, 'Yes, Lawd!' then came hurrying and jostling to sit behind the gathered men. Kunta was astonished at how much it reminded him of the way the people of Juffure sat at the Council of Elders' meetings once each moon.

The old man shouted again: 'I say – is y'all chilluns of JESUS?'

'Yes, Lawd!'

Now, the three other old men stepped out in front of the oldest one, and one after another, they cried out:

'Gon' come a time we be jes' GAWD's slaves!'

'Yes, Lawd!' shouted all who sat on the ground.

'You make youse'f ready, Jesus STAY ready!'

'Yes, Lawd!'

'Know what de Holy Father said to me jes' now? He say, "Ain't NOBODY strangers!" '

A massed shouting rose, all but drowning out what the oldest of the four had begun to say. In a strange way even Kunta felt some of the excitement. Finally the crowd quieted enough for him to hear what the greybeard was saying.

'Chilluns o' Gawd, dey is a PROMISE lan'! Dat's where ev'ybody b'lieve in Him gon' go! An' dem dat b'lieve, dat's where dey gon' LIVE – for all e-terni-ty! . . .'

Soon the old man was sweating profusely, his arms flailing the air, his body quivering with the intensity of his singsong exclamations, his voice rasping with emotion. 'It tell us in de Bible dat de lamb an' de lion gwine lay down TOGETHER!' The old man threw his head backwards, flinging his hands towards the sky. 'Ain't gon' be no massas an' slaves NO MO'! Jes' gon' be all GAWD's CHILLUNS!'

Then, suddenly, some woman leaped up and began shrieking, 'O Jesus! O Jesus! O Jesus! O Jesus!' It set off others around her, and within minutes two dozen or more women were screaming and jerking themselves about. It flashed into Kunta's mind how the fiddler had once told him that on some plantations where the massas forbade slaves to worship, they concealed a large iron pot in the woods nearby, where those who felt the spirit move them would stick their

343

heads inside and shout, the pot muffling the noise sufficiently for it not to be heard by the massa or the overseer.

It was in the middle of this thought that Kunta saw, with profound shock and embarrassment, that Bell was among the women who were staggering and screeching. Just then one of them shouted, 'I'se GAWD's chile!' toppled to the ground as if felled by a blow, and lay there quivering. Others joined her and began writhing and moaning on the grass. Another woman who had been flinging herself violently about now went as rigid as a post, screaming out, 'O Lawd! Jes' you, Jesus!'

Kunta could tell that none of them had planned whatever they were doing. It was just happening as they felt it – the way his own people danced to the spirits back at home, acting out what they felt inside. As the shouting and the twitching began to subside, it occurred to Kunta that this was the way the dancings in Juffure had ended – seemingly in exhaustion. And he could see that in some way, these people, too, seemed both spent and at peace with themselves.

Then, one after another, they began to get up from the ground and shout out to the others:

'My back pained me so bad till I talked to my Lawd. He say to me, "You stan' up straight," an' I ain't hurt since.'

'Didn't meet my Lawd Jesus till He saved my soul, an' now I puts my love for Him up against anybody's!'

There were others. Then, finally, one of the old men led a prayer, and when it was over everybody shouted 'A-MEN!' and began to sing loudly and with tremendous spirit: 'I got shoes, you got shoes, all Gawd's chilluns got shoes! When-uh gits to Heab'm, gon' put on mah shoes, gon' walk all ovah Gawd's Heab'm! Heab'm! Ev'body tellin' 'bout Heab'm ain't gwine dere! Heab'm! Heab'm! I'm gon' walk all ovah Gawd's Heab'm!'

As they sang the song, they had got up from the ground, one by one, and began to walk very slowly, following the grey-haired preacher, down from the knoll and across the meadow. By the time the song ended, they had reached the banks of a pond on the other side, where the preacher turned to face them, flanked by the other three elders, and held up his arms.

'An now, brothers an' sisters, de time is come fo' yo' sinners what ain't been cleansed to wash away yo' sins in de River JORDAN!'

'O yeah!' shouted a woman on the bank.

'It's time to squench out de fires o' Hell in de holy waters o' de Promise LAN'!'

'Say it!' came another shout.

'All dose ready to dive down fo' dey almighty soul an' rise up ag'in wid de Lawd, remain standin'. Res' o' you what done been baptize or ain't ready fo' Jesus yet, seddown!'

As Kunta watched in astonishment, all but twelve or fifteen of them sat down. While the others lined up at the water's edge, the preacher and the strongest of the four elders marched right into the pond, stopping and turning when they were immersed up to their hips.

Addressing himself to the teenage girl who was first in line, the preacher spoke. 'Is you ready, chile?' She nodded. 'Den come ahead!'

Grasping both of her arms, the two remaining elders led her into the pond, stumbling, to meet the others in the middle. Placing his right hand on the girl's forehead while the biggest elder grabbed her shoulders with both hands from behind and the other two men tightened their grip on her arms, the preacher said, 'O Lawd, let dis chile be wash clean,' and then he pushed her backwards while the man behind pulled her shoulders back and down until she was completely under water.

As the bubbles rose to the surface and her limbs began to thrash the water, they turned their gaze heavenwards and held on tight. Soon she started kicking wildly and heaving her body violently; it was all they could do to hold her under. 'ALMOST!' the preacher shouted, over the churning commotion beneath his arms. 'NOW!' They pulled her upwards from the water, gasping for breath, spewing water, struggling frantically as they half carried her back to shore – and into the arms of her waiting mother.

Then they turned to the next in line – a boy in his early twenties who stood staring at them, too terrified to move. They practically had to drag him in. Kunta watched with his mouth open wider as each person – next a middle-aged man, then another young girl around twelve, then an elderly woman who could barely walk – were led one by one into the pond and subjected to the same incredible ordeal. Why did they do it? What sort of cruel 'Gawd' demanded such suffering for those who wished to believe in him? How could half drowning someone wash away his evil? Kunta's mind teemed with questions – none of which he could answer – until finally the last one had been pulled spluttering from the water.

It must be over, he thought. But the preacher, wiping his face with his sopping sleeve, stood in the pond and spoke again: 'An' now, is dey any 'mongst y'all wishes to consecrate dey chilluns to JESUS dis holy day?' Four women stood up – the first of them Bell, holding Kizzy by the hand.

Kunta leaped up beside the wagon. Surely they wouldn't! But then he saw Bell leading the way to the bank of the pond, and began to walk – slowly, uncertainly at first, then faster and faster – towards the crowd at the water's edge. When the preacher beckoned to Bell, she leaned down to pick up Kizzy in her arms and strode vigorously into the water. For the first time in twenty-five years, since the day his foot had been chopped, Kunta began to run – but when he reached the pond, his foot throbbing, Bell was standing in the middle at the preacher's side. Gasping to catch his breath, Kunta opened his mouth to call out – just as the preacher began to speak:

'Dearly beloved, we's gathered here to welcome another lamb unto de fold! What de chile's name, sister?'

'Kizzy, reveren'.'

'Lawd . . .' he began, placing his left hand under Kizzy's head and squeezing his eyes shut.

'Naw!' Kunta shouted hoarsely.

Bell's head jerked around, her eyes were burning into his. The preacher stood looking from him to her and back again. Kizzy began to whimper. 'Hush, chile,' Bell whispered. Kunta felt the hostile stares surrounding him. Everything hung poised.

Bell broke the stillness. 'It's awright, reveren'. Dat's jes' my African husban'. He don' unnerstan'. I 'splain to him later. You go 'head.'

Kunta, too stunned to speak, saw the preacher shrug, turn back to Kizzy, shut his eyes, and start again.

'Lawd, wid his holy water, bless dis chile . . . What her name again, sister?'

'Kizzy.'

'Bless dis chile Kizzy and take her wid you safe into dat Promise Lan'!' With that the preacher dipped his right hand into the water, flicked a few drops into Kizzy's face, and shouted 'AMEN!'

Bell turned, carried Kizzy back to shore, trudged up out of the water, and stood dripping in front of Kunta. Feeling foolish and ashamed, he looked down at her muddy feet, then raised his eyes to meet hers, which were wet – with tears? She put Kizzy in his arms.

'It awright. She jes' wet,' he said, his rough hand caressing Kizzy's face.

'All dat runnin', you must be hungry. I sure is. Le's go eat. I brung fried chicken an' devil eggs an' dat sweet tater custard you can't never git enough of.'

'Sound good,' said Kunta.

Bell took his arm and they walked slowly back across the meadow to where their picnic basket sat on the grass in the shade of a walnut tree.

74

Bell told Kizzy one night in the cabin, 'You's gwine on seven years ol'! Fiel'-hand young'uns be awready out dere workin' ev'yday – like dat Noah – so you's gwine start bein' some use to me in de big house!' Knowing by now how her father felt about such things, Kizzy looked uncertainly at Kunta. 'You hear what yo' mammy say,' he said without conviction. Bell already had discussed it with him, and he had to agree that it was prudent for Kizzy to start doing some work that was visible to Massa Waller, rather than continue solely as a playmate for Missy Anne. He privately further liked the idea of her making herself useful, since in Juffure at her age mothers started teaching their daughters the skills that would later enable their fathers to demand a good bride price from a prospective husband. But he knew Bell didn't expect his enthusiasm about anything to bring Kizzy even closer to the toubob – and take her even farther away from him and the sense of dignity and heritage he was still determined to instil in her. When Bell reported a few mornings later that Kizzy was already learning to polish silverware, scrub floors, wax woodwork, even to make up the massa's bed, Kunta found it difficult to share her pride in such accomplishments. But when he saw his daughter emptying then washing the white-enamelled slop jar in which the massa relieved himself at night, Kunta recoiled in anger, convinced that his worst fears had been fulfilled.

He bridled, too, at the counsel he would hear Bell giving Kizzy about how to be a personal maid. 'Now, you listen to me good, gal! It ain't every nigger git chance to work fer quality white folks like massa. Right off, dat put you 'bove de rest o' young 'uns. Now, de big thing is to learn what massa want without him never havin' to tell you. You gwine start gittin' up an' out early wid me, 'way fo' massa do. Dat's how I gits a head start on 'im – done always b'lieve in dat. First thing, gwine show you how to whup de dus' out'n his coat an' pants when you hangs' em out to air on de clothesline. Jes' be sho' you don't break or scratch none o' de buttons—' and so on, sometimes for hours at a time.

Not a single evening passed, it seemed to Kunta, without more instructions down to the most ridiculous detail. 'For blackin' his shoes,' she told Kizzy one night, 'I shakes up in a jar li'l simmon beer an' lampblack wid li'l sweet oil an' rock candy. Dat stan' overnight, den shake it up good again, it make dem black shoes of his'n shine like glass.' Before he could stand no more of it and retreated for relief to the fiddler's hut, Kunta acquired such invaluable household hints as 'if you set a teaspoon o' black pepper an' brown sugar mashed to a paste wid a li'l cow's cream in a saucer in a room, ain't no flies comin' in dere nohow!' And that soiled wallpaper was best cleaned by rubbing it with the crumbly insides of two-day-old biscuits.

Kizzy seemed to be paying attention to her lessons, even if Kunta didn't, for Bell reported one day, weeks later, that the massa had mentioned to her that he was pleased with the way the andirons in the fireplace had been shining since Kizzy started polishing them.

But whenever Missy Anne came over for a visit, of course, the massa didn't have to say that Kizzy was excused from work for the duration of her stay. Then, as always, the two girls would go romping and skipping about, jumping rope, playing hide-and-seek and a few games they invented. 'Playing nigger', bursting open a ripe watermelon and jamming their faces down into its crisp wetness one afternoon, they ruined the fronts of their dresses, prompting Bell to send Kizzy yelping with a backhand slap, and to snap even at Missy Anne. 'You knows you's raised better'n dat! Ten years ol', gwine to school, an' fo' you knows it gwine be a high-class missy!'

Though Kunta no longer bothered to complain about it, he remained a most difficult mate for Bell to deal with during Missy Anne's visits and for at least another day afterwards. But whenever Kunta was told to drive Kizzy to Massa John's house, it was all he could do to keep from showing his eagerness to be alone again with his girlchild in the buggy. By this time, Kizzy had come to understand that whatever was said during their buggy rides was a matter between the two of them, so he considered it safer now to teach her more about his homeland without fear that Bell would find them out.

Rolling along the dusty Spotsylvania County roads, he would tell

her the Mandinka names of things they passed along the road. Pointing at a tree, he'd say '*yiro*,' then downwards at the road, '*silo*.' As
they passed a grazing cow, he'd say, '*ninsemuso*,' and went over a
small bridge, '*salo*.' Once when they got caught in a sudden shower,
Kunta shouted '*sanjio*,' waving out at the rain, and when the sun
reappeared, pointing at it, he said '*tilo*.' Kizzy would watch his
mouth intently as he said each word, then imitate what she saw with
her own lips, repeating it over and over until she got it right. Soon
she began pointing to things herself and asking him for their Mandinka names. One day they were hardly beyond the shadow of the
big house when Kizzy poked him in the ribs, tapped her finger above
an ear and whispered, 'What you call my head?' '*Kungo*,' Kunta
whispered back. She tweaked her hair; he said '*kuntinyo*.' She
pinched her nose; he told her '*nungo*'; she squeezed her ear; he said
'*tulo*.' Giggling, Kizzy jerked up her foot and tapped her large toe.
'*Sinkumba!*' exclaimed Kunta. Seizing her exploring forefinger, wiggling it, he said '*bulokonding*.' Touching her mouth, he said '*da*.'
Then Kizzy seized Kunta's forefinger and pointed it at him. 'Fa!' she
exclaimed. He felt overwhelmed with his love for her.

Pointing to a sluggish small river they were passing a little later,
Kunta said 'Dat a *bolongo*.' He told her that in his homeland he had
lived near a river called the Kamby Bolongo. That evening, when on
the way back home, passing by it again, Kizzy pointed and shouted,
'Kamby Bolongo!' Of course, she didn't understand when he tried to
explain that this was the Mattaponi River, not the Gambia River,
but he was so delighted that she had remembered the name at all that
it didn't seem to matter. The Kamby Bolongo, he said, was much
bigger, swifter, and more powerful than this puny specimen. He
wanted to tell her how the life-giving river was revered by his people
as a symbol of fertility, but he couldn't find a way to say it, so he told
her about the fish that teemed in it – including the powerful, succulent kujalo, which sometimes leaped right into a canoe – and about
the vast living carpet of birds that floated on it until some young boy
like himself would jump growling from the brush on the banks so
that he could watch them rise up and fill the sky like some feathery
snowstorm. Kunta said that reminded him of a time his Grandmother Yaisa had told him about when Allah sent The Gambia a
plague of locusts so terrible that they darkened the sun and devoured
everything green until the wind shifted and carried them out to sea,
where they finally fell and were eaten by the fish.

'Do I got a gran'ma?' asked Kizzy.

'You got two – my mammy and you' mammy's mammy.'

'How come dey ain't wid us?'

'Dey don't know where we is,' said Kunta. 'Does you know where we is?' he asked her a moment later.

'We's in de buggy,' Kizzy said.

'I means where does we live.'

'At Massa Waller's.'

'An' where dat is?'

'Dat way,' she said, pointing down the road. Disinterested in their subject, she said, 'Tell me some more 'bout dem bugs an' things where you come from.'

'Well, dey's big red ants knows how to cross rivers on leafs, dat fights wars an' marches like a army, an' builds hills dey lives in dat's taller dan a man.'

'Dey soun' scary. You step on 'em?'

'Not less'n you has to. Every critter got a right to be here same as you. Even de grass is live an' got a soul jes' like peoples does.'

'Won't walk on de grass no mo', den. I stay in de buggy.'

Kunta smiled. 'Wasn't no buggies where I come from. Walked wherever we was goin'. One time I walked four days wid my pappy all de way from Juffure to my uncles' new village.'

'What Joo-fah-ray?'

'Done tol' you don' know how many times, dat where I come from.'

'I thought you was from Africa. Dat Gambia you talks about in Africa?'

'Gambia a country in Africa. Juffure a village in Gambia.'

'Well, where dey at, Pappy?'

'Crost de big water.'

'How big dat big water?'

'So big it take near 'bout four moons to get crost it.'

'Four what?'

'Moons. Like you say "months".'

'How come *you* don't say months?'

''Cause moons my word for it.'

'What you call a "year"?'

'A rain.'

Kizzy mused briefly.

'How you get 'crost dat big water?'

'In a big boat.'

'Bigger dan dat rowboat we seen dem fo' mens fishin' in?'

'Big 'nough to hol' a hunnud mens.'

'How come it don't sink?'

'I use to wish it would of.'

'How come?'

' 'Cause we all so sick seem like we gon' die anyhow.'

'How you get sick?'

'Got sick from layin' in our own mess prac'ly on top each other.'

'Whyn't you go de toilet?'

'De toubob had us chained up.'

'Who "toubob"?'

'White folks.'

'How come you chained up? You done sump'n wrong?'

'Was jes' out in de woods near where I live – Juffure – lookin' fer a piece o' wood to make a drum wid, an' dey grab me an' take me off.'

'How ol' you was?'

'Sebenteen.'

'Dey ask yo' mammy an' pappy if'n you could go?'

Kunta looked incredulously at her. 'Woulda took *dem* too if'n dey could. To dis day my fam'ly don' know where I is.'

'You got brothers an' sisters?'

'Had three brothers. Maybe mo' by now. Anyways, dey's all growed up, prob'ly got chilluns like you.'

'We go see dem someday?'

'We cain't go nowhere.'

'We's gon' somewheres now.'

'Jes' Massa John's. We don't show up, dey have de dogs out at us by sundown.'

' 'Cause dey be worried 'bout us?'

' 'Cause we b'longs to dem, jes' like dese hosses pullin' us.'

'Like I b'longs to you an' mammy?

'You'se our young'un. Dat different.'

'Missy Anne say she want me fo' her own.'

'You ain't no doll fo' her to play wid.'

'I plays wid her, too. She done tole me she my bes' frien'.'

'You can't be nobody's frien' an' slave both.'

'How come, Pappy?'

' 'Cause frien's don't own one 'nother.'

'Don' mammy an' you b'long to one 'nother? Ain't y'all frien's?'

'Ain't de same. We b'longs to each other 'cause we *wants* to, 'cause we loves each other.'

'Well, I loves Missy Anne, so I wants to b'long to her.'

'Couldn't never work out.'

'What you mean?'

'You couldn't be happy when y'all grow up.'

'Would too. I bet you wouldn't be happy.'

'Yo' sho' right 'bout dat!'

'Aw, Pappy, I couldn't never leave you an' Mammy.'

'An' chile, speck we couldn't never let you go, neither!'

75

Late one afternoon, the driver for Massa Waller's parents at Enfield brought him their invitation to attend a dinner party in honour of an important Richmond businessman who had stopped for a night's lodging on his way to Fredericksburg. About a dozen buggies were already parked outside the Enfield big house when Kunta arrived with the massa soon after dark.

Though he had been there many times in the eight years since he and Bell were married, it had been only during the past few months that the fat black cook Hattie, who had been so smitten with Kunta, decided to begin speaking with him again – ever since he had brought Kizzy along with Missy Anne one day on a visit to her grandparents. Tonight, when he went to the kitchen door to say hello – and for something to eat – she invited him in to visit while she, her helper, and four serving women completed their preparations for dinner; Kunta thought that he had never seen so much food bubbling in so many pots and pans.

'How dat li'l puddin'-pie young'un o' your'n?' Hattie asked between sips and sniffs.

'She fine,' said Kunta. 'Bell got her learnin' how to cook now. S'prise me other night wid a apple betty she done made.'

'Dat li'l dickens. Nex' thing you know, I be eatin *her* cookies 'stead o' her eatin' mine. She musta put away half a jar o' my ginger snaps las' time she here.'

With a last look at the mouth-watering three or four kinds of breads that were baking in the oven, Hattie turned to the oldest of the serving women, in their starched yellow smocks, and said, 'We'se ready. Go tell missis.' As the woman disappeared through the swinging door, she told the other three, 'I come after y'all wid a ladle if'n yo' slops one drop o' soup on my bes' linen when you settin' down de bowls. Git to work now, Pearl,' she said to her teenage helper. 'Git dem turnip greens, de sweet cawn, squash, an' okra in de good china tureens whilst I wrestles dis here saddle o' mutton onto de carvin' bo'd.'

A few minutes later, one of the serving women came back in, whispered intently to Hattie at some length, and then hurried back out again. Hattie turned to Kunta.

'You 'members few months back when one dem tradin' boats got raided somewheres on de big water by dat France?

Kunta nodded. 'Fiddler say he heared dat Pres'dent Adams so mad he sent de whole Newnited States Navy to whup 'em.'

'Well, dey sho' did. Louvina jes' now tol' me dat man in dere from Richmon' say dey done took away *eighty* boats b'longin' to dat France. She say de white folks in dere act like dey nigh 'bout ready to start singin' an' dancin' 'bout teachin' dat France a lesson.'

As she spoke, Kunta had begun digging into the heaping plateful of food she had set before him, while he marvelled at the very sight of the roast beef, baked ham, turkey, chicken, and duck she was now busily arranging on big platters waiting to be served. He had just swallowed a mouthful of buttered sweet potato when the four serving women came bustling back into the kitchen – all loaded down with empty bowls and spoons. 'De soup's et!' Hattie announced to Kunta. A moment later the serving women were trooping out again with heaped trays, and Hattie mopped her face and said, 'Got 'bout fo'ty minutes befo' dey ready fo' dessert. You was gon' say sump'n befo'?'

'Jes' gon' say eighty boats don' make me no difference,' said Kunta, 'long's white folks messin' wid one 'nother 'stead o' us. Seem like dey ain't happy less'n dey's messin' wid somebody.'

' 'Pend who dey messin' wid, way I sees it,' said Hattie. 'Las' year was a *mulatto* led a re-volt 'gainst dat Toussaint, an' he mighta won if'n de Pres'dent hadn't of sent his boats down dere to he'p Toussaint.'

'Heared Massa Waller say Toussaint ain't got sense 'nough to be no gen'l, let alone run no country on his own,' said Kunta. 'He say jes' watch, all dem slaves dat done got free in dat Haiti gwine wind up whole lot wuss off dan dey was under dey ol' massas. 'Cose, dat's what white folks *hopin'*. But I specks dey's awready *better* off workin' de plantations deyselves.'

One of the serving women, who had returned to the kitchen and was listening to the conversation, spoke up: 'Dat what dey's talkin' 'bout in dere right now – free niggers. Say it's way too many, thirteen thousan' jes' here in Virginia. De jedge say he all fo' freein' niggers dat do sump'n outstandin', like dem what fit in dat Revolution 'long-side dey massas, or dem what tol' white folks 'bout any nigger up-risin' plan, or dat nigger dat come up wid dat herb medicine dat even white folks claim cure near 'bout everythin'. De jedge say he feel massas got de right in de wills to free ol' faithful niggers. But him an' ev'ybody in dere say dey's dead set 'gainst dem Quakers and some other white folks settin' dey niggers free fo' nothin'.' The serving woman headed for the door, adding, 'Jedge say mark his words, some new laws gwine be made to put a crimp in dat right soon.'

Hattie asked Kunta, 'What yo' think o' dat Massa Alexander Hamilton up Nawth sayin' all free niggers oughta be sent to Africa 'cause niggers an' white folks too different an' ain't gwine never git 'long?'

'He right, dat's what I thinks,' said Kunta. 'But white folks talks dat an' keeps bringin' mo' *from* Africa!'

'You know why well's I do,' said Hattie. 'Puts' 'em down in Georgia an' de Carolinas to keep up wid de cotton crop every since dat cotton gin come in few years back. Same reason plenty massas 'roun' here sellin' dey niggers off down South for much as two, three times what dey paid fo' dem.'

'Fiddler say de big massas down South got mean po'cracker ob-erseers drivin' niggers like mules clearin' lan' for new cottonfiel's,' said Kunta.

'Yeah, it's how come de papers lately so full o' notices 'bout runa-ways,' said Hattie.

Just then the serving women began returning to the kitchen with dirty plates and platters. Hattie beamed proudly. 'Look like dey's done et all dey can hol'. 'Bout now, massa pourin' de champagne whilst de table git cleared fo' dessert,' she told Kunta. 'See how you like dese plum puddin' tarts.' She set one on a saucer in front of him. ' 'sides dat dey's gittin' brandied peaches in dere, but I recollecks you don't touch no liquor.'

Enjoying the succulent tart, Kunta found himself recalling a run-away slave advertisement that Bell had read to him recently from the *Gazette*. 'Tall mulatto wench,' it said, 'very large breasts of which the right one has a deep scar. A sly liar and thief, who may be showing a large forged pass, since previous owner let her learn to write some, or who may be claiming herself a free nigger.'

Hattie sat down heavily, fingered a brandied peach from a jar and popped it into her mouth. Glancing across the kitchen at two high tubs filled with glasses, dishes, cutlery, and utensils yet to be washed and put away, she let out a loud sigh and said wearily, 'Know one thing, sho' be glad to see my bed dis night, 'cause Lawd, I jes' plum wo' out.'

76

For many years now, Kunta had got up every morning before dawn, earlier than anyone else on slave row – so early that some of the others were convinced that 'dat African' could see in the dark like a cat. Whatever they wanted to think was fine with him as long as he was left alone to slip away to the barn, where he would face the first faint streaking of the day prostrated between two large bundles of hay, offering up his daily suba prayer to Allah. Afterwards, by the time he had pitched some hay into the horses' feed trough, he knew that Bell and Kizzy would be washed, dressed, and ready to get things under way in the big house, and the boss field hand Cato would be up and out with Ada's son Noah, who would soon be ringing the bell to wake the other slaves.

Almost every morning, Noah would nod and say 'Mornin' ' with such solemn reserve that he reminded Kunta of the Jaloff people in Africa, of whom it was said that if one greeted you in the morning, he had uttered his last good word for the day. But although they had said little to each other, he liked Noah, perhaps because he reminded Kunta of himself at about the same age – the serious manner, the way he went about his work and minded his own business, the way he spoke little but watched everything. He had often noticed Noah doing a thing that he also did – standing somewhere with his eyes quietly following the rompings of Kizzy and Missy Anne around the plantation. Once when Kunta had been watching from the barn door as they rolled a hoop across the backyard, giggling and screaming, he had been about to go back inside when he saw Noah standing over by Cato's cabin, also watching. Their eyes met, and they looked at each other for a long moment before both turned away. Kunta wondered what had Noah been thinking – and had the feeling that, likewise, Noah was wondering what *he* was thinking. Kunta knew somehow that they were both thinking the same things.

At ten, Noah was two years older than Kizzy, but that difference wasn't great enough to explain why the two hadn't even become friends, let alone playmates, since they were the only slave children on the plantation. Kunta had noticed that whenever they passed near each other, each of them always acted as if they had not even seen the other, and he couldn't figure out why – unless it was because even at their age they had begun to sense the custom that house slaves and field slaves didn't mix with one another.

Whatever the reason, Noah spent his day out with others in the fields while Kizzy swept, dusted, polished the brass, and tidied up the massa's bedroom every day – for Bell to inspect later with a hickory switch in her hand. On Saturdays, when Missy Anne usually came to call, Kizzy would somehow miraculously manage to finish her chores in half the time it took her every other day, and the two of them would spend the rest of the day playing – excepting at midday if the massa happened to be home for lunch. Then he and Missy Anne would eat in the dining room with Kizzy standing behind them gently fanning a leafy branch to keep away flies, as Bell shuttled in and out serving the food and keeping a sharp eye on both girls, having warned them beforehand, 'Y'all lemme catch you even thinkin' 'bout gigglin' in dere wid massa, I'll tan both yo' hides!'

Kunta by now was pretty much resigned to sharing his Kizzy with Massa Waller, Bell, and Missy Anne. He tried not to think about what they must have her doing up there in the big house, and he spent as much time as possible in the barn when Missy Anne was around. But it was all he could do to wait until each Sunday afternoon, when church would be over and Missy Anne would go back home with her parents. Later on these afternoons, usually Massa Waller would be either resting or passing the time with company in the parlour, Bell would be off with Aunt Sukey and Sister Mandy at their weekly 'Jesus meetin's' – and Kunta would be free to spend another couple of treasured hours alone with his daughter.

When the weather was good, they'd go walking – usually along the vine-covered fencerow where he had gone almost nine years before to think of the name 'Kizzy' for his new girlchild. Out beyond where anyone would be likely to see them Kunta would clasp Kizzy's soft little hand in his own as, feeling no need to speak, they would stroll down to a little stream, and sitting closer together beneath a shade tree they would eat whatever Kizzy had brought along from the kitchen – usually cold buttered biscuits filled with his favourite blackberry preserves. Then they would begin talking.

Mostly he'd talk and she'd interrupt him constantly with questions, most of which would begin, 'How come ...' But one day Kunta didn't get to open his mouth before she piped up eagerly, 'You wanna hear what Missy Anne learned me yestiddy?'

He didn't care to hear of anything having to do with that giggling white creature, but not wishing to hurt his Kizzy's feelings, he said, 'I'm listenin'.'

'Peter, Peter, punkin eater,' she recited, 'had a wife an' couldn' keep 'er, put 'er in a punkin shell, dere he kep' 'er very well ...'

'Dat it?' he asked.

She nodded. 'You like it?'

He thought it was just what he would have expected from Missy Anne: completely asinine. 'You says it real good,' he hedged.

'Bet you can't say it good as me,' she said with a twinkle.

'Ain't tryin' to!'

'Come on, Pappy, say it fo' me jes' once.'

'Git 'way from me wid dat mess!' He sounded more exasperated than he really was. But she kept insisting and finally, feeling a bit foolish that his Kizzy was able to twine him around her finger so easily, he made a stumbling effort to repeat the ridiculous lines – just to make her leave him alone, he told himself.

Before she could urge him to try the rhyme again, the thought flashed to Kunta of reciting something else to her – perhaps a few verses from the Koran, so that she might know how beautiful they could sound – then he realized such verses would make no more sense to her than 'Peter, Peter' had to him. So he decided to tell her a story. She had already heard about the crocodile and the little boy, so he tried the one about the lazy turtle who talked the stupid leopard into giving him a ride by pleading that he was too sick to walk.

'Where you hears all dem stories you tells?' Kizzy asked when he was through.

'Heared 'em when I was yo' age – from a wise ol' gran'mammy name Nyo Boto.' Suddenly Kunta laughed with delight, remembering: 'She was bald-headed as a egg! Didn't have no teeth, neither, but dat sharp tongue o' her'n sho' made up fer it! Loved us young'uns like her own, though.'

'She ain't had none of 'er own?'

'Had two when she was real young, long time fo' she come to Juffure. But they got took away in a fight 'tween her village an' 'nother tribe. Reckon she never got over it.'

Kunta fell silent, stunned with a thought that had never occurred to him before: The same thing had happened to Bell when she was young. He wished he could tell Kizzy about her two half-sisters, but he knew it would only upset her – not to mention Bell, who hadn't spoken of it since she told him of her lost daughters on the night of Kizzy's birth. But hadn't he – hadn't all of those who had been chained beside him on the slave ship been torn away from their own mothers? Hadn't all the countless other thousands who had come before – and since?

'Dey brung us here naked!' he heard himself blurting. Kizzy jerked up her head, staring; but he couldn't stop. 'Even took our names away. Dem like you gits borned here don't even know who dey is! But you jes' much Kinte as I is! Don't never fo'git dat! Us'ns fo'fathers was traders, travellers, holy men – all de way back hunnuds o' rains into dat lan' call Ol' Mali! You unnerstan' what I'm talkin' 'bout, chile?'

'Yes, Pappy,' she said obediently, but he knew she didn't. He had an idea. Picking up a stick, smoothing a place in the dirt between them, he scratched some characters in Arabic.

'Dat my name – Kun-ta Kin-te,' he said, tracing the characters slowly with his finger.

She stared, fascinated. 'Pappy, now do my name.' He did. She laughed. 'Dat say Kizzy?' He nodded. 'Would you learn me to write like you does?' Kizzy asked.

'Wouldn't be fittin',' said Kunta sternly.

'Why not?' She sounded hurt.

'In Africa, only boys learns how to read an' write. Girls ain't got no use fer it – over here, neither.'

'How come mammy can read an' write, den?'

Sternly, he said, 'Don't you be talkin' dat! You hear me? Ain't nobody's business! White folks don' like none us doin' no readin' or writin'!'

'How come?'

' 'Cause dey figgers less we knows, less trouble we makes.'

'I wouldn't make no trouble,' she said, pouting.

'If'n we don't hurry up an' git back to de cabin, yo' mammy gon' make trouble fo' us both.'

Kunta got up and started walking, then stopped and turned, realizing that Kizzy was not behind him. She was still by the bank of the stream, gazing at a pebble she had seen.

'Come on now, it's time to go.' She looked up at him, and he walked over and reached out his hand. 'Tell you what,' he said. 'You pick up dat pebble an' bring it 'long an' hide it somewheres safe, an' if'n you keeps yo' mouth shet 'bout it, nex' new moon mornin' I let you drop it in my gourd.'

'Oh, Pappy!' She was beaming.

77

It was almost time for Kizzy to drop another pebble into Kunta's gourd – about a year later, in the summer of 1800 – when the massa told Bell he was going to Fredericksburg for about a week on business, and it was arranged that his brother would be coming over 'to look after things' while he was away. When Kunta heard the news, he was even more upset than the rest of slave row, for he hated leaving Bell and Kizzy exposed to his former owner even more than he disliked having to be away from them for so long. Of course, he said nothing about these concerns, but on the morning of departure, as he left the cabin to hitch up the horses, he was taken aback that it seemed almost as if Bell had read his mind. She said, 'Massa John sho' ain't like his brother, but I knows how to deal wid his kin'. An' it ain't but a week. So don't you worry none. We be fine.'

'I ain't worryin',' said Kunta, hoping she couldn't tell he was lying.

Kneeling to kiss Kizzy, he whispered in her ear, 'Don't forgit dat new moon pebble, now,' and she winked conspiratorially as Bell pretended not to have heard, although she had known what they were doing for almost nine months now.

For the next two days of the massa's absence, everything went on pretty much as usual, although Bell was mildly annoyed at nearly everything Massa John said or did. She particularly disliked how he sat up late in the study at night, drinking his brother's best whisky from the bottle, smoking his own big black, smelly cigars and flicking the ashes on the carpet. Still, Massa John didn't interfere too much with Bell's normal routine, and he stayed mostly to himself.

But the mid-morning of the third day, Bell was out sweeping off the front porch when a white man on a lathered horse came galloping up and leaped off, demanding to see the massa.

Ten minutes later, the man left as hurriedly as he had come. Massa

John barked down the hallway for Bell to come into the study. He looked deeply shaken, and it flashed in Bell's mind that something terrible had happened to Kunta and the massa. She was sure of it when he brusquely ordered her to assemble all the slaves in the backyard. They all gathered, standing in a line, tense with fear, as he flung open the back screen door and stalked out towards them; he had a revolver conspicuous in his belt.

Coldly scanning their faces, he said, 'I just got word of some Richmond niggers' plot to kidnap the governor, massacre the Richmond white people, and burn the city.' The slaves gawked at one another in astonishment as he went on. 'Thanks to God – an' a few smart niggers who found out and told their massas just in time – the plot's been crushed, and most of the niggers that started it already caught. Armed patrols are on the roads lookin' for the rest, an' I'm gonna make sure none of 'em decides to stop off here for the night. 'Case any o' you got uprising notions, I'm gonna be patrollin' day and night. None of you're to set foot off this property! I don't want no gatherin' of any kind; an' nobody outside their own cabin after dark!' Patting his revolver, he said, 'I'm not as patient an' soft with niggers as my brother! Any of you even looks like you're *thinkin'* about steppin' outa line, his doctorin' won't patch up a bullet 'tween your eyes. Now *git*!'

Massa John was as good as his word. For the next two days, he enraged Bell by insisting upon watching Kizzy taste his food before he'd eat it. He roamed the fields on horseback during the day and sat on the porch at night with a shotgun across his lap – his vigilance so absolute that the slave-row people dared not try even discussing the uprising, let alone plan one of their own. After receiving and reading the next issue of the *Gazette*, Massa John burned it in the fireplace; and when a neighbouring massa visited one afternoon, he ordered Bell to leave the house and they huddled talking in the study with the windows shut. So it was impossible for anyone even to find out more about the plot, or especially about its aftermath, which was what had Bell and the others worried sick – not about Kunta, since he'd be safe with the massa, but about the fiddler, who had left on the day before they had to play at a big society ball in Richmond. The slave-row people could only imagine what might be happening to black strangers in Richmond at the hands of enraged, panic-stricken whites.

The fiddler still hadn't returned when Kunta and the massa did – three days early – their trip cut short by the uprising. Upon Massa John's departure later that day, the restrictions he'd imposed were

360

relaxed somewhat, although not completely, and the massa was very cold towards everyone. It wasn't until Kunta and Bell were alone in their cabin that he could tell her of what he'd overheard in Fredericksburg: that the black revolters already captured had been tortured into helping the authorities round up others involved, and some had confessed that the revolt had been planned by a free blacksmith named Gabriel Prosser, who had recruited around two hundred hand-picked black men – butlers, gardeners, janitors, waiters, ironworkers, rope makers, coal miners, boatmen, even preachers – and trained them for more than a year. Prosser was still at large, and the militia was combing the countryside for suspects, said Kunta; poor-white 'paterollers' were terrorizing the roads; and there were rumours about some massas beating slaves, some to death, for little or no provocation.

'Look like our only hope is we's all dey got,' said Bell. 'If'n dey kills us off, dey won't have no slaves no mo'.'

'Fiddler back?' asked Kunta, ashamed that he'd been so engrossed in telling what had happened that he hadn't thought of his friend until now.

Bell shook her head. 'We all been mighty worried. But dat fiddler a crafty nigger. He get home awright.'

Kunta didn't fully agree. 'He ain't home yet.'

When the fiddler didn't return the next day, the massa wrote a message notifying the sheriff, and told Kunta to deliver it to the county seat. Kunta had done so – seeing the sheriff read the message and silently shake his head. Then returning homewards, Kunta had driven slowly for three or four miles, staring gloomily at the road ahead, wondering if he'd ever see the fiddler again, feeling badly that he had never actually expressed that he considered him a good friend – despite his drinking, his cussing, and other short-comings – when he heard a poor imitation of a white 'cracker' drawl, 'Hey, nigger!'

Kunta thought he must be hearing things. 'Where de hell you think you goin'?' the voice came again, and reining the horses, Kunta looked around and along both sides of the road, but saw nobody. Then, suddenly, 'You ain't got no travel pass, boy, you in a heap o' trouble' – and there, climbing from a ditch, ragged and torn, cut and bruised, covered with mud while carrying his battered case and grinning from ear to ear, was the fiddler.

Kunta let out a shout, jumping down from his seat, and within seconds he and the fiddler were hugging and whirling each other around, laughing.

'You de spittin' image of a African I knows,' exclaimed the

fiddler, 'but couldn't be him – he wouldn't never let nobody know he glad to see 'em.'

'Don' know why I is,' said Kunta, embarrassed at himself.

'Fine welcome fo' a frien' what crawled on his han's an' knees all de way back from Richmon' jes' to see yo' ugly face again.'

Kunta's seriousness conveyed the degree of his concern. 'Was it bad, Fiddler?'

'*Bad* ain't even close to it. Thought sho' I'd be playin' a duet wid angels fo' I got out'n dere!' As Kunta took the muddy fiddle case and they both clambered into the wagon, the fiddler continued talking, nonstop. 'Richmon' white folks jes' 'bout crazy scared. Militiamens ever'where stoppin' niggers, an' dem widout a travel pass next stop in jail wid a headache. An' dem de lucky ones. Packs o' po' crackers roamin' de streets like wil' dogs, jumpin' on niggers, beatin' some so bad can't hardly tell who dey was.

'De ball I'se playin' at break up halfway through when dey gits firs' word 'bout de uprisin', missies screamin' an' runnin' roun' in circles, massas pullin' guns on us niggers up on de ban'stan'. 'Midst all de ruckus, I slips into de kitchen an' hid in a garbage can till eve'ybody gone. Den I climbs out a window and took to de back streets, stayin' way from lights. I'd got to de edge o' town when all of a sudden I hears dis shoutin' behin' me, den a whole lotta feets runnin' same way I is. Sump'n tell me dey ain't black, but I ain't waitin' to fin' out. I cuts 'roun' de nex' corner flyin' low, but I hears 'em gainin' on me, an' I'se 'bout to say my prayers when I sees a real low porch dat I rolls right under.

'It's real tight under dere, an' I'se inchin' further back jes' when dem crackers goes runnin' by wid torches shoutin', 'Git dat nigger!' I bumps 'gainst sump'n big an' sof', an' a hand clap over my mouf, an' a nigger voice say, "Nex' time, knock!" Turns out it's a warehouse nightwatchman seen a mob tear a frien' o' his apart, an' he ain't got no 'tention o' comin' out from under dat porch 'til nex' spring, if'n it take dat long to blow over.

'Well, after a while I wishes 'im luck, an' heads out again an' makes it to de woods. Dat was five days ago. Would a made it here in fo', but so many paterollers on de roads, I had to keep to de woods, eatin' berries, sleepin' in de thickets wid de rabbits. Did all right 'till yestiddy a few miles east o' here, bunch o' real mean crackers cotched me in de open.

'Day's jes' spoilin' to whup deyselves a nigger, maybe even string 'im up – dey had a rope right dere wid 'em! Dey's shovin' me back an' fo'th, axin' whose nigger I is an' where I think I'se goin', but not

362

payin' no 'tention to what I tells 'em – 'til I says I'se a fiddler. Dey hol' on, dey thinks I'se lyin', an' hollers, "Well, le's hear you play, den!"

'African, le'me tell you sump'n. I open up dat fiddle case an' you ain't never heard no concert like I give right out dere in de middle o' de road. Played "Turkey in de Straw" – you know po' crackers loves dat – an' fo' I'm warmed up good, I had dem all a-hootin' an' clappin' an' tappin' dey feets, an' I ain't quit 'til dey's had dey fill an' tell me to go 'head an' don't dillydally gittin' my tail home. An' I ain't neither! Done hit de ditch whenever I seen a hoss or buggy, or wagon comin', until dis one was you! An' here I is!'

As they rolled into the narrow road leading to the big house, soon they heard shouting and then saw the people of slave row running to meet the wagon.

'Might think a body was missed 'round here' – although the fiddler was grinning, Kunta could sense how moved the man was, as grinning himself, he said, 'Look like you gon' have to tell de whole story all over again.'

'You ever knowed dat to stop me?' asked the fiddler. 'Leas'ways I'se here to tell it!'

78

In the months that followed, with the capture, trial, and execution of one conspirator after another, and finally of Gabriel Prosser himself, news of the Richmond uprising – and of the tensions it generated – gradually subsided, and once more politics became the chief discussion topic among the massa and his friends, and therefore also within the slave row. As best Kunta, Bell, and the fiddler could piece together what they overheard in various ways about the voting for the next President, a Massa Aaron Burr had run a tie with the famous Massa Thomas Jefferson – who finally had got the job, apparently since he was supported by the powerful Massa Alexander Hamilton; and Massa Burr, an arch-enemy of Massa Hamilton, had been made Vice President.

No one seemed to know much about Massa Burr, but Kunta

learned from a buggy driver who had been born in Virginia not far from Massa Jefferson's Monticello plantation that his slaves declared there couldn't be a better massa.

'Dat driver tol' me Massa Jefferson ain't never 'lowed his ob
erseers to whup nobody,' Kunta shared with the slave-row people. 'An' dey all eats good, an' he let de womens spin an' sew 'em all good clothes, an' he b'lieve in lettin' 'em learn different trades.' After Massa Jefferson returned home from one long trip, Kunta had heard, his slaves had met him two miles from the plantation, unhitched the horses, and gleefully pulled the carriage that long distance to the Monticello big house, where they carried him on their shoulders to the doorstep.

The fiddler snorted. 'Pret' near eve'ybody know plenty dem niggers Massa Jefferson's own chilluns by high-yaller woman he own, name o' Sally Hemings.' He was about to say more when Bell contributed the most interesting thing she knew. ''Cordin' to a kitchen maid he use to have dere,' she said, 'ain't nothin' Massa Jefferson ruther eat dan a rabbit soaked all night in oil, thyme, rosemary, an' garlic, den next day simmered down in wine till de meat fallin' off de bones.'

'You don' say!' exclaimed the fiddler sarcastically.

'See how soon you gits 'nother piece dat rhubarb pie you keeps axin' me to make!' snapped Bell.

'See how soon I axes you!' he shot back.

Refusing to get caught in the middle, as he had so often been in the past – in trying to make peace when his wife and the fiddler started in on each other, then turned on him for butting in – Kunta acted as if he hadn't heard, and simply continued where he'd left off before they interrupted.

'I heared Massa Jefferson say slavery jes' bad for white folks as for us'ns, an' he 'gree wid Massa Hamilton it's jes' too much nachel diff'rence fo' white an' black folks ever to learn to live wid one 'nother peaceful. Dey say Massa Jefferson want to see us sot free, but not stickin' roun' dis country takin' po' white folks' jobs – he favour shippin' us back to Africa, gradual, widout big fuss an' mess.'

'Massa Jefferson better talk to dem slave traders,' said the fiddler, ' 'cause look like dey got diff'rent ideas which way de ships oughta go.'

'Seem like lately when Massa go to other plantations, I hears 'bout lots of peoples gittin' sol',' said Kunta. 'Whole families dat's been all dey lives roun' here is gittin' sol' off down South by dey massas. Even passed one dem slave traders yestiddy on de road. He wave an' grin an' tip 'is hat, but massa ack like he ain't even seed 'im.'

'Humph! Dem slave traders gittin' thick as flies in de towns,' said the fiddler. 'Las' time I went to Fredericksburg, dey was buzzin' after sump'n ol' an' dried-up as me, 'til I flash my pass. I seed a po' ol' greybeard nigger git sol' off fo' six hunnud dollars. Young healthy buck use to fetch dat. But dat ol' nigger sho' didn't go quiet! Dey's jerkin' 'im off'n de auction block, an' he bawlin' out, "Y'all white folks done made Gawd's earth a livin' HELL fo' my peoples! But jes' sho' as JEDGMENT MAWNIN' gwine come, y'all's hell gwine bounce BACK on y'all dat brung it! Ain't no BEGGIN' gwine stop it from 'STROYIN' you! No MEDICINES y'all make ... no RUNNIN' y'all do ... none y'all's GUNS ... no PRAYIN', no NOTHIN' he'p y'all den!" By dat time dey'd drug 'im off. Ol' nigger soun' like a preacher or sump'n, de way he carry on.'

Kunta saw Bell's sudden agitation. 'Dat ol' man—' she asked, 'he real black an' skinny, kin' o' stooped over an' got a white beard an' had a big scar down his neck?'

The fiddler looked startled. 'Yeah! Sho' was! Sho' did. All dem things – you know who he was?'

Bell looked at Kunta as if she were ready to weep. 'Dat de preacher what christened Kizzy,' she said sombrely.

Kunta was visiting in the fiddler's cabin late the next day when Cato knocked at the open door. 'What you doin' out dere? Come on in!' the fiddler shouted.

Cato did. Both Kunta and the fiddler were very glad that he had come. Only recently they had expressed mutual wishing that the quiet, solid lead field hand Cato was closer to them, as the old gardener had been.

Cato seemed ill at ease. 'Jes' want to say I b'lieves it be good if y'all maybe don' tell de scaries' things y'all hears 'bout so many folks gittin' sol' off down South—' Cato hesitated. 'Reason why I'm tellin' y'all de truth, out in de fields de folks is gittin' so scairt dey gwine git sol', dey jes' can't hardly keep dey minds on no workin'.' Again he paused briefly. 'Leas'ways nobody 'ceptin' me an' dat boy Noah. I figgers if I gits sol', well, I'se jes' sol', ain't much I can do 'bout it. An' dat Noah – don't seem like he scairt o' nothin'.'

After several minutes of talk among the three of them – during which Kunta sensed Cato's warm response to their warm welcoming of his visit – they agreed that it would probably be best if only they, not even Bell, shared the news that was the most frightening, that could only alarm the others needlessly.

But one night in the cabin a week or so later, Bell looked up abruptly from her knitting and said, 'Seem like de cat got some tongues roun' here – either dat or white folks done quit sellin' niggers, an' I knows I got mo' sense dan dat!'

Grunting in embarrassment, Kunta was amazed that she – and probably all the other people on slave row – had guessed intuitively that he and the fiddler weren't telling them all they knew anymore. So he began reporting slave sale stories again – omitting the most unpleasant details. But he stressed news about successful runaways, featuring the black grapevine tales he had heard about wily, fast-talking slaves in the act of escaping and making fools of ignorant poor cracker 'paterollers'. One night he told them of a high-yaller butler and a black stablehand having stolen a buggy, horse, and fine clothing and a hat that the high yaller wore while he pretended to be a rich massa loudly cursing his black buggy driver whenever he drew within earshot of any white patrols they met along their rapid buggy ride into the North and automatic freedom. Another time Kunta told of a no less audacious slave who always galloped his mule almost into the 'paterollers'' faces before halting and unrolling with a flourish a large, fine-print document that he said would explain his urgent errand for his massa – gambling always correctly that the illiterate white crackers would wave him on rather than admit they couldn't read. Kunta often now set the slave-row people to laughing – telling such as how other escaping blacks had so perfected an act of chronic stuttering that disgusted 'paterollers' told them to get along their way rather than spend obvious hours trying to question them. He told of runaways' affected fearful reluctance before finally apologetically confiding how much their rich, powerful massas despised poor whites and how harshly they dealt with any interference with their servants. One night Kunta set slave row to roaring about a house slave he'd been told of who reached safety up North just a jump ahead of his hotly pursuing massa, who quickly summoned a policeman. 'You *know* you my nigger!' the massa screamed wildly at his slave, who simply looked blank and kept exclaiming, 'He'p me Gawd, I ain't never sot eyes on dat white man!' – convincing a gathered crowd, along with the policeman who ordered the furious white man to quiet down and move on or he'd have to arrest him for disturbing the peace.

For years now Kunta had managed to avoid going anywhere near any slave auction, ever since the one where the girl had futilely cried out to him for help. But a few months after his talk with Cato and the fiddler, one early afternoon Kunta drove the massa into the public square of the county seat just as a slave sale was beginning.

366

'Oyez, oyez, gentlemen of Spotsylvania, I offer the finest lot of niggers ever seen in y'all's lives!' As the auctioneer shouted to the crowd, his beefy, younger assistant jerked an old slave woman up onto the platform. 'A fine cook!' he began – but she began screaming, gesturing frantically to a white man in the crowd: 'Massa Philip! Philip! You act like you done forgot I worked fo' you an' yo' brudders' daddy when y'all was jes' young'uns! Knows I'se ol' an' ain't much now, but please, Lawd, keep me! I work for you hard, Massa Philip! *Please*, suh, don' let 'em whup me to death somewheres down South!'

'Stop the buggy, Toby!' the massa ordered.

Kunta's blood ran cold as he reined the horses to a halt. Why after all these years of showing no interest in slave auctions did Massa Waller want to watch one? Was he thinking of buying someone, or what? Was it the pitiful woman's heartbreaking outburst? Whomever she had appealed to yelled back some ridicule, and the crowd was still laughing when a trader bought her for seven hundred dollars.

'He'p me, Gawd, Jesus, Lawd, he'p me!' she cried as the trader's black helper began shoving her roughly towards the slave pen. 'Git yo' black hands off'n me, nigger!' she screamed, and the crowd rocked with laughter. Kunta bit his lip, blinking back tears.

'Prize buck o' the lot, gentlemen!' Next on the platform was a young black man, glaring baleful hatred, his barrel chest and thickly muscled body criss-crossed with the angry, reddish welts of a very recent, severe lashing. 'This one jes' needed some remindin'! He'll heal up quick! He can plough a mule into the ground! Pick you four hundred pounds of cotton any day! *Look* at 'im! A natural stud – if your wenches ain't bearin' every year like they ought! A steal at any price!' The chained young man brought fourteen hundred dollars.

Kunta's vision blurred anew as a weeping mulatto woman great with child was led onto the platform. 'Two for the price of one, or one for free, dependin' on how you look at it!' shouted the auctioneer. 'Pickaninnies today worth a hundred dollars soon's they draw breath!' She brought a thousand dollars.

It was becoming unendurable when the next one came, being pulled along by her chain – and Kunta nearly fell from his seat. The teenaged black girl, quaking with terror, in her build, her skin colour, even her facial features, might have been an older Kizzy! As if Kunta had been poleaxed, he heard the auctioneer start his spiel. 'A fine trained housemaid – or she's prime breedin' stock if you want one!' he added with a leering wink. Inviting closer inspection, he abruptly loosened the neckpiece of the girl's sack dress, which fell about her feet as she screamed, weeping, flinging her arms downwards in an effort to cover her nakedness from the ogling crowd, several of whom jostled forward, reaching out to poke and fondle her.

'That's enough! Let's get out of here!' the massa commanded – an instant before Kunta felt he would have done it anyway.

Kunta hardly saw the road before them as they rode back towards the plantation; his mind was reeling. What if the girl had really been his Kizzy? What if the cook had been his Bell? What if they both were sold away from him? Or he from them? It was too horrible to think about – but he could think of nothing else.

Even before the buggy reached the big house, Kunta intuitively sensed that something was wrong, perhaps because it was a warm summer evening, yet he saw none of the slave-row people strolling or sitting around outside. Dropping the massa off, Kunta hurriedly unhitched and stabled the horses, then headed straight for the kitchen, where he knew Bell now would be preparing the massa's supper. She didn't hear him until he asked through the screen door, 'You awright?'

'Oh, Kunta!' Whirling around, her eyes wide with shock, loudly she blurted, 'Slave trader done been here!' Then, lowering her voice, 'I heared Cato's whippoorwill whistle from out in de fiel' an' run to de front window. Minute I seed dat citified-lookin' white man gittin' off his hoss, I jes' smelt what he was! Lawd a mercy! I open de do' by time he got up de steps. He ax to see my massa or missis. I say my missis in de graveyard, an my massa a doctor off tendin' sick peoples, an' no tellin' what time o' night he git back. Den he throw me dis smirkin' look an' han' me a li'l card wid printin' on it an' say give dat to massa an' tell 'im he be back. Well, I'se feared not to give massa de card – finally jes' stuck it on his desk.'

'Bell!' a call came from the living-room.

She nearly dropped her spoon. She whispered, 'Wait! I be back!' Kunta waited – hardly daring to breathe, expecting the worst – until he saw the returning Bell's expression of immense relief.

'He say he want early supper! De card gone from de desk where I lef' it, but he don't say nothin' 'bout it, an' fo' sho' I ain't neither!'

After supper, Bell filled in the field hands on the developments after Cato's warning whistle, and Aunt Sukey started crying. 'Lawd, y'all think massa gwine sell some us?'

'Ain't nobody never gon' beat me no mo'!' declared Cato's big wife, Beulah.

A long, heavy silence fell. Kunta could think of nothing to say; but he knew he wasn't going to tell them about the auction.

'Well,' said the fiddler finally, 'massa ain't one o' dem wid a whole lotta spare niggers. An' he *is* one dem got plenty money, so ain't needin' to sell no niggers to pay debts, like a whole lot doin'.'

Kunta hoped the others found the fiddler's comforting effort more convincing than he did. Bell looked a little hopeful. 'I knows massa, or *anyhow*, I thinks I does. Long as we's all been here, he ain't never sol' off nobody – leas'ways nobody 'cept dat buggy driver Luther, an' dat 'cause Luther drawed dat map to he'p a gal try to 'scape.' Bell hesitated before continuing. 'Naw!' she said. 'Massa wouldn't git rid o' none us widout no good cause – any y'all speck he would?' But nobody answered.

79

Kunta's ears were riveted upon the massa's dialogue with a favourite one of his cousins, who was being brought home for dinner, as they sat in the rear of the rolling buggy.

'At a county seat auction the other day,' the massa was saying, 'I was astonished that everyday field hands are selling for twice to three times what they fetched just a few years ago. And from advertisements I read in the *Gazette*, carpenters, brickmasons, blacksmiths – in fact, slaves who are really experienced in about any trade, leatherworkers, sailmakers, musicians, whatever, are going for as much as twenty-five hundred dollars apiece.'

'It's the same everywhere since this new cotton gin!' exclaimed the massa's cousin. 'More than a million slaves already in the country, I've been told, yet the ships still can't seem to bring enough new ones to supply those Deep South bottomlands trying to meet the demands of the northern mills.'

'What's concerning me is that too many otherwise sensible planters, in their eagerness for quick profits, may be starting to see our state of Virginia eventually losing its best quality of slaves, even the best breeding stock,' said Massa Waller, 'and that's just plain foolishness!'

'Foolishness? Hasn't Virginia got more slaves than she needs? They cost more to maintain than most are worth in work.'

'Maybe today,' said the massa, 'but how do we know our needs five, ten years from today? Who would have predicted such a cotton boom as this ten years ago? And I've never gone along with your very popular talk of slaves' keep costing so much. It seems to me on any place that's just halfway well organized, don't they plant, raise, and harvest what they eat? And they're usually prolific – every pickaninny that's born is worth money to you, too. A lot are fully capable of learning skills to make them even more valuable. I'm convinced that slaves and land, in that order, are a man's best investments today. I'd never sell either of mine for the same reason – they're the backbone of our system.'

'The system may be starting to change without many realizing it,' said the massa's cousin. 'Look at these upstart rednecks strutting around as if they've entered the planter class just because they've bought one or two broken-down slaves to finish working them to death at building up their pitiful little crops of cotton and tobacco. They're beyond contempt, but rednecks seemed to breed even faster than niggers. Just in sheer numbers they may begin to encroach on our land before long as well as on our labour.'

'Well, I don't think we have much to worry about' – the massa chuckled, seemingly amused at his thought – 'not as long as poor whites are competing with free blacks to buy the cast-off slaves.'

His cousin joined him in laughter. 'Yes, isn't it unbelievable? I hear that half the free niggers in the cities work day and night to save enough money to buy their kinfolk, and then set them free.'

'It's why we have so many free blacks in the South,' said the massa.

'I think we're permitting too many of them in Virginia,' said his cousin. 'It's not just how they're sapping our labour supply by buying up their kin and creating *more* free blacks. They're also at the root of most uprisings. We don't ever want to forget that blacksmith in Richmond.'

'True!' said Massa Waller. 'But I still think that with enough good, strict laws to keep them in their places, and proper examples made of troublemakers, then most of them can serve useful purposes – in the cities. I'm told that right now, they just about dominate in most of the trades.'

'In the travelling I do, I've seen myself how widespread that is,' said his cousin. 'They're warehouse and waterfront workers, merchants, undertakers, gardeners. They're the best cooks, also musicians, of course! And I've heard there's not even one white barber in the whole city of Lynchburg. I'd have to grow a beard! I'd never let one of them near my throat with a razor!'

They both laughed. But then the massa grew serious. 'I think the cities may be spawning for us a bigger social problem than free blacks – I mean these slick-tongued con-man slave traders. I hear most are former tavern owners, speculators, jackleg teachers, lawyers, preachers and the like. Three or four have approached me in the county seat offering sight-unseen prices for my slaves, and one even had the nerve to leave his card here at the house! Far as I'm concerned, they're totally vultures without scruples.'

They had arrived at Massa Waller's house, and Kunta – seeming as if he hadn't heard a word they'd said – jumped down to help them out. By the time they'd gone inside, washed up after the dusty ride, then settled in the drawing-room and called Bell to bring them drinks, she and everyone else on the plantation knew from Kunta the vital fact that the massa had no plans to sell them. And not long after supper, Kunta repeated to his rapt slave-row audience the entire conversation, as best he could duplicate it.

There was silence for a moment. Then Sister Mandy spoke. 'Massa an' his cousin talkin' 'bout free niggers savin' up to buy kinfolks free. I wants to know how dem free niggers got *deyselves* free!'

'Well,' said the fiddler, 'whole lotta city slaves' massas lets 'em learn trades, den hires 'em out fo' pay an' gives 'em some de money, like massa do wid me. So wid ten, fi'teen years o' savin', if'n he real lucky, a hire-out nigger can maybe give his massa de money to buy hisself free.'

'Dat why you keeps so busy fiddlin'?' asked Cato.

'Ain't doin' it 'cause I loves to see white folks dance,' said the fiddler.

'You got 'nough to buy yo'self yet?'

'If I did, I wouldn' be here fo' you to ax dat question.' Everyone laughed.

'Is you close, anyways?' Cato persisted.

'Don' give up, does you?' said the fiddler, exasperated. 'I'se closer'n I was las' week, but not close I'se gwine be nex' week.'

'Awright, but when you *gits* it, what you gwine do?'

'Split de win', brudder! Headin' Nawth! Hear some dem northern free niggers livin' better'n plenty white folks, an' dat soun' good to me. Speck I move in nex' door to one dem high-tone mulattoes an' start talkin' high-toned an' dressin' up in silk like dey does, an' start to playin' de harp an' gwine to meetin's to 'scuss books an' raisin' flowers an' sich as dat.'

When the laughter lessened, Aunt Sukey asked, 'What y'all think 'bout what white folks always says dat dem mulattoes an' high yallers do so good 'cause de whole lot o' white blood dey got in 'em make 'em smarter'n we is?'

'Well, white mens sho' mixes roun' 'nough dey blood!' Bell said non-committally.

'Watch yo' talk 'bout my mammy's oberseer!' the fiddler exclaimed, trying to look insulted. Cato almost fell off his chair laughing till Beulah gave his head a whack with the back of her hand.

'Git serious here!' the fiddler went on. 'Aunt Sukey ax a question I 'tends to answer! If you judgin' by sich as *me*, den you *know* light-skinned niggers got to be smart! Or take dat brown-skin Benjamin Banneker what white folks calls a genius wid figgers, even studyin' de stars an' moon – but whole heap o' smart niggers black like y'all, too!'

Bell said, 'I done heared massa talk 'bout a James Derham nigger doctor in New Orleans. White doctor what teached 'im claim he know more 'n he do, an' he black as dey gits, too.'

'Tell you anudder one,' said the fiddler. 'Dat Prince Hall what started dat nigger Masonic Order! I seen pictures some dem big preachers what started dem nigger churches, most of 'em so black you couldn't hardly see 'em less'n dey eyes was open. An' what 'bout dat Phyllis Wheatley what writes dem pomes white folks say so fine, an' dat Gustavus Vassa what writes books?' The fiddler glanced in Kunta's direction. 'Dey's both straight-from-Africa niggers, not nary drop o' white folks' blood, an' dey sho' don't soun' all dat dumb to me!' Then laughing, the fiddler said, ' 'Cose, dey's always dumb black niggers – take Cato here . . .' He sprang up and ran with Cato two steps behind. 'Cotch you, I'll *dumb* you upside de head!' Cato shouted.

When the others stopped guffawing, Kunta spoke. 'Laugh all y'all want. All niggers de same to white folks. One drop o' nigger blood means nigger if you's even whiter'n dem – and I'se seed plenty dat is.'

It was about a month later when the fiddler returned from one of his trips bearing news that he had seen elating whites everywhere he'd been – and that plunged slave row into gloom. The French leader named Napoleon had sent across the big water a huge army which, after much fighting and bloodshed, had taken Haiti back from the blacks and their liberator, General Toussaint. Invited to dinner by the victorious French army's general, Toussaint had made the mistake of accepting; during the meal, the waiters seized and trussed him, and rushed him onto a ship bound for France, where he had been taken in chains before Napoleon, who had plotted the entire treachery.

Being the black General Toussaint's greatest admirer on the plantation, Kunta took the news harder than anyone else. He was still sitting dejectedly in the fiddler's cabin when the last of the others trudged silently out.

'I knows how you felt 'bout dat Toussaint,' said the fiddler, 'an' I don' want you to think I takes it light, but I got a piece o' news I jes' cain't hol' in another minute!'

Kunta glanced grimly at the fiddler, further offended that he looked ready to pop open with happiness. What news could be so good as to affect anyone's proper respect for the humiliation of the greatest black leader of all time?

'I done it!' The fiddler was a study of excitement. 'I didn't say nothin' jes' a month back when Cato axed how much I had saved up, but den I was jes' a few dollars short – an' now I jes' done made it wid dis trip! Took me playin' over nine hunnud times fo' white folks to dance, an' I sho' di'n't know if I'd ever make it, so I di'n't talk 'bout it wid nobody – not even you – 'til I done it! African, I got seven hunnud dollars what massa long time ago tol' me I'd have to earn to buy myself free!'

Kunta was too thunderstruck to speak.

'Looka here!' said the fiddler, ripping open his mattress and dumping the contents out onto the floor; hundreds of dollar bills eddied about their feet. 'An' looka here!' he said, dragging a gunny sack out from under the bed and emptying it, clinking, on top of the bills – hundreds of coins of every denomination.

'Well, African, you gwine say sump'n, or jes' stan' dere wid yo' mouf' open?'

'Don't know what to say,' said Kunta.

'How 'bout " 'gratulations"?'

'Jes' seem too good to be true.'

'It true awright. I done counted it a thousan' times. Even got 'nough extra to buy me a cardboard suitcase!'

Kunta just couldn't believe it. The fiddler was really going to be *free!* It wasn't just a dream. Kunta felt like laughing and crying – for himself as much as for his friend.

The fiddler knelt and began scooping up the money. 'Look, you deaf'n dumb 'bout dis till tomorrow mawnin', awright? Dat when I goes to see massa an' tell 'im he seven hunnud dollars richer! You gwine be glad as he is to see me go?'

'Glad fo' you. Not fo' me,' said Kunta.

'If you tryin' to make me feel so sorry for you, I buy *you* free, too, you gwine wait a spell! Done took me thutty-three years fiddlin' to freedom!'

By the time Kunta got back to his own cabin, he had begun to miss the fiddler already, and Bell mistook his sadness for grief about Toussaint, so he didn't have to hide – or explain – what he was feeling.

When he went by the fiddler's cabin the next morning after feeding the horses, he found it empty, so he went to ask Bell if he was in with the massa.

'He lef' an hour ago. Ack like he seen a ghost. What de matter wid 'im, an' what he want wid massa anyways?'

'What he say when he come out?' asked Kunta.

'Don' say nothin'. Tol' you he went pas' me like I wasn't dere.'

Without another word, Kunta walked out the screen door and back towards slave row – with Bell shouting after him, 'Now where *you* goin'?' And when he didn't answer: 'Dat right! Don't tell me nothin'! I'se jes' yo' wife!' Kunta had disappeared.

After asking around, knocking at every cabin door, even peeking inside the privy and shouting 'Fiddler!' in the barn, Kunta headed down along the fencerow. When he had gone a good way, he heard it – sad, slow strains of a song he had heard blacks at an 'O Lawd' camp meeting singing once . . . only this time it was being played on a fiddle. The fiddler's music was always rollicking and happy; this sounded almost as if the fiddle were sobbing, drifting up along the fencerow.

Quickening his stride, Kunta came within sight of an oak tree spreading half over a brook down near the edge of Massa Waller's property. Approaching closer, he saw the fiddler's shoes extending from behind the tree. Just then, the music stopped – and so did Kunta, feeling suddenly like an intruder. He stood still, waiting for the fiddling to resume, but the drone of bees and the burble of the stream were the only sounds that broke the silence. At last, almost sheepishly, Kunta moved around the tree and faced the fiddler. One glance was all he needed to know what had happened – the light was gone from his friend's face; the familiar sparkle in his eyes had been extinguished.

'You need some mattress stuffin'?' the fiddler's voice was cracking. Kunta said nothing. Tears began to drip down along the fiddler's

374

cheeks; he brushed them furiously away as if they were acid, and the words came in a rush: 'I tells 'im I finally got de money to buy me free – ev'y penny of it. He hem an' haw a minute, an' look at de ceilin'. Den he 'gratulate me on savin' up so much. But den he tell me if I wants to, de seven hunnud could be a down payment, 'cause in doin' business he got to consider how de slave prices done gone way up since dat cotton gin come in. He say now he couldn't 'cept no less'n fifteen hunnud at de leas' fo' a good money-makin' fiddler like me, dat he could git twenty-five hunnud fo' if he was to sell me to somebody else. He say he real sorry, but he hope I understan's business is business, an' he have to git fair return on his 'vestment.' The fiddler began openly sobbing now. 'He say bein' free ain't all it cracked up to be nohow, an' he wish me de bes' luck in comin' up wid de res' if I insists . . . an' he tell me keep up de good work . . . an' when I go out, would I ax Bell to bring 'im some coffee.'

He fell silent. Kunta just stood there.

'Dat son-of-a-bitch!' the fiddler screamed suddenly, and flinging back his arm, he hurled his fiddle into the stream.

Kunta waded in to get it, but even before he reached down, he could see it was broken.

80

When Kunta got home with the massa well into one night a few months later, Bell was less irritated than concerned that they were both too tired even to eat the good supper she'd prepared. For a strange fever had begun to strike throughout the county, and the two men had been leaving earlier each morning and coming back later each night in the massa's efforts as the county's doctor to keep up with the spreading contagion.

Kunta was so worn out, slumped in his rocking chair, staring vacantly at the fire, that he didn't even notice Bell feeling his forehead and taking off his shoes. And half an hour passed before he realized suddenly that Kizzy wasn't on his lap, as usual, showing him some new plaything she'd made or prattling about what she'd done that day.

'Where dat chile?' he asked finally.

'Put 'er to bed an hour ago,' said Bell.

'She ain't sick, is she?' he asked, sitting up.

'Naw, jes' tuckered out from play. Missy Anne come over today.' Kunta was too exhausted even to feel his customary annoyance, but Bell changed the subject anyway. 'While Roosby waitin' to take 'er home, he tell me he heared de fiddler playin' other night at a ball he took Massa John to over in Fredericksburg. He say he didn't hardly recognize de fiddlin', it jes' don't soun' de same. I didn't tell 'im de fiddler hisself ain't de same since he find out he ain't free.'

'Seem like he don't care 'bout *nothin'* no mo',' said Kunta.

'Sho' seem dat. He keep to hisself, don't hardly even nod to nobody no mo', 'ceptin Kizzy when she bring 'im supper an' set wid 'im whilst he eat it. She de onliest one he want anythin' to do wid. Don't even spen' no time wid *you* no mo'.'

'What wid dis fever goin' roun' lately,' said Kunta wearily, 'I ain't hardly had no time or stren'th for visitin' noways.'

'Yeah, I been noticin', an' you ain't gon' set up here half de night, you goin' straight to bed.'

'Leave me 'lone, woman. I'm fine.'

'Naw you ain't!' Bell said decisively, taking him by the hand, helping him up, and leading him into the bedroom without his further resistance. Kunta sat on the edge of the bed while she helped him out of his clothes; then he lay down, sighing.

'Roll over an' I gives you a back-rub.'

He obeyed, and she began kneading his back with her stiffened fingers.

He winced.

'What's de matter? I ain't rubbin' all dat hard.'

'Ain't nothin'.'

'Do dis hurt here, too?' she asked, pressing down farther towards the small of his back.

'*Ow!*'

'Don't like de looks o' dis,' she said, lightening her touch to a caress.

'I'se jes' tired. All I need's a night's sleep.'

'We'll see,' she said, blowing out the candle and climbing in beside him.

But when she had served the massa his breakfast the next morning, Bell had to tell him that Kunta had been unable to rise from his bed.

'Probably fever,' said the massa, trying to conceal his irritation.

376

'You know what to do. In the meanwhile, there's an epidemic going on and I've got to have a driver.'

'Yassa, Massa.' She thought for a moment. 'You got any objection to dat fiel'-hand boy Noah? He done growed up so fast he 'bout man-size now. Handle de mules good, he sho' could drive yo' hosses, too, suh.'

'How old is he now?'

'Well suh, Noah roun' two years older'n my Kizzy, so dat—' she paused to count on her fingers, '—dat make him thirteen or fo'teen, I b'lieve, suh.'

'Too young,' said the massa. 'You go tell that fiddler to take over. He's not doing that much in the garden, or with his fiddle either, lately. Have him hitch up the horses and get around front right away.'

On her way to the fiddler's cabin, Bell guessed that he'd be either very indifferent or very upset about the news. He was both. He didn't seem to care one way or the other about having to drive the massa, but when he learned that Kunta was ill, the fiddler got so concerned that she had to talk him out of stopping off at their cabin before picking up the massa.

From that day on, the fiddler was a changed man – certainly no happier than he'd been acting for the past few months, but caring, considerate, and tireless as he drove the massa all about the county day and night, and then came home to help Bell care for Kunta and others on slave row who also had come down with the fever.

Before long, so many people were sick – both on the plantation and off – that the massa pressed Bell into service as his assistant. While he attended the whites, the boy Noah drove her around in the mule-cart taking care of the blacks. 'Massa got his medicines, I got mine,' she confided to the fiddler. After administering the massa's drugs, she gave her patients her secret brew of dried, powdered herbs mixed with water from boiled persimmon tree bark – that she swore would work better and faster than any white folks' remedy. But what would really cure them, she confided to Sister Mandy and Aunt Sukey, was that always she knelt down at a patient's bedside and prayed for them. 'Whatever *He* bring on man, He can take away if He want to,' she said. But some of her patients died anyway – as well as Massa Waller's.

As Kunta's own condition steadily worsened, despite everything Bell and the massa could do, her prayers became more and more fervent. Kunta's strange, silent, stubborn ways had been entirely forgotten as herself too tired to sleep, she sat by his bed each night as he lay sweating heavily, tossing, moaning, or at times babbling in spells of delirium beneath the several quilts she'd piled on him. She would hold his hot, dry hand in hers, desperately afraid that she might never be able to tell him what had taken this, after all these years, for her fully to realize: that he was a man of calibre of strength, and of character, that she had never known the equal of, and she loved him very deeply.

He had been in a coma for three days when Missy Anne came to visit the massa and found Kizzy in the cabin, with Bell, Sister Mandy and Aunt Sukey, all of them weeping and praying. Tearful herself, Missy Anne returned to the big house and told the weary Massa Waller that she wanted to read something from the Bible for Kizzy's pappy. But she said she didn't know what would be a good place to read from, so would he please show her? The massa's eyes drank in the wet-eyed earnestness of his beloved niece, and getting up from the couch, he unlocked his bookcase and took out his big Bible. After a thoughtful moment, he turned to a page and pointed out with his forefinger the exact spot where she should begin.

As the word passed in slave row that Missy Anne was going to read something, everyone quickly assembled outside Bell and Kunta's cabin, and she started to read:

'The Lord is my shepherd; I shall not want. He maketh me to lie down in green pastures: He leadeth me beside the still waters. He restoreth my soul. He leadeth me in the paths of righteousness for His name's sake.' Missy Anne paused, frowning at the page, then went on. 'Yea, though I walk through the valley of the shadow of death, I will fear no evil: for Thou art with me; Thy rod and Thy staff they comfort me.' She paused again, this time for a deep breath, and looked up uncertainly at the faces watching her.

Deeply moved, Sister Mandy couldn't stop herself from exclaiming, 'Lawd, listen to dat chile! Done growed up an' learnt to read *so* good!'

Amid a hubbub of praises from others, Noah's mother Ada marvelled, 'Look like jes' yestiddy she runnin' roun' here in diapers! How ol' she now?'

'Ain't long turnt fo'teen!' said Bell as proudly as if she were her own. 'Please read us a li'l mo', honey!'

Flushed with their compliments, Missy Anne read the final verse of the Twenty-third Psalm.

Between treatment and prayer, a few days later Kunta showed signs of beginning to rally. Bell knew he was going to be all right when he glared at her and snatched from around his neck the dried rabbit's foot and the bag of asafoetida she had tied there to ward off further bad luck and sickness. And Kizzy knew it when she whispered into his ear that on the past new-moon morning she had put a pretty pebble into his gourd, and his drawn face found a broad smile. And Kunta knew that the fiddler was going to be all right when Kunta waked up one morning with a start to the sound of fiddling beside his bed.

'I mus' be dreamin',' said Kunta, opening his eyes.

'Not no mo', you ain't,' said the fiddler. 'I'se sick an' tired o' drivin' yo' massa all over hell an' gone. Got burn holes in my coat from his eyes at my back. Time you either git up or move over, nigger!'

81

Kunta was sitting up in bed the next day when he heard Kizzy enter the cabin laughing and chattering with Missy Anne, who was on vacation from school, and he heard them pulling back chairs to sit at the table in the next room.

'Kizzy, have you studied your lessons?' Missy Anne sternly demanded, playing teacher.

'Yes, ma'am,' snickered Kizzy.

'Very well, then – what's that?'

After a short silence, the intently listening Kunta heard Kizzy falter that she couldn't remember.

'It's a *D*,' said Missy Ann. 'Now what's *this* one?'

Almost instantly Kizzy cried triumphantly, 'Dat's dat circle, a *O!*'

Both girls laughed happily.

'Good! You ain't forgot it. Now, what's *that?*'

'Ah . . . uh . . . um . . .' Then Kizzy exulted, 'Dat's *G!*'

'Right!'

After another brief silence, Missy Anne said, 'Now, see that? *D-O-G*. What's that?'

Kizzy's silence told him that she didn't know – as neither did he.

'Dog!' Missy Anne exclaimed. 'You hear me? Don't forget,

D-O-G! You got to learn all the letters good, then we'll do some more about how they make words.'

After the girls left the cabin, Kunta lay thinking hard. He couldn't help feeling some pride in Kizzy's learning ability. On another hand, he couldn't stomach that it was toubob things her head was being stuffed with. It maybe explained why lately she had seemed to show less interest in their conversations about Africa. It might be too late, but he wondered if he should reconsider his decision not to teach her how to read in Arabic. But then he thought that would be as foolish as encouraging her to continue her lessons with Missy Anne. Suppose Massa Waller were to discover that Kizzy could read – in any language! That would be a good way to end the white girl's 'school-teaching', and yet better, it might even end their relationship. But the trouble was that Kunta couldn't be sure the massa would let the matter stop at that. So Kizzy's 'school' continued at least two or three times weekly, until Missy Anne had to return to her own daily studies – about the time that Kunta, now adequately recovered, returned to relieve the happy fiddler of driving the massa in his buggy.

But even after Missy Anne was gone, night after night, as Bell sewed or knitted and Kunta rocked in his chair before the fireplace, Kizzy would sit bent over the table, her pencil almost touching her cheek, carefully copying words from a book Missy Anne had given her or from a torn piece of one of the massa's discarded newspapers. Sitting with his back to them, Kunta sometimes would hear Kizzy involve Bell, although Kizzy knew of her mother's ability to read and write a bit herself.

'Naw, dat's a *A*, Mammy,' Kizzy might explain, 'an' dat's a *O*. It ain't nothin' but a li'l circle.'

In time, she began to move on to words, just as Missy Anne did with *her*. 'Dat's "dog", an dat's "cat" . . . an' dat dere's "Kizzy" . . . an' dis here's yo' name, *B-E-L-L*. How you like dat? You write it now.' And Bell would make a great pretence of struggling with the pencil as she scrawled it out, deliberately making some mistakes so that Kizzy would have a chance to correct her. 'You does like I shows you, Mammy, you can write good as me,' said Kizzy, proud of having something to teach her mother for a change.

One night a few weeks later, after Kizzy had fallen asleep at the table after hours of copying her latest writing lesson from Missy Anne, Bell sent her daughter to bed and soon after herself lay alongside Kunta and said quietly, 'Ain't no game no mo'. Dat chile awready know more'n I does. I jes' hopes it be's awright, Lawd have mercy!'

Over the months that followed, Kizzy and Missy Anne continued to visit one another, mostly on weekends, but not every weekend, and after a while, Kunta began to detect – or wishfully felt that he did – if not exactly a cooling between the two of them, at least some slow, subtle ebbing in their closeness, a gradual growing apart as Missy Anne began to ripen towards young womanhood four years ahead of Kizzy.

Finally the milestone of her long-awaited sixteenth birthday was about to arrive, but three days before the party that was being planned, the wilful, hot-headed Missy Anne galloped angrily over to Massa Waller's house – bareback on their buggy horse – and told him, amid copious tears, that her sickly mother was affecting one of her week-long headaches as an effort to call it off. And with much pouting, eyelash fluttering and tugging his sleeve, she implored him to let her party be at his house instead. Unable to refuse her anything she'd ever asked, he said yes, of course, and as Roosby rushed all over the county informing the dozens of teenaged guests about the change of address, Bell and Kizzy helped Missy Anne with all of the frantic last-minute preparations. They were completed barely in time for Kizzy to help Missy Anne into her party gown and downstairs to greet her guests.

But then, as Bell told Kunta later, from the moment the first carriage arrived, Missy Anne suddenly had acted as if she didn't even know the starchly uniformed aproned Kizzy, who kept circulating among the guests bearing trays of refreshments, 'till de po' chile come bustin' in de kitchen cryin' her eyes out.' That night in the cabin, Kizzy was still weeping as Bell tried to comfort her. 'She jes' done growed up into a young missy, now, honey, an' her mind on dem kind o' things. Ain't she think no less o' you, or really meant no harm. Dis time always come, fo' any us dat's growed up real close wid white young'uns, when you jes' got to go yo' own way, an' dey goes dere's.'

Kunta sat seething with the same emotions he had felt when he had first seen Missy Anne playing with the infant Kizzy in her basket. Across the twelve rains since then, he had asked Allah many times to end the toubob girl's closeness to his Kizzy – and though finally his prayers had been answered, still it both hurt and angered him to see her so deeply wounded. But it had been necessary, and surely from this experience she would learn and remember. Moreover, from the tightness that Kunta had seen in Bell's face as she had been talking to Kizzy, he felt some hope that even Bell might have got cured of at least some of her sickening great affection for the obviously treacherous, conniving 'young missy'.

Missy Anne still continued to visit at Massa Waller's, although much less often than before since – as Roosby confided to Bell – young massas had begun to occupy her time. When she visited, she always saw Kizzy; and usually she'd bring along an old dress for Bell to 'let out' for Kizzy, who was physically bigger, despite being years younger. But now, as if by some unspoken agreement, the two of them would spend around a half hour together, walking and talking quietly in the backyard near slave row, and then Missy Anne would leave.

Kizzy would always stand looking after her, then very quickly she would walk back into the cabin and bury herself in study, often reading and writing until suppertime. Kunta still didn't like the idea of her increasing abilities to do either, but he accepted that she must have something to occupy herself with now that she'd lost her life-long friend. His Kizzy was herself now approaching adolescence, he reflected, which likely was going to present them both with a whole new area of worries.

Just after Christmas of the next year – 1803 – the winds blew the snow into deep, feathery drifts until in places the roads were hidden and impassable for all but the biggest wagons. When the massa went out – in response to only the most desperate summons – he had to ride on one of the horses, and Kunta stayed behind, busily helping Cato, Noah and the fiddler to keep the driveway clear and to chop wood to keep all of the fireplaces steadily going.

Cut off as they were – even from Massa Waller's *Gazette*, which had stopped arriving about a month before with the first big snow – the slave-row people were still talking about the last bits of news that had got through to them: how pleased the white massas were with the way President Jefferson was 'runnin' the gubmint', despite the massas' initial reservations towards his views regarding slaves. Since taking office, President Jefferson had reduced the size of the army and navy, lowered the public debt, even abolished the personal property tax – that last act, the fiddler said, particularly having impressed those of the massa class with his greatness.

But Kunta said that when he had made his last trip to the county seat before they had got snowed in, white folks had seemed to him even more excited about President Jefferson's purchase of the huge 'Louisiana Territory' for but three cents an acre. 'What I likes 'bout it,' he said, ' 'cordin' to what I heared, dat Massa Napoleon had to sell it so cheap 'cause he in sich hot water in France over what it cost 'im in money, 'long wid fifty thousan' Frenchmans got killed or died fo' dey beat dat Toussaint in Haiti.'

They were all still warming themselves in the glow of that thought a later afternoon when a black rider arrived amid a snow-storm with an urgently ill patient's message for the massa – and another of dismal news for the slave row: in a damp dungeon on a remote French mountain where Napoleon had sent him, Haiti's General Toussaint had died of cold and starvation.

Three days later, Kunta was still feeling stricken and depressed when he trudged back to the cabin one afternoon for a mug of hot soup, and stamping snow from his shoes, then entering pulling off his gloves, he found Kizzy stretched out on her pallet in the front room, her face drawn and frightened. 'She feelin' po'ly,' was the explana- tion that Bell offered as she strained a cup of her herb tea and ordered Kizzy to sit up and drink it. Kunta sensed that something more was being kept from him; then when he was a few more minutes there in the over-warm, tightly closed, mud-chinked cabin, his nostrils helped him to guess that Kizzy was experiencing her first time of the bloodiness.

He had watched his Kizzy growing and maturing almost every day now for nearly thirteen rains, and he had lately come to accept within himself that her ripening into womanhood would be only a matter of time; yet somehow he felt completely unprepared for this pungent evidence. After another day abed, though, the hardy Kizzy was back up and about in the cabin, then back at work in the big house – and it was as if overnight that Kunta began actually noticing for the first time how his girlchild's always previously narrow body had budded. With a kind of embarrassed awe, he saw that somehow she had got mango-sized breasts and that her buttocks had begun to swell and curve. She even seemed to be walking in a less girlish way. Now, whenever he came through the bedroom separator curtain into the front room where Kizzy slept, he began to avert his eyes, and whenever Kizzy happened not to be clothed fully, he sensed that she felt the same.

In Africa now, he thought – Africa had sometimes seemed so distantly in the past – Bell would be instructing Kizzy in how to make her skin shine using shea-tree butter, and how to fashionably beautifully blacken her mouth, palms and soles, using the powdered crust from the bottom of cooking pots. And Kizzy would at her present age already be starting to attract men who were seeking for themselves a finely raised, well-trained, virginal young wife. Kunta felt jolted even by the thought of some man's *foto* entering Kizzy's thighs; then he felt better after reassuring himself that this would happen only after a proper wedding. In his homeland at this time, as Kizzy's *fa*, he would be assuming his responsibility to appraise very closely the personal qualities as well as the family backgrounds of whatever men began to show marriageable interest in Kizzy – in order to select the most ideal of them for her; and he would also be deciding now what proper bride price would be asked for her hand.

But after a while, as he continued to shovel snow along with the fiddler, young Noah, and Cato, Kunta found himself gradually feeling increasingly ridiculous that he was even thinking about these African customs and traditions any more; for not only would they never be observed here, nor respected – indeed, he would also be hooted at if he so much as mentioned them, even to other blacks. And anyway, he couldn't think of any likely, well-qualified suitor for Kizzy who was of proper marriageable age – between thirty and thirty-five rains – but there he was doing it again! He was going to have to force himself to start thinking along lines of the marrying customs here in the toubob's country – where girls generally married – 'jumpin' de broom', it was called – someone who was around their same age.

Immediately then Kunta began thinking about Noah. He had always liked the boy. At fifteen, two years older than Kizzy, Noah seemed to be no less mature, serious and responsible than he was big and strong. The more Kunta thought about it, the only thing he could find lacking with Noah, in fact, was that he had never seemed to show the slightest personal interest in Kizzy – not to mention that Kizzy herself seemed to act as if Noah didn't exist. Kunta pondered: *Why* weren't they any more interested than that in each other, at the least in being friends? After all, Noah was very much as he himself had been as a young man, and therefore he was highly worthy of Kizzy's attention, if not her admiration. He wondered: Wasn't there something he could do to influence them into each other's paths? But then Kunta sensed that probably would be the best way to insure their never getting together. He decided, as usual, that it was wisest that he mind his own business – and, as he had heard Bell put it, with 'de sap startin' to rise' within the young pair of them who were living right there in the same slave row, he privately would ask if Allah would consider helping nature to take its course.

82

'You listen here, gal, don' you never lemme hear 'bout you fannin' yo' tail roun' dat Noah no mo'! I take a hik'ry stick to you in a minute.' Headed home, Kunta stopped in his tracks two or three steps from the door of the cabin and stood listening as Bell went on: 'Why, you ain't even turned sixteen yet! What yo' pappy think, you carryin' on like dat?'

He quietly turned and went back down along the path to the privacy of the barn, to consider the implications of what he had heard. 'Fannin' her tail' – around Noah! Bell personally hadn't seen whatever it was, but someone had told her. No doubt it had been Aunt Sukey or Sister Mandy: knowing those old biddies, it wouldn't surprise him if either or both of them had witnessed something completely innocent and made it sound suggestive just to have something to cluck about. But what? From what he'd overheard, Bell probably wouldn't tell him unless it was repeated and she needed him to put a stop to it. It was a kind of thing he'd never dream of querying Bell about, for that was too much like women's gossip.

But what if it *hadn't* been so innocent? Had Kizzy been flaunting herself before Noah? And if she had, what had he done to encourage it? He had seemed to be a young man of honour, of good character – but you never knew.

Kunta wasn't sure how to feel or what to think. In any case, as Bell had said, their daughter was only fifteen, which in the customs of the toubob's land was still too young for her to be thinking about getting married. He realized that he wasn't feeling very African about it, but somehow he just didn't feel ready to think about Kizzy walking around with a big belly as he'd seen on so many girls her age, even younger.

If she *did* marry Noah, though, he thought, at least their child would be black and not one of those pale sasso-borro babies, products of the mothers having been raped by lusting massas or overseers. Kunta thanked Allah that neither his Kizzy nor any other slave-row women ever had faced that horrifying experience, or at least not since he had been there, for countless times he had heard Massa Waller strongly expressing among friends his convictions against white and black bloods being mixed.

The next few weeks, as the opportunity would present, Kunta covertly watched Kizzy's bottom for any signs of wiggling. He never caught her at it, but once or twice both he and she were startled when he came upon her in the cabin twirling round and round, tossing her head and humming dreamily to herself. Kunta also kept a close eye on Noah; he noticed that now – unlike before – Noah and Kizzy would nod and smile whenever they passed each other within the sight of anyone else. The more he mused on it, the more strongly he speculated that they were skilfully concealing their ardour. After a while Kunta decided that there should be no harm in Noah and Kizzy's publicly taking conversational walks together; in his accompanying her to camp meetings, or to the 'dance-ol'-Jenny-down' frolics that were held each summer, where Noah as her partner would surely be preferable to some impudent stranger. Indeed, it was possible that, after another rain or so for them both, Noah might even make Kizzy a good mate.

An awareness began to dawn within Kunta that Noah had begun to observe *him*, just as closely as the other way around, and now Kunta anticipated, nervously, that the boy was trying to muster the nerve to ask if he could marry Kizzy. It was on a Sunday afternoon in early April – Massa Waller had brought a family of guests home with him after church, and Kunta was outside the barn polishing the guests' buggy – when something told him to glance up, and he saw the dark, slender Noah walking purposefully down along the path from slave row.

Reaching Kunta, he spoke without hesitation, as if his words were rehearsed: 'Ol' suh, you's de onliest one I feels like I can trust. I got to tell somebody. I can't live no mo' like dis. I got to run away.'

Kunta was so astounded that at first he could think of nothing to say – he just stood there staring at Noah.

Kunta finally found some words. 'You ain't gon' run nowhere wid Kizzy!' It wasn't a question but a statement.

'Nawsuh, wouldn't want to git 'er in no trouble.'

Kunta felt embarrassed. After a while he said non-committally, 'Reckon sometime ever'body feel like runnin'.'

Noah's eyes inspected his. 'Kizzy tol' me Miss Bell say you run off fo' times.'

Kunta nodded, his face still showing nothing of how he was thinking back on himself at the same age, freshly arrived, so desperately obsessed with *run, run, run* that every day spent waiting and watching for the next half-decent opportunity was an unbearable torment. A swift realization thrust itself into his head that if Kizzy didn't know, as Noah's earlier statement could be interpreted she didn't, then whenever her loved one suddenly disappeared, she was sure to be utterly devastated – so soon again after her crushing heart-break involving the toubob girl. He thought that it just couldn't be helped. He thought that, for numerous reasons, whatever he said to Noah must be considered carefully.

He said gravely, 'Ain't gwine tell you run or don't run. But less'n you ready to die if you gits caught, you ain't ready.'

'Ain't plannin' to git caught,' said Noah. 'I'se heared de main thing is you follows de Nawth Star, an' it's different Quaker white folks an' free niggers he'ps you hide in de daytimes. Den you's free once you hits dat Ohio.'

How little he knows, thought Kunta. How could escaping seem anywhere near so simple? But then he realized that Noah was young – as he had been; also that like most slaves, Noah had seldom set foot beyond the boundaries of his plantation. This was why most of those who ran, field hands especially, were usually captured so soon, bleeding from briar cuts, half starved and stumbling around in forests and swamps full of water moccasins and rattlesnakes. In a rush, Kunta remembered the running, the dogs, the guns, the whips – the axe.

'You don't know what you talkin' 'bout, boy!' he rasped, re-gretting his words almost as they were uttered. 'What I mean to say – it jes' ain't dat easy! You know 'bout dem bloodhounds dey uses to cotch you?'

Noah's right hand slid into his pocket and withdrew a knife. He flicked it open, the blade honed until it gleamed dully. 'I figgers dead dogs don't eat nobody.' Cato had said that Noah feared nothing. 'Jes' can't let nothin' stop me,' Noah said, closing the knife and returning it into his pocket.

'Well, if you gwine run, you gwine run,' said Kunta.

'Don't know 'zactly when,' said Noah. 'Jes' knows I got to go.'

Kunta re-emphasized awkwardly, 'Jes' make sho' Kizzy ain't in none o' dis.'

Noah didn't seem offended. His eyes met Kunta's squarely. 'Naw-suh.' He hesitated. 'But when I gits Nawth, I means to work an' buy her free.' He paused. 'You ain't gon' tell her none o' dis, is you?'

Now Kunta hesitated. Then he said, 'Dat 'tween you and her.'

'I tell her in good time,' said Noah.

Impulsively, Kunta grasped the young man's hand between both of his own. 'I hopes you makes it.'

'Well, I see you!' said Noah, and he turned to walk back towards slave row.

Sitting that night in the cabin's front room, staring into the low flames of the hickory log burning in the fireplace, Kunta wore a faraway expression that made both Bell and Kizzy know out of past experiences that it would be futile to make any effort to talk with him. Quietly Bell knitted. Kizzy was as usual hunched over the table practising her writing. At sun-up, Kunta decided he would ask Allah to grant Noah good luck. He thought afresh that if Noah did get away, it would yet again crush utterly Kizzy's trusting faith that already had been wounded so badly by Missy Anne. He glanced up and watched his precious Kizzy's face as her lips moved silently, following her finger across a page. The lives of all black people in the toubob land seemed full of suffering, but he wished he could spare her some of it.

83

It was a week after Kizzy's sixteenth birthday, the early morning of the first Monday of October, when the slave-row field hands were gathering as usual to leave for their day's work, when someone asked curiously, 'Where Noah at?' Kunta, who happened to be standing near by talking to Cato, knew immediately that he was gone. He saw heads glancing around, Kizzy's among them, straining to maintain a mask of casual surprise. Their eyes met – she had to look away.

'Thought he was out here early wid you,' said Noah's mother Ada to Cato.

'Naw, I was aimin' to give 'im de debbil fo' sleepin' late,' said Cato.

Cato went banging his fist at the closed door of the cabin, once occupied by the old gardener, but which Noah had inherited recently on his eighteenth birthday. Jerking the door open, Cato charged inside, shouting angrily, 'Noah!' He came out looking worried. 'Ain't like 'im,' he said quietly. Then he ordered everyone to go quickly and search their cabins, the toilet, the store-rooms, the fields.

All the others ran off in all directions; Kunta volunteered to search the barn. 'NOAH! NOAH!' he called loudly for the benefit of any who might hear, although he knew there was no need of it, as the animals in their stalls stopped chewing their morning hay to look at him oddly. Then, peering from the door and seeing no one coming that way, Kunta hastened back inside to climb quickly to the hayloft, where he prostrated himself and made his second appeal to Allah for Noah's successful escape.

Cato worriedly dispatched the rest of the field hands off to their work, telling them that he and the fiddler would join them shortly; the fiddler had wisely volunteered to help with the fieldwork ever since his income from playing for dances had fallen off.

'B'lieve he done run,' the fiddler muttered to Kunta as they stood in the backyard.

As Kunta grunted, Bell said, 'He ain't never been missin', an' he don't slip off nights.'

Then Cato said what was uppermost in all of their minds. 'Gwine have to tell massa, Lawd have mercy!' After a hurried consultation, Bell recommended that Massa Waller not be told until after he had eaten his breakfast, ' 'case de boy done jes' eased off somewhere an' got scairt to slip back fo' it's dark again, less'n dem road paterollers cotches 'im.'

Bell served the massa his favourite breakfast – canned peaches in heavy cream, hickory-smoked fried ham, scrambled eggs, grits, heated apple butter and buttermilk biscuits – and waited for him to ask for his second cup of coffee before speaking.

'Massa—' she swallowed, '—Massa, Cato ax me to tell you look like dat boy Noah ain't here dis mawnin'!'

The massa set down his cup, frowning. 'Where is he, then? Are you trying to tell me he's off drunk or tomcatting somewhere, and you think he'll slip back today, or are you saying you think he's trying to run?'

'All us sayin', Massa,' Bell quavered, 'is seem like he ain't here, an' us done searched eve'ywheres.'

Massa Waller studied his coffee cup. 'I'll give him until tonight – no, tomorrow morning – before I take action.'

'Massa, he a good boy, born and bred right here on yo' place, an' work good all his life, ain't never give you or nobody a minute's trouble—'

He looked levelly at Bell. 'If he's trying to run, he'll be sorry.'

'Yassuh, Massa.' Bell fled to the yard, where she told the others what the massa had said. But no sooner had Cato and the fiddler hurried off towards the fields than Massa Waller called Bell back and ordered the buggy.

All day long, as he drove him from one patient to the next, Kunta soared from exhilaration – as he thought of Noah running – to anguish as he thought of the thorns and the briars and the dogs. And he felt what hope and suffering Kizzy must be enduring.

At that night's huddled gathering, everyone spoke barely above whispers.

'Dat boy done lef' here. Fo' now, I done seed it in his eyes,' Aunt Sukey said.

'Well, I knows he ain't no young'un to jes' steal off gittin' drunk, no suh!' said Sister Mandy.

Noah's mother Ada was hoarse from a day of weeping. 'My baby sho' ain't never talked to me nothin' 'bout no runnin'! Lawd, y'all reckon massa gwine sell 'im?' No one chose to reply.

When they returned to their cabin, Kizzy burst into tears the moment she got inside; Kunta felt helpless and tongue-tied. But without a word, Bell went over to the table, put her arms around her sobbing daughter, and pulled her head against her stomach.

Tuesday morning came, still with no sign of Noah, and Massa Waller ordered Kunta to drive him to the county seat, where he went directly to the Spotsylvania jailhouse. After about half an hour, he came out with the sheriff, ordering Kunta brusquely to tie the sheriff's horse behind the buggy and then to drive them home. 'We'll be dropping the sheriff off at the Creek Road,' said the massa.

'So many niggers runnin' these days, can't hardly keep track – they'd ruther take their chances in the woods than get sold down South—' The sheriff was talking from when the buggy started rolling.

'Since I've had a plantation,' said Massa Waller, 'I've never sold one of mine unless my rules were broken, and they know that well.'

'But it's mighty rare niggers appreciate good masters, Doctor, you know that,' said the sheriff. 'You say this boy around eighteen? Well, I'd guess if he's like most field hands his age, there's fair odds he's tryin' to make it North.' Kunta stiffened. 'If he was a house nigger, they're generally slicker, faster talkers, they like to try passin' themselves off as free niggers or tell the road patrollers they're on their master's errands and lost their travelling passes, tryin' to make it to Richmond or some other big city where they can easier hide among so many niggers and maybe find jobs.' The sheriff paused. 'Besides his mammy on your place, this boy of yours got any other kin livin' anywheres he might be tryin' to get to?'

'None that I know of.'

'Well, would you happen to know if he's got some gal somewhere, because these young bucks get their sap risin', they'll leave your mule in the field and take off.'

'Not to my knowledge,' said the massa. 'But there's a gal on my place, my cook's young'un, she's still fairly young, fifteen or sixteen, if I guess correctly. I don't know if they've been haystacking or not.'

Kunta nearly quit breathing.

'I've known 'em to have pickaninnies at the age of twelve!' the sheriff chortled. 'Plenty of these young nigger wenches even draw white men, and nigger boys'll do anything!'

Through churning outrage, Kunta heard Massa Waller's abrupt chilliness. 'I have the least possible personal contact with my slaves, and neither know nor concern myself regarding their personal affairs!'

'Yes, yes, of course,' said the sheriff quickly.

But then the massa's tone eased. 'Along your line of thinking, though, this boy could have slipped off to see some other plantation gal. I don't know, and of course the others wouldn't say if they did. In fact, anything might have happened – some fight, perhaps; he could be half dead somewhere. It's even possible that some of these slave-stealing poor whites could have grabbed him. That's been going on around here, as you know; even some of the more un-scrupulous traders engage in it. Again, I don't know. But I'm told this is the boy's first time being unaccounted for.'

His general manner now more careful, the sheriff said. 'You told me he was born on your place and never travelled much?'

'I'd guess he wouldn't have any idea how to get even to Richmond, let alone North,' said the massa.

'Niggers exchange a lot of information, though,' the sheriff said. 'We've picked up some and beat it out of them that they practically had maps in their heads of where they'd been told to run and where to hide. A lot of this can be traced to nigger-loving white people like the Quakers and Methodists. But since he ain't never been nowhere, ain't never tried runnin' before, and ain't never give you no other trouble to now, sounds like to me a good bet a couple more nights in the woods might bring him back, scared to death and half starved. A nigger's powerfully moved by a hungry belly. And that'll save you spending to advertise in the *Gazette* or hiring some of these nigger catchers with their dogs to track him. He just don't sound to my experience like one of them hard, outlaw niggers that's slipping around in and out of the swamps and woods right now, killing people's cattle and hogs like they would rabbits.'

'I hope you're right,' said Massa Waller, 'but whatever the case, he's broken my rules by leaving without permission to begin with, so I'll be selling him South immediately.' Kunta's firsts squeezed the reins so tightly that his nails dug into his palms. 'Then that's a good twelve to fifteen hundred dollars you've got runnin' around loose somewhere,' said the sheriff. 'You've written me his description, I'll sure get it to the county road patrollers, and if we pick 'im up – or we hear anything – I'll let you know right away.'

Saturday morning after breakfast, Kunta was curry-combing a horse outside the barn when he thought he heard Cato's whip-poorwill whistle. Cocking his head, he heard it again. He tied the horse quickly to a nearby post and cripped rapidly up the path to the cabin. From its front window he could see almost from where the main road intersected with the big-house driveway. Inside the big house, he knew that Cato's call had also alerted Bell and Kizzy.

Then he saw the wagon rolling down the driveway – and with surging alarm recognized the sheriff at the reins. Merciful Allah, had Noah been caught? As he watched the sheriff dismount, Kunta's long-trained instincts tugged at him to hasten out and provide the visitor's winded horse with water and a rubdown, but it was as if he were paralysed where he stood, staring, from the cabin window, as the sheriff hurried up the big-house front steps two at a time.

Only a few minutes passed before Kunta saw Bell almost stumbling out the back door. She started running – and Kunta was seized with a horrible premonition the instant before she nearly snatched their cabin door off its hinges.

Her face was twisted, tear-streaked. 'Sheriff an' massa talkin' to Kizzy!' she squealed.

The words numbed him. For a moment he just stared disbelievingly at her, but then violently seizing and shaking her, he demanded, 'What he want?'

Her voice rising, choking, breaking, she managed to tell him that the sheriff was scarcely in the house before the massa had yelled for Kizzy to come from tidying his room upstairs. When I heard him holler at her from de kitchen, I flew to git in de drawin' room hall-way where I always listen from, but I couldn't make out nothin' clear 'cept he was mighty mad—' Bell gasped and swallowed. 'Den heared massa ringin' my bell, an' I run back to look like I was comin' from de cookhouse. But massa was a waitin' in de do'way, wid his hand' holdin' de knob behin' him. Ain't never seed 'im look like he did at me. He tol' me col' as ice to git out'n de house an' stay out 'til I'm sent for!' Bell moved to the small window, staring at the big house, unable to believe that what she had just said had really happened. 'Lawd Gawd, what in de worl' sheriff want wid my chile?' she asked incredulously.

Kunta's mind was clawing desperately for something to do. Could he rush out to the fields, at least to alert those who were chopping there? But his instincts said that anything could happen with him gone.

As Bell went through the curtains, into their bedroom, beseeching Jesus at the top of her lungs, he could barely restrain himself from raging in and yelling that she must see now what he had been trying to tell her for nearly forty rains about being so gullible, deluded, and deceived about the goodness of the massa – or any other touob.

'Gwine back in dere!' cried Bell suddenly. She came charging through the curtain and out the door.

Kunta watched as she disappeared inside the kitchen. What was she going to do? He ran out after her and peered in through the screen door. The kitchen was empty and the inside door was swinging shut. He went inside, silencing the screen door as it closed, and tiptoed across the kitchen. Standing there with one hand on the door, the other clenched, he strained his ears for the slightest sound – but all he could hear was his own laboured breathing.

Then he heard. 'Massa?' Bell had called softly. There was no answer.

'*Massa?*' she called again, louder, sharply.

He heard the drawing-room door open.

'Where my Kizzy, Massa?'

'She's in my safekeeping,' he said stonily. 'We're not having another one running off.'

'I jes' don't understan' you, Massa.' Bell spoke so softly that Kunta could hardly hear her. 'De chile ain't been out'n yo' yard, hardly.'

The massa started to say something, then stopped. 'It's possible you really don't know what she's done,' he said. 'The boy Noah has been captured, but not before severely knifing the two road patrolmen who challenged a false travelling pass he was carrying. After being subdued by force, he finally confessed that the pass had been written not by me but by your daughter. She has admitted it to the sheriff.'

There was silence for a long, agonizing moment, then Kunta heard a scream and running footsteps. As he whipped open the door, Bell came bolting past him – shoving him aside with the force of a man – and out the back door. The hall was empty, the drawing-room door shut. He ran out after her, catching up with her at the cabin door.

'Massa gon' sell Kizzy, I knows it!' Bell started screaming, and inside him something snapped. 'Gwine git 'er!' he choked out, cripping back towards the big house and into the kitchen as fast as he could go, with Bell not far behind. Wild with fury, he snatched open the inside door and went charging down the unspeakably forbidden hallway.

The massa and the sheriff spun with disbelieving faces as the drawing-room door came jerking open. Kunta halted there abruptly, his eyes burning with murder. Bell screamed from behind him, 'Where our baby at? We come to git 'er!'

Kunta saw the sheriff's right hand sliding towards his holstered gun as the massa seethed, '*Get out!*'

'You niggers can't hear?' The sheriff's hand was withdrawing the pistol, and Kunta was tensed to plunge for it – just as Bell's voice trembled behind him 'Yassa' – and he felt her desperately pulling his arm. Then his feet were moving backwards through the doorway – and suddenly the door was slammed behind them, a key clicking sharply in the lock.

As Kunta crouched with his wife in the hall, drowning in his shame, they heard some tense, muted conversation between the massa and the sheriff ... then the sound of feet moving, scuffling faintly ... then Kizzy's crying, and the sound of the front door slamming shut.

'Kizzy! Kizzy chile! Lawd Gawd, don't let 'em sell my Kizzy!' As she burst out the back door with Kunta behind her, Bell's screams reached away out to where the field hands were, who came racing. Cato arrived in time to see Bell screeching insanely, springing up and down with Kunta bear-hugging her to the ground. Massa Waller was descending the front steps ahead of the sheriff, who was hauling Kizzy after him – weeping and jerking herself backwards – at the end of a chain.

'*Mammy! Maaaaaaamy!*' Kizzy screamed.

Bell and Kunta leaped up from the ground and went raging around the side of the house like two charging lions. The sheriff drew his gun and pointed it straight at Bell: she stopped in her tracks. She stared at Kizzy. Bell tore the question from her throat: 'You done dis thing deys says?' They all watched Kizzy's agony as her reddened, weeping eyes gave her answer in a mute way – darting imploringly from Bell and Kunta to the sheriff and the massa – but she said nothing.

'O my Lawd Gawd!' Bell shrieked. 'Massa, please have mercy! She ain't meant to do it! She ain't knowed what she was doin'! Missy Anne de one teached 'er to write!'

Massa Waller spoke glacially. 'The law is the law. She's broken my rules. She's committed a felony. She may have aided in a murder. I'm told one of those white men may die.'

'Ain't *her* cut de man, Massa! Massa, she worked for you ever since she big 'nough to carry your slop jar! An' I done cooked an' waited on you han' an' foot over forty years, an' he ...' gesturing at Kunta, she stuttered, 'he done driv you eve'ywhere you been for near 'bout dat long. Massa, don' all dat count for sump'n?'

Massa Waller would not look directly at her. 'You were doing your jobs. She's going to be sold – that's all there is to it.'

'Jes' cheap, low-class white folks splits up families!' shouted Bell. 'You ain't dat kin'!'

Angrily, Massa Waller gestured to the sheriff, who began to wrench Kizzy roughly towards the wagon.

Bell blocked their path. 'Den sell me an' 'er pappy wid 'er! Don' split us up!'

'Get out of the way!' barked the sheriff, roughly shoving her aside.

Bellowing, Kunta sprang forwards like a leopard, pummelling the sheriff to the ground with his fists.

'Save me, Fa!' Kizzy screamed. He grabbed her around the waist and began pulling frantically at her chain.

When the sheriff's pistol butt crashed above his ear, Kunta's head seemed to explode as he crumpled to his knees. Bell lunged towards the sheriff, but his outflung arm threw her off balance, falling heavily as he dumped Kizzy into the back of his wagon and snapped a lock on her chain. Leaping nimbly onto the seat, the sheriff lashed the horse, whose forward jerk sent the wagon lurching as Kunta clambered up. Dazed, head pounding, ignoring the pistol, he went scrambling after the wagon as it gathered speed.

'*Missy Anne! ... Missy Annnnnnnnnnnne!*' Kizzy was screeching it at the top of her voice. '*Missy Annnnnnnnnnnnnnnnnne!*' Again and again, the screams came; they seemed to hang in the air behind the wagon swiftly rolling towards the main road.

When Kunta began stumbling, gasping for breath, the wagon was a half mile away; when he halted, for a long time he stood looking after it until the dust had settled and the road stretched empty as far as he could see.

The massa turned and walked very quickly with his head down back into the house, past Bell huddled sobbing by the bottom step. As if Kunta were sleepwalking, he came cripping slowly back up the driveway – when an African remembrance flashed into his mind, and near the front of the house he bent down and started peering around. Determining the clearest prints that Kizzy's bare feet had left in the dust, scooping up the double handful containing those footprints, he went rushing towards the cabin: the ancient forefathers said that precious dust kept in some safe place would insure Kizzy's return to where she made the footprints. He burst through the cabin's open door, his eyes sweeping the room and falling upon his gourd on a shelf containing his pebbles. Springing over there, in the instant before opening his cupped hands to drop in the dirt, suddenly he knew the truth: his Kizzy was gone; she would not return. He would never see his Kizzy again.

His face contorting, Kunta flung his dust towards the cabin's roof. Tears bursting from his eyes, snatching his heavy gourd up high over his head, his mouth wide in a soundless scream, he hurtled the gourd down with all his strength, and it shattered against the packed-earth floor, his 662 pebbles representing each month of his 55 rains flying out, ricocheting wildly in all directions.

84

Weak and dazed, Kizzy lay in the darkness, on some burlap sacks, in the cabin where she had been pushed when the mulecart arrived shortly after dusk. She wondered vaguely what time it was; it seemed that night had gone on forever. She began tossing and twisting, trying to force herself to think of something – anything – that didn't terrify her. Finally, for the hundredth time, she tried to concentrate on figuring out how to get 'up Nawth', where she had heard so often that black people could find freedom if they escaped. If she went the wrong way, she might wind up 'deep Souf', where people said massas and overseers were even worse than Massa Waller. Which way was 'nawth'? She didn't know. I'm going to escape anyway, she swore bitterly.

It was as if a pin pricked her spine when she heard the first creaking of the cabin's door. Springing upright and backwards in the dark, she saw the figure entering furtively, with a cupped hand shielding a candle's flame. Above it she recognized the face of the white man who had purchased her, and she saw that his other hand was holding up a short-handled whip, cocked ready for use. But it was the glazed leer on the white man's face that froze her where she stood.

'Rather not have to hurt you none,' he said, the smell of his liquored breath nearly suffocating her. She sensed his intent. He wanted to do with her what Pappy did with Mammy when she heard strange sounds from their curtained-off room after they thought she was asleep. He wanted to do what Noah had urged her to do when they had gone walking down along the fencerow, and which she almost had given in to, several times, especially the night before he had left, but he had frightened her too much when he exclaimed hoarsely, 'I wants you wid my baby!' She thought that this white man must be insane to think that she was going to permit him to do that with her.

'Ain't got no time to play with you now!' The white man's words were slurred. Kizzy's eyes were judging how to bolt past him to flee into the night – but he seemed to read that impulse, moving a little bit sideways, not taking his gaze off her as he leaned over and tilted the candle to drain its melted wax onto the seat of the cabin's single broken chair; then the small flame flickered upright. Inching slowly backwards, Kizzy felt her shoulders brushing the cabin's wall. 'Ain't you got sense enough to know I'm your new massa?' He watched her, grimacing some kind of a smile. 'You a fair-lookin' wench. Might even set you free, if I like you enough—'

When he sprang, seizing Kizzy, she wrenched loose, shrieking, as with an angry curse he brought the whip cracking down across the back of her neck. 'I'll take the hide off you!' Lunging like a wild woman, Kizzy clawed at his contorted face, but slowly he forced her roughly to the floor. Pushing back upwards, she was shoved down again. Then the man was on his knees beside her, one of his hands choking back her screams – 'Please, Massa, please!' – the other stuffing dirty burlap sacking into her mouth until she gagged. As she flailed her arms in agony and arched her back to shake him off, he banged her head against the floor, again, again, again, then began slapping her – more and more excitedly – until Kizzy felt her dress being snatched upwards, her undergarments being ripped. Frantically thrashing, the sack in her mouth muffling her cries, she felt his hands fumbling upwards between her thighs, finding, fingering her private parts, squeezing and spreading them. Striking her another numbing blow, the man jerked down his suspenders, made motions at his trousers' front. Then came the searing pain as he forced his way into her, and Kizzy's senses seemed to explode. On and on it went, until finally she lost consciousness.

In the early dawn, Kizzy blinked her eyes open. She was engulfed in shame to find a young black woman bending over her and sponging her private parts gently with a rag and warm, soapy water. When

Kizzy's nose told her that she had also soiled herself, she shut her eyes in embarrassment, soon feeling the woman cleaning her there as well. When Kizzy slitted her eyes open again, she saw that the woman's face seemed as expressionless as if she were washing clothes, as if this were but another of the many tasks she had been called upon to perform in her life. Finally laying a clean towel over Kizzy's loins, she glanced up at Kizzy's face. 'Reckon you ain't feel like talkin' none now,' the woman said quietly, gathering up the dirty rags and her waterpail, preparing to leave. Clutching these things in the crook of one arm, she bent again and used her free hand to draw up a burlap sack to cover most of Kizzy's body. ' 'Fore long, I bring you sump'n to eat—' she said, and went on out of the cabin door.

Kizzy lay there feeling as if she were suspended in midair. She tried to deny to herself that the unspeakable, unthinkable thing had really happened, but the lancing pains of her torn privates reminded her that it had. She felt a deep uncleanness, a disgrace that could never be erased. She tried shifting her position, but the pains seemed to spread. Holding her body still, she clutched the sack tightly about her, as if somehow to cocoon herself against any more outrage, but the pains grew worse.

Kizzy's mind raced back across the past four days and nights. She could still see her parents' terrified faces, still hear their helpless cries as she was rushed away. She could still feel herself struggling to escape from the white trader whom the Spotsylvania County sheriff had turned her over to; she had nearly slipped free after pleading that she had to relieve herself. Finally they had reached some small town where – after long, bitterly angry haggling – the trader at last had sold her to this new massa, who had awaited the nightfall to violate her. Mammy! Pappy! If only screaming for them could reach them – but they didn't even know where she was. And who knows what might have happened to them? She knew that Massa Waller would never sell anyone he owned *'less'n dey breaks his rules'*. But in trying to stop the massa from selling *her*, they must have broken a dozen of those rules.

And Noah, what of Noah? Somewhere beaten to death? Again, it came back to Kizzy vividly, Noah demanding angrily that to prove her love, she must use her writing ability to forge a travelling pass for him to show if he should be seen, stopped, and questioned by patrollers or any other suspicious whites. She remembered the grim determination etched on his face as he pledged to her that once he got up North, with just a little money saved from a job he would quickly find, 'Gwine steal back here an' slip you Nawth, too, fo' de res' our days togedder.' She sobbed anew. She knew she would never see him again. Or her parents. Unless . . .

Her thoughts leaped with a sudden hope! Missy Anne had sworn since girlhood that when she married some handsome, rich young massa, Kizzy alone must be her personal maid, later to care for the houseful of children. Was it *possible* that when she found out Kizzy was gone, she had gone screaming, ranting, pleading to Massa Waller? Missy Anne could sway him more than anyone else on earth! Could the massa have sent out some men searching for the slave dealer, to learn where he had sold her, to buy her back?

But soon now a new freshet of grief poured from Kizzy. She realized that the sheriff knew exactly who the slave dealer was; they would certainly have traced her by now! She felt even more desperately lost, even more totally abandoned. Later, when she had no more tears left to shed, she lay imploring God to destroy her, if He felt she deserved all this, just because she loved Noah. Feeling some slickness seeping between her upper legs, Kizzy knew that she was continuing to bleed. But the pain had subsided to a throbbing.

When the cabin's door came creaking open again, Kizzy had sprung up and was rearing backwards against the wall before she realized that it was the woman. She was carrying a steaming small pot, with a bowl and spoon, and Kizzy slumped back down onto the dirt floor as the woman put the pot on the table, then spooned some food into the bowl, which she placed down alongside Kizzy. Kizzy acted as if she saw neither the food nor the woman, who squatted beside her and began talking as matter-of-factly as if they had known each other for years.

'I'se de big-house cook. My name Malizy. What your'n?'

Finally Kizzy felt stupid not to answer. 'It Kizzy, Miss Malizy.'

The woman made an approving grunt. 'You sounds well-raised.' She glanced at the untouched stew in the bowl. 'I reckon you know you let vittles git cold dey don't do you no good.' Miss Malizy sounded almost like Sister Mandy or Aunt Sukey.

Hesitantly picking up the spoon, Kizzy tasted the stew, then began to eat some of it, slowly.

'How ol' you is?' asked Miss Malizy.

'I'se sixteen, ma'am.'

'Massa boun' for hell jes' sho's he born!' exclaimed Miss Malizy, half under her breath. Looking at Kizzy, she said, 'Jes' well's to tell you massa one dem what loves nigger womens, 'specially young'uns like you is. He use to mess wid me, I ain't but roun' nine years older'n you, but he quit after he brung missy here an' made me de cook, workin' right dere in de house where she is, thanks be to Gawd!' Miss Malizy grimaced. 'Speck you gwine be seein' 'im in here regular.'

Seeing Kizzy's hand fly to her mouth, Miss Malizy said, 'Honey, you jes' well's realize you's a nigger woman. De kind of white man massa, is, you either give in, or he gwine make you wish you had, one way or 'nother. An' lemme tell you, dis massa a mean thing if you cross 'im. Fact, ain't never knowed nobody git mad de way he do. Ever'thing can be gwine 'long jes' fine, den let jes' anythin' happen dat rile 'im,' Miss Malizy snapped her fingers, 'quick as dat he can fly red hot an' ack like he done gone crazy!'

Kizzy's thoughts were racing. Once darkness fell, before he came again, she must escape. But it was as if Miss Malizy read her mind. 'Don't you even start thinkin' 'bout runnin' nowhere, honey! He jes' have you hunted down wid dem blood dogs, an' you in a worser mess. Jes' calm yo'self. De next fo', five days he ain't gon' be here nohow. Him an' his ol' nigger chicken trainer already done left for one dem big chicken fights halfway crost de state.' Miss Malizy paused. 'Massa don't care 'bout nothin' much as dem fightin' chickens o' his'n.'

She went on talking nonstop – about how the massa, who had grown to adulthood as a po' cracker, bought a twenty-five-cent raffle ticket that won him a good fighting rooster, which got him started on the road to becoming one of the area's more successful game-cock owners.

Kizzy finally interrupted. 'Don't he sleep wid his missis?'

'Sho' he do!' said Miss Malizy. 'He jes' love womens. You won't never see much o' her 'cause she scairt to death o' 'im, an' she keep real quiet an' stay close. She whole lot younger'n he is; she was jes' fo'teen, same kind of po' cracker he was, when he married 'er an' brung 'er here. But she done foun' out he don't care much for her as he do his chickens—' As Miss Malizy continued talking about the massa, his wife, and his chickens, Kizzy's thoughts drifted away once again to thoughts of escape.

'Gal! Is you payin' me 'tention?'

'Yes'm,' she replied quickly. Miss Malizy's frown eased. 'Well, I specks you better, since I'se 'quaintin you wid where you is!'

Briefly she studied Kizzy. 'Where you come from, anyhow?' Kizzy said from Spotsylvania County, Virginia. 'Ain't never heared of it! Anyhow, dis here's Caswell County in North Ca'liny.' Kizzy's expression showed that she had no idea where that was, though she had often heard of North Carolina, and she had the impression that it was somewhere near Virginia.

'Look here, does you even know massa's name?' asked Miss Malizy. Kizzy looked blank. 'Him's Massa Tom Lea—' She reflected a moment. 'Reckon now dat make you Kizzy Lea.'

'My name Kizzy Waller!' Kizzy exclaimed in protest. Then, with a flash, she remembered that all of this had happened to her at the hands of Massa Waller, whose name she bore, and she began weeping. 'Don't take on so, honey!' exclaimed Miss Malizy. 'You sho' knows niggers takes whoever's dey massa's name. Nigger names don't make no difference nohow, jes' sump'n to call 'em—'

Kizzy said, 'My pappy real name Kunta Kinte. He a African.'

'You don't say!' Miss Malizy appeared taken aback. 'I'se heared my great-gran-daddy was one dem Africans, too! My mammy say her mammy told her he was blacker'n tar, wid scars zigzaggin' down both cheeks. But my mammy never said his name—' Miss Malizy paused. 'You know yo' mammy, too?'

' 'Cose I does. My mammy name Bell. She a big-house cook like you is. An' my pappy drive de massa's buggy – leas' he did.'

'You jes' come from bein' wid yo' mammy an' pappy both?' Miss Malizy couldn't believe it. 'Lawd, ain't many us gits to know *both* our folks fo' somebody git sol' away!'

Sensing that Miss Malizy was preparing to leave, suddenly dreading being left alone again, Kizzy sought a way to extend the conversation. 'You talks a whole lot like my mammy,' she offered. Miss Malizy seemed startled, then very pleased. 'I specks she a good Christian woman like I is.' Hesitantly, Kizzy asked something that had crossed her mind. 'What kin' of work dey gwine have me doin' here, Miss Malizy?'

Miss Malizy seemed astounded at the question. 'What you gon' *do*?' she demanded. 'Massa ain't tol' you how many niggers here?' Kizzy shook her head. 'Honeychile, you makin' zactly five! An' dat's countin' Mingo, de ol' nigger dat live down 'mongst de chickens. So it's me cookin', washin', an' housekeepin', an' Sister Sarah an' Uncle Pompey workin' in de fiel', where you sho' gwine go too – dat you is!'

Miss Malizy's brows lifted at the dismay on Kizzy's face. 'What work you done where you was?'

'Cleanin' in de big house, an' helpin' my mammy in de kitchen,' Kizzy answered in a faltering voice.

'Figgered sump'n like dat when I seen dem soft hands of your'n! Well, you sho' better git ready for some calluses an' corns soon's massa git back!' Miss Malizy then seemed to feel that she should soften a bit. 'Po' thing! Listen here to me, you been used to one dem rich massa's places. But dis here one dem po' crackers what scrabbled an' scraped till he got holt a li'l lan' an' built a house dat ain't nothin' but a big front to make 'em look better off dan dey is. Plenty crackers like dat roun' here. Dey got a sayin', "Farm a hunnud acres wid fo' niggers." Well, he too tight to buy even dat many. 'Cose, he ain't got but eighty-some acres, an' farmin' jes' 'nough of dat to lay claim to bein' a massa. His big thing is his hunnud an' some fightin' chickens dat Mingo nigger helpin' him raise an' train to bet on in fights. Only thing massa spen' any money on is dem chickens. He always swearin' to missy one day dem chickens gwine see 'em rich. He git drunk an' tell 'er one dese days he gwine buil' her a house so big it have six columns crost de front, an' be two stories tall, an' even finer'n de houses o' dese real rich massas hereabouts what snubs 'em so bad, like dey still de po' crackers dey started out! Fact, massa claim he savin' up for de day he buil' dat fine house. *Humph!* Might, for all I know. I know he too tight even to have a stableboy, let alone a nigger to drive 'im places like near 'bout all massas has. He hitch up his own buggy an' wagon both, saddle his own hoss, an' he drive hisself. Honey, de only reason *I* ain't out in de fiel' is missis can't hardly cook water, an' he love to eat. 'Sides dat, he likes de looks of havin' a house servin nigger for when dey guests come. When he git to drinkin' out somewhere, he *love* 'vitin' in guests for dinner, tryin' to put on de dog, an' 'specially if he been winnin' pretty good, bettin' on his roosters at dem cockfights. But anyhow, he finally had to see wasn't no way jes' Uncle Pompey an' Sister Sarah could farm much as he like to plant, an' he *had* to git somebody else. Dat's how come he bought you—' Miss Malizy paused. 'You know how much you cost?'

Kizzy said weakly, 'No'm.'

'Well, I reckon six to seb'n hundred dollars, considerin' de prices I'se heard him say niggers costin' nowdays, an' you bein' strong an' young, lookin' like a good breeder, too, dat'll bring 'im free pickaninnies.'

With Kizzy again speechless, Miss Malizy moved closer to the door and stopped. 'Fact, I wouldn't o' been surprised if massa stuck you in wid one dem stud niggers some rich massas keeps on dey places an' hires out. But it look like to me he figgerin' on breedin' you hisself.'

85

The conversation was short.

'Massa, I gwine have a baby.'

'Well, what you expectin' me to do about it? I know you better not start playin' sick, tryin' to get out of workin'!'

But he did start coming to Kizzy's cabin less often as her belly began to grow. Slaving out under the hot sun, Kizzy went through dizzy spells as well as morning sickness in the course of her painful initiation to fieldwork. Torturous blisters on both her palms would burst, fill with fluid again, then burst again from their steady friction against the rough, heavy handle of her hoe. Chopping along, trying to keep not too far behind the experienced, short, stout, black Uncle Pompey, and the wiry, light-brown-skinned Sister Sarah – both of whom she felt were still deciding what to think of her – she would strain to recall everything she had ever heard her mammy say about the having of young'uns. She felt she'd give anything if Bell could be here beside her now. Despite her humiliation at being great with child and having to face her mammy – who had warned repeatedly of the disgrace that could befall her 'if'n you keeps messin' roun' wid dat Noah an' winds up too close' – Kizzy knew she'd understand that it hadn't been her fault, and she'd let her know the things she needed to know.

She could almost hear Bell's voice telling her sadly, as she had so often, what she believed had caused the tragic deaths of both the wife and baby of Massa Waller: 'Po' li'l thing was jes' built too small to birth dat great big baby!' Was she herself built big enough? Kizzy wondered frantically. Was there any way to tell? She remembered once when she and Missy Anne had stood goggle-eyed, watching a cow deliver a calf, then their whispering that despite what grown-ups told them about storks bringing babies, maybe mothers had to squeeze them out through their privates in the same gruesome way.

The older women, Miss Malizy and Sister Sarah, seemed to take hardly any notice of her steadily enlarging belly – and breasts – so Kizzy decided angrily that it would be as big a waste of time to confide her fears to them as it would to Massa Lea. Certainly he couldn't have been less concerned as he rode around the plantation on his horse, yelling threats at anyone he felt wasn't working fast enough.

When the baby came – in the winter of 1806 – Sister Sarah served as the midwife. After what seemed an eternity of moaning, screaming, feeling as she were ripping apart, Kizzy lay bathed in sweat, staring in wonder at the wriggling infant grinning Sister Sarah was holding up. It was a boy – but his skin seemed to be almost high yaller.

Seeing Kizzy's alarm, Sister Sarah assured her, 'New babies takes leas' a month to darken to dey full colour, honey!' But Kizzy's apprehension deepened as she examined her baby several times every day; when a full month passed, she knew that the child's permanent colour was going to be at best a pecan-coloured brown.

She remembered her mammy's proud boast, 'Ain't nothin' but black niggers here on massa's place.' And she tried not to think about 'sasso-borro', the name her ebony-black father – his mouth curled in scorn – used to call those with mulatto skin. She was grateful that they weren't there to see – and share – her shame. But she knew that she'd never be able to hold her head up again even if they never saw the child, for all anyone had to do was compare her colour and the baby's to know what had happened – and with whom. She thought of Noah and felt even more ashamed. 'Dis our *las'* chance fo' I leaves, baby, how *come* you can't?' she heard him say again. She wished desperately that she had, that this was Noah's baby; at least it would be black.

'Gal, what's de *matter* you ain't happy, great big ol' fine chile like dat!' said Miss Malizy one morning, noticing how sad Kizzy looked and how awkwardly she was holding the baby, almost at her side, as if she found it hard even to *look* at her child. In a rush of understanding, Miss Malizy blurted, 'Honey, what you lettin' bother you ain't no need to worry 'bout. Don't make no difference, 'cause des days an' times don't nobody care, ain't even pay no 'tention. It gittin' to be near 'bout many mulattoes as it is black niggers like us. It's jes' de way things is, dat's all—' Miss Malizy's eyes were pleading with Kizzy. 'An' you can be sho' massa ain't never gwine claim de chile, not no way atall. He jes' see a young'un he glad he ain't had to pay for, dat he gwine stick out in de fields same as you is. So de only thing for you to feel is dat big, fine baby's *your'n*, honey – dat's all it is to it!'

That way of seeing things helped Kizzy to collect herself, at least somewhat. 'But what gwine happen,' she asked, 'when sometimes or 'nother missis sho' catch sight dis chile, Miss Malizy?'

'She know he ain't no good! I wisht I had a penny for every white woman knows dey husbands got chilluns by niggers. Main thing, I speck missis be jealous 'cause seem like *she* ain't able to have none.'

The next night Massa Lea came to the cabin – about a month after the baby was born – he bent over the bed and held his candle close to the face of the sleeping baby. 'Hmmmm. Ain't bad-looking. Good-sized, too.' With his forefinger, he jiggled one of the clenched, tiny fists and said, turning to Kizzy, 'All right. This weekend will make enough time off. Monday you go back to the field.'

'But Massa, I ought to stay to nuss 'im!' she said foolishly.

His rage exploded in her ears. 'Shut up and do as you're told! You're through being pampered by some fancy Virginia blueblood! Take that pickaninny with you to the field, or I'll keep that baby and sell you out of here so quick your head swims!'

Scared silly, Kizzy burst into weeping at even the thought of being sold away from her child. '*Yassuh*, Massa!' she cried, cringing. Seeing her crushed submission, his anger quickly abated, but then Kizzy began to sense – with disbelief – that he had actually come intending to use her again, even now, with the baby sleeping right beside them.

'Massa, Massa, it too soon,' she pleaded tearfully. 'I ain't healed up right yet, Massa!' But when he simply ignored her, she struggled only long enough to put out the candle, after which she endured the ordeal quietly, terrified that the baby would awaken. She was relieved that he still seemed to be sleeping even when the massa spent himself, and then was clambering up, preparing to go. In the darkness, as he snapped his suspenders onto his shoulders, he said, 'Well, got to call him something—' Kizzy lay with her breath sucked in. After another moment, he said, 'Call him George – that's after the hardest-working nigger I ever saw.' After another pause, the massa continued, as if talking to himself, 'George. Yeah. Tomorrow I'll write it in my Bible. Yeah, that's a good name – George!' And he went on out.

Kizzy cleaned herself off and then lay back down, unsure which outrage to be most furious about. She had thought earlier of either 'Kunta' or 'Kinte' as ideal names, though uncertain of what the massa's reaction might be to their uncommon sounds. But she dared not risk igniting his temper with any objection to the name he'd chosen. She thought with a new horror of what her African pappy would think of it, knowing what importance he attached to names. Kizzy remembered how her pappy had told her that in his homeland, the naming of sons was the most important thing of all, '*'cause de sons becomes dey families' mens!*'

She lay thinking of how she had never understood why her pappy had always felt so bitter against the world of white people – 'toubob' was his word for them. She thought of Bell's saying to her, 'You's so lucky it scare me, chile, 'cause you don't really know what bein' a nigger is, an' I hopes to de good Lawd you don't never have to fin' out.' Well, she had found out – and there seemed no limit to the anguish whites were capable of wreaking upon black people. But the worst thing they did, Kunta had said, was to keep them ignorant of who they are, to keep them from being fully human.

'De reason yo' pappy took holt of my feelin's from de firs',' her mammy had told her, 'was he de proudest black man I ever seed!' Before she fell asleep, Kizzy decided that however base her baby's origins, however light his colour, whatever name the massa forced upon him, she would never regard him as other than the grandson of an African.

86

Since Uncle Pompey had never said much beyond 'How do?' to Kizzy when he saw her in the mornings, she was surprised and deeply touched when she arrived in the field with her baby on her first day back at work. Uncle Pompey approached her shyly and, touching the brim of his sweat-stained straw hat, pointed towards the trees at the edge of the field. 'Figgered you could put de baby under dere,' he said. Not sure what he meant, Kizzy squinted and saw something beneath one of the trees. Her eyes were soon glistening with tears, for when she walked over to it, she saw that it was a little lean-to, its top thatched with freshly cut long grass, thick-stemmed weeds, and green leaves.

Gratefully Kizzy spread her clean crocus sack upon the sheltered leafy cushion and laid the baby on it. He cried briefly, but with her comforting sounds and pats, soon he was gurgling and inspecting his fingers. Rejoining her two companions, who were working in the tobacco, she said, 'Sho' 'preciates dat, Uncle Pompey.' He grunted and chopped faster, trying to conceal his embarrassment. At intervals Kizzy would hurry over and check on her baby, and about every three hours, when it began crying, she would sit down and let it nurse at one of her breasts, which were taut with milk.

'Yo' baby jes' perkin' us all up, 'cause sho' ain't nothin' else roun' here to pay no 'tention,' Sister Sarah said a few days later, addressing Kizzy but casting a sly eye at Uncle Pompey, whose return look was as if at some persistent mosquito. By now, when each workday ended with the setting sun, Sister Sarah insisted on carrying the baby as Kizzy took their two hoes for the tired trudge back to slave row, which was nothing more than four small box-like, one-windowed cabins near a large chinquapin tree. Usually the early darkness would have fallen by the time Kizzy hurriedly lighted sticks in her small fireplace to cook something from her remaining rations, which were issued each Saturday morning by Massa Lea. Eating quickly, she would lie down on her cornshuck mattress, playing with George but not nursing him until hunger made him start bawling. Then, encouraging him to drink to his fullest, she would hold him over her shoulder, rubbing his back to help him burp, and then she would play with him again. She kept them both awake as late as she could, wanting the baby to sleep as long as possible before he would awaken for his next night feeding. It was during this interim that – twice or three times weekly – the massa would come to force himself upon her. He would always smell of liquor, but she had decided – for the sake of the baby as well as her own – not to try resisting him anymore. Filled with loathing, she would lie cold and still, with her legs apart, as he took of her his grunting pleasure. When it ended and he got up, she would keep lying there with her eyes closed – hearing the dime or sometimes the quarter that he would always drop on her table – until he left. Kizzy would wonder if the missis, too, was lying awake in the big house, which was close enough to be within earshot; what must she think, how must she feel, when the massa came to their bed still smelling of another woman?

Finally, after nursing George twice again before daybreak, she fell into a deep sleep – just in time to be roused by Uncle Pompey knocking at the door to wake her up. Kizzy ate breakfast and nursed the baby again before Sister Sarah arrived to carry him out to one of the fields. There was a separate field for corn, tobacco and cotton, and Uncle Pompey had by now constructed a little tree-shaded shelter at the edge of each one.

When the massa and missis finished their midday meal on Sunday, they always left soon after for their weekly buggy ride, and while they were gone, slave row's handful of folk would gather round the chinquapin tree for an hour of visiting. Now that Kizzy and her son had joined them, Miss Malizy and Sister Sarah would promptly begin their tug-of-war over who would get to hold the restless George. Uncle Pompey, who sat puffing his pipe, seemed to enjoy talking to Kizzy, perhaps because she'd listen to him with far fewer interruptions and far more respect than the two older women would.

'Dis place weren't nothin' but jes' woods worth 'bout fifty cents a acre,' said Pompey one afternoon, 'when massa got his firs' thirty acres an' his firs' nigger name George, same as yo' young'un here. He jes' plain worked dat nigger to death.' Seeing Kizzy gasp, Uncle Pompey halted. 'Sump'n de matter?' he asked.

'Nawsuh, nothin'!' Kizzy quickly collected herself, and Uncle Pompey continued.

'When I come here, massa'd done had dat po' nigger a year, cuttin' trees, gougin' up stumps, clearin' brush enough to plough an' plant to make his first crop. Den one day me an' dat nigger was sawin' logs into de very planks in dat big house yonder.' Uncle Pompey pointed. 'Lawd, I heard dis 'culiar sound an' glanced up from my end o' de saw. Dis George nigger's eyes was rollin', he grab at his chest, an' drop down dead – jes' like dat.'

Kizzy changed the subject. 'Every since I come here, been hearin' y'all go on 'bout fightin' chickens. Ain't hardly heared 'bout none befo'—'

'Well, I'se sho' heared massa say dey fights a-plenty o' 'em in dat Virginia,' said Miss Malizy. 'Reckon it jes' wasn't nowhere close where you was at.'

'Don't none us know no whole lot 'bout 'em here, neither,' said Uncle Pompey. ' 'Ceptin' dey's jes' some special kin' of roosters born an' bred to kill one 'nother, an' mens gambles whole lots of money on 'em.'

Sister Sarah chimed in. 'Onliest somebody could tell you mo' 'bout 'em is dat ol' Mingo nigger what live down dere wid dem chickens.'

Seeing Kizzy's open-mouthed surprise, Miss Malizy exclaimed, 'Done tol' you dat firs day you got here. You jes' ain't seed 'im yet.' She laughed. 'And you might not *never* see 'im!'

'I been here fo'teen years,' said Sister Sarah, 'an' I ain't seed dat nigger mo'n eight, ten times! He jes' ruther be 'mongst chickens dan peoples! Hmph!' she snorted. 'Fact, I specks his mammy *hatched* him!'

While Kizzy joined in the laughter, Sister Sarah leaned towards Miss Malizy, her arms outstretched. 'Here, lemme hol' dat chile awhile.' Grudgingly, Miss Malizy relinquished the baby.

'Well, anyhow,' she said, 'dem chickens sho' took massa an' missis from bein' raggedy to ridin' roun' here puttin' on sich big airs now.'

She made a mimicking grand gesture. 'Dat's massa throwin' up his hand when dey buggy passin' some rich massas' carriages!' Her finger resembled a butterfly in motion. 'Dat's missis' handkerchief a-flutterin' 'til she 'bout to fall out'n de buggy!'

Amid the loud guffawing, Miss Malizy needed a while to recover herself. Then, as she reached out to take the baby back, Sister Sarah snapped, 'You wait! I ain't had 'im but a minute!'

It delighted Kizzy to see them compete over her child, and to watch Uncle Pompey watching quietly, then beaming instantly if the baby happened to look his way, when he would make funny faces or movements with his fingers to hold the child's attention. George was crawling around one Sunday a few months later when he started crying to nurse. Kizzy was about to lift him when Miss Malizy said, 'Let 'im hol' on jes' a bit, honey. Dat boy big enough to start eatin' sump'n now.' Hurrying to her cabin, Miss Malizy returned in a few moments, and they all watched as she used the back of a teaspoon to mash a half teacup of cornbread and potlikker into a mush. Then, lifting George onto her ample lap, she spooned a tiny portion into his mouth. They all beamed as he wolfed it down and smacked his lips in eagerness for more.

With George now starting to explore on all fours when they were out in the fields, Kizzy tied a length of small rope about his waist to limit his range, but she soon discovered that even within its reach, he was picking up and eating dirt and crawling insects. They all agreed that something had to be done. 'Since he ain' got to nuss no mo',' Miss Malizy suggested, 'seem like if you leaves 'im wid me, I can keep a good eye on 'im whilst you's in de fiel'.' Even Sister Sarah thought that made sense, and as much as Kizzy hated to, she began delivering George to the big-house kitchen before she left each morning, then retrieving him when she returned. She almost wavered about her decision when George's first recognizable word was 'Mi'lize,' but soon after he clearly said 'Mammy,' thrilling Kizzy to the core. Then his next word was 'Unka'pomp,' which made the old man look like he'd swallowed the sunshine. And that was soon followed by 'Sis'sira.'

At one year, George was walking without assistance. By fifteen months he was even romping about, clearly revelling in the sheer joy of being at last independent and on his own. Now he seldom permitted any of them to hold him, unless he was sleepy or didn't feel well, which was rare, for he was fairly bursting with health and growth, thanks in no small part to his daily stuffing by Miss Malizy with the best fare that the kitchen could afford. Now during Sunday afternoons, as Kizzy and the other three doting adults carried on their conversation, they feasted their eyes on the boy waddling around, playing happily alone, with his soon baggy-wet diapers shortly matching the dirt in colour. George was as delighted with tasting a twig as with catching a beetle or with chasing a dragonfly, the yard cat, or the chickens – which he sent clucking off in alarm to find another scratching place. One Sunday the three women held their sides in laughter at the spectacle of the usually sombre Uncle Pompey loping awkwardly for short distances trying to get a light breeze to lift the kite he had made for the fascinated boy. 'Lem'me tell you, gal, you don't really know what you seein' yonder,' Sister Sarah remarked to Kizzy. 'Fo' dat chile come here, once Pompey got in his cabin, we wouldn't hardly see 'im no mo' 'til de mornin'.'

'De truth!' said Miss Malizy. 'I ain't even knowed Pompey had no fun in 'im!'

'Well, I know I sho' felt good when he put up dem l'il shelters for George when I first brung 'im to de fiel's,' said Kizzy.

'*You* feel good! Dat chile doin' us *all* good!' said Sister Sarah.

Uncle Pompey further claimed George's attention when he began telling him stories at the age of two. With the Sunday sun setting and the evening turning cool, Pompey would build a small, smoky fire of green wood to discourage the mosquitoes as the three women would position their chairs around the fire. Then George would find his most comfortable position to watch the mobile face and gesturing hands of Uncle Pompey as he told of 'Br'er Rabbit' and 'Br'er Bear', in time drawing upon such a seeming endless wealth of tales that once Sister Sarah was moved to exclaim, 'Ain't never dreamt you knowed all dem stories!' Uncle Pompey gave her a cryptic glance and said, 'Whole *heap* o' things 'bout me you don't know.' Sister Sarah, flouncing her head, affected great disgust. 'Hmph! Sho' ain't nobody tryin' to fin' out!' Uncle Pompey puffed solemnly at his pipe, his crinkled eyes laughing.

'Miss Malizy, I gwine say sump'n to you,' Kizzy declared one day. 'Sister Sarah an' Uncle Pompey always carryin' on like dey gits on each other's nerves. But sometimes I gits de feelin' it's sump'n like dey way of courtin' one 'nother—'

'Chile, I don't know. I know neither of 'em wouldn't never say if it was. But I speck dey jes' makin' some fun to pass de time, dat's all. You git ol' as we is an' ain't got yo'self nobody, you done jes' got used to it, since seem like ain't nothin' you can do 'bout it nohow,'

Miss Malizy's eyes searched Kizzy before she went on. 'We's ol', an' dat's dat, but bein' young like you, honey, an' ain't got nobody, dat's different! I'se jes' *wished* massa'd buy somebody dat y'all could jes' kin' of nachel git together!'

'Yes'm, Miss Malizy, ain't no need me actin' like I don't think 'bout it, neither, 'cause I sho do.' Kizzy paused. She then said what she was certain they both knew. 'But massa ain't gwine do dat.' She felt a flash of appreciation that none of them had ever mentioned, or even hinted at, what they all must know still went on between her and the massa; at least they never mentioned it in her presence. 'Since we's talkin' close,' she went on, 'it was a man I knowed where I come from. I still thinks 'bout him a-plenty. We was gwine git married, but den everything got messed up. Fact, dat's how come I got here.'

Forcing more brightness into her tone, sensing Miss Malizy's genuinely affectionate concern, Kizzy told her how it had been with Noah, ending finally, 'I tells myself he jes' steady gwine 'bout lookin' fo' me, an' we's gwine turn up face-to-face somewhere one dese days.' Kizzy's expression might have been of someone praying. 'If dat was to happen, Miss Malizy, I tell you de truth, I b'lieve neither one us would say nary word. I b'lieve we jes' take one 'nother's hand an' I slip on in here and tell y'all goodbye, an' git George, an' we leave. I wouldn't even ax or care whereabouts. Ain't never gwine forgit de las' thing he said to me. He say, "We spen' de res' our days togedder, baby!"' Kizzy's voice broke and then both she and Miss Malizy were weeping, and soon afterwards Kizzy went back to her cabin.

One Sunday morning, a few weeks later, George was in the big house 'helping' Miss Malizy prepare the noon meal when Sister Sarah invited Kizzy into her cabin for the first time since she had come to the Lea plantation. Kizzy stared at the much-chinked walls; they were all but covered with bunches of dried roots and herbs hanging from pegs and nails, attesting to Sister Sarah's claim that she could supply the nature cure for nearly any ailment. Pointing to her only chair, she said, 'Set yo'self down, gal.' Kizzy sat, and Sister Sarah went on, 'I gwine tell you sump'n ever'body don't know. My mammy was a Louisiana Cajun woman what teached me how to tell fortunes good.' She studied Kizzy's startled face. 'You want me to tell your'n?'

Instantly Kizzy remembered times when both Uncle Pompey and Miss Malizy had mentioned that Sister Sarah had a gift for fortune-telling. Kizzy heard herself saying, 'I reckon I would, Sister Sarah.'

Squatting on the floor, Sister Sarah drew a large box from under the bed. Removing from it a smaller box, she picked out two palmfuls of mysterious-looking dried objects and slowly turned towards Kizzy. Carefully arranging her objects into a symmetrical design, she produced a thin, wand-like stick from within the bosom of her dress and began vigorously stirring them around. Bending forwards until her forehead actually touched the objects on the floor, she seemed to be straining to straighten back upwards when she spoke in an unnaturally high tone, 'I hates to tell you what de sperrits says. You ain't never gwine see yo' mammy an' yo' pappy no mo', leas'ways not in dis worl'—'

Kizzy burst into sobs. Ignoring her entirely, Sister Sarah carefully rearranged her objects, then stirred and stirred again, much longer than before, until Kizzy regained some control and her weeping had diminished. Through misty eyes, she stared in awe as the wand trembled and quivered. Then Sister Sarah began a mumbling that was barely audible: 'Look like jes' ain't dis chile's good-luck time . . . onlies' man she gwine ever love . . . he had a mighty hard road . . . an' he love her, too . . . but de sperrits done tol' 'im it's de bes' to know de truth . . . an' to give up jes' even hopin' . . .'

Kizzy sprang upright, shrieking, this time highly agitating Sister Sarah '*Shhhhh! Shhhhh! Shhhhh!* Don't 'sturb de sperrits, daughter! SHHHHH! SHHHHH! SHHHHH!' But Kizzy continued to scream, bolting outside and across into her own cabin and slamming her door, as Uncle Pompey's cabin door jerked open and the faces of Massa and Missis Lea, Miss Malizy, and George appeared abruptly at windows of the big house and its kitchen. Kizzy was thrashing and wailing on her cornshuck mattress when George came bursting in. '*Mammy! Mammy!* what de matter?' Her face tear-streaked and contorted, she screamed hysterically at him, 'SHUT UP!'

87

By George's third year, he had begun to demonstrate a determination to 'help' the slave-row grown-ups. 'Lawd, tryin' to carry some water for me, an' can't hardly lif' up de bucket!' Miss Malizy said laughing. And another time: 'Dog if he ain't toted a stick at a time 'til he fill up my woodbox, den he raked de ashes out'n de fireplace!' Proud as Kizzy was, she took pains not to repeat Miss Malizy's praises to George, whom she felt was giving her headaches enough already.

'How come I ain't black like you is, Mammy?' he asked one night when they were alone in the cabin, and gulping, Kizzy said, 'Peoples jes' born what colour dey is, dat's all.' But not many nights passed before he raised the subject again. 'Mammy, who my pappy was? Why ain't I never seed 'im? Where he at?' Kizzy affected a threatening tone: 'Jes' shut yo' mouth up!' But hours later, she lay awake beside him, still seeing his hurt, confused expression; and the next morning delivering him to Miss Malizy, she apologized in a lame way. 'I jes' gits frazzled, you ax me so many questions.'

But she knew that something better than that had to be told to her highly alert, inquisitive son, something that he both could understand and would accept. 'He tall, an' black as de night, an' didn't hardly never smile,' she offered finally. 'He b'longst to you same as me, 'cept you calls him Gran'pappy!' George seemed interested and curious to hear more. Telling him that his gran'pappy had come on a ship from Africa 'to a place my mammy said dey calls 'Naplis,' she said that a brother of her Massa Waller had brought him to a plantation in Spotsylvania County, but he tried to escape. Uncertain how to soften the next part of the story, she decided to make it brief: '—an' when he kept on runnin' 'way, dey chopped off half his foot.'

A grimace twisted George's small face. 'How come dey done dat, Mammy?'

'He near 'bout kilt some nigger catchers.'

'Catchin' niggers fo' what?'

'Well, niggers dat had runned 'way.'

'What dey was runnin' from?'

'From dey white massas.'

'What de white massas done to 'em?'

In frustration, she shrilled, 'Heish yo' mouf! Git on 'way from me, worryin' me to death!'

413

But George never was silenced for long, any more than his appetite to know more of his African gran'pappy ever was fully satisfied. 'Where 'bouts is dat Africa, Mammy?' ... 'Any li'l boys in dat Africa?' ... 'What my gran'pappy's name was again?'

Even beyond what she had hoped, George seemed to be building up his own image of his gran'pappy, and – to the limits of her endurance – Kizzy tried to help it along with tales from her own rich store of memories. 'Boy, I wish you could o' heared 'im singin' some o' dem African songs to me when we be ridin' in de massa's buggy, an' I was a li'l gal, right roun' de age you is now.' Kizzy would find herself smiling as she remembered with what delight she used to sit on the high, narrow buggy seat alongside her pappy as they went rolling along the hot, dusty Spotsylvania County roads; how at other times she and Kunta would walk hand-in-hand along the fencerow that led to the stream where later she would walk hand-in-hand with Noah. She said to George, 'Yo' gran'pappy like to tell me things in de African tongue. Like he call a fiddle a *ko*, or he call a river *Kamby Bolongo*, whole lotsa different, funny-soundin' words like dat.' She thought how much it would please her pappy, wherever he was, for his grandson also to know the African words.

'*Ko!*' she said sharply. 'Can you say dat?'

'*Ko*,' said George.

'All right, you so smart: *Kamby Bolongo!*' George repeated it perfectly the first time. Sensing that she didn't intend to continue, he demanded, 'Say me some mo', Mammy!' Overwhelmed with love for him, Kizzy promised him more – later on – and then she put him, protesting, to bed.

88

When George's sixth year came – meaning that he must start working in the fields – Miss Malizy was heartsick to lose his company in the kitchen, but Kizzy and Sister Sarah rejoiced to be getting him back at last. From George's first day of fieldwork, he seemed to relish it as a new realm of adventure, and their loving eyes followed him as he ran around picking up rocks that might break the point of Uncle

Pompey's oncoming plough. He scurried about bringing to each of them a bucket of cool drinking water that he had trudged to get from the spring at the other end of the field. He even 'helped' them with the corn and cotton planting, dropping at least some of the seeds more or less where they should have gone along the mounded rows. When the three grown-ups laughed at his clumsy but determined efforts to wield a hoe whose handle was longer than he was, George's own broad smile displayed his characteristic good spirits. They had a further laugh when George insisted to Uncle Pompey that he could plough, and then discovered that he wasn't tall enough to hold the plough handles; but he promptly wrapped his arms around the sides and hollered to the mule, '*Git up!*'

When they finally got back into their cabin in the late evenings, Kizzy immediately began the next chore of cooking them a meal, as hungry as she knew George must be. But one night he proposed that the routine be changed. 'Mammy, you done worked hard all day. How come you don't lay down an' res' some fo' you cooks?' He would even try to order her around if she felt like letting him get away with it. At times it seemed to Kizzy as if her son was trying to fill in for a man whom she felt he sensed was missing in both of their lives. George was so independent and self-sufficient for a small boy that now or then when he got a cold or some small injury, Sister Sarah would insist upon all but smothering him with her herb cures; and Kizzy would finish the job with a plentiful salving of her love. Sometimes, as they both lay before sleeping, he would set Kizzy smiling to herself with the fantasies he'd share with her there in the darkness. 'I'se gwine down dis big road,' he whispered one night, 'an' I looks up, an' I sees dis great big ol' bear a-runnin' . . . seem like he taller'n a hoss . . . an' I hollers, "*Mr Bear! Hey, Mr Bear!* You jes' well's to git ready for me to turn you inside out, cause you sho' ain't gwine hurt *my* mammy!"' Or sometimes he would urge and urge and finally persuade his tired mammy to join him in singing some of the songs that he had heard Miss Malizy sing when he had spent his days with her in the big-house kitchen. And the little cabin would resound softly with their duets: 'Oh, Mary, don't 'cha weep, don't 'cha moan! Oh, Mary, don't 'cha weep, don't 'cha moan! 'Cause ol' Pharaoh's army done got drown-ded! Oh, Mary, don't 'cha weep!'

Sometimes when nothing else attracted George within the cabin, the restless six-year-old would stretch out before the fireplace. Whittling a finger-sized stick to a point at one end, which he then charred in the flames to make a sort of pencil, he would then draw on a piece of white pine board the simple outline figures of people or animals.

Every time he did it, Kizzy all but held her breath, fearing that George would next want to learn to write or read. But apparently the idea never occurred to him, and Kizzy took great care never to mention writing or reading, which she felt had forever scarred her life. In fact, during all of Kizzy's years on the Lea plantation, she had not once held a pen or pencil, a book or newspaper, nor had she mentioned to anyone that she once read and wrote. When she thought about it, she would wonder if she still could, should she ever want to, for any reason. Then she would spell out in her head some words she felt she still remembered correctly, and with intense concentration she would mentally picture what those words would look like written – not that she was sure what her handwriting would look like anymore. Sometimes she'd be tempted – but still she kept her sworn pact with herself never to write again.

Far more than she missed writing or reading, Kizzy felt the absence of news about what was happening in the world beyond the plantation. She remembered how her pappy would tell what he had heard and seen when he returned from his trips with Massa Waller. But any outside news was almost a rarity here on this modest and isolated plantation, where the massa rode his own horse and drove his own buggy. This slave row found out what was going on outside only when Massa and Missis Lea had guests for dinner – sometimes months apart. During one such dinner on a Sunday afternoon in 1812, Miss Malizy ran down from the house to them, 'Dey's eatin' now an' I got to hurry right back, but dey's talkin' in dere 'bout some new war done started up wid dat England! Seem like de England is sendin' whole shiploads of dey so'jers over here at us!'

'Ain't sendin' 'em over here at *me*!' said Sister Sarah. 'Dem's white folks fightin'!'

'Where dey fightin' dis war at?' asked Uncle Pompey, and Miss Malizy said she hadn't heard. 'Well,' he replied, 'long as it's somewheres up Nawth an' not nowhere roun' here, don't make me no difference.'

That night in the cabin, sharp-eared little George asked Kizzy, 'What a war is, Mammy?'

She thought a moment before answering. 'Well, I reckon it's whole lots of mens fightin' 'gainst one 'nother.'

'Fightin' 'bout what?'

'Fightin' 'bout anything dey feels like.'

'Well, what de white folks an' dat England feelin' 'gainst one 'nother 'bout?'

'Boy, jes' ain't never no end to 'splainin' you nothin'.'

A half hour later, Kizzy had to start smiling to herself in the darkness when George began singing one of Miss Malizy's songs, barely audibly, as if just for himself, 'Gon' put on my long white robe! Down by de ribberside! Down by de ribberside! Ain't gon' stud-dy de war no mo'!'

After a very long time without further news, during another big-house dinner, Miss Malizy reported, 'Dey sayin' dem Englands done took some city up Nawth dey calls "Detroit".' Then again, months later, she said the massa, missis, and guests were jubilantly discussing, 'some great big Newnited States ship dey's callin' 'Ol' Ironsides'. Dey's sayin' it done sunk plenty dem England ships wid its fo'ty-fo' guns!'

'*Whoowee!*' exclaimed Uncle Pompey. 'Dat's 'nough to sink de ark!'

Then one Sunday in 1814, Miss Malizy had George 'helping' her in the kitchen when he came flying down to slave row, breathless with a message: 'Miss Malizy say tell y'all dat England's army done whupped five thousan' Newnited States so'jers, an' done burnt up both dat Capitol an' de White House.'

'Lawd, where dat at?' said Kizzy.

'In dat Washington Deecee,' said Uncle Pompey. 'Dat's a fur piece from here.'

'Jes' long as dey keeps killin' an' burnin' one 'nother 'stead of us!' exclaimed Sister Sarah.

Then during a dinner later that year, Miss Malizy came hurrying to tell them, 'Be dog if dey ain't all in dere a singin' sump'n 'bout dem England's ships shootin' at some big fort near roun' Baltimore.' And Miss Malizy half talked and half sang what she had heard. Later that afternoon, there was an odd noise outside, and the grown-ups hurried to open their cabin doors and stood astonished: George had stuck a long turkey feather through his hair and was high-stepping along, banging a stick against a dried gourd and singing loudly his own version of what he had overheard from Miss Malizy: 'Oh, hey, can you see by dat dawn early light ... an' dem rockets' red glare ... oh, dat star-spangle banner wavin' ... oh, de lan' o' de free, an' de home o' de brave—'

Within another year the boy's gift for mimicry had become slave row's favourite entertainment, and one of George's most popular requests was for his impression of Massa Lea. First making sure that the massa was nowhere near, then slitting his eyes and grimacing, George drawled angrily, 'Less'n you niggers pick dis fiel' o' cotton clean fo' dat sun set, y'all ain't gon' git no mo' rations to eat!' Shaking with laughter, the adults exclaimed among themselves, 'Is you ever seed anything like dat young'un?' ... 'I sho' ain't!' ... 'He jes' a caution!' George needed but a brief observation of anyone to mock them in a highly comical way – including one big-house dinner guest, a white preacher, whom the massa had taken afterwards to preach briefly to the slaves down by the chinquapin tree. And when George caught his first good glimpse of the mysterious old Mingo who trained the massa's fighting gamefowl, George was soon aping perfectly the old man's peculiar hitching gait. Catching two squawking barnyard chickens and holding them tightly by their legs, he thrust them rapidly back and forth as if they were menacing each other while he supplied their dialogue: 'Big ol' ugly buzzard-lookin' rascal, I'm gon' scratch yo' eyes out!' to which the second chicken replied scornfully, 'You ain't nothing' but half a mouthful o' feathers!'

The following Saturday morning, as Massa Lea routinely distributed the slave row's weekly rations, Kizzy, Sister Sarah, Miss Malizy, and Uncle Pompey were standing dutifully before their cabin doors to receive their share when George came tearing around a corner chasing a rat, then screeched to a stop, having only narrowly missed colliding with the massa. Massa Lea, half amused, affected a gruff tone: 'What do you do to earn your rations around here, boy?' The four grown-ups all but collapsed as nine-year-old George, squaring his shoulders confidently and looking the massa straight in the eye, declared, 'I works in yo' fields an' I preaches, Massa!' Astounded, Massa Lea said, 'Well, let's hear you preach, then!' With five pairs of eyes upon him, George took a step backwards and announced, 'Dis dat white preacher you brung down here, Massa—' and suddenly he was flailing his arms and ranting, 'If you specks Uncle Pompey done took massa's hog, tell massa! If you sees Miss Malizy takin' missis' flour, tell missis! 'Cause if y'all's dat kin' o' good niggers, an' doin' well by yo' good massa an' missis, den when y'all die, y'all might git into de kitchen of heab'n!'

Massa Lea was doubled over with laughter even before George finished – whereupon, flashing his strong white teeth, the boy launched into one of Miss Malizy's favourite songs, 'It's me, it's me, it's me, O Lawd, a-standin' in de need o' prayer! Not my mammy, not my pappy, but it's me, O Lawd, a-standin' in de need o' prayer! Not de preacher, not de deacon, but me, O Lawd, a-standin' in de need o' prayer!'

None of the adults had ever seen Massa Lea laugh so hard. Obviously captivated, he clapped George across the shoulders, 'Boy, you preach around here anytime you want to!' Leaving the basket of

418

rations for them to divide among themselves, the massa went off back towards the big house with his shoulders shaking, glancing back over his shoulder at George, who stood there happily grinning.

Within weeks that summer, Massa Lea returned from a trip bringing two long peacock plumes. Sending Miss Malizy out to the fields to get George, he carefully instructed the boy how he wanted the plumes waved gently back and forth behind the guests he was inviting for dinner on the following Sunday afternoon.

'Jes' puttin' on airs, tryin' to act like dey's rich white folks!' scoffed Miss Malizy, after she had given Kizzy Missis Lea's instructions that the boy must come to the big house scrubbed thoroughly and with his clothes freshly washed, starched, and ironed. George was so excited about his new role, and about all the attention that was being paid to him – even by the massa and missis – that he could scarcely contain himself.

The guests were still in the big house when Miss Malizy slipped from the kitchen and ran to slave row, no longer able to keep from reporting to her anxiously awaiting audience. 'Lemme tell y'all, dat young'un too much!' Then she described George waving the peacock plumes, 'a-twistin' his wrists an' bendin' hisself back an' forth, puttin' on mo' airs dan massa an' missis! An' after dessert, massa was pourin' de wine, when seem like de idea jes' hit 'im, an' he say, "Hey, boy, let's hear some preachin'!" An' I declares I b'lieves dat young'un been practicin'! 'Cause quick as dat he ax massa for some book to be his Bible, an' massa got 'im one. *Lawd!* Dat young'un jumped on missis' prettiest 'broidered footstool! Chile, he lit *up* dat dinin' room preachin'! Den ain't nobody ax 'im, he commence to singin' his head off. Dat was when I jes' run out!' She fled back to the big house, leaving Kizzy. Sister Sarah, and Uncle Pompey wagging their heads and grinning in incredulous pride.

George had been such a success that Missis Lea began returning from her and the massa's Sunday afternoon buggy rides telling Miss Malizy that previous dinner guests whom they had met always asked about George. After a while the usually withdrawn Missis Lea even began to express her own fondness for him, 'an' Lawd knows, she ain't never liked no nigger!' exclaimed Miss Malizy. Gradually Missis Lea began finding chores for George to do in or around the big house, until by his eleventh year it seemed to Kizzy that he spent hardly half of his time out with them in the fields any more.

And because waving his plumes at every dinner kept George in the dining-room hearing the white people's conversation, he began picking up more news than Miss Malizy had ever been able to with her having to keep running back and forth between the dining-room and the kitchen. Soon after the dinner guests left, George would proudly tell all he had heard to the waiting ears in slave row. They were astonished to hear how one guest had said that 'roun' 'bout three thousan' free niggers from lots o' different places held a big meetin' in dat Philadelphia. Dis white man say dem niggers sent some res'lution to dat Pres'dent Madison dat both slave an' free niggers done helped build dis country, well as to help fight all its wars, an' de Newnited States ain't what it claim to be less'n niggers shares in all its blessin's.' And George added, 'Massa say any fool can see free niggers ought to be run out'n de country!'

George reported that during a later dinner 'dem white folks was so mad dey turned red' in discussing recent news of huge slave revolts in the West Indies. 'Lawd, y'all ought to o' heared 'em gwine on in dere 'bout ship sailors tellin' dat Wes' Indian slave niggers is burnin' crops an' buildin's, even beatin' an' choppin' up an' hangin' white folks dat was dey massas!' After subsequent dinners, George reported that a new ten-mile-an-hour speed record had been achieved by a six-horse 'Concord Coach' between Boston and New York City, including rest stops; that 'a Massa Robert Fulton's new paddle-wheel steamboat done crost some 'Lantic Ocean inside 'o twelve days!' Later, a dinner guest had described a showboat sensation. 'Bes' I could git it, dey calls it "de minstrels" – soun' like to me he say white mens blackin' dey faces wid burnt corks an' singin' an' dancin' like niggers.' Another Sunday dinner's conversation concerned Indians, George said. 'One dem mens said de Cherokees is takin' up sump'n like eighty million acres de white mens needs. He say de gubmint would o' took care dem Injuns long fo' now if wasn't for some interferin' big white mans, 'specially two name of Massa Davy Crockett an' Massa Daniel Webster.'

One Sunday in 1818, George reported 'sump'n dem guests was callin' de "Merican Colonize Society" tryin' to send shiploads o' free niggers off to a "Liberia" somewheres in dat Africa. De white folks was a-laughin' 'bout de free niggers being' tol' dat Liberia got bacon trees, wid de slices hangin' down likes leaves, an' 'lasses trees you jes' cuts to drain out all you can drink!' George said, 'Massa swear far's he concerned, dey can't put dem free niggers on ships fas' enough!'

'Hmph!' snorted Sister Sarah. 'I sho' wouldn't go to no Africa wid all dem niggers up in trees wid monkeys—'

'Where you git dat at?' demanded Kizzy sharply. 'My pappy come from Africa, an' he sho' ain't never been in no trees!'

Indignantly, Sister Sarah spluttered, taken aback, 'Well, *ever*-body grow up hearin' dat!'

'Don't make it right,' said Uncle Pompey, casting her a sidewise glance. 'Ain't no ship take you nohow, you ain't no free nigger.'

'Well, I wouldn't go if I was!' snapped Sister Sarah, flouncing her head and squirting an amber stream of snuff into the dust, annoyed now at both Uncle Pompey and Kizzy, whom she made a point of not bidding goodnight when the little gathering retired to their cabins. Kizzy, in turn, was no less seething at Sister Sarah's demeaning implication about her wise, stiffly dignified father and his beloved African homeland.

She was surprised and pleased to discover that even George was irritated at what he felt was ridicule of his African gran'pappy. Though he seemed reluctant to say anything, he couldn't help himself. But when he finally did, she saw his concern about seeming disrespectful. 'Mammy, jes' seem like Sister Sarah maybe talk what ain't so, don't she?'

'*Dat* de truth!' Kizzy emphatically agreed.

George sat quietly for a while before he spoke again. 'Mammy,' he said hesitantly, 'is it maybe any li'l mo' you could tell me 'bout 'im?'

Kizzy felt a flooding of remorse that during the previous winter she had got so exasperated with George's unending questions one night that she had forbidden him to question her any further about his grandfather. She said softly now, 'Whole lot o' times I done tried to scrape in my min' if it's sump'n 'bout yo' gran'pappy I ain't tol' you, an' seem like jes' ain't no mo'—' she paused. 'I knows you don't forgit nothin' – but I tell you again any part of it if you says so.'

George was again quiet for a moment. 'Mammy,' he said, 'one time you tol' me gran'pappy give you de feelin' dat de main thing he kep' on his mind was tellin' you dem Africa things—'

'Yeah, it sho' seem like dat, plenty time,' Kizzy said reflectively.

After another silence, George said, 'Mammy, I been thinkin'. Same as you done fo' me, I gwine tell my chilluns 'bout gran'pappy.' Kizzy smiled, it being so typical of her singular son to be discussing at twelve his children of the future.

As George's favour continued to rise with the massa and the missis, he was permitted increasing liberties without their ever really having to grant them. Now and then, especially during Sunday afternoons when they took buggy rides, he would go wandering off somewhere on his own, sometimes for hours, leaving the slave-row adults talking among themselves, as he curiously explored every corner of the Lea plantation. One such Sunday it was nearly dusk when he returned and told Kizzy that he had spent the afternoon visiting with the old man who took care of the massa's fighting chickens.

'I he'ped him catch a big ol' rooster dat got loose, an' after dat me an' de ol' man got to talkin'. He don't seem all dat 'culiar to me, like y'all says, Mammy. An' I ain't never see sich chickens! It's roosters he said ain't even grown yet jes' a-crowin' an jumpin' in dey pens, trying' to git at one 'nother to fight! Ol' man let me pick some grass an' feed 'em, an' I did. He tol' me he take mo' pains raisin' dem chickens dan mos' mammies does raisin' dey babies!' Kizzy's hackles raised a bit at that but she made no response, half amused at her son's being so excited about some chickens. 'He showed me how he rub dey backs an' necks an' legs, to help 'em fight de bes'!'

'You better stay 'way from down dere, boy!' she cautioned. 'You know massa don't 'low nobody but dat ol' man down dere messin' wid dem chickens!'

'Uncle Mingo say he gwine ax massa to let me come down dere an' help 'im feed dem chickens!'

On their way out to the field the next morning, Kizzy told Sister Sarah of George's latest adventure. Sarah walked on in thoughtful silence. Then she said, 'I know you don't hardly want me tellin' you no mo' fortunes, but I'm gwine tell you jes' a li'l 'bout dat George, anyhow.' She paused. 'He ain't never gwine be what nobody would call no ordinary nigger! He always gwine keep gittin' into sump'n new an' different jes' long as he draw breath.'

89

'He act like he well-raised, an' he seem like he handy, Massa,' said Uncle Mingo, concluding his description of the boy who lived up on slave row but whose name he had neglected to ask.

When Massa Lea immediately agreed to give him a try-out, Mingo was greatly pleased – since he had been wanting a helper for several years – but not really surprised. He was well aware that the massa was concerned about his gamecock trainer's advancing age and uncertain health; for the past five or six months he had fallen prey to increasingly frequent spells of bad coughing. He also knew that the massa's efforts to buy a promising young slave apprentice trainer had come to nought among the area's other gamecock owners, who were quite naturally disinclined to help him out. 'If I had any boy showing any signs of ability,' the massa told him one had said, 'you got to have more sense than to think I'd sell him. With that old Mingo of yours training him, five or ten years from now I'd see him helping you beat me!' But the likeliest reason for Massa Lea's quick approval, Mingo knew, was that Caswell County's annual cockfighting season would be opening shortly with the big New Year 'main' fight, and if the boy simply fed the younger birds, Mingo would be able to spend that much more time conditioning and training the freshly matured two-year-olds that soon would be brought in from their open rangewalks.

On the morning of George's first day on the job, Mingo showed him how to feed the scores of cockerels that were kept in several pens, each containing young birds of roughly the same ages and sizes. Seeing that the boy performed that trial task acceptably, the old man next let him feed the more matured 'stags', not quite a year old but already trying to fight each other from their triangular pens within the zigs and zags of a split-rail fence. Through the days that followed, Mingo kept George practically on the run, feeding the birds their cracked corn, giving them clean grit, oyster shell, and charcoal, and changing the sweet spring water in their drinking tins three times daily.

George had never dreamed that he could feel awe for chickens – especially the stags, which were starting to grow spurs and to develop bright feather colours as they strutted fearlessly about with their lustrous eyes flashing defiance. If he was away from Uncle Mingo's immediate scrutiny, sometimes George would laugh aloud at how some of the stags would suddenly rear back their heads and crow awkwardly and throatily, as if they were trying to compete with the frequent raucous cries of Mingo's six-or seven-old roosters – each bearing the scars of many past battles – that Uncle Mingo called 'catchcocks' and always fed himself. George pictured himself as one of the stags and Uncle Mingo as one of the old roosters.

At least once every day, when Massa Lea came riding on his horse down the sandy road into the gamecock training area, George would make himself as inconspicuous as possible, having quickly sensed how much chillier the massa was acting towards him. George had heard Miss Malizy saying that the massa didn't even permit the missus to come down where his chickens were, but she had indignantly assured him that was the last thing she'd want to do.

The massa and Mingo would go walking around, inspecting the pens of gamefowl, with Mingo always keeping exactly one step behind, close enough to hear and respond to whatever the massa said between the crowings of the scarred old catchcock roosters. George noticed that the massa spoke almost companionably with Uncle Mingo, in sharp contrast to his brusque and cold manner with Uncle Pompey, Sister Sarah, and his mammy, who were only field hands. Sometimes when their inspection tour brought them close enough to wherever George was working, he would then overhear what they were saying. 'I figure to fight thirty cocks this season, Mingo, so we've got to bring in around sixty or more from the rangewalk,' said the massa one day.

'Yassuh, Massa. By de time we culls 'em out, we oughta have a good forty birds dat'll train good.'

George's head became more and more filled with questions every day, but he had the feeling it would be best not to ask Uncle Mingo anything he didn't have to. Mingo scored it as a point in the boy's favour that he could keep from talking too much, since wise game-cockers kept many secrets to themselves. Mingo's small, quick, deeply squinting eyes, meanwhile, missed no detail of how George performed his work. Deliberately he gave his orders briefly and then quickly walked away, to test how quickly and well the boy would grasp and remember instructions; Mingo was pleased that George seemed to need to be told most things only once.

After a while, Mingo told Massa Lea that he approved of George's care and attention to the game-fowl – but he carefully qualified himself: 'Lease'ways far as I been able to tell in jes' dis little bit o' time, Massa.'

Mingo was totally unprepared for Massa Lea's reply: 'I've been thinking you need that boy down here all the time. Your cabin's not big enough, so you and him put up a shack somewhere so he'll be handy to you all the time.' Mingo was appalled at the prospect of anyone's sudden and total invasion of the privacy that only he and the game-fowl had shared for over twenty years, but he wasn't about to voice openly any disagreement.

After the massa had left, he spoke to George in a sour tone. 'Massa say I needs you down here all de time. I reckon he must know sump'n I don't.'

'Yassuh,' said George, struggling to keep his expression blank. 'But where I gwine stay at, Uncle Mingo?'

'We got to buil' you a shack.'

As much as he enjoyed the gamecocks and Uncle Mingo, George

knew this would mean the end of his enjoyable times in the big house, waving the peacock plumes and preaching for the massa and the missis and their guests. Even Missis Lea had just begun to show that she'd taken a liking to him. And he thought of the good things he wouldn't get to eat from Miss Malizy in the kitchen anymore. But the worst part about leaving slave row was going to be breaking the news to his mammy.

Kizzy was soaking her tired feet in a washpan full of hot water when George came in, his face unusually sombre. 'Mammy, sump'n I got to tell you.'

'Well, tired as I is, choppin' all day long, I don't want to hear no mo' 'bout dem chickens, tell you dat!'

'Well, ain't zackly dat.' He took a deep breath. 'Mammy, massa done tol' me an' Uncle Mingo to buil' a shack an' move me down dere.'

Kizzy sent some of the water splattering out of the pan as she leaped up seemingly ready to spring on George. 'Move you fo' what? What you can't do stayin' up here where you always been?'

'Weren't my doin', Mammy! It was massa!' He stepped back from the fury on her face, voice rising to a high-pitched cry, 'I ain't wantin' to leave you, Mammy!'

'You ain't ol' enough to be movin' nowhere! I bet it's dat ol' Mingo nigger put massa up to it!'

'No'm, he didn't Mammy! 'Cause I can tell he don't like it neither! He don't like nobody roun' him all de time. He done tol' me he ruther be by hisself,' George wished he could think of something to say that would calm her down. 'Massa feel like he bein' good to me, Mammy. He treat Uncle Mingo an' me nice, ain't like he acts to fiel' hands—' Too late, he gulped sickly, remembering that his mammy was a field hand. Jealousy and bitterness twisted her face as she grabbed George and shook him like a rag, screaming, 'Massa don't care nothin' bout you. He may be yo' pappy, but he don't care nothin' 'bout nobody but dem chickens!'

She was almost as stunned as he was by what she had said.

'It's true! An' jes' well you know it fo' you's figgerin' he doin' you sich favours! Only thing massa wants is you's helpin' dat ol' crazy nigger take care his chickens dat he figger gwine make him rich!'

George stood dumbfounded.

She went pummelling at George with both fists. 'Well, what you hangin' on roun' here fo'?' Whirling, she snatched up his few items of clothing and flung them towards him. 'G'wan! Git out'n dis cabin!'

425

George stood there as if he had been poleaxed. Feeling her tears flooding up and spilling out, Kizzy ran from the cabin and went bolting across to Miss Malizy's.

George's own tears trickled down his face. After a while, unsure what else to do, he stuffed his few pieces of clothing into a sack and went stumbling back down the road to the gamecock area. He slept near one of the stag pens, using his sack for his pillow.

In the predawn, the early-rising Mingo came upon him asleep there and guessed what had happened. Throughout the day, he went out of his way to be gentle with the boy, who went about his tasks silent and withdrawn.

During their two days of building the tiny shack, Mingo began speaking to him as if he had only just now really become aware of George's presence. 'Yo' life got to be dese chickens, til dey's like yo' family, boy,' he said abruptly one morning – that being the foremost thing that he wanted to plant in his mind.

But George made no response. He couldn't think of anything but what his mother had told him. His massa was his pappy. His pappy was his massa. He couldn't deal with it either way.

When the boy still said nothing, Mingo spoke again. 'I knows dem niggers up yonder thinks I'se peculiar—' He hesitated. 'I reckon I is.' Now he fell silent.

George realized that Uncle Mingo expected him to respond. But he couldn't admit that that was exactly what he had heard about the old man. So he asked a question that had been on his mind since the first day he came to visit. 'Uncle Mingo, how come dese chickens ain't like de rest?'

'You' talkin' 'bout tame chickens ain't fit for nothin' 'cept eatin',' said Uncle Mingo scornfully. 'Dese here birds near 'bout same as dey was back in dem jungles massa say dey come from in ancient times. Fact, I b'leeves you stick one dese cocks in de jungle, he jes' fight to take over de hens an' kill any other roosters jes' like he ain't never left.'

George had other questions he'd been saving up to ask, but he hardly got the chance to open his mouth once Uncle Mingo got going. Any gamecockerel that crowed before reaching the stag stage, he said, should promptly have its neck wrung, for crowing too early was a sure signal of cowardice later on. 'De true birds come out'n de egg wid de fightin' already in dey blood from dey gran'daddies and great-gran'daddies. Massa say 'way back, a man an' his gamechickens was like a man an' his dogs is now. But dese birds got mo' fightin' in 'em dan you fin' in dogs, or bulls, or bears, or 'coons, or whole lots of mens! Massa say it's all de way up to kings an' pres'dents fights gamebirds, 'cause it's de greatest sport dey is.'

Uncle Mingo noticed George staring at the latticework of small, livid scars on his black hands, wrists, and forearms. Going over to his cabin, Mingo returned shortly with a pair of curving steel spurs that tapered to needle sharpness. 'De day you starts to handlin' birds, yo' hands gon' be lookin' like mine, less'n you's mighty careful,' said Uncle Mingo, and George was thrilled that the old man seemed to consider it possible that *he* might put spurs on the massa's gamefowl one day.

Through the following weeks, though, long intervals would pass when Uncle Mingo wouldn't permit much conversation, for it had been years since he had talked with anyone except for the massa and the gamechickens. But the more he began to get used to having George around – and thinking of the boy as his assistant – the oftener he would break his silence to address him, almost always abruptly, about something he felt would help George to understand that only the most superbly bred, conditioned, and trained gamefowl could consistently win fights and money for Massa Lea.

'Massa don't fear no man in de cockpit,' Uncle Mingo told him one night. 'Fact, he love to match up 'gainst dem real rich massas dat can 'ford dem flocks o' much as a thousand birds so dey can pick out maybe dey bes' hundred to fight wid ever' year. You see we ain't got no great big flock, but massa still win plenty bettin' 'gainst dem rich ones. Dey don't like it cause he done come up in de world from startin' out as a po'cracker. But wid 'nough real fine birds an' 'nough luck, massa could git to be jes' big an rich as dey is—' Uncle Mingo squinted at George. 'You hear me, boy? Whole lots of peoples ain't realize how much money can be winned in cock fightin'. I knows one thing, if somebody was to offer me a hunnud-acre cotton or tobacco field, or a real good fightin' cock, I take de bird every time. Dat's how massa feel, too. Dat's how come he ain't put his money in no whole big lot of land or ownin' no big passel o' niggers.'

By the time George turned fourteen, he began his Sundays off by visiting with his slave-row family, which he felt included Miss Malizy, Sister Sarah, and Uncle Pompey no less than his own mammy. Even after all this time, he would have to reassure her that he harboured no ill will over the way she told him about his father. But he still thought a lot about his pappy, though he never discussed it with anyone, least of all the massa. Everyone on slave row by now was openly awed by his new status, though they tried to seem as if they weren't.

'I diapered yo' messy behind, an' you jes' let me catch you puttin' on any airs, I still beat it in a minute!' exclaimed Sister Sarah with affectionate mock ferocity one Sunday morning.

George grinned. 'No'm, Sister Sarah, ain't got no airs.'

But they were all consumed with curiosity about the mysterious things that took place down in the forbidden area where he lived with the gamecocks. George told them only things of a routine nature. He said he had seen gamecocks kill a rat, drive off a cat, even attack a fox. But the gamehens could be as bad-tempered as the roosters, he told them, and sometimes even crowed like the roosters. He said that the massa was vigilant against trespassers because of the high prices one could get for even the stolen eggs of championship birds, not to mention for the birds themselves, which thieves could easily take into another state and sell – or even fight as their own. When George said that Uncle Mingo had spoken of as much as three thousand dollars having been paid for one bird by the very rich gamecocking Massa Jewett, Miss Malizy exclaimed, 'Lawd, could o' bought three-four niggers for less'n dat chicken!'

After he had talked with them at length, George would begin to grow restless and fidgety by early Sunday afternoon. And soon he would go hurrying back down the sandy road to his chickens. Slowing down as he passed their pens along the road, he would pluck fresh tender green grass, drop a handful into each one, and sometimes stand awhile, enjoying the stags' contented *gluck, gluck, gluck* as they gobbled it down. About a year old now, they were maturing into glossy full feather, with fire in their eyes, and entering a stage of sudden explosive crowing and vicious flurrying efforts to get at each other. 'De quicker de better we gits 'em out to de rangewalks to start matin'!' Uncle Mingo had said not long ago.

George knew that would happen when the fully matured roosters already out on the rangewalks would be brought in to be conditioned and trained for the coming cockfighting season.

After visiting with the stags, George would usually spend the rest of his afternoon off wandering farther down the road into the pine groves where the rangewalks were. Occasionally he caught a glimpse of one of the fully grown birds there ruling a covey of hens in total liberty. Grass, seeds, grasshoppers, and other insects, he knew, were plentiful there, along with good gravel for their craws and as much sweet, fresh water as they wanted from the grove's several natural springs.

One chilly morning in early November, when Massa Lea arrived in the mulecart, Uncle Mingo and George were waiting with the

428

crowing, viciously pecking stags already collected in covered wicker baskets. After loading them into the cart, George helped Uncle Mingo catch his favourite old scarred, squawking catchcock.

'He's just like you, Mingo,' said Massa Lea with a laugh. 'Done all his fightin' an breedin' in his young days. Fit for nothin' but to eat and crow now!'

Grinning, Uncle Mingo said, 'I ain't hardly even crowin' no mo' now, Massa.'

Since George was as much in awe of Uncle Mingo as he was afraid of the massa, he was happy to see them both in such rare good spirits. Then the three of them climbed onto the mulecart, Uncle Mingo seated alongside the massa holding his old catchcock, and George balancing himself in the back behind the baskets.

Finally Massa Lea stopped the cart deep in the pine grove. He and Uncle Mingo cocked their heads, listening carefully. Then Mingo spoke softly. 'I hears 'em back in dere!' Abruptly puffing his cheeks, he blew hard on the head of the old catchcock, which promptly crowed vigorously.

Within seconds came a loud crowing from among the trees, and again the old catchcock rooster crowed, its hackles rising. Then goose-pimples broke out over George when he saw the magnificent game-cock that came bursting from the edge of the grove. Iridescent feathers were bristled high over the solid body; the glossy tail feathers were arched. A covey of about nine hens came hurrying up nervously, scratching and clucking, as the rangewalk cock powerfully beat its wings and gave a shattering crow, jerking its head about, looking for the intruder.

Massa Lea spoke in a low tone. 'Let him see the catchcock, Mingo!'

Uncle Mingo hoisted it high, and the rangewalk cock seemed almost to explode into the air straight after the old rooster. Massa Lea moved swiftly, grabbing the thrashing rangewalk cock in flight, deftly avoiding the wickedly long natural spurs that George glimpsed as the massa thrust it into a basket and closed the top.

'What you gawkin' for, boy? Loose one dem stags!' barked Uncle Mingo, as if George had done it before. He fumbled open the nearest basket, and the released stag flapped out beyond the mulecart and to the ground. After no more than a moment's hesitation, it flapped its wings, crowed loudly, dropped one wing, and went strutting stiffly around one hen. Then the new cock o' the walk started chasing all the other hens back into the pine grove.

Twenty-eight mature two-year-olds had been replaced with year-old stags when the mulecart returned just before dusk. After doing it all over again to get thirty-two more the next day, George felt he had been retrieving gamecocks from rangewalks all his life. He now busily fed and watered the sixty cocks. When they weren't eating, it seemed to him, they were crowing and pecking angrily at the sides of their pens, constructed so as to prevent their seeing each other, which would have caused some of them to get injured in their violent efforts to fight. With wonder, George beheld these majestically wild, vicious, and beautiful birds. They embodied everything that Uncle Mingo ever had told him about their ancient bloodlines of courage, about how both their physical design and their instincts made them ready to fight any other gamecock to the death anytime, anywhere.

The massa believed in training twice as many birds as he planned to fight during the season. 'Some birds jes' don't never pink up an' feed an' work like de rest,' Uncle Mingo explained to George, 'an' dem what don't we's gwine to cull out.' Massa Lea began to arrive earlier than before to work along with Uncle Mingo, studying the sixty birds, one by one, for several hours each day. Overhearing snatches of their conversations, George gathered that they would be culling out birds with any sores on their heads or bodies; or with what they judged to be less than perfect beaks, necks, wings, legs, or over-all configuration. But the worst sin of all was not showing enough aggressiveness.

One morning the massa arrived with a carton from the big house. George watched as Uncle Mingo measured out quantities of wheat-meal and oatmeal and mixed them into a paste with butter, a bottle of beer, the whites of twelve gamehen eggs, some wood sorrel, ground ivy, and a little liquorice. The resulting dough was patted into thin, round cakes, which were baked to crispness in a small earth oven. 'Dis bread give 'em strength,' said Uncle Mingo, instructing George to break the cakes into small bits, feed each bird three hand-fuls daily, and put a little sand in their waterpans each time he refilled them.

'I want 'em exercised down to nothin' but muscle and bone, Mingo! I don't want one ounce of fat in that cockpit!' George heard the massa order. 'Gwine run dey tails off, Massa!' Starting the next day, George was sprinting back and forth tightly holding under an arm one of Uncle Mingo's old catchcocks as it was hotly pursued by one after another of the cocks in training. As Mingo had instructed, George would occasionally let the pursuing cock get close enough to spring up with its beak snapping and legs scissoring at the furiously squawking catchcock.

Catching the panting aggressor, Uncle Mingo would quickly let it hungrily peck up a walnut-sized ball of unsalted butter mixed with beaten herbs. Then he would put the tired bird on some soft straw within a deep basket, piling more straw over the bird, up to the top, then closing the lid. 'It gwine sweat good down in dere now,' he explained. After exercising the last of the cocks, George began removing the sweating birds from their baskets. Before he returned them to their pens, Uncle Mingo licked each bird's head and eyes with his tongue, explaining to George, 'Dat git 'em used to it if I has to suck blood clots out'n dey beaks to help 'em keep breathin' when dey done got bad hurt fightin'.'

By the end of a week, so many sharp, natural cockspurs had nicked George's hands and forearms that Uncle Mingo grunted, 'You gwine git mistook fo' a gamecocker, you don't watch out!' Except for George's brief Christmas-morning visit to slave row, the holiday season passed for him almost unnoticed. Now, as the opening of the cockfighting season approached, the birds' killer instincts were at such a fever pitch that they crowed and pecked furiously at *anything*, beating their wings with a loud whumping noise. George found himself thinking how often he heard his mammy, Miss Malizy, Sister Sarah, and Uncle Pompey bemoaning their lot; little did they dream what an exciting life existed just a short walk down the road.

Two days after the New Year, George grasped each gamecock in turn as Massa Lea and Uncle Mingo closely snipped each bird's head feathers, shortened the neck, wing, and rump feathers, then shaped the tail feathers into short, curving fans. George found it hard to believe how much the trimming accentuated the birds' slim, compact bodies, snake-like necks, and big, strong-beaked heads with their shining eyes. Some of the birds' lower beaks had to be trimmed, too, 'For when dey has to grab a mouth holt,' explained Uncle Mingo. Finally, their natural spurs were scraped smooth and clean.

At the first light of opening day, Mingo and George were stowing the finally selected twelve birds in square travelling coops woven of hickory strips. Uncle Mingo fed each bird a walnut-sized lump of butter mixed with powered brown-sugar candy, then Massa Lea arrived in the wagon, carrying a peck of red apples. After George and Mingo loaded the twelve cock coops, Mingo climbed up on the seat beside the massa, and the wagon began rolling.

Glancing back, Uncle Mingo rasped, 'You gwine or not?'

Leaping after them, George reached the wagon's tailgate and

vaulted up and in. No one had *said* he was going! After catching his breath, he hunkered down into a squatting position. The wagon's squeakings mingled in his ears with the gamecocks' crowing, cluckings, and peckings. He felt deep gratitude and respect for Uncle Mingo and Massa Lea. And he thought again – always with perplexity and surprise – about his mammy's having said that the massa was his daddy, or his daddy was the massa, whichever it was.

Farther along the road, George began seeing either ahead or emerging from side roads other wagons, carts, carriages, and buggies, as well as horsemen, and poor crackers on foot carrying bulging crocus sacks that George knew contained gamecocks bedded in straw. He wondered if Massa Lea had once walked to cockfights like that with his first bird, which people said he had won with a raffle ticket. George saw that most of the vehicles carried one or more white men and slaves, and every vehicle carried some cockpens. He remembered Uncle Mingo's saying, 'Cockfightin' folks don't care nothin' 'bout time or distance when a big main gwine happen.' George wondered if maybe some of those poor crackers afoot would someday come to own a farm and a big house like the massa did.

After about two hours, George began hearing what could only be the crowing of many gamecocks faintly in the distance. The incredible chorus grew steadily louder as the wagon drew nearer to a heavy thicket of tall forest pines. He smelled the aroma of barbecuing meat; then the wagon was among others manoeuvring for places to park. All around, horses and mules were tied to hitching posts, snorting, stomping, swishing their tails, and many men were talking.

'Tawm Lea!'

The massa had just stood up in the wagon, flexing his knees to relieve the stiffness. George saw that the cry had come from several poor crackers standing nearby exchanging a bottle among themselves, and was thrilled at the instant recognition of his massa. Waving at those men, Massa Lea jumped to the ground and soon had joined the crowd. Hundreds of white people – from small boys holding their fathers' pants legs to old, wrinkled men – were all milling about in conversational clusters. Glancing around, George saw that nearly all the slave people remained in vehicles, seemingly attending to their cooped gamecocks, and the hundreds of birds sounded as if they were staging a crowing contest. George saw bedrolls under various nearby wagons and guessed that the owners had come from such long distances that they were going to have to stay overnight. He could smell the pungent aroma of corn liquor.

'Quit settin' dere gapin', boy! We got to limber up dese birds!' said

Uncle Mingo, who had just got the wagon parked. Blocking out the unbelievable excitement as best he could, George began opening the travel coops and handing one after another angrily pecking bird into Uncle Mingo's gnarled black hands, which proceeded to massage each bird's legs and wings. Receiving the final bird, Uncle Mingo said, 'Chop up half dozen dem apples good an' fine. Dey's de bes' las' eatin' fo' dese birds gits to fightin'.' Then the old man's glance happened to catch the boy's glazed stare at the crowd, and Uncle Mingo remembered how it had been for him at *his* first cockfight, longer ago than he cared to think about any more. '*G'wan!*' he barked, 'git out'n here an' run roun' li'l bit if you want to, but be back fo' dey starts, you hear me?'

By the time his 'Yassuh' reached Uncle Mingo, George had vaulted over the wagon's side and was gone. Slithering among the jostling, drinking crowd, he darted this way and that, the carpeting of pine needles springy under his bare feet. He passed dozens of cock coops containing crowing birds in an incredible array of plumage from snow-white to coal-black, with every imaginable combination of colours in between.

George stopped short when he saw it. It was a large sunken circle, about two feet deep, with padded sides, and its packed sandy clay floor was marked with a small circle in its exact centre and two straight lines equally distant from each side. The cockpit! Looking up, he saw boisterous men finding seats on a natural sloping rise behind it, a lot of them exchanging bottles. Then he all but jumped from his skin at the nearby bellow of a reddish-faced official, 'Gentlemen, let's get started fighting these birds!'

George sped back like a hare, reaching the wagon only an instant before Massa Lea did. Then the massa and Uncle Mingo went walking around the wagon talking in low tones as they glanced at the cooped birds. Standing up on the wagon's front seat, George could see over men's heads to the cockpit. Four men there were talking closely together as two others came towards them, each cradling a gamecock under an arm. Suddenly cries rose among the spectators: 'Ten on the red!' ... 'Taken!' ... 'Twenty on the blue!' ... 'Five of it!' ... 'Five more!' ... 'Covered!' The cries grew louder and more numerous as George saw the two birds being weighed and then fitted by their owners with what George knew must be the needle-sharp steel gaffs. His memory flashed to Uncle Mingo once telling him that birds were seldom fought if either of them was more than two ounces lighter or heavier than the other.

'Bill your cocks!' cried someone at the edge of the cockpit. Then quickly he and two other men squatted outside the ring, as the two owners squatted, within the circle, holding their birds closely enough to let them peck briefly at each other.

'Get ready!' Backing to their opposite starting marks, the two owners held their birds onto the ground, straining to get at each other.

'Pit your cocks!'

With blurring speed, the gamecocks lunged against each other so hard that each of them went bouncing backwards, but recovering within a second, they were up into the air shuffling their steelgaffed legs. Dropping back onto the pit floor, instantly they were airborne again, a flurry of feathers.

'The red's cut!' someone hollered, and George watched breathlessly as each owner snatched his bird as it came down, examining the bird quickly, then set it back on its start mark. The cut, desperate red bird somehow sprang higher than its opponent, and suddenly one of its scissoring legs had driven a steel gaff into the brain of the blue bird. It fell with its wings fluttering convulsively in death. Amid a welter of excited shouting and coarse cursing, George heard the referee's loud announcement, 'The winner is Mr Grayson's bird – a minute and ten seconds in the second pitting!'

George's breath came in gasps. He saw the next fight and even more quickly, one owner angrily flinging aside his losing bird's bloody body as if it were a rag. 'Dead bird jes' a mess of feathers,' said Uncle Mingo close behind George. The sixth or the seventh fight had ended when an official cried out, 'Mr Lea!' . . .

The massa walked hurriedly away from the wagon cradling a bird under his arm. George remembered feeding that bird, exercising it, holding it in his arms; he felt dizzy with pride. Then the massa and his opponent were by the cockpit, weighing in their birds, then fitting on the steel gaffs amid a clamour of betting cries.

At 'Pit your cocks!' the two birds smashed head-on; taking to the air, they dropped back to the floor, furiously pecking, feinting, their snakelike necks manoeuvring, seeking any opening. Again bursting upwards, they beat at each other with their wings – and then they fell with Massa Lea's bird reeling, obviously gaffed! But within seconds, in the next aerial flurry, the massa's bird fatally sank his own gaff.

Massa Lea snatched up his bird – which was still crowing in triumph – and came running back to the wagon. Only vaguely George heard, 'The winner is Mr Lea's' – as Uncle Mingo seized the bleeding bird, his fingers flying over its body to locate the deep slash wound in the rib cage. Clamping his lips over it, Uncle Mingo's cheeks puckered inward with his force of sucking out the clotted blood. Suddenly thrusting the bird down before George's knees, Mingo barked, 'Piss on it! Right there!' The thunderstruck George gaped. *'Piss!* Keep it from 'fectin'!' Fumbling, George did so, his strong stream splattering against the wounded bird and Uncle Mingo's hands. Then Uncle Mingo was packing the bird lightly between soft straw in a deep basket. 'B'lieve we save 'im, Massa! What one you fightin' next?' Massa Lea gestured towards a coop. 'Git dat bird out, boy!' George nearly fell over himself complying, and Massa Lea went hurrying back towards the shouting crowd as another fight's winner was announced. Faintly, beneath the raucous crowing of hundreds of cocks crowing, of men shouting new bets, George could hear the injured bird clucking weakly in his basket. He was sad, exultant, frightened; he had never been so excited. And on that crisp morning, a new gamecocker had been born.

90

'Look at 'im tryin' to outstrut dem roosters!' exclaimed Kizzy to Miss Malizy, Sister Sarah, and Uncle Pompey. George came striding up the road to spend his Sunday morning with them.

'Hmph!' Sister Sarah snorted with a glance at Kizzy. 'Aw, heish up, woman, we's jes' proud of 'im as you is!'

As George came on, still well beyond earshot, Miss Malizy told the others that only the previous evening she had overheard Massa Lea declare tipsily to some gamecocker dinner guests that he had a boy who after four years of apprenticeship seemed as 'natural born' to become, in time, 'the equal of any white or black gamecock trainer in Caswell County.'

'Massa say de ol' Mingo nigger say dat boy jes' live an' breathe chickens! 'Cordin' to massa, Mingo swear one evenin' late he was walkin' roun' down dere an' seed George settin' hunched over kind of funny on a stump. Mingo say he ease up behin' real slow, an' he be dog if'n George wasn't talkin' to some hens settin' on dey eggs. He swear dat boy was tellin' dem hens all 'bout fights gwine be winned by de baby chicks de hens 'bout to hatch.'

'Do Lawd!' said Kizzy, her eyes bathing in the sight of her approaching son. After the usual kissing and hugging with the women and handshaking with Uncle Pompey, they all settled onto stools brought quickly from their cabins. First they told George the latest white folks' news that Miss Malizy had managed to overhear during the week. The scant news this time was that more and more strange-talking white folks from across the big water were said to be arriving by the shiploads up North, swelling the numbers of those already fighting to take the jobs previously held by free blacks, and there was also steadily increasing talk of sending the free blacks on ships to Africa. Living as he did in such isolation with that strange old man, they kidded George, he couldn't be expected to know about any of this, or about anything else that was going on in the rest of the world – 'less'n it git told to you by some dem chickens' – and George laughingly agreed.

These weekly visits offered not only the pleasure of seeing his mammy and the others but also of getting some relief from Uncle Mingo's cooking, which was more suitable for chickens than for people. Miss Malizy and Kizzy knew enough by now to prepare at least two or three platefuls of George's favourite dishes.

When his conversation began to lag – around noon, as usual – they knew he was getting restless to leave, and after they had exacted his promise to pray regularly, and after another round of huggings and kissings and pumping of hands, George went hurrying back down the road with his basket of food to share with Uncle Mingo.

In the summertime, George often spent the rest of his Sunday afternoon 'off' in a grassy pasture where Mingo could see him spring about catching grasshoppers, which he would then feed as tidbits to the penned-up cockerels and stags. But this was early winter, and the two-year-old birds had just been retrieved from the rangewalks for training, and George was trying to salvage one of the several birds that Mingo and the massa felt were probably too wild and man-shy to respond properly to training and were likely to be culled out as discards. Mingo watched with affection and amusement as George forcibly restrained the pecking, squawking, struggling stag and started crooning to it, blowing gently on its head and neck, rubbing his face against the brilliant feathers, massaging its body, legs, and wings – until it actually began to settle down.

Mingo wished him luck, but he hoped George remembered what he had told him about taking chances with an unreliable bird. A gamecocker's breeding and development of a fine game-flock could represent a lifetime investment, and it could all be lost in a single emotional gamble. You simply couldn't risk fighting a bird unless every detectable flaw had been permanently corrected. And if it wasn't well, George had learned by now to quite calmly wring a gamecock's neck. He had come to share fully the massa's and Uncle Mingo's view that the only worthwhile birds were those whose intense training and conditioning, coupled with instinctive aggressiveness and courage, would drive them to drop dead in a cockpit before they would quit fighting.

George loved it when the massa's birds killed their opponents swiftly and without injury, sometimes within as little as thirty or forty seconds, but privately – though he never would have breathed this to Mingo or Massa Lea – nothing could match the thrill of watching a bird he had helped raise from a baby chick battle to the death with another equally game champion, each of them staggering, torn and bleeding, beaks lolling open, tongues hanging out, wings dragging on the cockpit floor, bodies and legs trembling, until finally both simply collapsed; then with the referee counting towards ten, the massa's bird would find somehow one more ounce of strength to struggle up and drive in a fatal spur.

George understood very well Mingo's deep attachment to the five or six scarred old catchcocks that he treated almost as pets – especially the one he said had won the biggest bet of the massa's career. 'Terriblest fight I ever seed!' said Uncle Mingo, nodding towards that one-eyed veteran. 'It was back dere in his prime, reckon three-four years fo' you come here. Somehow or 'nother massa had got in dis great big New Year's main bein' backed by some real rich massa clear over in Surrey County, Virginia. Dey 'nounced no less'n two hunnud cocks was to fight for a ten thousand dollars' main stake, wid no less'n hunnud-dollar side bets. Well, massa an' me took twenty birds. You lemme tell you, dem twenty birds was *ready!* We driv days in de wagon to git dere, feedin', waterin', an' massagin' dem birds in dey coops as we went. Well, gittin' on near de end o' de fightin', we'd winned some, but we'd lost too many to git at dat main purse, an' massa was plenty mad. Den he foun' out he was gwine be matched 'gainst what folks claimin' was de meanest mess o' feathers in Virginia. You oughta heared de hollerin' of bets on dat bird!

'Well, now! Massa'd done hit his bottle a couple good licks, an' got all red in de face as he could git! An' out'n de birds we had left, he pick dat ol' buzzard you's lookin' at right over dere. Massa stuck dat bird under one arm, an' commence walkin' roun' dat cockpit swearin' loud he weren't backin' off nobody's bets! He say he started wid nothin', if he win' up wid nothin' again, he sho' wouldn't be no stranger to it! Boy, lemme tell you! Dat tough ol' meat an' pin-feathers over yonder went in dat cockpit, an' he come out jes' barely, but dat other bird was dead! Dem referees 'nounced dey'd been steady tryin' to kill one 'nother for nigh fo'teen minutes!' Uncle Mingo looked with warm nostalgia across at the old rooster. 'So bad cut up an' bleedin' he was s'posed to die, but I ain't slept a wink 'til I saved 'im!'

Uncle Mingo turned towards George. 'Fact, boy, dis sump'n I'se got to 'press on you mo'n I'se done – you got to do everything you can to save hurt birds. Even dem dat's been lucky 'nough to kill quick, an' standin' up dere crowin' big an' actin' ready to fight again, well, dey can fool you! Soon's you git 'im back in yo' wagon, be sho' you checks 'im good all over, real close! Maybe he got jes' some l'il spur cuts, or nicks, dat can easy git 'fected. Any sich cut, piss on it good. If it's any bleedin', put on a spider web compress, or li'l bit o' de soft belly fur of a rabbit. If you don't, two-three days later yo' bird can start lookin' like it's shrinkin' up, like a limp rag, den next thing you know yo' bird dead. Gamebirds is like I hears racehosses is. Dey's tough, but same time dey's mighty delicate critters.'

It seemed to George that Uncle Mingo must have taught him a thousand things, yet thousands more were still in Uncle Mingo's head. As hard as George had tried to understand, he still couldn't comprehend how Mingo – and the massa – could seem to *sense* which birds would prove to be the smartest, boldest, and proudest in the cockpit. It wasn't simply the assets you could see, which by now even George had learned to recognize: the ideal short, broad backs with the full-rounded chests tapering to a fine, straight keelbone and a small, compact belly. He knew that good, solid, roundboned wings should have hard-quilled, wide, glossy feathers that tended to meet under a median-angled tail; that short, thick, muscular legs should be spaced well apart, with stout spurs evenly spaced above strong feet whose long back toe should spread well backwards and flat to the ground.

Uncle Mingo would chide George for becoming so fond of some birds that he seemed to forget their jungle instincts. Now or then some gamecock docilely being petted in George's lap would glimpse one of Uncle Mingo's old catchcocks and with a shattering crow burst from George's grasp in violent pursuit of the old bird, with George racing to stop them before one killed the other. Uncle Mingo also repeatedly cautioned George to control his emotions better when some bird of George's got killed in the cockpit; on several occasions the big, strapping George had burst into tears. 'Nobody can't speck to win every fight, don' know how many times I got to tell you dat!' said Mingo.

Mingo also decided to let the boy know that for several months he had been aware that George had been disappearing not long after full darkness fell, then returning very late, recently close to daybreak. Uncle Mingo was sure it had a connection with George's having once mentioned, with elaborate casualness, that while he had been at the gristmill with Massa Lea one day, he had met a pretty and nearly high-yaller big-house maid named Charity from the adjacent plantation. 'All dese years down here, dese ol' ears an' eyes o' mine's like a cat's. I knowed de first night you slipped off,' Uncle Mingo said to his astounded apprentice. 'Now, I ain't one to poke in nobody's business, but I'se gwine tell you sump'n. You jes' be mighty sho' you ain't cotched by some dese po' white paterollers, 'cause if dey don't beat you half to death deyself, dey'll bring you back, an' don't you think massa won't lay his whip crost yo' ass!' Uncle Mingo stared for a while across the grassy pasture before he spoke again. 'You notice I ain't said *quit* slippin' off?'

'Yassuh,' said George humbly.

During another silence, Mingo sat down on a favourite stump of his, leaned slightly forwards, and crossed his legs, with his hands clasped around his knees. 'Boy! I 'members back when I first foun' out what gals was, too—' and a new light crept into Uncle Mingo's eyes as the aged features softened. 'It was dis here long, tall gal, she was still new to de county when her massa bought a place right next to my massa's.' Uncle Mingo paused, smiling. 'Bes' I can 'scribe 'er, well, de niggers older'n me commence to callin' 'er "Blacksnake"—' Uncle Mingo went on, his smile growing wider and wider the more he remembered – and he remembered plenty. But George was too chagrined at being caught to be embarrassed by anything Mingo was telling him. It was pretty clear though that he had underestimated the old man in more ways than one.

91

Walking up the road towards slave row one Sunday morning, George sensed that something was wrong when he saw that neither his mammy nor any of the others were standing around Kizzy's cabin to greet him, as they had never failed to do before in the four years he'd spent with Uncle Mingo. Quickening his pace, he reached his mammy's cabin and was about to knock when the door was snatched open and Kizzy practically jerked him inside, quickly shutting the door behind them, her face taut with fear.

'Is missis seed you?'

'Ain't seed her, Mammy! What's the *matter*?'

'Lawd, boy! Massa got word some free nigger over in Charleston, South Ca'liny, name o' Denmark Vesey, had hunnuds o' niggers ready to kill no tellin' how many white folks right tonight, if dey hadn't o' got caught. Massa ain't long lef' here actin' like he gone wild, a-wavin' his shotgun an' threatenin' to kill anybody missy see outside dey cabins fo' he git back from some big organizin' meetin'!'

Kizzy slid alongside the cabin's wall until she could look through the cabin's single window towards the big house. 'She ain't still where she was peepin' from! Maybe she seen you comin' an' went an' hid!' The absurdity of Missis Lea *hiding* from him struck some of Kizzy's alarm into George. 'Run back down wid dem chickens, boy. No tellin' *what* massa do he catch you up here!'

'I gwine stay here an' talk to massa, Mammy!' He was thinking that in such an extremity as this, he would even somehow indirectly remind the massa whose father he was, which should curb his anger, at least somewhat.

'You plum crazy? Git outa here!' Kizzy was shoving George towards the cabin door. '*G'wan! Git!* Mad as he was, he catch you here, jes' make it wuss on us. Slip through dem bushes behin' de toilet 'til you's out'n sight o' missy!'

Kizzy seemed on the verge of hysteria. The massa must have been worse than he'd ever been before to terrify her so. 'Awright, Mammy,' he said finally. 'But I ain't slippin' through no bushes. I ain't done nothin' to nobody. I'se gwine back down de road jes' same as I come up it.'

'Awright, awright, jes' go '*head!*'

Returning to the gamefowl area, George had barely finished telling Uncle Mingo what he had heard, fearing that he sounded foolish, when they heard a horse galloping up. Within moments Massa Lea sat glowering down at them from his saddle, the reins in one hand, his shotgun in the other, and he directed the cold fury of his words at George. 'My wife saw you, so y'all know what happened!'

'Yassuh—' gulped George, staring at the shotgun.

Then, starting to dismount, Massa Lea changed his mind, and staying on his horse, his face mottled with his anger, he told them, 'Plenty good white people would be dyin' tonight if one nigger hadn't told his massa just in time. Proves you never can trust none of you niggers!' Massa Lea gestured with the shotgun. 'Ain't no tellin' what's in y'all's heads off down here by yourselves! But you just let me *half* think anything funny, I'll blow your heads off quick as a rabbit's!' Glaring balefully at Uncle Mingo and George, Massa Lea wheeled his horse and galloped back up the road.

A few minutes passed before Uncle Mingo even moved. Then he spat viciously and kicked away the hickory strips he had been weaving into a gamecock carrying basket. 'Work a thousan' years for a white man you still any nigger!' he exclaimed bitterly. George didn't know what to say. Opening his mouth to speak again, then closing it, Mingo went towards his cabin, but turning at the door, he looked back at George. 'Hear me, boy! You thinks you's sump'n special wid massa, but nothin' don't make no difference to mad, scared white folks! Don't you be no fool an' slip off nowhere till this blow over, you hear me? I mean *don't!*'

George picked up the basket Mingo had been working on and sat down on a nearby stump. His fingers began to weave the hickory strips together as he tried to collect his thoughts. Once again Uncle Mingo had managed to divine exactly what was going on inside his head.

George grew angry for permitting himself to believe that Massa Lea would ever act like anything but a massa towards him. He should have known better by now how anguishing – and fruitless – it was to even *think* about the massa as his pappy. But he wished desperately that he knew someone he felt he could talk with about it. Not Uncle Mingo – for that would involve admitting to Uncle Mingo that he knew the massa was his pappy. For the same reason, he could never talk to Miss Malizy, Sister Sarah, or Uncle Pompey. He wasn't sure if they knew about the massa and his mammy, but if one did, then they all would, because whatever anyone knew got told, even when it was about each other, behind each other's backs, and he and Kizzy would be no exception.

He couldn't even raise the agonizing subject with his mammy –

not after her fervently remorseful apologies for telling him about it in the first place.

After all these years, George wondered what his mammy really felt about the whole excruciating thing, for by now, as far as he could see, she and the massa acted as if they were no longer aware that the other existed, at least in that way. It shamed George even to think about his mammy having been with the massa as Charity – and more recently Beulah – would be with him on those nights when he slipped away from the plantation.

But then, seeping up from the recesses of his memory, came the recollection of a night long ago, when he was three or four years old and awakened one night feeling that the bed was moving, then lying still and terrified with his eyes staring wide in the darkness, listening to the rustle of the cornshucks and the grunting of the man who lay there beside him jerking up and down on top of his mammy. He had lain there in horror until the man got up; heard the dull *plink* of a coin on the tabletop, the sound of footfalls, the slam of the cabin door. For a seemingly interminable time, George had fought back scalding tears, keeping his eyes tightly closed, as if to shut out what he had heard and seen. But it would always come back like a wave of nausea whenever he happened to notice on a shelf in his mother's cabin a glass jar containing maybe an inch of coins. As time passed, the depth of coins increased, until finally he no longer could bring himself to look directly at the jar. Then when he was around ten years old, he noticed one day that the jar was no longer there. His mammy had never suspected that he knew anything about it, and he vowed that she never would.

Though he was too proud ever to mention it, George had once considered talking with Charity about his white father. He thought she might understand. The opposite of Beulah, who was as black as charcoal, Charity was a considerably lighter mulatto than George; in fact, she had the tan skin that very black people liked to call 'high yaller'. Not only did Charity seem to harbour no distress whatever about her colour, she had laughingly volunteered to George that her pappy was the white overseer on a big South Carolina rice and indigo plantation with over a hundred slaves where she had been born and reared until at eighteen she was sold at auction and bought by Massa Teague to be their big-house maid. On the subject of skin colour, about all that Charity had ever expressed any concern about was that in South Carolina she had left behind her mammy and a younger brother who was practically white. She said that black-skinned young'uns had unmercifully teased him until their mammy told him

442

to yell back at his tormentors, 'Turkey buzza.d laid me! Hot sun hatched me! Gawd gim'me dis colour dat ain't none o' y'all black niggers' business!' From that time on, Charity said, her brother had been let alone.

But the problem of George's own colour – and how he got it – was eclipsed for the moment by his frustration at realizing that the near-uprising in faraway Charleston was surely going to delay his following through with an idea he had been developing carefully in his head for a long time. In fact, nearly two years had gone into his finally reaching a decision to try it out on Uncle Mingo. But there was no sense in telling him about it now, since the whole thing would hang on whether or not Massa Lea would approve of the idea, and he knew Massa Lea was going to remain angrily unapproachable about anything for quite a while. Though the massa stopped carrying the shotgun after a week or so, he would inspect the gamefowl only briefly every day, and after terse instructions to Uncle Mingo, would ride off as grim-faced as he had come.

George didn't really realize the full gravity of what had almost happened in Charleston until, after another two weeks – despite Uncle Mingo's warning – he found himself unable to resist any longer the temptation to slip out for a visit with one of his girl-friends. Impulsively, he decided to favour Charity this time, swayed by memories of what a tigress she always was with him. After waiting to hear Uncle Mingo's snoring, he went loping for nearly an hour across the fields until he reached the concealing pecan grove from which he always whistled his whippoorwill call to her. When he'd whistled four times without seeing the familiar 'come ahead' signal of a lighted candle waved briefly in Charity's window, he began to worry. Just when he was about to leave his hiding place and sneak on in anyway, he saw movement in the trees ahead of him. It was Charity. George rushed forwards to embrace her, but she permitted him only the briefest hug and kiss before pushing him away.

'What'sa *matter*, baby?' he demanded, so aroused by her musky body aroma that he hardly heard the quavering in her voice.

'You de bigges' fool, slippin' roun' now, many niggers as gittin' shot by paterollers!'

'Well, le's git on in yo' cabin, den!' said George, throwing an arm around her waist. But she moved away again.

'You act like you ain't even heared 'bout no uprisin'!'

'I know was one, dat's all—'

'I tell you 'bout it, den', and Charity said she overheard her massa and missis saying that the ringleader, a Bible-reading, free-black

Charleston carpenter named Denmark Vesey, had spent years in planning before confiding in four close friends who helped him to recruit and organize hundreds of the city's free and slave blacks. Four heavily armed groups of them had only awaited the signal to seize arsenals and other key buildings, while others would burn all they could of the city and kill every white they saw. Even a horse company of black drivers would go dashing wildly about in drays, carts, and wagons to confuse and obstruct white people from assembling. 'But dat Sunday mornin' some scairt nigger tol' his massa what s'posed to happen dat midnight, den white mens was all over, catchin', beatin', an' torturin' niggers to tell who was de uprisers. Dey's done hung over thirty of 'em by now, an' ever'where dey's throwin' de fear o' Gawd into niggers, jes' like dey's doin' roun' here now, but especially in South Ca'liny. Done run out Charleston's free niggers an' burnt dey houses, de nigger preachers, too, an' locked up dey churches, claimin' dat 'stid o' preachin', dey's been teachin' niggers to read an' write—'

George had renewed his efforts to start her moving towards the cabin. 'Ain't you been listenin' to me?' she said, highly agitated. 'You git home fo' you's seed an' shot by some dese paterollers!'

George protested that inside her cabin was safety from any paterollers, as well as relief of his passion for her, which had caused him to risk being shot already.

'Done tol' you, NAW!'

Exasperated, George finally shoved her roughly backwards. 'Well, g'wan, den!' And bitterly he went loping back the way he had come, wishing furiously that he had gone to Beulah's instead, because it was too late to go there now.

In the morning, George said to Mingo, 'Went up to see my mammy las' night, an' Miss Malizy was tellin' me what she been hearin' massa tellin' missis 'bout dat uprisin'—' Unsure if Mingo would believe that story, he went on anyway, telling what Charity had said, and the old man listened intently. Finishing, George asked, 'How come niggers herebouts gittin' shot at 'bout sump'n clear in South Ca'liny, Uncle Mingo?'

Uncle Mingo thought awhile before he said, 'All white folks scairt us niggers sometime gwine organize an' rise up together—' He snorted derisively. 'But niggers ain't gwine never do *nothin'* together.' He reflected for another moment. 'But dis here shootin' an' killin' you talk 'bout gwine ease up like it always do, soon's dey's kilt an' scairt niggers enough, an' soon's dey makes whole passel o' new laws, an' soon's dey gits sick of payin' whole bunch o' peckerwood paterollers.'

'How long all dat take?' asked George, realizing as soon as he had said it what a foolish question it was, and Uncle Mingo's quick look at him affirmed the opinion.

'Well, I sho' ain't got no answer to dat!' George fell silent, deciding not to tell Uncle Mingo his idea until things had returned to normal with Massa Lea.

In the course of the next couple of months, Massa Lea gradually did begin to act more or less like his old self – surly, most of the time, but not dangerous. And one day soon afterwards George decided that the time was right.

'Uncle Mingo, I been studyin' a long time on sump'n—' he began. 'I b'lieves I got a idea might help massa's birds win mo' fights dan dey does.' Mingo looked as if some special form of insanity had struck his strapping seventeen-year-old assistant, who continued talking. 'I been five years gwine to de big chicken fights wid y'all. Reckon two seasons back, I commence noticin' sump'n I been watchin' real close every since. Seem like every different gamecocker massa's set o' birds got dey own fightin' style—' Scuffing the toe of one brogan against the other, George avoided looking at the man who had been training gamefowl since long before he was born. 'We trains massa's birds to be real strong, wid real long wind, to win a lot dey fights jes' by outlastin' de other birds. But I done kept a count – de mos' times we loses is when some bird flies up over massa's bird an' gaffs 'im from de top, gin'ly in de head. Uncle Mingo, I b'lieves if'n massa's birds got stronger wings, like I b'lieves we could give 'em wid whole lot o' special wing exercise, I b'lieves dey'd gin'ly fly higher'n other birds, an' kill even mo' dan dey does now.'

Beneath his wrinkled brow, Mingo's deep-set eyes searched the grass between George's and his own shoes. It was a while before he spoke. 'I sees what you means. I b'lieves you needs to tell massa.'

'If you feels so, cain't you tell 'im?'

'Naw. You thunk it up. Massa hear it from you good as me.'

George felt an immense sense of relief that at least Uncle Mingo didn't laugh at the idea, but lying awake on his narrow cornshuck mattress that night, George felt uneasy and afraid about telling Massa Lea.

Bracing himself on Monday morning when the massa appeared, George took a deep breath and repeated almost calmly what he had said to Uncle Mingo, and he added more detail about different game-flocks' characteristic fighting styles. '—An' when you notices, Massa, dem birds o' Massa Graham's fights in a fast, feisty way. But Massa MacGregor's birds fights real cautious an' wary-like. Or Cap'n Peabody's strikes wid dey feets an' spurs close together, but Massa Howard's scissors wid dey legs pretty wide apart. Dat rich Massa Jewett's birds, dey gin'ly fights low in de air, an' dey pecks hard when dey's on de groun', an' any bird dey catches a good beakhold o' jes' liable to git gaffed right dere—' Avoiding the massa's face, George missed his intensely attentive expression. 'Reckon what I'se tryin' to say, Massa, if you 'grees wid me an' Uncle Mingo givin' yo' birds some whole lotsa strong wing exercisin' dat we oughta be able to figger out, seem like dat help 'em to fly up higher'n de res' to gaff 'em from on top, an' speck nobody wouldn't quick catch on.'

Massa Lea was staring at George as if he had never seen him before.

In the months that remained before the next cockfighting season, Massa Lea spent more time than ever before in the gamefowl training area, observing and sometimes even joining Uncle Mingo and George as they tossed gamecocks higher and higher into the air. Descending with a frantic flapping of their wings, trying to support their five-to-six-pound weights, their wings grew steadily stronger.

As George had prophesied, the 1823 cockfighting season opened and progressed through one after another 'main' contest, with no one seeming to detect how or why the Lea birds were managing to win an even higher percentage of their fights than the year before. Their steel gaffs had sunk fatally into thirty-nine of their fifty-two opponents by the end of the season.

One morning about a week later, Massa Lea arrived – in high spirits – to check on the recovery of the half dozen of his prime birds that had been injured seriously during the season.

'Don't b'lieve dis'n gwine pull through, Massa,' said Uncle Mingo, indicating one so drooping and battered that Massa Lea's head quickly shook in agreement. 'But I speck dese in dese next two cages gwine heal up so good you be fightin' 'em again next season.' Mingo gestured next at the last three convalescing birds. 'Dese here ain't gwine never be perfect enough fo' de big main fights no mo', but we can use 'em as catchcocks if you wants to, Massa, or dey be good cull birds anyhow.' Massa Lea expressed his satisfaction with the prognosis and had started towards his horse when, turning, he spoke casually to George. 'These nights you slip out of here tomcattin' you'd better be mighty careful about that bad nigger that's sweet on the same gal—'

George was so dumbfounded it took a full second before anger flared within him at Uncle Mingo's obvious treachery. But then he saw that Uncle Mingo's face was no less astounded, as the massa continued. 'Missis Teague told my wife at their quilting club meeting she couldn't figure out what had come over her yaller housemaid until lately some of the other niggers told her the gal's wore out from two-timing you and some bad buck older nigger—' Massa Lea chuckled. 'Reckon the two of y'all sure must be tearin' up that gal!'

Charity! *Two*-timing! As George recalled furiously with what insistence she had blocked him from her cabin that night, he forced himself to smile and laugh nervously; Uncle Mingo joined in just as hollowly. George felt stricken. Now that the massa had discovered that he had been slipping off nights, what was he going to do to him?

Having paused to let George expect his anger, Massa Lea said instead – in an incredible, almost man-to-man way – 'Hell, long as you do your work, go on and chase you some tail. Just don't let some buck slice you to pieces – and don't get caught out on that road where the patrol is shootin' people's niggers.'

'*Nawsuh!* Sho' ain't—' George was so confused he didn't know what to say. '*Sho*' 'preciates, Massa—'

Massa Lea climbed on his horse, a discernible shaking of his shoulders suggesting to his gamecock trainers that he was laughing to himself as he cantered on up the road.

Finally alone in his shack that night, after enduring Uncle Mingo's frostiness through the rest of the day, free at last to vent his outrage at Charity, George cursed her – and vowed that he would turn his attentions, which she obviously didn't deserve, to the surely more faithful, if less hotly passionate, Beulah. He also remembered that tall, cinnamon-coloured girl who had given him the eye at a secret frolic he had stumbled on in the woods while hurrying homewards one night. The only reason he hadn't tried her then and there was he got so drunk on the white lightning she offered him that he was barely able to stagger home by dawn. But he remembered she said her name was Ophelia and that she belonged to the very rich Massa Jewett, who owned over a thousand gamefowl, or so it was said, and whose family had huge plantations in Georgia and South Carolina as well as the one there in Caswell County. It was a long way to walk, but first chance he got, George decided he was going to get better acquainted with that tasty-looking field girl Massa Jewett probably didn't even know he owned.

92

One Sunday morning George had left for his weekly visit on slave row by the time Massa Lea showed up for daily inspection of the flock. It was the perfect moment. After walking about and talking of game-cocking for a while, Uncle Mingo said, as if it had just occurred to him, 'Massa, you knows how every season we culls out dese fifteen or twenty good birds dat's better'n a whole lots o' folks fights wid. I b'lieves you can make good side money if'n you lets dat boy fight yo' culls in hackfights.'

Uncle Mingo knew well that the name of Tom Lea, throughout the length and breadth of Caswell County, symbolized the rise of a poor white man to eminence and a major gamecocker who started out as a hackfighter with one good bird. Many a time he had told Uncle Mingo how fondly he looked back upon those early, hungry days, declaring that their excitements were at least the equal of those he had enjoyed in all of the major 'mains' he had competed in ever since. The only significant differences, Massa Lea said, were that the big 'main' fights involved a better class of people as well as of game-cocks, and much higher amounts of money were wagered; one might see really rich gamecockers winning – and losing – fortunes in the course of a single fight. Hackfights were for those who were able to fight only one or two or three usually second- or third-rate birds – the poor whites, free blacks, or slaves whose pocketbooks could afford bets ranging from twenty-five cents, to a dollar, with as much as perhaps twenty dollars being bet only when some hackfighter went out of his head and put on the line everything he had in the world.

'What makes you think he can handle birds in a cockpit?' asked Massa Lea.

Uncle Mingo was relieved to hear no objections to his proposal. 'Well, suh, close as you know dat boy watch fights, reckon he ain't missed a move you made in de cockpits for five, six years, Massa. An' put dat togedder wid jes' how na'chel born he is wid roosters, I sho' b'lieves he'd need no mo'n a little teachin'. Even fights he'd lose be jes' cull birds we has roun' here dat you don't never hardly use nohow, suh.'

'Uh-huh,' the massa murmured, rubbing his chin thoughtfully. 'Well, I don't see nothin' wrong with it. Why don't you buff the spurs of some culls and help him practice fights across the summer? If he looks any good by next season, yeah, I'll stake him a little for some bets.'

'Sho' will, yassuh!' Uncle Mingo was exultant, since for months now in the gamefowl area's woodsy privacy, he and George had been mock-fighting culled birds, their spurs harmlessly covered with a light leather pouch Uncle Mingo had devised. Being the cautious man he was, the old man hadn't ventured his suggestion to the massa without first ascertaining for himself that his able apprentice showed genuine potential to develop into a really good fight handler. With enough hackfighting experience, he thought privately that George might someday become as expert as Massa Lea at handling birds at a cockpit. As Uncle Mingo had said, even the culls from a flock as good as the massa's were superior to the ones usually pitted in the many hackfights that were staged each season in various impromptu and informal settings around the county. All in all, it seemed to Uncle Mingo that there was practically no way George would miss.

'Well, boy, you jes' gwine stand dere wid yo' mouth open?' asked Uncle Mingo when he broke the news that afternoon.

'Don't know what to say.'

'Never thought I'd live to see de day when you ain't got nothin' to say.'

'I . . . jes' don't know how to thank you.'

'Wid all dem teeth showin', you don' need to. Le's get to work.'

Every day that summer, he and Uncle Mingo spent at least an hour in the late afternoons squatting on opposite sides of a make-shift cockpit, smaller in diameter and shallower than the regular size, but still sufficient for training. After several weeks, the massa came down to observe one of the sessions. Impressed with the pit-side agility and keen reflexes George showed in handling his bird, he gave him a few cockfight pointers of his own.

'You want your bird to get the jump. Now watch me—' Taking over Mingo's bird, he said, 'Okay, your referee's already hollered "Get ready!" You're down here holding your bird – but don't watch it! Keep your eyes on that referee's lips! You want to tell the split second he's going to say "Pit!" It's when his lips press together tight—' Massa Lea compressed his own lips. 'Right *then* snatch up your hand – you'll hear "Pit" just as your bird gets out there first!'

Some afternoons, after their training session was done and the cull birds they had used had been put back in their pens, Uncle Mingo would sit and tell George about the glory and the money that could be earned in hackfights. 'Jes' like de po' peckerwoods hollers for massa to win, I'se seed niggers dat gits hollered for at de big hackfights. An' it's much as ten, twelve, even mo' dollars can be winned in one fight, boy!'

'Ain't never *had* a dollar, Uncle Mingo! Don't hardly know what a dollar look like!'

'I ain't never had many neither. Fact, ain't got no use for none no mo'. But massa say he gwine stake you some bettin' money, an' if you wins' any, he jes' might let you have some of it—'

'You reckon he do dat?'

'I specks, 'cause I know he got to be feelin' pretty good 'bout dat wing-strengthenin' idea of your'n what done put good money in his pocket. Thing is if he do, is you gwine have sense enough to save up what you git?'

'Sho' do dat! I sho' would!'

'I'se even heared o' niggers winnin' an' savin' enough from hackfightin' to buy deyselves free from dey massas.'

'Buy me an' my mammy both!'

Immediately Uncle Mingo rose from the stump he had been sitting on; the lancing of jealousy that he had just experienced had not only come entirely unexpectedly, but it was also so unsettling deep within him that he found it hard to make any reply. Then he heard himself snapping, 'Well – reckon ain't nothin' impossible!' Wanting suddenly to get away from a feeling that his own sense of sharing a truly close affection wasn't being equally reciprocated, he walked quickly off towards his cabin, leaving George staring after him, puzzled.

At a big cockfight main with Massa Lea early during the 1824 season, Uncle Mingo heard from an old trainer he had known for years that a hackfight was due to be held that coming Saturday afternoon behind the large barn of a local plantation. 'Reckon he 'bout ready as he ever gwine be, Massa,' Mingo told the massa later. On Saturday morning, as he had promised, Massa Lea came down and counted out twenty dollars in small bills and coins to Uncle Mingo. 'Now, you know my policy,' he said to both of them. 'Don't get in there fightin' a bird if you're afraid to bet on him! If you bet nothin' you'll never win nothin'! I'm willin' to lose whatever you lose, but I'm puttin' up the money and you're fightin' my chickens, so I want half of any winnin's, you understand that? And if I even *think* there's any messin' around with my money, I'll take it out of *both* your black hides!' But they could clearly see that he was only putting on a gruff act when he was really in a good humour as they chorused, 'Yassuh, Massa!'

Rounding the corner of the large grey-painted barn, trying not to show how excited he was, George saw about twenty black hackfighters moving around, laughing and talking on one side of a wide, shallow cockpit. Recognizing about half of them from the big fights they'd attended with their massas, as he had, he waved and smiled his greetings, exchanging nods with others whose colourful dress and cockily independent air made him guess that they must be free blacks. Flicking glances at about an equal number of poor whites just across the cockpit, he was surprised to find that he knew some of them, too, and pridefully, he overheard one telling another, 'Them two's Tom Lea's niggers.' Both the black and white hackfighters soon began untying their hay-filled crocus bags, withdrawing their crowing, clucking birds and starting to limber them up as Uncle Mingo stepped around the cockpit and said something to the stout, ruddy-faced referee, who nodded with a glance across at George.

The boy was diligently massaging his stag when Mingo returned and began working on the other bird they'd brought along. George felt vaguely uneasy at being physically closer than ever before to poor whites, who generally meant nothing but trouble for blacks, but he reminded himself that Uncle Mingo had told him on their way over here that hackfighting was the only thing he knew of that poor whites and blacks did together. The rule was that only two whites or two blacks fought their birds against each other, but anyone freely could bet on or against any bird in any fight.

With his bird well massaged and limbered up and nestled back in its sack, George drank in more of the surrounding hubbub, and he saw yet more hackfighters with filled sacks hurrying towards the barn when the referee began waving his arms.

'All right, all right now! Let's get started fightin' these birds! Jim Carter! Ben Spence! Get over here and heel 'em up!'

Two gaunt, shabbily dressed white men came forward, weighed in their birds, then fitted on the steel gaffs amid sporadic shouted bets of twenty-five and fifty cents. As far as George was concerned, neither bird looked any better than medicore compared to the two culls from the massa's flock in his and Uncle Mingo's sacks.

At the cry '*Pit!*' the birds rushed out, burst into the air, and dropped back down, flurrying and feinting – fighting conventionally, George felt, and without the quality of drama he always sensed with Uncle Mingo and the massa at the big fights. When at last one bird hung a gaff that badly wounded the other in the neck, it took minutes more to finish the kill that George knew would have taken a top-class bird only seconds. He watched the losing owner stalk off bitterly cursing his bad luck and holding his dead bird by the legs. In a second fight, then in a third, neither the winning nor losing birds showed George the fight fire and style he was used to seeing, so diminishing his nervousness that as the fourth fight wore on, he all but cockily anticipated his own turn in the cockpit. But when it came, his heart immediately started pounding faster.

'All right, all right! Now Mr Roames' nigger with a speckled grey, and Mr Lea's nigger with a red bird! Y'all boys heel 'em up!' George had recognized his stocky black opponent when they arrived; in fact, several times over the past few years they had talked briefly at the big main fights. Now, feeling Uncle Mingo's eyes fastened on him, George went through the weighing-in and then kneeled, unbuttoning the bib pocket of his overalls and pulling out the wrapped gaffs. Tying them onto his rooster's legs, he remembered Mingo's admonition, 'not too loose or dey can git looser an' slide down, an' not too tight less'n dey numbs and cramps his legs.' Hoping that he was achieving just the right tightness, George heard around him the cries, 'Fifty cents on de red!' ... 'Covered!' ... 'Dollar on de grey!' ... 'Got dat!' 'Fo' dollars on de red!' It was Uncle Mingo, barking out by far the biggest bet, triggering a quick rash of cries to cover him. George could feel the excitement of the crowd increasing along with his own. 'Get ready!'

George kneeled, holding his rooster firmly against the ground, feeling its body vibrating in its anxiety to burst into attack.

'Pit!'

He had forgotten to watch the referee's lips! By the time his hands jerked up, the other bird was already blurring into motion. Scrambling backwards, George watched in horror as his bird got hit broadside and knocked tumbling off balance, then gaffed in the right side with such swiftness and force that it was sent reeling. But recovering quickly, it turned to the attack as a patch of feathers began to darken with blood. The two birds flurried upwards, his own flying higher, but its gaffs somehow missed on the way down. Feinting, they went up again, about evenly high this time, both of their gaffs flashing faster than anyone's eyes could follow. George's heart skipped beats for endless minutes as the birds pecked, feinted, lunged, and leaped all over the cockpit. He knew his rooster had to be weakening from its steady loss of blood, even as it kept countering the rushes of the spangled grey. Then suddenly, with the flash of a spur, it was all over, and George's bird lay quivering and fluttering in its final throes. He scarcely heard the bettors' shouts and curses as he snatched his dying bird from the cockpit. Tears bursting forth, he had pushed through the crowd of astonished, staring men when Uncle Mingo roughly seized his elbow and propelled him on beyond where anyone else could hear.

'You's actin' like a fool!' he rasped. 'Go git dat other bird fo' yo' next fight!'

'I ain't no good at it, Uncle Mingo. Done got massa's bird kilt!'

Mingo seemed incredulous. 'Any time birds fight one gwine lose! Ain't you never seen massa lose? Now git on back out dere!' But neither his threats nor urgings were sufficient to move the boy, and finally he stopped trying. 'Awright! I ain't gwine back tellin' massa we was scared to try winnin' his money back!'

Angrily, Uncle Mingo turned back towards the crowd around the cockpit. Humiliated, George was surprised and grateful that he was hardly noticed by the other hackfighters, who had turned their attention to the next contest. Two more fights passed before the referee cried out again, 'Tom Lea's nigger!' In deeper shame, he heard Mingo bet *ten* dollars and get it covered before the old man pitted the second of the massa's cull birds. It expertly killed its opponent in less than two minutes.

Uncle Mingo's efforts to console George as they trudged back towards the plantation did little good. 'We done made two dollars, so how come you actin' like sump'n dyin'?'

'Jes' so shame o' losin' – an' reckon massa won't hardly want me losin' no mo' his birds—'

Mingo was so upset that his boy seemed determined to become a loser even before he got started that after George had moped around for three days, acting as if he wanted the earth to open up and swallow him whole, he spoke to Massa Lea about it. 'Would you have a word with dat boy, Massa? Seem like he think it a disgrace to lose one fight!' When the massa next visited the gamefowl area, he accosted George. 'What's this I hear you can't lose a fight?'

'Massa, jes' feel terrible gittin' yo' bird kilt!'

'Well, I've got twenty more I want you to fight!'

'Yassuh.' He was half-hearted even with the massa's reassurance.

But when George won with both birds in his next hackfight, he began to preen and crow like one of his winning roosters. After proudly collecting his bets, Uncle Mingo took him aside and whispered, 'Git yo' head big, you be losin' again!'

'Jes' lemme hol' all dat money, Uncle Mingo!' he exclaimed, holding out his cupped hands.

As he stared at the pile of crumpled one-dollar bills and more in coins, Mingo said laughingly, 'You take de money to massa. Do y'all both good!'

On their way home, George tried for what seemed the hundredth time to persuade Uncle Mingo to visit the slave row to meet his mammy, Miss Malizy, Sister Sarah, and Uncle Pompey. 'Massa ain't got but de six o' us niggers, Uncle Mingo, look like de leas' we could do is know one 'nother! Dey sho' like to meet you. I talks 'bout you all de time when I'se dere, but dey feels like you don't like 'em or sump'n!'

'You an' dem both ought to know I can't be 'gainst nobody I don't even know!' said Mingo. 'Les' jes' keep it like it been, den dey ain't got to worry wid me, an' me neither wid dem!' And once again, when they reached the plantation, Mingo took the path that would give him a wide berth around slave row.

Kizzy's eyes fairly bugged when she saw the bills and coins in George's palm. 'Lawdy, boy, where you git all dat?' she demanded, calling Sister Sarah to take a look.

'How much *is* dat, anyhow?' asked Sarah.

'Don't know, ma'am, but plenty mo' where it come from.'

Sister Sarah towed George by his free hand to show the windfall to Uncle Pompey.

'Speck I better git *me* a rooster,' said the old man. 'But looka here, boy, dat's massa's money!'

'He gimme half!' George explained proudly. 'Fact, I got to go give him his share right now.'

Presenting himself at the kitchen, George showed Miss Malizy the money, then asked to see the massa.

When Massa Lea pocketed his nine dollars' winnings, he laughed. 'Hell, I think Mingo's slippin' you my best birds and me the culls!'

George was beside himself!

In the next hackfight, George won with two birds he had won with before, and Massa Lea grew so intrigued by George's string of victories that he finally ignored his self-imposed objections to attending a hackfight.

The massa's unexpected arrival prompted hasty nudges and whispers among both the white and black hackfighters. Seeing even Uncle Mingo and George nervous and uncertain, Massa Lea began to feel misgivings that he had come. Then, realizing that any initiative must be his own, he began grinning and waving at one of the older poor whites. 'Hi, Jim.' Then to another: 'Hey there, Pete!' They grinned back, astounded that he even remembered their names. 'Hey, Dave!' he went on. 'See your wife kicked out the rest of your teeth – or was it that bad whisky?' Amid uproarious laughter, the hackfight seemed nearly forgotten as they crowded around the man

454

who had started out as poor as any of them and then became a legend for them.

Bursting with pride, George cradled his bird under one arm, and astonishing Uncle Mingo as well as Massa Lea, he was suddenly strutting around the edges of the cockpit. 'All right! All right!' he cried out loudly, 'any y'all got any money, git it on de line! Don't care what you bets, if I cain't cover it, my massa sho' can, rich as he is!' Seeing the massa smiling, George grew yet louder. 'Dis here jes' his *cull* bird I's fightin', an' he beat anything out here! C'mon!'

An hour later, after ballyhooing a second winning fight, George had won twenty-two dollars and Massa Lea nearly forty from accepting side bets pressed upon him. He really hated to take the money from men whom he knew to be as dirt poor as he once had been, but he knew they would go the rest of the year boastfully lying how they had lost ten times as much as they had in betting against Tom Lea.

The cocky, self-proclaiming George was missed when he didn't show up at four of Caswell County's next hackfights, for Uncle Mingo was suffering from another siege of severe coughing spells. George saw how they came on him suddenly, without warning, and then persisted, and he felt he shouldn't leave his old teacher alone with the gamefowl, nor did he wish to go by himself. But even when Mingo had improved somewhat, he said he still didn't feel quite up to walking all the way to the next hackfight – but he demanded that George go anyway.

'You ain't no baby! You sho' be gone quick enough if it was some gals dere!'

So George went alone, carrying in each hand a bulging bag containing a gamecock cull. As he came into view of the gamecockers who had been missing his recently colourful presence, one of them cried loudly, 'Look out! Here come dat "Chicken George"!' There was a burst of laughter from them all, and he heartily joined in.

The more he thought of it on his way home – with still more winnings in his pocket – the better he liked the sound of that name. It had a certain *flair*.

'Betcha none y'all can't guess what dey done name me at de hackfight!' he said the moment he arrived on slave row.

'Naw, what?'

'*Chicken George!*'

'Do Lawd!' exclaimed Sister Sarah.

Kizzy's love and pride shone from her eyes. 'Well,' she said, 'it's sho' 'bout close as anybody gwine git to 'scribin' you nowdays!'

The nickname even amused Massa Lea when he was told it by

Uncle Mingo, who added wryly, 'Wonder to me dey ain't callin' 'im "Cryin' George", de way he still bust out cryin' any time a bird he fightin' git kilt. Much as he winnin' nowdays, don't make no difference! Jes' let a killin' gaff hit his rooster an' he gushin' and blubberin' an' huggin' dat bird like it his own chile. Is you ever heared or seed de like of dat befo', Massa?'

Massa Lea laughed. 'Well, plenty times I've felt like crying myself when I'd bet a lot more'n I ought to and my bird caught a gaff! But, no, I guess he's the only one I've heard of takin' on like you say. I think he just gets too attached to chickens.'

Not long afterwards, at the biggest 'Main' of the year, the massa was returning to the wagon carrying his bird, which had just won in the final contest, when he heard someone shout, '*Oh, Mr Lea!*' Turning, he was astonished to see the gamecocker aristocrat George Jewett striding towards him, smiling.

Massa Lea managed to make himself sound casual. 'Oh, yes, Mr Jewett!'

Then they were shaking hands. 'Mr Lea, I'll be very frank, as one gentleman and gamecocker to another. I've recently lost my trainer. The road patrol stopped him without a pass the other night. Unfortunately, he tried to run and was shot, badly. It's not likely he'll pull through.'

'Sorry to hear it – for you, I mean, not the nigger.' Massa Lea cursed his confusion, guessing at what was coming. The aristocrat wanted Mingo.

'Of course,' said Jewett. 'So I find myself needing at least a temporary trainer, one who knows at least something about birds—' He paused. 'I've noticed at our cockfights you've got two of them. I wouldn't think of wanting your experienced older one, but I wonder if you would entertain a fair offer for the other, the young one who's sparkin' one of the gals on my place, my niggers tell me—'

Massa Lea's astonishment mixed with fury at this evidence of treachery by Chicken George. He sounded choked: 'Oh, I see!'

Massa Jewett smiled again, knowing he'd drawn blood. 'Let me prove I'm not wishing to engage us in bargaining.' He paused. 'Would three thousand be all right?'

Massa Lea was staggered, not sure if he had heard right. 'I'm sorry, Mr Jewett,' he heard himself say flatly. He felt the thrill of refusing a rich blueblood.

'All right.' Jewett's voice tightened. 'My final offer: four!'

'I'm just not selling my trainers, Mr Jewett.'

The rich gamecocker's face fell, his eyes had gone cold. 'I understand. Of course! Good day to you, sir!'

'The same to you, sir,' said Massa Lea, and they strode away in opposite directions.

The massa returned to the wagon as quickly as he could without running, his rage rising. Uncle Mingo and Chicken George, seeing his face, sat with their own carefully blank. Reaching the wagon, he brandished his fist at George, his voice trembling with fury. 'I'll bash your brains in! What the hell are you doin' over at Jewett's – tellin' him how we train chickens?'

Chicken George turned ashen. 'Ain't tol' Massa Jewett *nothin*', Massa—' He could hardly speak. 'Ain't spoke nary word to him, *never*, Massa!' His total astonishment and fright half convinced Massa Lea. 'You tryin' to tell me you're goin' way the hell over there just to tomcat with Jewett's wench?' Even if it was innocent, he knew how every visit exposed his apprentice trainer to Jewett's cunning, which could lead to anything.

'*Massa, Lawdy mercy—*'

Another wagon now was pulling close by, with men calling and waving to the massa. Returning their waves, Massa Lea slitted his mouth into a smile and went clambering up onto the fartherest edge of the wagon's seat, snapping at the terrified Uncle Mingo out of the corners of his mouth, 'Drive, goddammit!' A knife could have cut the tension during the seemingly endless trip back to the plantation. Nor was the tension much less taut between Uncle Mingo and Chicken George during the rest of the day. That night a sleepless George lay in a sweat of anticipation over the punishment he knew was coming.

But none came. And a few days later the massa said to Uncle Mingo, as if nothing had happened, 'Next week I've got a bid to fight birds just over the state line in Virginia. I know that long ride wouldn't do your coughing spells any good, so I'll just take the boy.'

'Yassuh, Massa.'

Uncle Mingo had long known this day was coming; that's why the massa had trained the boy to replace him. But he hadn't dreamed it would come so soon.

93

'What you thinkin' about so hard, boy?'

After more than an hour sharing the wagon's seat and watching the warm February morning's fleecy clouds, the dusty road stretching ahead, or the monotonously flexing muscles of the mules' rumps, Massa Lea's sudden question startled Chicken George.

'Nothin',' he replied. 'Wasn't thinkin' 'bout nothin', Massa.'

'Somethin' I ain't never understood about you niggers!' There was an edge in Massa Lea's voice. 'Man try to talk to y'all decent, you right away start acting stupid. Makes me maddern' hell, especially a nigger like you that talks his head off if he wants to. Don't you reckon white people would respect you more if you acted like you had some sense?'

Chicken George's lulled mind had sprung to keen alertness. 'Dey might, den again some might not, Massa,' he said carefully. 'It all depen'.'

'There you go with that round-the-mulberry-bush talk. Depend on what?'

Still parrying until he got a better idea of what the massa was up to, Chicken George offered yet another meringue of words. 'Well, suh, I means like it depen' on what white folks you talkin' to, Massa, leas'ways dat's what I gits de impression.'

Massa Lea spat disgustedly over the side of the wagon. 'Feed and clothe a nigger, put a roof over his head, give him everything else he needs in this world, and that nigger'll never give you one straight answer!'

Chicken George risked a guess that the massa had simply decided upon impulse to open some sort of conversation with him, hoping to enliven what had become a boring and seemingly endless wagon ride.

In order to stop irritating Massa Lea, he tested the water by saying, 'You wants de straight up-an'-down truth, Massa, I b'lieves mos' niggers figger deys' bein' smart to act maybe dumber'n dey really is, 'cause mos' niggers is scairt o' white folks.'

'Scared!' exclaimed Massa Lea. 'Niggers slick as eels, that's what! I guess it's scared niggers plottin' uprisings to kill us every time we turn around! Poisonin' white people's food, even killin' babies! Anything you can name against white people, niggers doin' it all the time, and when white people act to protect themselves, niggers hollerin' they so scared!'

Chicken George thought it would be wise to stop fiddling with the massa's hair-trigger temper. 'Don't b'lieve none on yo' place ever done nothin' like dat, Massa,' he said quietly.

'You niggers know I'd kill you if you did!' A gamecock crowed loudly in its coop behind them, and some others clucked in response.

George said nothing. They were passing a large plantation, and he glanced across at a group of slaves beating down the dead cornstalks in preparation for ploughing before the next planting.

Massa Lea spoke again. 'It makes me sick to think how tough niggers can make it for a man that's worked hard all his life tryin' to build up somethin'.'

The wagon rolled on in silence for a while, but Chicken George could feel the massa's anger rising. Finally the massa exclaimed, 'Boy, let me tell you somethin'! You been all your life on my place with your belly full. You don't know nothin' about what it's like to grow up scufflin' and half starvin' with ten brothers and sisters and your mama and papa all sleeping in two hot, leaky rooms!'

Chicken George was astonished at such an admission from the massa, who went on heatedly as if he had to get the painful memories out of his system. 'Boy, I can't remember when my mama's belly wasn't big with another baby. And my papa chawin' his tobacco and half drunk forever hollerin' and cussin' that none of us was workin' hard enough to suit him on ten rocky acres that I wouldn't give fifty cents an acre for, where he called himself a farmer!' Glaring at Chicken George, he said angrily, 'You want to know what changed my life?'

'Yassuh,' said George.

'This big faith-healer came. Everybody was runnin' around excited about his big tent bein' put up. The openin' night everybody who could walk, even those who needed to be carried, were overflowin' that tent. Later on, people said there had never been such a hellfire sermon and such miracle cures in Caswell County. I never will forget the sight of those hundreds of white people leapin', screamin', shoutin', and testifyin'. People fallin' out in one 'nother's arms, moanin' and twitchin' and havin' the jerks. Worse than you'll see at any nigger camp meetin'. But midst all that ruckus and hoorah, there was one thing that somehow or 'nother really hit me.' Massa Lea looked at Chicken George. 'You know anything about the Bible'

'Not – well, nawsuh, not to speak of.'

'Bet you wouldn't of thought I know nothin' about it, either! It was from the Psalms. I've got that place marked in my own Bible. It says, "I have been young and now am old; yet have I not seen the righteous forsaken, nor His seed beggin' bread."

'After that preacher was long gone, that sayin' stuck in my head. I turned it up and down and sideways tryin' to figure out what meanin' it had for me. Everything I saw in my family just translated to beggin' bread. We didn't have nothin', and we wasn't goin' go *get* nothin'. Finally it seemed like that sayin' meant if I made myself to get righteous – in other words, if I worked hard, and lived the best I knew how – I'd never have to beg for bread when I was old.' The massa looked at Chicken George defiantly.

'Yassuh,' said Chicken George, not knowing what else to say.

'That's when I left home,' Massa Lea went on. 'I was eleven years old. I hit the road, askin' any and everybody for a job, doing anything, includin' nigger work. I was ragged. I ate scraps. I saved every cent I got, I mean for years, until I finally bought my first twenty-five woodsland acres, along with my first nigger, name of George. Fact, that's who I named you for—'

The massa seemed to expect some response. 'Uncle Pompey tol' me 'bout 'im,' said Chicken George.

'Yeah. Pompey came along later, my second nigger. Boy, you hear what I tell you, I worked shoulder to shoulder alongside that George nigger, we slaved from can to can't, rootin' up stumps and brush and rocks to plant my first crop. It wasn't nothin' but the Lord that made me buy a twenty-five-cent lottery ticket, and that ticket won me my first gamecock. Boy, that was the best bird I ever had! Even when he got cut bad, I'd patch him up and he went on to win more hackfights than anyone ever heard of one rooster doin'.'

He paused. 'Don't know how come I'm sittin' up here talkin' this way to a nigger. But I guess a man just need to talk to somebody sometime.'

He paused again. 'Can't do no talkin' to your wife, much. Seem like once a woman catches a husband to take care of them, they spend the rest of their lives either sick, restin', or complainin' about somethin', with niggers waitin' on them hand and foot. Or they're forever pattin' their faces with powder till they look like ghosts—'

Chicken George couldn't believe his ears. But the massa couldn't seem to stop himself. 'Or then you can get the other kind, like my family. I've wondered a lot of times why none of my nine brothers and sisters didn't fight to get away like I did. They're still scufflin' and starvin' just the same as the day I left – only now they've all got their own families.'

460

Chicken George decided that he had best not acknowledge with even a 'Yassuh' anything the massa was saying about his family, some of whom George had seen briefly talking with the massa when they were at cockfights or in town. Massa Lea's brothers were dirt-poor crackers of the sort that not only the rich planters but also even their slaves sneered at. Time and again he had seen how embarrassed the massa was to meet any of them. He had overheard their constant whining about hard times and their begging for money, and he had seen the hatred on their faces when the massa gave them the fifty cents or a dollar that he knew they were going to spend on white lightning. Chicken George thought of how many times he had heard Miss Malizy tell how, when the massa used to invite members of his family home for dinner, they would eat and drink enough to glut three times their own number, and the moment he was out of ear-shot, would heap scorn on him as if he were a dog.

'Any one of them could have done what I did!' Massa Lea exclaimed beside him on the wagon seat. 'But they didn't have the gumption, so the hell with them!' He fell silent again – but not for long.

'One way or another, I've got things goin' along pretty good now – a respectable roof to live under, my hundred or so gamebirds and eighty-five acres with over half of it in crops, along with the horse, mules, cows, and hogs. And I've got you few lazy niggers.'

'Yassuh,' said Chicken George, thinking that it might be reasonably safe to express in a mild way another point of view. 'But us niggers works hard for you, too, Massa. Long as I been knowin' my mammy an' Miss Malizy an' Sister Sarah an' Uncle Pompey an' Uncle Mingo – ain't dey been workin' fo' you hard as dey can?' And before the massa could reply, he tacked on something Sister Sarah had mentioned during his visit to slave row the previous Sunday. 'Fact, Massa, 'ceptin' for my mammy, ain't none of 'em less'n fifty years ol'–' He stopped himself, not about to add Sister Sarah's conclusion that the massa was simply too cheap to buy any younger slaves, apparently expecting to work the few he had until they dropped dead.

'You must not have been payin' attention to all I've been tellin' you, boy! Ain't a nigger I got worked as hard as me! So don't come tellin' *me* how hard niggers work!'

'Yassuh.'

' "Yassuh" *what?*'

'Jes' yassuh. You sho' work hard, too, Massa.'

'Damn right! You think it's easy being responsible for everything and everybody on my place? You think it's easy keepin' up a big flock of chickens?'

'Nawsuh, I know for sho' dat's hard on you, Massa.' George thought of Uncle Mingo's having attended the game-flock every day for more than thirty years – not to mention his own seven. Then, as a ploy to emphasize Mingo's decades of service, he asked innocently, 'Massa, is you got any idea how ol' is Uncle Mingo?'

Massa Lea paused, rubbing his chin. 'Hell, I really don't know. Let's see, I once figured he's around fifteen years older'n I am – that would put him somewhere up in his early sixties. And gettin' older every day. Seems like he's gettin' sick more and more every year. How does he seem to you? You're livin' down there around him.'

Chicken George's mind flashed to Uncle Mingo's recent bout of coughing, the worst one he had ever yet suffered, as far as he knew. Remembering how Miss Malizy and Sister Sarah often declared that the massa viewed any claim of sickness on their part as sheer laziness, he said finally, 'Well, Massa, mos' de time seem like he feelin' fine, but I b'lieves you really ought to know he do git real bad coughin' spells sometimes – so bad I gits scared, 'cause he jes' like a daddy to me.'

Catching himself too late, instantly he sensed a hostile reaction. A bump in the road set the cooped gamecocks clucking again, and for several moments the wagon rolled on before Massa Lea demanded, 'What's Mingo done so much for you? Was it him took you out of the fields and sent you down there with a shack for yourself?'

'Nawsuh, you done all dat, Massa.'

They rode on in silence for a while until the massa decided to speak again. 'I hadn't much thought about what you said there back a ways, but now that you mention it, I really got me a bunch of old niggers. Some of 'em bound to start breakin' down on me anytime now, goddammit! Much as niggers cost nowadays, I'm goin' to have to buy one or two younger field hands!' He turned as if accosting Chicken George. 'You see what I'm talking about, the kind of things I have to worry about all the time?'

'Yassuh, Massa.'

' "Yassuh, Massa!" ' That's the nigger answer to everything!'

'You sho' wouldn't want no nigger disagreein' wid you, suh.'

'Well, can't you find somethin' to say besides "Yassuh, Massa"?'

'Nawsuh – I means, well, suh, leas' you got some money to buy niggers wid, Massa. Dis season you winned so good in de cockfights.' Chicken George was hoping to move the conversation on to a safer subject. 'Massa,' he asked guilelessly, 'is it any gamecockers ain't got no farm atall? I means don't raise no crops, jes' nothin' but chickens?'

'Hmmmm. Not that I know of, unless it's some of those city slickers, but I never heard of any of them with enough birds to be called serious gamecockers.' He thought for a moment. 'In fact, it's usually the more gamecocks, the bigger the farm – like that Mr Jewett's place where you've been tomcattin'.'

Chicken George could have kicked himself for handing the massa that kind of an opening, and he quickly sought to close it. 'Ain't been over dere no mo', Massa.'

After a pause, Massa Lea said, 'Found you another wench somewhere else, huh?'

Chicken George hesitated before replying. 'I stays close now, Massa.' Which avoided a direct lie.

Massa Lea scoffed. 'Big, strapping twenty-year-old buck like you? Boy, don't tell *me* you're not slippin' around nights gettin' plenty of that good hot tail! Hell, I could hire you out to stud; bet you'd like that!' The massa's face creased into a half leer. 'Good friend of mine says them black wenches got plenty good hot tail, now tell me the truth, ain't that right, boy?'

Chicken George thought of the massa with his mammy. Steaming inside, he said slowly, almost coldly, 'Maybe dey is, Massa—' Then, defensively, 'I don't know dat many—'

'Well, okay, you don't want to tell you've been slippin' off my place at night, but I know it's time, and I know *where* you go and how *often* you go. I don't want that road patrol maybe shooting you like happened to that Mr Jewett's trainer nigger, so I'll tell you what I'm going to do, boy. When we get back, I'm goin' to write you out a travellin' pass to go chase tail *every* night if you want to! Ain't never thought I'd do that for no nigger!'

Massa Lea seemed almost embarrassed, then covered it with a frown. 'But I'm going to tell you one thing. First time you mess up, don't get back by daybreak, or too wore out to work, or I find out you've been on that Jewett place again, or anything else you know you're not supposed to do, I'm tearin' up the pass for good – and you along with it. Got that?'

Chicken George was incredulous. 'Massa, I sho' 'preciate dat! *Sho'* do, Massa!'

Expansively, Massa Lea waved away the thanks. 'All right now, you see I'm not half bad as you niggers make out. You can tell 'em I know how to treat a nigger good if I want to.'

The leering grin returned, 'Okay, what about them hot black wenches, boy? How many can you mount in a night?'

Chicken George was squirming in his seat. 'Suh, like I said, ain't know many—'

But his words seemed unheard as Massa Lea went on. 'I hear tell whole lots of white men go and find nigger women for their pleasure. You know what happens, don't you, boy?'

'I'se heared of it, Massa,' he said, trying not to think about the fact that he was talking to his own father. But apart from what went on in plantation cabins, George knew that in Burlington, Greenboro, and Durham there were 'special houses', spoken of only in hushed tones, usually run by some free black woman, where he had heard that white men paid from fifty cents to a dollar to couple with women in their choice of colours from sooty black to high yaller.

'Hell,' the massa persisted, 'I'm just talkin' to you sittin' up here by ourselves in this wagon. From what I hear tell, they're nigger women, all right, but by God they're women! Especially if it's one of the kind that lets a man know she wants it as much as he does. I hear tell they can be as hot as firecrackers, not always claimin' they're sick and whinin' about everythin' under the sun.' The massa looked inquisitively at Chicken George. 'Fellow I know told me you nigger boys can't never get enough of that hot black tail, that your experience?'

'Massa, nawsuh – leas'ways, I means jes' now sho' ain't—'

'There you go talkin' round the maypole again!'

'Don't mean roun' no pole, Massa.' Chicken George was trying his best to project his seriousness. 'I'se tryin' to say sump'n to you I ain't never tol' nobody, Massa! You know dat Massa MacGregor wid dem spangle yellow birds in de cockfights?'

'Of course. He and I talk a lot. What's he got to do with it?'

'Well, you done give yo' word you gon' give me a pass, so ain't no need me lyin'. Well, yassuh, lately I been slippin' out jes' like you say, visitin' dis here gal over at Massa MacGregor's—' His face was a study of earnestness.

'Dis here's sump'n I really been needin' to talk wid somebody I really can talk to, Massa. Jes' cain't figger 'er out! She name Matilda, she work in dey fiel', an' fill in if dey needs 'er in dey big house. Massa, she de firs' gal don't care what I'se said or tried, won't let herself be touched, nawsuh! Bes' I can git, she say she like me all right, 'cept she cain't stan' my ways – an' I tol' 'er I sho' ain't got no use for her'n neither. I tol' her I can git all de womens I wants, she jes' say go git 'em den, leave her alone.'

464

Massa Lea was listening to Chicken George as incredulously as he had to the massa.

'An' 'nother thing,' he went on. 'Every time I goes back she keep quotin' de Bible on me! How come she read de Bible, a preacher massa raised 'er till his 'ligion made 'im sell his niggers. Fact, I tell you how 'ligious *she* is! She heard 'bout bunch o' free niggers givin' a big night frolic wid eatin' an' liquor an' dancin' somewheres in de woods roun' over dere. Well, dis gal, ain't but seb'nteen, slip 'way from Massa MacGregor's an' bust in on dat frolic while it gwine on hot an' heavy! Dey says she commence sich a carryin' on, shoutin' for de Lawd to come save dem sinners 'fo' de devil git dere an' burn 'em up, dat every one dem free niggers near 'bout run over one 'nother leavin' dere, dey fiddler hard behin' 'em!'

Massa Lea laughed uproariously. 'Sounds like a hell of a gal! I'll say that!'

'Massa—' Chicken George hesitated. ' 'Fo' I met her, I is been catchin' jes' much tail as you says – but *dog* if she ain't got me to feelin' mo' to it dan jes' tail. Man git to thinkin' 'bout jumpin' de broom wid a good woman—'

Chicken George was astounded at himself. 'Dat is, if she have me,' he said in a weak voice. Then even more weakly, 'An' if'n you wouldn't make no objections—'

They rode on quite a way amid the wagon's squeakings and the gamecocks' cluckings before Massa Lea spoke again. 'Does Mr MacGregor knows you've been courtin' this gal of his?'

'Well, she bein' a field han', don't imagine she never say nothin' to him directly, nawsuh. But de big-house niggers knows, I speck some dem done tol' it.'

After another lull, Massa Lea asked, 'How many niggers has Mr MacGregor got?'

'He got pretty big place, Massa. Seem like from de size his slave row, I'd reckon twenty or mo' niggers, Massa.' George was confused by the questions.

'Been thinking,' said the massa after another silence. 'Since you were born, you never give me any real trouble – in fact, you've helped me around the place a lot, and I'm goin' to do somethin' for you. You just heard me sayin' a while back I need some younger field-hand niggers. Well, if that gal's big enough fool to jump the broom with somebody loves runnin' tail as much as I expect you won't never quit doin', then I'll ride over and talk with Mr MacGregor. If he's got as many niggers as you say, he ought not to miss one field gal all that much – if we can come to a decent price. Then you could move that gal – what's her name?'

' 'Tilda – Matilda, Massa,' breathed Chicken George, unsure if he was hearing right.

'Then you could move her over to my place, build y'all a cabin—'

George's mouth worked, but no sound came out. Finally he blurted, 'Nothin' but *high*-class massa do dat!'

Massa Lea grunted. He gestured. 'Long as you understand your first place remains down with Mingo!'

' *'Cose,* suh!'

Mustering a scowl, Massa Lea directed a stabbing forefinger at his driver. 'After you get hitched, I'm takin' back that travellin' pass! Help that what's her name, Matilda, keep your black ass home where it belongs!'

Chicken George was beyond words.

94

When the sun rose on the morning of Chicken George's wedding in August of 1827, the groom was frantically fastening iron hinges onto the cured-oak door jamb of his still uncompleted two-room cabin. Loping to the barn when that was done, he hurried back carrying over his head the new door that Uncle Pompey had carved and stained with the juice of crushed black walnut hulls, and mounted it in place. Then, casting a worried glance at the rising sun, he stopped long enough to wolf down the sausage and biscuit sandwich that had been practically thrown at him by his mammy late the previous evening in her fury at his long succession of put-offs, excuses, interruptions, and excursions. He had waited so long, and worked so slowly, that she had finally commanded everyone else not only to stop helping him anymore, but also even to stop offering him any encouragement.

Chicken George next quickly filled a large keg with slaked lime and water, stirred it vigorously, and – as fast as he could – dipped his large brush into the mess and began slathering whitewash over the outside of the rough-sawn planking. It was about ten o'clock when he finally backed away, almost as whitened as the cabin, to survey the completed job. There was plenty of time to spare, he told himself. All he had to do was bathe and dress, then take the two-hour wagon ride to the MacGregor plantation, where the wedding was due to start at one.

Bounding between the cabin and the well, he dashed three bucketfuls of water into the new galvanized tub in the cabin's front room. Humming loudly as he scrubbed himself, he dried himself off briskly and then wrapped himself in the bleached-sacking towel to run into the bedroom. After climbing into his cotton long drawers, he slipped on his blue stiff-front shirt, red socks, yellow pants, and yellow belt-backed suitcoat, and finally his brand-new bright-orange shoes, all of which he had bought with hackfighting winnings, an item at a time, over the past few months while he and Massa Lea were travelling to various North Carolina cities. Squeaking in his stiff shoes over to the bedroom table and sitting down on Uncle Mingo's wedding present, a carved stool with a sea of woven hickory strips, Chicken George smiled widely at himself in the long-handled mirror that was going to be one of his surprise presents for Matilda. With the mirror's help, he carefully arranged around his neck the green woollen scarf Matilda had knitted for him. Lookin' good, he had to admit. There remained only the crowning touch. Pulling a round cardboard box out from under the bed, he removed the top and with almost reverent gentleness lifted out the black derby hat that was his wedding present from Massa Lea. Turning it slowly around and around on stiff forefingers, he savoured its stylish shape almost sensuously before returning to the mirror and positioning the derby at just the right rakish tilt over one eye.

'Git out'n dere! We been sittin' a hour in dis wagon!' His mammy Kizzy's shout from just outside the window left no doubt that her rage was undiminished.

'Comin', Mammy!' he hollered back. After one last appreciation of his ensemble in the mirror, he slipped a flat, small bottle of white lightning into his inside coat pocket and emerged from the new cabin as if expecting applause. He was going to flash his biggest smile and tip his hat until he got a look at the baleful glares of his mammy, Miss Malizy, Sister Sarah, and Uncle Pompey, all sitting frozenly in their Sunday best in the wagon. Averting his glance and whistling as breezily as he could manage, he climbed up onto the driver's seat – careful not to disturb a crease – slapped the reins against the backs of the two mules, and they were under way – only an hour late.

Along the road, Chicken George sneaked several fortifying nips from his bottle, and the wagon arrived at the MacGregor place shortly after two. Kizzy, Sister Sarah, and Miss Malizy descended amid profuse apologies to the visibly worried and upset Matilda in her white gown. Uncle Pompey unloaded the food baskets they had brought, and after pecking at Matilda's cheek, Chicken George went swaggering about slapping backs and breathing liquor in the faces of the guests as he introduced himself. Apart from those he already knew who lived in Matilda's slave row, they were mostly prayer-meeting folk she had recruited from among the slaves of two nearby plantations and whom she had got permission to invite. She wanted them to meet her intended, and so did they. Though most of them had heard a lot about him from sources other than herself, their first actual sight of Chicken George evoked reactions ranging from muttering to open-mouthed astonishment. As he cut his swath through the wedding party, he gave a wide berth to Kizzy, Sister Sarah, and Miss Malizy, whose dagger stares were being sharpened by every remark each was overhearing about the dubiousness of Matilda's 'catch'. Uncle Pompey had chosen simply to merge with the other guests as if he were unaware of who the bridegroom was.

Finally, the hired white preacher came out of the big house, followed by the massas and Missis MacGregor and Lea. They stopped in the backyard, the preacher clutching his Bible like a shield, and the suddenly quiet crowd of black people grouped stiffly a respectful distance away. As Matilda's missis had planned it, the wedding would combine some of the white Christian wedding service with jumping the broom afterwards. Guiding her rapidly sobering groom by one yellow sleeve, Matilda positioned them before the preacher, who cleared his throat and proceeded to read a few solemn passages from his Bible. Then he asked, 'Matilda and George, do you solemnly swear to take each other, for better or worse, the rest of your lives?'

'I does,' said Matilda softly.

'Yassuh!' said Chicken George, much too loudly.

Flinching, the preacher paused and then said, 'I pronounce you man and wife!'

Among the black guests, someone sobbed.

'Now you may kiss the bride!'

Seizing Matilda, Chicken George crushed her in his arms and gave her a resounding smack. Amid the ensuing gasps and tongue-clucking, it occurred to him that he might not be making the best impression, and while they locked arms and jumped the broom, he racked his brains for something to say that would lend some dignity to the occasion, something that would placate his slave row family and win over the rest of those Bible toters. He had it!

'De Lawd is my shepherd!' he proclaimed. 'He done give me what I wants!'

When he saw the stares and glares that greeted this announcement, he decided to give up on them, and the first chance he got, he slipped the bottle from his pocket and drained it dry. The rest of the festivities – a wedding feast and reception – passed in a blur, and it was Uncle Pompey who drove the Lea plantation's wagon homewards through the sunset. Grim and mortified, Mammy Kizzy, Miss Malizy, and Sister Sarah cast malevolent glances at the spectacle behind them: the bridegroom snoring soundly with his head in the lap of his tearful bride, his green scarf askew and most of his face concealed under his black derby.

Chicken George snorted awake when the wagon jerked to a stop alongside their new cabin. Sensing groggily that he should beg everyone's forgiveness, he began to try, but the doors of three cabins slammed like gunshots. But he wouldn't be denied a last courtly gesture. Picking up his bride, he pushed open the door with one foot and somehow manoeuvred both of them inside without injury – only to stumble with her over the tub of bathwater that still stood in the middle of the room. It was the final humiliation – but all was forgotten and forgiven when Matilda, with a shriek of joy, caught sight of her special wedding present: the highly lacquered, eight-day-winding grandfather clock, as tall as herself, that Chicken George had purchased with the last of his hackfight savings and hauled in the back of the wagon all the way from Greensboro.

As he sat bleary-eyed on the floor where he'd fallen, bathwater soaking his brand-new orange shoes, Matilda went over to him and reached out her hand to help him up.

'You come wid me now, George. I'm gwine put you to bed.'

95

By daybreak, Chicken George was gone back down the road to his gamefowl. Then, about an hour after breakfast, Miss Malizy heard someone calling her name and, going to the kitchen door, she was startled to see the new bride, whom she greeted and invited inside.

'No'm, thank you,' said Matilda. 'I jes' wanted to ax whichaway is de fiel' dey's workin' in today, an' whereabouts can I fin' me a hoe?'

A few minutes later, Matilda simply appeared and joined Kizzy, Sister Sarah, and Uncle Pompey in the day's field work. Late that evening they all gathered about her in slave row, keeping her company until her husband got home. In the course of conversation, Matilda asked if any slave-row prayer meetings were held regularly, and when she was told that none were, proposed that one be made a part of each Sunday afternoon.

'Tell you de truth, I'se shame to say I ain't done nowhere near de prayin' I ought to,' said Kizzy.

'Me neither,' confessed Sister Sarah.

'Jes' ain't never seem to me no 'mount of prayin' is did nothin' to change white folks,' said Uncle Pompey.

'De Bible say Joseph was sol' a slave to de Egyptians, but de Lawd was wid Joseph, an' de Lawd blessed de Egyptians' house for Joseph's sake,' Matilda said in a matter-of-fact manner.

Three glances, quickly exchanged, expressed their steadily mounting respect for the young woman.

'Dat George tol' us yo' first massa a preacher,' said Sister Sarah. 'You soun' like a preacher yo'se'f!'

'I'se a servant o' de Lawd, dat's all,' replied Matilda.

Her prayer meetings began the following Sunday, two days after Chicken George and Massa Lea had gone off in the wagon with twelve gamecocks.

'Massa say he finally got de right birds to go fight where de big money is,' he explained, saying that this time the Lea birds would be competing in an important 'main' somewhere near Goldsboro.

One morning when they were out in the field, carefully employing a gentle tone that suggested the sympathy of a forty-seven-year-old woman for a new bride of eighteen, Sister Sarah said, 'Lawdy, honey, I 'spect yo' married life gwine be split up twixt you an' dem chickens.'

Matilda looked at her squarely. 'What I done always heared, an' b'lieved, is anybody's marriage jes' what dey makes it. An' I reckon he know what kin' he want our'n to be.'

But having established her stand about marriage, Matilda would readily share in any conversation about her colourful husband, whether it was humorous or serious in nature.

'He done had itchy foots since he was a crawlin' baby,' Kizzy told her one night, visiting in the new cabin.

'Yes, ma'am,' said Matilda, 'I figgered dat when he come a-courtin'. He wouldn't talk 'bout hardly nothin' 'cept rooster fightin' an' him an' de massa travellin' somewheres.' Hesitating, she then added in her frank way, 'But when he foun' out weren't no man gwine have his way wid me 'fo' we'd jumped a broom, Lawd, he had a fit! Fact, one time I give up on seein' 'im again. Don't know what hit 'im, but I like to fell out de night he come a-rushin' in an' say, "Look, let's us get hitched!" '

'Well, I'se sho' glad he had de sense!' said Kizzy. 'But now you's hitched, gal, I'se gwine tell you straight what's on my min'. I wants me some gran'chilluns!'

'Ain't nothin' wrong wid dat, Miss Kizzy, 'Cause I wants me some young'uns, too, same as other womens haves.'

When Matilda announced two months later that she was in a family way, Kizzy was beside herself. Thinking about her son becoming a father made her think about *her* father – more than she had in many years – and one evening when Chicken George was away again, Kizzy asked, 'Is he ever mentioned anything to you 'bout his gran'pappy?'

'No'm, he ain't.' Matilda looked puzzled.

'He *ain't?*' Seeing the old woman's disappointment, Matilda added quickly, 'Reckon he jes' ain't got to it yet, Mammy Kizzy.'

Deciding that she'd better do it herself, since she remembered more than he did anyway, Kizzy began telling Matilda of her life at Massa Waller's for sixteen years until her sale to Massa Lea, and most of what she had to say was about her African pappy and the many things he had told her. ' 'Tilda, how come I'se tellin' you all dis, I jes' wants you to understan' how I wants dat chile in yo' belly an' any mo' you has to know all 'bout 'im, too, on 'count of he's dey great-gran'daddy.'

'I sho' does understan', Mammy Kizzy,' said Matilda, whereupon her mother-in-law told yet more of her memories, with both of them feeling their closeness growing throughout the rest of the evening.

Chicken George's and Matilda's baby boy was born during the spring of 1828, with Sister Sarah serving as the midwife, assisted by a nervous Kizzy. Her joy about having a grandchild at last tempered her anger that the boy's father was yet again off somewhere for a week with Massa Lea. The following evening, when the new mother felt up to it, everyone on slave row gathered at the cabin to celebrate the birth of the second baby that had been born there on the Lea plantation.

'You's finally "Gran-mammy Kizzy" now!' said Matilda, propped up in bed against some pillows, nestling the baby and weakly smiling at her visitors.

'Lawd, yes! Don't it soun' pretty!' exclaimed Kizzy, her whole face one big grin.

'Soun' like to me Kizzy gittin' ol', dat's wat!' said Uncle Pompey with a twinkle in his eye.

'*Hmph!* Ain't no woman here ol' as some we knows!' snorted Sister Sarah.

Finally, Miss Malizy commanded, 'Awright, time us all git out'n here an' let 'em res'!' And they all did, except for Kizzy.

After being quietly thoughtful for a while, Matilda said, 'Ma'am, I been thinkin' 'bout what you tol' me 'bout yo' pappy. Since I never even got to see mine, I b'lieves George wouldn't care if dis child have my pappy's name. It was Virgil, my mammy say.'

The name instantly had Chicken George's hearty approval when he returned, filled with such jubilance at the birth of a son that he could hardly contain himself. Black derby awry as his big hands swooped the infant up in the air, he exclaimed, 'Mammy, 'member what I tol' you, I gwine tell my young'uns what you tol' me?' His face alight, he made a little ceremony of seating himself before the fireplace with Virgil held upright in his lap as he spoke to him in grand tones. 'Listen here, boy! Gwine tell you 'bout yo' great-gran'daddy. He were a African dat say he name "Kunta Kinte". He call a guitar a *ko*, an' a river "Kamby Bolongo", an' lot mo' things wid African names. He say he was choppin' a tree to make his l'il brother a drum when it was fo' mens come up an' grabbed 'im from behin'. Den a big ship brung 'im crost de big water to a place call 'Naplis. An' he had runned off fo' times when he try to kill dem dat cotched 'im an' dey cut half his foot off!'

Lifting the infant, he turned his face towards Kizzy. 'An' he jumped de broom wid de big-house cook name Miss Bell, an' dey had a l'il ol' gal – an' dere she is, yo' gran'mammy grinnin' at you right dere!' Matilda was beaming her approval as widely as Kizzy, whose eyes were moist with love and pride.

With her husband away as much as he was, Matilda began spend-

472

ing more of her time in the evenings with Gran'mammy Kizzy, and after a while they were pooling their rations and eating their supper together. Always Matilda would say the grace as Kizzy sat quietly with her hands folded and her head bowed. Afterwards Matilda would nurse the baby, and then Kizzy would sit proudly with little Virgil clasped against her body, rocking him back and forth, either humming or singing to him softly as the grandfather clock ticked and Matilda sat reading her worn Bible. Even though it wasn't against the massa's rules, Kizzy still disapproved of reading – but it *was* the Bible, so she guessed no harm could come of it. Usually, not too long after the baby was asleep, Kizzy's head would begin bobbing, and often she would begin murmuring to herself as she dozed. When she leaned over to retrieve the sleeping Virgil from Kizzy's arms, Matilda sometimes heard snatches of the things she was mumbling. They were always the same: 'Mammy . . . Pappy . . . Don't let 'em take me! . . . My people's los' . . . Ain't never see 'em no mo' dis worl' . . .' Deeply touched, Matilda would whisper something like, 'We's yo' people now, Gran'mammy Kizzy,' and after putting Virgil to bed, she would gently rouse the older woman – whom she was growing to love as she had her own mother – and after accompanying her to her own cabin, Matilda would often be wiping at her eyes on her way back.

On Sunday afternoons, only the three women attended Matilda's prayer services at first – until Sister Sarah's sharp tongue finally shamed Uncle Pompey into joining them. No one ever even thought about inviting Chicken George, for even when he was at home, by Sunday noon he would have returned to the gamefowl area. With the little group of five seated solemnly on chairs brought from their cabins and placed in a half circle under the chinquapin tree, Matilda would read some biblical passages she had selected. Then, with her serious brown eyes searching each face, she would ask if any among them would care to lead in prayer, and seeing that none of them did, she would always say, 'Well, den, will y'all jine me on bended knee?' As they all kneeled facing her, she would offer a moving, unpretentious prayer. And afterwards she'd lead them in singing some spirited song; even Uncle Pompey's cracked, raspy baritone joined in as they made slave row resound with such rousing spirituals as 'Joshua fit de battle o' Jericho! Jericho! Jericho! . . . An' de walls come a-tumblin' down!' The meeting turned then into a group discussion on the general subject of faith.

'Dis is de Lawd's day. We all got a soul to save an' a heab'n to maintain,' Matilda might offer in her matter-of-fact way. 'We needs to keep in our minds who it was made us, an' dat was Gawd. Den who it was redeemed us, an' dat was Christ Jesus. Christ Jesus teached us to be humble, an' mindful, dat we can be reborn in de sperrit.'

'I loves Lawd Jesus good as anybody,' Kizzy testified humbly, 'but y'all see, I jes' ain't never knowed dat much 'bout 'im 'till I was up some size, even though my mammy say she had me christened when I was jes' a l'il thing, at one dem big camp meetin's.'

'Seem like to me we does be bes' if we's been put next to Gawd when we's young'uns,' said Sister Sarah. She gestured at Virgil in his gran'mammy's lap. ' 'Cause dat way we starts out early soakin' up some 'ligion an' settin' sto' by it.'

Miss Malizy spoke to Uncle Pompey. 'You don't know, if you'd of started out early, you might of made a preacher. You even got de look of one as it is.'

'Preacher! How I'm gwine preach an' cain't even read!' he exclaimed.

'De Lawd put things to say in yo' mouth if He call you to preach,' Mat'ida said.

'Dat husban' of your'n call hisself preachin' roun' here once!' said Miss Malizy. 'He ever tol' you 'bout dat?' They all laughed and Kizzy said, 'He sho' could of made some kin' o' preacher! Much as he love to show off an' run his mouth!'

'He'd o' been one dem trickin' an' trancin' preachers holdin' big revivals!' said Sister Sarah.

They talked for a while about powerful preachers they had all either seen or heard about. Then Uncle Pompey told of his powerfully religious mother, whom he remembered from boyhood on the plantation where he was born. 'She was big an' fat an' I reckon de shoutin'est woman anybody ever heared of.'

'Remind me of ol' maid Sister Bessie on de plantation I was raised on,' said Miss Malizy. 'She was 'nother one dem shoutin' womens. She'd got ol' widout no husban' till it come one dem big camp meetin's. Well, she shouted till she went in a trance. She come out'n it sayin' she jes' had a talk wid de Lawd. She say He say her mission on de earth was to save ol' Br'er Timmons from goin' to hell by him jumpin' de broom wid sich a Christian woman as her! Scared 'im so bad he jumped it, too!'

Though few of those he ran into on his trips would have guessed from the way he acted that Chicken George had jumped the broom — or ever would — he surprised the women on slave row at home with how warmly he took to marriage and how well he treated his wife and family. Never did he return from a cockfight – wearing his scarf and derby, which had become his costume, rain or shine, summer or winter – without winnings to put away. Most of the time, giving Matilda a few dollars, he didn't have much money left after paying for the gifts he, of course, always brought along not only for Matilda and his mammy, but also for Miss Malizy, Sister Sarah, and Uncle Pompey as well as for young Virgil. He always came home, too, with at least an hour's worth of news about whatever he had seen or heard about on his travels. As his slave-row family gathered around him, Kizzy would nearly always think how her African pappy had brought another slave row most of its news, and now it was her son.

Returning once from a long journey that had taken him to Charleston, Chicken George described 'so many dem great big sailin' ships dey poles look like a thicket! An' niggers like ants packin' an' polin' out dem great big tobacco hogsheads an' all kinds o' other stuff to sail de water to dat England an' different mo' places. Look like wherever me an' massa travels nowdays, it's niggers diggin' canals, an' layin' dem gravel highways, an' buildin' railroads! Niggers jes' buildin' dis country wid dey muscles!'

Another time he had heard that 'de white folks threatenin' de Indians 'bout takin' in so many niggers on dey reservations. Plenty dem Creeks and Seminoles done married niggers. It's even some nigger Indian chiefs! But I hears dem Chocktaws, Chickasaws, an' Cherokees hate niggers even worse'n white folks does.'

He would be asked far fewer questions than they really wanted to know the answers to, and soon, making polite excuses, Kizzy, Miss Malizy, Sister Sarah, and Uncle Pompey would disappear into their cabins to let him and Matilda be alone.

'Done tol' myself you never gwine hear me wid no whole lot of complainin', George,' she told him one such night as they lay in bed, 'but I sho' do feel like I ain't hardly got no husban' a lot o' times.'

'Knows what you means, honey, I sho' does,' he said easily. 'Out dere travellin' wid massa, or sometimes me and Uncle Mingo up all night wid some dem sick chickens, I be's jes' thinkin' 'bout you an' de young'un.'

Matilda bit her tongue, choosing not to voice her doubts, even her suspicions about some of the things he said. Instead she asked, 'You figger it's ever gwine git any better, George?'

'Ever git massa rich enough! So he be willin' to stay home hisself. But look, it ain't hurtin' us none, baby! Look how we's savin' if I can keep bringin' in winnin's like I is.'

'Money ain't you!' said Matilda flatly, and then she made her tone

475

softer. 'An' we'd save a lot mo' if you jes' ease up buyin' presents for ever'body! We all 'preciates 'em, you knows dat! But George, where I ever gwine wear sich as dat fine silk dress I specks better'n any missy got!'

'Baby you can jes' put dat dress on right in here, den pull it off fo' me!'

'You's terrible!'

He was the most exciting man – beyond anyone she had even dreamed of knowing, at least in that way. And he certainly was a fine provider. But she didn't really trust him, and she couldn't help wondering whether he loved her and their baby as much as he did travelling with the massa. Was there anything in the Scriptures about chickens? Vaguely she recalled something – in Matthew, if she wasn't mistaken – about 'a hen gathereth her chickens beneath her wings . . .' I must look that up, she told herself.

When she did have a husband at home, though, Matilda submerged her doubts and disappointments and tried to be the best wife she knew how. If she knew he was coming, a big meal was waiting; if he came unexpectedly, she prepared one right away, day or night. After a while she quit trying to get him to bless a meal, simply saying a short grace herself, then delighting in watching him eat while he held the gurgling Virgil in his lap. Then afterwards, with the boy put to bed, examining George's face, she pinched out blackheads; or heating water to half fill the tin tub, she would wash his hair and his back; and if he arrived complaining of aching feet, she would rub them with a warm paste of roasted onions and homemade soap. Finally, whenever the candles were blown out and they were again between her fresh sheets, Chicken George would make up for his absences to the utmost. About the time Virgil began to walk, Matilda was great with child again; she was surprised it hadn't happened sooner.

With another child on the way, Gran'mammy Kizzy decided the time had come to take her son aside and tell him a thing or two that had been on her mind for a long time. He arrived home from a trip one Sunday morning to find her minding Virgil while Matilda was up in the big house helping Miss Malizy prepare dinner for guests who were soon to arrive.

'You set down right dere!' she said, wasting no time. He did, eyebrows risen. 'I don't care if you's grown now, I still brought you in dis worl', an' you gwine listen! God done give you a real good woman you ain't noways treatin' right! I ain't foolin' wid you now! You hear me? I still take a stick to your behin' in a minute! You got to spen' mo' time wid yo' wife an' young'un, an' her awready big wid yo' nex' one, too!'

'Mammy, what you 'speck?' he said as irritably as he dared. 'When massa say "Go", tell him I ain't?'

Kizzy's eyes were blazing. 'Ain't talkin' 'bout dat an' you know it! Tellin' dat po' gal you settin' up nights tendin' sick chickens an' sich as dat! Where you *git* all dis lyin' an' drinkin' an' gamblin' an' runnin' roun'? You *knows* I ain't raised you like dat! An' don't think dis jes' me talkin'! 'Tilda ain't no fool, she jes' ain't let you know she seein' right through you, too!' Without another word, Gran'mammy Kizzy stalked angrily from the cabin.

With Massa Lea being among the entrants for the great 1830 cockfighting tournament in Charleston, no one could criticize Chicken George for being away when the baby was born. He returned as ecstatic to learn about his second son – whom Matilda had already named Ashford, after her brother – as he was aglow with his good luck. 'Massa winned over a thousan' dollars, an' I winned fifty in de hackfights! Y'all ought to hear how white folks an' niggers both has started to hollerin', "I'm bettin' on dat Chicken George!"' He told her how in Charleston, Massa Lea had learned that President Andrew Jackson was a man after their own style. 'Ain't nobody love cockfightin' mo'n he do! He call in dem big congressmens an' senators an' he show 'em a *time* fightin' dem Tennessee birds o' his'n right dere in dat White House! Massa say dat Jackson gamble an' drink wid any man. Dey say when dem matchin' chestnut hosses pullin' 'im in dat fine Pres'dent's coach, he be settin' up dere wid his velvet-lined suitcase o' liquor right beside 'im! Massa say far as southern white men's concerned, he can stay Pres'dent till he git tired!' Matilda was unimpressed.

But Chicken George had seen something in Charleston that shook her – and the others on slave row – as deeply as it had him. 'I bet you I seen a mile long o' niggers bein' driv' along in chains!'

'*Lawdy!* Niggers from where?' asked Miss Malizy.

'Some sol' out'n Nawth an' South Ca'liny, but mainly out'n Virginia was what I heared!' he said. 'Different Charleston niggers tol' me it's thousan's o' niggers a month gittin' took to great big cotton plantations steady bein' cleared out'n de woods in Alabama, Mississippi, Louisiana, Arkansas, an' Texas. Dey say de ol'-style nigger traders on a hoss is gone, done become big companies wid offices in big hotels! Dey say it's even big paddle-wheel ships carryin' nothin' but chained-up Virginia niggers down to New Orleans! An' dey says—'

'Jes' *heish!*' Kizzy sprang upright. 'HEISH!' She went bolting towards her cabin in tears.

'What come *over* her?' George asked Matilda after the others had left in embarrassment.

'Ain't you know?' she snapped. 'Her mammy an' pappy in Virginia las' she know, an' you scare her half to death!'

Chicken George looked sick. His face told her he hadn't realized, but Matilda refused to let him off that easily. She had become convinced that for all of his worldliness, he was sorely lacking in sensitivity about too many things. 'You knows well as I does Mammy Kizzy been sol' herself! Jes' like I was!' she told him. 'Anybody ever sol' ain't gwine never forget it! An' won't never be de same no mo'!' She looked at him significantly. 'You ain't never been. Dat's how come you don't understan' no massa cain't never be trusted – includin' your'n!'

'What you rilin' at *me* fo'?' he demanded testily.

'You ax me what upset Mammy Kizzy an' I tol' you. Ain't got no mo' to say 'bout it!' Matilda caught herself. She didn't want harshness between her and her husband. After a moment's silence, she managed a small smile. 'George, I knows what make Mammy Kizzy feel better! Go make 'er come on over here to hear you tell dis baby 'bout his African gran'pappy like you tol' Virgil.' And that's just what he did.

96

It was near dawn, and Chicken George was standing in the doorway swaying slightly and grinning at Matilda, who was sitting up waiting for him. His black derby was askew. 'Fox got 'mongst de chickens,' he slurred. 'Me an' Uncle Mingo been all night catchin' 'em—'

Matilda's upraised hand silenced him, and her tone was cold. 'Reckon de fox give you liquor an' sprinkled you wid dat rosewater I smells—' Chicken George's mouth opened. 'Naw, George, you *listen!* Look here, long as I'se yo' wife, an' mammy to our chilluns, I be here when you leaves an' I be here when you gits back, 'cause ain't us much as yo'self you's doin' wrong. It right in de Bible: "You sows what you reaps" – sow single, you reaps double! An' Matthew sebenth chapter say, "Wid whatsoever measure you metes out to others, dat shall be measured out to you again!"'

He tried to pretend that he was too outraged to speak, but he just couldn't think of anything to say. Turning, he reeled back out the door and staggered down the road to sleep with the chickens.

But he was back the next day, derby hat in hand, and dutifully spent all but a few nights with his family through the rest of that fall and winter, and those few only when he and the massa were away briefly on some trip. And when Matilda's next labour pains quickened early one morning in January of 1831, although it was the height of gamecocking season, he persuaded the massa to let him stay home – and to take the ailing Uncle Mingo along with him to that day's fights.

Anxiously, he paced outside the cabin door, wincing and frowning as he listened to Matilda's anguished moans and cries. Then, hearing other voices, he tiptoed gingerly close and heard his Mammy Kizzy urging, 'Keep pullin' 'gainst my hand – *hard*, honey! ... Another breath ... deep! ... dat's right! ... *Hold!* ... Hold!' Then Sister Sarah commanded, 'Bear *down*, you hear me! ... Now PUSH! ... PUSH!'

Then, soon: 'Here it come ... Yes, Lawd—'

When he heard sharp slaps, then an infant's shrill cries, Chicken George backed away several steps, dazed by what he had just heard. It wasn't long before Gran'mammy Kizzy emerged, her face creasing into a grin. 'Well, look like all y'all got in you is boys!'

He began leaping and springing about, whooping so boisterously that Miss Malizy came bolting out the back door of the big house. He ran to meet her, scooped her up off her feet, whirled her around and around, and shouted, 'Dis one be name after me!'

The next evening, for the third time, he gathered everyone around to listen as he told his family's newest member about the African great-gran'daddy who called himself Kunta Kinte.

At the end of a routine Caswell County landholders' meeting late that August, the county courthouse was resounding with the parting calls of the local planters as they began to disperse and head homewards. Massa Lea was driving his wagon – Chicken George squatting in the back with his pocket clasp knife, gutting and scaling the string of hand-sized perch that the massa had just bought from a vendor – when the wagon stopped abruptly. George's eyes widened as he sat up in time to see Massa Lea already on the ground hurrying along with many other massas towards a white man who had just dismounted from a heaving, lathered horse. He was shouting wildly to his swiftly enlarging crowd. Snatches of his words reached Chicken George and the other blacks who listened gaping: 'Don't know how many whole families dead' ... 'women, babies' ... 'sleepin' in their beds when the murderin' niggers broke in' ... 'axes, swords, clubs' ... 'nigger preacher named Nat Turner...'

The faces of the other blacks mirrored his own dread foreboding as the white men cursed and gestured with flushed, furious faces. His mind flashed back to those terror-filled months after that revolt in Charleston had been foiled with no one hurt. What on earth would happen now? Slit-eyed, the massa returned to the wagon, his face frozen with rage. Never looking back, he drove homewards at a mad gallop with Chicken George hanging on in the wagon-bed with both hands.

Reaching the big house, Massa Lea sprang from the wagon, leaving George staring at the cleaned fish. Moments later, Miss Malizy ran out the kitchen door and rushed across the backyard towards slave row, flailing her hands over her bandannaed head. Then the massa reappeared carrying his shotgun, his voice rasping at George, 'Get to your cabin!'

Ordering everyone on slave row out of their quarters, Massa Lea told them icily what Chicken George had already heard. Knowing that he alone might possibly temper the massa's wrath, George found his voice. '*Please*, Massa—' he said, quavering. The shotgun jerked directly towards him.

'*Git!* Everything out of your cabins! *All* you niggers, GIT!' For the next hour, carrying, dragging, heaping their meagre belongings outside, under the massa's searching eyes and abusive threats of what he would do to whomever he found concealing any weapons or suspicious objects, they shook out every cloth, opened every container, cut and tore apart every cornshuck mattress – and still his fury seemed beyond any bounds.

With his boot he shattered Sister Sarah's box of nature remedies, sending her dried roots and herbs flying while he yelled at her, 'Get rid of that damn voodoo!' Before other cabins he flung away treasured possessions and smashed others with his fists or his feet. The four women were weeping, old Uncle Pompey seemed paralysed, the frightened children clutched tearfully about Matilda's skirts. Chicken George's own fury boiled as Matilda cried out, almost in pain, when the shotgun's butt smashed the front panelling of her precious grandfather clock. 'Let me find a sharpened nail in there, some nigger'll die!'

Leaving slave row in a shambles, the massa rode in the wagon-bed holding his shotgun as George drove them down to the gamefowl training area.

Faced with the gun and the barked command for all of their belongings to be emptied out, the terrified old Uncle Mingo began blurting, 'Ain't done nothin', Massa—'

'Trustin' niggers got whole families dead now!' yelled Massa Lea. Confiscating the axe, the hatchet, the thin wedge, a metal frame, and both of their pocket knives, the massa loaded them all into the wagon as Chicken George and Uncle Mingo stood watching. 'In case you niggers try to break in, I'm sleepin' with this shotgun!' he shouted at them, lashing the horse into a gallop and disappearing up the road in a cloud of dust.

97

'Hear you've got four boys in a row now!' The massa was getting off his horse in the gamefowl training area. It had taken a full year for the white South's mingled fear and fury – including Massa Lea's – to fully subside. Though he had resumed taking Chicken George with him to cockfights a month or two after the revolt, the massa's obvious coldness had taken the rest of a year to thaw. But for reasons unknown to either man, their relationship had seemed to grow closer than ever before ever since then. Neither one ever mentioned it, but they both hoped fervently that there would be no more black uprisings.

'Yassuh! Big ol' fat boy borned fo' daybreak, Massa!' said Chicken George, who was mixing a dozen gamehen egg whites and a pint of beer with oatmeal, cracked wheat, and a variety of crushed herbs to bake a fresh supply of the gamecocks' special bread. He had learned the 'secret' recipe only that morning, grudgingly, from ailing old Uncle Mingo, whom Massa Lea had ordered to rest in his cabin until his unpredictable and increasingly severe coughing spells eased off. In the meanwhile, Chicken George alone was intensely training twenty-odd top-prime gamecocks after almost ruthless cullings from among the seventy-six freshly matured birds recently brought in off the rangewalks.

It was but nine weeks from the day that he and Massa Lea were to leave for New Orleans. His years of local victories, plus no few in statewide competitions, had finally emboldened the massa to pit his topmost dozen birds in that city's renowned New Year's Day season-opening 'main'. If the Lea birds could win as many as half of their pittings against the calibre of championship fighting cocks assembled there, the massa would not only win a fortune but also find himself elevated overnight into recognition among the entire South's major gamecockers. Just the possibility was so exciting that Chicken George had been able to think of almost nothing else.

Massa Lea had walked his horse over and tied a small rope from its halter onto the split-rail fence. Ambling back over near George, the massa scuffed the toe of his boot against a clump of grass and said, 'Mighty funny, four boy young'uns, an' you ain't never named none after me.'

Chicken George was surprised, delighted – and embarrassed. 'You sho' right, Massa!' he exclaimed lamely. 'Dat 'zactly what to name dat boy – *Tom!* Yassuh, *Tom!*'

The massa looked gratified. Then he glanced towards the small cabin beneath a tree, his expression serious. 'How's the old man?'

'Tell you de truth, Massa, middle of las' night, he had a *bad* coughin' spell. Dat was 'fo' dey sent Uncle Pompey down here to git me up dere when 'Tilda havin' de baby. But when I cooked 'im sump'n to eat dis mo'nin', he set up an' et it all, an' swear he feel fine. He got mad when I tol' 'im he got to stay in de bed till you say he can come out.'

'Well, let the old buzzard stay in there another day, anyhow,' said the massa. 'Maybe I ought to get a doctor to come down here and look him over. That bad coughing off and on, for long as it's been, it's no good!'

'Nawsuh. But he sho' don' b'lieve in no doctors, Massa—'

'I don't care what he believes! But we'll see how he does the rest of the week—'

For the next hour, Massa Lea inspected the cockerels and the stags in their fencerow pens, and finally the magnificent birds that Chicken George was conditioning and training. Massa Lea was pleased with what he saw. Then, for a while, he talked about the forthcoming trip. It would take almost six weeks to reach New Orleans, he said, in the heavy new wagon he was having custom-built in Greensboro. It would have an extended bed with twelve fitted removable cock coops, a special padded workbench for daily exercising of birds during travel, along with special shelves, racks, and bins that Massa Lea had specified to hold all necessary items and supplies for any long trips carrying gamecocks. It would be ready in ten days.

When Massa Lea left, Chicken George immersed himself in the day's remaining tasks. He was driving the gamecocks to the limit. The massa had given him the authority to use his own judgment in further culling out any birds in which he discovered the slightest flaw of any sort, as only the most comprehensively superb birds could stand a chance in the level of competition awaiting them in New Orleans. Working with the birds, he kept thinking about the music he had been told he was going to hear in New Orleans, including big brass bands marching in the streets. The black sailor he had met in Charleston had also said that early every Sunday afternoon, thousands of people would gather in a large public square called 'Place Congo' to watch hundreds of slaves perform the dances of the African places and peoples they had come from. And the sailor had sworn that the New Orleans waterfront surpassed any other he had ever seen. And the women! An unending supply of them said the sailor, as exotic as they were willing, of every kind and colour, known as 'creoles', 'octoroons', and 'quadroons'. He could hardly wait to get there.

Late that afternoon, after having meant to do so several times before when some chore had detained him, George finally knocked, then stepped on inside the cluttered, musty cabin of Uncle Mingo.

'How you feelin'?' George asked. 'Is it anything I can git you?' But he didn't need to wait for an answer.

The old man was shockingly wan and weak – but as irritable as ever about his enforced inactivity.

'Git on out'n here! Go ax *massa* how I feels! He know better'n *I* does!' Since Uncle Mingo clearly wished to be left alone, Chicken George did leave, thinking that Mingo was getting to be like his leathery, pin-feathered old catchcocks – tough old veterans of many battles, but with age catching up and taking its toll, leaving mostly the instincts.

By the time the last of the birds had been given their extra wing-strengthening exercise and returned to their coops, it was shortly after sundown, and Chicken George at last felt free to pay at least a brief visit home. Upon reaching his cabin, delighted to find Kizzy visiting with Matilda, he told them with much chuckling about the morning's exchange with the massa about naming the new baby

Tom. When he was through, he noticed with great surprise that they seemed not to be sharing his enjoyment.

It was Matilda who spoke first, her words flat and noncommittal, 'Well, I reckon lotsa Toms in dis worl'.'

His mammy looked as if she had just had to chew a bar of soap. 'I 'speck me an' 'Tilda feelin' de same thing, an' she ruther spare yo' feelings 'bout yo' precious massa. Ain't nothin' wrong wid de name Tom. Jes' sho' wish it was some *other* Tom dis po' chile git named after—' She hesitated, then added quickly, ' 'Cose, dat's jes' my 'pinion – ain't my young'un, or my business!'

'Well, it's de Lawd's business!' snapped Matilda, stepping across to get her Bible. 'Fo' de chile was born, I was huntin' in de Scriptures to see what it say 'bout names.' Hurriedly she thumbed pages, finding the section, page and verse she sought, and read it aloud; 'De mem'ry of de jes' is blessed; but de name of de wicked shall rot!'

'Have mercy!' exclaimed Gran'mammy Kizzy.

Chicken George rose, incensed. 'Awright den! Which one y'all gwine tell massa we ain't?' He stood glaring at them. He was getting sick of so many goadings when he came in his own house! And he was fed up *past* the limit with Matilda's never-ending damnation from the Bible. He raked his mind for something he once heard, then it came. 'Y'all call 'im for Tom de *Baptis'*, den!' He shouted it so loudly that the faces of his three sons appeared in the bedroom doorway, and the day-old infant began crying as Chicken George stomped out.

At that very moment, at the living-room writing desk in the big house, Massa Lea dipped his pen, then scrawled carefully inside his Bible's front cover a fifth date-and-birth line below the four names already recorded there – Chicken George and his first three sons: '20 September 1833 . . . boy born to Matilda . . . name Tom Lea.'

Returning angrily down the road, George fumed that it wasn't that he didn't care for Matilda. She was the finest, most loyal woman he ever had met. A fine wife, however, was not necessarily one who piously chastized her husband every time he turned around just for being human. A man had a *right* now and then to enjoy the company of the kind of women who wanted only to enjoy laughter, liquor, wit, and the body's urgencies. And from their past year's travels together, he knew that Massa Lea felt the same. After fighting their gamecock near any sizable town, they always stayed on an extra day, with the mules in a stable and some local gamecocker's helper paid well to care for the cooped birds, while he and Massa Lea went their separate ways. Meeting at the stable early the next morning, they would collect their gamecocks and ride on homewards, each nursing hangovers, and neither one saying a word about the fact that he knew the other one had been tomcattin'.

It was five days before Chicken George's exasperation had diminished enough for him to think about returning home. Ready to forgive them, he strode up the road to slave row and opened the cabin door.

'Lawd! Is dat you, George?' said Matilda. 'De chilluns be so glad to see dey pappy again! 'Specially dis one – his eyes wasn't open yet when you was here las'!'

Instantly furious, he was about to stalk right back outside when his glance fell upon his older three sons – aged five, three, and two – huddled awkwardly together, staring at him almost fearfully. He felt an urge to grab them and hug them close. Soon he wouldn't be seeing them for three months when he went to New Orleans; he must bring them some really nice presents.

Reluctantly, he sat down at the table when Matilda laid out a meal for him and sat down to bless the food. Then, standing back up, she said, 'Virgil, go ax Gran'mammy to come over here.'

Chicken George stopped chewing, merely swallowing what he had in his mouth. What did the two of them have planned to plague him with this time?

Kizzy knocked and came in hugging Matilda, kissing, petting, and clucking over the three boys before glancing at her son. 'How do? Ain't seen you so long!'

'How *you* do, Mammy?' Though he was fuming, he tried to make a weak joke of it.

Settling in a chair and accepting the baby from Matilda, his mammy spoke almost conversationally. 'George, yo' chilluns been wantin' to ax you sump'n—' She turned. 'Ain't you, Virgil?'

Chicken George saw the oldest boy hanging back. What had they primed him to say?

'Pappy,' he said finally in his piping voice, 'you gwine tell us 'bout our great-gran'daddy?'

Matilda's eyes reached out to him.

'You's a good man, George,' said Kizzy softly. 'Don't never let nobody tell you no different! An' don't never git to feelin' we don't love you. I b'lieves maybe you gits mixed up 'bout who you is, an' sometime who *we* is. We's yo' *blood*, jes' like dese chilluns' great-gran'pappy.'

'It's right in de Scriptures—' said Matilda. Seeing George's apprehensive glance, she added, 'Everything in de Bible ain't sump'n hard. De Scriptures have plenty 'bout love.'

Overwhelmed with emotion, Chicken George moved his chair near the hearth. The three boys squatted down before him, their eyes glistened with anticipation, and Kizzy handed him the baby. Composing himself, he cleared his throat and began to tell his four sons their gran'mammy's story of their great-gran'pappy.

'Pappy, I knows de story, too!' Virgil broke in. Making a face at his younger brothers, he went ahead and told it himself – including even the African words.

'He done heared it three times from you, and gran'mammy don't cross de do'sill widout tellin' it again!' said Matilda with a laugh. George thought: How long had it been since he last heard his wife laughing?

Trying to recapture the centre of attention, Virgil jumped up and down. 'Gran'mammy say de African make us know who we is!'

'He do *dat!*' said Gran'mammy Kizzy, beaming.

For the first time in a long time, Chicken George felt that his cabin was his home again.

98

Four weeks late, the new wagon was ready to be picked up in Greensboro. How right the massa had been to have it built, Chicken George reflected as they drove there, for they must arrive in New Orleans not creaking and squeaking in this battered old heap, but in the finest wagon money could buy – looking the parts of a great gamecocker and his trainer. For the same reason, before they left Greensboro, he must borrow a dollar and a half from the massa to buy a new black derby to go with the new green scarf that Matilda had almost finished knitting. He would also make sure that Matilda packed both his green and yellow suits, his wide-webbed best red suspenders, and plenty of shirts, drawers, socks, and handkerchiefs, for after the cockfighting, he knew he'd have to look *right* when they were out on the town.

Within moments after they arrived at the wagon-maker's shop, as he waited outside, George began hearing snatches of loud argument behind the closed door. He'd known the massa long enough to expect that sort of thing, so he didn't bother to listen; he was too busy sifting in his mind through the tasks he had to take care of at home before they left. The toughest one, he knew, would be the job of culling seven more birds from the nineteen magnificent specimens he had already trained to lethal keenness. There was room in the wagon for only a dozen, and selecting them would challenge not only his own judgment and the massa's but also that of Uncle Mingo, who was once again up, out and about, as vinegary and tart-tongued as ever.

Inside the shop, Massa Lea's voice had risen to a shout: The inexcusable delay in finishing the wagon had cost him money, which should be deducted from the price. The wagon-maker was yelling back that he had rushed the job as fast as he could, and the price should really be higher because cost of materials had risen along with his free black workmen's outrageous salary demands. Listening now, Chicken George guessed that the massa was actually less angry than he seemed and was simply testing the wagon-maker to see if an argument might succeed in cutting at least a few dollars off the cost of the wagon.

After a while something must have worked out inside, for the altercation seemed to end, and soon Massa Lea and the wagon-maker came out, still red-faced but acting and talking now in a friendly way. The tradesman shouted towards the area behind his shop, and a few more minutes later, four blacks hove into view, bent nearly double pulling the heavy new custom-built wagon behind them. George's eyes went wide at its sheer craftsmanship and beauty. He could feel the strength in its oaken frame and body. The centre section of the luxuriously long bed showed the tops of the twelve removable cock coops. The iron axles and the hubs were obviously superbly balanced and greased, for despite the vehicle's imposing weight, he could hear no creaking or even rubbing sounds at all. Nor had he ever seen Massa Lea's face split into such a grin.

'She's one of the best we've ever turned out!' exclaimed the wagon-master. 'Nearly too pretty to drive!' Expansively, Massa Lea said, 'Well, she's about to roll a long way!' The wagon-maker's head wagged. 'New Orleans! That's a six-week trip. Who all's goin' with you?'

Massa Lea turned, gesturing at Chicken George on the old wagon-driver's seat. 'My nigger there and twelve chickens!'

Anticipating the massa's command, Chicken George jumped

down and went back to untie the pair of rented mules they'd brought along and led them over to the new wagon. One of the four blacks helped him hitch them up, then went back to join the others, who were paying Chicken George no more attention than he was to them; after all, they were free blacks, whom Massa Lea often said he couldn't stand the sight of. After walking around the wagon a few times with his eyes shining and a big smile on his face, the massa shook hands with the wagon-maker, thanked him, and climbed proudly up onto the seat of the new wagon. Wishing him good luck, the wagon-maker stood there shaking his head in admiration for his own work as Massa Lea led the way out of the lot with Chicken George following in the old wagon.

On the long drive home – his new derby on the seat beside him, along with a pair of elegant grey felt spats that had set him back a dollar – George finished his mental checklist of chores that he had to take care of before they left for New Orleans, and started thinking about what had to be done to make sure things would keep running smoothly while they were gone. As difficult as he knew it would be to get along without him at home, he was confident that Matilda and Kizzy would be equal to the task; and though Uncle Mingo didn't get around quite as spryly any more, and he was becoming increasingly forgetful with each passing year, George was sure the old man would be able to mind the chickens adequately until his return. But sooner or later, he knew he was going to need more help than Mingo would be able to offer any more.

Somehow he must find a way around his wife's and his mammy's blindness to the rare opportunity he felt he could open for young Virgil, especially since at nearly six years of age the boy would soon have to start working in the fields. During his absence, it had occurred to him that Virgil could be assigned to help Uncle Mingo with the gamecocks – and then simply kept on in the job after they returned – but he had hardly brought up the idea before Matilda had flared, 'Let massa buy somebody to help 'im, den!' and Kizzy had put in hotly, 'Dem chickens done stole 'nough from dis family!' Wanting no new fights with them, he hadn't tried to force the matter, but certainly didn't intend to see the massa possibly buy some total stranger to intrude in his and Uncle Mingo's private province.

Even if the massa knew better than to bring in an outsider, though, George couldn't be sure if Virgil's help would be accepted by Uncle Mingo, who seemed to be rankling more and more ever since his first helper had developed with the massa a relationship closer than his own. Only recently, in his bitterness about not being allowed to come along with them to New Orleans, Mingo had snapped, 'You an' massa figger y'all can trust me to feed de chickens while you's gone?' George wished that Uncle Mingo would realize that he had nothing to do with the massa's decisions. At the same time, he wondered why the old man wouldn't simply face the fact that at seventy-odd years of age, he just wasn't in any kind of shape to travel for six weeks in either direction; almost surely he would fall sick somewhere, with all of the extra problems that would present to him and the massa. George wished hard that he knew some way to make Uncle Mingo feel better about the whole thing or at least that Uncle Mingo would stop blaming *him* for everything.

Finally the two wagons turned off the big road and were rolling down the driveway. They were almost halfway to the big house when, to his amazement, he saw Missis Lea come onto the front porch and down the steps. A moment later, out the back door, came Miss Malizy. Then, hurrying from their cabins, he saw Matilda and their boys, Mammy Kizzy, Sister Sarah, and Uncle Pompey. What are they all doing here Thursday afternoon, wondered George, when they should be out in the fields? Were they so anxious to see the fine new wagon that they had risked the massa's anger? Then he saw their faces, and he knew that none of them cared anything about any new wagon.

When Missis Lea kept walking on to meet the massa's wagon, George reined to a halt and leaned far over from his high driver's seat to hear better what she said to the massa. George saw the massa's body jerk upright as the missis fled back towards the house. Dumbfounded, George watched as Massa Lea clambered down from the new wagon and walked slowly, heavily back towards him. He saw the face, pale with shock – and suddenly he knew! The massa's words reached him as if from a distance: 'Mingo's dead.'

Slumping sideways against the wagon-seat, George was bawling as he never had before. He hardly felt the massa and Uncle Pompey half wrestling him onto the ground. Then Pompey on one side and Matilda on the other were guiding him towards slave row with others around them weeping afresh at seeing his grief. Matilda helped him to lurch inside their cabin, followed by Kizzy with the baby.

When he had recovered himself, they told him what had happened. 'Y'all left Monday mornin',' said Matilda, 'an' dat night nobody here slept no good. Seem like Tuesday morning we all got up feelin' like we'd heared whole lots' hoot owls an' barkin' dogs. Den we heared de screamin'—'

'Was Malizy!' exclaimed Kizzy. 'Lawd, she hollered! Us all jes' flew out dere where she'd done gone to slop de hogs. An' dere he was. Po' ol' soul layin' out on de road, look like some pile o' rags!'

'He was still alive,' said Matilda, 'but t'was jes' one side o' his mouth movin'. I got right down close on my knees an' could jes' barely make out he was whisperin'. "B'lieve I done had a stroke," he say. "He'p me wid de chickens . . . I ain't able—"'

'Lawd have mercy, none us knowed what to do!' said Kizzy, but Uncle Pompey tried to lift the limp, heavy form. When he failed, their combined efforts finally succeeded in lugging Uncle Mingo back to slave row and onto Pompey's bed.

'George, he stunk so bad, wid dat sick smell on 'im!' said Matilda. 'We commence fannin' his face, an' he kept whisperin', "de chickens . . . got to git back—"'

'Miss Malizy done run an' tol' missis by den,' said Kizzy, 'an' she come a-wringin' her hands an' cryin' an' carryin' on! But not 'bout Br'er Mingo! Naw! First thing she hollerin' was somebody better git to dem chickens less'n massa have a fit! So Matilda called Virgil—'

'I sho' didn't want to!' said Matilda. 'You know how I feels 'bout dat. One of us *'nough* down wid dem chickens. 'Sides, I done heared you talkin' 'bout stray dogs an' foxes, even wildcats be's roun' trying' to eat dem birds! But bless de chile's heart! His eyes was bucked scairt, but he say, "Mammy, I go, I jes' don' know what to do!" Uncle Pompey got a sack o' corn an' say, "You throw han'ful dis to any chickens you sees, an' I be down dere soon's I can—"'

With no way to reach him and the massa, and Sister Sarah's telling them that she feared Uncle Mingo was beyond what her roots could cure, and not even the missis knowing how to contact any doctor, 'weren't nothin' else us could do 'cept jes' wait on y'all—' they told him. Matilda began weeping, and George reached out to hold her hand.

'She cryin' 'cause when we got back in Pompey's cabin after talkin' to the missis, Mingo gone,' said Kizzy. '*Lawd!* Knowed it jes' to look at 'im!' She began sobbing herself. 'Po' ol' soul done died all by hisself.'

When Missis Lea was told, said Matilda, 'She commence hollerin' she jes' don't know what to do wid dead peoples, 'cept she done heared massa say dey starts to rottin' if dey's kept out mo'n a day. She say be 'way past dat fo' y'all git back, so us gwine have to dig a hole—'

'*Lawd!*' exclaimed Kizzy. 'Below de willow grove de groun' kin' o' sof'. We took de shovel, Pompey an' us wimmins dug an' dug, one at de time, 'til we had a hole enough to put 'im in. We come back, den Pompey bathed 'im up.'

'He rubbed some glycerin on 'im Miss Malizy got from missy,' said Matilda, 'den sprinkled on some dat perfume you brung me las' year.'

'Weren't no decent clothes to put 'im in,' continued Kizzy. 'De ones he had on stunk too bad, an' what l'il Pompey have was 'way too tight, so jes' rolled 'im up in two sheets.' She said Uncle Pompey then had cut two straight green limbs while the women found old planks, and they had fashioned a litter. 'Have to say for missis dat when she seen us all bearin' 'im over to de hole,' said Matilda, 'she did come a-runnin' wid dey Bible. When we got 'im dere, she read some Scripture from de Psalms, an' den I prayed, axin' de Lawd to please res' an' keep Mr Mingo's soul—' Then they had put the body in the grave and covered it.

'We done 'im de bes' we could! Don't care if you's mad,' Matilda burst out, misreading the anguish on her husband's face.

Grabbing her and squeezing her fiercely, he rasped, 'Nobody mad—' too stifled by his emotions to convey in words his anger with himself and the massa for not being there that morning. There might have been *something* they could have done to save him.

A little later, he left his cabin thinking about what concern, care, even love had been shown to Uncle Mingo by those who had always claimed to dislike him so. Seeing Uncle Pompey, he walked over and wrung his hands, and they talked a little while. Nearly as old as Uncle Mingo had been, Pompey said he had just come up from the gamefowl area, leaving Virgil watching the chickens. 'Dat a good boy y'all got, he sho' is!' Then he said, 'When you goes down dere, since it ain't been no rain, you can still see in de dus' o' de road de crooked trail where Br'er Mingo dragged hisself all de way up here in de night.'

George didn't want to see that. Leaving Uncle Pompey, he walked slowly to below the willow grove. A while passed before he could look directly at the freshly mounded earth. Moving about as if in a daze, picking up some rocks, he arranged them in a design around the grave. He felt unworthy.

In order to avoid Mingo's dust trail in the road, he cut through a field of broken cornstalks to reach the gamefowl area.

'You done a good job, boy. Now you better go on back up to your mammy,' he said, patting Virgil roughly on the head, thrilling the boy with his first compliment. After he was gone, George sat down and stared at nothing, his mind tumbling with scenes from the past fifteen years, listening to echoes of his teacher, his friend, his nearest to a father he ever had known. He could almost hear the cracked voice barking orders, speaking more gently of gamecocking; complaining bitterly about being cast aside: *'You an' massa figger y'all can trust me to feed de chickens whilst y'all's gone?'* George felt himself drowning in remorse.

Questions came to him: Where was Uncle Mingo from before Massa Lea bought him? Who had been his family? He had never mentioned any. Had he a wife or children somewhere? George had been the closest person in the world to Uncle Mingo, yet he knew so little about the man who had taught him everything he knew.

Chicken George paced: Dear God, where was the beloved old shambling companion with whom he had so many times trod every inch of this familiar place?

He stayed there alone through the next day and night. It was Saturday morning before Massa Lea showed up. His face bleak and sombre, he went directly to the point. 'I've been thinking through this whole thing. To start with, just burn Mingo's cabin, now. That's the best way to get rid of it.'

A few minutes later they stood and watched as the flames consumed the small cabin that for over forty years had been home to Uncle Mingo. Chicken George sensed that the massa had something else on his mind; he was unprepared for it when it came.

'I've been thinking about New Orleans,' said the massa. 'There's too much at stake unless everything's right—' He spoke slowly, almost as if he were talking to himself. 'Can't leave without somebody here to mind these chickens. Take too much time to find somebody, maybe have to teach them to boot. No point in me goin' by myself, that much driving and twelve birds to look after. No point goin' to a chicken fight unless you aim to win. Just foolish to make the trip now—'

Chicken George swallowed. All those months of planning ... all the massa's spending ... all of the massa's hopes to join the South's most élite gamecocking circles ... those birds so magnificently trained to beat anything with wings. Swallowing a second time, he said, 'Yassuh.'

99

Working by himself down there with the gamefowl was so strange and lonely that Chicken George wondered how in the world Uncle Mingo had managed to do it for over twenty-five years before he came to join him. 'When massa bought me,' the old man had told him, 'an' de flock got to growin', he kept sayin he gwine buy me some he'p, but he never did, an' I reckon I jes' fin' out chickens maybe better company dan peoples is.' Though George felt that he, too, loved the birds about as much as any man could, with him they could never take the place of people. But he needed someone to *help* him, he told himself, not to keep him company.

As far as he was concerned, Virgil still seemed the most sensible choice. It would keep things all in the family, and he could train the boy just as Uncle Mingo had trained him. But since he wasn't anxious to deal with Matilda and Kizzy in order to get him, George tried to think of some gamefowl trainer acquaintance whom he might be able to persuade the massa to buy away from his present owner. But he knew that any real gamecocker massa would have to be in some truly desperate fix for money to even think about selling his trainer, especially to such a competitor as Massa Lea. So he began considering black hackfighters, but a good half of them were trainers like himself fighting their massa's cull birds; and most of the others, like their birds, were third-raters or shady characters who fought very good birds that had been suspiciously acquired. There were a number of free-black hackfighters he had seen who were really good, and were available for hire by the day, the week, the month, or even the year, but he knew there was no way Massa Lea would ever permit even the best free-black trainer in North Carolina on his place. So George had no choice. And finally one evening he mustered his nerve to bring it up at home.

'Fo' you tells me ag'in why you won't stan' fo' it, woman, you listen to me. Nex' time massa want me to travel wid 'im somewhere, dat's when he sho' gwine say "Go git dat oldes' young'un of your'n down here!" An' once dat happen, Virgil be wid chickens to *stay*, less'n massa say different, which might be never, an' you or me neither can't say a mumblin' word—' He gestured to stop Matilda from interrupting. 'Wait! Ain't wantin' no back talk! I'se tryin' to git you to see de boy need to come on down dere now. If'n *I* bring 'im, den he can stay jes' long 'nough fo' me to teach 'im how to feed de birds when I has to leave, an' he'p me exercise 'em durin' trainin' season. Den res' de time, mos' de year, he can be wid y'all in de fiel'.' Seeing Matilda's tight expression, he shrugged elaborately and said with mock resignation, 'Awright, I jes' leave it up to you an' massa, den!'

'What git me is you talk like Virgil grown awready,' said Matilda. 'Don' you realize dat chile ain't but six years ol'? Jes' *half* de twelve you was when dey drug you off down dere.' She paused. 'But I knows he got to work now he's six. So reckon can't do nothin' 'cept what you says, much as I jes' git mad every time I thinks 'bout how dem chickens stole you!'

'Anybody listen to you an' mammy! Y'all soun' like chickens done snatched me up an' off crost de ocean somewheres!'

'Jes' well's to, mos' de time, much as you's gone.'

'Gone! Who settin' up here talkin' to you? Who been here every day dis month?'

'Dis month maybe, but where you gwine be fo' long?'

'If you's talkin' 'bout de fighting season, I be wherever massa tell me we's gwine. If you talkin' 'bout right now, soon's I eats, I sho' ain't gwine set here 'til some varmints creeps roun' down dere an' eats some chickens, or den I *really* be gone!'

'Oh! You's finally 'greein' he'd sell you, too!'

'I b'lieves he sell missis, she let his chickens git et!'

'Look,' she said, 'we done got by widout no big fallin' out 'bout Virgil, so let's sho' don't start none 'bout nothin' else.'

'I ain't arguin' in de firs' place, it's you de one!'

'Awright, George, I'se through wid it,' Matilda said, setting steaming bowls on the table. 'Jes' eat yo' supper an' git on back, an' I sen' Virgil down dere in de mornin'. Less'n you wants to take 'im back wid you now. I can go git 'im from over at 'is gran'mammy's.'

'Naw, tomorrow be fine.'

But within a week it became clear to Chicken George that his eldest son lacked totally what had been his own boyhood fascination with gamebirds. Six years old or not, it seemed inconceivable to George that after completing an assigned task, Virgil would either wander off and play alone, or just sit down somewhere and do nothing. Then Virgil would leap up as his father angrily exclaimed, 'Git up from dere! What you think dis is? Dese ain't no pigs down dere, dese fightin' chickens!' Then Virgil would do acceptably well whatever new task he was set to, but then once more, as George watched from the corner of his eye, he would see his son soon either sitting down again or going off to play. Fuming, he remembered how,

494

as a boy, he had spent what little free time he had scampering around admiring the cockerels and the stags, plucking grass and catching grasshoppers to feed them, finding it all incredibly exciting.

Though Uncle Mingo's way of training had been cool and businesslike – an order given, a watchful silence, then another order – George decided to try another approach with Virgil in hopes that he'd snap out of it. He'd *talk* to him.

'What you been doin' wid yo'self up yonder?'

'Nothin', Pappy.'

'Well, is you an' de other young'uns gittin' 'long all right an' mindin' yo' mammy an' gran'mammy?'

'Yassuh.'

'Reckon dey feeds you pretty good, huh?'

'Yassuh.'

'What you like to eat de mos'?'

'Anythin' Mammy cooks us, yassuh.'

The boy seemed to lack even the faintest imagination. He'd try a different tack.

'Lemme hear you tell de story 'bout yo' great-gran'daddy like you done once.'

Virgil obediently did so, rather woodenly. George's heart sank. But after standing there thoughtfully for a moment, the boy asked, 'Pappy, is you seed my great-gran'pappy?'

'Naw, I ain't,' he replied hopefully. 'I knows 'bout 'im same as you does, from yo' gran'mammy.'

'She used to ride in de buggy wid 'im!'

'Sho' she did! It was her pappy. Jes' like one dese days you tell yo' chilluns you used to set down here 'mongst de chickens wid yo' pappy.'

That seemed to confuse Virgil, who fell silent.

After a few more such lame efforts, George reluctantly gave up, hoping that he'd have better luck with Ashford, George and Tom, Without communicating to anyone his disappointment in Virgil, he regretfully decided to use the boy for the simple part-time duties he had discussed with Matilda, rather than try futilely to train him as a full-time permanent helper as he had actually intended.

So when Chicken George felt Virgil had mastered the task of feeding and watering the cockerels and stags in their pens three times daily, he sent him back up to Matilda to begin working with them in the fields – which seemed to suit the boy just fine. Chicken George would never have breathed it to Matilda, Kizzy, or the others, but George had always felt a deep disdain for field work, which he saw as nothing more than a ceaseless drudge of wielding hoes under hot sun, dragging cotton sacks, picking endless tobacco worms, and beating cornstalks down for fodder, in relentless seasonal succession. With a chuckle he remembered Uncle Mingo's saying, 'Gimmme a good corn or cotton field or a good fightin' bird, I'll take de bird every time!' It was exhilarating just to think of how anywhere a cockfight had been announced – if it was in a wood, an open cow pasture, or behind some massa's barn – the very air would become charged as gamecockers began converging on it with their birds raucously crowing in their lust to win or die.

In this summertime off-season, with the gamecocks moulting off their old feathers, there was only routine work to be done, and Chicken George gradually became accustomed to not having anyone around to talk with, except for the chickens – in particular the pin-feathered veteran catchcock that had been practically Uncle Mingo's pet.

'You could o' tol' us how sick he was, you ol' wall-eyed devil!' he told the old bird one afternoon, at which it cocked its head for a second, as if aware that it was being addressed, and then went on pecking and scratching in its ever-hungry way. 'You hears me talkin' to you!' George said with amiable gruffness. 'You must o' knowed he was real bad off!' For a while he let his eyes idly follow the foraging bird. 'Well, I reckon you knows he's gone now. I wonders if you's missin' de ol' man de way I is.' But the old catchcock, pecking and scratching away, seemed not to be missing anyone, and finally Chicken George sent him squawking off with a tossed pebble.

In another year or so, George reflected, the old bird will probably join Uncle Mingo, wherever it is that old gamecockers and their birds go when they die. He wondered what had ever happened to the massa's very first bird – that twenty-five-cent, raffle-ticket gamecock that had got him started more than forty years ago. Did it finally catch a fatal gaff? Or did it die an honoured catchcock's death of old age? Why hadn't he ever asked Uncle Mingo about that? He must remember to ask the massa. Over forty years back! The massa had told him he was only seventeen when he had won the bird. That would make him around fifty-six or fifty-seven now – around thirty years older than Chicken George. Thinking of the massa, and of how he owned people, as well as chickens, all their lives, he found himself pondering what it must be like *not* to belong to someone. What would it feel like to be 'free'? It must not be all that good or Massa Lea, like most whites, wouldn't hate free blacks so much. But then he remembered what a free black woman who had sold him some white lightning in Greensboro had told him once. 'Every one us free show y'all plantation niggers livin' proof dat jes' bein' a nigger don' mean you have to be no slave. Yo' massa don' never want you thinkin' nothin' 'bout dat.' During his long solitudes in the gamefowl area, Chicken George began to think about that at length. He decided he was going to strike up conversation with some of the free blacks he always saw but had always ignored when he and the massa went to the cities.

Walking along the split-rail fence, feeding and watering the cockerels and stags, Chicken George enjoyed as always the stags' immature clucking angrily at him, as if they were rehearsing their coming savagery in the cockpits. He found himself thinking a lot about being *owned*.

One afternoon, while he was on one of his periodic inspections of the birds that were maturing out on the rangewalk, he decided to amuse himself by trying out his nearly perfect imitation of a challenging cock's crow. Almost always in the past, it would bring instantly forth a furious defender crowing angrily in reply and jerking its head this way and that in search of the intruding rival he was sure he had just heard. Today was no exception. But the magnificent gamecock that burst from the underbrush in response to his call stood beating its wings explosively against its body for almost half a minute before its crow seemed to shatter the autumn afternoon. The bright sunlight glinted off its iridescent plumage. Its carriage was powerful and ferocious, from the glittering eyes to the stout yellow legs with their lethal spurs. Every ounce, every inch of him symbolized its boldness, spirit, and freedom so dramatically that Chicken George left vowing this bird must never be caught and trained and trimmed. It must remain there with its hens among the pines – untouched and *free!*

100

The new cockfighting season was fast approaching, but Massa Lea
hadn't mentioned New Orleans. Chicken George hadn't really expected him to; somehow he had known that trip was never going to
happen. But he and the massa made a very big impression at the
local 'mains' when they showed up in their gleaming, custom-built,
twelve-coop wagon. And their luck was running good. Massa Lea
averaged almost four wins out of five, and George, using the best of
the culls, did just about as well in the Caswell County hackfights. It
was a busy season as well as a profitable one, but George happened
to be home again when his fifth son was born late that year. Matilda
said she wanted to name this one James. She said 'James somehow
'nother always been my fav'rite 'mongst all de Disciples.' Chicken
George agreed, with a private grimace.

Wherever he and Massa Lea travelled for any distance now, it
seemed that he would hear of increasing bitterness against white
people. On their most recent trip, a free black had told George about
Osceola, chief of the Seminole Indians in the state called Florida.
When white men recaptured Osceola's black wife, an escaped slave,
he had organized a war party of two thousand Seminoles and escaped black slaves to track and ambush a detachment of the U.S.
Army. Over a hundred soldiers were killed, according to the story,
and a much larger Army force was hard after Osceola's men, who
were running, hiding, and sniping from their trails and recesses in the
Florida swamps.

And the cockfight season of 1836 hadn't long ended when
Chicken George heard that at some place called 'The Alamo', a
band of Mexicans had massacred a garrison of white Texans, including a woodsman named Davey Crockett, who was famous as a
friend and defender of the Indians. Later that year, he heard of
greater white losses to the Mexicans, under a General Santa Anna,
who was said to boast of himself as the greatest cockfighter in the
world; if that was true, George wondered why he'd never heard of
him till now.

It was during the spring of the next year when George returned
from a trip to tell slave row still another extraordinary piece of news.
'Done heard it from de co'thouse janitor nigger at de county seat,
dat new Pres'dent Van Buren done ordered de Army to drive all de
Indians wes' de Mis'sippi River!'

'Soun' for sho' now like gwine be dem Indians' River Jordan!' said Matilda.

'Dat's what Indians gittin' for lettin' in white folks in dis country, in de firs' place,' said Uncle Pompey. 'Whole heap o' folks, 'cludin' me till I got grown, ain't knowed at firs' weren't nobody in dis country *but* Indians, fishin' an' huntin' an' fightin' one 'nother, jes' mindin' dey own business. Den here come l'il ol' boat o' white folks a-wavin' an' grinnin'. "Hey, y'all red mens! How 'bout let us come catch a bite an' a nap 'mongst y'all an' le's be friends!" Huh! I betcha nowadays dem Indians wish dey's made dat boat look like a porcupine wid dey arrows!'

After the massa attended the next Caswell County landholders' meeting, Chicken George came back with still more news about the Indians. 'Hear tell it's a Gen'l Winfield Scott done warned 'em dat white folks bein' Christians ain't wantin' to shed no mo' Indians' blood, so dem wid any sense best to hurry up an' git to movin'! Hear tell if an Indian even *look* like he wanted to fight, de sojers shot 'im in 'is tracks! An' den de Army commence drivin' jes' thousan's dem Indians towards somewheres called Oklahoma. Say ain't no tellin' *how* many 'long de way was kilt or took sick an' died—'

'Jes' evil, *evil!*' exclaimed Matilda.

But there was some good news, too – only this time it was waiting for him when he got home from one of his trips in 1837: his sixth son in a row was born. Matilda named him Lewis, but after finding out where she got the name for James, Chicken George decided not even to inquire why. Less exuberant than she'd been at the birth of each previous grandchild, Kizzy said, 'Look like to me y'all ain't gwine never have nothin' *but* boys!'

'Mammy Kizzy, bad as I'se layin' up here hurtin' an' you soundin' disappointed!' cried Matilda from the bed.

'Ain't neither! I loves my gran'boys an' y'all knows it. But jes' seem like y'all could have *one* gal!'

Chicken George laughed. 'We git right to work on a gal for you, Mammy!'

'You git *out'n* here!' exclaimed Matilda.

But only a few months passed before a look at Matilda made it clear that George intended to be a man of his word.

'*Hmph!* Sho' can tell when dat man been spendin' reg'lar time home!' commented Sister Sarah. 'Seem like he wuss'n dem roosters!' Miss Malizy agreed.

When her pains of labour came once again, the waiting, pacing George heard – amid his wife's anguished moans and cries – his mother's yelps of *'Thank you, Jesus! Thank you, Jesus!'* and he needed no further advisement that at last he had fathered a girl.

Even before the baby was cleaned off, Matilda told her mother-in-law that she and George had agreed years before that their first girl would be named Kizzy.

'Ain't done lived in vain!' Gran'mammy cried at intervals throughout the rest of the day. Nothing would do for her then but that the following afternoon Chicken George would come up from the gamefowl area and tell once again about the African great-gran'pappy Kunta Kinte for the six boys and the infant Kizzy in his lap.

One night about two months later, with all of the children finally asleep, George asked, ''Tilda, how much money is we got saved up?'

She looked at him, surprised. 'L'il over a hunnud dollars.'

'*Dat* all?'

'Dat *all!* It's a wonder it's dat much! Ain't I been tellin' you all dese years de way you spends ain't hardly no point even do no talkin' 'bout no *savin'!*'

'Awright, awright,' he said guiltily.

But Matilda pursued the point. 'Not countin' what you winned an' spent what I ain't never seed, which was yo' business, you want to guess 'bout how much you done give me to *save* since we been married, den you borrowin' back?'

'Awright, how much?'

Matilda paused for effect. 'Twixt three-fo' thousan' dollars.'

'*Wheeeew!*' he whistled. 'I *is?*'

Watching his expression change, she sensed that she had never observed him grow more serious in all their twelve years together. 'Off down yonder by myself so much,' he said finally, 'I been thinkin' 'bout whole heap o' things—' He paused. She thought he seemed almost embarrassed by whatever he was about to say. 'One thing I been thinkin', if'n us could save 'nough dese nex' comin' years, maybe us could buy ourselves free.'

Matilda was too astounded to speak.

He gestured impatiently. 'I wish you git yo' pencil to figger some, an' quit buckin' yo' eyes at me like you ain't got no sense!'

Still stunned, Matilda got her pencil and a piece of paper and sat back down at the table.

'Trouble to start wid,' he said, 'jes' can't do nothin' but guess roun' what massa'd ax for us all. Me an' you an' de passel o' young'uns. Start wid you. Round de county seat, I knows men fiel' han's is bringin' 'bout a thousan' dollars apiece. Wimmins is worth less, so le's call you 'bout eight hunnud—' Getting up, bending to inspect Matilda's moving pencil, he sat back down. 'Den let's say massa let us have our chilluns, all eight, 'bout three hunnud apiece—'

'Ain't but seb'n!' said Matilda.

'Dat new one you say started in yo' belly ag'in make eight!'

'Oh!' she said, smiling. She figured at length. 'Dat makes twenty-fo' hunnud—'

'Jes' for chilluns?' His tone mingled doubt with outrage. Matilda refigured. 'Eight threes is twenty-fo'. Plus de eight hunnud fo' me, dat make 'zactly thirty hunnud – dat's same as three thousan'.'

'Wheeeew!'

'Don't carry on so yet! De big one you!' She looked at him. 'How much you figger fo' you?'

Serious as it was, he couldn't resist asking, 'What *you* think I'se worth?'

'If I'd o' knowed, I'd o' tried to buy you from massa myself.' They both laughed. 'George, I don' even know how come we's talkin' sich as dis, nohow. You know good an' well massa ain't gwine never sell you!'

He didn't answer right away. But then he said, ' 'Tilda, I ain't never mentioned dis, reckon since I know you don't hardly even like to hear massa's name called. But I betcha twenty-five different times, one or 'nother, he done talk to me 'bout whenever he git 'nough together to buil' de fine big house he want, wid six columns crost de front, he say him an' missis could live off'n what de crops make, an' he 'speck he be gittin' out'n de chicken-fightin' business, he say he steady gittin' too ol' to keep puttin' up wid all de worries.'

'I have to see dat to b'lieve it, George. Him or you neither ain't gwine never give up messin' wid chickens!'

'I'm tellin' you what he say! If you can listen! Looka here, Uncle Pompey say massa 'bout sixty-three years ol' right now. Give 'im another five, six years – it ain't *easy* fo' no real ol' man to keep runnin' here an' yonder fightin' no birds! I didn't pay 'im much 'tention neither till I kept thinkin' dat, yeah, he really might let us buy ourselves, an 'specially if we be payin' him 'nough would he'p 'im buil' dat big house he want.'

'Hmph,' Matilda grunted without conviction. 'Awright, let's talk 'bout it. What you reckon he'd want for you?'

'Well—' His expression seemed to mingle pride in one way and pain in another at what he was about to say. 'Well – nigger buggy driver o' dat rich Massa Jewett done swo' up an' down to me one time dat he overheard his massa tellin' somebody he'd offered Massa Lea fo' thousan' dollars fo' me—'

'*Whoooooooee!*' Matilda was flabbergasted.

'See, you ain't never knowed de valuable nigger you sleeps wid!' But quickly he was serious again. 'I don't really b'lieve dat nigger. I 'speck he jes' made up dat lie tryin' to see if I'd be fool 'nough to swallow it. Anyhow, I go by what's gittin' paid nowdays for niggers wid de bes' trades, like de carpenters an' blacksmiths, sich as dem. Dey's sellin' twix two-three thousan', I know dat fo' a fac'—' He paused, peering at her waiting pencil. 'Put down three thousan'—' He paused again. 'How much dat be?'

Matilda figured. She said then that the total estimated cost to buy their family would be sixty-two hundred dollars. 'But what 'bout Mammy Kizzy?'

'I git to Mammy!' he said impatiently. He thought. 'Mammy gittin' pretty ol' now, dat he'p her cost less—'

'Dis year she turnin' fifty,' said Matilda.

'Put down six hunnud dollars.' He watched the pencil move. 'Now what dat?'

Matilda's face strained with concentration. 'Now it's sixty-*eight* hunnud dollars.'

'Whew! Sho' make you start to see niggers is money to white folks.' George spoke very slowly. 'But I 'clare I b'lieves I can hackfight an' do it. 'Cose, gon' mean waitin' an' savin' up a long time—' He noticed that Matilda seemed discomfited. 'I knows right what's on yo' mind,' he said. 'Miss Malizy, Sister Sarah, an' Uncle Pompey.'

Matilda looked grateful that he knew. He said, 'Dey's family to me even fo' dey was to you—'

'Lawd, George!' she exclaimed, 'jes' don't see how jes' one man s'posed to be tryin' to buy ever'body, but I sho' jes' couldn't walk off an' leave dem!'

'We got plenty time, 'Tilda. Let's us jes' cross dat bridge when we gits to it.'

'Dat's de truth, you right.' She looked down at the figures that she had written. 'George, I jes' can't hardly b'lieve we's talkin' 'bout what we is—' She felt herself beginning to dare to believe it, that the two of them, together, were actually engaging for the first time in a monumental family discussion. She felt an intense urge to spring around the table and embrace him as tightly as she could. But she felt too much to move – or even speak for a few moments. Then she asked, 'George, how come you got to thinkin' dis?'

He was quiet for a moment. 'I got by myself, an' seem like I jes' got to thinkin' mo', like I tol' you—'

'Well,' she said softly, 'sho' is nice.'

'We ain't gittin' nowhere!' he exclaimed. 'All we ever doin' is gittin' *massa* somewhere!' Matilda felt like shouting 'Jubilee!' but made herself keep still. 'I been talkin' wid free niggers when me an' massa go to cities,' George went on. 'Dey say de free niggers up Nawth is de bes' off. Say dem lives 'mongst one 'nother in dey own houses an' gits good jobs. Well, I *know* I can git *me* a job! Plenty cockfightin' up Nawth! Even famous cockfightin' niggers I'se heared live right in dat New Yawk City, a Uncle Billy Roger, a Uncle Pete what got a big flock an' own a great big gamblin' joint, an' another one call "Nigger Jackson" dey say don't nobody beat his birds, hardly!' He further astounded Matilda. 'An' 'nother thing – I wants to see our young'uns learnin' to read an' write, like you can.'

'Lawd, better'n me, I hope!' Matilda exclaimed, her eyes shining.

'An' I wants 'em to learn trades.' Abruptly he grinned, pausing for effect. 'How you reckon you look settin' in yo' own house, yo' own stuffed furniture, an' all dem li'l knick-knacks? How 'bout Miss 'Tilda be axin' de other free nigger womens over for tea in de mornin's, an' y'all jes' settin' roun' talkin' 'bout rangin' y'all's flowers, an sich as dat?'

Matilda burst into nearly shrieking laughter. 'Lawd, man, you is jes' *crazy!*' When she stopped laughing, she felt more love for him than she'd ever felt before. 'I reckon de Lawd is done give me what I needs dis night.' Eyes welling, she put her hand on his. 'You really think we can do it, George?'

'What you think I'se been settin' up here talkin' 'bout, woman?'

'You 'member de night we 'greed to marry, what I tol' you?' His face said that he didn't. 'I tol' you sump'n out'n de first chapter o' Ruth. Tol' you, "Whither thou goes', I will go, an' where thou lodgest, I will lodge; thy people shall be my people—" You don't 'member me sayin' dat?'

'Yeah, I reckon.'

'Well, I ain't never felt dat way more'n I does right now.'

101

Removing his derby with one hand, with the other Chicken George held out to Massa Lea a small water pitcher that looked as if it were woven tightly of thick strands of wire. 'My boy, Tom, de one we done name for you, Massa, he done made dis for his gran'mammy, but I jes' want you to see it.'

Looking dubious, Massa Lea took the pitcher by its carved cow-horn handle and gave it a cursory inspection. 'Uh-huh,' he grunted non-committally.

George realized that he'd have to try harder. 'Yassuh, made dat out'n jes' ol' rusty scrap barb wire, Massa. Built 'im a real hot charcoal fire an' kept bendin' an' meltin' one wire 'gainst 'nother 'til he got de shape, den give it a kin' o' brazin' all over. Dat Tom always been real handy, Massa—'

He halted again, wanting some response, but none came.

Seeing that he'd have to reveal his real intent without gaining the tactical advantage of some advance positive reaction to Tom's craftsmanship, George took the plunge. 'Yassuh, dis boy been so proud o' carryin' yo' name all his life, Massa, us all really b'lieves he jes' git de chance, he make you a good blacksmith—'

An instantly disapproving expression came upon Massa Lea's face, as if by reflex, and it fuelled George's determination not to fail Matilda and Kizzy in his promise to help Tom. He saw that he'd have to make what he knew would be the strongest appeal to Massa Lea – picturing the financial advantages.

'Massa, every year money you's spendin' on blacksmithin' you could be savin'! Ain't none us never tol' you how Tom awready been savin' you some, sharpenin' hoe blades an' sickles an' different other tools – well as fixin' lot o' things gits broken roun' here. Reason I brings it up, when you sent me over for dat Isaiah nigger blacksmith to put de new wheel rims on de wagon, he was tellin' me Massa Askew been years promisin' him a helper dat he need real bad, much work as he doin' to make money fo' his massa. He tol' me he sho' be glad to make a blacksmith out'n any good boy he could git holt of, so I thought right 'way 'bout Tom. If he was to learn, Masa, ain't jes' he could do ever'thing we needs roun' here, but he could be takin' in work to make you plenty money jes' like dat Isaiah nigger doin' for Massa Askew.'

George felt sure he'd struck a nerve, but he couldn't be sure, for the massa carefully showed no sign. 'Looks to me this boy of yours is spending more time making this kind of stuff instead of working,' said Massa Lea, thrusting the metal pitcher back into George's hands.

'Tom ain't missed a day since he started workin' in yo' fiel's, Massa! He do sich as dis jes' on Sundays when he off! Ever since he been any size, seem like he got fixin' an' makin' things in 'is blood! Every Sunday he out in dat l'il ol' lean-to shed he done fixed hisself behin' de barn, a-burnin' an bangin', on sump'n 'nother. Fact, we's been scairt he 'sturb you an' de missis.'

'Well, I'll think about it,' Massa Lea said, turning abruptly and walking away, leaving Chicken George standing there confused and frustrated – purposely, he felt sure – holding the metal pitcher.

Miss Malizy was seated in the kitchen peeling turnips when the massa walked in. She half turned around, no longer springing to her feet as she would have done in years past, but she didn't think he'd mind, since she had reached that point in age and service where some small infractions could be permitted.

Massa Lea went straight to the point. 'What about this boy named Tom?'

'Tom? You means 'Tilda's Tom, Massa?'

'Well, how many Toms out there? You know the one I mean, what about him?'

Miss Malizy knew exactly why he was asking. Just a few minutes before, Gran'mammy Kizzy had told her of Chicken George's uncertainty about how Massa Lea had reacted to his proposal. Well, now she knew. But her opinion of young Tom was so high – and not just because he'd made her new S-curved pot-hooks – that she decided to hesitate a few seconds before answering, in order to sound impartial.

'Well,' she said finally, 'a body wouldn't pick 'im out of a crowd to talk to, Massa, 'cause de boy ain't never been much wid words. But I sho' can tell you fo' fac' he de smartes' young'un out dere, an' de goodest o' dem big boys, to boot!' Miss Malizy paused meaningfully. 'An' I 'speck he gwine grow up to be mo' *man* in whole lot o' ways dan his pappy is.'

'What are you talking about? What kind of ways?'

'Jes' *man* ways, Massa. Mo' solid, an' 'pendable, an' not fo' no foolishness no kin' o' way, an' like dat. He gwine be de kin' o' man make some woman a mighty good husban'.'

'Well, I hope he hasn't got matin' on his mind,' said Massa Lea, probing, ' 'cause I just permitted it with that oldest one – what's his name?'

'Virgil, Massa.'

'Right. And every weekend he's runnin' off to bed down with her over at the Curry plantation when he ought to be here workin'!'

'Nawsuh, not Tom. He too young for sich as dat on his min', an' I 'speck he won't be too quick 'bout it even when he git grown, leas' not 'til he fin' jes' de right gal he want.'

'You're too old to know about young bucks nowadays,' said Massa Lea. 'Wouldn't surprise me if one left my plough and mule in the field to go chasin' some gal.'

''Gree wid you if you talkin' 'about dat Ashford, Massa, 'cause he took to woman chasin' jes' like his pappy. But Tom jes' ain't dat kin', dat's all.'

'Well, all right. If I go on what you say, the boy sounds like he might be fit for something.'

'Go on what any us say 'bout him, Massa.' Miss Malizy concealed her jubilation. 'Don' know what you axin' 'bout Tom fo', but he sho' de pick o' dem big boys.'

Massa Lea broke the news to Chicken George five days later.

'I've worked out an arrangement to board your Tom over at the Askew plantation,' he announced solemnly, 'for a three-year apprenticeship with that nigger blacksmith Isaiah.'

George was so elated that it was all he could do to keep from picking up the massa and spinning him around. Instead, he just grinned from ear to ear and began to sputter his appreciation.

'You'd better be right about that boy, George. On the strength of your assurances, I recommended him very highly to Massa Askew. If he isn't as good as you say, I'll have him back here so fast it'll make your head spin, and if he gets out of line, if he betrays my trust in any way, I'll take it out of your hide as his. Do you understand?'

'He won't let you down, Massa. You got my promise on dat. Dat boy a chip off de ol' block.'

'That's what I'm afraid of. Have him packed and ready to leave in the mornin'.'

'Yassuh. An' thank you, suh. You won't never regret it.'

Racing up to slave row as soon as the massa was gone, Chicken George was so near to bursting with pride in his achievement when he told them the great news that he didn't see the wry smiles exchanged by Matilda and Kizzy, who had been the ones responsible for urging him to approach the massa in the first place. Soon he stood in the doorway hollering, 'Tom! Tom! *You* Tom!'

'Yaaay, Pappy!' His reply came from behind the barn.

'Boy, *c'mere!*'

A moment later Tom's mouth was open as wide as his eyes. The incredible news had come as a total surprise – for they hadn't wanted him to be disappointed if the effort hadn't worked. But as overjoyed as he was, their heaped congratulations so embarrassed him that Tom got back outside as quickly as he could – partly to give himself the chance to realize that his dream had actually come true. He hadn't noticed while he was in the cabin that his little sisters, Kizzy and Mary, had scampered outside and breathlessly spread the news among their brothers.

The lanky Virgil was just trotting up from his chores in the barn before leaving for the plantation of his recent bride; he merely grunted something non-committal under his breath and hurried on past Tom, who smiled, since Virgil had been in a daze ever since he had jumped the broom.

But Tom tensed when he saw stocky, powerful eighteen-year-old Ashford approaching, trailed by their younger brothers James and Lewis. After nearly a lifetime of unaccountable hostility between him and Ashford, Tom wasn't surprised at his snarling bitterness.

'You always been dey pet! Butterin' up eve'ybody so you gits de favours! Now you gwine off laughin' at us still in de fiel'!' He made a swift feint as if to strike Tom, drawing gasps from James and Lewis. 'I'm gon' git you yet, jes' watch!' And Ashford stalked off, Tom staring levelly after him, certain that someday he and Ashford were going to have a showdown.

What Tom heard from 'L'il George' was another kind of bitterness. 'Sho' wish I was you gittin' way from here, fo' pappy work me to death down dere! Jes' cause I got his name, he figger I'se s'posed to be crazy as he is 'bout chickens. I *hates* dem stinkin' things!'

As for the ten-year-old Kizzy and eight-year-old Mary, having spread the news, they now trailed Tom around the rest of the afternoon, their shy looks making it clear that he was their adored and favourite big brother.

The next morning, after seeing Tom off in the mule cart with Virgil, Kizzy, Sister Sarah, and Matilda had just begun the day's chopping in the field when Gran'mammy Kizzy observed, 'Anybody seen us all up dere snifflin' an' cryin' an' gwine on would o' thought we weren't gwine never see dat chile ag'in.'

'Hmph! No mo' *chile*, honey!' exclaimed Sister Sarah. 'Dat Tom de nex' *man* roun' dis place!'

102

With a special travelling pass supplied by Massa Lea, Virgil had hung a lantern on the mulecart and driven it through the night before Thanksgiving in order to get Tom home from the Askew plantation in time for the big dinner, after an absence of nine months. As the cart rolled back into the Lea driveway in the chilly November afternoon and Virgil quickened the mule to a brisk trot, Tom had to press back tears as the familiar slave row came into view and he saw all of those whom he had missed so much standing there waiting for him. Then they began waving and shouting, and moments later, grasping his bag of the gifts that he had made with his own hands for each of them, he jumped to the ground amid the huggings and kissings of the womenfolk.

'Bless 'is heart' ... 'He look so good!' ... 'Don't he now! See how dem shoulders an' arms done filled out!' ... 'Gran'mammy, leave me kiss Tom!' ... 'Don't squeeze 'im all day, lem'me git holt of 'im too, chile!'

Over their shoulders, Tom caught a glimpse of his two younger brothers, James and Lewis, wearing awed expressions; he knew that L'il George was down among the gamecocks with his father, and Virgil had told him that Ashford had got the massa's permission to visit a girl on another plantation.

Then he saw the usually bedridden Uncle Pompey sitting outside his cabin in an old cane chair, bundled in a heavy quilt. As soon as he could manoeuvre clear, Tom hurried over to shake the old man's puffy, trembling hand, bending closer to hear the cracked and almost whispery voice.

'Jes' wants to make sho's you's really back to see us, boy—'

'Yassuh, Uncle Pompey, mighty glad to git back!'

'Awright, see you later on,' the old man quavered.

Tom was having trouble with his emotions. In his now sixteen years, not only had he never been treated so much like a man, but also he had never before felt such an outpouring of his slave-row family's love and respect.

His two little sisters were still pulling and clamouring over him when they heard a familiar voice trumpeting in the distance.

'Lawd, here come Mr Rooster!' exclaimed Matilda, and the women went scurrying to set the Thanksgiving meal on the table.

When Chicken George came striding into the slave-row area.

seeing Tom, he beamed. 'Well, look what done got loose an' come home!' He clapped Tom heavily across the shoulders with his hand. 'Is you makin' any money yet?'

'Nawsuh, not yet, Pappy.'

'What kin' of blacksmith you is ain't makin' no money?' demanded George in mock astonishment.

Tom remembered that he had always felt caught in a windstorm whenever closely exposed to his father's bombastic way of expressing himself. 'Long ways yet from bein' no blacksmith, Pappy, jes' tryin' to learn,' he said.

'Well, you tell dat Isaiah nigger I say hurry up an' learn you sump'n!'

'Yassuh,' said Tom mechanically, his mind flashing that he could probably never master even so much as half of what Mr Isaiah was patiently making every effort to help him learn. He asked, 'Ain't L'il George comin' up here fo' dinner?'

'He might git here in time, an' he might not,' said Chicken George. 'He too lazy to finish what I give 'im to do firs' thing dis mornin', an' I tol' 'im I don't want to see his face up here 'til he git it done!' Chicken George was moving over to Uncle Pompey. 'Sho' glad to see you out'n yo' cabin, Uncle Pompey. How's you doin'?'

'Po'ly, son, mighty po'ly. Ol' man jes' ain't no mo' good, dat's all.'

'Don't give me dat stuff, nary bit!' boomed Chicken George, and laughing, he turned to Tom, 'Yo' ol' Uncle Pompey one dem ol' lizard kin' o' niggers gwine live to be a hunnud! Done got real low sick reckon two, three times since you been gone, but every time de wimminfolks all snifflin' ready to bury 'im, he git right back up ag'in!'

The three of them were laughing when the voice of Gran'mammy Kizzy shrilled at them, 'Y'all bring Pompey on over here to de table now!' Though the day was crisp, the women had set up a long table under the chinquapin tree so that everybody could enjoy their Thanksgiving dinner together.

James and Lewis seized Uncle Pompey's chair, with Sister Sarah running up solicitously behind them.

'Don' drop 'im, now, he still ain't too ol' to fan y'all's britches!' called Chicken George.

When they were all seated, though Chicken George was at the head of the table, it was pointedly to Tom that Matilda said, 'Son, grace de table.' The startled Tom wished he had anticipated this, to have given advance thought to some prayer that would express the emotions he was feeling about the warmth and strength of a family.

But with everyone's head already bowed, all he could think of now was, 'O Lawd, bless dis food we's 'bout to eat, we ax in de name de Father, de Son, an' de Holy Ghos'. Amen.'

'Amen! ... Amen!' others echoed up and down the table. Then Matilda, Gran'mammy Kizzy, and Sister Sarah began shuttling back and forth, setting heaped and steaming bowls and platters at intervals along the table, and urging all to help themselves, before they also finally sat back down. For several minutes not a word was spoken as everyone ate as if they were starving, with appreciative grunts and smacking noises. Then, after a while, with either Matilda or Kizzy refilling his glass with fresh buttermilk or putting more hot meat, vegetables, and cornbread on his plate, they began plying Tom with questions.

'Po' thing, is dey feedin' you any good over yonder? Who cook fo' you anyhow?' asked Matilda.

Tom chewed his mouthful enough to reply, 'Mr Isaiah's wife, Miss Emma.'

'What colour she is, what she look like?' asked Kizzy.

'She black, sorta fat.'

'Dat ain't got nothin' to do wid 'er cookin'!' guffawed Chicken George. 'She cook any good, boy?'

'Pretty fair, Pappy, yassuh,' Tom nodded affirmatively.

'Well, ain't like yo' own mammy's nohow!' snapped Sister Sarah. Tom murmured agreeably, 'No'm,' thinking how indignant Miss Emma would have been to hear them, and how indignant they'd be to know that she was a better cook.

'Her an' dat blacksmith man, is dey good Christian folks?'

'Yes'm, dey is,' he said. ' 'Specially Miss Emma, she read de Bible a whole lots.'

Tom was just finishing his third plateful when his mammy and gran'mammy descended on him with still more, despite his vigorous headshaking. He managed a muffled protest: 'Save sump'n for L'il George when he come!'

'Plenty lef' for 'im an' you knows it!' said Matilda. 'Have 'nother piece dis fried rabbit ... l'il mo' dese collard greens ... an' dis stewed winter squash. An' Malizy done sent down a great big sweet 'tater custard from de dinner she servin' in de big house. Y'all knows how good dat is—'

Tom had started forking into the custard when Uncle Pompey cleared his throat to speak, and everyone hushed up to hear him. 'Boy, is you hoein' mules an' hosses yet?'

'Dey lets me pull off de ol' shoes, but I ain't put none on yet,' said

510

Tom, thinking how only the previous day it had been necessary to hobble a vicious mule before it could be shod. Loudly Chicken George hooted. ''Speck he ain't got 'nough good hard mules kicks yet to be broke in good! Mighty easy to mess up hosses' foots less'n somebody know what he doin'! Heared 'bout one blacksmith nigger put de shoes on backwards, an' dat hoss wouldn't do nothin' but back up!' When he quit laughing at his own joke, Chicken George asked, 'How much y'all git for shoein' hosses an' mules?'

'B'lieves de mens pays Massa Askew fo'teen cents a shoe,' said Tom.

'Sho' ain't no money in it like fightin' chickens!' Chicken George exclaimed.

'Well, it's sho' plenty mo' use o' blacksmithin' dan it is dem chickens!' snapped Gran'mammy Kizzy, her tone so cutting that Tom wanted to jump up and hug her. Then she went on, her voice suddenly tender, 'Son, what de man have you doin' in learnin' you how to blacksmith?'

Tom was glad she asked, for he wanted to share with his family some idea of what he was doing. 'Well, Gran'mammy, early every mornin' I has de forge fire goin' good by time Mr Isaiah gits dere. Den I lays out de tools I knows he gwine need for de jobs he gwine be doin'. 'Cause when you shapin' red-hot iron, can't let it be coolin' down while you hunts for de right hammers to hit it wid—'

'Lawd, de chile blacksmithin' already!' exclaimed Sister Sarah.

'No'm,' said Tom. 'I be's what dey calls a "striker". If Mr Isaiah makin' sump'n heavy, like wagon axles or ploughshares, den I hits wid de sledge wherever he tap his hammer. An' sometime l'il simple jobs he'll let me finish while he start sump'n else.'

'When he gwine let you start shoein' de hosses?' asked Chicken George, still pushing, seeming almost as if he wanted to embarrass his blacksmithing son, but Tom grinned. 'Dunno, Pappy, but I reckon soon's he feel like I kin do it widout 'is he'p. Jes' like you said, I sho' has got kicked aplenty times. Fact, some dem bad ones git to rarin' up, dey won't only kick, dey'll bite a plug out'n you if you ain't careful.'

'Do white folks come roun' dat blacksmith shop, son?' asked Sister Sarah.

'Yes, ma'am, whole lots of 'em. Ain't hardly no day don't see leas' a dozen or mo' standin' roun' talkin' while dey's waiting for Mr Isaiah to finish whatever work dey done brung.'

'Well, den what kind o' news is you done heared 'em talkin' 'bout dat maybe we ain't, bein' stuck off like we is here?'

Tom thought a moment, trying to remember what had Mr Isaiah and Miss Emma felt were the most important things they'd recently heard white people talking about. 'Well, one thing was sump'n dey calls "telegraph". It was some Massa Morse in Washington, D.C., dat talked to somebody clear in Baltimore. Dey say he say, "What have God wrought?" But I ain't never got de straight of what it s'posed to mean.'

Every head around the dinner table turned towards Matilda as their Bible expert, but she seemed perplexed. 'I – well, I can't be sho',' she said uncertainly, 'but b'lieve I ain't never read nothin' 'bout dat in de Bible.'

'Somehow or 'nother, Mammy,' said Tom, 'seem like it weren't to do wid de Bible. Was jes' sump'n talked a long ways through de air.'

He asked then if any of them were aware that a few months before, President Polk had died of diarrhoea in Nashville, Tennessee, and had been succeeded by President Zachary Taylor.

'Everybody know dat!' exclaimed Chicken George.

'Well, you know so much, you ain't never told it in my hearin',' said Sister Sarah sharply.

Tom said, 'White folks, 'specially dey young'uns, is been comin' roun' singing songs s'posed to soun' like us, but dey was writ by a Massa Stephen Foster.' Tom sang the little that he could remember of 'Ol' Black Joe', 'My Ol' Kentucky Home', and 'Massa's in de Col', Col' Ground'.

'Sho' do soun' sump'n like niggers!' Gran'mammy Kizzy exclaimed.

'Mr Isaiah say dat Massa Foster growed up spendin' a lotta time lissenin' to nigger singin' in churches an' roun' de steamboats an' wharves,' said Tom.

'Dat 'splain it!' said Matilda. 'But ain't you heared of no doin's by none o' us?'

'Well, yas'm,' said Tom, and he said that free blacks who brought work to Mr Isaiah had been talking a lot about famous northern blacks who were fighting against slavery, travelling around, lecturing large mixed audiences to tears and cheers by telling their life stories as slaves before they had escaped to freedom. 'Like it's one named Frederick Douglass,' Tom said. 'Dey says he was raised a slave boy in Maryland, an' he teached hisself to read an' write an' finally worked an' saved up enough to buy hisself free from his massa.' Matilda cast a meaningful glance at Chicken George as Tom went on. 'Dey says people gathers by de hunnuds anywhere he speak, an' he done writ a book an' even started up a newspaper.

'It's famous womens, too, Mammy.' Tom looked at Matilda, Gran'mammy Kizzy, and Sister Sarah, and he told them of a former slave named Sojourner Truth, said to be over six feet tall, who also lectured before huge crowds of white and black people, though she could neither read nor write.

Springing up from her seat, Gran'mammy Kizzy began wildly gesturing. 'Sees right now I needs to git up Nawth an' do *me* some talkin'.' She mimicked as if she were facing a big audience, 'Y'all white folks listen here to Kizzy! Ain't gwine have dis mess no mo'! Us niggers sick an' tired o' slavin'!'

'Mammy, de boy say dat woman six feet! You ain't tall enough!' Chicken George said, roaring with laughter, as the others around the table glared at him in mock indignation. Chagrined, Gran'mammy Kizzy sat back down.

Tom told them of another famous escaped slave woman. 'She named Harriet Tubman. Ain't no tellin' how many times she come back South an' led out different whole bunches o' folks like us to freedom up Nawth on sump'n deys callin' de "unnergroun' railroad". Fac', she done it so much dey claims by now white folks got out forty thousand dollars' worth o' rewards fo' her, alive or dead.'

'Lawd have mercy, wouldn't o' thought white folks pay dat much to catch no nigger in de worl'!' said Sister Sarah.

He told them that in a far-distant state called California, two white men were said to have been building a sawmill when they discovered an unbelievable wealth of gold in the ground, and thousands of people were said to be rushing in wagons, on mules, even afoot to reach the place where it was claimed that gold could be dug up by the shovelful.

He said finally that in the North great debates on the subject of slavery were being held between two white men named Stephen Douglas and Abraham Lincoln.

'Which one 'em for de niggers?' asked Gran'mammy Kizzy.

'Well, soun' like de Massa Lincoln, leas'ways de bes' I can tell,' said Tom.

'Well, praise de Lawd an' give 'im stren'th!' said Kizzy.

Sucking his teeth, Chicken George got up patting his ample belly and turned to Tom. 'Looka here, boy, why'n't you'n me stretch our legs, walk off some dat meal?'

'Yassuh, Pappy,' Tom almost stammered, scarcely able to conceal his amazement and trying to act casual.

The women, who were no less startled, exchanged quizzical, significant glances when Chicken George and Tom set off together down the road. Sister Sarah exclaimed softly, 'Lawd, y'all realize dat boy done growed nigh big as his daddy!' James and Lewis stared after their father and older brother nearly sick with envy, but they knew better than to invite themselves along. But the two younger girls, L'il Kizzy and Mary, couldn't resist leaping up and happily starting to hop-skip along eight or ten steps behind them.

Without even looking back at them, Chicken George ordered, 'Git on back yonder an' he'p y'all's mammy wid dem dishes!'

'Aw, Pappy!' they whined in unison.

'*Git*, done tol' you!'

Half turning around with his eyes loving his little sisters, Tom chided them gently, 'Ain't y'all hear Pappy? We see you later on.'

With the girls' complaining sounds behind them, they walked on in silence for a little way and Chicken George spoke almost gruffly, 'Looka here, reckon you know I ain't meant no harm jes' teasin' you a l'il at dinner.'

'Aw, nawsuh,' Tom said, privately astounded at what amounted to an apology from his father. 'I knowed you was jes' teasin'.'

Grunting, Chicken George said, 'What say we head on down an' look in on dem chickens? See what keepin' dat no-count L'il George down dere so long. All I knows, he mighta cooked an' et up some dem chickens fo' his Thanksgivin' by now.'

Tom laughed. 'L'il George mean well, Pappy. He jes' a l'il slow. He done tol' me he jes' don' love dem birds like you does.' Tom paused, then decided to venture his accompanying thought. 'I 'speck nobody in de *worl'* loves dem birds like you does.'

But Chicken George agreed readily enough. 'Nobody in dis family, anyways. I done tried 'em all – 'ceptin' you. Seem like all de res' my boys willin' to spend dey lives draggin' from one end of a fiel' to de other, lookin' up a mule's butt!' He considered for a moment. 'Yo' blacksmithin', wouldn't 'zackly call dat no high livin' neither – nothin' like gamecockin' – but leas'ways it's a man's work.'

Tom wondered if his father ever seriously respected anything excepting fighting chickens. He felt deeply grateful that somehow he had escaped into the solid, stable trade of blacksmithing. But he expressed his thoughts in an oblique way. 'Don't see nothin' wrong wid farmin', Pappy. If some folks wasn't farmin', 'speck nobody wouldn' be eatin'. I jes' took to blacksmithin' same as you wid gamecockin', 'cause I loves it, an' de Lawd gimme a knack fo' it. Jes' ever'body don' love de same things.'

'Well leas' you an' me got sense to make *money* doin' what we likes,' said Chicken George.

Tom replied, 'You does, anyway. I won't make no money fo' couple mo' years, 'til I'se finished 'prenticin' an' goes to work for massa – dat is, if he gimme some de money, like he do o' what you wins hackfightin'!'

'Sho' he will!' said Chicken George. 'Massa ain't bad as yo' mammy an' gran'mammy an' dem likes to claim. He got 'is ornery ways, sho' is! You jes' have to learn how to git to massa's good side, like I does – keep 'im b'leevin' you considers 'im one dem high-class massas what do good by dey niggers.' Chicken George paused. 'Dat Massa Askew whose place you over dere workin' on – you got any idea what 'mount o' money he give dat Isaiah nigger fo' his black-smithin'?'

'I b'leeves dollar a week,' said Tom. 'I'se heared Mr Isaiah's wife says dat's what he give her every week to save, an' she do, every penny.'

'Less'n a minute win mo'n dat fightin' chickens!' Chicken George exclaimed, and then contained himself.

'Well, anyhow, you jes' leave de money part to me when you comes back here to blacksmith fo' massa. I talk to 'im good 'bout how cheap dat Massa Askew is wid 'is nigger.'

'Yassuh.'

Chicken George was experiencing a peculiar feeling that he really wished to insure having the alliance, even the approval of this particular one among his six sons – not that anything was wrong with the other five, and despite the fact that this one was by far the least likely ever to sport anything like a green scarf and black derby with a long feather in it; it was just that very clearly this Tom possessed qualities of responsibleness not encountered every day, as well as an unusual individual durability and strength.

They had walked on in silence for a while when Chicken George said abruptly, 'You ever think 'bout blacksmithin' fo' yo'self, boy?'

'What you mean? How in de worl' I gwine do *dat*, Pappy?'

'You ever think 'bout savin' de money you gwine be makin' an' buyin' yo'self *free?*'

Seeing Tom too thunderstruck to reply, Chicken George kept talking.

'Few years back, roun' when L'il Kizzy born, one night me an' yo' mammy set down an' figgered 'bout how much it cost to buy us whole family free, 'cordin' to prices fo' niggers dem days. Come to roun' sixty-eight hunnud dollars—'

'*Whew!*' Tom was shaking his head.

'Hear me out!' George said. 'Sho' it's a *lot!* But ever since den, I been hackfightin' my butt off, wid yo' mammy savin' my share o' de winnins. Ain't winned as much as I'd figured when I started out, but all de same don' nobody know but yo' mammy an' me – an' now you – she got mo'n a thousan' dollars buried in jars roun' de back-yard!' Chicken George looked at Tom. 'Boy, I'se jes' thinkin' . . .

'Me, too, Pappy!' A gleam was in Tom's eyes.

'Lissen here, boy!' The urgency increased in Chicken George's tone. 'If'n I keeps winnin' 'bout de same as in de past few seasons, I oughta have three, fo' hunnud mo' stashed away time you starts blacksmithin' fo' massa.'

Tom was eagerly nodding his head. 'An', Pappy, wid *bofe* us makin' money, mammy could bury maybe five, six hunnud a year!' he said excitedly.

'Yeah!' Chicken George exclaimed. 'An' dat rate, less'n nigger prices is riz a lot higher, we ought to have 'nough to buy us whole fam'ly free inside o' – lemme see now . . .'

They both figured, using their fingers. After a while, Tom exclaimed, ' 'Bout fifteen years!'

'Where you learn to count so fas'? What you think 'bout my idea, boy?'

'Pappy, gwine blacksmith my head off! I jes' wish you'd o' said somethin' fo' now.'

'Wid two us, I *knows* we can do it!' said George, beaming. 'Make dis family '*mount* to sump'n! Us all git up Nawth, raisin' chilluns an' gran'chilluns *free*, like folks was meant to! What you say, boy?'

Both deeply moved, Tom and Chicken George had impulsively grasped each other about the shoulders when just then they turned to see the stout, pudgy figure of L'il George approaching at a lumbering trot, shouting '*Tom! Tom!*' and wearing a grin seeming almost as wide as himself. Reaching them breathless, his chest heaving, he grabbed and pumped Tom's hands, clapped him on the back, and stood there alternately wheezing and grinning, with sweat making his plump cheeks shine. 'Glad . . . to . . . see . . . you . . . Tom!' he gasped finally.

'Take it easy dere, boy!' said Chicken George. 'You won't have strength to git to yo' dinner.'

'Never . . . too . . . tired . . . fo' . . . dat . . . Pappy!'

'Whyn't you git on up dere an' eat, den,' said Tom, 'an' we jine you by and by. Pappy and me got things to talk 'bout.'

'Awright . . . I . . . see . . . y'all . . . later,' said L'il George, needing no further encouragement as he turned to head for slave row.

'Better *hurry!*' Chicken George shouted after him. 'Don' know how long yo' mammy can hol' off yo' brothers from eatin' up what's lef'!'

Watching L'il George break into a waddling run, Tom and his father stood holding their sides from laughter until he disappeared around the bend, still gaining momentum.

'We better figger *sixteen* years fo' we gits free,' Chicken George gasped.

'How come?' asked Tom, quickly concerned.

'Way dat boy eat, gwine cost a year's pay jes' keepin' 'im fed 'til den!'

103

In the memory of Chicken George, nothing had ever generated such excitement among North Carolina gamecockers as the news that spread swiftly during late November of 1855 that the wealthy Massa Jewett was entertaining as his house guest a titled, equally rich gamecocker from England who had brought with him across the ocean thirty of his purebred 'Old English' gamebirds, said to be the finest breed of fighting cocks in existence. According to the news, the Englishman, Sir C. Eric Russell, had accepted Massa Jewett's written invitation to pit his birds against some of the best in the United States. Since as longtime friends they preferred not to fight their gamecocks against one another, each of them would supply twenty birds to fight any forty challenger birds whose collective owners would be expected to ante up their half of a $30,000 main pot, and $250 side bets would be the minimum permitted on each cockfight. Another wealthy local gamecocker volunteered to organize the forty competitors – accepting only five birds apiece from seven other owners besides himself.

It had not been really necessary for Massa Lea to tell his veteran trainer that he was going after a share of such a huge pot.

'Well,' he said upon return to the plantation after posting his $1,875 bond, 'we've got six weeks to train five birds.' 'Yassuh, ought to be able to do dat, I reckon,' Chicken George replied, trying as hard – and as unsuccessfully – not to seem excited. Apart from his own deep thrill just to think of such a contest, Chicken George exulted to the assembled slave-row family that it seemed to him that sheer excitement had rolled twenty-five years off Massa Lea. 'Dey's sho' pricin' out any hackfighters!' he exclaimed. 'Massa say it's sho' de bigges' money fight he ever got anywheres near to – fac', de secon' bigges' he ever even heared of!'

'Phew! What bigger fight was *dat?*' exclaimed Uncle Pompey.

Chicken George said, 'Reckon maybe twenty years back dis double-rich Massa Nicholas Arrington what live near Nashville, Tennessee, took 'leben covered wagons, twenty-two mens, and three hunnud birds clear crost no tellin' how many states, through bandits an' Indians an' everythin', 'til dey got to Mexico. Dey fought 'gainst 'nother three hunnud birds belongin' to de Pres'dent o' Mexico, a Gen'l Santa Anna, what had so much money he couldn' even count it, an' swo' he raised de world's greatest gamecocks. Well, Massa say de fightin' jes' dem two men's birds went on a solid *week!* De stake was so big dey main purse was a chest apiece full o' money! Massa say even dey side bets could o' broke mos' rich mens. In de end, dis Tennessee Massa Arrington won roun' half a million dollars! His birds he called "Cripple Tonys" after his crippled nigger trainer named Tony. An' dat Mexican Gen'l Santa Anna wanted one dem "Cripple Tonys" so bad fo' a breedin' cock he paid its weight in gol'!'

'I see right now I better git in de chicken business,' said Uncle Pompey.

For most of the next six weeks, Chicken George and Massa Lea were seldom seen by anyone else on the plantation. 'It's a good thing massa keepin' off down dere wid dem chickens, mad as ol' missis is!' Miss Malizy told the others on slave row at the end of the third week. 'I heard her jes' screechin' at him 'bout takin' five thousan' dollars out'n de bank. Heared her say it near 'bout half what dey got saved up from all dey lives, an' she jes' hollered an' carried on 'bout 'im tryin' to keep up wid dem real rich massas what got a thousan' times mo' money dan he is.' After shouting at the missis to shut up and mind her own damn business, the massa had stalked out of the house, said Miss Malizy.

Listening grimly, but saying nothing, were Matilda and twenty-two-year-old Tom, who four years before had returned to the plantation and built a blacksmith shop behind the barn, where by now he was serving a thriving trade of customers for Massa Lea. Fit to burst with anger, Matilda had confided to her son how Chicken George had furiously demanded and got their own two-thousand-dollar cache of savings, which he was going to turn over to the massa to be bet on the Lea birds. Matilda, too, had screeched and wept in desperate effort to reason with Chicken George, 'but he act like he gone crazy!' she had told Tom. 'Hollered at me, "Woman, I knows every bird we got from when dey was eggs. Three or fo' ain't nothin' wid wings can beat! Ain't 'bout to pass up dis chance to zackly double what we got saved no quicker'n it take one our chickens to kill another'n! Two minutes can save us eight, nine mo' years o 'scrapin' an' savin' to buy us free!"'

'Mammy, I know you tol' Pappy de savin' have to start over ag'in if de chicken lose!' Tom had exclaimed.

'Ain't only tol' 'im dat! Tried my bes' to press on 'im he ain't got no right to gamble wid our freedom! But he got real mad, hollerin', "Ain't no *way* we kin lose! You gimme my money, woman!"' And Matilda had done so, she had told Tom, her face stricken.

In the gamefowl area, Chicken George and Massa Lea finished culling seventeen of the best rangewalk birds down to ten of the finest gamecocks either of them had ever seen. Then they began airtraining those ten birds, tossing them higher and higher, until finally eight of them flew as much as a dozen yards before their feet touched the ground. 'I 'clare look like we's trainin' wil' turkeys, Massa!' chortled Chicken George.

'They're going to need to be hawks up against Jewett's and that Englishman's birds,' said the massa.

When the great cockfight was but a week away, the massa rode off, and late the following day he returned with six pairs of the finest obtainable Swedish steel gaffs, their lengths as sharp as razors tapering to needle points.

After a final critical appraisal two days before the fight, each of the eight birds seemed so perfect that there was simply no way to say which five were best. So the massa decided to take all eight and choose among them at the last minute.

He told Chicken George that they would leave the following midnight in order to arrive early enough for both the gamecocks and themselves to rest from the long ride and be fresh for the big fights. Chicken George knew that the massa was itching as bad as he was just to get there.

The long ride through the darkness was uneventful. As he drove, his gaze idly upon the lantern glowing and bobbing at the end of the wagon's tongue between the two mules, Chicken George thought with mingled feelings of his and Matilda's recent emotional altercation about the money. He told himself resentfully that he knew better than she did how many years of patient saving it represented; after all, hadn't it been his own perennial scores upon scores of hackfights that had earned it? He'd never feel for a moment that Matilda wasn't as good as wives came, so he regretted he'd had to shout her down, upsetting her so badly, as apparently the massa had also been forced to do within the big house, but on the other hand there were those times when the head of a family simply had to make the important, hard decisions. He again heard Matilda's tearful cry, 'George, you ain't got no right to gamble wid all our freedom!' How quickly she'd forgotten that it had been he in the first place who had introduced the idea of accumulating enough to buy their freedom. And after all those slow years of saving, it was now nothing but a godsend that the massa had confided that he needed more cash for side betting during the forthcoming fights, not only to make a good showing before those snobby, rich massas, but to win their money as well. Chicken George grinned to himself, remembering with relish Massa Lea's utterly astounded expression at hearing him say, 'I got 'bout two thousand dollars saved dat you can use to bet wid, Massa.' Upon recovering from his shock, Massa Lea had actually grabbed and shaken his trainer's hand, pledging his word that Chicken George would receive every cent that was won in bets using his money, declaring, 'You ought to double it, anyhow!' The massa hesitated. 'Boy, what you gonna do with four thousand dollars?'

In that instant Chicken George had decided to take an even bigger gamble – to reveal why he had been saving so long and so hard, 'Massa, don't mistake me none, ain't got nothin' but de bes' kin' o' feelin's 'bout you, Massa. But me an' 'Tilda jes' got to talkin', an' Massa we jes' 'cided we gwine try see couldn' us buy us an' our chilluns from you, an' spen' out de res' our days free!' Seeing Massa Lea clearly taken aback, Chicken George again implored, 'Please Lawd don't take us wrong, Massa—'

But then in one of Chicken George's most richly warming life experiences, Massa Lea had said, 'Boy, I'm gonna tell you what's been on *my* mind about this chicken-fight we're going into. I'm figuring for it to be my last big one. Don't think you even realize, I'm seventy-eight years old. I've been over fifty years of dragging back and forth every season worrying with raising and fighting these chickens. I'm *sick* of it. You hear me! I tell you what, boy! With my cut of that main pot and side bets, I'm figgerin' to win enough to build me and my wife another house – not no great big mansion like I wanted one time, but just five, six rooms, *new*, that's all we need. And I hadn't thought about it until you just brought it up, but then won't be no more point in owning a whole passel of y'all niggers to have to fend for. Just Sarah and Malizy could cook and keep a good garden we can live off, and have enough money in the bank not to never have to beg nobody for nothin'—'

Chicken George was barely breathing as Massa Lea went on. 'So I'm gonna tell you what, boy! Y'all have served me well an' ain't never give me no real trouble. We win this chickenfight big, at least double both our money, yeah, you just give me what you'll have, four thousand dollars, and we'll call it square! And you know good as I do all y'all niggers are worth twice that! Fact, I never told you, but once that rich Jewett offered me four thousand just for you, an' I turned him down! Yeah, an y'all can go on free if that's what you want!'

Suddenly in tears, Chicken George had lunged to embrace Massa Lea, who quickly moved aside in embarrassment. 'Oh Lawdy, Massa, you don' know what you's sayin'! Us wants to be free *so* bad!' Massa Lea's reply was strangely hoarse. 'Well, I don't know what y'all niggers'll *do*, free, without somebody lookin' out for you. An' I know my wife's going to raise all manners of hell about me just the same as giving y'all away. Hell, that blacksmith boy Tom alone is worth a good twenty-five hundred plus he's making me good money to boot!'

Roughly the massa had shoved Chicken George. 'Git, nigger, before I change my mind! Hell! I must be crazy! But I hope your woman an' mammy and the rest y'all niggers find out I ain't bad as I know they always make me out to be!'

'Aw nawsuh, nawsuh, Massa, thank you, Massa!' Chicken George went scrambling backwards, as Massa Lea hastily departed up the road towards the big house.

Chicken George wished now more than ever that the bitter encounter with Matilda had never occurred. Now he decided it best to keep his triumphant secret, to let Matilda, his mammy Kizzy, and the whole family learn of their freedom as an absolutely total surprise. Still, fit to burst with such a secret, several times he nearly told Tom, but then always at the last moment he didn't, for even as solid a man as Tom was, he was so close with both his mammy and gran'mammy that he might swear them to secrecy, which would ruin it. Also that would activate among them the very sticky issue that according to what the massa had said, Sister Sarah, Miss Malizy, and Uncle Pompey were going to have to be left behind, though they were as much family as anybody else.

So across the interim weeks, Chicken George, pent up with his secret, had submerged himself body and soul into honing into absolute perfection the final eight gamecocks that now were riding quietly in their coops behind him and Massa Lea in the big custom-built wagon rolling along the lonely road through the dark. At intervals Chicken George wondered what the uncommonly silent Massa Lea was thinking.

It was in the early daylight when they caught sight of the vast and motley throng that even this early had not only overrun the cockfighting area but had also spilled into an adjoining pasture that was quickly filling with other wagons, carriages, buggies, carts, and snorting mules and horses.

'*Tawm Lea!*' A group of poor crackers cried out upon seeing the massa climb down from his huge wagon. 'Go *git* 'em, Tawm! As he adjusted his black derby, Chicken George saw the massa nodding at them in a friendly manner, but he kept on walking. He knew that the massa wavered between pride and embarrassment at his notoriety among the crackers. After half a century as a gamecocker in fact, Massa Lea was a legend wherever chickens were fought locally, since even at his age of seventy-eight, his ability to handle birds in a cockpit seemed undiminished.

Chicken George had never heard such a din of crowing gamecocks as he began unpacking things for action. A passing slave trainer stopped and told him that among the crowd were many who had travelled for days from other states, even as distant as Florida. Glancing about as they talked, Chicken George saw that the usual spectator area was more than doubled, but already was crawling with men guaranteeing themselves a seat. Among those moving steadily past the wagon, he saw as many strange faces both white and black as he did familiar ones, and he felt pride when numerous among both races obviously recognized him, usually nudging their companions and whispering.

The sprawling crowd's buzzing excitement rose to a yet higher pitch when three judges came to the cockpit and began measuring and marking the starting lines. Another buzz arose when someone's gamecock fluttered loose and went furiously attacking men in its path, even sending a dog yelping, until the bird was cornered and caught. And the crowd's noises swelled with each arrival and identification of any of the area's well-known gamecockers – especially the rest of the eight who would be competing against the sponsoring Massas Jewett and Russell.

'I ain't never seed no Englishman, is you?' Chicken George overheard one poor white man ask another, who said he hadn't either. He also heard talk about the titled Englishman's wealth, that he had not only a huge English estate, but also rich holdings in places called Scotland, Ireland, and Jamaica. And he heard that Massa Jewett had proudly boasted among friends of how his guest was known for fighting his birds anytime, anywhere, against any competition, for any amount.

Chicken George was chopping a few apples into small bits to feed the birds when suddenly the crowd noise rose to a roar – and standing up quickly in the wagon he recognized the approaching canopied surrey driven by Massa Jewett's always poker-faced black coachman. In the back were the two rich massas, smiling and waving down at the crowd, surging so thickly around them that the carriage's finely matched horses had a hard time progressing. And not far behind came six wagons, each filled with tall cock coops, the lead wagon driven by Massa Jewett's white trainer, alongside of whom sat a thin and keen-nosed white man whom Chicken George overheard someone nearby exclaim that the titled, wealthy Englishman had brought clear across the ocean just to care for his birds.

But the oddly dressed, short, stockily built, and ruddy-complexioned English nobleman himself was the milling crowd's major focus of attention as he rode alongside Massa Jewett in the surrey, both of them looking every inch the important, even lordly men they were, the Englishman seeming to display just an extra touch of disdain and hauteur towards the jostling throng on the ground.

Chicken George had attended so many cockfights that he turned to his work of massaging the legs and wings of his birds, knowing out of experience that different sounds of the crowd would tell him whatever was going on, without his even looking. Soon a referee shouted for a quieting of the hoots, catcalls, and rebel yells that said that many in the crowd had already been hard at their bottles.

Then he heard the first announcement: 'Mr Fred Rudolph of Williamstown is pitting his red bird against Sir C. Eric Russell of England with his speckled grey.'

Then: 'Bill your cocks!'

And then: '*Pit!*' And the crowd's shouting, followed by a sudden awed hush, told him as clearly as if he had been watching that the fight had quickly been won by the Englishman's bird.

As each of the eight challengers in turn fought their string of five birds alternately against one belonging either to Massa Jewett or the Englishman, Chicken George had never heard such a roar of side betting in his life, and the battles within the pit were often matched by the verbal contests between the crowd and the referees shouting for quiet. Now and then the crowd noises would tell the busy

Chicken George that both birds had been hurt badly enough for the referees to stop the fight to let the owners doctor them up before the fight continued. George could tell from a special roaring of the crowd each time one of the wealthy men's birds was beaten, which wasn't often, and he wondered nervously how soon Massa Lea's turn was going to come. George guessed that the judges must be picking the order of challengers by plucking their names on slips from a hat.

He would have loved to see at least some of the actual fighting, but *so* much was at stake: he was not going to interrupt his massaging, not even for one moment. He thought fleetingly about what a fortune of money, some of it his own years of savings, the massa was only waiting to bet on the very birds whose muscles he was gently kneading under his fingers. Although only some chosen five among them would fight, there was no way to guess which five, so every one of the eight had to be in the very ultimate of physical readiness and condition. Chicken George had not often prayed in his life, but now he did so. He tried to picture what Matilda's face was going to look like, first when he returned and dropped into her apron their money at least doubled, and next when he would ask her to assemble the whole family, when he would announce they were FREE.

Then he heard the shout of the referee: 'The next five challenging birds are owned and will be handled by Mr Tom Lea of Caswell County!'

George's heart leaped up into his throat! Clapping his derby tighter on his head, he sprang down from the wagon, knowing the massa would be coming now to select his first bird.

'*Taaaaawm Lea!*' Above the crowd noise he heard the name being squalled out by the poor crackers. Then came advancing raucous rebel yells as a group of men surged out of the crowd, surrounding the massa. Reaching the wagon amid them, he cupped his hand over his mouth and over the din shouted in George's ear, 'These fellas will help us take 'em all over by the cockpit.'

'Yassuh, Massa.

George went leaping back onto the wagon, handing down the eight cock coops to the massa's poor-white companions, his thoughts flashing that in his thirty-seven years of gamecocking he never had ceased to marvel at Massa Lea's appearance of a totally detached calm in such tense times as now. Then they were all trooping back towards the cockpit through the crowd, Massa Lea carrying the splendid dark buff bird he had chosen to fight first, and Chicken George bringing up the rear carrying his woven basket of emergency injury medications, rabbit underbelly fur, some leaves of fresh ivy, glycerin, a ball of spider's web, and turpentine. It was a worsening push-and-shove progress the closer they got towards the cockpit, with the alcoholic cries of 'Tawm Lea!' ringing in their ears, as well as sometimes 'That's his Chicken George nigger!' and George could feel the eyes on him as if they were fingers, and it felt good, but kept both moving and looking straight ahead, trying to appear as cool as the massa.

And then Chicken George saw the short, squat, titled Englishman standing casually near the cockpit, holding a magnificent bird within the crook of his left arm, as his eyes watchfully appraised the little procession of them arriving with the challenger birds. After exchanging curt nods with Massa Lea, Russell set his bird on the scales and the referee sang out, 'Five pounds and fifteen ounces!' The beautiful bird's silvery blue plumage reflected brilliantly in the sunlight.

Then the massa stepped up with his dark buff bird, which was one of Chicken George's particular favourites. It was powerful, savage, its neck jerking about like a rattlesnake, murder in its eyes, and it was seething to be released. When the referee shouted 'Six pounds even!' the hard-drinking poor-white fans started yelling as if the extra ounce meant the fight was won already. '*Taaaaawm Lea!* Go git that Britisher Tawm! Act like he mighty stuck up! Take 'im down a peg!'

It was plain that Massa Lea's special fans were really well liquored, and Chicken George saw the darkening flush of embarrassment on both the massa's and the Englishman's faces as, pretending not to hear, they kneeled to tie on their birds' steel gaffs. But the cries grew more loud and rude: 'Them chickens or ducks he fightin'?' . . . 'Naw, it's swimmin' chickens!' . . . 'Yeah! He feed 'em fishes!' The Englishman's face was angry. The referee had begun dashing back and forth, furiously waving his arms, shouting, 'Gentlemen! Please!' But the derisive laughter only spread and the wisecracks became more cutting: 'Where's his red coat at?' . . . 'Do he fight foxes, too?' . . . 'Naw, too slow, waddle like a possum!' . . . 'More like a bullfrog!' . . . 'He look to me like a bloodhound!'

Massa Jewett strode out, angrily confronting the referee, his hands hacking the air, but with his words drowned out by the chanting chorus, '*Tawmmm Lea!*' . . . '*Tawmmmmm LEA!*' Now even the judges joined the referee, dashing this way and that, flailing their arms, brandishing their fists and barking repeatedly, 'The cockfight will stop unless there's quiet!' . . . 'Y'all want that, keep it up!' Slowly, the drunken cries and laughter began subsiding. Chicken George saw Massa Lea's face sick with his embarrassment, and that both the Englishman and Massa Jewett were absolutely livid.

'*Mr Lea!*' When the Englishman loudly and abruptly snapped out the words, almost instantly the crowd fell silent.

'Mr Lea, we both have such superb birds here, I wonder if you'd care to join me in a special personal side bet?'

Chicken George knew that every man among the hundreds present sensed just as he did the Englishman's tone of vengefulness and condescension behind his manner of civility. The back of the massa's neck, he saw, had suddenly become flushed with his anger.

A few seconds brought Massa Lea's stiff reply: 'That will suit me, sir. What is your proposition?'

The Englishman paused. He appeared to be pondering the matter before he spoke. 'Would ten thousand dollars be sufficient?'

He let the wave of gasps sweep the crowd, and then, 'That is, unless you haven't that much faith in your bird's chances, Mr Lea.' He stood looking at the massa, his thin smile clearly contemptuous.

The crowd's brief exclamatory rumbling quickly faded into a deathly stillness; those who had been seated were standing up now. Chicken George's heart seemed to have stopped beating. Like a distant echo he heard Miss Malizy's report of Missis Lea's fury that the five thousand dollars the massa had withdrawn from the bank was 'near 'bout half dey life savin's.' So Chicken George knew Massa Lea couldn't dare to call that bet. But what possible response could he make not to be utterly humiliated before this throng including practically everyone he knew? Sharing his massa's agony, Chicken George couldn't even bring himself to look at him. An eternity seemed to pass, then George doubted his ears.

Massa Lea's voice was strained. 'Sir, would you care to double that? *Twenty* thousand!'

The whole crowd vented exclamations of incredulity amid rustling, agitated movements. In sheer horror Chicken George realized that sum represented Massa Lea's total assets in the world, his home, his land, his slaves, plus Chicken George's savings. He saw the Englishman's expression of utter astonishment, before quickly he collected himself, his face now set and grim. 'A true sportsman!' he exclaimed, extending his hand to Massa Lea. 'A bet, sir! Let us heel up our birds!'

Suddenly then Chicken George understood: Massa Lea *knew* that his magnificent dark buff bird would win. Not only would the massa become instantly rich, but this one crucial victory would make him forever a heroic legend for all poor crackers, a symbol that even the snobbish, rich blueblood massas could be challenged and beaten! None of them could ever again look down their noses at Tom Lea!

Massa Lea and the Englishman now bent down on their opposite sides of the cockpit, and in that instant it seemed to Chicken George that the entire life of the massa's bird flashed through his mind. Even as a cockerel, its unbelievably quick reflexes at first had caught his attention; then as a stag its amazing viciousness saw it constantly trying to attack others through the cracks in their fence-row pen; and when recently retrieved from the rangewalk, within seconds it had nearly killed the old catchcock before it could be stopped. The massa had picked that bird knowing how smart, aggressive, and deep game it was. For just a split second Chicken George seemed again to hear an outraged Matilda, 'You's crazier even dan massa! Wors' can happen to 'im is endin' up jes' a po' cracker again, but you's gamblin' yo' whole fam'ly's freedom on some chicken!'

Then the three judges stepped out, positioning themselves evenly around the cockpit. The referee poised as if he stood on eggs. An atmosphere seemed to be hovering that everyone there knew they were about to witness something to talk about for the rest of their days. Chicken George saw his massa and the Englishman holding down their straining birds, both of their faces raised to watch the referee's lips.

'*Pit!*'

The silvery blue and dark buff birds blurred towards each other, crashing violently and bouncing backwards. Landing on their feet, both were instantly again in the air, tearing to reach each other's vitals. Beaks snapping, spurs flashing were moving at a blinding speed, attacking with ferocity that Chicken George had seldom seen equalled by any two birds in a cockpit. Suddenly the Englishman's silvery blue was hit, the massa's bird had sunk a spur deeply into one of its wing bones; they fell off balance, both struggling to loosen the stuck spur while pecking viciously at each other's heads.

'Handle! Thirty seconds!' The referee's shout was barely uttered before both the Englishman and Massa Lea sprang in; the spur freed, both men licked their birds' disarrayed head feathers to smoothness again, then set them back down on their starting lines, this time holding them by the tails. 'Get ready . . . '*Pit!*'

Again the cocks met evenly high in mid-air, both sets of spurs seeking a lethal strike, but failing to do so before they dropped back to the ground. The massa's bird dashed trying to knock its enemy off balance, but the English bird feinted brilliantly sidewise, drawing the crowd's gasps as the massa's bird lunged harmlessly past at full force. Before he whirled about, the English bird was upon him; they rolled furiously on the ground, then regained their feet, battling furi-

527

ously beak to beak, parting, beating at each other with powerful wing blows above a flurry of slashing legs. Again they took to the air, dropping back again, ground-fighting with new fury.

A cry rose! The English bird had drawn blood. A spreading darkening area showed on the breast of the massa's bird. But he violently buffeted his enemy with wing blows until it stumbled and he sprang above it for a kill. But again the English bird brilliantly crouched, dodged, escaped. Chicken George had never witnessed such incredibly swift reflexes. But the massa's bird now whirled forcefully enough to knock the English bird onto its back. He hit it twice in the chest, drawing blood, but the English bird managed to flap into the air, and came down, striking the massa's bird in the neck.

Chicken George had quit breathing as the bleeding birds sparred, circling, heads low, each seeking an opening. In a sudden blinding flurry, the English bird was overpowering the massa's bird, battering with its wings, its striking spurs drawing more blood, then incredibly the massa's bird burst into the air and as it came down sinking a spur into the English bird's heart; it collapsed in a feathery heap, its beak gushing blood.

It came so swiftly that a second or so seemed to pass before the huge din rose. Screaming, red-faced men were springing up and down, 'Tawm! Tawm! He done it!' Chicken George, beyond happiness, saw them mobbing the massa, pounding his back, pumping his hand 'Tawm *Lea!* Tawm *Lea!* Tom LEA!'

We's gwine be free, Chicken George kept thinking. The actuality of soon telling his family seemed unbelievable, inconceivable. He glimpsed the Englishman with his jaw set in a way that made one think of a bulldog.

'Mr LEA!' Probably nothing else could have so quickly quieted the crowd.

The Englishman was walking, he stopped about three yards distant from the massa. He said, 'Your bird fought brilliantly. Either one could have won it. They were the most perfectly matched pair I've ever seen. I'm told you're a kind of sportsman who might care to let your winnings ride on another contest between birds of ours.'

Massa Lea stood there, his face blanched.

For seconds cooped gamécocks' cluckings and crowings were the only sounds heard as thronged men tried to comprehend the potential of two gamecocks battling with eighty thousand dollars at stake, winner take all . . .

Heads had swivelled towards Massa Lea. He seemed bewildered, uncertain. For one split second his glance brushed Chicken George, working feverishly on the injured bird. Chicken George was as startled as others to hear his own voice, 'Yo' birds whup anything wid feathers, Massa!' The sea of white faces swivelled towards him.

'I've heard that your faithful darky is among the best trainers, but I wouldn't rely too much on his advice. I also have other very good birds.'

The words had come as if the rich Englishman regarded his previous loss about as he might have a game of marbles, as if he were taunting Massa Lea.

Then Massa Lea sounded elaborately formal: 'Yes, sir, As you propose, I'll take pleasure in letting the sum ride on another fight.'

The next several minutes of preparatory activities passed almost as a blur for Chicken George. Not a sound came from the surrounding crowd. There had never been anything like this. All of Chicken George's instincts approved when Massa Lea indicated with a forefinger the coop containing the bird that Chicken George had previously given a nickname. 'De Hawk, yassuh,' he breathed, knowing precisely that bird's tendency for seizing and holding an enemy with its beak while slashing with its spurs. It would be the countermeasure for birds trained to feint expertly, as the previous contest had suggested was characteristic within the Englishman's flock.

Cradling 'De Hawk' in his arm, Massa Lea went out to where the Englishman held a solid dark grey bird. The birds weighed in at six pounds even.

When '*Pit!*' came, bringing the anticipated rushing impact, somehow instead of either bird taking to the air, they exchanged furious wing blows and Chicken George could hear 'De Hawk's' beak snapping after a proper hold . . . when somehow amid mutual buffeting an English spur struck in savagely. The massa's bird stumbled and its head dropped limply for an instant before it collapsed, its opened mouth streaming blood.

'O Lawd! O Lawd! O Lawd!' Chicken George went bolting, knocking aside men in his lunge into the circular cockpit. Bellowing like a baby, scooping up the obviously mortally wounded 'Hawk', he sucked clotting blood from its beak as it weakly fluttered, dying in his hands. He struggled to his feet with the nearest men drawing back from his bawling anguish as he stumbled back through the crowd and towards the wagon cradling the dead bird.

Back about the pit a gathering of planters were wildly back-slapping and congratulating the Englishman and Massa Jewett. All of their backs were turned to the stricken, solitary figure of Massa Lea, who stood rooted, staring down with a glazed look at the bloodstains in the cockpit.

Turning finally, Sir C. Eric Russell walked over to where Massa Lea was, and Massa Lea slowly raised his eyes.

'What'd you say?' he mumbled.

'I said, sir, it just wasn't your lucky day.'

Massa Lea managed a trace of a smile.

Sir C. Eric Russell said, 'Concerning the wager. Of course, no one carries about such sums in his pocket. Why don't we settle up tomorrow? Say, sometime in the afternoon—' He paused. '*After* the tea hour, at Mr Jewett's home.'

Numbly, Massa Lea nodded. 'Yes, sir.'

The trip home took two hours. Neither the massa nor Chicken George spoke a word. It was the longest ride Chicken George had ever taken. But it had not been long enough, as the wagon pulled into the driveway . . .

When Massa Lea returned from Massa Jewett's during the next day's dusk, he found Chicken George mixing meal for the cockerels in the supply hut, where he had spent most of the hours since Matilda's screams, wails, and shouting during the previous night had finally driven him from their cabin.

'George,' the massa said, 'I got somethin' hard to tell you.' He paused, groping for words. 'Don't know how to say it hardly. But you already know I ain't had nowhere near the money folks thinks I did. Fact is, 'cept for a few thousand, 'bout all I own is the house, this land, and you few niggers.'

He's going to sell us, George sensed.

'Trouble is,' the massa went on, 'even all that ain't but roun' half what I owe that goddamned sonofabitch. But he's offered me a break—' The massa hesitated again. 'You heard him say what he's heard about you. And he said today he could see how good you train in both the birds fought—'

The massa took a deep breath. George held his. 'Well, seems like he needs to replace a trainer he lost over in England awhile back, and he thinks bringing back a nigger trainer would be fun.' The massa couldn't look into George's disbelieving eyes and became more abrupt. 'Not to drag out this mess, he'll call us square for all I've got in cash, a first and second mortgage on the house, and using you over in England long enough to train somebody else. He says no more'n a couple of years.'

The massa forced himself to look Chicken George in the face. 'Can't tell you how bad I feel about this, George ... I ain't got no choice. He's lettin' me off light. If I don't do it, I'm ruint, everything I ever worked for.'

George couldn't find words. What *could* he say? After all, he was the massa's slave.

'Now, I know you're wiped out, too, and I mean to make it up to you. So I pledge you my word right here and now while you're gone I'll take care of your woman and young'uns. And the day you get home—'

Massa Lea paused, sliding a hand into his pocket, withdrawing it, and holding a folded paper that he unfolded and thrust before Chicken George.

'Know what that is? Sat down an' wrote it out last night. You're looking right at your legal freedom paper, boy! I'm gonna keep it in my strongbox to hand you the day you come back!'

But after momentarily staring at the mysterious writing that covered most of the square, white sheet of paper, Chicken George continued struggling to control his fury. 'Massa,' he said quietly, 'I was gwine *buy* us all free! Now all I had gone, an' you sendin' *me* off crost de water somewheres 'way from my wife an' chilluns besides. How come you can't leas' free *dem* now, den me when I gits back?'

Massa Lea's eyes narrowed. 'I don't need you tellin' me what to do, boy! Ain't my fault you lost that money! I'm offerin' to do too much for you anyhow, that's the trouble with niggers! You better be careful of your mouth!' The massa's face was reddening. 'If it wasn't for you bein' all your life here, I'd just go ahead an' sell your ass!'

George looked at him, then shook his head. 'If all my life mean anythin' to you, Massa, how come you's jes' messin' it up mo'?'

The massa's face set into hardness. 'Pack whatever you intend to take with you! You leave for England Saturday.'

104

With Chicken George gone, his luck gone, and perhaps his nerve gone as well, the fortunes of Massa Lea continued to decline. At first, he ordered L'il George into full-time daily care of the chickens, but towards the end of only a third day, the massa found some of the cockerel pens' waterpans empty and the chubby, slow L'il George was sent fleeing with dire threats. The youngest boy, Lewis, nineteen, was next transferred from field work to take on the job. In preparation for the season's several remaining gamecocking matches, Massa Lea now was forced to take over most of the pre-fight training and conditioning chores himself, since Lewis as yet simply did not know how. He accompanied the massa to the various local contests, and each of those days, the rest of the family gathering in the evenings awaited the return of Lewis to tell them whatever had happened.

The massa's birds had lost more fights than they won, Lewis always said, and after a while that he had overheard men openly talking that Tom Lea was trying to borrow money to make bets. 'Ain't many seem like dey wants to talk wid massa. Dey jes' speaks or waves quick an' keeps goin' like he got de plague.'

'Yeah, de plague o' dem knowin' now he po',' said Matilda. 'Po' cracker's all he *ever* been!' Sister Sarah snapped.

It became slave row's common knowledge that Massa Lea had taken to drinking heavily, almost every day, between his shouting matches with Missis Lea.

'Dat ol' man ain't never been *dis* evil!' Miss Malizy told her grimly listening audience one night. 'He hit de house actin' jes' like a snake, hollerin' an' cussin' if'n missy even look at 'im. An' all day long when he gone, she in dere cryin' she don't even never want to *hear* no more 'bout no chickens!'

Matilda listened, emotionally drained from her own weeping and praying since her Chicken George had been gone. Briefly her glances reviewed their teenaged daughters and six strong grown sons, three of them now with mates and children. Then her eyes came back to rest upon her blacksmith son, Tom, as if she wished he would say something. But who spoke instead was Lilly Sue, Virgil's pregnant mate, who was briefly visiting from the nearby Curry plantation where she lived, and fear was thick in her tone. 'I don' know y'all's massa good as you do, but I jes' *feels* he gwine do somethin' terrible.

sho's we born.' A silence fell among them, no one being willing to express their own guess, at least not aloud.

After the next morning's breakfast, Miss Malizy waddled hurriedly from the kitchen down to the blacksmith shop. 'Massa say tell you saddle his hoss and git it roun' to de front porch, Tom,' she urged, her large eyes visibly moist. 'Lawd, please hurry up, 'cause de things he been saying to po' ol' missis jes' ain't hardly fittin'.' Without a word Tom soon tied the saddled horse to a gatepost, and he had just started back around the side of the big house when Massa Lea came lurching through the front door. Already red-faced from drinking, he struggled up onto the horse's back and galloped away, weaving in the saddle.

Through a half-opened window, Tom could overhear Missis Lea weeping as if her heart would break. Feeling embarrassment for her, he continued across the backyard to the blacksmith shed where he was just starting to beat a dulled plough point into sharpness when Miss Malizy came again.

'Tom,' she said, 'I 'clare seem like massa jes' win' up killin' hisself, he keep on like he goin', man nigh onto eighty years ol'.'

'You want to know the truth, Miss Malizy,' he replied, 'I b'lieve one way or 'nother dat's what he tryin' to do.'

Massa Lea returned during the mid-afternoon, accompanied by another white man on horseback, and from their respective kitchen and blacksmith shop observation posts, both Miss Malizy and Tom saw with surprise that the pair didn't dismount and enter the big house to freshen up and share a drink, as was always previously done with any guests. Instead, the horses were kept trotting on down the back road towards the gamecock area. Not half an hour later, Tom and Miss Malizy saw the visitor come back riding rapidly alone, holding under one arm a frightened, clucking gamehen, and Tom being outside was able to catch a fairly close glimpse of the man's furious expression as he rode by.

It was at that night's usual slave-row gathering when Lewis told what actually had happened. 'When I heared de hosses comin',' he said, 'I jes' made sho' massa seed me workin' fo' I made myself scarce, over behin' some bushes where I knowed I could see an' hear

'Well, after some pretty hot bargainin', dey come to a hunnud-dollar 'greement fo' dis gamehen settin' on a clutch o' eggs. An' I seen de man count out de money, den massa count it again fo' puttin' it in his pocket. Right after den a misunderstandin' commence 'bout de eggs under de hen went wid de deal. Well, massa commence to cussin' like he crazy! He run, grab up de hen an' wid his foot stomped an' squashed dat nest o' eggs into one mess! Dem two was nigh fightin' when all o' a sudden de odder man snatched de hen an' jumped on his hoss, yellin' he'd bus' massa's head if he wasn't so damn ol'!'

The uneasiness of the slave-row family deepened with each passing day, and nights were spent in fitful sleep resultant from worry of whatever might be the next frightful development. Across that 1855 summer and into the fall, with every angry outburst from the massa, with his every departure or arrival, the rest of the family's eyes involuntarily would turn to the twenty-two-year-old blacksmith Tom, as if appealing for his direction, but Tom offered none. By the crisp November, when there had been a fine harvest from the massa's roughly sixty-five acres in cotton and tobacco, which they knew he had been able to sell for a good price, one Saturday dusk Matilda watched from her cabin window until she saw Tom's last blacksmithing customer leave, and she hurried out there, her expression telling him from long experience that something special was on her mind.

'Yas'm, Mammy?' he asked, starting to bank the fire in his forge.

'I been thinkin', Tom. All six you boys done growed up to be mens now. You ain't my oldes', but I'se yo' mammy an' knows you's got de levellest head,' Matilda said. 'Plus dat, you's de blacksmith an' dey's fiel' han's. So look like you's got to be de main man o' dis fam'ly since yo' daddy gone 'bout eight months now—' Matilda hesitated, then added loyally, 'leas' ways, 'til he git back.'

Tom was frankly startled, for ever since his boyhood he had been his family's most reserved member. Although he and his brothers had all been born and reared on Massa Lea's plantation, he had never become very close with any of them, principally because he had been away for years as a blacksmithing apprentice, and since his return as a man, he was at the blacksmith shed, while the rest of his brothers were out in the fields. He had especially little contact anymore with Virgil, Ashford, and L'il George, for differing reasons. Virgil, now twenty-six, spent all his free time over on the adjoining plantation with his wife Lilly Sue and their recently born son, whom they had named Uriah, As for Ashford, twenty-five, he and Tom had always disliked and avoided each other, and Ashford had become more bitter at the world than ever since a girl he desperately wanted to marry had a massa who refused to let them jump the broom, calling Ashford an 'uppity nigger'. And the twenty-four-year-old L'il George, now just plain fat, was also deep in courtship with an adjoining plantation's cook, twice his age, which evoked wry family comments that he would woo anyone who would fill his stomach.

Matilda's telling Tom that she saw him as the family leader startled him the more since it implied his becoming their intermediary with Massa Lea, with whom he intentionally had very little actual contact. From when the equipment had been bought to establish a blacksmith shop, the massa somehow had always seemed to respect Tom's quiet reserve, along with his obvious competence at blacksmithing, which brought in an increasing flow of customers. They always paid the massa at the big house for whatever jobs Tom had done, and each Sunday the massa gave Tom two dollars for his week's work.

Along with Tom's ingrained reticence to talk very much with anyone was his equal tendency to ponder deeply on private thoughts. No one ever would have dreamed that for two years or more he had turned over and over again in his mind his father's descriptions of exciting potentials that 'up Nawth' offered to free black people, and Tom had weighed at great length proposing to the whole slave-row family that instead of waiting more endless years trying to buy their freedom, they should carefully plan and attempt a mass escape to the North. He had reluctantly abandoned the idea in realization that Gran'mammy Kizzy must be well into her sixties, and old Sister Sarah and Miss Malizy, who seemed the same as family, were in their seventies. He felt that those three would have been the quickest to leave, but he seriously doubted if any of them would survive the risks and rigours of such a desperate gamble.

More recently, Tom had privately deduced that the massa's recent cockfight loss must have been even greater than he had fully revealed. Tom had closely watched Massa Lea becoming more strained, haggard, and aged with each passing day and each emptied bottle of whisky. But Tom knew that the most disturbing evidence of something deeply amiss was that by now Lewis declared, the massa had sold off at least half of his chickens, whose bloodlines represented at least half a century of careful breeding.

Then Christmas came, and ushered in the New Year of 1856, as a heavy pall seemed to hang over not only the slave row, but also the entire plantation. Then an early spring afternoon, another rider came up the entry lane. At first Miss Malizy appraised him as another chicken buyer. But then, seeing how differently the massa greeted this one, she grew apprehensive. Smiling and chitchatting with the man as he dismounted, the massa yelled to the nearby L'il George to feed, water, and stable the horse for the night, then graciously Massa Lea squired his visitor inside.

Before Miss Malizy even began serving the big-house supper, outside in slave row the family members were exchanging fearful questions. 'Who dat man anyhow?' . . . 'Ain't never seen 'im befo'!' . . . 'Massa ain't acted like dat no time recent!' . . . 'Well, what you reckon him here fo'?' They could hardly await the later arrival and report of Miss Malizy.

'Dey ain't talked in my hearin' nothin' 'mount to nothin',' she said. 'Could be 'cause ol' missis was right dere.' Then Miss Malizy went on emphatically, 'But somehow or 'nother, I jes' don't nohow like dat odder man's looks! Seed too many like 'im befo', shifty-eyed an' tryin' to act like dey's sump'n dey *ain't*!'

A dozen pairs of slave-row eyes were monitoring the big-house windows from slave row when the obvious movements of a lamp told that Missis Lea had left the men in the living-room and made her way upstairs to bed. The living-room's lamp was still burning when the last of the slave-row family gave up the vigil and went to bed, dreading the daybreak wake-up bell.

Matilda took her blacksmith son aside at her first chance, before breakfast. 'Tom, las' night wasn't no chance to tell you private, and ain't wanted to scare ever'body to death, but Malizy tol' me she heared massa say he got to pay two mor'gage notes on dey house, an' Malizy know dey ain't hardly got a penny! I jes' feels to my feets dat white man's a nigger buyer!'

'Me too,' Tom said simply. He was silent for a moment. 'Mammy, I been thinkin', wid some different massa we jes' might fin' ourselves better off. Dat is, long's we all stays together. Dat' my big worry.'

As others began to come out of their cabins for the morning, Matilda hurried away rather than unduly alarm them by continuing the conversation.

After Missis Lea told Miss Malizy that she had a headache and wanted no breakfast, the massa and his visitor ate a hearty one, and then set out walking in the front yard, busily talking, their heads close together. Before very long, they sauntered alongside the big house, into the backyard, and finally over to where Tom was pumping his homemade bellows, sending yellowish sparks flying up from his forge in which two flat sheets of iron were approaching the heating necessary for their conversion into door hinges. For several minutes the two men stood closely watching Tom use long-handled tongs to remove the cherry-red iron sheets. Deftly folding their middles tightly about a shaping rod fixed into the hardy hole of his Fisher & Norris anvil, forming the channel for hinge pins, he then steel-punched three screw holes into each leaf. Taking up his short-shanked cold chisel and his favourite homemade four-pound

536

hammer, he cut the leaves into the H-shaped hinges that a customer had ordered, working all the while as if unaware of his observers' presence.

Massa Lea finally spoke. 'He's a pretty fair blacksmith, if I do say so myself,' he said casually.

The other man grunted affirmatively. Then he began moving around under the little blacksmithing shed, eyeing the many examples of Tom's craftsmanship that hung from nails and pegs. Abruptly, the man addressed Tom directly. 'How old are you, boy?'

'Gwine on twenty-three now, suh.'

'How many young'uns you got?'

'Ain't got no wife yet, suh.'

'Big, strong boy like you don't need no wife to have young'uns scattered everywhere.'

Tom said nothing, thinking how many white men's young'uns were scattered in slave rows.

'You maybe one of these real religious niggers?'

Tom knew the man was trying to draw him out for a reason – almost certainly to size him up for purchase. He said pointedly, 'I 'magines Massa Lea done tol' you we's mostly a family here, my mammy, gran'mammy, an' brothers an' sisters an' young'uns. We's all been raised to believe in de Lawd an' de Bible, suh.'

The man's eyes narrowed. 'Which one of y'all reads the Bible to the rest?'

Tom wasn't about to tell this ominous stranger that both his gran'mammy and mammy could read. He said, 'Reckon we all jes' growed up hearin' de Scriptures so much we knows 'em by heart, suh.'

Seeming to relax, the man returned to his original subject. 'You think you could handle the blacksmithing on a much bigger place than this one?'

Tom felt ready to explode with the further confirmation that his sale was planned, but he had to know if the family also was to be included. Through his rage to be dangled in suspense like this, again he probed, 'Well, suh, me an' de res' us here can raise crops an' do pret' near ever'thing a place need, I guess—'

Leaving the seething Tom as calmly as they had come, the massa and his guest had no more than headed out towards the fields when old Miss Malizy came hurrying from the kitchen. 'What dem mens sayin', Tom? Missis can't even look me in de eye.'

Trying to control his voice, Tom said, 'It's gwine be some sellin', Miss Malizy, maybe all us, but could be jes' me.' Miss Malizy burst into tears, and Tom roughly shook her shoulders. 'Miss Malizy, ain't no need o' cryin'! Jes' like I tol' mammy, I 'speck some new place see us better off dan here wid 'im.' But try as Tom would, he couldn't ease the aged Miss Malizy's grief.

Late that day the rest of them returned from the fields, Tom's brothers wearing grim, stricken faces amid the women's copious weeping and wailing. All of them were trying at once to tell how the massa and his visitor also had come out watching them as they worked, with the stranger then moving from one to another asking questions that left no doubt that they were being appraised for sale.

Until into the wee hours, there was no way that the three people within the big house could have missed hearing the rising pandemonium of grief and terror that arose among the seventeen people in the slave row, most of the men eventually reacting as hysterically as the women as they all became seized in the contagion of grabbing and hugging whomever was nearest, screaming that they would soon never see each other again. 'Lawd, deliver us from dis *eeeeevil*!' shrieked Matilda in prayer.

Tom rang the next morning's wake-up bell with a prescience of doom.

Aged Miss Malizy had passed by him, making her way to the big-house kitchen to prepare breakfast. Not ten minutes later she heavily returned to slave row, her black face taut with fresh shock and glistening with fresh tears: 'Massa say don't nobody go nowhere. He say when he finish breakfas', he want *ever'body* 'sembled out here . . .'

Even sick, ancient Uncle Pompey was brought from his cabin in his chair as all of them assembled, terrified.

When Massa Lea and his visitor came around the side of the big house, Massa Lea's lurching walk told seventeen pairs of eyes that he had been drinking even more heavily than usual, and when the pair of them stopped about four yards before the slave-row people, the massa's voice was loud, angry, and slurred.

'Y'all niggers keep your noses always stuck in my business, so ain't no news to you this place goin' broke. Y'all too much burden for me to carry no more, so I'm doin' some sellin' to this gentleman here—'

At the chorus of shrieks and groans, the other man gestured roughly. '*Shut up!* All this carryin' on since last night!' He glared up and down the line until they quieted down. 'I ain't no ordinary nigger trader. I represent one of the biggest, finest firms in the business. We got branch offices, and boats delivering niggers to order between Richmond, Charleston, Memphis, and New Orleans—'

538

Matilda cried out the first anguish in all their minds. 'We gwine git sol' together, Massa?'

'I told you *shut up*! You'll find out! I ought not to have to say your massa here's a true gentleman, same as that fine lady up in that house cryin' her heart out about your black hides. They could get more to sell y'all apiece, *plenty* more!' He glanced at the quaking L'il Kizzy and Mary. 'You two wenches ready right now to start breedin' pickaninnies worth four hundred an' up apiece.' His glance fell on Matilda. 'Even if you gittin' pretty old, you said you know how to cook. Down South a good cook'll bring twelve to fifteen hundred nowadays.' He looked at Tom. 'The way prices up now, reckon a prime stud blacksmith can easy fetch twenty-five hundred, much as three thousand from somebody wants you to take in customers like you doin' here.' His eyes scanned across Tom's five brothers between twenty and twenty-eight years of age. 'And y'all field-hand bucks ought to be worth nine hundred to a thousan' apiece—' The slave trader paused for effect. 'But y'all one lucky bunch of niggers! Your missis *insists* y'all got to be sold together, and your massa's goin' along with that!'

'*Thank* you, Missis! *Thank* you, Jesus!' Gran'mammy Kizzy cried out. 'Praise *God*!' shrieked Matilda.

'SHUT UP!' The slave trader angrily gestured. 'I've done my best to convince 'em different, but I ain't been able. And it just happen my firm's got some customers with a tobacco plantation ain't too far from here! Right near the North Carolina Railroad Company over in Alamance County. They're wantin' a family of niggers that's been together an' won't give no trouble, no runaways or nothin' like that, an' with experience to handle everything on their place. Won't need no auctionin' you off. I'm told won't need no chainin' you up, nothin' like that, less'n I have some trouble!' He surveyed them coldly. 'All right, startin' right now, y'all I've spoke to consider yourselves *my* niggers 'til I get you where you're goin'. I'm givin' you four days to put your stuff together. Saturday morning we'll get you moving over to Alamance County in some wagons.'

Virgil was the first to find a stricken voice: 'What 'bout my Lilly Sue an' chile over at the Curry place? You gwine buy dem too, ain't you, suh?'

Tom burst out, 'An' what 'bout our gran'mammy, Sister Sarah, Miss Malizy, an' Uncle Pompey? Dey's fam'ly you ain't mentioned—'

'Ain't meant to! Can't be buyin' every wench some buck's laid with, so he won't feel *lonely*!' the slave trader exclaimed sarcastically. 'As for these old wrecks here, they can't hardly walk, let alone work, no customers gonna buy *them*! But Mr Lea's being good enough to let 'em keep dragging on around here.'

Amid an outburst of exclamations and weeping, Gran'mammy Kizzy sprang squarely before Massa Lea, words ripping from her throat, 'You done sent off yo' own boy, can't I *leas*' have gran'chilluns?' As Massa Lea quickly looked away, she slumped towards the ground, young, strong arms grabbing and supporting her, while old Miss Malizy and Sister Sarah screamed almost as one, 'Dey's all de fam'ly I got, Massa!' ... 'Me, too, Massa! We's fifty-some years togedder!' The invalid ancient Uncle Pompey just sat, unable to rise from his chair, tears streaming down his cheeks, staring blankly straight ahead, his lips moving as in prayer.

'SHUT UP!' the slave trader yelled. 'I'm tellin' you the last time! You find out quick I know how to handle niggers!'

Tom's eyes sought and locked for a fleeting instant with those of Massa Lea, and Tom hoarsely fully chose words, 'Massa, we's sho' sorry you's met bad luck, an' we knows only reason you's sellin' us is you got to—'

Massa Lea seemed almost grateful before his eyes again bent downwards, and they had to strain to hear him. 'Naw, I ain't got nothin' 'gainst none of y'all, boy—' He hesitated. 'Fact, I'd even call y'all good niggers, most of y'all born and bred up right on my place.'

'Massa,' gently Tom begged, 'if dem Alamance County peoples won't take our family's ol' folks, ain't it some way you lemme buy 'em from you? Dis man done jes' say dey ain't worth much in money, an' I pay you good price. I git on my knees an' beg de new massa lemme fin' some hire-out blacksmithin', maybe for dat railroad, an' my brothers hire out and he'p too, suh.' Tom was abjectly pleading, tears now starting down his cheeks, 'Massa, *all* we makes we sends you 'til we pays whatever you ax fo' Gran'mammy and dese three mo' dat's fam'ly to us. All we's been through togedder, we sho' 'preciate stayin' togedder, Massa—'

Massa Lea had stiffened. But he said, 'Awright! Get me three hundred dollars apiece, you can have 'em—' His palm shot up before their exultation could fully erupt. '*Hol' on!* They stay here 'til the money's in my hand!'

Amid the groans and sobs, Tom's voice came, bleak, 'Us kinda 'spected mo'n dat from you, Massa, 'siderin' everything.'

'Get 'em out of here, trader!' the massa snapped. Turning on his heel, he walked rapidly towards the big house.

Back in the desperately despairing slave row, even old Miss

540

Malizy and Sister Sarah were among those comforting Gran'mammy Kizzy. She sat in her rocking chair, that Tom had made for her, amid the welter of her family hugging, kissing her, wetting her with their tears. Everyone was crying.

From somewhere she found the strength, the courage to rasp hoarsely, 'Don' y'all take on so! Me an' Sarah, Malizy, an' Pompey jes' wait here for George 'til he gits back. Ain't gwine be dat long, it's aweady gwine on de two years. If'n he ain't got de money to buy us, den I 'speck won't take much mo' time fo' Tom an' res' y'all boys will—'

Ashford gulped, 'Yes'm, we *sho'* will!' Wanly she smiled at him, at them all. ' 'Nother thing,' Gran'mammy Kizzy went on, 'any y'all gits mo' chilluns fo' I sees you ag'in, don't forgit to tell 'em 'bout my folks, my mammy Bell, an' my African pappy name Kunta Kinte, what be yo' chillun's great-great gran'pappy! *Hear* me, now! Tell 'em 'bout me, 'bout my George, 'bout yo'selves, too! An' 'bout what we been through 'midst differen' massas. Tell de chilluns all de res' about who we is!'

Amid a snuffling chorus of 'We sho' will' ... 'Ain't gon' *never* fo'git, Gran'mammy,' she brushed the nearest faces with her hand, 'SHUSH, now! Ever'thing gwine be fine! *Heish up,* done tol' you! Y'all gwine flood me right out de do'!'

Four days somehow passed with those who were leaving getting packed, and finally Saturday morning came. Everyone had been up through most of the night. With scarcely a word uttered, they gathered, holding each other's hands, watching the sun come up. Finally the wagons arrived. One by one those who were leaving turned silently to embrace those who were to remain behind.

'Where's Uncle Pompey?' asked someone.

Miss Malizy said, 'Po' ol' soul tol' me las' night he couldn't stan' to see y'all go—'

'I run kiss 'im, anyhow!' exclaimed L'il Kizzy, and went running towards the cabin.

In a little while, they heard her: 'Oh, NO!'

Others already on the ground, or leaping from the wagon, went dashing. The old man sat there in his chair. And he was dead.

105

On the new plantation, it wasn't until the next Sunday, when Massa and Missis Murray drove off in their buggy to attend church services, that the whole family had a chance to sit down together for a talk.

'Well, I sho' ain't want to judge too quick,' said Matilda, looking around at all of her brood, 'but all through de week me an' Missis Murray done plenty talkin' in de kitchen whilst I been cookin'. I got to say she an' dis new massa soun's like good Christian peoples. I feels like we's gwine be whole lot better off here, 'cept yo' pappy still ain't back, an' Gran'mammy an' dem still at Massa Lea's.' Again studying her children's faces, she asked, 'Well, from what y'all's seed an' heared, how y'all feel?'

Virgil spoke. 'Well, dis Massa Murray don't seem like he know much 'bout farmin', or bein' no massa, neither.'

Matilda interrupted. 'Dat's 'cause dey was town folks runnin' a sto' in Burlington, 'til his uncle died an' in 'is will lef' 'em dis place.'

Virgil said, 'Ever' time he done talked to me, he's said he lookin' fo' a white oberseer to work us. I done kept tellin' 'im ain't no need to spend dat money, dat worse'n a oberseer he needed leas' five, six mo' fiel' han's. Tol' 'im jes' give us chance, we raise 'im good tobacco crops by ourself—'

Ashford broke in, 'I ain't stayin' long nowhere wid no cracker oberseer trackin' every move!'

After a pointed look at Ashford, Virgil went on. 'Massa Murray say he watch awhile an' see how we do.' He paused. 'I jes' 'bout begged 'im to buy my Lilly Sue an' young'un from Massa Curry back yonder an' bring 'em here. Tol' 'im Lilly Sue work hard as anybody he ever gon' git. He say he think 'bout it, but to buy us, dey already done had to take out a bank mor'gage on de big house, an' he see how much 'baccy he sell dis year.' Virgil paused. 'So we all got to pitch in! I can tell odder white folks been givin' 'im plenty advisin' niggers won't half work by deyselves. Let 'im see any hangin' back an' playin' roun', we sho' liable win' up wid some oberseer.' Glancing again at the sullen Ashford, Virgil added, 'Fac', I 'speck it be good when Massa Murray ride out where we's workin' I'll holler at y'all some, but y'all know why.'

'Sho'!' burst out Ashford, 'you an' somebody else I knows always tries to be massa's special nigger!'

Tom tensed, but managed to seem as if he totally ignored

Ashford's remark while Virgil half rose, lancing forward a work-cal-loused forefinger, 'Boy, lemme tell you, sump'n wrong anybody don' git 'long wid *nobody*! Gwine git you in big trouble one dese days! Jes' speakin' fo' myself, if'n it be's wid me, somebody gwine carry off one us!'

'*Heish!* Bofe y'all *heish* up dat mess!' Matilda glared at them both, then particularly at Ashford, before turning an entreating look onto Tom, clearly seeking an easing of the sudden tension. 'Tom, whole lot o' times I seen you an' Massa Murray talkin' down dere while you puttin' up yo' shop. What's yo' feelin's?'

Slowly, thoughtfully, Tom said, 'I 'gree we ought to be better off here. But 'pend a lot on how we handles it. Like you said, Massa Murray don' 'pear no mean, lowdown white man. I feel like Virgil say, he jes' ain't had much 'sperience to put no trus' in us. Even mo'n dat, I b'leeve he worried we git to figgerin' he's *easy*, dat's how come he make hisself act an' soun' harder'n he na'chly is, an' dat's how come de oberseer talk.' Tom paused. 'Way I sees it, mammy handle de missis. Res' us needs to teach de massa he do fine jes' leave us 'lone.'

After murmurs of approval, Matilda's tone was vibrant with her joy at clearly a potentially promising family future, 'Well, now, linin' it up, 'long wid what y'all says, we's got to 'suade Massa Murray to buy Lilly Sue an' dat l'il Uriah, too. 'Bout y'all's pappy, ain't nothin' we can do but jes' wait. He walk in here one dese days—'

Giggling, Mary interrupted, 'Wid dat green scarf trailin', an' black derby settin' upon his head!'

'Sho' right 'bout dat, daughter,' Matilda smiled with the others. She went on. 'An' 'cose I ain't even got to say 'bout gittin' Gran'mammy, Sarah, an' Malizy. I already got Missis Murray prom-ised to he'p wid dat. 'Scribed to 'er stronges' I could how it jes' 'bout tore us all up to have to leave 'em. Lawd! Missis got to cryin' hard as I was! She say weren't no use nobody includin' her axin' Massa Murray to buy no three real ol' womens, but she promise faithful she ax massa to git Tom hire-out jobs, an' de res' y'all boys, too. So le's all keep in mind we ain't jes' here workin' for 'nother massa, we's workin' to git our fam'ly back togedder.'

With that resolve, the family settled into the planting season of 1856, with Matilda commanding the increasing trust and appreci-ation of both Missis and Massa Murray through her clear loyalty and sincerity, her excellent cooking, and her spotless housekeeping. The massa saw how Virgil steadily urged and pressed his brothers and sisters towards a bumper tobacco crop. He saw Tom visibly putting the plantation into an enviable state of repair, his talented hands wielding his mostly homemade tools, transforming foraged old rusted, discarded, scrap iron into eventually scores of sturdy new farming tools and implements, along with both functional and decorative household items.

Nearly every Sunday afternoon, unless the Murrays had gone off somewhere themselves, various of the local plantation families would pay them welcoming visits, along with their old friends from Burlington, Graham, Haw River, Mebane, and other towns around. In showing their guests about the big house and yards, the Murrays always proudly pointed out different examples of Tom's craftsmanship. Few of their farm or township guests left without urging that the massa permit Tom to make or repair something for them, and Massa Murray would agree. Gradually more of Tom's custommade articles appeared about Alamance County, as word of mouth further advertised him, and Missis Murray's original request that the massa seek hire-out jobs for Tom became entirely unnecessary. Soon, every day saw slave men, young and old, come riding on mules, or sometimes afoot, bringing broken tools or other items for Tom to fix. Some massas or missis sketched decorative items they wanted made for their homes. Or sometimes customers' requests required that Massa Murray write out a travelling pass for Tom to ride a mule to other plantations, or into local towns, to make on-site repairs or installations. By 1857, Tom was working from dawn to dark every day excepting Sundays, his overall volume of work at least equalling that of Mr Isaiah, who had taught him. The customers would pay Massa Murray, either at the big house or when they saw him at church, such rates as fourteen cents a hoof for the shoeing of horses, mules, or oxen, thirty-seven cents for a new wagon tyre, eighteen cents to mend a pitchfork, or six cents to sharpen a pick. Prices for customer-designed decorative work were specially negotiated, such as five dollars for a trellis-shaped front gate adorned with oak leaves. And each weekend Massa Murray figured out for Tom's pay ten cents of each dollar that his work had brought in during the previous week. After thanking the massa, Tom gave the weekly sum to his mother Matilda, who soon had it buried in one of her glass jars whose locations only she and Tom knew.

On Saturday noons the work-week ended for the family's field hands. L'il Kizzy and Mary, now nineteen and seventeen, respectively, quickly bathed, wrapped their short, kinky braids tightly with string, and rubbed their faces to shiny blackness with beeswax. Then donning their best starchily ironed cotton-print dresses, they soon appeared at the blacksmith shop, one bringing a pitcher of water, or sometimes 'lemonegg', with the other carrying a gourd dipper. Once Tom had quenched his thirst, they next offered welcomed gourdfuls among each Saturday afternoon's invariable small gathering of slave men whose massas had sent them to pick up items that Tom had promised to complete by the weekend. Tom noted, with wry amusement, how his sisters' lightest, gayest banter was always with the better-looking younger men. One Saturday night he was not surprised to overhear Matilda shrilly voicing chastisement: 'I ain't blin'! Sees y'all down dere flouncin' yo' tails 'mongst dem mens!' L'il Kizzy came back defiantly, 'Well, Mammy, we's wimmins! Ain't met *no* mens at Massa Lea's!' Matilda loudly muttered something that Tom couldn't distinguish, but he suspected that she was privately less disapproving than she was trying to act. It was confirmed when, shortly after, Matilda said to him, 'Look like you lettin' dem two gals go to courtin' right under yo' nose. Reckon de leas' you can do is keep out a eye it ain't de wrong ones dey hooks up wid!'

To the entire family's astonishment, not the particularly 'flouncy' L'il Kizzy but the much quieter Mary soon quietly announced her wish to 'jump de broom' with a stablehand from a plantation near the village of Mebane. She pleaded to Matilda, 'I knows you can he'p 'suade massa to sell me reasonable when Nicodemus' massa ax 'im 'bout it, Mammy, so us can live togedder!' But Matilda only muttered vaguely, sending Mary into tears.

'Lawd, Tom, I jes' don't know how to feel!' Matilda said. ' 'Cose I'se happy fo' de gal, I see she so happy. But jes' hates to see any us sol' off no mo'.'

'You's wrong, Mammy. You knows you is!' Tom said. 'I sho' wouldn't want to be married wid nobody livin' somewhere else. Look what happened to Virgil. Ever since we got sol', you can see he *sick* 'bout Lilly Sue lef' back yonder.'

'Son,' she said, 'don't tell *me* 'bout bein' married to somebody you don' never hardly see! Whole lot o' times, lookin' at y'all chilluns he'p me know I got a husban'—' Matilda hesitated. 'But gittin' back to Mary leavin', ain't jes' her on my min', it's all y'all. You workin' so much guess you ain't paid no 'tention, but on Sundays off nowdays don' hardly never see yo' brudders roun' here no mo', jes' you an' Virgil. De res' all off co'tin' heavy—'

'Mammy,' Tom sharply interrupted, 'we's grown mens!'

'Sho' you is!' retorted Matilda. 'Ain't what I'm gittin' at! I'se meanin' it look like dis fam'ly gwine split to de winds fo' we ever gits it back togedder!'

In a silent moment between them, Tom was trying to think of what comforting thing he might say, sensing that underlying his mother's recent quick irritability or unaccustomed depressions were the months now passed beyond when his father should have returned. As she had just mentioned, she was again living with his absence.

Tom was shocked when abruptly Matilda glanced at him, 'When you gwine git married?'

'Ain't thinkin' 'bout dat now—' Embarrassed, he hesitated, and changed the subject. 'Thinkin' 'bout us gittin' back Gran'mammy, Sister Sarah, an' Miss Malizy. Mammy, 'bout how much we got saved up now?'

'No 'bout! Tell you 'zactly! Dat two dollars an' fo' cents you give me las' Sunday make it eighty-seben dollars an' fi'ty-two cents.'

Tom shook his head. 'I'se got to do better—'

'Sho' wish Virgil an' dem was he'pin' mo'.'

'Can't blame dem. Hire-out fiel' work jes' hard to fin', 'cause mos' massas needin' it hires free niggers what works fit to kill deyselves to git dat twenty-five cents a day less'n dey starves. I jes' got to make mo'! Gran'mammy, Sister Sarah, an' Miss Malizy, dey's all gittin' ol'!'

'Yo' gran'mammy right roun' sebenty now, an' Sarah an' Malizy nigh 'bout eighty.'

A sudden thought struck Matilda; her features took on a faraway expression. 'Tom, you know what jes' come to me? Yo' gran'mammy use to say her African pappy kep' up wid how ol' he was by droppin' l'il rocks in a gourd. You 'member her sayin' dat?'

'Yas'm, sho' does.' He paused. 'Wonder how ol' was he?'

'Ain't never heard, leas' not to my recollection.' A puzzlement grew on her face. 'Would 'pend when was you talkin' 'bout. He'd o' been one age when Gran'mammy Kizzy was sol' from him an' her mammy. Den he'd o' been 'nother age whenever de Lawd claimed 'im—' She hesitated. 'Wid Gran'mammy pushin' seb'nty, you know her pappy got to be long dead'n gone. Her mammy, too. Po' souls!'

'Yeah—' said Tom, musing. 'Sometime I wonders what dey looked like. Done heared so much 'bout 'em.'

Matilda said, 'Me, too, son.' She straightened in her chair. 'But gittin' back to yo' gran'mammy, Sarah, an' Malizy, every night down on my knees, I jes' ax de Lawd to be wid 'em an' I prays any day yo' pappy git dere wid lump o' money in 'is pocket an' buy 'em.' She laughed brightly. 'One mawnin' we looks up an' dere all fo' be, free as birds!'

'Dat be sho' one sight to see!' grinned Tom.

A silence fell between them, each in their private thoughts. Tom was pondering that now was as good a time and atmosphere as any to confide in his mother something he had kept carefully guarded from anyone, but which now did seem likely to develop further.

He used as his avenue an earlier query of Matilda's. 'Mammy, while back you ax if'n I ever think maybe 'bout gittin' married?'

Matilda jerked upright, her face and eyes alight. 'Yeah, son?'

Tom could have kicked himself for ever having brought it up. He all but squirmed seeking how to go on. Then, firmly, 'Well, I'se kinda met a gal, an' we been talkin' some—'

'Lawd-a-mussy, Tom! *Who?*'

'Ain't nobody you knows! Her name Irene. Some calls 'er "Reeny". She b'longst to dat Massa Edwin Holt, work in dey big house—'

'De rich Massa Holt massa and missis talks 'bout own dat cotton mill on Alamance Creek?'

'Yas'm—'

'Dey big house where you put up dem pretty window grilles?'

'Yas'm—' Tom's expression was rather like that of a small boy caught taking cookies.

'*Lawd!*' A beaming spread across Matilda's face. 'Somebody cotched ol' coon at las'!' Springing up, suddenly embracing her embarrassed son, she burbled, 'I'se *so* happy fo' y'all, Tom, *sho'* is!'

'*Hol'* on! Hol' *on*, Mammy!' Extricating himself, he gestured her back towards her chair. 'I jes' say we been talkin'.'

'Boy, you's my close-mouthdes' young'un since you first drawed breath! If you 'mits you's much as *seed* a gal, I know it mo' to it dan dat!'

He all but glared at her. 'Don' want no whisperin' to *nobody*, you hear me?'

'I *know* massa buy 'er fo' *you*, boy! Tell me mo' 'bout 'er, Tom!' So much was tumbling in Matilda's head that it poured out together ... across the back of her mind flashed a vision of the wedding cakes she would bake ...

'Gittin' late, got to go—' But she beat him to the door. 'So glad somebody be catchin' all y'all young'uns fo' long! You's jes' my bes'!' Matilda's laughter was the happiest Tom had seen her in a long time. 'Gittin' older, guess I'se same as Gran'mammy Kizzy, wantin' mo' gran-chilluns!' Tom brushed past, hearing her as he strode outside, 'I live long 'nough, might even see some great-gran'chilluns!'

106

A Sunday several months before, Massa and Missis Murray had returned home from church, and the massa almost immediately rang the bell for Matilda, whom he told to have Tom come around to the front porch.

The massa's pleasure was showing both in his face and in his tone as he told Tom that Mr Edwin Holt, who owned the Holt Cotton Mill, had sent him a message that Missis Holt had recently been highly impressed with seeing some of Tom's delicate ironwork; that she had already sketched a design for decorative window grilles that they hoped that Tom could soon make and install at their 'Locust Grove' home.

With a travelling pass from Massa Murray, Tom left on a mule early the next morning to see the sketches and measure the windows. Massa Murray had told him not to worry about whatever jobs awaited doing in his shop, and the massa said that the best route was to follow the Haw River Road to the town of Graham, then the Graham Road to Bellemont Church, where after a right turn and about another two miles, the elegant Holt mansion would be impossible to miss.

Arriving and identifying himself to a black gardener, Tom was told to wait near the front steps. Missis Holt herself soon came pleasantly congratulating Tom's previous work that she had seen, and showing him her sketches, which he carefully studied for an iron window grille having the visual effect of a trellis amply covered with vines and leaves. 'B'leeves I can do dem, leas' I try my bes', Missis,' he said, but he pointed out that with so many windows needing the grilles, each of which would require much patiently tedious work, the completing of the task might take two months. Missis Holt said she would be delighted if it could be done in that time, and handing Tom her sketches to keep and work by, she left him to go about his necessary starting job of carefully measuring the many windows' dimensions.

By the early afternoon, Tom was working on the upstairs windows opening onto a veranda when his instincts registered someone watching him, and glancing about, he blinked at the striking prettiness of the coppery-complexioned girl holding a dust rag who stood quietly just within the next opened window. Wearing a simple housemaid's uniform, her straight black hair coiled into a large bun at the back of her head, she was evenly but warmly returning Tom's stare. Only his lifelong innate reserve enabled him to mask his jolting inner reaction as, collecting himself, and quickly removing his hat, he blurted, 'Hidy, miss.'

'Hidy do, suh!' she replied, flashing a bright smile, and with that she disappeared.

Finally riding back to the Murray plantation, Tom was surprised, and unsettled, that he couldn't rid his mind of her. Lying in his bed that night, it hit him like a bolt that he hadn't even got her name. He guessed her age at nineteen or maybe twenty. At last he slept, fitfully, and awakened torturing himself that her prettiness guaranteed that she was married, or surely was courting with somebody.

Making the basic grille frames, smoothly lap-welding four precut flat iron bars into window-sized rectangles was only a routine job. After six days of doing that, Tom began forcing white-hot rods through his set of successively smaller steel reducing dies until he had long rods no thicker than ivy or honeysuckle vines. After Tom had experimentally heated and variously bent several of these, dissatisfied, he began taking early-morning walks, closely inspecting actual growing vines' graceful curvings and junctures. Then he had a sense that his efforts to simulate them improved.

The work went along well, with Massa Murray explaining daily to sometimes irate customers that Tom could attend only the most urgent emergency repair jobs until he had finished a major job for Mr Edwin Holt, which blunted the indignance of most. Massa Murray, then Missis Murray came to the shop to observe, then they brought visiting friends, until sometimes eight or ten of them stood silently watching Tom work. Plying his craft, he thought how blessed he was that all people seemed even to expect being ignored by blacksmiths engrossed in what they were doing. He reflected upon how most slave men who brought him their massas' repairing jobs usually seemed either morose, or they big-talked among other slaves about the shop. But if any white people appeared, in the instant, all of the slaves grinned, shuffled, and otherwise began acting the clown, as in fact Tom often previously had felt embarrassed to conclude privately of his own derby-wearing, bombastic-talking father, Chicken George.

Tom felt further blessed with how sincerely he enjoyed feeling immersed, to a degree even isolated, within his world of blacksmithing. As he worked on the window grilles from the daylights until he could no longer see, his private random musings would occupy his mind sometimes for hours before he again caught himself thinking of the pretty housemaid he had met.

Making the leaves for the window grilles would be his toughest test, he had realized from when Missis Holt first showed him her sketches. Again Tom walked, now intently studying nature's leaves. Heating and reheating inch-square iron pieces, beating them with his heavy, square-faced hammer into delicately thin sheets, with his trimming shears he cut out eventually scores of oversized heart-shaped patterns. Since such thin metal could quickly burn and ruin if a forge was too hot, he pumped his homemade bellows with utmost care, hastily tonging each red-hot thin sheet onto his anvil and deftly shaping it into leafy contours with quick tappings of his lightest ball-point hammer.

With intricate welding, Tom delicately veined his leaves, and next stemmed them onto the vines. He felt it good that no two looked exactly the same, as he had observed in nature. Finally in his seventh intensive week, Tom spot-welded his leafy vines onto their waiting window-grille frames.

'Tom, I 'clare look like dey jes' growin' somewheres!' Matilda exclaimed it, staring in awe at her son's craftsmanship. Scarcely less demonstrative was L'il Kizzy, who by now was flirting openly with three local young slave swains. Even Tom's brothers and their wives – only Ashford and Tom were single now – cast glances that mirrored their further heightened respect for him. Massa and Missis Murray could hardly contain the extent of their pleasure, as well as their pride, that they owned such a blacksmith.

In the wagon laden with window grilles, Tom drove alone to the Holt big house to install them. When he held up one for Missis Holt to inspect, exclaiming and clapping her hands, ecstatic with pleasure, she called outside her teenaged daughter and several grown young sons who happened to be there, and all of them joined instantly in congratulating Tom.

Right away, he began the installations. After two hours, the downstairs window grilles were in place, being further admired by the Holt family members, as well as several of their slaves; he guessed that their grapevine must have sped word of their missis' delight and they had come running to see for themselves. Where *was* she? Tom was tense from wondering it as one of the Holt sons directed him through the polished downstairs foyer to mount the curving stairs to install the remaining grilles at the second-floor veranda windows.

It was the very area where she had been before. How, whom, might he query, without seeming more than curiously interested, as

550

to who she was, where she was, and what was her status? In his frustration, Tom went at his work even faster; he must finish quickly and leave, he told himself.

He was installing the third upstairs window grille when after a rush of footsteps there she was, flushed, nearly breathless from hurrying. He stood just tongue-tied.

'Hidy, Mr Murray!' It jolted him to realize she wouldn't know of Lea, only that a Massa Murray owned him now. He fumbled off his straw hat.

'Hidy, Miss Holt...'

'Was down in de smokehouse smokin' meat, jes' heared you was here—' Her gaze swept to the last window grille he had fixed into place. 'Ooh, it jes' beautiful!' she breathed. 'Passed Missis Emily downstairs jes' havin' a fit 'bout what you done.'

His glance flicked her field-hand head-rag. 'I thought you was a housemaid—' It sounded such an inane thing to say.

'I loves doin' different things, an' dey lets me,' she said, glancing about. 'I jes' run up here a minute. Better git back to workin', an' you, too—'

He had to know more, at least her name. He asked her.

'Irene,' she said. 'Dey calls me 'Reeny. What your'n?'

'Tom,' he said. As she had said, they had to get back to work. He had to gamble. 'Miss Irene, is – is you keepin' company wid anybody?'

She looked at him so long, so hard, he knew he had terribly blundered. 'I ain't never been knowed for not speakin' my mind, Mr Murray. When I seed befo' how shy you was, I was scairt you wouldn't come talk wid me no mo'.'

Tom could have fallen off the veranda.

From then, he had begun asking Massa Murray for an all-day travelling pass each Sunday, along with permission to use the mule-cart. He told his family as well that he searched the roadsides for discarded metal objects to freshly supply his blacksmith shop scrap pile. He nearly always did find something useful while driving different routes in the round trip of about two hours each way to see Irene.

Not only she, but the others whom he met at the Holts' slave row could not have received or treated him more warmly. 'You's so shy, smart as you is, folks jes' likes you,' Irene candidly told him. They would ride usually to some reasonably private fairly nearby place where Tom would unhitch the mule to let it graze on a long tether as they walked, with Irene doing by far the most talking.

'My pappy a Injun. He name Hillian, my mammy say. Dat 'count fo' de 'culiar colour I is,' Irene volunteered matter-of-factly. 'Way back, my mammy run off from a real mean massa, an' in de woods some Injuns cotched her an' took her to dey village where her an' my pappy got togedder an' I got borned. I weren't much size when some white mens 'tacked de village, an' 'mongst de killin' captured my mammy an' brung us back to her massa. She say he beat her bad an' sol' us to some nigger trader, an' Massa Holt bought us, what was lucky, 'cause dey's high-quality folks—' Her eyes narrowed. 'Well, leas' mos'ly. Anyhow, Mammy was dey washin' an' ironin' woman, right up 'til she took sick an' died 'bout fo' years back, an' I been here ever since. I'se eighteen now, gwine turn nineteen New Year's Day—' She looked at Tom in her frank way. 'How ol' is you?'

'Twenty-fo',' Tom said.

Telling Irene in turn the essential facts about his family, Tom said that as yet they had but little knowledge of this new region of North Carolina into which they had been sold.

'Well,' she said, 'I'se picked up a heap 'cause de Holts is mighty 'portant folks, so nigh ever'body big comes visitin', an' gin'ly I be's servin', an' I got ears.'

'Dey says mos' dese Alamance County white folks' great-great-gran'daddies come here from Pennsylvania long fo' dat Revolution War, when wasn't much nobody herebouts 'cept Sissipaw Injuns. Some calls 'em Saxapaws. But English white so'jers kilt dem out 'ti Saxapaw River de only thing even got dey name now—' Irene grimaced. 'My massa say dey'd run from hard times crost de water an was crowdin' Pennsylvania so bad dem Englishmans runnin' de Colonies 'nounced all de lan' dey wanted be sellin' in dis part Nawth Ca'liny fo' less'n two cents a acre. Well, massa say no end o Quakers, Presbyterian Scotch-Irishers, an' German Lutheran squeezed ever'thin' dey could in covered wagons an' crost dem Cumberlan' an' Shenando' valleys. Massa say sump'n like fo' hundred miles. Dey bought what lan' dey could an' commence diggin' clearin', an' farmin', jes' mos'ly small farms dey worked deyselves like mos' dis county's white folks herebouts still does. Dat's how come ain't many niggers as where it's great big plantations.'

Irene toured Tom on the following Sunday to her massa's cotton mill on a bank of Alamance Creek, prideful as if both the mill and the Holt family were her own.

After his hard work attending weekly scores of blacksmithin jobs, Tom coveted each next Sunday when the cart rolled past th miles of split-rail fences enclosing crops of corn, wheat, tobacco, an cotton, with an occasional apple or peach orchard and modest farm-houses. Passing other blacks, who were nearly always afoot, they exchanged waves, Tom hoping they understood that if he offered a ride, it would rob his privacy with Irene. Abruptly stopping the mule sometimes, he would jump out and throw into the cart's rear some rusty discarded metal he had spied while driving. Once Irene startled him, also jumping out, picking a wild rose. 'Ever since I was a l'il gal I'se loved roses,' she told him.

Meeting white people also out driving, or on horseback, Tom and Irene would become as two statues, with both them and the white people staring straight ahead. Tom commented after a while that since in Alamance County he felt he had seen fewer 'po' cracker' type of whites than abounded where he previously lived.

'I knows dem turkey-gobbler rednecks kin' you mean,' she said. 'Naw, ain't many roun' here. Any you sees be's gin'ly jes passin' through. De big white folks have less use fo' 'em dan dey does niggers.'

Tom expressed surprise at how Irene seemed to know something of every crossroads store they passed, or church, schoolhouse, wagon shop, or whatever. 'Well, I jes' hears massa tellin' guests how his folks had sump'n to do wid pret' near ever'thin' in Alamance County,' was how Irene explained it; then identifying a gristmill that they were passing as belonging to her massa, she said, 'He turn lotta his wheat into flour, an' his cawn into whisky to sell in Fayetteville.'

Privately, Tom gradually wearied of what began to sound to him as if Irene relished a running chronology of implied praises of her owner and his family. A Sunday when they ventured into the county-seat town of Graham, she said, 'De year dat big California gol' rush, my massa's daddy 'mongst de big mens what bought de lan' an' built dis town to be de county seat.' The next Sunday, as they drove along the Salisbury Road, she pointed out a prominent rock marker, 'Right dere on massa's gran'daddy's plantation dey fought de Battle o' Alamance. Folks sick o' dat king's bad treatments took dey guns to his redcoats, an' massa say dat battle what lit de fuse fo 'de 'Merican Revolution War roun' five years later on.'

By this time, Matilda had grown irate. It had strained her patience to the limit to suppress the exciting secret for so long. 'What's de matter wid you? Ack like you don't want nobody to see yo' Injun gal!'

Checking his irritance, Tom only mumbled something unintel-ligible, and an exasperated Matilda hit below the belt. 'Maybe she too good fo' us' cause she b'longst to sich big-shot folks!'

For the first time Tom had ever done such a thing, he stalked away from his mother, refusing to dignify that with a reply.

He wished there was someone, anyone, with whom he could talk about what had become his deep uncertainties regarding his continuing to keep company with Irene.

He had finally admitted to himself how much he loved her. Along with her pretty mixed black and Indian features, unquestionably she was as charming, tantalizing, and smart a potential mate as he would have dreamed for. Yet being as inherently deliberate and careful as he was, Tom felt that unless two vital worries he had developed about Irene got solved, they could never enjoy a truly successful union.

For one thing, deep within, Tom neither completely liked, nor completely trusted any white person, his own Massa and Missis Murray included. It seriously bothered him that Irene seemed actually to adore if not worship the whites who owned her; it strongly suggested that they would never see eye to eye on a vital matter.

His second concern, seeming even less soluble, was that the Holt family seemed scarcely less devoted to Irene, in the way that some prosperous massa families often came to regard certain household slaves. He knew that he could never survive the charade of mating with any woman, then living apart on different plantations, involving the steady indignity of their having to ask their respective massas to approve occasional marital visits.

Tom had even given thought to what might be the most honourable way, though he knew that any would be excruciating, to withdraw from seeing Irene any further.

'What de matter, Tom?' she asked him on the next Sunday, her tone full of concern.

'Ain't nothin'.'

They rode on silently for a while. Then she said in her candid open manner, 'Well, ain't gwine press you if you don' want to say jes' long as you knows I knows sump'n workin' hard on you.'

Hardly aware of the reins in his hands, Tom thought that among Irene's qualities that he most admired were her frankness and honesty, yet for weeks, months, he had been actually dishonest with her in the sense that he had evaded telling her his true thoughts, however painful it might prove to them both. And the longer he delayed would be continued dishonesty, as well as dragging out his bitter frustrations.

Tom strained to sound casual. 'While back, 'member I tol' you how my brudder Virgil's wife had to stay wid her massa when us go sol'?' It being unconnected with his point, he did not speak of how after his own recent personal appeal, Massa Murray had travelled to Caswell County and successfully had purchased Lilly Sue and her son Uriah.

Forcing himself to go on, Tom said, 'Jes' feel like if I was ever maybe git thinkin' 'bout matin' up wid anybody . . . well, jes' don't b'leeve I could if'n we s'pose to be livin' on different massas' plantations.'

'*Me neither!*' Her response was so quickly emphatic that Tom nearly dropped the reins, doubting his ears. He jerked about towards her, agape. 'What you mean?' he stammered.

'Same as you jes' said!'

He practically accosted her, 'You know Massa an' Missis Holt ain't gwine sell you!'

'I git sol' whenever I gits ready!' She looked at him calmly.

Tom felt a weakness coursing throughout his body. 'How you talkin' 'bout?'

'Not meanin' to soun' short, dat ain't yo' worry, it be's mine.'

Limply, Tom heard himself saying, 'Well, whyn't you git sol' den—'

She seemed hesitant. He nearly panicked.

She said, 'Awright. You got any special time?'

'Reckon dat up to you, too—'

His mind was racing. What earthly sum would her massa demand for such a prize as she was . . . if this was not all some wild dream in the first place?

'You got to ax yo' massa if he buy me.'

'He buy you,' he said with more certainty than he felt. He felt like a fool then, asking, 'How much you reckon you be costin'? Reckon he need to have a idea o' dat.'

' 'Speck dey'll take whatever he offer, reasonable.'

Tom just stared at her, and Irene at him.

'Tom Murray, you's in some ways de 'zasperatines' man I'se ever seed! I could o' tol' you dat since de day we firs' met! Long as I been waitin' fo' you to say sump'n! You jes' wait 'til I gits hol' o' you, gwine knock out some dat stubbornness!' He scarcely felt her small fists pummelling his head, his shoulders, as he took his first woman into his arms, the mule walking without guidance.

That night, lying abed, Tom began to see in his mind's eye how he was going to make for her a rose of iron. In a trip to the county seat he must buy only a small bar of the finest newly wrought iron. He must closely study a rose, how its stem and base were joined, how the petals spread, each curving outwards in its own way . . . how to heat the iron bar to just the orange redness for its quickest hammering to the wafer thinness from which he would trim the rose petals' patterns that once reheated and tenderly, lovingly shaped, would be dipped into brine mixed with oil, insuring her rose petals' delicate temper . . .

107

First hearing the sound, then rapidly advancing upon the totally startling sight of her treasured housemaid Irene huddled down and heavily sobbing behind where the lower staircase curved into an arc, Missis Emily Holt instantly reacted in alarm. 'What *is* it, Irene?' Missis Emily bent, grasping and shaking the heaving shoulders. 'Get yourself up from there this *minute* and tell me! What *is* it?'

Irene managed to stumble upright while gasping to her missis of her love for Tom, whom she said she wished to marry, rather than continuing her struggle to resist her regular pursuit by certain young massas. Pressed by a suddenly agitated Missis Holt to reveal their identities, Irene through her tears blurted out two names.

That evening before dinner, a shaken Massa and Missis Holt agreed that it was clearly in the best interests of the immediate family circle for her to be sold to Massa Murray and quickly.

Still, because Missis and Massa Holt genuinely liked Irene, and highly approved of her choice of Tom for a mate, they insisted that Massa and Missis Murray let them host the wedding and reception dinner. All members of both the white and black Holt and Murray families would attend in the Holt big-house front yard, with their minister performing the ceremony and Massa Holt himself giving away the bride.

But amid the lovely, moving occasion, the outstanding sensation was the delicately hand-wrought, perfect long-stemmed rose of iron that the groom Tom withdrew from inside his coat pocket and tenderly presented to his radiant bride. Amid the '*oohs*' and '*ahhs*' of the rest of the wedding assembly, Irene embraced it with her eyes, then pressing it to her breast she breathed, 'Tom, it's jes' too beautiful! Ain't gwine never be far from dis rose – or you neither!'

During the lavish reception dinner there in the yard after the beaming white families had retired to their meal served within the big house, after Matilda's third glass of the fine wine, she burbled to Irene, 'You's mo'n jes' a pretty daughter! You's done saved me from worryin' if Tom too shy ever to ax a gal to git married—' Irene loudly and promptly responded, 'He didn't!' And the guests within earshot joined them in uproarious laughter.

After the first week back at the Murray place, Tom's family soon joked among themselves that ever since the wedding, his hammer had seemed to start singing against his anvil. Certainly no one had ever seen him talk so much, or smile at so many people as often, or work as hard as he had since Irene came. Her treasured rose of iron graced the mantelpiece in their new cabin, which he left at dawn and went out to kindle his forge, whereafter the sounds of his tools shaping metals seldom went interrupted until the dusk's final red-hot object was plunged into the stale water of his slake tub to hiss and bubble as it cooled. Customers who came for some minor repair or merely to get a tool sharpened, he would usually ask if they could wait. Some slaves liked to sit on foot-high sections of logs off to one side, though most preferred shifting about in a loose group exchanging talk of common interest. On the opposite side, the waiting white customers generally sat on the split-log benches that Tom had set up for them, positioned carefully just within his earshot, though far enough away that the whites didn't suspect that as Tom worked, he was monitoring their conversations. Smoking and whittling and now or then taking nips from their pocket flasks as they talked, they had come to regard Tom's shop as a locally popular meeting place, supplying him now with a daily flow of small talk and sometimes with fresh, important news that he told to his Irene, his mother Matilda, and the rest of his slave-row family after their suppertimes.

Tom told his family what deep bitterness the white men expressed about northern Abolitionists' mounting campaign against slavery. 'Dey's sayin' dat Pres'dent Buchanan better keep 'way from dat no-good bunch o' nigger lovers if he 'speck any backin' here in de South.' But his white customers vented their worst hatred, he said, ' 'gainst Massa Abraham Lincoln what been talkin' 'bout freein' us slaves—'

'Sho' is de truth,' said Irene. 'Reckon leas' a year I been hearin' how if he don' shut up, gwine git de Nawth an' de South in a war!'

'Y'all ought to of heared my ol' massa rantin' an' cussin'!' exclaimed Lilly Sue. 'He say dis Massa Lincoln got sich gangly legs an' arms an' a long, ugly, hairy face can't nobody hardly tell if he look de mos' like a ape or gorilla! Say he borned an' growed up dirt po' in some log cabin, an' cotched bears an' polecats to git anythin' to eat, twixt splittin' logs into fence-rails like a nigger.'

'Tom, ain't you tol' us Massa Lincoln a lawyer nowdays?' asked L'il Kizzy, and Tom affirmatively grunted and nodded.

'Well, I don' care what dese white folks says!' declared Matilda. 'Massa Lincoln doin' good fo' us if he git dem so upset. Fact, mo' I hear 'bout 'im, soun' to me he like Moses tryin' to free us chilluns o' Israel!'

'Well, he sho' can't do it too fas' to suit me,' said Irene.

Both she and Lilly Sue had been bought by Massa Murray to increase his field workers, as she dutifully did in the beginning. But not many months had passed when Irene asked her doting husband if he would build her a handloom – and she had one in the shortest time that his skilled hands could make it. Then the steady *frump frump* of her loom could be heard from three cabins away as she worked into the nights until well beyond the rest of the slave-row family's bedtime. Before very long the visibly proud Tom was somewhat self-consciously wearing a shirt that Irene had cut and sewn from the cloth that she had made herself. 'I jes' loves doin' what my mammy teached me,' she modestly responded to congratulations. She next carded, spun, wove, and sewed matching ruffled dresses for an ecstatic Lilly Sue and L'il Kizzy – who now approaching the age of twenty was demonstrating absolutely no interest in settling down, seeming to prefer only successive flirtatious courtships, her newest swain, Amos, being a general worker at the North Carolina Railroad Company's newly completed hotel, ten miles distant at Company Shops.

Irene then made shirts for each of her brothers-in-law – which genuinely moved them, even Ashford – and finally matching aprons, smocks, and bonnets for Matilda and herself. Nor were Missis and next Massa Murray any less openly delighted with the amazingly finely stitched dress and shirt she made for them, from cotton grown right on their own plantation.

'Why, it's just beautiful!' Missis Murray exclaimed, turning around displaying her dress to a beaming Matilda. 'I'll never figure out why the Holts sold her to us at all, and even at a reasonable price!' Glibly avoiding the truth that Irene had confided, Matilda said, 'Bes' I can reckon, Missis, is dey liked Tom so much.'

Having a great love of colours, Irene avidly collected plants and leaves that she needed for cloth dyeing, and the weekends of 1859's early autumn saw cloth swatches in red, green, purple, blue, brown, and her favourite yellow hanging out to dry on the rattan clothes-lines. Without anyone's formally deciding or even seeming to much notice it, Irene gradually withdrew from doing further field work. From the massa and missis on down to Virgil's and Lilly Sue's peculiar-acting four-year-old Uriah, everyone was far more aware of the increasing ways in which Irene was contributing a new brightness to all of their lives.

'Reckon good part of what made me want Tom so much was 'cause I seed we both jes' loves makin' things fo' folks,' she told Matilda, who was rocking comfortably in her chair before her dully glowing fireplace one chilly late October evening. After a pause, Irene looked at her mother-in-law in a sly, under-eyed manner. 'Knowin' Tom,' she said, 'ain't no need me axin' if he done tol 'you we's makin' sump'n else—'

It took a second to register. Shrieking happily, springing up and tightly embracing Irene, Matilda was beside herself with joy. 'Make a l'il gal firs', honey, so I can hug an' rock 'er jes' like a doll!'

Irene did an incredible range of things across the winter months as her pregnancy advanced. Her hands seemed all but able to wreak a magic that soon was being enjoyed within the big house as well as in every slave-row cabin. She plaited rugs of cloth scraps; she made both tinted and scented Christmas-New Year holiday season candles; she carved dried cow's horns into pretty combs, and gourds into water dippers and birds' nests in fancy designs. She insisted until Matilda let her take over the weekly chore of boiling, washing, and ironing everyone's clothes. She put some of her fragrant dried-rose leaves or sweet basil between the folded garments, making the black and white Murrays alike smell about as fine as they felt.

That February Irene got urged into a three-way conspiracy by Matilda, who had already enlisted an amused Ashford's assistance. After explaining her plan, Matilda fiercely cautioned, 'Don't'cha breathe nary word to Tom, you know how stiff an' proper *he* is!' Privately seeing no harm in carrying out her instructions, Irene used her first chance to draw aside her openly adoring sister-in-law L'il Kizzy, and speak solemnly: 'I'se done heared sump'n I kinda 'speck you'd want to. Dat Ashford whispin' it roun' dat look like some real pretty gal beatin' yo' time wid dat railroad hotel man Amos—' Irene hesitated just enough to confirm L'il Kizzy's jealously narrowing eyes, then continued, 'Ashford say de gal right on de same plantation wid one o' his'n. He claim Amos go see her some week-nights, twixt seein' you Sundays. De gal say fo' long she gwine have Amos jumpin' de broom fo' sho'—'

L'il Kizzy gulped the bait like a hungry blue catfish, a report that was immensely gratifying to Matilda, who had concluded that after her covert observations of her fickle daughter's previous swains, Amos seemed the most solid, sincere prospect for L'il Kizzy to quit flirting and settle down with.

Irene saw even her stoic Tom raise his brows during the following Sunday afternoon after Amos arrived on his borrowed mule for his usual faithful visit. None of the family ever had seen L'il Kizzy in such a display of effervescing gaiety, wit, and discreetly suggestive wiles as she practically showered on the practically tongue-tied Amos, with whom she had previously acted more or less bored. After a few more of such Sundays, L'il Kizzy confessed to her heroine Irene that she finally had fallen in love, which Irene promptly told the deeply pleased Matilda.

But then when more Sundays had passed without any mention of jumping the broom, Matilda confided to Irene, 'I'se worried. Knows ain't gwine be long fo' dey does sump'n. You sees how ever' time he come here, dey goes walkin', right 'way from all us, an' dey heads close togedder—' Matilda paused, 'Irene, I'se worried 'bout two things. Firs' thing, dey fool roun' an' git too close, de gal liable to win' up in a fam'ly way. Other thing, dat boy so used to railroads an' folks travellin', I wonders is dey maybe figgerin' to run off to up Nawth? 'Cause L'il Kizzy jes' wil' 'nough to try anythin', an' you know it!'

Upon Amos' arrival the next Sunday, Matilda promptly appeared bearing a frosted layer cake and a large jug of lemonade. In loud, pointed invitation, she exclaimed to Amos that if she couldn't cook as well as L'il Kizzy, perhaps Amos would be willing to suffer through a bit of the cake and conversation. 'Fac', us don't never hardly even git to see you no mo,' seem like!'

An audible groan from L'il Kizzy instantly squelched with her catching a hard glance from Tom, as Amos, without much acceptable alternative, took an offered seat. Then as the family small talk accompanied the refreshments, Amos contributed a few strained, self-conscious syllables. After a while, apparently L'il Kizzy decided that her man was much more interesting than her family was being enabled to appreciate.

'Amos, how come you don't tell 'em 'bout dem tall poles an' wires dem railroad white folks ain't long put up?' Her tone was less a request than a demand.

Fidgeting some, then Amos said, 'Well, ain't rightly know if'n I can 'zackly 'scribe whatever it is. But jes' las' month dey got through

560

wid stringin' wires crost de tops o' real tall poles stretchin' fur as you can see—'

'Well, what de poles an' wires fo'?' Matilda demanded.

'He gittin' to dat, Mammy!'

Amos looked embarrassed. 'Telegraph. B'leeve dat's what dey calls it, ma'am. I been an' looked at how de wires leads down inside de railroad station where de station agent got on his desk dis contraption wid a funny kin' o' sideways handle. Sometime he makin' it click wid his finger. But mo' times de contraption git to clickin' by itself. It mighty 'citin' to de white folks. Now every mornin' a good-size bunch 'em comes an' ties up dey hosses to jes' be roun' waitin' fo' dat thing to git to clickin'. Dey says it's news from different places comin' over dem wires 'way up on dem poles.'

'Amos, wait a minute, now—' Tom spoke slowly. 'You's sayin' it bringin' news but ain't no talkin', jes' de clickin'?'

'Yassuh, Mr Tom, like a great big cricket. Seem like to me some-how or 'nother de station agent be's gittin' words out'n dat, 'til it stop. Den pretty soon he step outside an' tell dem odder mens what-all was said.'

'Ain't dese white folks sump'n?' exclaimed Matilda. 'De Lawd do tell!' She beamed upon Amos almost as broadly as L'il Kizzy was.

Amos, obviously feeling much more at ease than before, elected now without any prompting to tell them of another wonder. 'Mr Tom, is you ever been in any dem railroad repair shops?'

Tom was privately deciding that he liked this young man who appeared to be, at last, his sister's choice to jump the broom with; he had manners. He seemed sincere, solid.

'Naw, son, I ain't,' Tom said. 'Me an' my wife used to drive by de Company Shops village, but I ain't never been inside none de buildin's.'

'Well suh, I'se took plenty meals on trays from de hotel to de mens in all twelve dem different shops, an' I reckon de busies' one de blacksmith shop. Dey be's doin' sich in dere as straightening' dem great big train axles what's got bent, fixin' all manners o' other train troubles, an' makin' all kinds o' parts dat keeps de trains runnin'. It's cranes in dere big as logs, bolted to de ceilin', an' de reckon twelve, fifteen blacksmith's each got a nigger helper swingin' mauls an' sledges bigger'n I ever seen. Dey got forges big enough to roas' two, three whole cows in, an' one dem nigger helpers tol' me dey anvils weighs much as eight hundred pounds!'

'*Whew!*' whistled Tom, obviously much impressed.

'How much yo' anvil weigh, Tom?' Irene asked.

'Right roun' two hundred pounds, an ain't ever'body could lif' it.'

'Amos—' L'il Kizzy exclaimed, 'you ain't tol' 'em nothin' 'bout yo' new hotel where you works!'

'Hol' on, none o' *my* hotel!' Amos widely grinned. 'Sho' *whist* it was! Dey takes in money han' over fis'! Lawd! Well, 'magines y'all knows de hotel ain't long built. Folks says some mens pretty hot under de collar 'cause de railroad pres'dent talked wid dem, but den picked Miss Nancy Hillard to manage it. She de one hired me, 'memberin' me workin' hard fo' her fam'ly, growin' up. Anyhow, de hotel got thirty rooms, wid six toilets out in de backyard. Folks pays a dollar a day fo' room an' washbowl an' towel, 'long wid breakfas', dinner, supper, an' a settin' chair on de front porch. Sometime I hears Miss Nancy jes' acarryin' on 'bout how mos' de railroad workmens leaves her nice clean white sheets all grease an' soot-streaked, but den she say well leas' dey spends ever'thin dey makes, so deys he'pin' de Company Shops village git better off!'

Again L'il Kizzy cued her Amos: 'How 'bout y'all feedin' dem trainloads o' folks?'

Amos smiled. 'Well, den's 'bout busy as us ever gits! See, every day it be's de two passenger trains, one runnin' eas', de odder wes'. Gittin' to McLeansville or Hillsboro, 'pendin' which way it gwine, de train's conductor he telegraphs 'head to de hotel how many passengers an' crew he got. An' by time dat train git to our station, lemme tell y'all, Miss Nancy's got all de stuff out on dem long tables hot an' steamin', an' all us helpers jes' rarin' to go to feed dem folks! I means it be's quail an' hams, chickens, guineas, rabbit, beef; it's all kinds o' salads, an' 'bout any vegetable you can name, 'long wid a whole table nothin' but desserts! De peoples piles off dat big ol' train dat sets dere waitin' twenty minutes to give 'em time to eat fo' dey gits back on boa'd an' it commence achuffin' out an' gone again!'

'De drummers, Amos!' cried L'il Kizzy, with everyone smiling at her pride.

'Yeah,' said Amos. 'Dey's de ones Miss Nancy purely love to have put up in de hotel! Sometime two, three 'em git off'n de same train, an' me an' 'nother nigger hurries up carryin' 'head o' 'em to de hotel dey suit bag an' big heavy black web-strap cases what we knows is full o' samples whatever dat 'ticular drummer's sellin'. Miss Nancy says dey's real gen'lmens, keeps deyselves clean as pins, an' really 'preciates bein' took good care of, an' I likes 'em, too. Some jes' quick to give you a dime as a nickel fo' carryin' dey bags, shinin' dey shoes, or doin' nigh 'bout anythin'! Gin'ly dey washes up an' walks roun' town talkin' wid folks. After eatin' dinner, dey'll set on de porch, smokin' or chawin' 'baccy an' jes' lookin', or talkin' 'til dey goes on upstairs to bed. Den nex' mornin' after breakfas', dey calls one us niggers to tote dey samples cases over crost to dat blacksmith's what fo' a dollar a day rents 'em a hoss an' buggy, an' off dey drives to sell stuff at I reckon 'bout all de stores 'long de roads in dis county—'

In a spontaneity of sheer admiration that Amos worked amid such wonders, the chubby L'il George exclaimed, 'Amos, boy, I ain't realized you is leadin' some life!'

'Miss Nancy say de railroad bigges' thing since de hoss,' Amos modestly observed. 'She say soon's some mo' railroads gits dey tracks jines togedder, things ain't gwine never be de same no mo'.'

108

Chicken George slowed his galloping, lathered horse barely enough for its sharp turning off the main road into the lane, then abruptly his hands jerked the reins taut. It *was* the right place, but since he had seen it last: unbelievable! Beyond the weed-choked lane ahead, the once buff-coloured Lea home looked a mottled grey of peeling old paint; rags were stuffed where some window panes had been; one side of the now heavily patched roof seemed almost sagging. Even the adjacent fields were barren, containing nothing but old dried weathered stalks within the collapsing split-log fences.

Shocked, bewildered, he relaxed the reins to continue with the horse now picking its way through the weeds. Yet closer, he saw the big-house porch aslant, the broken-down front steps; and the slave-row cabins' roof were all caving in. Not a cat, dog, or chicken was to be seen as he slid off the horse, leading it now by its bridle alongside the house to the backyard.

He was no more prepared for the sight of the heavy old woman sitting bent over on a piece of log, picking poke salad greens, dropping the stems about her feet and the leaves into a cracked, rusting wash-basin. He recognized that she had to be Miss Malizy, but so incredibly different it seemed impossible. His unnecessary loud '*Whoa!*' caught her attention.

Miss Malizy quit picking the greens. Raising her head, looking about, then she saw him, but he could tell she didn't yet realize who he was.

'*Miss Malizy!*' He ran over closer, halting uncertainly as he saw her face still querying. Her eyes squinting, she got him into better focus ... suddenly pushing one hand heavily down against the log, she helped herself upwards. 'George ... ain't'cha dat boy George?'

'Yes'm, Miss Malizy!' He rushed to her now, grasping and embracing her large flabbiness within his arms, close to crying. 'Lawd, boy, where you *been* at? Used to be you were roun' here all de time!'

Her tone and words held some vacantness, as if she were unaware of nearly five years' time lapse. 'Been crost de water in dat Englan', Miss Malizy. Been fightin' chickens over dere – Miss Malizy, where my wife an' mammy an' chilluns at?'

So was her face blankness, as if beyond any more emotion no matter whatever else might happen. 'Ain't nobody hardly here no mo', boy!' She sounded surprised that he didn't know it. 'Dey's all gone. Jes' me an' massa's lef—'

'Gone *where*, Miss Malizy?' He knew now that her mind had weakened.

With a puffy hand she gestured towards the small willow grove still below the slave row. 'Yo' mammy ... Kizzy her name ... layin' down yonder—'

A whooping sob rose and burst from Chicken George's throat. His hand flew up to muffle it.

'Sarah, too, she down dere .. an' ol' missy ... in de front yard – ain't you seed 'er when you rid by?'

'Miss Malizy, where 'Tilda an' my chilluns?'

He didn't want to rattle her. She had to think a moment.

''Tilda? Yeh. 'Tilda good gal, sho' was, Whole lotta chilluns, too. Yeh. Boy, you oughta knowed massa sol' off all 'em long time ago—'

'*Where*, Miss Malizy, where *to*?' Rage flooded him. 'Where *massa*, Miss Malizy?'

Her head turned towards the house. 'Up in dere still 'sleep, I reckons. Git so drunk don' git up 'til late, hollerin' he want to eat ... ain't no vittles, hardly ... boy, you bring anything to cook?'

His 'No'm' floating back to the confused old lady, Chicken George burst through the shambles of the kitchen and down the peeling hallway into the smelly, messy living-room to stop at the foot of the short staircase, bellowing angrily '*Massa Lea!*'

He waited briefly.

'MASSA LEA!'

About to go stomping up the stairs, he heard activity sounds.

After a moment, from the right doorway the dishevelled figure emerged, peering downwards.

Chicken George through his anger stood shocked to muteness at the shell of his remembered massa, gaunt, unshaven, unkempt; obviously he had slept in those clothes. 'Massa Lea?'

'*George!*' The old man's body physically jerked. '*George!*' He came stumbling down the creaking staircase, stopping at its foot; they stood staring at each other. In Massa Lea's hollowed face, his eyes were rheumy, then with high, cackling laughter he rushed with widening arms to hug Chicken George, who sidestepped. Catching Massa Lea's bony hands, he shook them vigorously.

'George, so glad you're back! Where all you been? You due back here long time ago!'

'Yassuh, yassuh. Lawd Russell jes' lemme loose. An' I been eight days gittin' here from de ship in Richmon'.'

'Boy, come on in here in the kitchen!' Massa Lea was tugging Chicken George's wrists. And when they reached there, he scraped back the broken table's two chairs. '*Set*, boy! 'LIZY! Where my jug? 'LIZY!'

'Comin', Massa—' the old woman's voice came from outside. 'She's done got addled since you left, don't know yesterday from tomorrow,' said Massa Lea.

'Massa, where my fam'ly?'

'Boy, less us have a drink fore we talk! Long as we been together, we ain't *never* had a drink together! So glad you back here, finally somebody to talk to!'

'Ain't fo' talkin', Massa! Where my fam'ly—'

' 'LIZY!'

'Yassuh—' Her bulk moved through the door frame and she found and put a jug and glasses on the table and then went back outside as if unaware of Chicken George and Massa Lea there talking.

'Yeah, boy, I sure am sorry 'bout your mammy. She just got too old, didn't suffer much, and she went quick. Put 'er in a good grave—' Massa Lea was pouring them drinks.

On purpose ain't mentionin' 'Tilda an' de chilluns, it flashed through Chicken George's mind. *Ain't changed none ... still tricky an' dangerous as a snake ... got to keep from gittin' 'im real mad ...*

' 'Member de las' things you said to me, Massa? Said you be settin' me free jes' soon's I git back. Well, here I is!'

But Massa Lea gave no sign he'd even heard as he shoved a glass three-quarters filled across the table. Then, lifting his own, 'Here y'are, boy. Le's drink to you bein' back—'

I needs dis . . . quaffing of the liquor, Chicken George felt it searing down and warming within him.

He tried again, obliquely. 'Sho' sorry to hear from Miss Malizy you los' missis, Massa.'

Finishing his liquor, grunting, Massa Lea said, 'She just didn't wake up one mornin'. Hated to see her go. She never give me any peace since that cockfight. But I hated to see her go. Hate to see anybody go.' He belched. 'We all got to go—'

He ain't bad off as Miss Malizy, but he 'long de way. He went now directly to the point.

'My 'Tilda an' young'uns, Massa, Miss Malizy say you sol' 'em—'

Massa Lea glanced at him. 'Yeah, had to, boy. Had to! Bad luck got me down so bad. Had to sell off near 'bout the last of my land, everything, hell, even the chickens!'

About to flare, Chicken George got cut off.

'Boy, I'm so po' now, me an' Malizy's eatin' 'bout what we can pick an' catch!' Suddenly he cackled. 'Hell, sure ain't nothin' new! I was borned po'!' He got serious again. 'But now you're back, you and me can get this place agoin' again, you hear me? I know we can do 'er, boy!'

All that repressed Chicken George from lunging up at Massa Lea was his lifelong conditioning knowledge of what would automatically follow physically attacking any white man. But his rasping anger contained his closeness to it. 'Massa, you sent me 'way from here wid yo' word to free me! But I git back, you done even sol' my fam'ly. I wants my papers an' know where my wife and chilluns is, Massa!'

'Thought I tol' you that! They over in Alamance County, tobacco planter name Murray, live not far from the railroad shops—' Massa Lea's eyes were narrowed. 'Don't you raise your voice at me, boy!'

Alamance . . . Murray . . . railroad shops. Inking into memory those key words, Chicken George now managed a seeming contriteness, 'I'se sorry, jes' got excited, sho' ain't meant to, Massa—'

The massa's expression wavered, then forgave. *I got to ease out'n 'im dat piece o' paper he writ dat free me.* 'I been *down*, boy!' Hunching forwards across the table, the massa squinted fiercely, 'You hear me? Nobody never know how down I been! Ain't jes' meaning' money—' He gestured at his chest, 'Down in *here*!' He seemed wanting a response—

'Yassuh.'

'Seen *hard* days, boy! Them sonsabitches used to holler my name crossin' the street when I'm comin'. Heared 'em laughin' 'hin' my

566

back. *Sonsabitches!*' A bony fist banged the tabletop. 'Swore in my heart Tom Lea show 'em! Now you back. Git 'nother set of chickens! Don't *care* I'm eighty-three . . . we can do 'er, boy!'

'Massa—'

Massa Lea squinted closely, 'Forget how old you now, boy?'

'Fifty-fo' now, Massa.'

'You *ain't!*'

'Is, too, Massa. Fo' long, be fifty-five—'

'Hell, I seen you the same mornin' you birthed! L'il ol' wrinkled-up straw-coloured nigger—' Massa Lea cackled. 'Hell, I give you your name!'

Pouring himself another smaller drink after Chicken George had waved his hand negatively, quickly Massa Lea peered around as if to insure that only they were there. 'Reckon ain't no sense keepin' you 'mongst all them I got fooled! They think I ain't got nothin' no more—' He gave Chicken George a conspiratorial look. 'I got money! Ain't much . . . I got it *hid!* Don't nobody but me know where!' He looked longer at Chicken George. 'Boy, when I go, you know who git what I got? Still ownin' ten acres, too! Lan' like money at the bank! Whatever I got go to *you!* You the closest I got now, boy.'

He seemed to be wrestling with something. Furtively he leaned yet closer. 'Hell, ain't no need not to face the fact. It's *blood* 'tween us, boy!'

He done hit bottom fo' sho', sayin' dat. His insides contracting, Chicken George sat mutely.

'Jes' stay on even if a l'il while, George—' The whiskied face petitioned. 'I know you ain't the kin' go turnin' your back 'gainst them what helped you in this worl'—'

Jes' fo' I lef' he showed me my freedom paper he'd writ an' signed an' said he gwine keep in 'is strongbox. Chicken George realized that he was going to have to get Massa Lea yet drunker. He studied the face across the table, thinking *bein' white de only thing he got lef'* . . .

'Massa, never will fo'git how you bring me up – mighty few white men's good as dat—'

The watery eyes lighted. 'You was jes' l'il shirt-tail nigger, I shore remember—'

'Yassuh, you an' Uncle Mingo—'

'Ol' Mingo! Damn his time! Bes' nigger trainer it was—' The wavering eyes found a focus on Chicken George '. . . 'til you learnt good . . . started takin' you to fights an' leavin' Mingo—'

'... *hope you an' massa trus' me to feed de chickens*—' The memory of old Uncle Mingo's bitterness hurt even yet.

' 'Member, Massa, we was gwine to a big fight in New Orleans?'

'Shore was! An' never did make it—' His brow wrinkled.

'Uncle Mingo died jes befo' was how come.'

'Yeah! Ol' Mingo over under them willow trees now.' *Along with my mammy and Sister Sarah, and Miss Malizy whenever she go, pending which one y'all goes first.* He wondered what either would do without the other.

'Boy, you 'member me givin' you the travellin' pass to go catch all the tail you wanted?'

Making himself simulate guffawing laughter, Chicken George pounded the tabletop himself, the massa continuing, 'Damn right I did, 'cause you was horny buck if I ever seen one. An' we both catched aplenty tail them trips we made, boy! I knowed you was an' you knowed I was—'

'Yassuh! Sho' did, Massa!'

'An' you commence hackfightin' an' I give you money to bet, an' you win your ass off!'

'Sho' did, suh, de truth! De *truth!*'

'Boy, we was a *team,* we was!'

Chicken George caught himself almost starting to share a thrilling in the reminiscings; he also felt a little giddy from the whisky. He reminded himself of his objective. Reaching across the table, taking up the liquor jug, he poured into his glass about an inch, closing a fist quickly around the glass to mask the small amount as extending the jug across the table, he poured for Massa Lea about three-quarters of a glassful. Raising his glass within his fist, appearing to lurch, his voice sounded slurring, 'Drink to gooda massa as is anywhere! Like dem Englishmans says, "Down de hawtch!" '

Sipping of his, he watched Massa Lea quaff, 'Boy, it do me good you feel thataway—'

' 'Nother toas'!' The two glasses elevated. 'Fines' nigger I ever had!' They drained their glasses.

Wiping his mouth with the back of a veiny hand, coughing from the whisky's impact, Massa Lea also slurred, 'You ain't tol' me nothin' 'bout that Englishman, boy – what's his name?'

'Lawd Russell, Massa. He got mo' money'n he can count. Got mo'n fo' hunnud bloodline roosters to pick from to fight wid—' Then after a purposeful pause, 'But ain't nowhere de gamecocker you is, Massa.'

'You mean that, boy?'

'Ain't as smart, one thing. An' ain't de *man* you is! He jes' rich an' lucky. Ain't yo' *quality* o' white folks, Massa!' Chicken George thought of having overheard Sir C. Eric Russell say to friends, *'George's mawster's a glorified hackfighter.'*

Massa Lea's head lolled, he jerked it back upwards, his eyes trying to focus on Chicken George. *Where would he keep his strongbox?* Chicken George thought how the rest of his life's condition would hang upon his obtaining the vividly remembered square sheet of paper containing maybe three times more writing than a travelling pass, over the signature.

'Massa, could I have l'il mo' yo' liquor?'

'You know better'n ask, boy . . . all you wan'—'

'I tol' amany dem English folks bes' massa in de worl's what I got . . . ain't nobody never hear me talkin' 'bout stayin' over dere . . . hey, yo' glass gittin' low, Massa—'

'. . . Jes' l'il be 'nough . . . naw, you ain't that kin', boy . . . never give no real trouble—'

'Nawsuh . . . well, drinkin' to you 'gin, suh—' They did, some of the massa's liquor wetting his chin. Chicken George, feeling more of the whisky's effect, suddenly sat up straighter, seeing the massa's head lowering towards the tabletop . . .

'Y'always good to y'other niggers, too, Massa . . .'

The head wavered, stayed down. 'Tried to, boy . . . tried to—' It was muffled.

B'leeve he good'n drunk now. 'Yessuh, you'n missis bofe—'

'Good woman . . . lotta ways—'

The massa's chest now also met the table. Lifting his chair with minimal sound, Chicken George waited a suspenseful moment. Moving to the entrance, he halted, then not overloudly, 'Massa! . . . Massa!'

Suddenly turning, catlike, within seconds he was searching every drawer within any front-room furniture. Halting, hearing only his breathing, he hastened up the steps, cursing their creaking.

The impact of entering a white man's bedroom hit him. He stopped . . . involuntarily stepping backwards, he glimpsed the conglomerate mess. Sobering rapidly, he went back inside, assaulted by the mingled strong odours of stale whisky, urine, sweat, and unwashed clothes among the emptied bottles. Then as if possessed, he was pulling open, flinging aside things, searching futilely. *Maybe under the bed.* Frantically dropping onto his knees, peering, he saw the strongbox.

Seizing it, in a trice he was back downstairs, tripping in the hallway.

Seeing the massa still slumped over on the table, turning, he hastened through the front door. Around at the side of the house, with his hands he wrested to open the locked, metal box. *Git on de hoss an' go – bus' it open later.* But he had to be sure he had the freedom paper.

The backyard wood-chopping block caught his eyes, with the old axe near it on the ground. Nearly leaping there, jerking up the axe, setting the box lockside up, with one smashing blow it burst open. Bills, coins, folded papers spilled out, and snatching open papers he instantly recognized it.

'What'cha doin', boy?'

He nearly jumped from his skin. But it was Miss Malizy sitting on her log, unperturbed, quietly staring.

'What massa say?' she asked vacantly.

'I got to go, Miss Malizy!'

'Well, I reckon you better go 'head, den—'

'Gwine tell 'Tilda an' de chilluns you wishes 'em well—'

'That be nice, boy . . . y'all take care—'

'Yes'm—' Swiftly moving, he embraced her tightly. *Oughta run see de graves.* Then thinking it better to remember his mammy Kizzy and Sister Sarah as he remembered them living, Chicken George swept a last look over the crumbling place where he was born and raised; unexpectedly blubbering, clutching the freedom paper, he went running, and vaulting onto his horse ahead of the two double saddle rolls containing his belongings, he went galloping back up through the high weeds of the lane, not looking back.

109

Near the fencerow that flanked the main road, Irene was busily picking leaves to press into dry perfumes when she looked up, hearing the sound of a galloping horse's hoofs. She gasped, seeing the horseman wearing a flowing green scarf and a black derby with a curving rooster tail feather jutting up from the hatband.

Waving her arms wildly, she raced towards the road, crying out at the top of her lungs, '*Chicken George! Chicken George!*' The rider reined up just beyond the fence, his lathered horse heaving with relief.

'Do I know you, gal?' he called, returning her smile.

'Nawsuh! We ain't never seen one 'nother, but Tom, Mammy, 'Tilda, an' de fam'ly talk 'bout you so much I knows what you look like.'

He stared at her. '*My* Tom and 'Tilda?'

'Yassuh! Yo' wife an' my husban' – my baby's daddy!'

It took him a few seconds to register it. 'You an' Tom got a *chile?*' She nodded, beaming and patting her protruding stomach. 'It due 'nother month!' He shook his head. 'Lawd God! Lawd God Amighty! What's yo' name?'

'Irene, suh!'

Telling him to ride on, she hurried clumsily as fast as she dared until she reached within vocal range of where Virgil, Ashford, L'il George, James, Lewis, L'il Kizzy, and Lilly Sue were planting in another section of the plantation. Her loud hallooing quickly brought a worried L'il Kizzy, who raced back to relay the incredible news. They all breathlessly reached the slave row, shouting and surging about their father, mother, and Tom, and all trying at once to embrace him, until a pummelled and disarrayed Chicken George was entirely overwhelmed with his reception.

'Guess bes' y'all hears de bad news firs',' he told them, and then of the deaths of Gran'mammy Kizzy and Sister Sarah. 'Ol' Missis Lea, she gone, too—'

When their griefs at their losses had abated somewhat, he described Miss Malizy's condition, and then his experience with Massa Lea, finally resulting in the freedom paper that he triumphantly displayed. Supper was eaten and the night fell upon the family grouped raptly about him as he entered the topic of his nearly five years in England.

'Gwine tell y'all de truth, reckon I'd need 'nother year tryin' tell all I'se seed an' done over 'way crost all dat water! My Lawd!' But he gave them now at least a few highlights of Sir C. Eric Russell's great wealth and social prestige; of his long purebred lineage and consistently winning game-flock, and how as an expert black trainer from America he had proved fascinating to lovers of gamecocking in England, where fine ladies would go strolling leading their small African boys dressed in silks and velvet by golden chains about their necks.

'Ain't gwine lie, I'se glad I had all de 'speriences I is. But Lawd knows I'se missed y'all sump'n terrible!'

'Sho' don' look it to me – stretchin' two years out to mo'n fo'!' Matilda snapped.

'Ol' biddy ain't changed a bit, is she?' observed Chicken George to his amused children.

'*Hmph! Who* so ol'?' Matilda shot back. 'Yo' head done got to showin' mo' grey dan mine is!'

He laughingly patted Matilda's shoulder as she feigned great indignance. 'T'wan't me ain't wanted to git back! I commence 'mindin' Lawd Russell soon's dem two years done. But one day after a while he come an' say I'se trainin' his chickens so good, well as de young white feller was my helper dat he done 'cided sen' nudder som o' money to Massa Lea, tellin' 'im he need me one mo' year – an' I nearly had a fit! But what I'm gwine do? Done de bes' I could – I got in 'is letter fo' Massa Lea be sho' an' 'splain to y'all what happen—'

'He ain't tol' us nary word!' exclaimed Matilda, and Tom spoke.

'You know why? He'd done sol' us off by dat time.'

'Sho' right! It's why us ain't heared!'

'Umh-huh! Umh-huh! See? T'warn't me!' Chicken George sounded pleased to be vindicated.

After his bitter disappointment, he said he had extracted Sir Russell's pledge that it would be the last year. 'Den I went 'head an' he'ped his chickens win dey bigges' season ever – leas' dat's what he tol' me. Den fin'ly he said he feel like I done teached de young white feller 'nough dat he could take over, an' I jes' 'bout lit up dat place carryin' on, I was so happy!

'Lemme tell y'all sump'n – it's a mighty few niggers ever has two whole carriage-loads of English folks 'companyin' 'em like dey did me, to Souf'hampton. Dat's great big city by de water wid ain't no tellin' how many ships gwine in an' out. Lawd Russell had 'ranged for me ridin' steerage in dis ship crost de ocean.

'Lawd! De scardes' I ever been! We ain't got all dat far out dere fo' commence to buckin' an' rearin' like a wil' hoss! Talk 'bout prayin'!' – he ignored Matilda's '*Hmph!*' – 'seem like de whole ocean gone crazy, tryin' to wrench us to pieces! But den fin'ly it got ca'med down pretty fair an' it was even restful by time we come in New Yawk where ever'body got off—'

'New Yawk!' L'il Kizzy exclaimed. 'What'cha do dere, Pappy?'

'Gal, ain't I tellin' it fas' as I can? Well, Lawd Russell had give one de ship officers money wid 'structions to put me on nudder ship dat'd git me to Richmon'. But de ship de officer made 'rangements wid weren't leavin' fo' five, six days. So I jes' walked up an' down in dat New Yawk, lissenin' an' lookin—'

'Where you stay at?' asked Matilda.

'Roomin' house for coloured – dat's same as niggers, where you *think?* I had money. I *got* money, out in my saddlebags right now. Gwine show it y'all in de mawnin'.' He glanced devilishly at Matilda. 'Might even give you hundred dollars, y'act right!' As she snorted, he went on, 'Dat Lawd Russell turnt out to be a real good man. Gimme dis pretty fair piece o'money jes' fo' I lef'. Say it strictly fo' *me*, not even to mention it to Massa Lea, an' you knows fo' sho' I ain't.

'Really main thing I done was talked wid plenty dem New Yawk free niggers. Seem like to me mos' 'em tryin' to keep from starvin', worse off'n we is. But it is like we's heared. Some of 'em is livin' good! Got different kinds dey own businesses, or nice-payin' jobs. Few owns dey own homes, an' more pays rents in sump'n dey calls 'partments, an' some de young'uns gittin' some schoolin', sich as dat.

'But whatever nigger I talked to mad as yellowjackets 'bout is all dem 'migratin' white folks ever'where you looks—' 'Dem Abolitions?' yelped L'il Kizzy. 'You tellin' it or me? Naw! Sho' ain't! Way I unnerstan', de Abolitions is pret' much white folks what been in dis country leas' long as niggers is. But dese I'se speakin' 'bout is pilin' off'n ships into New Yawk, in fact all over de Nawth. Dey's Irishers, mainly, you can't unnerstan' what dey's sayin', an' lotta odder 'culiar kinds can't even speak English. Fact, I heared dey steps off de ships an firs' word dey learns is "nagur", den next thing deys claimin' niggers takin' *dey* jobs! Dey's startin' fights an' riots all de time – dey's wusser'n po' crackers!'

'Well, Lawd, I hope dey stays 'way from down here!' said Irene.

'Look here, y'all, it'd take me 'nother week to tell *half* de goin's on I seed an' heared fo' dat ship brung me to Richmon—'

'S'prise to me you even got on it!'

'Woman, ain't you gon' *never* let me 'lone! Man gone fo' years an' you actin' like I lef' yestiddy!' The slightest suggestion of an edge was in Chicken George's voice.

Tom asked quickly, 'You bought yo' hoss in Richmon'?'

'Dat's right! Sebenty dollars! She a real fas' speckle mare. I figgered free man gwine need a good hos. I rid 'er hard as she could stan' it to Massa Lea's—'

It being early April, everyone *else* was extremely busy. Most of the family were in the planting season's height. Among cleaning, cooking, and serving in the big house, Matilda had very little available free time. Tom's customers kept him going at his hardest from daylight into deepening dusk, and the nearly eight months' pregnant

Irene was scarcely less occupied among her diverse tasks.

No matter, across the next week, Chicken George visited with them all. But out in the fields, it soon was as uncomfortably clear to them as to himself that he and anything connected with field work were alien. Matilda and Irene's faces made quick smiles when he came near, then they made equally quick apologies that they knew he understood that they had to get back to what they were doing. Several times, he dropped by to have some chat with Tom while he blacksmithed. But each time the atmosphere would grow tense. The slaves who were waiting grew visibly nervous on seeing whatever as yet unattended white customers abruptly quit their conversations, spit emphatically and shift their bodies about on the log benches, while eyeing the wearer of the green scarf and the black derby with obvious silent suspicion.

Twice during these times, Tom happened to glance and see Massa Murray starting down towards the shop, then turn back, and Tom knew why. Matilda had said that when the Murrays first learned of Chicken George's arrival, 'dey seem happy fo' us, but Tom, I worries, I knows dey's since had dey heads togedder whole lot, den quits talkin' soon's I comes in.'

What was going to be Chicken George's 'free' status there on the Murray plantation? What was he going to do? The questions hung like a cloud in the minds of every individual among them . . . excepting Virgil's and Lilly Sue's four-year-old Uriah.

'You's my gran'pappy?' Uriah seized his chance to say something directly to the intriguing man who had seemed to occasion such a stir among all of the other adults ever since his arrival several days before.

'*What?*'

The startled Chicken George had just wandered back into the slave row, deeply rankled by his feeling of being rejected. He eyed the child who stared at him with large, curious eyes. 'Well, reckon I is.' About to walk on, George turned. 'What dey say yo' name?'

'Uriah, suh. Gran'pappy, wherebouts you work at?'

'What you talkin' 'bout?' He glared down at the boy. 'Who tol' you to ax me dat?'

'Nobody. Jes' ax you.'

He decided that the boy told the truth. 'Don' work nowheres. I'se free.'

The boy hesitated. 'Gran'pappy, what free is?'

Feeling ridiculous standing there being interrogated by a young'un, Chicken George started on, but then he thought of what Matilda had confided of the boy. 'Seem like he tend to be sickly, even

574

maybe a l'il quare in de head. Next time you roun' 'im, notice how he apt to jes' keep starin' at somebody even after dey's quit talkin'.' Turning about, Chicken George searched the face of Uriah, and he saw what Matilda meant. The boy did project an impression of physical weakness and, except for his blinking, the large eyes were as if they had fastened onto Chicken George, assessing his every utterance or movement. George felt uncomfortable. The boy repeated his question. 'Suh, what free is?'

'Free mean ain't nobody own you no mo'.' He had a sense that he was speaking to the eyes. He started off again.

'Mammy say you fights chickens. What you fight 'em wid?'

Wheeling about, a retort on his tongue, Chicken George perceived the earnest, curious face of only a small boy. And it stirred something within him: gran'chile.

Critically he studied Uriah, thinking that there must be something appropriate to say to him. And finally, 'Yo' mammy or anybody tol' you where you comes from?'

'Suh? Comes from where?' He had not been told, Chicken George saw, or if he had, not in a way that he remembered.

'C'mon 'long wid me here, boy.'

Also, it was something for him to do. Followed by Uriah, Chicken George led the way over to the cabin that he was sharing with Matilda. 'Now set yo'self down in dat chair an' don't be axin' no whole lotta questions. Jes' set an' lissen to what I tells you.'

'Yassuh.'

'Yo' pappy born of me an' yo' Gran'mammy 'Tilda.' He eyed the boy. 'You unnerstans dat?'

'My pappy y'all young'un.'

'Dat's right. You ain't dum' as you looks. Den my mammy name Kizzy. So she yo' great-gran'mammy. Gran'mammy Kizzy. Say dat.'

'Yassuh. Gran'mammy Kizzy.'

'Yeah. Den her mammy name Bell.'

He looked at the boy.

'Name Bell.'

Chicken George grunted. 'Awright. An' Kizzy's pappy name Kunta Kinte—'

'Kunta Kinte.'

'Dat's right. Well, him an' Bell yo' great-great-gran'folks—'

Nearly an hour later, when Matilda came hurrying nervously into the cabin, wondering what on earth had happened to Uriah, she found him dutifully repeating such sounds as 'Kunta Kinte' and 'ko' and 'Kamby Bolongo'. And Matilda decided that she had the time to sit down, and beaming with satisfaction, she listened as Chicken George told their rapt grandson the story of how his African great-great-gran'daddy had said he was not far from his village, chopping some wood to make a drum, when he had been surprised, overwhelmed, and stolen into slavery by four men, '—den a ship brung 'im crost de big water to a place call 'Naplis, an' he was bought dere by a Massa John Waller what took 'im to his plantation dat was in Spotsylvania County, Virginia . . .'

The following Monday, Chicken George rode with Tom in the mulecart to buy supplies in the county-seat town of Graham. Little was said between them, each seeming mostly immersed in his own thoughts. As they went from one to another store, Chicken George keenly relished the quiet dignity with which his twenty-seven-year-old son dealt with the various white merchants. Then they went into a feed store that Tom said had recently been bought by a former county sheriff named J. D. Cates.

The heavy-set Cates was seeming to ignore them as he moved about serving his few white customers. Some sense of warning rose within Tom; glancing, he saw Cates looking covertly at the green-scarfed, black-derbied Chicken George, who was stepping about in a cocky manner visually inspecting items of merchandise. Intuitively Tom was heading towards his father to accomplish a quick exit when Cates' voice cut through the store: 'Hey, boy, fetch me a dipper of water from that bucket over there!'

Cates was gazing directly at Tom, the eyes taunting, menacing. Tom's insides congealed as, under the threat of a white man's direct order, he walked stony-faced to the bucket and returned with a dipper of water. Cates drank it at a gulp, his small eyes over the dipper's rim now on Chicken George, who stood with his head slowly shaking. Cates thrust the dipper towards him. 'I'm still thirsty!'

Avoiding any quick moves, Chicken George drew from his pocket his carefully folded freedom paper and handed it to Cates. Cates unfolded it and read. 'What're you doin' in our county?' he asked coldly.

'He my pappy,' Tom put in quickly. Above all, he did not want his father attempting any defiant talk. 'He jes' been give his freedom.'

'Livin' with y'all now over at Mr Murray's place?'

'Yassuh.'

Glancing about at his white customers, Cates exclaimed, 'Mr Murray ought to know the laws of this state better'n that!'

Uncertain what he meant, neither Tom nor George said anything.

Suddenly Cates' manner was almost affable. 'Well, when y'all boys get home, be shore to tell Mr Murray I'll be out to talk with him 'fore long.' With the sound of white men's laughter behind them, Tom and Chicken George quickly left the store.

It was the next afternoon when Cates galloped down the driveway of the Murray big house. A few minutes later, Tom glanced up from his forge and saw Irene running towards the shop. Hurrying past his few waiting customers, he went to meet her.

'Mammy 'Tilda say let you know massa an' dat white man on de porch steady talkin'. Leas' de man keep talkin' an' massa jes' noddin' an' noddin'.'

'Awright, honey,' said Tom. 'Don' be scairt. You git on back now.' Irene fled.

Then, after about another half hour, she brought word that Cates had left, 'an' now massa an' missis got dey heads togedder.'

But nothing happened until Matilda was serving supper to Massa and Missis Murray, whom she saw were eating in a strained silence. Finally, when she brought their dessert and coffee, Massa Murray said, in a tight voice, 'Matilda, tell your husband I want to see him out on the porch right away.'

'Yassuh, Massa.'

She found Chicken George with Tom down at the blacksmith shop. Chicken George forced a laugh when he got the message. 'Reckon he might want to see if I git 'im some fightin' roosters!'

Adjusting his scarf and tilting his derby to a jauntier angle, he walked briskly towards the big house. Massa Murray was waiting there, seated in a rocker on the porch. Chicken George stopped in the yard at the foot of the stairs.

' 'Tilda say you wants to see me, suh.'

'Yes, I do, George. I'll come right to the point. Your family has brought Missis Murray and me much happiness here—'

'Yassuh,' George put in, 'an' dey sho' speaks de highes' of y'all, too, Massa!'

The massa firmed his voice. 'But I'm afraid we're going to have to solve a problem – concerning you.' He paused. 'I understand that in Burlington yesterday you met Mr J. D. Cates, our former county sheriff—'

'Yassa, reckon could say I met 'im, yassa.'

'Well, you probably know Mr Cates has visited me today. He brought to my attention a North Carolina law that forbids any freed black from staying within the state for more than sixty days, or he must be re-enslaved.'

It took a moment to sink in. Chicken George stared disbelievingly at Massa Murray. He couldn't speak.

'I'm really sorry, boy. I know it don't seem fair to you.'

'Do it seem fair to you, Massa Murray?'

The massa hesitated. 'No, to tell you the truth. But the law is the law.' He paused. 'But if you would want to choose to stay here, I'll guarantee you'll be treated well. You have my word on that.'

'Yo' word, Massa Murray?' George's eyes were impassive.

That night George and Matilda lay under their quilt, hands touching, both staring up at the ceiling. ' 'Tilda,' he said after a long while, 'guess ain't nothin' to do but stay. Seem like runnin's all I ever done.'

'Naw, George.' She shook her head slowly back and forth. ' 'Cause you de firs' one us ever free. You got to *stay* free, so us have somebody free in dis family. You jes' can't go back to bein' a slave!'

Chicken George began to cry. And Matilda was weeping with him. Two evenings later, she was not feeling well enough to join him in having supper with Tom and Irene in their small cabin. The conversation turned to their child, which was due within two weeks, and Chicken George grew solemn.

'Be sho' y'all tells dat chile 'bout our fam'ly, y'all hear me?'

'Pappy, ain't none my chilluns gon' grow up widdout knowin'.' Tom strained a smile. 'I reckon if I don' tell 'em, Gran'mammy Kizzy come back to set me straight.'

There was silence for a while as the three of them sat staring at the fire.

Finally Chicken George spoke again.

'Me an' 'Tilda was countin'. I got forty more days 'fo' I has to leave, 'cordin' to what de law say. But I been thinkin' ain't no good time to go. Ain't no point keep jes' puttin' off—'

He sprang up from his chair, fiercely embracing Tom and Irene. 'I be back!' he rasped brokenly. 'Take care one 'nother!' He bolted through the door.

110

It was early in November of 1860, and Tom was hurrying to finish his last blacksmithing task before darkness fell. He made it. Then, banking the fire in his forge, he trudged wearily home to have supper with Irene, who was nursing their baby girl, Maria, now half a year old. But they ate wordlessly, because Irene elected not to interrupt his thoughtful silence. And afterwards they joined the rest of the family crowded into Matilda's cabin, cracking and shelling hickory nuts that she and Irene – who was again pregnant – had ben collecting for use in the special cakes and pies they planned to bake for Christmas and New Year.

Tom sat listening to the light conversation without comment – or even seeming to hear – and then, finally, during a lull, he leaned forwards in his chair and spoke: 'Y'all 'member different times I'se said white mens talkin' 'roun' my shop done been cussin' an' carryin' on 'bout dat Massa Lincoln? Well, wish y'all coulda heared 'em today, 'cause he been 'lected Pres'dent. Dey claim now he gon' be up dere in de White House 'gainst de South an anybody keepin' slaves.'

'Well,' said Matilda, 'I be primed to hear whatever Massa Murray got to say 'bout it. He sho' been steady tellin' missis gwine be big trouble less'n de North an' South git dey differences settled, one way or 'nother.'

'Different things I've heared,' Tom went on, 'whole lots mo' folks dan we thinks is 'gainst slavin'. Ain't all of 'em up Nawth, neither. I couldn't hardly keep my min' on what I was doin' today, I been studyin' on it so hard. Seem like too much to b'lieve, but it could come a day won't *be* no mo' slaves.'

'Well, *we* sho' won't live to see it,' said Ashford sourly.

'But maybe *she* will,' said Virgil, nodding towards Irene's baby.

'Don't seem likely,' said Irene, 'much as I like to b'lieve it. You put together all de slaves in de South, wid even jes' fiel' hands bringin' eight an' nine hunnud dollars apiece, dat's mo' money'n God's got! Plus dat, we does all de work.' She looked at Tom. 'You know white folks ain't gwine give dat up.'

'Not widdout a fight,' said Ashford. 'An' dey's lot's more dem dan us. So how we gwine win?'

'But if'n you talkin' 'bout de whole country,' said Tom, 'it might be jes' many folks 'gainst slavery as fo' it.'

'Trouble is dem what's 'gainst it ain't here where we is,' Virgil said, and Ashford nodded, agreeing with someone for a change.

'Well, if'n Ashford right 'bout a fight, all dat could change real fast,' said Tom.

In early December, soon after Massa and Missis Murray returned home in their buggy from dinner at a neighbouring big house one night, Matilda hurried from the big house to Tom and Irene's cabin. 'What do "seceded" mean?' she asked, and when they shrugged their

shoulders, she went on. 'Well, massa says dat's what South Ca'liny jes'
done. Massa soun' like it mean dey's pullin' out'n de Newnited States.'

'How dey gon' pull out de country dey's in?' Tom said.

'White folks do anythin',' said Irene.

Tom hadn't told them, but throughout the day, he had been listening to his white customers fuming that they would be 'wadin' knee deep in blood' before they'd give in to the North on something they called 'states' rights', along with the right to own slaves.

'I ain't wantin' to scare y'all none,' he told Matilda and Irene, 'but I really b'leeves it gon' be a war.'

'Oh, my Lawd! Where'bouts it gon' be, Tom?'

'Mammy, ain't no special war grounds, like church or picnic grounds!'

'Well, I sho' hope don't be nowhere roun' here!'

Irene scoffed at them both. 'Don't y'all ax me to b'lieve no white folks gwine git to killin' one 'nother over niggers.'

But as the days passed, the things Tom overheard at his shop convinced him that he was right. Some of it he told his family about, but some not, for he didn't want to alarm them unnecessarily, and he hadn't decided himself whether he dreaded the events he saw coming – or hoped for them. But he could sense the family's uneasiness increasing anyway, along with the traffic on the main road, as white riders and buggies raced back and forth past the plantation faster and faster and in ever-growing numbers. Almost every day someone would turn into the driveway and engage Massa Murray in conversation, Matilda employed every ruse to mop and dust where she could listen in. And slowly, over the next few weeks, in the nightly family exchanges, the white people's frightened, angry talk gradually encouraged all of them to dare to believe that if there *was* a war – and the 'Yankees' won – it was just possible that they might really be set free.

An increasing number of the blacks who delivered blacksmithing jobs to Tom told him that their massas and missies were becoming suspicious and secretive, lowering their voices and even spelling out words when even their oldest and closest servants entered a room.

'Is dey actin' anyways 'culiar in de big house roun' you, Mammy?' Tom asked Matilda.

'Not no whisperin' or spellin' or sich as dat,' she said. 'But dey sho' is done commence to shift off sudden to talkin' 'bout crops or dinner parties jes' soon's I come in.'

'Bes' thing for us all to do,' said Tom, 'is act dumb as we can, like we ain't even heard 'bout what gwine on.'

Matilda considered that – but decided against it. And one evening after she had served the Murrays their desserts, she came into the dining-room and exclaimed, wringing her hands, 'Lawd, Massa an' Missy, y'all 'scuse me, jes' got to say my chilluns an' me is hearin' all dis talk goin' roun', an' we be's mighty scared o' dem Yankees, an' we sho' hopes you gwine take care of us if'n dey's trouble.' With satisfaction, she noted the swift expressions of approval and relief crossing their faces.

'Well, you're right to be scared, for those Yankees are certainly no friends of yours!' said Missis Murray.

'But don't you worry,' said the massa reassuringly, 'there's not going to be any trouble.'

Even Tom had to laugh when Matilda described the scene. And he shared with the family another laugh when he told them how he had heard that a stablehand in Melville Township had handled the ticklish matter. Asked by his massa whose side he'd be on if a war came, the stablehand had said, 'You's seed two dogs fightin' over a bone, Massa? Well, us niggers be's dat bone.'

Christmas, then New Year came and went with hardly any thought of festivity throughout Alamance County. Every few days Tom's customers would arrive with news of secessions by still more among the southern states – first Mississippi, then Florida, Alabama, Georgia, and Louisiana, all during the month of January 1861, and on the first day of February, Texas. And all of them proceeded to join a 'confederacy' of southern states headed by their own President, a man named Jefferson Davis.

'Dat Massa Davis an' whole passels of other southern senators, congressmens, an' high mens in de Army,' Tom reported to the family, 'is resignin' to come on back home.'

'Tom, it's done got closer'n dat to us,' exclaimed Matilda. 'A man come today an' tol' massa dat Ol' Jedge Ruffin leavin' Haw River tomorrow to 'tend a big peace conference in dat Washington, D.C.!'

But a few days later, Tom heard his blacksmithing customers saying that Judge Ruffin had returned sadly reporting the peace conference a failure, ending in explosive arguments between the younger delegates from the North and the South. A black buggy driver then told Tom that he had learned firsthand from the Alamance County courthouse janitor that a mass meeting of nearly fourteen hundred local white men had been held – with Massa Murray among them, Tom knew – and that Massa Holt, Irene's former owner, and others as important, had shouted that war must be averted and pounded

581

tables calling anyone who would join the Confederates 'traitors'. The janitor also told him that a Massa Giles Mebane was elected to take to a state secession convention the four-to-one vote in Alamance County to remain within the Union.

It became hard for the family to keep up with all that was reported each night either by Tom or Matilda. On a single day in March, news came that President Lincoln had been sworn in, that a Confederate flag had been unveiled at a huge ceremony in Montgomery, Alabama, and that the Confederacy's President, Jeff Davis, had declared the African slave trade abolished; feeling as they knew he did about slavery, the family couldn't understand why. Only days later, tension rose to a fever pitch with the announcement that the North Carolina legislature had called for an immediate twenty thousand military volunteers.

Early on the Friday morning of 12 April 1861 Massa Murray had driven off to a meeting in the town of Mebane, and Lewis, James, Ashford, L'il Kizzy, and Mary were out in the field busily transplanting young tobacco shoots when they began to notice an unusually large number of white riders passing along the main road at full gallop. When one rider briefly slowed, angrily shaking his fist in their direction and shouting at them something they couldn't understand, Virgil sent L'il Kizzy racing from the field to tell Tom, Matilda, and Irene that something big must have happened.

The usually calm Tom lost his temper when Kizzy could tell him no more than she did. 'Shouted *what* at y'all?' he demanded. But she could only repeat that the horseman had been too far away for them to hear clearly.

'I better take de mule an' go fin' out!' Tom said.

'But you ain't got a travellin' pass!' shouted Virgil as he went riding down the driveway.

'Got to take dat chance!' Tom shouted back.

By the time he reached the main road, it was starting to resemble a racetrack, and he knew that the riders must be headed for Company Shops, where the telegraph office received important news over wires strung high atop poles. As they raced along, some of the horsemen were exchanging shouts with each other; but they didn't seem to know much more than he did. As he passed poor whites and blacks running on foot, Tom *knew* the worst had happened, but his heart clenched anyway when he reached the railroad repair yard settlement and saw the great jostling crowd around the telegraph office.

Leaping to the ground and tethering his mule, he ran in a wide circle around the edge of the mob of angrily gesturing white men

582

who kept glancing up at the telegraph wires as if they expected to see something coming over the wires. Off to one side, he reached a cluster of blacks and heard what they were jabbering: 'Massa Linkum sho' gon' fight over us now!' ... 'Look like de Lawd care sump'n 'bout niggers after all!' ... 'Jes' can't b'lieve it! ... 'Free, Lawd, free!'

Drawing one old man aside, Tom learned what had happened. South Carolina troops were firing on the Federal Fort Sumter in Charleston Harbor, and twenty-nine other Federal bases in the South had been seized on the orders of President Davis. The war had actually begun. Even after Tom returned home with the news – arriving safely before the massa got home – the black grapevine was almost choked with bulletins for weeks. After two days of siege, they learned, Fort Sumter had surrendered with fifteen dead on both sides, and over a thousand slaves were sandbagging the entrances to Charleston Harbor. After informing President Lincoln that he would get no North Carolina troops, North Carolina Governor John Ellis had pledged thousands with muskets to the Confederate Army. President Davis asked all southern white men between eighteen and thirty-five to volunteer to fight for up to three years, and ordered that of each ten male slaves on any plantation, one should be turned over for unpaid war labour. General Robert E. Lee resigned from the army of the United States to command the army of Virginia. And it was claimed that every government building in Washington, D.C., was thick with armed soldiers and iron and cement barricades in fear of southern invasion forces.

White men throughout Alamance County, meanwhile, were lining up by the scores to sign up and fight. Tom heard from a black wagon-driver that his massa had called in his most trusted big-house servant and told him, 'Now, boy, I'm expectin' you to look out after missis and the children till I get back, you hear?' And a number of neighbouring whites dropped in to shoe up their horses before assembling at Mebane Township with the rest of the newly formed 'Hawfields Company' of Alamance County to board the train that waited to take them to a training camp at Charlotte. A black buggy-driver who had taken his massa and his missy there to see off their eldest son described the scene for Tom: the womenfolk bitterly weeping, their boys leaning from the train's windows, making the air ring with rebel yells, many of them shouting 'Goin' to ship those sonsabitchin' Yankees an' be back 'fore breakfast!' 'Young massa,' said the buggy-driver, 'had on his new grey uniform, an' he was a-cryin' jes' hard as ol' massa and missy was, an' dey commence to kissin' and huggin' till dey finally jes' kind o' broke apart from one 'nother, jes' standin' in de road clearin' dey throats an' snifflin'. Ain't no need me telling no lie, I was acryin', too!'

111

Within their lamplit cabin late that night, now for a second time Tom sat by the bed with Irene convulsively gripping his hand and when abruptly her moans of suffering in labour advanced to a piercing scream, he went bolting outside to get his mother. But despite the hour, intuitively Matilda had not been asleep and also had heard the scream. He met her already rushing from her cabin, shouting back over her shoulder at a bug-eyed L'il Kizzy and Mary. 'Bile some kittles o' water an' git it to me quick!' Within the next few moments, the other adults of the family had also popped from their cabins, and Tom's five brothers joined his nervous pacing and wincing while the sounds of Irene's anguish continued. In the first streaks of dawn when an infant's shrill cry was heard, Tom's brothers converged upon him, pounding his back, wringing his hands – even Ashford – then in a little while a grinning Matilda stepped through the cabin door, exclaiming, 'Tom, y'all got anudder li'l ol' gal!'

After a while there in the brightening morning, first Tom, then the rest of the family became a procession trooping in to see the wan but smiling Irene and the crinkly-faced brown infant. Matilda had taken the news into the big house, where she hurriedly cooked breakfast, and right after Massa and Missis Murray finished eating, they also came to the slave row to see with delight the new infant born into their ownership. Tom readily agreed to Irene's wish to name this second daughter 'Ellen' after Irene's mother. He was so jubilant that he had become a father again that he didn't remember until later how much he had wanted a boy.

Matilda waited until the next afternoon to drop by the blacksmithing shop. 'Now, Tom, you know what I'm thinkin' 'bout?' she asked, Smiling at her, Tom said, 'You late, Mammy. I done already tol' eve'ybody – an' was fixin' to tell you – to come squeeze in de cabin dis comin' Sadday night an' I'se gwine tell dis chile de fam'ly story jes' like I done wid Maria, when she born.' As planned, the family did gather, and Tom continued the tradition that had been passed down from the late Gran'mammy Kizzy and Chicken George, and there was much joking afterwards that if ever anyone among them should neglect to relate the family chronicle to any new infant, they could surely expect to hear from the ghost of Gran'mammy Kizzy.

But even the excitement of Tom and Irene's second child soon diminished as a war's swiftly paced events gained momentum. As Tom busily shod horses and mules and made and repaired tools, he kept his ears strained to hear every possible scrap of the exchanges of talk among the white customers gathered before his shop, and he winced with disappointment at their successive jubilant reports of Confederate triumphs. Particularly a battle the white men called 'Bull Run' had set the white customers hollering, beating each others' backs and throwing their hats into the air as they shouted such things as 'What Yankees wasn't left dead or hurt run for their lives!' The jubilance was repeated over a big Yankee loss at a 'Wilson's Creek' in Missouri, then not long after when at a 'Ball's Bluff' in Virginia, hundreds of Yankees were left dead, including a bullet-riddled general who had been a close personal friend of President Lincoln. 'Dem white mens was all jumpin' up an down an' laughin' dat Pres'dent Lincoln heared it an' commence to cryin' like a baby,' Tom told his sombre family. By the end of 1861 – when Alamance County had sent twelve companies off into the various fighting – he hated to report more than a little of what he was continuing to hear, for it only deepened his family's gloom, along with his own. 'Lawd knows sho' don't soun' like we's gwine git free, keep gwine like dis!' said Matilda, glancing about one late Sunday afternoon's semicircle of downcast faces. No one made any comment for a long while; then Lilly Sue said, as she nursed her sickly son Uriah, 'All dat freedom talk! I done jes' give up any mo' hope!'

Then a spring 1862 afternoon, when a rider came cantering down the Murray driveway, wearing the Confederate officer's grey uniform, even from some distance he seemed vaguely familiar to Tom. As the rider drew nearer, with a shock Tom realized that it was the former County Sheriff Cates, the feed-store owner, whose counsel to Massa Murray had forced Chicken George to leave the state. With growing apprehension, Tom saw Cates dismount and disappear within the big house; then before long Matilda came hurrying to the blacksmith shop, her brows furrowed with worry. 'Massa want you, Tom. He talkin' wid dat no-good feed-store Massa Cates. What you reckon dey wants?'

Tom's mind had been racing with possibilities, including having heard his customers saying that many planters had taken slaves to battles with them, and others had volunteered the war services of their slaves who knew trades, especially such as carpentry, leather-working, and blacksmithing. But he said as calmly as he could, 'Jes' don' know, Mammy. I go find out is de bes' thing, I reckon.' Composing himself, Tom walked heavily towards the big house.

Massa Murray said, 'Tom, you know Major Cates.'

'Yassuh.' Tom did not look at Cates, whose gaze he could feel upon him.

'Major Cates tells me he's commanding a new cavalry unit being trained at Company Shops, and they need you to do their horse-shoeing.'

Tom swallowed. He heard his words come with a hollow sound. 'Massa, dat mean I go to de war?'

It was Cates who scornfully answered. 'No niggers will go any-where I'm fighting, to fly if they as much as hear a bullet! We just need you to shoe horses where we're training.'

Tom gulped his relief. 'Yassuh.'

'The major and I have discussed it,' said Massa Murray. 'You'll work a week for his cavalry, then a week here for me, for the dur-ation of the war, which it looks like won't be long.' Massa Murray looked at Major Cates. 'When would you want him to start?'

'Tomorrow morning, if that's all right, Mr Murray.'

'Why, certainly, it's our duty for the South!' said Massa Murray briskly, seeming pleased at his chance to help the war effort.

'I hope the nigger understands his place,' said Cates. 'The military is no soft plantation.'

'Tom knows how to conduct himself, I'm sure.' Massa Murray looked his confidence at Tom. 'Tonight I'll write out a travelling pass and let Tom take one of my mules and report to you tomorrow morning.'

'That's fine!' Cates said, then he glanced at Tom. 'We've got horseshoes, but you bring your tools, and I'll tell you now we want good, quick work. We've got no time to waste!'

'Yassuh.'

Carrying a hastily assembled portable horseshoeing kit on the mule's back, when Tom approached the railroad repair settlement at Company Shops, he saw the previously lightly wooded surrounding acres now dotted with long, orderly rows of small tents. Closer, he heard bugles sounding and the flat cracking of muskets being fired; then he tensed when he saw a mounted guard galloping towards him.

'Don't you see this is the Army, nigger? Where do you think you're headed?' the soldier demanded.

'Major Cates done tol' me come here an' shoe hosses,' Tom said nervously.

'Well, the cavalry's over yonder—' the guard pointed. 'Git! Before you git shot!'

Booting the mule away, Tom soon came over a small rise and saw four lines of horsemen executing manouvres and formations, and behind the officers who were shouting orders, he distinguished Major Cates wheeling and prancing on his horse. He was aware when the major saw him there on the mule and made a gesture, whereupon another mounted soldier came galloping in his direction. Tom reined up and waited.

'You the blacksmith nigger?'

'Yassuh.'

The guard pointed towards a small cluster of tents. 'You'll stay and work down by those garbage tents. Soon as you get set up, we'll be sending horses.'

The horses in dire need of new metal shoes came in an unending procession across Tom's first week of serving the Confederate cavalry, and from first dawn until darkness fell, he shod them until the underside of hooves seemed to become a blur in his mind. Everything he overheard the young cavalrymen say made it sound even more certain that the Yankees were being routed in every battle, and it was a weary, disconsolate Tom who returned home to spend a week serving the regular customers for Massa Murray.

He found the women of slave row in a great state of upset. Through the previous full night and morning, Lilly Sue's sickly son Uriah had been thought lost. Only shortly before Tom's return Matilda, while sweeping the front porch, had heard strange noises, and investigating she had found the tearful, hungry boy hiding under the big house. 'I was jes' tryin' to hear what massa an' missy was sayin' 'bout freein' us niggers, but under dere I couldn't hear nothin' atall,' Uriah had said, and now both Matilda and Irene were busily trying to comfort the embarrassed and distraught Lilly Sue, whose always strange child had caused such a commotion. Tom helped to calm her, then described to the family his own week's experience. 'Ain't hardly nothin' I seed or heared make it look no better,' he concluded. Irene tried a futile effort to make them all feel at least a little better. 'Ain't never been free, so ain't gwine miss it nohow,' she said. But Matilda said, 'Tell y'all de truth, I'se jes' plain scairt somehow us gwine wind up worse off'n we was befo'.'

The same sense of foreboding pervaded Tom as he began his second week of horseshoeing for the Confederate cavalry. During the third night, as he lay awake, thinking, he heard a noise that seemed to be coming from one of the adjoining garbage tents. Nervously Tom groped, and his fingers grasped his blacksmithing hammer. He tipped out into the faint moonlight to investigate. He was about to conclude that he had heard some foraging small animal when he glimpsed the shadowy human figure backing from the garbage tent starting to eat something in his hands. Tipping closer, Tom completely surprised a thin, sallow-faced white youth. In the moonlight for a second, they stared at each other, before the white youth went bolting away. But not ten yards distant, the fleeing figure stumbled over something that made a great clatter as he recovered himself and disappeared into the night. Then armed guards who came rushing with muskets and lanterns saw Tom standing there holding his hammer.

'What you stealin', nigger?'

Tom sensed instantly the trouble he was in. To directly deny the accusation would call a white man a liar – even more dangerous than stealing. Tom all but babbled in his urgency of knowing that he had to make them believe him. 'Heared sump'n an' come lookin' an' seed a white man in de garbage, Massa, an' he broke an' run.'

Exchanging incredulous expressions, the two guards broke into scornful laughter. 'We look that dumb to you, nigger?' demanded one. 'Major Cates said keep special eye on you! You're going to meet him soon's he wakes up in the morning, boy!' Keeping their gazes fixed on Tom, the guards held a whispered consultation.

The second guard said, 'Boy, drop that hammer!' Tom's fist instinctively clenched the hammer's handle. Advancing a step, the guard levelled his musket at Tom's belly. 'Drop it!'

Tom's fingers loosed and he heard the hammer thud against the ground. The guards motioned him to march ahead of them for quite a distance before commanding him to stop in a small clearing before a large tent where another armed guard stood. 'We're on patrol an' caught this nigger stealin',' said one of the first two and nodded towards the large tent. 'We'd of took care of him, but the major told us to watch him an' report anything to him personal. We'll come back time the major gets up.'

The two guards left Tom being scowled at by the new one, who rasped, 'Lay down flat on your back, nigger. If you move you're dead.' Tom lay down as directed. The ground was cold. He speculated on what might happen, pondered his chances of escape, then the consequences if he did. He watched the dawn come; then the first two guards returned as noises within the tent said that Major Cates had risen. One of the guards called out, 'Permission to see you, Major?'

'What about?' Tom heard the voice growl from within.

'Last night caught that blacksmith nigger stealing, sir!'

There was a pause. 'Where is he now?'

'Prisoner right outside, sir!'

'Coming right out!'

After another minute, the tent flap opened and Major Cates stepped outside and stood eyeing Tom as a cat would a bird. 'Well, highfalutin' nigger, tell me you been stealin'! You know how we feel about that in the Army?'

'Massa—' Passionately Tom told the truth of what had happened, ending, 'He was mighty hungry, Massa, rummagin' in de garbage.'

'Now you got a white man eating garbage! You forget we've met before, plus I know your kind, nigger! Took care of that no-good free nigger pappy of yours, but you slipped loose. Well, this time I got you under the rules of war.'

With incredulous eyes, Tom saw Cates go striding to snatch a horse-whip hanging from the pommel of his saddle atop a nearby post. Tom's eyes darted, weighing escape, but all three guards levelled their muskets at him as Cates advanced; his face contorted, raising the braided whip, he brought it down lashing like fire across Tom's shoulders again, again . . .

When Tom went stumbling back in humiliation and fury to where he had been shoeing the horses, uncaring what might happen if he was challenged, he seized his kit of tools, sprang onto his mule, and did not stop until he reached the big house. Massa Murray listened to what had happened, and he was reddened with anger as Tom finished. 'Don't care what, Massa, I ain't gwine back.'

'You all right now, Tom?'

'I ain't hurt none, 'cept in my mind, if dat's what you means, suh.'

'Well, I'm going to give you my word. If the major shows up wanting trouble, I'm prepared to go to his commanding general, if necessary. I'm truly sorry this has happened. Just go back out to the shop and do your work.' Massa Murray hesitated. 'Tom, I know you're not the oldest, but Missis Murray and I regard you as the head of your family. And we want you to tell them that we look forward to us all enjoying the rest of our lives together just as soon as we get these Yankees whipped. They're nothing but human devils!'

'Yassuh,' Tom said. He thought that it was impossible for a massa to perceive that being owned by anyone could never be enjoyable. As the weeks advanced into the spring of 1862, Irene again became pregnant, and the news that Tom heard daily from the local white men who were his customers gave him a feeling that Alamance County seemed within the quiet centre of a hurricane of war being fought in other places. He heard of a Battle of Shiloh where Yankees and Confederates had killed or injured nearly forty thousand apiece of each other, until survivors had to pick their way among the dead, and so many wounded needed amputations that a huge pile of severed human limbs grew in the yard of the nearest Mississippi hospital. That one sounded like a draw, but there seemed no question that the Yankees were losing most of the major battles. Near the end of August Tom heard jubilant descriptions of how in a second Battle of Bull Run, the Yankees had retreated with two generals among their dead, and thousands of their troops straggling back into Washington, D.C., where civilians were said to be fleeing in panic as clerks barricaded federal buildings, and both the Treasury's and the banks' money was being shipped to New York City while a gunboat lay under steam in the Potomac River, ready to evacuate President Lincoln and his staff. Then at Harpers Ferry hardly two weeks later, a Confederate force under General Stonewall Jackson took eleven thousand Yankee prisoners.

'Tom, I jes' don' want to hear no mo' 'bout dis terrible war,' said Irene one evening in September as they sat staring into their fireplace after he had told her of two three-mile-long rows of Confederate and Yankee soldiers having faced and killed each other at a place called Antietam. 'I sets here wid my belly full of our third young'un, an' it somehow jes' don' seem right dat all us ever talks 'bout any mo' is jes' fightin' an' killin'—'

Simultaneously then they both glanced behind them at the cabin door, having heard a sound so slight that neither of them paid it any further attention. But when the sound came again, now clearly a faint knock, Irene, who sat closer, got up and opened the door, and Tom's brow raised hearing a white man's pleading voice. 'Begging pardon. You got anything I can eat? I'm hungry.' Turning about, Tom all but fell from his chair, recognizing the face of the white youth he had surprised among the garbage cans at the cavalry post. Quickly controlling himself, suspicious of some trick, Tom sat rigidly, hearing his unsuspecting wife say, 'Well, we ain't got nothin' but some cold cornbread left from supper.'

'Sho' would 'preciate that, I ain't hardly et in two days.'

Deciding that it was only bizarre coincidence, Tom now rose from his chair and moved to the door. 'Been doin' a l'il mo'n jes' beggin', ain't you?'

For half a moment the youth stared quizzically at Tom, then his eyes flew wide; he disappeared so fast that Irene stood astounded – and she was even more so when Tom told her whom she had been about to feed.

The whole of slave row became aware of the incredible occurrence on the next night when – with both Tom and Irene among the family gathering – Matilda mentioned that just after breakfast, 'some scrawny po' white boy' had suddenly appeared at the kitchen screen door piteously begging for food; she had given him a bowl of leftover cold stew for which he had thanked her profusely before disappearing, then later she had found the cleaned bowl sitting on the kitchen steps. After Tom explained who the youth was, he said, 'Since you feedin' 'im, I 'speck he still hangin' roun'. Probably jes' sleepin' somewhere out in de woods. I don't trust him nohow; first thing we know, somebody be in trouble.'

'Ain't it de truth!' exclaimed Matilda. 'Well, I tell you one thing, if he show me his face ag'in, I gwine ax him to wait an' let 'im b'leeve I'se fixin' 'im sump'n while I goes an' tells massa.'

The trap was sprung perfectly when the youth reappeared the following morning. Alerted by Matilda, Massa Murray hurried through the front door and around the side of the house as Matilda hastened back to the kitchen in time to overhear the waiting youth caught by total surprise. 'What are you hanging around here for?' demanded Massa Murray. But the youth neither panicked nor even seemed flustered. 'Mister, I'm just wore out from travellin' an' stayin' hungry. You can't hold that 'gainst no man, an' your niggers been good enough to feed me something.' Massa Murray hesitated, then said, 'Well, I can sympathize, but you ought to know how hard the times are now, so we can't be feeding extra mouths. You just have to move on.' Then Matilda heard the youth's voice abjectly pleading, 'Mister, please let me stay. I ain't scared of no work. I just don't want to starve. I'll do any work you got.'

Massa Murray said, 'There's nothing for you here to do. My niggers work the fields.'

'I was born and raised in the fields. I'll work harder'n your niggers, Mister – to just eat regular,' the youth insisted.

'What's your name and where you come here from, boy?'

'George Johnson. From South Carolina, sir. The war pretty near tore up where I lived. I tried to join up but they said I'm too young, I'm just turned sixteen. War ruint our crops an' everything so bad, look like even no rabbits left. An' I left, too, figgered somewhere – anywhere else – had to be better. But seem like the only somebody even give me the time of day been your niggers.'

Matilda could sense that the youth's story had moved Massa Murray. Incredulously then she heard, 'Would you know anything at all about being an overseer?'

'Ain't never tried that.' The George Johnson youth sounded startled. Then he added hesitantly, 'But I told you ain't nothin' I won't try.'

Matilda eased yet closer to the edge of the screen door to hear better in her horror.

'I've always liked the idea of an overseer, even though my niggers do a good job raising my crops. I'd be willing to try you out for just bed and board to start – to see how it works out.'

'Mister – sir, what's your name?'

'Murray,' the massa said.

'Well, you got yourself an overseer, Mr Murray.'

Matilda heard the massa chuckle. He said, 'There's an empty shed over behind the barn you can move into. Where's your stuff?'

'Sir, all the stuff I've got, I've got on,' said George Johnson.

The shocking news spread through the family with a thunderbolt's force. 'Jes' couldn't b'leeve what I was hearin'!' exclaimed Matilda, ending her incredible report, and the family's members fairly exploded. 'Massa mus' be goin' crazy!' . . . 'Ain't we run his place fine ourselves?' . . . 'Jes' 'cause dey both white, dat's all!' . . . ' 'Speck he gwine see dat po' cracker different time we sees to it 'nough things go wrong!'

But as furious as they were, from their first direct confrontation with the impostor out in the field on the following morning, he immediately made it difficult for their anger to remain at a fever pitch. Already out in the field when they arrived led by Virgil, the scrawny, sallow George Johnson came walking to meet them. His thin face was reddened and his Adam's apple bobbed as he said, 'I can't blame y'all none for hatin' me, but I can ask y'all to wait a little to see if I turn out bad as y'all think. You the first niggers I ever had anything to do with, but seem like to me y'all got black same as I got white, an' I judge anybody by how they act. I know one thing, y'all fed me when I was hungry, and it was plenty of white folks hadn't. Now seem like Mr Murray got his mind set on having a overseer, and I know y'all could help him git rid of me, but I figger you do that, you be takin' your chances the next one he git might be a whole lot worse.'

None of the family seemed to know what to say in response. There seemed nothing to do except filter away and set to work, all of them covertly observing George Johnson proceeding to work as hard as they, if not harder – in fact, he seemed obsessed to prove his sincerity.

Tom's and Irene's third daughter – Viney – was born at the end of the newcomer's first week. By now out in the field, George Johnson boldly sat down with the members of the family at lunchtimes, appearing not to notice how Ashford conspicuously got up, scowling, and moved elsewhere. 'Y'all see I don't know nothin' 'bout overseein', so y'all needs to help me along,' George Johnson told them frankly. 'It would be no good for Mr Murray to come out here an' figger I ain't doin' the job like he want.'

The idea of training their overseer amused even the usually solemn Tom when it was discussed in the slave row that night, and all agreed that the responsibility naturally belonged to Virgil, since he had always run the field work. 'First thing,' he said to George Johnson, 'you gon' have to change whole lot o' yo' ways. 'Cose, wid all us lookin' all de time, massa ain't likely to git close fo' us can give you a signal. Den you have to hurry up an' git 'way from too close roun' us. Reckon you knows white folks an' 'specially oberseers ain't s'posed to seem like deys close wid niggers.'

'Well, in South Carolina where I come from, seem like the niggers never got too close to white folks,' George Johnson said.

'Well, dem niggers is smart!' said Virgil. 'De nex' thing, a massa want to feel like his oberseer makin' his niggers work harder'n dey did befo' de oberseer come. You got to learn how to holler, "Git to work, you niggers!" an' sich as dat. An' anytime you's roun' massa or any mo' white folks, don' never call us by our names de way you does. You got to learn how to growl an' cuss an' soun' real mean, to make massa feel like you ain't too easy an' got us goin'.'

When Massa Murray did next visit his fields. George Johnson made strong efforts, hollering, cursing, even threatening everyone in the field, from Virgil down. 'Well, how they doing?' asked Massa Murray. 'Pretty fair for niggers been on their own,' George Johnson drawled, 'but I 'speck another week or two ought to git 'em shaped up awright.'

The family rocked with laughter that night, imitating George Johnson, along with Massa Murray's evident pleasure. Afterwards when the mirth had waned, George Johnson quietly told them how it had been to be dirt-poor for all of his earlier life, even before his family had been routed with their fields ruined by the war, until he had sought some new, better life. 'He 'bout de only white man we ever gwine meet dat's jes' plain honest 'bout hisself,' Virgil expressed their collective appraisal.

'I tell de truth, I 'joys listenin' to 'im talk,' said Lilly Sue, and L'il George scoffed, 'He talk like any other cracker. What make him different he de firs' one I ever seen ain't try to act like sump'n he wasn't. De mos' is so shame of what dey is.' Mary laughed. 'Well, dis one ain't shame, not long as he keep eatin' de way he is.'

'Soun' like to me y'all done really taken a likenin' to Ol' George,' said Matilda. More laughter rose at their homemade overseer's new nickname, 'Ol' George', since he was so ridiculously young. And Matilda was correct: incredibly enough, they had come to like him genuinely.

112

The North and the South seemed locked together like stags in mortal combat. Neither seemed able to mount a successful campaign to put the other away. Tom began to notice some despondency in his customers' conversations. It was a buoy to the hope yet strong in him for freedom.

The family plunged into intense speculation when Ol' George Johnson said mysteriously, 'Mr Murray done said I could go 'tend to some business. I be back jes' quick as I can.' Then the next morning he was gone.

'What you reckon it is?'

'Way he always talked, wasn't nothin' lef' to take care of where he come from.'

'Maybe sump'n to do wid his folks—'

'But he ain't mentioned no folks – leas'ways, not partic'lar.'

'He bound to got some somewhere.'

'Maybe he done 'cided to go jine de war.'

'Well, I sho' cain't see Ol' George wantin' to shoot nobody.'

' 'Speck he jes' finally got his belly full an' we done seen de las' o' him.'

'Oh, heish up, Ashford! You ain't never got nothin' good to say 'bout him or nobody else!'

Nearly a month had passed when one Sunday a whooping and hollering arose – for Ol' George was back, grinning shamefacedly, and with him was a painfully shy creature of a girl as sallow and scrawny as himself, and her eight-months pregnancy made her seem as if she had swallowed a pumpkin.

'This is my wife, Miss Martha,' Ol' George Johnson told them. 'Jes' befo' I left, we'd got married, an' I tol' 'er I'd be back when I found us somewhere. How come I hadn't said nothin' 'bout a wife was it was hard enough to find anybody willing to have jes' me.' He grinned at his Martha. 'Whyn't you say hello to the folks?'

Martha dutifully said hello to them all, and it seemed a long speech for her when she added, 'George tol' me a lot 'bout y'all.'

'Well, I hope whatever he tol' you was good!' Matilda said brightly, and Ol' George saw her glance a second time at Martha's extreme pregnancy.

'I ain't knowed when I left we had a baby comin'. I jes' kept havin' a feelin' I better git back. An' there she was in a family way.'

The fragile Martha seemed such a perfect match for Ol' George Johnson that the family felt their hearts going out to the pair of them.

'You mean you ain't even tol' Massa Murray?' asked Irene.

'Naw, I ain't. Jes' said I had some business same as I tol' y'all. If he want to run us off, we jes' have to go, that's all.'

'Well, I know massa ain't gwine feel like dat,' said Irene, and Matilda echoed, ' 'Cose he ain't. Massa ain't dat kind o' man.'

'Well, tell him I got to see him first chance,' said Ol' George Johnson to Matilda.

Leaving nothing to chance, Matilda first informed Missis Murray, somewhat dramatizing the situation. 'Missy, I know he a oberseer an' all dat, but him an' dat po' l'il wife o' his'n jes' scairt to death massa gwine make 'em leave 'cause he hadn't mentioned no wife befo' an' times is so hard an' all. An' her time ain't far off, neither.'

'Well, of course I can't make my husband's decisions, but I'm sure he'll not put them out—'

'Yes'm, I knowed y'all wouldn't, 'specially bein's how I 'speck she ain't no mo'n thirteen or fo'teen years ol', Missis, an' lookin' ready to have dat baby any minute, an' done jes' got here an' don't know nobody 'ceptin us – an' y'all.'

Missis Murray said, 'Well, as I say, it's not my affair, it's Mr Murray's decision. But I do feel certain they can stay on.'

Returning to the slave row, Matilda told a grateful Ol' George Johnson not to worry, that Missis Murray had expressed certainty there would be no problem. Then she hurried to Irene's cabin, where after quick consultation, the two of them ambled over to the converted small shed behind the barn where the Ol' George Johnsons were.

Irene knocked, and when Ol' George Johnson came to the door, she said. 'We worried 'bout yo' wife. Tell 'er we do y'alls cookin' an' washin', 'cause she got to save up what strength she got fo' her to have y'all's baby.'

'She sleep now. Sho' 'preciate it,' he said. ' 'Cause she been throwin' up a lot ever since we got here.'

'Ain't no wonder. She don't look to have hardly de strength of a bird,' said Irene. 'You ain't had no business bringin' her all dat long way right dis time nohow,' Matilda added severely.

'Tried my best to tell 'er that when I went back. But she wouldn't have it no other way.'

'S'pose sump'n would o' happened. You don't know nothin' in de worl' 'bout 'liverin' no baby!' exclaimed Matilda.

He said, 'I can't hardly believe I'm gon' be no daddy nohow.'

'Well, you sho' 'bout to!' Irene nearly laughed at Ol' George's worried expression, then she and Matilda turned and headed back to their cabins.

She and Matilda worried privately. 'De po' gal don' look noways right to me,' Matilda muttered in confidence. 'Can nigh see her bones. An' speck it 'way too late to git her built up right.'

'Feel like she gwine have a mighty hard time,' Irene prophesied. 'Lawd! I sho' ain't never thought I'd end up likin' no po' white folks!'

Less than two more weeks had passed when one midday Martha's pains began. The whole slave-row family heard her agony from within the shed, as Matilda and Irene laboured with her on through the night until shortly before the next noon. Finally when Irene emerged, her face told the haggard Ol' George Johnson even before her mouth could form the words. 'B'leeve Miss Martha gon' pull through. Yo' baby was a gal – but she dead.'

113

The late afternoon of the 1863 New Year's Day, Matilda came almost flying into the slave row. 'Y'all seen dat white man jes' rid in here? Y'all ain't gon' *b'leeve*! He is dere cussin' to massa it jes' come over de railroad telegraph wire Pres'dent Lincoln done signed 'Mancipation Proclamation dat set us *free*!'

The galvanizing news thrust the black Murrays among the millions more like them exulting wildly within the privacy of their cabins ... but with each passing week the joyous awaiting of the freedom dwindled, diminished, and finally receded into a new despair the more it became clear that within the steadily more bloodied, ravaged Confederacy the presidential order had activated nothing but even more bitter despising of President Lincoln.

So deep was the despair in the Murray slave row that despite Tom's intermittent reports of the Yankees winning major battles, including even the capture of Atlanta, they refused to build up their freedom hopes any more until towards the end of 1864, when they had not seen Tom so excited for almost two years. He said that his white customers were describing how untold thousands of murderous, pillaging Yankees, marching five miles abreast under some insane General Sherman, were laying waste to the state of Georgia. However often the family's hopes had previously been dashed, they scarcely could suppress their renewed hope of freedom as Tom brought subsequent nightly reports.

'Soun' like de Yankees ain't leavin' nothin'! Dem white mens swears dey's burnin' de fiel's, de big houses, de barns! Dey's killin' de mules an' cookin' de cows an' everythin' else dey can eat! Whatever dey ain't burnin' an' eatin' dey's jes' ruinin', plus stealin' anythin' dey can tote off! An' dey says it's niggers all out in de woods an' roads thick as ants dat done lef' dey massas an' plantations to follow dem Yankees 'til dat Gen'l Sherman hisself beggin' 'em to go back where dey come fum!'

Then not long after the Yankees' triumphal march had reached the sea, Tom breathlessly reported 'Charleston done fell!' ... and next 'Gen'l Grant done took Richmon'!' ... and finally in April of 1865, 'Gen'l Lee done surrendered de whole 'Federacy Army! De South done give up!'

The jubilance in the slave row was beyond any measure now as they poured out across the big-house front yard and up the entry lane to reach the big road to join the hundreds already there, milling about, leaping and springing up and down, whooping, shouting, singing, preaching, praying. 'Free, Lawd, free!' ... 'Thank Gawd A'mighty, free at las'!'

But then within a few days the spirit of celebration plunged into deep grief and mourning with the shattering news of the assassination of President Lincoln. '*Eeeeeeevil!*' shrieked Matilda as the family wept around her, among the millions like them who had revered the fallen President as their Moses.

Then in May, as it was happening all across the defeated South, Massa Murray summoned all of his slaves into the front yard that faced the big house. When they were all assembled in a line, they found it hard to look levelly at the drawn, shocked faces of the massa, the weeping Missis Murray, and the Ol' George Johnsons, who, too, were white. In an anguished voice then, Massa Murray read slowly from the paper in his hand that the South had lost the war. Finding it very hard not to choke up before the black family standing there on the earth before him, he said, 'I guess it means y'all as free as us. You can go if you want to, stay on if you want, an' whoever stays, we'll try to pay you something—'

The black Murrays began leaping, singing, praying, screaming anew, 'We's free!' ... 'Free at las'!' ... 'Thank you, Jesus!' The wild celebration's sounds carried through the opened door of the small cabin where Lilly Sue's son, Uriah, now eight years of age, had lain for weeks suffering a delirium of fever. 'Freedom! Freedom!' Hearing it, Uriah came boiling up off his cot, his nightshirt flapping; he raced first for the pigpen shouting, 'Ol' pigs quit gruntin', you's free!' He coursed to the barn, 'Ol' cows, quit givin' milk, you's free!' The boy raced to the chickens next, 'Ol' hens quit layin', you's free! – and so's ME!'

But that night, with their celebration having ended in their sheer exhaustion, Tom Murray assembled his large family within the barn to discuss what they should do now that this long-awaited 'freedom' had arrived. 'Freedom ain't gwine feed us, it just let us 'cide what we wants to do to eat,' said Tom. 'We ain't got much money, and 'sides me blacksmithin' an' Mammy cookin', de only workin' we knows is in de fiel's,' he appraised their dilemma.

Matilda reported that Massa Murray had asked her to urge them all to consider his offer to parcel out the plantation, and he would go halves with anyone interested in sharecropping. There was a heated debate. Several of the family's adults wished to leave as quickly as possible. Matilda protested, 'I wants dis family to stay togedder.

Now 'bout dis talk o' movin', s'pose we did an' y'all's pappy Chicken George git back, an' nobody couldn't even tell him whichaway we'd gone!'

Quiet fell when Tom made it clear he wished to speak. 'Gwine tell y'all how come we can't leave yet – it's 'cause we jes' ain't noways ready. Whenever we git ourselves ready, I'll be de firs' one to want to go.' Most were finally convinced that Tom talked 'good sense', and the family meeting broke up.

Taking Irene by the hand, Tom went walking with her in the moonlight towards the fields. Vaulting lightly over a fence, he took long strides, made a right-angle turn, and paced off a square, then striding back towards the rail fence, he said, 'Irene, that's going to be *ours*!' She echoed him, softly. 'Ours.'

Within a week, the family's separate units were each working their fields. A morning when Tom had left his blacksmith shop to help his brothers, he recognized a lone rider along the road as the former cavalry major Cates, his uniform tattered and his horse spavined. Cates also recognized Tom, and riding near the fence, he reined up. 'Hey, nigger, bring me a dipperful of your water!' he called. Tom looked at the nearby water bucket, then he studied Cates' face for a long moment before moving to the bucket. He filled the dipper and walked to hand it to Cates. 'Things is changed now, Mr Cates,' Tom spoke evenly. 'The only reason I brought you this water is because I'd bring any thirsty man a drink, not because you hollered. I jes' want you to know that.'

Cates handed back the dipper. 'Git me another one, nigger.'

Tom took the dipper and dropped it back into the bucket and walked off, never once looking back.

But when another rider came galloping and hallooing along the road with a battered black derby distinguishable above a faded green scarf, those out in the fields erupted into a mass footrace back towards the old slave row. 'Mammy, he's back! He's back!' When the horse reached the yard, Chicken George's sons hauled him off onto their shoulders and went trooping with him to the weeping Matilda.

'What you bellerin' fo,' woman?' he demanded in mock indignation, hugging her as if he would never let go, but finally he did, yelling to his family to assemble and be quiet. 'Tell y'all later 'bout all de places I been an' things I done since we las' seen one 'nother,' hollered Chicken George. 'But right now I got to 'quaint you wid where we's all gwine togedder!' In pin-drop quiet and with his born sense of drama, Chicken George told them now that he had found for them all a western Tennessee settlement whose white people anxiously awaited their arrival to help build a town.

'Lemme tell y'all sump'n! De lan' where we goin' so black an' rich, you plant a pig's tail an' a hog'll grow . . . you can't hardly sleep nights for de watermelons growin' so fas' dey cracks open like firecrackers! I'm tellin' you it's possum layin' under 'simmon trees too fat to move, wid de 'simmon sugar drippin' down on 'em thick as 'lasses . . .!'

The family never let him finish in their wild excitement. As some went dashing off to boast to others on adjacent plantations, Tom began planning that afternoon how to alter a farm wagon into a covered 'Rockaway', of which about ten could move all of the units of the family to this new place. But by that sundown a dozen other heads of newly freed families had come – not asking, but demanding that their families, too, were going – they were black Holts, Fitzpatricks, Perms, Taylors, Wrights, Lakes, MacGregors, and others, from local Alamance County plantations.

Amid the next two months of feverish activity, the men built the Rockaways. The women butchered, cooked, canned, and smoked foodstuffs for travel and selected what other vital things to take. Old Chicken George strode about, supervising every activity, loving his hero role. Tom Murray was thronged with volunteered assistance from yet more newly freed families, and with assurances that they would swiftly obtain their own wagons to become their family's Rockaways. Finally he announced that all who wished could go – but that there must be but one Rockaway per family unit. When at last twenty-eight wagons were packed and ready to roll on the following sun-up, in a strange calm sense of sadness, the freed people went about gently touching the familiar things, wash pots, the fence posts, knowing that it was for the last time.

For days, the black Murrays had caught only glimpses of the white Murrays. Matilda wept, 'Lawd, I hates to think what dey's goin' through, I swears I does!'

Tom Murray had retired for the night within his wagon when he heard the light knocking at the tailgate. Somehow he knew who was there even before he opened the end flap. Ol' George Johnson stood there, his face working with emotion, his hands wringing his hat. 'Tom – like a word with you, if you got time—'

Climbing down from the wagon, Tom Murray followed Ol' George Johnson off a way in the moonlight. When finally Ol' George stopped, he was so choked with embarrassment and emotion that he could hardly talk. 'Me and Martha been talkin' . . . jes' seem like y'all the only folks we got. Tom, we been wonderin' if y'all let us go along where you goin'?'

It was a while before Tom spoke. 'If it was jes' my family, I could tell you right now. But it's a lot mo'. I jes' have to talk it over wid 'em all. I let you know—'

Tom went to each other wagon, knocking gently, calling out the men. Gathering them, he told them what happened. There was a moment of heavy quiet. Tom Murray offered, 'He was 'bout de bes' obserseer for us I ever heard of 'cause he wasn't no real obserseer at all, he worked wid us shoulder to shoulder.'

There was sharp opposition from some, some of it anti-white. But after a while someone spoke quietly, 'He can't help it if he white—' Finally, a vote was taken, and a majority said that the Johnsons could go.

One day's delay was necessary to build a 'Rockaway' for Ol' George and Martha. Then the next sun-up, a single-file caravan of twenty-nine covered Rockaways went creaking and groaning off the Murray place into the dawn. Ahead of the wagons rode the derbied and scarfed sixty-seven-year-old Chicken George, carrying his old one-eyed fighting rooster atop his horse 'Old Bob'. Behind him, Tom Murray drove the first wagon, with Irene beside him, and behind them, goggle-eyed in excitement, were their children, the youngest of them the two-year-old Cynthia. And after twenty-seven more wagons whose front seats held black or mulatto men and their wives, finally the anchor wagon's seat held Ol' George and Martha Johnson, who soon were peering to see clearly through the haze of dust raised by all the hoofs and wheels moving ahead of them towards what Chicken George had sworn would prove to be the promised land.

114

'Dis is it?' asked Tom.

'De promised lan'?' asked Matilda.

'Where dem pigs an' watermelons poppin' out'n de groun'?' asked one of the children, as Chicken George reined his horse to a halt.

Ahead of them was a clearing in the woods with a few wooden storefronts at the intersection of the rutted road they were on and another one crossing it at right angles. Three white men – one sitting on a nail keg, another in a rocker, the third propped on the back legs of a stool with his back to a clapboard wall and his feet on a hitching post – nudged one another and nodded at the line of dusty wagons and their passengers. A couple of white boys rolling a hoop stopped in their tracks and stared, the hoop rolling on beyond them into the middle of the road, where it twirled a few times and fell. An elderly black man sweeping off a stoop looked at them impassively for a long moment and then broke into a small, slow smile. A large dog that was scratching himself beside a rain barrel paused, leg in the air, to cock his head at them, then went back to scratching.

'I done tol' y'all dis here a new settlement,' said Chicken George, talking fast. 'Dey's only a hundred or so white folks livin' roun' here yet, an' even wid jes' our fifteen wagons lef' after all dem dat dropped off to settle on de way here, we's jes' 'bout gon' double de pop'lation. We's gittin' in on de groun' flo' of a growin' town.'

'Well, ain't nothin' it can do but grow, dat's sho',' said L'il George without smiling.

'Jes' wait'll y'all sees de prime farmlan' dey got,' said his father brightly, rubbing his hands with anticipation.

'Prob'ly swamp,' muttered Ashford, wisely not loud enough for Chicken George to hear.

But it *was* prime – rich and loamy, thirty acres of it for every family, scattered on checkerboard plots from the outskirts of town all the way to the white-owned farms that already occupied the best land in Lauderdale County, on the banks of the Hatchie River six miles to the north. Many of the white farms were as large as all of their property put together, but thirty acres was thirty more than any of them had ever owned before, and they had their hands full with *that*.

Still living in their cramped wagons, the families began grubbing up stumps and clearing brush the next morning. Soon the furrows had been ploughed and their first crops planted – mostly cotton, some corn, with plots for vegetables and a patch for flowers. As they set about the next task of sawing down trees and splitting logs to build their cabins, Chicken George circulated from one farm to another on his horse, volunteering his advice on construction and trumpeting how he had changed their lives. Even among Henning's white settlers he boasted about how those he had brought with him were going to help the town grow and prosper, not failing to mention that his middle son Tom would soon be opening the area's first blacksmith shop.

One day soon afterwards, three white men rode up to Tom's plot as he and his sons were mixing a load of mud with hog bristles to chink the walls of his half-built cabin.

'Which one of you is the blacksmith?' one called from his horse.

Sure that his first customers had arrived even before he could get set up for business, Tom stepped out proudly.

'We hear you're figurin' to open a blacksmith shop here in town,' one said.

'Yassuh. Been lookin' fo' de bes' spot to build it. Was thinkin' maybe dat empty lot nex' to de sawmill if'n nobody else got his eye on it.'

The three men exchanged glances. 'Well, boy,' the second man went on, 'no need of wasting time, we'll get right to the point. You can blacksmith, that's fine. But if you want to do it in this town, you'll have to work for a white man that owns the shop. Had you figured on that?'

Such a rage flooded up in Tom that nearly a minute passed before he could trust himself to speak. 'Nawsuh, I ain't,' he said slowly. 'Me an' my family's free peoples now, we's jes' lookin' to make our livin's like anybody else, by workin' hard at what we knows to do.' He looked directly into the men's eyes. 'If I cain't own what I do wid my own hands, den dis ain't no place fo' us.'

The third white man said, 'If that's the way you feel, I 'speck you're going to be ridin' a long way in this state, boy.'

'Well, we's used to travellin',' said Tom. 'Ain't wantin' to cause no trouble nowhere, but I got to be a man. I just wisht I could o' knowed how y'all felt here so my family wouldn't of troubled y'all by stoppin' atall.'

'Well, think about it, boy,' said the second white man. 'It's up to you.'

'You people got to learn not to let all this freedom talk go to your heads,' said the first man.

Turning their horses around without another word, they rode off.

When the news went flashing among the farm plots, the heads of each family came hurrying to see Tom.

'Son,' said Chicken George, 'you's knowed all yo' life how white folks is. Cain't you jes' start out dey way? Den good as you black-smiths, won't take hardly no time to get 'em to turn roun'.'

'All dat travellin' an' now pack up an' go again!' exclaimed Matilda. 'Don't do dat to yo' fam'ly, son!'

Irene joined the chorus 'Tom, please! I'se jes' tired! Tired!'

But Tom's face was grim. 'Things don't never git better less'n you makes 'em better!' he said. 'Ain't stayin' nowhere I can't do what a free man got a right to do. Ain't axin' nobody else to go wid us, but we packin' our wagon an' leavin' tomorrow.'

'I'm comin', too!' said Ashford angrily.

That night Tom went out walking by himself, weighed down by guilt at the new hardship he was imposing upon his family. He played back in his mind the ordeal they had all endured in the wagons, rolling for weeks on end ... and he thought of something Matilda had said often: 'You search hard enough in sump'n bad, you's jes' liable to find sump'n good.'

When the idea struck him, he kept walking for another hour, letting the plan become a picture in his mind. Then he strode quickly back to the wagon where his family was sleeping and went to bed.

In the morning, Tom told James and Lewis to build temporary lean-tos for Irene and the children to sleep in, for he would need the wagon. As the family stood around watching him in amazement – Ashford with rising disbelief and fury – he unloaded the heavy anvil with Virgil's help, and mounted it atop a newly sawed stump. By noon he had set up a makeshift forge. With everyone still staring, he next removed the canvas top of the wagon, then its wooden sides, leaving the bare flatbed, on which he now went to work with his heaviest tools. Gradually they began to perceive the astounding idea that Tom was turning into a reality.

By the end of that week, Tom drove right through town with his rolling blacksmith shop, and there wasn't a man, woman, or child who didn't stand there gaping at the anvil, forge, and cooling tub, with racks holding a neat array of blacksmithing tools, all mounted sturdily on a wagon bed reinforced with heavy timbers.

Nodding politely at all the men he met – white and black – Tom asked if they had blacksmithing jobs he could do at reasonable rates. Within days, his services were being requested at more and more farms around the new settlement, for no one could think of a good reason why a black man shouldn't do business from a wagon. By the time they realized that he was doing far better with his rolling shop than he ever could have done with a stationary one, Tom had made himself so indispensable around town that they couldn't afford to raise any objections even if they'd wanted to. But they didn't really want to, because Tom seemed to them the kind of man who did his job and minded his own business, and they couldn't help respecting that. In fact, the whole family soon established themselves as decent Christian folk who paid their bills and kept to themselves – and 'stayed in their place', as Ol' George Johnson said a group of white men had put it in a conversation he'd overheard down at the general store.

But Ol' George, too, was treated as one of 'them' – shunned socially, kept waiting in stores till all the other white customers had been taken care of, even informed once by a merchant that he'd 'bought' a hat that he'd tried on and put back on the shelf when he found it was too small. He told the family about it later, perching the hat atop his head for them, and everybody laughed as hard as he did. 'I'se surprised dat hat don't fit,' cracked L'il George, 'dumb as you is to try it on in dat sto'.' Ashford, of course, got so angry that he threatened – emptily – to 'go down dere an' stuff it down dat peckerwood's throat.'

However little use the white community had for them – and vice versa – Tom and the others knew very well that the town's tradesmen could hardly contain their elation at the brisk increase in business they'd been responsible for. Though they made most of their own clothes, raised most of their own food, and cut most of their own lumber, the quantities of nails, corrugated tin, and barbed wire they bought over the next couple of years testified to the rate at which their own community was growing.

With all their houses, barns, sheds, and fences built by 1874, the family – led by Matilda – turned its attention to an enterprise they considered no less important to their welfare: the construction of a church to replace the makeshift bush arbours that had been serving as their place of worship. It took almost a year, and much of their savings, but when Tom, his brothers, and their boys had finished building the last pew and Irene's beautiful white handwoven cloth – emblazoned with a purple cross – had been draped over the pulpit in front of the $250 stained-glass window they'd ordered from Sears, Roebuck, everyone agreed that the New Hope Coloured Methodist Episcopal Church was well worth the time, effort, and expense it represented.

So many people attended the service that first Sunday – just about every black person within twenty miles who could walk or be carried – that the crowd spilled out the doors and windows and across the lawn surrounding it. But nobody had any trouble hearing every word of the ringing sermon delivered by the Reverend Sylus Henning, a former slave of Dr D. C. Henning, an Illinois Central Railroad executive with extensive land holdings around town. In the course of his oration, L'il George whispered to Virgil that the Reverend seemed to be under the impression that *he* was Dr Henning, but no one within earshot would have dared to question the fervour of his preaching.

After the last heartrending chorus of 'The Old Rugged Cross', again – led by Matilda, looking more radiant than Chicken George had ever seen her – the congregation dried their eyes and filed out past the preacher, pumping his hand and slapping him on the back. Retrieving their picnic baskets on the porch, they spread sheets on the lawn and proceeded to relish the fried chicken, pork chop sandwiches, devilled eggs, potato salad, coleslaw, pickles, cornbread, lemonade, and so many cakes and pies that even L'il George was gasping for breath when he finished the last slice.

As they all sat chatting, or strolled around – the men and boys in coat and tie, the older women all in white, the girls in bright-coloured dresses with a ribbon at the waist – Matilda watched misty-eyed as her brood of grandchildren ran about tirelessly playing tag and catch. Turning finally to her husband and putting her hand on his, gnarled and scarred with gamecock scratches, she said quietly, 'I won't never forget dis day, George. We done come a long way since you first come courtin' me wid dat derby hat o' yours. Our fam'ly done growed up an' had chilluns of dey own, an' de Lawd seen fit to keep us all togedder. De onliest thing I wish is you Mammy Kizzy could be here to see it wid us.'

Eyes brimming, Chicken George looked back at her. 'She lookin', baby. She *sho'* is!'

115

Promptly at the noon hour on Monday, during their break from the fields, the children started filing into church for their first day of school indoors. For the past two years, ever since she came to town after being one among the first graduating class from Lane College in Jackson, Tennessee, Sister Carrie White had been teaching out under the brush arbours, and this use of the church was a great occasion. The New Hope CME stewards – Chicken George, Tom, and his brothers – had contributed the money to buy pencils, tablets, and primers on 'readin', writing', an' 'rithmetic'. Since she taught all the children of school age at the same time, in her six grades Sister Carrie had pupils ranging from five to fifteen, including Tom's oldest five: Maria Jane, who was twelve; Ellen; Viney; L'il Matilda; and

Elizabeth, who was six. Young Tom, next in line, began the year after that, and then Cynthia, the youngest.

By the time Cynthia was graduated in 1883, Maria Jane had dropped out, got married, and given birth to her first child; and Elizabeth, who was the best student in the family, had taught their father Tom Murray how to write his name and had even become his blacksmithing book-keeper. He needed one, for by this time he had become so successful with his rolling blacksmith shop that he had also built a stationary one – without a murmur of objection – and was among the more prosperous men in town.

About a year after Elizabeth went to work for her father, she fell in love with John Toland, a newcomer to Henning who had gone to work sharecropping on the six-hundred-acre farm of a white family out near the Hatchie River. She had met him in town one day at the general store and been impressed, she told her mother Irene, not only by his good looks and muscular build but also by his dignified manner and obvious intelligence. He could even write a little, she noticed, when he signed for a receipt. Over the next several weeks, during the walks she'd take with him in the woods once or twice each week, she also found out that he was a young man of fine reputation, a church-goer, who had ambitions of saving up enough to start a farm of his own; and that he was as gentle as he was strong.

It wasn't until they'd seen each other regularly for almost two months – and had begun to talk secretly about marriage – that Tom Murray, who had known about them from the start, ordered her to stop skulking around and bring him home from church the following Sunday. Elizabeth did as she was told. John Toland couldn't have been friendlier or more respectful when he was introduced to Tom Murray, who was even more taciturn than usual, and excused himself after only a few minutes of painful pleasantries. After John Toland left, Elizabeth was called by Tom Murray, who said sternly: 'It's plain to see from de way you act roun' dat boy dat you's stuck on 'im. You two got anythin' in mind?'

'What you mean, Pappy?' she stuttered, flushing hotly.

'Gittin' married! Dat's on your mind, ain't it?'

She couldn't speak.

'You done tol' me. Well, I'd like to give you my blessin's, 'cause I wants you to be happy much as you does. He seem like a good man – but I can't let you hitch up wid 'im.'

Elizabeth looked at him uncomprehendingly.

'He's too high-yaller. He could nigh 'bout pass fo' white – jes' not quite. He ain't fish or fowl. Y'unnerstan' what I'se sayin'? He too light fo' black folks, too dark fo' white folks. He cain't he'p what he look like, but don't care how hard he try, he never gon' b'long nowhere. An' you got to think 'bout what yo' chilluns might look like! I don't want dat kinda life fo' you, 'Lizabeth.'

'But Pappy, ever'body *like* John! If'n we gits 'long wid Ol' George Johnson, why can't we git 'long wid him?'

'Ain't de same!'

'But Pappy!' she was desperate. 'You talk 'bout people not 'ceptin' 'im! *You's* de one ain't!'

'Dat's 'nough! You done said all I'm gon' hear 'bout it. You ain't got de sense to keep 'way from dat kinda grief, I gotta do it fo' you. I don' want you seein' 'im no mo'.'

'But Pappy . . .' She was sobbing.

'It's over wid! Dat's all is to it!'

'If'n I cain't marry John, ain't never gon' marry nobody!' Elizabeth screamed.

Tom Murray turned and strode from the room, slamming the door. In the next room, he stopped.

'Tom, what do you . . .' Irene began, sitting up rigidly in her rocker.

'Ain't got no mo' to say 'bout it!' he snapped, marching out the front door.

When Matilda found out about it, she got so angry that Irene had to restrain her from confronting Tom. 'Dat boy's pappy got white blood in 'im!' she shouted. Suddenly wincing, then clutching at her chest, Matilda lurched against a table. Irene caught her as she toppled to the floor.

'O my God!' she moaned, her face contorted with pain. 'Sweet Jesus! O Lawd, no!' Her eyelids fluttered and closed.

'Grandmammy!' Irene shouted, seizing her around the shoulders. '*Grandmammy!*' She put her head to her chest and listened. There was still a heartbeat. But two days later it stopped.

Chicken George didn't cry. But there was something heartbreaking about his stoniness, the deadness in his eyes. From that day on, no one could remember him ever smiling again or saying a civil word to anyone. He and Matilda had never seemed really close – but when she died, somehow his own warmth died with her. And he began to shrink, dry up, grow old almost overnight – not turning feeble and weak-minded but hard and mean-tempered. Refusing to live anymore in the cabin he had shared with Matilda, he began to roost with one son or daughter after another until both he and they were fed up, when old grey-headed Chicken George moved on.

When he wasn't complaining, he'd usually sit on the porch in the rocker he took along with him and stare fiercely out across the fields for hours at a time.

He had just turned eighty-three – having cantankerously refused to touch a bite of the birthday cake that was baked for him – and was sitting late in the winter of 1890 in front of the fire at his eldest granddaughter Maria Jane's house. She had ordered him to sit still and rest his bad leg while she hurried out to the adjacent field with her husband's lunch. When she returned as quickly as she could, she found him lying on the hearth, where he'd dragged himself after falling into the fire. Maria Jane's screams brought her husband running. The derby hat, scarf, and sweater were smouldering, and Chicken George was burned horribly from his head to his waist. Late that night he died.

Nearly everyone black in Henning attended his funeral, dozens of them his children, grandchildren, or great-grandchildren. Standing there by the grave as he was lowered into the ground beside Matilda, his son L'il George leaned to Virgil and whispered: 'Pappy so tough 'spec he wouldn't o' never died natural.'

Virgil turned and looked sadly at his brother. 'I loved 'im,' he said quietly. 'You too, an' all us.'

' 'Cose we did,' said L'il George. 'Nobody couldn't stan' livin' wid de cockadoodlin' ol' rascal, an' look now at ever'body snufflin' cause he gone!'

116

'Mama!' Cynthia breathlessly exclaimed to Irene, 'Will Palmer done axed to walk me home from church nex' Sunday!'

'He ain't 'zackly one to rush into things, is he? Leas' two years I seen 'im watchin' you in church every Sunday—' said Irene.

'Who?' Tom asked.

'Will Palmer! Is it awright for him to walk her home?'

After a while Tom Murray said dryly, 'I think 'bout it.'

Cynthia went off looking as if she had been stabbed, leaving Irene studying her husband's face. 'Tom, ain't *nobody* good 'nough fo' yo' gals? Anybody in town know dat youn' Will jes' 'bout *run* de lumber company fo' dat ol' stay-drunk Mr James. Folks all over Henning seen 'im unload de lumber off de freight cars hisself, sell it an' deliver it hisself, den write out de bills, colleck de money, an 'posit it in de bank hisself. Even do different l'il carpenterin' de customers needs an' ax nothin' fo' it. An' wid all dat fo' whatever l'il he make, he don't never speak a hard word 'gainst ol' Mr James.'

'De way I sees it, doin' his job an' mindin' his own business,' said Tom Murray. 'I sees 'im in church, too, half de gals in dere battin' dey eyes at 'im.'

' 'Cose dey is!' said Irene, ' 'cause he de bes' catch in Henning. But he ain't never yet ax to walk none home.'

'How 'bout dat Lula Carter he gave dem flowers to?'

Astonished that Tom even knew, Irene said, 'Dat more'n a year ago, Tom, an' if you knows so much, reckon you also know she carried on like sich a fool after dat. fawnin' roun' 'im like a shadow, he finally quit talkin' to her at all!'

'He done it once, he could do it ag'in.'

'Not to Cynthia, he ain't, not much sense as *she* got, 'long wid bein' pretty an' well raised. She done tol' me much as she like Will, she ain't never let on to 'im how *she* feel! Mos' she ever say is howdy an' smile back when he do. Don't care how many gals buzzin' after 'im, you see who *he* buzzin' after!'

'See you got everythin' worked out,' said Tom.

Irene pleaded, 'Aw, Tom, let 'im walk de child home. Leas' let 'em git togedder. Dey stays togedder's up to dem.'

'An' *me*!' Tom said sternly. He did not want to seem too easy to any of his daughters, his wife either. Above all, he did not want Irene aware that before now he had seen the potential, had weighed it, and thoroughly approved of Will Palmer if the time came. Having watched young Will since he had come to Henning, Tom privately had often wished that either of his two sons showed half of young Will's gumption. In fact, the deviously serious, ambitious, highly capable Will Palmer reminded Tom of a younger himself.

No one had expected that the courtship would develop so fast. Ten months later, in the 'company room' of Tom and Irene's new four-room house, Will proposed to Cynthia, who barely could restrain her 'Yes!' until he had finished speaking. The third Sunday from then, they were married in the New Hope CME Church in a ceremony attended by well over two hundred people, about half of whom had come from North Carolina on the wagon train, and their children – and who now lived on farms scattered throughout Lauderdale County.

610

Will with his own hands and tools built their small home where, a year later, in 1894, their first child, a son, was born, who died within a few days. By now Will Palmer never took off a weekday from work, the lumber company's hard-drinking owner being so far gone into the bottle that Will practically *was* running the entire business. Going over the company's books one stormy late Friday afternoon, Will discovered a bank payment overdue that day at People's Bank. He rode his horse eight miles through drenching rains to knock at the bank president's back porch.

'Mr Vaughan,' he said, 'this payment slipped Mr James' mind, and I know he wouldn't want to keep you waitin' till Monday.'

Invited inside to dry, he said, 'No, thank you, sir. Cynthia'll be wonderin' where I am.' And wishing the banker a good night, he rode back off in the rain.

The banker, deeply impressed, told the incident all over town.

In the fall of 1893, someone came and told Will he was wanted at the bank. Puzzled throughout the few minutes' walk there, Will found inside, waiting for him, Henning's ten leading white businessmen, all seeming red-faced and embarrassed. Banker Vaughan explained, speaking rapidly, that the lumber company's owner had declared bankruptcy, with plans to move elsewhere with his family. 'Henning needs the lumber company,' said the banker. 'All of us you see here have been weeks discussing it, and we can't think of anyone better to run it than you, Will. We've agreed to co-sign a note to pay off the company's debts for you to take over as the new owner.'

Tears trickling down his cheeks, Will Palmer walked wordlessly along the line of white men. As he double-gripped and squeezed each hand, then that man hurriedly signed the note and even more quickly left with tears in his own eyes. When they had all gone, Will wrung the banker's hand for a long moment. 'Mr Vaughan, I've got one more favour to ask. Would you take half of my savings and make out a cheque for Mr James, without his ever knowing where it came from?'

Within a year, Will's credo – to provide the best possible goods and service for the lowest possible price – was drawing customers even from adjoining towns, and wagonloads of people, mostly black, were coming from as far away as Memphis – forty-eight miles to the South – to see with their own eyes western Tennessee's first black-owned business of its kind, where Cynthia had hung ruffled, starched curtains in the windows and Will had painted the sign on the front: W. E. PALMER LUMBER COMPANY.

117

Cynthia's and Will's prayers were answered in 1895 with the birth of the sound, healthy girl whom they named Bertha George – the 'George' after Will's father. Cynthia insisted on assembling a houseful of family before whom she told the gurgling infant the whole story back to the African, Kunta Kinte, just as Tom Murray had told it to all of his children at intervals when they had been young.

Will Palmer respected Cynthia's devotion to her ancestors' memory, but it irritated his own deep pride to be considered as having married into Cynthia's family rather than the other way around. It was probably why he began to monopolize little Bertha even before she could walk. Every morning he carried her about before he left for work. Every night he tucked her into the little crib that he had made with his hands for her.

By the time Bertha was five, the rest of the family and much of the town's black community quoted Cynthia, and speaking for themselves echoed her opinion. 'Will Palmer jes' spilin' dat gal to pieces!' He had arranged that she had credit at every Henning store that sold candy, and he paid the bill each month, though he made her keep an accounting, which he solemnly checked 'to teach her business.' As her fifteenth-birthday present, when he opened a Sears, Roebuck mail-order account in her name, the people shook and wagged their heads in mingled astonishment, dismay and pride. 'All dat young un got to do is pick what she like out'n dat pitcher catalogue, an' write off de order blank, an' firs' thing you knows dem Sears, Roebuck white folks way yonder in Chicago done sent it – seen it wid dese here eyes . . . an' her daddy pays fo' it . . . you hearin' what I'm tellin' you, chile? Anythin' dat Bertha *want*!'

Later that same year, Will hired a teacher to come weekly all the way from Memphis to give Bertha piano lessons. She was a gifted pupil, and before long was playing for the choir in the New Hope Coloured Methodist Episcopal Church, of which Will was the senior trustee and Cynthia was the perennial president of the Stewardess Board.

When Bertha finished the local eighth grade in June of 1909, there was no question that she would be leaving Henning to attend the CME Church-supported Lane Institute thirty miles to the east in Jackson, Tennessee, which went from ninth grade through two years of college.

'Gal, jes' no way you can know ... what it mean, you bein' dis fam'ly's firs' one headin' fo' a college—'

'Maw, if I can *ever* git you and Paw to *please* quit saying such as "*dis*" and "*fo'* "! I keep telling you they're pronounced "*this*" and "*for*"! Anyway, isn't that why colleges are there? For people to go to?'

Cynthia wept when she got alone with her husband. 'Lawd God he'p us wid 'er, Will, she jes' don unnerstan'.'

'Maybe she best don't,' he tried to console. 'I jes' know I'll draw my last breath seein' she have better chance'n us did.'

As was only expected of her, Bertha achieved consistently high grades – studying pedagogy, to become a teacher – and she both played the piano and sang in the school choir. On one of her two weekend visits back home every month, she persuaded her father to have a sign painted on both doors of his delivery truck: 'Henning 121 – Your Lumber Number'. Telephones recently had come to Henning; it was typical of Bertha's ready wit, which got quoted often around town.

On later visits, Bertha began to speak about a young man whom she had met in the college choir, his name, Simon Alexander Haley, and he was from a town named Savannah, Tennessee. Being very poor, she said, he was working at as many as four odd jobs at the time in order to stay in school, where he was studying agriculture. When Bertha continued to talk about him, a year later, in 1913, Will and Cynthia suggested that she invite him to visit with them in Henning, so they could appraise him in person.

The New Hope CME Church was packed on the Sunday it had been circulated that 'Bertha's beau from college' would be in attendance. He arrived under the searching scrutiny not only of Will and Cynthia Palmer, but also of the total black community. But he seemed a very self-assured young man. After singing a baritone solo, 'In the Garden', accompanied by Bertha at the piano, he talked easily with all who crowded about him later out in the churchyard, he looked everyone squarely in the eyes, firmly gripping all of the men's hands, and tipping his hat to all of the ladies.

Bertha and her Simon Alexander Haley – his full name – returned to Lane College together on the bus that evening. No one had a thing to say against him publicly – in the ensuing community discussions. Privately, though, some queasy uncertainties were expressed concerning his very nearly high-yaller complexion. (He had told dark brown Bertha in confidence that his parents, former slaves, had both told him of having slave mothers and Irish white fathers, paternally an overseer named Jim Baugh, of whom little else was known, and maternally a Marion County, Alabama, plantation scion and later Civil War colonel named James Jackson.) But it was agreed by all that he sang well; that he seemed to have been well raised; and he showed no signs of trying to put on airs just because he was educated.

Haley landed a summer's work as a Pullman porter, saving every possible penny to enable his transferring to the four-year A & T College in Greensboro, North Carolina, exchanging weekly letters with Bertha. When World War I came, he and all other males in their senior class enlisted en masse in the U.S. Army, and before long his letters to Bertha came from France, where in the Argonne Forest in 1918, he was gassed. After treatment for several months in a hospital overseas, he was returned home to convalesce, and in 1919, fully recovered, he came again to Henning and he and Bertha announced their engagement.

Their wedding in the New Hope CME Church in the summer of 1920 was Henning's first social event attended by both black and white – not only since Will Palmer by now was among the town's most prominent citizens, but also because in her own right the accomplished, irrepressible Bertha was someone whom all in Henning regarded with pride. The reception was held on the wide, sloping lawn of the Palmers' brand-new home of ten rooms, including a music parlour and a library. A banquet of food was served; more presents were heaped than were normally seen at an average three weddings; there was even a recital by the full Lane College Choir – in whose ranks the ecstatic newlyweds had met – which had come in the bus that Will Palmer had chartered from Jackson.

Late that day, Henning's little railroad depot was overrun as Simon and Bertha boarded the Illinois Central train that took them through the night to Chicago, where they changed onto another bound for somewhere called Ithaca, New York. Simon was going to study for his master's degree in agriculture at some 'Cornell University', and Bertha would be enrolling at a nearby 'Ithaca Conservatory of Music'.

For about nine months, Bertha wrote home regularly, reporting their exciting experiences so far away and telling how happy they were with each other. But then, in the early summer of 1921, Bertha's letters began to arrive less and less often, until finally Cynthia and Will grew deeply concerned that something was wrong that Bertha wasn't telling them about. Will gave Cynthia five hundred dollars to send to Bertha, telling Bertha to use it however they might need it, without mentioning it to Simon. But their daughter's letters came even more seldom, until by late August, Cynthia told Will and their closest friends that she was going to New York herself to find out what was the matter.

Two days before Cynthia was due to leave, a midnight knocking at the front door awakened them in alarm. Cynthia was first out of bed, snatching on her robe, with Will close behind. At their bedroom's doorway, she could see through the living room's glass-panelled french doors the moonlit silhouettes of Bertha and Simon on the front porch. Cynthia went shrieking and bounding to snatch open the door.

Bertha said calmly, 'Sorry we didn't write. We wanted to bring you a surprise present—' She handed to Cynthia the blanketed bundle in her arms. Her heart pounding, and with Will gazing incredulously over her shoulder, Cynthia pulled back the blanket's top fold – revealing a round brown face ...

The baby boy, six weeks old, was *me*.

118

I used to be told later by Dad, laughing in recalling that night of big surprise as he loved to do, 'Seemed I'd nearly lost a son a little while there—' Dad declared Grandpa Will Palmer walked around and lifted me out of Grandma's arms 'and without a word took you out to the yard and around the rear of the house somewhere. Why, he must have stayed gone I believe as long as half an hour' before returning, 'with Cynthia, Bertha, or me saying not a word to him of it, either, I guess for one reason just because he was Will Palmer, and the other thing was all of us knew how badly for many years he'd wanted to have a son to raise – I guess in your being Bertha's boy, you'd become it.'

After a week or so, Dad went back alone to Ithaca, leaving Mama and me in Henning; they had decided it would be better while he finished pushing for his master's degree. Grandpa and Grandma proceeded to just about adopt me as their own – especially Grandpa.

Even before I could talk Grandma would say years later, he would carry me in his arms down to the lumber company, where he built a crib to put me in while he took care of business. After I had learned to walk, we would go together downtown, me taking three steps to each of his, my small fist tightly grasped about his extended left forefinger. Looming over me like a black, tall, strong tree, Grandpa would stop and chat with people we met along the way. Grandpa taught me to look anyone right in their eyes, to speak to them clearly and politely. Sometimes people exclaimed how well raised I was and how fine I was growing up. 'Well, I guess he'll do,' Grandpa would respond.

Down at the W. E. Palmer Lumber Company, he would let me play around among the big stacks of oak, cedar, pine, and hickory all in planks of different lengths and widths, and with their mingling of good smells, and I would imagine myself involved in all kinds of exciting adventures, almost always in faraway times or places. And sometimes Grandpa would let me sit in his office in his big, high-backed swivel chair with his green-visored eyeshade on my head, swivelling around and back and forth until I'd get so dizzy my head seemed to keep going after I'd stopped. I enjoyed myself anywhere I ever went with Grandpa.

Then, when I was going on five, he died. I was so hysterical that Dr. Dillard had to give me a glass of something milky to make me sleep that night. But before I did, I remember drowsily glimpsing many people, black and white, gathering in a ragged line along the dusty road that ran nearby the house, all of their heads bowed, the women wearing headscarves, the men holding their hats in their hands. For the next several days it seemed to me as if everybody in the world was crying.

Dad, who had by now nearly completed his master's thesis, came home from Cornell to take over the lumber mill, as Mama started teaching in our local school. Having loved Grandpa so deeply myself, and having seen Grandma's terrible grief, she and I soon became extremely close, and there weren't many places she went that she didn't take me along with her.

I suppose it was somehow to try to fill the void of Grandpa's absence that now during each springtime, Grandma began to invite various ones among the Murray family female relatives to spend some, if not all, of the summers with us. Averaging in her age range, the later forties and early fifties, they came from exotic-sounding places to me, such as Dyersburg, Tennessee; Inkster, Michigan; St Louis and Kansas City – and they had names like Aunt Plus, Aunt Liz, Aunt Till, Aunt Viney, and Cousin Georgia. With the supper dishes washed, they all would go out on the front porch and sit in

616

cane-bottomed rocking chairs, and I would be among them and sort of scrunch myself down behind the white-painted rocker holding Grandma. The time would be just about as the dusk was deepening into the night, with the lightning bugs flickering on and off around the honeysuckle vines, and every evening I can remember, unless there was some local priority gossip, always they would talk about the same things – snatches and patches of what later I'd learn was the long, cumulative family narrative that had been passed down across the generations.

It was the talk, I knew, that always had generated my only memories of any open friction between Mama and Grandma. Grandma would get on that subject sometimes without her older women summer guests there, and Mama always before long would abruptly snap something like, 'Oh, Maw, I *wish* you'd stop all that old-timey slavery stuff, it's entirely embarrassing!' Grandma would snap right back, 'If *you* don't care who and where you come from, well, *I* does!' And they might go around avoiding speaking to each other for a whole day, maybe even longer.

But anyway, I know I gained my initial impression that whatever Grandma and the other greying ladies talked about was something that went a very long way back when one or another of them would be recalling something of girlhood and suddenly thrusting a finger down towards me say, 'I wasn't any bigger'n this here young'un!' The very idea that anyone as old and wrinkled as they had once been my age strained my comprehension. But as I say, it was this that caused me to realize that the things they were discussing must have happened a very long time ago.

Being just a little boy, I couldn't really follow most of what they said. I didn't know what an 'ol' massa' or an 'ol' missis' was; I didn't know what a 'plantation' was, though it seemed something resembling a farm. But slowly, from hearing the stories each passing summer, I began to recognize frequently repeated names among the people they talked about and to remember things they told about those people. The farthest-back person they ever talked about was a man they called 'the African', whom they always said had been brought to this country on a ship to some place that they pronounced ' 'Naplis'. They said he was bought off this ship by a 'Massa John Waller', who had a plantation in a place called 'Spotsylvania County, Virginia'. They would tell how the African kept trying to escape, and how on the fourth effort he had the misfortune to be captured by two white professional slave catchers, who apparently decided to make an example of him. This African was given the choice either of being castrated or having a foot cut off, and – 'thanks to Jesus, or we wouldn't be here tellin' it' – the African chose his foot. I couldn't figure out why white folks would do anything as mean and low-down as that.

But this African's life, the old ladies said, had been saved by Massa John's brother, a Dr William Waller, who was so mad about the entirely unnecessary maiming that he bought the African for his own plantation. Though now the African was crippled, he could do limited work, and the doctor assigned him in the vegetable garden. That was how it happened that this particular African was kept on one plantation for quite a long time – in a time when slaves, especially male slaves, were sold back and forth so much that slave children grew up often without even knowledge of who their parents were.

Grandma and the others said that Africans fresh off slave ships were given some name by their massas. In this particular African's case the name was 'Toby'. But they said anytime any of the other slaves called him that, he would strenuously rebuff them, declaring that his name was 'Kin-tay'.

Hobbling about, doing his gardening work, then later becoming his massa's buggy-driver, 'Toby' – or 'Kin-tay' – met and eventually mated with a woman slave there whom Grandma and the other ladies called 'Bell, the big-house cook'. They had a little girl who was given the name 'Kizzy'. When she was around four to five years old, her African father began to take her by the hand and lead her around, whenever he got the chance, pointing out different things to her and repeating to her their names in his own native tongue. He would point at a guitar, for example, and say something that sounded like 'ko'. Or he would point at the river that ran near the plantation – actually the Mattaponi River – and say what sounded like 'Kamby Bolongo', along with many more things and sounds. As Kizzy grew older, and her African father learned English better, he began telling her stories about himself, his people, and his homeland – and how he was taken away from it. He said that he had been out in the forest not far from his village, chopping wood to make a drum, when he had been surprised by four men, overwhelmed, and kidnapped into slavery.

When Kizzy was sixteen years old, Grandma Palmer and the other Murray family ladies said, she was sold away to a new master named Tom Lea, who owned a smaller plantation in North Carolina. And it was on this plantation that Kizzy gave birth to a boy, whose father was Tom Lea, who gave the boy the name of George.

When George got around four or five years old, his mother began to tell him her African father's sounds and stories, until he came to know them well. Then when George got to be the age of twelve, I learned there on Grandma's front porch, he was apprenticed to an old 'Uncle Mingo', who trained the master's fighting gamecocks, and by the mid-teens, the youth had earned such a reputation as a gamecock trainer that he'd been given by others the nickname he'd take to his grave: 'Chicken George'.

Chicken George when around eighteen met and mated with a slave girl named Matilda, who in time bore him eight children. With each new child's birth, said Grandma and the others, Chicken George would gather his family within their slave cabin, telling them afresh about their African great-grandfather named 'Kin-tay', who called a guitar a 'ko', a river in Virginia 'Kamby Bolongo', and other sounds for other things, and who had said he was chopping wood to make a drum when he was captured into slavery.

The eight children grew up, took mates, and had their own children. The fourth son, Tom, was a blacksmith when he was sold along with the rest of his family to a 'Massa Murray', who owned a tobacco plantation in Alamance County, North Carolina. There, Tom met and mated with a half-Indian slave girl named Irene, who came from the plantation of a 'Massa Holt', who owned a cotton mill. Irene eventually also bore eight children, and with each new birth, Tom continued the tradition his father, Chicken George, had begun, gathering his family around the hearth and telling them about their African great-great-grandfather and all those descending from him.

Of that second set of eight children, the youngest was a little girl named Cynthia, who was two years old when her father, Tom, and grandfather, Chicken George, led a wagon-train of recently freed slaves westward to Henning, Tennessee, where Cynthia met and at the age of twenty-two married Will Palmer.

When I had been thoroughly immersed in listening to accounts of all those people unseen who had lived away back yonder, invariably it would astonish me when the long narrative finally got down to Cynthia ... and there I sat looking right at Grandma! As well as Aunt Viney, Aunt Matilda, and Aunt Liz, who had ridden right along with Grandma – her older sisters – in the wagon-train.

I was there at Grandma's in Henning until two younger brothers had been born, George in 1925, then Julius in 1929. Dad sold the lumber company for Grandma, and moved now into being a professor of agriculture with Mama and we three boys living wherever he taught, the longest period being at A & M College at Normal, Alabama, where I was in some class a morning in 1931 and someone came with a message for me to hurry home, and I did, hearing Dad's great wracking sobs as I burst into the door. Mama – who had been sick off and on since we had left Henning – lay in their bed, dying. She was thirty-six.

Every summer, George, Julius, and I spent in Henning with Grandma. Noticeably something of her old spirit seemed to have gone, along with both Grandpa and Mama. People passing would greet her in her white-painted rocker there on the front porch, 'Sister Cynthy, how's you doin'?' and she generally would answer them, 'Jes' settin'—'

After two years, Dad married again to a colleague professor who was named Zeona Hatcher, from Columbus, where she had got her master's degree at Ohio State University. She busied herself with the further raising and training of we three rapidly growing boys, then she gave us a sister named Lois.

I had finished a second year in college and at seventeen years of age enlisted into the US Coast Guard as a messboy when World War II happened. On my cargo-ammunition ship plying the Southwest Pacific, I stumbled onto the long road that has taken me finally to the writing of this *Roots*.

At sea sometimes as long as three months, our crew's really most incessant fighting wasn't of enemy aerial bombers or submarines, but our fighting of sheer boredom. At Dad's insistence, I'd learned to type in high school, and my most precious shipboard possession was my portable typewriter. I wrote letters to everyone I could think of. And I read every book in the ship's small library or that was owned and loaned by shipmates; from boyhood, I'd loved reading, especially stories of adventure. Having read everything on board a third time, I guess simply in frustration I decided I'd try writing some stories myself. The idea that one could roll a blank sheet of paper into a typewriter and write something on it that other people would care to read challenged, intrigued, exhilarated me – and does to this day. I don't know what else motivated and sustained me through trying to write, every single night, seven nights a week – mailing off my efforts to magazines and collecting literally hundreds of their rejection slips – across the next eight years before my first story was bought.

After the war, with one or another editor accepting a story now or then, the US Coast Guard's hierarchy created for me a new rating – 'journalist'. Writing every hour I could, I got published more; finally in 1959 at age thirty-seven, I'd been in the service for twenty years, making me eligible to retire, which I did, determined to try now for a new career as a full-time writer.

At first I sold some articles to men's adventure magazines, mostly about historic maritime dramas, because I love the sea. Then *Reader's Digest* began giving me assignments to write mostly biographical stories of people who'd had dramatic experiences or lived exciting lives.

Then, in 1962, I happened to record a conversation with famous jazz trumpeter Miles Davis that became the first of the *Playboy* 'interviews'. Among my subsequent interview subjects was the then Nation of Islam spokesman Malcolm X. A publisher reading the interview asked for a book portraying his life. Malcolm X asked me to work with him as his collaborator, and I did. The next year was mostly spent intensively interviewing him, then the next year in actually writing *The Autobiography of Malcolm X*, which, as he had predicted, he hadn't lived to read, for he was assassinated about two weeks after the manuscript was finished.

Soon, a magazine sent me on assignment to London. Between appointments, utterly fascinated with a wealth of history everywhere, I missed scarcely a guided tour anywhere within London's area during the next several days. Poking about one day in the British Museum, I found myself looking at something I'd heard of vaguely: the Rosetta Stone. I don't know why, it just about entranced me. I got a book there in the museum library to learn more about it.

Discovered in the Nile delta, I learned the stone's face had chiselled into it three separate texts: one in known Greek characters, the second in a then-unknown set of characters, the third in the ancient hieroglyphics, which it had been assumed no one ever would be able to translate. But a French scholar, Jean Champollion, successively matched, character for character, both the unknown text and the hieroglyphics with the known Greek text, and he offered a thesis that the texts read the same. Essentially, he had cracked the mystery of the previously undeciphered hieroglyphics in which much of mankind's earliest history was recorded.

The key that had unlocked a door into the past fascinated me. I seemed to feel it had some special personal significance, but I couldn't imagine what. It was on a plane returning to the United States when an idea hit me. Using language chiselled into stone, the French scholar had deciphered a historic unknown by matching it with that which was known. That presented me a rough analogy: in the oral history that Grandma, Aunt Liz, Aunt Plus, Cousin Georgia, and the others had always told on the boyhood Henning front porch, I had an unknown quotient in those strange words or sounds passed on by the African. I got to thinking about them: 'Kin-tay', he had said, was his name. 'Ko' he had called a guitar. 'Kamby Bolongo' he had called a river in Virginia. They were mostly sharp, angular sounds, with 'k' predominating. These sounds probably had undergone some changes across the generations of being passed down, yet unquestionably they represented phonetic snatches of whatever was the specific tongue spoken by my African ancestor who was a family legend. My plane from London was circling to land at New York with me wondering: What specific African tongue was it? Was there any way in the world that maybe I could find out?

119

Now over thirty years later the sole surviving one of the old ladies who had talked the family narrative on the Henning front porch was the youngest among them, Cousin Georgia Anderson. Grandma was gone, and all of the others too. In her eighties now, Cousin Georgia lived with her son and daughter, Floyd Anderson and Bea Neely, at 1200 Everett Avenue, Kansas City, Kansas. I hadn't seen her since my frequent visits there of a few years before, then to offer what help I could to my politically oriented brother, George. Successively out of the U.S. Army Air Force, Morehouse College, then the University of Arkansas Law School, George was hotly campaigning to become a Kansas state senator. The night of his victory party, laughter flourished that actually why he'd won was ... Cousin Georgia. Having repetitively heard her campaign director son, Floyd, tell people of George's widely recognized integrity, our beloved grey, bent, feisty Cousin Georgia had taken to the local sidewalks. Rapping her walking cane at people's doors, she had thrust before their startled faces a picture of her grandnephew candidate, declaring, 'Dat boy got mo' 'teggity dan you can shake a stick at!'

Now I flew to Kansas City again, to see Cousin Georgia.

I think that I will never quite get over her instant response when I raised the subject of the family story. Wrinkled and ailing, she jerked upright in her bed, her excitement like boyhood front-porch echoes:

'Yeah, boy, dat African say his name was "Kin-tay"! ... He say de guitar a "ko", de river "Kamby Bolongo", an' he was choppin' wood

622

to make hisself a drum when dey cotched 'im!'

Cousin Georgia became so emotionally full of the old family story that Floyd, Bea, and I had a time trying to calm her down. I explained to her that I wanted to try to see if there was any way that I could possibly find where our 'Kin-tay' had come from ... which could reveal *our* ancestral tribe.

'You go 'head, boy!' exclaimed Cousin Georgia. 'Yo' sweet grandma an' all of 'em – dey up dere *watchin'* you!'

The thought made me feel something like ... *My God!*

120

Soon after, I went to the National Archives in Washington, D.C., and told a reading-room desk attendant that I was interested in Alamance County, North Carolina, census records just after the Civil War. Rolls of microfilm were delivered. I began turning film through the machine, feeling a mounting sense of intrigue while viewing an endless parade of names recorded in that old-fashioned penmanship of different 1800s census takers. After several of the long microfilm rolls, tiring, suddenly in utter astonishment I found myself looking down there on: 'Tom Murray, black, blacksmith—', 'Irene Murray, black, housewife' ... followed by the names of Grandma's older sisters – most of whom I'd listened to countless times on Grandma's front porch. 'Elizabeth, age 6' – nobody in the world but my Great Aunt Liz! At the time of that census, Grandma wasn't even born yet!

It wasn't that I hadn't believed the stories of Grandma and the rest of them. You just *didn't* not believe my grandma. It was simply so uncanny sitting staring at those names actually right there in official US Government records.

Then living in New York, I returned to Washington as often as I could manage it – searching in the National Archives, in the Library of Congress, in the Daughters of the American Revolution Library. Wherever I was, whenever black library attendants perceived the nature of my search, documents I'd requested would reach me with a miraculous speed. From one or another source during 1966, I was able to document at least the highlights of the cherished family story;

I would have given anything to be able to tell Grandma – then I would remember what Cousin Georgia had said, that she, all of them, were 'up there watchin'.'

Now the thing was where, what, how could I pursue those strange phonetic sounds that it was always said our African ancestor had spoken. It seemed obvious that I had to reach as wide a range of actual Africans as I possibly could, simply because so many different tribal tongues are spoken in Africa. There in New York City, I began doing what seemed logical: I began arriving at the United Nations around quitting time; the elevators were spilling out people who were thronging through the lobby on their way home. It wasn't hard to spot the Africans, and every one I was able to stop, I'd tell my sounds to. Within a couple of weeks, I guess I had stopped about two dozen Africans, each of whom had given me a quick look, a quick listen, and then took off. I can't say I blame them – me trying to communicate some African sounds in a Tennessee accent.

Increasingly frustrated, I had a long talk with George Sims, with whom I'd grown up in Henning, and who is a master researcher. After a few days, George brought me a list of about a dozen people academically renowned for their knowledge of African linguistics. One whose background intrigued me quickly was a Belgian Dr Jan Vansina. After study at the University of London's School of African and Oriental Studies, he had done his early work living in African villages and written a book called *La Tradition Orale*. I telephoned Dr Vansina where he now taught at the University of Wisconsin, and he gave me an appointment to see him. It was a Wednesday morning that I flew to Madison, Wisconsin, motivated by my intense curiosity about some strange phonetic sounds . . . and with no dream in this world of what was about to start happening . . .

That evening in the Vansinas' living room, I told him every syllable I could remember of the family narrative heard since little boyhood – recently buttressed by Cousin Georgia in Kansas City. Dr Vansina, after listening intently throughout, then began asking me questions. Being an oral historian, he was particularly interested in the physical transmission of the narrative down across generations.

We talked so late that he invited me to spend the night, and the next morning Dr Vansina, with a very serious expression on his face, said, 'I wanted to sleep on it. The ramifications of phonetic sounds preserved down across your family's generations can be immense.' He said that he had been on the phone with a colleague Africanist, Dr Philip Curtin; they both felt certain that the sounds I'd conveyed to him were from the 'Mandinka' tongue. I'd never heard that word;

he told me that it was the language spoken by the Mandingo people. Then he guess translated certain of the sounds. One of them probably meant cow or cattle; another probably meant the baobab tree, generic in West Africa. The word 'ko', he said, could refer to the *kora*, one of the Mandingo people's oldest stringed instruments, made of a halved large dried gourd covered with goatskin, with a long neck, and twenty-one strings with a bridge. An enslaved Mandingo might relate the *kora* visually to some among the types of stringed instruments that US slaves had.

The most involved sound I had heard and brought was 'Kamby Bolongo', my ancestor's sound to his daughter Kizzy as he had pointed to the Mattaponi River in Spotsylvania County, Virginia. Dr Vansina said that without question, *bolongo* meant, in the Mandinka tongue, a moving water, as a river; preceded by 'Kamby', it could indicate the Gambia River.

I'd never heard of it.

An incident happened that would build my feeling – especially as more uncanny things occurred – that, yes, they were up there watchin' ...

I was asked to speak at a seminar held at Utica College, Utica, New York. Walking down a hallway with the professor who had invited me, I said I'd just flown in from Washington and why I'd been there. 'The Gambia? If I'm not mistaken, someone mentioned recently that an outstanding student from that country is over at Hamilton.'

The old, distinguished Hamilton College was maybe a half hour's drive away, in Clinton, New York. Before I could finish asking, a Professor Charles Todd said, 'You're talking about Ebou Manga.' Consulting a course roster, he told me where I could find him in an agricultural economics class. Ebou Manga was small of build, with careful eyes, a reserved manner, and black as soot. He tentatively confirmed my sounds, clearly startled to have heard me uttering them. Was Mandinka his home tongue? 'No, although I am familiar with it.' He was a Wolof, he said. In his dormitory room, I told him about my quest. We left for The Gambia at the end of the following week.

Arriving in Dakar, Senegal, the next morning, we caught a light plane to the small Yundum Airport in The Gambia. In a passenger van, we rode into the capital city of Banjul (then Bathurst). Ebou and his father, Alhaji Manga – Gambians are mostly Moslem – assembled a small group of men knowledgeable in their small country's history, who met with me in the lounge of the Atlantic Hotel. As I had told Dr Vansina in Wisconsin, I told these men the family narrative that had come down across the generations. I told them in a reverse progression, backwards from Grandma through Tom, Chicken George, then Kizzy saying how her African father insisted to other slaves that his name was 'Kin-tay', and repetitively told her phonetic sounds identifying various things, along with stories such as that he had been attacked and seized while not far from his village, chopping wood.

When I had finished, they said almost with wry amusement, 'Well, of course "Kamby Bolongo" would mean Gambia River; anyone would know that.' I told them hotly that no, a great many people *wouldn't* know it! Then they showed a much greater interest that my 1760s ancestor had insisted his name was 'Kin-tay'. 'Our country's oldest villages tend to be named for the families that settled those villages centuries ago,' they said. Sending for a map, pointing, they said, 'Look, here is the village of Kinte-Kundah. And not too far from it, the village of Kinte-Kundah Janneh-Ya.'

Then they told me something of which I'd never have dreamed: of very old men, called 'griots', still to be found in the older back-country villages, men who were in effect living, walking archives of oral history. A senior griot would be a man usually in his late sixties or early seventies; below him would be progressively younger griots – and apprenticing boys, so a boy would be exposed to those griots' particular line of narrative for forty or fifty years before he could qualify as a senior griot, who told on special occasions the centuries-old histories of villages, of clans, of families, of great heroes. Throughout the whole of black Africa such oral chronicles had been handed down since the time of the ancient forefathers, I was informed, and there were certain legendary griots who could narrate facets of African history literally for as long as three days without ever repeating themselves.

Seeing how astounded I was, these Gambian men reminded me that every living person ancestrally goes back to some time and some place where no writing existed; and then human memories and mouths and ears were the only ways those human beings could store and relay information. They said that we who live in the Western culture are so conditioned to the 'crutch of print' that few among us comprehend what a trained memory is capable of.

Since my forefather had said his name was 'Kin-tay' – properly spelled 'Kinte', they said – and since the Kinte clan was old and well known in The Gambia, they promised to do what they could to find a griot who might be able to assist my search.

Back in the United States, I began devouring books on African

626

history. It grew quickly into some kind of obsession to correct my ignorance concerning the earth's second-largest continent. It embarrasses me to this day that up to then my images about Africa had been largely derived or inferred from Tarzan movies and my very little authentic knowledge had come from only occasional leafings through the *National Geographic*. All of a sudden now, after reading all day, I'd sit on the edge of my bed at night studying a map of Africa, memorizing the different countries' relative positions and the principal waters where slave ships had operated.

After some weeks, a registered letter came from The Gambia; it suggested that when possible, I should come back. But by now I was stony broke – especially because I'd been investing very little of my time in writing.

Once at a *Reader's Digest* lawn party, co-founder Mrs Dewitt Wallace had told me how much she liked an 'Unforgettable Character' I had written – about a tough old seadog cook who had once been my boss in the US Coast Guard – and before leaving, Mrs Wallace volunteered that I should let her know if I ever needed some help. Now I wrote to Mrs Wallace a rather embarrassed letter, briefly telling her the compulsive quest I'd gotten myself into. She asked some editors to meet with me and see what they felt, and invited to lunch with them, I talked about nonstop for nearly three hours. Shortly afterwards, a letter told me that the *Reader's Digest* would provide me with a three-hundred-dollar monthly cheque for one year, and plus that – my really vital need – 'reasonable necessary travel expenses'.

I again visited Cousin Georgia in Kansas City – something had urged me to do so, and I found her quite ill. But she was thrilled to hear both what I had learned and what I hoped to learn. She wished me Godspeed, and I flew then to Africa.

The same men with whom I had previously talked told me now in a rather matter-of-fact manner that they had caused word to be put out in the back country, and that a griot very knowledgeable of the Kinte clan had indeed been found – his name, they said, was 'Kebba Kanji Fofana'. I was ready to have a fit. 'Where *is* he?' They looked at me oddly: 'He's in his village.'

I discovered that if I intended to see this griot, I was going to have to do something I'd never have dreamed I'd ever be doing – organizing what seemed, at least to me then, a kind of mini safari! It took me three days of negotiating through unaccustomed endless African palaver finally to hire a launch to get upriver; to rent a lorry and a Land-Rover to take supplies by a roundabout land route; to hire finally a total of fourteen people, including three interpreters and four musicians, who had told me that the old griots in the back country wouldn't talk without music in the background.

In the launch *Baddibu*, vibrating up the wide, swift 'Kamby Bolongo', I felt queasily, uncomfortably alien. Did they all have me appraised as merely another pith helmet? Finally ahead was James Island, for two centuries the site of a fort over which England and France waged war back and forth for the ideal vantage point to trade in slaves. Asking if we might land there awhile, I trudged amid the crumbling ruins yet guarded by ghostly cannon. Picturing in my mind the kinds of atrocities that would have happened there, I felt as if I would like to go flailing an axe back through that facet of black Africa's history. Without luck I tried to find for myself some symbol remnant of an ancient chain, but I took a chunk of mortar and a brick. In the next minutes before we returned to the *Baddibu*, I just gazed up and down that river that my ancestor had named for his daughter far across the Atlantic Ocean in Spotsylvania County, Virginia. Then we went on, and upon arriving at a little village called Albreda, we put ashore, our destination now on foot the yet smaller village of Juffure, where the men had been told that this griot lived.

There is an expression called 'the peak experience' – that which emotionally, nothing in your life ever transcends. I've had mine, that first day in the back country of black West Africa.

When we got within sight of Juffure, the children who were playing outside gave the alert, and the people came flocking from their huts. It's a village of only about seventy people. Like most back country villages, it was still very much as it was two hundred years ago, with its circular mud houses and their conical thatched roofs. Among the people as they gathered was a small man wearing an off white robe, a pillbox hat over an aquiline-featured black face, and about him was an aura of 'somebodiness' until I knew he was the man we had come to see and hear.

As the three interpreters left our party to converge upon him, the seventy-odd other villagers gathered closely around me, in a kind of horseshoe pattern, three or four deep all around; had I stuck out my arms, my fingers would have touched the nearest ones on either side. They were all staring at me. The eyes just raked me. Their foreheads were furrowed with their very intensity of staring. A kind of visceral surging or a churning sensation started up deep inside me; bewildered, I was wondering what on earth was this ... then in a little while it was rather as if some full-gale force of realization rolled in on me: many times in my life I had been among crowds of people, but never where *every one was jet black!*

Rocked emotionally, my eyes dropped downwards as we tend to do when we're uncertain, insecure, and my glance fell upon my own hands' brown complexion. This time more quickly than before, and even harder, another gale-force emotion hit me: I felt myself some variety of a hybrid... I felt somehow impure among the pure; it was a terribly shaming feeling. About then, abruptly the old man left the interpreters. The people immediately also left me now to go crowding about him.

One of my interpreters came up quickly and whispered in my ears, 'They stare at you so much because they have never here seen a black American.' When I grasped the significance, I believe that hit me harder than what had already happened. They hadn't been looking at me as an individual, but I represented in their eyes a symbol of the twenty-five millions of us black people whom they had never seen, who lived beyond an ocean.

The people were clustered thickly about the old man, all of them intermittently flicking glances towards me as they talked animatedly in their Mandinka tongue. After a while, the old man turned, walked briskly through the people, past my three interpreters, and right up to me. His eyes piercing into mine, seeming to feel I should understand his Mandinka, he expressed what they had all decided they *felt* concerning those unseen millions of us who lived in those places that had been slave ships' destinations – and the translation came: 'We have been told by the forefathers that there are many of us from this place who are in exile in that place called America – and in other places.'

The old man sat down, facing me, as the people hurriedly gathered behind him. Then he began to recite for me the ancestral history of the Kinte clan, as it had been passed along orally down across centuries from the forefathers' time. It was not merely conversational, but more as if a scroll were being read; for the still, silent villagers, it was clearly a formal occasion. The griot would speak, bending forwards from the waist, his body rigid, his neck cords standing out, his words seeming almost physical objects. After a sentence or two, seeming to go limp, he would lean back, listening to an interpreter's translation. Spilling from the griot's head came an incredibly complex Kinte clan lineage that reached back across many generations: who married whom; who had what children; what children then married whom; then their offspring. It was all just unbelievable. I was struck not only by the profusion of details, but also by the narrative's biblical style, something like: '—and so-and-so took as a wife so-and-so, and begat ... and begat ... and begat ...' He would next name each begat's eventual spouse, or spouses, and their averagely numerous offspring, and so on. To date things the griot linked them to events, such as '—in the year of the big water' – a flood – 'he slew a water buffalo.' To determine the calendar date, you'd have to find out when that particular flood occurred.

Simplifying to its essence the encyclopedic saga that I was told, the griot said that the Kinte clan had begun in the country called Old Mali. Then the Kinte men traditionally were blacksmiths, 'who had conquered fire,' and the women mostly were potters and weavers. In time, one branch of the clan moved into the country called Mauretania; and it was from Mauretania that one son of this clan, whose name was Kairaba Kunta Kinte – a 'marabout', or holy man of the Moslem faith – journeyed down into the country called The Gambia. He went first to a village called Pakali N'Ding, stayed there for a while, then went to a village called Jiffarong, and then to the village of Juffure.

In Juffure, Kairaba Kunta Kinte took his first wife, a Mandinka maiden whose name was Sireng. And by her he begot two sons, whose names were Janneh and Saloum. Then he took a second wife; her name was Yaisa. And by Yaisa, he begot a son named Omoro.

Those three sons grew up in Juffure until they became of age. Then the elder two, Janneh and Saloum, went away and founded a new village called Kinte-Kundah Janneh-Ya. The youngest son, Omoro, stayed on in Juffure village until he had thirty rains – years – of age, then he took as his wife a Mandinka maiden named Binta Kebba. And by Binta Kebba, roughly between the years 1750 and 1760, Omoro Kinte begot four sons, whose names were, in the order of their birth, Kunta, Lamin, Suwadu, and Madi.

The old griot had talked for nearly two hours up to then, and perhaps fifty times the narrative had included some detail about someone whom he had named. Now after he had just named those four sons, again he appended a detail, and the interpreter translated—

'About the time the King's soldiers came' – another of the griot's time-fixing references – 'the eldest of these four sons, Kunta, went away from his village to chop wood ... and he was never seen again ...' And the griot went on with his narrative.

I sat as if I were carved of stone. My blood seemed to have congealed. This man whose lifetime had been in this back-country African village had no way in the world to know that he had just echoed what I had heard all through my boyhood years on my grandma's front porch in Henning, Tennessee . . . of an African who always had insisted that his name was 'Kin-tay'; who had called a guitar a 'ko', and a river within the state of Virginia, 'Kamby Bolongo'; and who had been kidnapped into slavery while not far from his village, chopping wood, to make himself a drum.

I managed to fumble from my dufflebag my basic notebook, whose first pages containing grandma's story I showed to an interpreter. After briefly reading, clearly astounded, he spoke rapidly while showing it to the old griot, who became agitated; he got up, exclaiming to the people, gesturing at my notebook in the interpreter's hands, and *they* all got agitated.

I don't remember hearing anyone giving an order, I only recall becoming aware that those seventy-odd people had formed a wide human ring around me, moving counterclockwise, chanting softly, loudly, softly; their bodies close together, they were lifting their knees high, stamping up reddish puffs of the dust . . .

The woman who broke from the moving circle was one of about a dozen whose infant children were within cloth slings across their backs. Her jet-black face deeply contorting, the woman came charging towards me, her bare feet slapping the earth, and snatching her baby free, she thrust it at me almost roughly, the gesture saying 'Take it!' . . . and I did, clasping the baby to me. Then she snatched away her baby; and another woman was thrusting her baby, then another, and another . . . until I had embraced probably a dozen babies. I wouldn't learn until maybe a year later, from a Harvard University professor, Dr Jerome Bruner, a scholar of such matters, 'You didn't know you were participating in one of the oldest ceremonies of humankind, called "The laying on of hands"! In their way, they were telling you "Through this flesh, which is us, we are you, and you are us!"'

Later the men of Juffure took me into their mosque built of bamboo and thatch, and they prayed around me in Arabic. I remember thinking, down on my knees, 'After I've found out where I came from, I can't understand a word they're saying.' Later the crux of their prayer was translated for me: 'Praise be to Allah for one long lost from us whom Allah has returned.'

Since we had come by the river, I wanted to return by land. As I sat beside the wiry young Mandingo driver who was leaving dust pluming behind us on the hot, rough, pitted, back-country road toward Banjul, there came from somewhere into my head a staggering awareness . . . that *if* any black American could be so blessed as I had been to know only a few ancestral clues – could he or she know *who* was either the paternal or maternal African ancestor or finally about *when* the ancestor was taken – then only those few clues might well see that black American able to locate some wizened old black griot whose narrative could reveal the black American's ancestral clan, perhaps even the very village.

In my mind's eye, rather as if it were mistily being projected on a screen, I began envisioning descriptions I had read of how collectively millions of our ancestors had been enslaved. Many thousands were individually kidnapped, as my own forebear Kunta had been, but millions had come awake screaming in the night, dashing out into the bedlam of raided villages, which were often in flames. The captured able survivors were linked neck-by-neck with thongs into processions called 'coffles', which were sometimes as much as a mile in length. I envisioned the many dying, or left to die when they were too weak to continue the torturous march towards the coast, and those who made it to the beach were greased, shaved, probed in every orifice, often branded with sizzling irons; I envisioned them being lashed and dragged towards the longboats; their spasms of screaming and clawing with their hands into the beach, biting up great choking mouthfuls of the sand in their desperate efforts for one last hold on the Africa that had been their home; I envisioned them shoved, beaten, jerked down into slave ships' stinking holds and chained onto shelves, often packed so tightly that they had to lie on their sides like spoons in a drawer . . .

My mind reeled with it all as we approached another, much larger village. Staring ahead, I realized that word of what had happened in Juffure must have left there well before I did. The driver slowing down, I could see this village's people thronging the road ahead; they were waving, amid their cacophony of crying out something; I stood up in the Land-Rover, waving back as they seemed grudging to open a path for the Land-Rover.

I guess we had moved a third of the way through the village when it suddenly registered in my brain what they were all crying out . . . the wizened, robed elders and younger men, the mothers and the naked tar-black children, they were all waving up at me; their expressions buoyant, beaming, all were crying out together, '*Meester Kinte! Meester Kinte!*'

Let me tell you something: I am a man. A sob hit me somewhere around my ankles; it came surging upwards, and flinging my hands over my face, I was just bawling, as I hadn't since I was a baby. '*Meester Kinte!*' I just felt like I was weeping for all of history's incredible atrocities against fellowmen, which seems to be mankind's greatest flaw ...

Flying homewards from Dakar, I decided to write a book. My own ancestors' would automatically also be a symbolic saga of all African-descent people – who are without exception the seeds of someone like Kunta who was born and grew up in some black African village, someone who was captured and chained down in one of those slave ships that sailed them across the same ocean, into some succession of plantations, and since then a struggle for freedom.

In New York, my waiting telephone messages included that in a Kansas City Hospital our eighty-three-year-old Cousin Georgia had died. Later, making a time-zone adjustment, I discovered that she passed away within the very hour that I had walked into Juffure Village. I think that as the last of the old ladies who talked the story on Grandma's front porch, it had been her job to get me to Africa, then she went to join the others up there watchin'.

In fact, I see starting from my little boyhood, a succession of related occurrences that finally when they all joined have caused this book to exist. Grandma and the others drilled the family story into me. Then, purely by the fluke of circumstances, when I was cooking on US Coast Guard ships at sea, I began the long trial-and-error process of teaching myself to write. And because I had come to love the sea, my early writing was about dramatic sea adventures gleaned out of yellowing old maritime records in the US Coast Guard's archives. I couldn't have acquired a much better preparation to meet the maritime research challenges that this book would bring.

Always, Grandma and the other old ladies had said that a ship brought the African to 'somewhere called 'Naplis'. I knew they had to have been referring to Annapolis, Maryland. So I felt now that I had to try to see if I could find *what* ship had sailed to Annapolis from the Gambia River, with her human cargo including 'the African', who would later insist that 'Kin-tay' was his name, after his massa John Waller had given him the name 'Toby'.

I needed to determine a time around which to focus the search for this ship. Months earlier, in the village of Juffure, the griot had timed Kunta Kinte's capture with 'about the time the King's soldiers came'.

Returning to London, midway during a second week of searching in records of movement assignments for British military units during the 1760s, I finally found that 'King's soldiers' *had* to refer to a unit called 'Colonel O'Hare's forces'. The unit was sent from London in 1767 to guard the then British-operated Fort James Slave Fort in the Gambia River. The griot had been so correct that I felt embarrassed that, in effect, I had been checking behind him.

I went to Lloyds of London. In the office of an executive named Mr R. C. E. Landers, it just poured out of me what I was trying to do. He got up from behind his desk and he said, 'Young man, Lloyds of London will give you all of the help that we can.' It was a blessing, for through Lloyds, doors began to be opened for me to search among myriad old English maritime records.

I can't remember any more exhausting experience than my first six weeks of seemingly endless, futile, day-after-day searching in an effort to isolate and then pin down a specific slave ship on a specific voyage, from within cartons upon cartons, files upon files of old records of thousands of slave-ship triangular voyages among England, Africa, and America. Along with my frustration, the more a rage grew within me the more I perceived to what degree the slave trade, in its time, was regarded by most of its participants simply as another major industry, rather like the buying, selling, and shipment of livestock today. Many records seemed never to have been opened after their original storage; apparently no one had felt occasion to go through them.

I hadn't found a single ship bound from The Gambia to Annapolis, when in the seventh week, one afternoon about two-thirty, I was studying the 1,023rd sheet of slave-ship records. A wide rectangular sheet, it recorded the Gambia River entrances and exits of some thirty ships during the years 1766 and 1767. Moving down the list, my eyes reached ship No. 18, and automatically scanned across its various data heading entries.

On 5 July 1767 – the year 'the King's soldiers came' – a ship named *Lord Ligonier*, her captain, a Thomas E. Davies, had sailed from the Gambia River, her destination Annapolis ...

I don't know why, but oddly my internal emotional reaction was delayed. I recall passively writing down the information, I turned in the records, and walked outside. Around the corner was a little tea shop. I went in and ordered a tea and cruller. Sitting, sipping my tea, it suddenly hit me that quite possibly that ship brought Kunta Kinte!

I still owe the lady for the tea and cruller. By telephone, Pan American confirmed their last seat available that day to New York. There simply wasn't time to go by the hotel where I was staying; I told a taxi driver, 'Heathrow Airport!' Sleepless through that night's crossing of the Atlantic, I was seeing in my mind's eye the book in the Library of Congress, Washington, D.C., that I had to get my hands on again. It had a light brown cover, with darker brown letters

– Shipping in the Port of Annapolis, by Vaughan W. Brown.

From New York, the Eastern Airlines shuttle took me to Washington; I taxied to the Library of Congress, ordered the book, almost yanked it from the young man who brought it, and went riffling through it . . . and there it was, confirmation! The *Lord Ligonier* had cleared Annapolis' customs officials on 29 September 1767.

Renting a car, speeding to Annapolis, I went to the Maryland Hall of Records and asked archivist Mrs Phebe Jacobsen for copies of any local newspaper published around the first week of October 1767. She soon produced a microfilm roll of the Maryland *Gazette.* At the projection machine, I was halfway through the 1 October issue when I saw the advertisement in the antique typeface: 'JUST IMPORTED, In the ship *Lord Ligonier*, Capt. Davies, from the River Gambia, in Africa, and to be sold by the subscribers, in Annapolis, for cash, or good bills of exchange on Wednesday the 7th of October next, A Cargo of CHOICE HEALTHY SLAVES. The said ship will take tobacco to London on liberty at 6s. Sterling per ton.' The advertisement was signed by John Ridout and Daniel of St Thos. Jenifer.

On 29 September 1967 I felt I should be nowhere else in the world except standing on a pier at Annapolis – and I was; it was two hundred years to the day after the *Lord Ligonier* had landed. Staring out to seaward across those waters over which my great-great-great-great-grandfather had been brought, again I found myself weeping.

The 1766–67 document compiled at James Fort in the Gambia River had included that the *Lord Ligonier* had sailed with 140 slaves in her hold. How many of them had lived through the voyage? Now on a second mission in the Maryland Hall of Records, I searched to find a record of the ship's cargo listed upon her arrival in Annapolis – and found it, the following inventory, in old-fashioned script: 3,265 'elephants' teeth', as ivory tusks were called; 3,700 pounds of beeswax; 800 pounds of raw cotton; 32 ounces of Gambian gold; and 98 'Negroes'. Her loss of 42 Africans en route, or around one third, was average for slaving voyages.

I realized by this time that Grandma, Aunt Liz, Aunt Plus, and Cousin Georgia also had been griots in their own ways. My notebooks contained their centuries-old story that our African had been sold to 'Massa John Waller', who had given him the name 'Toby'. During his fourth escape effort, when cornered he had wounded with a rock one of the pair of professional slave-catchers who caught him, and they had cut his foot off. 'Massa John's brother, Dr William Waller', had saved the slave's life, then indignant at the maiming, had bought him from his brother. I dared to hope there might actually exist some kind of an actual documenting record.

I went to Richmond, Virginia. I pored through microfilmed legal deeds filed within Spotsylvania County, Virginia, after September 1767, when the *Lord Ligonier* had landed. In time, I found a lengthy deed dated 5 September 1768 in which John Waller and his wife Ann transferred to William Waller land and goods, including 240 acres of farmland ... and then on the second page, 'and also one Negro man slave named Toby.'

My God!

In the twelve years since my visit to the Rosetta Stone, I have travelled half a million miles, I suppose, searching, sifting, checking, crosschecking, finding out more and more about the people whose respective oral histories had proved not only to be correct, but even to connect on both sides of the ocean. Finally I managed to tear away from yet more researching in order to push myself into actually writing this book. To develop Kunta Kinte's boyhood and youth took me a long time, and having come to know him well, I anguished upon his capture. When I began trying to write of his, or all of those Gambians' slave-ship crossing, finally I flew to Africa and canvassed among shipping lines to obtain passage on the first possible freighter sailing from any black African port directly to the United States. It turned out to be the Farrell Lines' *African Star*. When we put to sea, I explained what I hoped to do that might help me write of my ancestor's crossing. After each late evening's dinner, I climbed down successive metal ladders into her deep, dark, cold cargo hold. Stripping to my underwear, I lay on my back on a wide rough bare dunnage plank and forced myself to stay there through all ten nights of the crossing, trying to imagine what did he see, hear, feel, smell, taste – and above all, in knowing Kunta, what things did he think? My crossing of course was ludicrously luxurious by any comparison to the ghastly ordeal endured by Kunta Kinte, his companions, and all those other millions who lay chained and shackled in terror and their own filth for an average of eighty to ninety days, at the end of which awaited new physical and psychic horrors. But anyway, finally I wrote of the ocean crossing – from the perspective of the human cargo.

Finally I've woven our whole seven generations into this book that is in your hands. In the years of the writing, I have also spoken before many audiences of how *Roots* came to be, naturally now and then someone asks, 'How much of *Roots* is fact and how much is fiction?' To the best of my knowledge and of my effort, every lineage

636

statement within *Roots* is from either my African or American families' carefully preserved oral history, much of which I have been able conventionally to corroborate with documents. Those documents, along with the myriad textural details of what were contemporary indigenous lifestyles, cultural history, and such that give *Roots* flesh have come from years of intensive research in fifty-odd libraries, archives, and other repositories on three continents.

Since I wasn't yet around when most of the story occurred, by far most of the dialogue and most of the incidents are of necessity a novelized amalgam of what I *know* took place together with what my researching led me to plausibly *feel* took place.

I think now that not only are Grandma, Cousin Georgia, and those other ladies 'up there watchin',' but so are all of the others: Kunta and Bell; Kizzy; Chicken George and Matilda; Tom and Irene; Grandpa Will Palmer; Bertha; Mama – and now, as well, the most recent one to join them, Dad . . .

He was eighty-three. When his children – George, Julius, Lois, and I – had discussed the funeral arrangements, some one of us expressed that Dad had lived both a full life and a rich one in the way that he interpreted richness. Moreover, he had gone quickly without suffering, and knowing Dad as well as we all did, we agreed that he would not have wanted us going about crying. And we agreed that we would not.

I found myself so full of memories that when the mortician said 'the deceased', it startled me that he meant our dad, around whom things rarely got dull. Shortly before the first service that was held for him in a Washington, D.C. chapel, thick with family friends, my brother George told the Reverend Boyd, who was in charge, that at an appropriate point, we sons would like to share some memories of Dad with the friends there.

So after brief conventional services, a favourite song of Dad's was sung, then George got up and stood near the open casket. He said he vividly recalled that wherever Dad had taught, our home was always shared with at least one youth whose rural farmer father Dad had talked into letting his son attend college, the 'no money' protest being solved by Dad's saying, 'He'll live with us.' As a result, George estimated that about the South were around eighteen county agricultural agents, high school principals, and teachers who proudly call themselves ' 'Fessor Haley's boys'.

George said that among earlier memory was once when we lived in Alabama and at breakfast Dad said, 'You boys come on, there's a great man I want you to meet.' And just like that Dad drove us three boys the several hours to Tuskeegee, Alabama, where we visited the mysterious laboratory of the small, dark genius scientist, Dr George Washington Carver, who talked to us about the need to study hard and gave us each a small flower. George said that in Dad's later years, he had been irked that we did not hold annual large family reunions as he would have liked, and George asked the audience now to join us in feeling that really we were holding a reunion both for and with our dad.

I got up as George took his seat, and going over, looking at Dad, I said to the people that being the oldest child, I could remember things farther back about the gentleman lying there. For instance, my first distinct boyhood impression of love was noticing how Dad's and Mama's eyes would look at each other over the piano top when Mama was playing some little introduction as Dad stood near waiting to sing in our church. Another early memory was of how I could always get a nickel or even a dime from Dad, no matter how tight people were going around saying things were. All I had to do was catch him alone and start begging him to tell me just one more time about how his AEF 92nd Division, 366th Infantry, fought in the Meuse Argonne Forest. 'Why, we were ferocious, son!' Dad would exclaim. By the time he gave me the dime it was clear that whenever things would look really grim to General Blackjack Pershing, once again he would send a courier to bring Savannah, Tennessee's, Sergeant Simon A. Haley (No. 2816106), whereupon the lurking German spies sped that news to their highest command, throwing fright into the Kaiser himself.

But it seemed to me, I told the people, that after Dad's having met Mama at Lane College, his next most fateful meeting for all of us had been when Dad had transferred to A & T College in Greensboro, North Carolina, and was about to drop out of school and return home to sharecrop, 'Because, boys, working four odd jobs, I just never had time to study.' But before he left, word came of his acceptance as a temporary summer-season Pullman porter. On a night train from Buffalo to Pittsburgh, at about 2 a.m., his buzzer rang, and a sleepless white man and his wife each wanted a glass of warm milk. Dad brought the milk, he said, 'and I tried to leave, but the man was just talkative and seemed surprised that I was a working college student. He asked lots of questions, then he tipped well in Pittsburgh.' After saving every possible cent, when Dad returned to college that September of 1916, the college president showed him correspondence from the man on the train – a retired Curtis Publishing Company executive named R. S. M. Boyce – who had written

638